the joy of
seafood

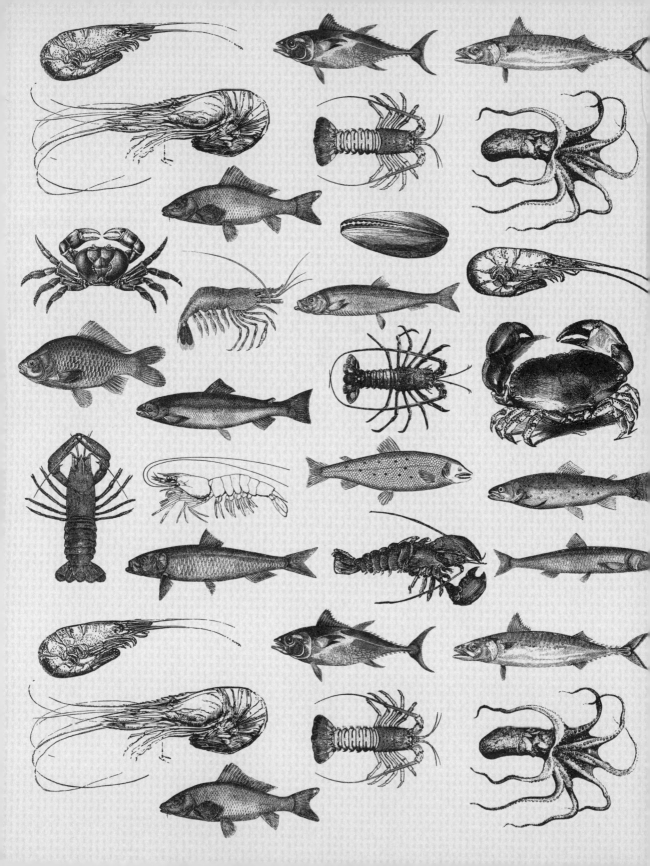

the joy of
seafood

the all-purpose seafood cookbook
with more than 900 recipes

barton
seaver

STERLING EPICURE
New York

STERLING EPICURE
New York

An Imprint of Sterling Publishing Co., Inc.
1166 Avenue of the Americas
New York, NY 10036

ISBN 978-1-4549-2198-1
ISBN 978-1-4549-3810-1(signed edition)

Distributed in Canada by Sterling Publishing Co., Inc.
c/o Canadian Manda Group, 664 Annette Street
Toronto, Ontario, Canada M6S 2C8
Distributed in the United Kingdom by GMC Distribution Services
Castle Place, 166 High Street, Lewes, East Sussex, England BN7 1XU
Distributed in Australia by NewSouth Books
University of New South Wales, Sydney, NSW 2052, Australia

For information about custom editions, special sales,
and premium and corporate purchases, please
contact Sterling Special Sales at 800-805-5489
or specialsales@sterlingpublishing.com.

Manufactured in China

2 4 6 8 10 9 7 5 3 1

sterlingpublishing.com

Interior design by Christine Heun
Cover design by Scott Russo

Image Credits

Getty Images: Alhontess: 396; antiqueimgnet: 233, 451; asmakar: 151; TonyBaggett: 108; bauhaus1000:
121; channarongsds: 345; duncan1890: 74, 177, 409; gameover2012: 234; Grafissimo: 238; IADA: 67, 437;
ilbusca: 159, 162, 180, 213, 216, 223, 445; mecaleha: 391; nicoolay: ii, 190; GeorgePeters: 85; Ruskpp: 171;
THEPALMER: 89, 97, 133, 199, 207, 247, 252; ZU_09: 194
Michael Piazza: 486

To all the cooks who have ever said,
"I'd love to eat more seafood, but
I don't know how to cook it."

CONTENTS

INTRODUCTION

Seafood cookery is the art of simplicity: the delicate flavors and textures of all types of seafood shine when they are given a simple platform. There is, of course, leeway to have some fun combining exciting flavors that add spice and contrast to the final dish. The cook merely provides a context in which the seafood can be most appreciated. And therein lies the beauty of seafood.

Myriad flavors, textures, shapes, sizes, and colors of seafood swim or settle in our oceans. I have been cooking and eating seafood my entire life, and I am still constantly amazed by the "newness" I discover in each meal. A single species of fish can have regional nuances that are as subtle and fluctuating as any wine-grape varietal. Seasonality also changes seafood. A familiar favorite pulled from the water in the fall can taste like an altogether different culinary creature if it is harvested in the spring. It will be delicious but different all the same.

For too long we have thought of seafood as a product without provenance, a commodity that is ever the same, from places other than where we are. But just as farmers markets have reintroduced us to the wonders of diversity in the world of produce, so, too, are we beginning to rediscover seafood, once so dearly prized in our culinary culture, from sea to shining sea, and then forgotten by later generations.

Who among us would prefer to return to a world in which lettuce is synonymous with iceberg? We wouldn't accept only apples in the Delicious (are they, though?) varieties of Golden or Red these days. And we were comfortable with pink, hard, flavorless tomatoes until varieties like Sungold and Cherokee Purple and Green Zebra and Brandywine awakened in us the memory of what a tomato should be. It is because of these changes in our perception of the ingredient landscape that I suggest the next culinary horizon lies below the waterline. There are oceans, seas, lakes, ponds, and rivers of culinary opportunity to discover, each delicious in its own unique way.

Some cooks are hesitant about cooking seafood, a hang-up that prevents them from eating seafood as often as they would like. Much of the fear is based on a lack of fundamental comfort with seafood as an ingredient. We might overcook it. The process might leave a lingering smell in the house. Seafood is too expensive, and shopping can be inconvenient. These are real concerns, but they are concerns that can be overcome with just a little bit of effort.

Building up your confidence to cook seafood properly takes only a small amount of practice. But even before you bring anything salty, scaled, or shelled into the kitchen, you can address any lingering concerns or worries by following the very first rule of seafood cookery: buy the best-quality seafood available, even if you are not totally familiar with the specific species.

When the success of a meal is based on the preordained selection of a certain type of seafood, then the very best outcome will be limited by the unavailability of quality. But if you switch the order of operations to first buy quality, regardless of the species, and then choose an appropriate recipe for what you've bought, you will have dramatically increased the likelihood of success and enjoyment. When you're at the fish counter, don't demand only the fish you know and have eaten in the past. Instead, make your selection from the freshest available options. It's a pretty simple concept: buy the catch of the day.

Good-quality seafood doesn't smell like fish; it smells like fresh salt breezes, violets, cucumbers. As the great writer M. F. K. Fisher opined, fresh smells right. Also, know that quality is not an inverse function of price. As a measure of wholesomeness and deliciousness, quality is not determined by the popularity of a species. In fact, popularity plays a significant role in driving up the cost of some species. Just because you might not have heard of a particular kind of seafood doesn't mean that it isn't tasty. It just means that you haven't yet realized how tasty it is.

Some options in the seafood case may be priced economically, due to seasonal abundance and increased regional availability. Seasonal seafood that doesn't have to travel far to reach your table is likely to be high-quality seafood, and there will be less risk of overcooking it because it will still retain its original resilience, moisture, and integrity.

If you shop once a week, as many Americans do, the decision to buy fresh seafood, with its relatively short shelf life, can be fraught, since you may feel compelled to cook it as soon as you bring it home, but some seafood, like trout, tilapia, farmed salmon, and mussels, is often so fresh when it lands in the seafood case that it can easily deliver delicious meals later in the week if it is properly stored at home.

It is also important to understand that quality is no longer confined to the fresh seafood case. Both frozen and canned seafood are worthy of our attention because of their longer shelf life (more on this a bit later, on page 3), and they can really deliver on taste.

So what is the cook to do once quality seafood is in hand?

This book offers many suggestions.

It is important that all people eat at least two servings of seafood per week. This is particularly true for children and pregnant and nursing mothers, though one should be mindful that a small number of species have an associated risk of toxicity. For more information visit seafoodnutrition.org.

Acknowledgments

Special thank-you to Christine Burns-Rudalevige for all that she added to this effort. Thanks to my business partner, Katy Kennedy Rivera, for keeping the ship upright while I was below deck buried in this task. And as always to my Ladyfish and Kidsquid for making everything worthwhile.

PART ONE

HOW TO BUY, STORE, AND PREPARE SEAFOOD

In my hectic household, which includes a very active three-year-old, we eat seafood ten or more times per week (and I'm not including fish-shaped cheddar cheese crackers in this tally). It can be exhausting to prepare so many lunches and dinners—and be creative each time—but the recipes in this book help overcome that hurdle.

The Joy of Seafood is designed to help you feel confident about cooking seafood, using recipes that don't require much more than a reasonably well-stocked pantry.

The recipes are also simply meant to be channel markers to help cooks navigate their journey to seafood literacy. They were developed from a broad spectrum of cultural influences, regional ingredients, classic dishes, and modernized techniques. Traditional French preparations share these pages with dishes that pay homage to the vast influence of Asian cuisines, along with regional soups and stews. Many of these recipes result in simple meals that can be brought to the table in less than 30 minutes, while others deliver elegant appetizers and jazzy Saturday night options.

Most types of seafood have flavor partners and methods of preparation that are particularly flattering to their culinary character. You'll learn a lot about the personalities of various kinds of seafood by reading the species introductions in this book. Spend even a little time with both the species introductions and the recipes and you will see some patterns emerge.

Recipes for fish of a certain shape and size are interchangeable for the most part. As such, many basic recipes are repeated throughout the book with minor variations to accommodate the subtle nuances of the particular seafood being prepared. Once you know how to make a Sautéed Snapper with Brown Butter, Thyme, and Orange (page 390), you'll know how to prepare more than half the fish you're likely to see at the store. And if your family likes Roasted Tilapia in Marinara (page 420), you can apply it to almost any similar seafood. For example, many of the recipes for snapper are equally delicious with striped bass or black bass. So don't take these recipes to be strictly prescriptive by any means. When you are comfortable cooking one species, you'll gain the confidence to cook another. Buy the freshest piece of fish available and then find a recipe that can be made with whatever you have in your pantry and within your schedule. Once you've gained competencey in a couple of techniques and have developed your own canon of basic recipes, your newfound seafood literacy will inspire further seafood cooking and eating adventures.

That is the joy of seafood.

How to Buy Seafood

Shopping is the most important step in any seafood recipe. There are a few easy steps to ensuring that you take home the best seafood possible.

First, inspect the general cleanliness of the store: Is it well lit, clean, and odorless (or, even better, pleasantly sea-breeze perfumed)? Is the counter staff wearing clean aprons, gloves, a smile? If the answer to these questions is yes, you're more than halfway there. And don't forget, seafood is in three different parts of the store, so be sure to check the canned and frozen food aisles, as they are sure to offer good options.

Second, buy fresh seafood from a knowledgeable person whenever possible. The power of a personal relationship with your fishmonger is not to be underestimated. Simply introducing yourself and interacting on a named basis creates a dynamic of responsibility. The expert attending to you will steer you toward the right choice for that day. As the consumer, your responsibility is to take the advice you sought from him or her.

Most fish is bought in fillet form. However, you can still determine the high quality and freshness of fillets by observing these visual cues:

+ The fillets smell right.
+ The fillets are nicely presented and not heaped on top of each other.
+ There is no gaping or torn flesh.
+ The fillets are not sitting in any liquid but rather are perched above ice, arranged in pans, or displayed on cold blocks, such as marble.
+ The flesh and skin (if present) have a lustrous quality and a moist sheen.

- The color of the fillets is uniform, showing no signs of age, oxidation (discoloration), or bleaching because of prolonged contact with water.
- The flesh is resilient when the fillet is gently pressed. (Ask the attendant to do this for you.)
- If the fillets were previously frozen, they were thawed within the last 12 hours (if not, ask for frozen fillets).

Most of these cues for freshness also apply to shellfish such as shrimp and scallops.

If you get the opportunity to purchase whole fish, I highly recommend it; I've included several recipes to help you prepare it. When you are purchasing whole fish, many of the same cues as those above apply, but there are additional telltale signs of quality to look for:

- The fish smells right. (It gives no sense of doubt.)
- The eyes are vibrant.
- The gills should be moist and bright in color (ask the attendant to show you).
- The scales firmly adhere to the skin.
- The fins are mostly intact and pliable.
- The outside of the fish has a moist sheen.
- The belly cavity is clean and free of blood and green bile stains (almost all whole fish is gutted before it is sold).
- The flesh is resilient to pressure and bounces back after a light touch (ask the attendant to do this for you).

If you are purchasing bivalves, such as mussels and clams, make sure that the shells are firmly closed or that they close immediately when given a gentle knock. This means the shellfish is alive and will last several days under the proper conditions.

How to Store Seafood

Once you have bought fresh seafood it is imperative to keep it cold before using it.

It is best to store seafood on ice (but never in direct contact with it), just as it was at the store. Frankly, I find this method too burdensome and inconvenient. I simply place the fish, in its wrapping, in a dish that is just large enough to hold it, and then place the dish in the coldest part of the refrigerator, away from the door or in a drawer, in order to avoid temperature swings each time the refrigerator is opened and closed.

The best way to store fresh shellfish, such as mussels and clams, is to place them in a dish or bowl and cover them with moist paper towels or a clean, damp dishcloth. They'll keep in the fridge for several days, if you periodically drain off any liquid exuded by the shellfish and check for any that may have opened and will not immediately close when given a gentle knock. Remoisten the towels as needed.

Frozen Seafood

I have become a big proponent of quality frozen seafood. On the whole it offers a major win for sustainability, as it has a smaller carbon footprint because of slower and more efficient routes to market, helps decrease the amount of wasted seafood because it has significantly decreased perishability, and takes advantage of seasonal bounty by making it available throughout the year.

Frozen seafood rightly earned its bad reputation in past years, as it was often frozen at or near the point of sale, using less-than-optimal technology to freeze already aging fish. For the most part, seafood is now processed quickly and frozen at sea. Sometimes this process happens even before a fish can enter rigor mortis. Freezing seafood closer to the time when it is pulled from the water has really changed the process from simply being a method to arrest spoilage to a means of capturing pristine quality. The quality of frozen seafood has also benefited from modern techniques that range from micromisting seafood with water, which forms a protective sheath, to using rapid deep-freeze technologies.

These days, frozen seafood is sometimes referred to as "fresh frozen" or "frozen fresh," terms I find completely accurate and quite descriptive of the quality of these products. In fact, when they are properly stored and thawed, fresh-frozen products are even better than "fresh" seafood that has been sitting in a fishmonger's case longer than it should have been.

A lot of trepidation about buying fish can be reduced by buying frozen instead of fresh. For Americans, many of whom often shop for one or even two weeks' worth of meals at a time, frozen seafood doesn't demand its own timeline; instead, it has become a convenience protein in its own right. Frozen seafood can be taken directly from the freezer just a few hours before it is needed. And because it doesn't require rapid transport to keep it fresh, there is less expense involved in bringing it to market and less waste due to spoilage, all of which contribute to bringing down the cost of frozen seafood and making it accessible to more people. This is especially important in communities where access to fresh, healthy food is limited. Nowadays, frozen seafood purchased from a corner bodega can be just as good as the product you buy from top-quality full-service grocers.

Properly Stored Frozen Seafood

All frozen seafood should be held below 32°F at every point in the supply chain. Signs that seafood has been poorly handled or improperly stored at some point in the supply chain include:

* Packaging is torn or crushed on the edges.

* Individual quick-frozen pieces are frozen together in a single mass.

* Excessive ice crystals or frost are present on the fish or in the package.

How to Thaw Frozen Seafood

Knowing how to properly thaw frozen seafood before cooking it is just as essential as sourcing high-quality frozen products.

Fresh-frozen seafood should be solidly frozen when you buy it and placed in your freezer as soon as possible. This is the key to preserving the quality that you've worked so hard to find. The great advantage of fresh-frozen seafood is that you do not need to thaw it until just a few hours before you are ready to use it.

Seafood is best thawed under refrigeration. Depending on the thickness of the fish, thawing can take 2–8 hours. Simply put the fillets or portions on a plate and place it in an open area in the refrigerator where air can circulate around it.

If you need to thaw seafood quickly, you can place individually wrapped seafood portions in a bowl of cold water, but only do so if it is wrapped in plastic to prevent the fish from touching the water, which will rob it of flavor and alter its texture when it is cooked.

For food safety and quality reasons, seafood should not be thawed at room temperature for more than an hour or two. It should never be thawed in warm or hot water. A properly thawed piece of seafood will look and cook like a fresh piece from the same species. Avoid refreezing seafood, as this can severely alter the flavor and quality.

Equipment

A reasonably well-equipped kitchen is sufficient for basically all forms of fish cookery. Sure, you can buy fancy pans and a bucketful of specialized seafood gadgets, but you really don't need them. There's nothing you can't do with fish if you're set up to cook chicken. All you need is a good nonstick pan, a baking dish, heavy-bottomed pots for braising, casserole dishes, zip-top plastic bags for storing and marinating, and a sharp knife.

There is one item that does help: a thin metal fish spatula that can easily slide under fish is the best tool to use when flipping delicate fillets in a pan or turning them on the grill. A metal fish spatula is useful for making pancakes, too, so I think you should have one anyway.

Pantry

Below is a list of ingredients I commonly use in seafood cooking. Many of the recipes that follow are based on various uses of these mostly staple items.

+ **Citrus:** lemons, limes, oranges
+ **Spices:** mace, smoked sweet paprika, black pepper, crushed chile flakes, allspice, fennel seeds
+ **Fresh soft herbs:** tarragon, chervil, parsley, mint, chives, cilantro, dill
+ **Fresh hard herbs:** thyme, rosemary
+ **Condiments:** soy sauce, Worcestershire sauce, fish sauce, whole grain and ground mustard, prepared horseradish, mayonnaise, red/white/sherry vinegars
+ **Cured and canned ingredients:** anchovies in oil, green olives, capers, canned fire-roasted diced tomatoes, canned peeled San Marzano tomatoes
+ **Alcohol:** red and white wines, sherry (drier styles such as Amontillado, Palo Cortado), Madeira (drier styles), anise-flavored liquors (Pernod, Herbsaint, Anisette, Ricard), dark rum, brandy
+ **Fats:** butter (unsalted), extra-virgin olive oil (nothing too fancy), vegetable or peanut oil, cold-pressed nut oils (occasionally)
+ **Dry goods:** nuts (pecans, peanuts, pistachios, almonds, walnuts), panko bread crumbs, raisins

Salt

When I cook seafood I use kosher salt. Nearly every recipe calls for it, very often at the outset of the preparation, to season the seafood before cooking it. Because this step takes place so early in the process it allows the salt to penetrate the flesh rather than simply sit on top of it. I've found that less salt applied early yields better results than more salt applied later.

One of the most important skills to learn as a cook is to properly season foods. The key to this skill is an awareness of how salt will both season the ingredient it is applied to as well as how it will manifest in the larger dish.

Different salts have different salinities, volumes, textures, associated flavors, and rates at which they dissolve. I can't claim that any one salt is better than another for total overall effect, but I do know that practice makes perfect, and practice is best if it is consistent: the fewer the variables, the more likely you are to achieve success. Therefore, when I cook I always use the same type of salt, as I have learned by physical memory exactly what effect a given pinch will have on a dish. However, salts can vary even within the same category, such as kosher salt. For example, there are noticeable differences in salinity by volume between two leading brands, Morton® and Diamond Crystal®. My advice is to pick your favorite salt—any salt—and use only that salt.

Pairing Wine with Seafood

There are only two rules I follow for pairing wine with food: drink what you want and eat what you want. There are simply no strict formulas, and your enjoyment is the ultimate measure of a successful pairing. That said, just as wearing plaids and stripes makes for an odd ensemble, pairing syrah with flounder makes for a tumultuous relationship. Syrah and salmon, however, can be a different story. So while no strict formula applies to pairing wine with seafood, I do have a few suggestions to make in the section below, as selecting the right wine to drink with seafood is similar to selecting the right wine to use for cooking seafood.

Cooking Seafood with Wine

The most important thing to keep in mind when you are cooking seafood with wine is to use good-quality wine (which does not have to mean expensive). This applies to everything you cook, whether it is seafood, chicken, meat, quinoa, or any other ingredient. Wine is reduced when it is cooked, a process that magnifies the wine's impact on the finished dish.

I cook with the wine that I plan to drink with the meal. Not only does this guideline help unite the flavors of the food and the wine, it pretty much guarantees that you'll appreciate the resulting concentrated flavors of the wine in the food. The wine you use to cook the meal doesn't even have to be the same variety that you are drinking. A half glass or so left over from a previous meal will work just as well.

It is worth paying attention to the character of a wine before you use it in a dish. Acidic wines, for example, will add a tart element, while buttery, luscious wines will add weight and richness to a dish. A bright, lemony pan sauce is best made with a richer style to provide balance, and the flavor of a seafood stock can be made all the more focused by a lighter, tart wine.

Where the style of wine matters the most is in poached and braised preparations, because ultimately it will exert the most influence over the personality of the dish. There is really no wrong wine to use, but it is generally best to try to contrast the wine with other ingredients in the preparation, for example, using an acidic wine in a creamy sauce, rather than trying to match styles, such as an acidic wine with acidic tomatoes. Pairing and cooking with red wines is a fun way to add extra dimension to seafood. Lighter reds, with their typical berry/woodsy/cherry flavors and light tannins, can punctuate seafood flavors in interesting ways and add sweet fruit flavors without bringing any actual sweetness to a dish, while wines with a more earthy character can supply a wonderful contrast to the sea brine of a fish dish (think surf and turf). I tend to shy away from cooking with heavy red styles, as the tannins typical of these wines can be too bitter and prevent the subtle flavors of seafood from shining through a dish, and they can also draw out unwanted metallic flavors from fish. However, a reduction of an angular cabernet or muscled malbec, swirled with butter in a rich sauce for salmon or other flavor-forward seafood, makes the most of a good heavy red wine.

Sherry and Madeira wines are classic accompaniments to seafood cookery. Each of them imparts a nutty, oxidized flavor and a gentle sweetness, making them perfect partners for just about anything that ever swam anywhere. It's best to stick to light-to-medium styles, however, as heavier, super-sweet Madeira and sherry wines simply don't pair evenly with seafood and can easily overpower it.

Cooking with Booze

Either spirits are generally too potent and highly flavored (e.g., bourbon) to work well with seafood or they are not flavored enough to make much impact (e.g., vodka). But there are a few spirits, such as brandy, that are well suited to pairing with seafood. Much like sherry or Madeira, brandy gives a dish a light, nutty punctuation while also lending some depth with a toasty, woody flavor.

The usefulness of big-flavored booze also depends on the dish, such as Broiled Bluefish with Oregano and Raisin Flambé with dark rum. Almost universally, though, anise- or licorice-flavored spirits partner perfectly with seafood. You'll see that I commonly call for a dash (or shot) of Pernod or Herbsaint to finish a dish. The soaring aroma of anise works magic for all forms of seafood and integrates into a dish seamlessly. One anise-flavored spirit, Sambuca, though, is far too heavily flavored and sweet, and it overpowers anything it's partnered with.

PART TWO

TECHNIQUES

Seafood cookery employs just about every technique used to cook all other proteins, so you don't need to know much outside of the basics to feel confident about preparing seafood. The following are descriptions of the most common techniques as they apply to the unique qualities of seafood.

Muscle Structure

You've probably sautéed a chicken breast, grilled a pork chop, roasted a leg of lamb, and braised a pot roast in your time as a cook, but using those techniques to prepare seafood requires a few adjustments, mainly because of gravity. Land animals deal with it; fish don't. Because fish live in a buoyant environment, their muscles are more delicately structured and contain less connective tissue than those of chickens, pigs, lambs, and cows. This delicate composition is why cooked fish flakes apart rather than requiring a knife to be cut.

Braising or Stewing

The technique of braising or stewing generally conjures scenes in which large, tough cuts of beef or pork simmer and break down over low heat for long periods of time, in heavy sauces and in even heavier enameled pots. Even seafood, with its typically delicate structure, can also be prepared using this moist-heat cooking technique. In fact, braised fish is featured prominently in French cuisine and across regional Chinese culinary traditions. In Malaysia, seafood is braised in coconut milk, and in the West (in Spain, for example) it is simmered in juicy chopped tomatoes.

Braising fish is an easy means of getting a one-pot meal on the table on a Tuesday night and an elegant way to prepare fish for a dinner party on a Saturday night.

The biggest difference between braising fish and braising tougher land-animal proteins is that fish requires a shorter cooking time in the braising liquid. As with most methods of cooking fish, whether it is whole, filleted, or cut into steaks, you can count on about 8 minutes of cooking time for every inch of thickness. Since the cooking time for fish is so short, make sure the braising liquid is highly flavored with herbs, spices, and aromatic vegetables before you add the fish, which makes the finished dish much more exciting. The aromatics used to flavor the dish can be a mix of vegetables or an elegant layered mix of spices, butter, and wine. Once the fish is cooked, though, transfer it to a warm dish and reduce the braising liquid to thicken it and intensify its impact. It's also important that all other ingredients are parcooked so they are done when the seafood is. There is no 3-hour simmer time to cook carrots as there would be with beef stew.

Many types of seafood are suitable for braising: flaky fish such as cod, halibut, salmon, trout, and snapper all braise well, as do the denser varieties such as carp, catfish, cobia, eel, grouper, monkfish, swordfish, tilefish, and wolffish—my personal favorite. Other seafood that takes well to braising includes conch, octopus, squid, and whelks.

Broiling

Broiling, the process of applying heat from above to food in the oven, below a gas burner or electric coil, adds flavor and texture to seafood dishes because it produces a bit of charring and caramelization on the exterior of the fish, while the tender flesh underneath stays moist. Broiling, like grilling, is a technique that is typically applied to fish that are rich in luxurious and healthy fats, like salmon or swordfish. Leaner seafood like tilapia, catfish, haddock, and flounder, however, can become just as succulent when broiling is combined with a rich, brightly flavored topping, such as mayonnaise, yogurt, or flavored butter (see pages 18–23). In New England cookbooks, I often see recipes that call for coating fish in mayonnaise before broiling it. The process struck me as old-fashioned and a bit boring until I tried it. For so little effort, you reap really great results—a moist, flavorful piece of fish every time.

In principle, broiling is a versatile cross between grilling and roasting, because you apply extreme heat for one aspect of the cooking process and then use the ambient temperature of the oven (or toaster oven) to cook the fish completely. High broiler heat can be used in combination with other techniques to start seafood dishes, finish them, or cook them in their entirety.

Start cooking fish in a skillet on the stovetop and then slide the whole pan under the broiler in the oven. This is particularly useful when cooking fish with other ingredients, as the flavors of the fish meld with the other ingredients in the pan. When you place the skillet under the broiler first and let it sit there until you've achieved the char you want for flavor, you can then turn off

the broiler and the fish will roast to completion as the oven cools down.

Oh, and did I mention you can make all kinds of broiled fish in 10 minutes flat in a toaster oven? In fact, a toaster oven works even better than a larger oven broiler because the smaller compartment makes it easier to efficiently manage the overall ambient temperature, and the fish cooks faster.

The broiler should be turned on well before placing seafood under it. As in most recipes, any fillet, steak, or butterflied fish should be placed as close to the broiler unit as possible, never more than 3–4 inches below it. Any lower than that will cause the fish to sweat moisture before the top can get a good char.

The length of time any fish needs to cook under the broiler depends on its thickness. Very thin fillets will require no more than 5–7 minutes to cook through. As a rule of thumb, the total cooking time under the broiler for thicker fillets should be 8–10 minutes per inch of thickness.

Frying

Deep-fried foods are first coated and then submerged in hot fat to cook until the exterior has crisped and turned brown. Oils that have a high smoke point, such as soybean or peanut oil, work best for frying. (Avoid olive oil, which has a lower smoke point.) Batters can range from heavy beer batters to light tempura-style coating, while breading runs the gamut from cornmeal to panko.

When making bread crumbs, it's important not to use the crust of the bread, because it is already browned and will only cook further (or burn) in the fryer. The most popular bread crumb for frying is panko. These Japanese-style crumbs have lots of texture, which I like to tone down a bit by crushing half of the crumbs with my hands before dredging the fish in them.

There are several different methods you can use to apply bread crumbs. The standard French method is a three-step process, in which you first dip the food in flour, and then in egg (sometimes egg and milk), before finally dredging the food in bread crumbs. My favorite method for coating fish is to dip it in a mixture of two parts vinegar to one part water, shake it dry, and then roll it in finely ground cornmeal. Many Southern cooks call for a dip in buttermilk prior to applying a coating of fine flour. Or you can keep it really simple and just roll the food in flour or cornmeal.

The key to getting a crisp crust and a properly cooked interior is to make sure that the coating is dry, which will prevent it from absorbing oil in the cooking process. To accomplish this, items should be breaded immediately prior to frying. All seafood should be fried with the skin off, as the skin can prevent breading from adhering.

Properly fried foods are crisp textured but not greasy to the touch. Use a narrow, deep pan so there is enough oil for the food to be fully submerged. When frying, you want to avoid overcrowding the pan with food or cooking it at too low a temperature, as this is what causes food to become greasy. A deep-fry thermometer, available at any kitchen supply shop or grocery store, is vital to this process, as oil gives little indication of its temperature the way water does. I think seafood is best deep-fried between 350°F and 375°F.

Knowing when fried foods are done requires a bit of practice, although it is not complicated. When frying seafood, generally you are cooking small pieces, and once the crust has turned golden brown and crisp, and the vigorous bubbling has subsided, the seafood is usually done. You can always test a piece as you go to get a sense of timing.

NOTE *Basically all types of seafood are well suited to deep frying.*

Grilling

Grilling is one of the best ways to cook seafood. When spring heralds the return of grilling season, I use my trusted 20-year-old Weber® grill almost daily to tap into the perfect union of seafood and live fire. Cooking over charcoal or gas flatters almost all types of seafood by imparting to the fish a smoky charm and slightly bitter char.

Seafood rarely benefits from prolonged application of high heat, so when it comes to grilling seafood, a combination of direct and indirect heat is best.

To prepare charcoal to grill seafood indirectly, arrange all briquettes on one side of the grill basin and set them alight. Burn the coals down to red embers and add wood chips, if you like. Place seasoned seafood on the grill grate directly above the smoking, hot embers. Once the skin or flesh touching the grates begins to char around the edges, pick up the entire grill grate and rotate it 180° so the seafood sits opposite the hot coals. Cover the grill. From this position, the seafood will cook slowly from all sides while absorbing the smoky notes of the live fire.

You don't need to flip seafood, so the chances of a delicate fillet breaking apart or sticking to the grill grate are greatly reduced. But you do still need to lift the fish off the grill. It's best to keep that fact in mind as you are placing it on the grate. Positioning a fillet or whole fish, head-to-tail, parallel to the grate lets you easily slide a fish spatula under it and lift it off the grill.

To grill seafood on a gas grill, preheat all burners to the heat level called for in the recipe. Place the seafood (skin side down if you are leaving the skin on) on one side of the grate, directly over the heat. When the skin or flesh touching the grate begins to char around the edges, turn off the burner directly under the food, but leave the other burner on; cover the grill and let the seafood cook through. As with a charcoal grill, cooking times will vary based on the thickness of the seafood.

Cooking time will vary between 3 minutes for thin fillets and 45 minutes for larger, whole fish, but the rule of thumb is 8 minutes of cooking time for every inch of thickness. Grilled fish is cooked when the flesh flakes under gentle pressure from your thumb.

Categorically, when choosing seafood for the grill it is best to go with varieties that have a higher fat content. Lean seafood such as flounder can take on a slightly tinny flavor when grilled, and its delicate texture can be a problem when maneuvering the fish on the grill.

Most seafood destined for the grill can—and I argue *should*—be salted or brined ahead of time. Given the delicate nature of seafood and its fragile muscular structures, pre-seasoning flavors seafood more evenly, as salt from the brine passes through osmosis into the cells of the seafood. The salt strengthens the cell walls, and thus less moisture is lost during the cooking process. Brining also slightly stiffens the fragile flesh, giving it a bit more structural integrity during the grilling process.

Poaching

This low-heat method of cooking seafood lets a cook's imagination run a little wild. You can add ingredients to the poaching liquid that are not usually found in seafood dishes, such as red wine, almond milk, apples, and pistachios (to name just a few), and that provide a dash of creative flair without necessarily complicating either the process or the character of the dish. Not only do you end up with a moist, flavorful piece of fish, but the poaching liquid becomes the basis of a rich, easy-to-make sauce. When poached seafood is served over slices of toasted bread, the contrast of the crunchy, slightly charred bread and the delicate sauce makes for inspired eating.

Both delicate seafood (like squid and halibut) and more robustly flavored varieties (like salmon and mackerel), including all forms of fish (whether it is whole, a fillet, or a steak), benefit from poaching. As a general rule of thumb, seafood is poached at a rate of 8–10 minutes per inch of thickness.

Poaching is a very simple method, in which you maintain the temperature of a flavored liquid at around 170°F, while the seafood sits in it, to gently cook. There are two ways to poach seafood. With **shallow poaching**, known as *cuisson* in French cooking, seafood is partially submerged in a gently flavored broth known as a cuisson, which is then reduced and used as sauce. The seafood can be kept warm at a very low temperature in the oven while you finish the sauce. Shallow poached seafood is not a piping-hot prospect, so it benefits from being served alongside other components that maintain a lot of heat, such as risotto, pilaf, or lentil stew. **Deep poaching**, on the other hand, requires seafood to be fully submerged in a very flavorful liquid to cook. An accompanying sauce is typically made separately, although the poaching liquid can be strained and saved to flavor soups and stews. Deep-poached seafood is a great way to prepare a dish for serving cold or at room temperature, especially if it is chilled in the broth to fully develop the flavor before serving.

While the liquid for shallow poaching should be lightly seasoned with salt, since it will be reduced, deep poaching calls for an aggressively seasoned liquid. No matter which poaching style you use, lightly season the seafood for at least 5 minutes before cooking to firm the fillets. Wine is typically used in poaching liquids, but if you don't want to use it, you can use just water for poaching seafood. However, the liquid should have a bit of acid in the mix, so add a splash of lemon or orange juice, as well as a 2-inch piece of zest.

As the right temperature is key to this technique, it's best to use a digital thermometer, perched on the side of the pan, to make sure it's not too hot. But if you don't have a digital thermometer on hand, you'll know the poaching liquid has hit about 170°F when it is just barely simmering.

When removing fish from poaching liquid, use a slotted spatula that both supports the flaky, cooked fillet and allows the liquid to drain back into the pan to be saved or reduced. Though it is not customary to serve poached seafood with the skin on, it adds complexity and richness to the poaching liquid in the end, especially when using the shallow poaching method. The skin can be easily removed after cooking.

Roasting

Roasting fish affords cooks the luxury of time: Time to prep the rest of the meal. Time to sit with a glass of wine and chat about the day's events with your spouse, while also feeling confident that the fish roasting in the oven will come out perfectly—neither undercooked nor overcooked.

Roasting is a dry-heat method of cooking that typically takes place inside an oven, although it can be done over a spit. The term *roasting* has evolved to describe the process of using an oven to cook food that already has a relatively firm structure, like red meat, fish, and root vegetables. The goal of roasting raw products like those is to soften their texture. *Baking* is the term used to describe the cooking process for ingredients, like batter or dough, that lack structure and require dry heat to make them firm up into cake or bread.

Several roasting methods can be used to cook seafood, such as slow roasting fillets at low temperatures, using very high heat to roast whole fish, or employing a hybrid technique in which you start the dish atop the stove in a pan or on the grill and finish it in the oven. When you are cooking at home, slow roasting is the best method for preserving the succulence and texture that is so admired in pristine seafood. The key to slow roasting is maintaining an even, constant temperature. To me, slow roasting means cooking at 300°F or less; I prefer going as low as 275°F. The gentle heat gives the cooked fish a delicate texture, full of natural juices. Of course, this technique dictates that it takes longer for the seafood to go from raw to cooked, but by the same principle, it also takes more time to go from cooked perfectly to overcooked.

Slow roasting is applicable to all sorts of fish fillets, from softly flaked flounder to the perennial favorite: salmon. Slow roasting yields custard-like halibut, tender tilapia, and succulent sea bass.

To prepare fillets for slow roasting, simply season them with salt and a drizzle of olive oil or pat of butter, and arrange them skin side down (if you are cooking the fish skin on), in a pan that is big enough to accommodate the portions without crowding them—a good amount of space between each of them will ensure even cooking. If the portions have a thin end, fold them under to make the thickness of the fillets as uniform as possible.

My general guideline is 20 minutes of slow roasting time per inch of thickness. If your fish is ½ inch or ¾ inch thick, check it after 10 and 15 minutes, respectively. This method, like broiling, is a perfect technique to pull off in a toaster oven. The smaller space gives home cooks better control of the ambient temperature so the fillets roast evenly. The fish is done when it flakes apart under the gentle pressure of your thumb. The color of the fish does not change drastically as it cooks, but be confident that if it flakes, it is done. During the last few minutes of cooking, it is a good idea to set the serving plates in the oven to warm. Slow roasting never gets the fish really hot, so warming the plates is key to keeping the fillets from cooling too quickly. If you cooked the fillet with the skin on, you can remove it by simply sliding a fish spatula between the flesh and the skin before transferring the fillet to a plate for serving. The texture of slow-roasted fish is soft because of the retained moisture, so pair the fish with something crunchy—an herb salad, a raw cucumber relish, or a garden-fresh pico de gallo—for a delicious, texturally interesting meal.

When roasting whole fish, I prefer to use both higher heat (350°F–375°F), to sear the skin and give it a bit of textural contrast, and a bed of partially cooked vegetables, as a makeshift rack, to elevate the fish and allow heat to circulate around the whole portion. The skin of the whole fish is scored on both sides and stuffed with herbs and citrus slices, and then placed on the bed of vegetables to roast at a rate of 10 minutes for every inch of thickness. The best way to check if the whole roasted fish is done is to gently wiggle a knife into the flesh at the backbone. Lever the knife to give you a peek at the flesh and check that it is an even color throughout. Another method used to check for doneness in professional kitchens is to stick a toothpick into the flesh and push it all the way down to the spine. Hold it there for a few seconds, and then pull it out. Immediately place the toothpick under your lower lip. If it feels hot, the fish is done.

While I don't believe it's appropriate to deeply caramelize fish, a slight singe to the flesh or skin can be quite pleasant, especially if it is a fatty fish. Cooking a fillet skin-side down in a super-hot pan and then finishing it in the oven at a low temperature will allow the skin to continue to crisp while letting the fish cook evenly all the way through. Pan roasting works well for many fish, notably those with a rich texture that will retain their moist, luxurious mouthfeel in contrast to the crisp skin. My favorite species for cooking with this method are trout, sablefish, salmon, bluefish, and mackerel.

Sautéing

Sautéing is a quick and easy method for cooking all kinds of fish, from mild, white fillets to orange-fleshed fish, to meaty, dense fish. It also provides an opportunity to make an almost endless number of complementary pan sauces.

If you are drawn to sautéing seafood for any, or all, of these reasons, there are ways to best manage the process. First, turn down the heat. Sautéing a fillet over medium to medium-high heat takes just a few minutes longer than sautéing the fish over screamingly high heat; in fact, it can yield crispier skin and a juicier fillet.

Second, understand that skin-on seafood is prone to curling when it is placed in a medium-hot pan, because the connective tissues just beneath the skin contract, forcing the fillet to arch away from the heat. To prevent this, use a sharp knife to score the skin with shallow slashes, about every inch or so, prior to cooking.

Third, do not overcrowd the pan. Doing so reduces the heat of the pan and results in soggy fish with limp skin. Typically, it works best to cook two portions at a time, or four if the pan is heavy enough to retain heat.

Finally, avoid fiddling with the fish. It's the pan that cooks the fish, not impatient pokes and prods from the cook.

For the best results, place fillets in the pan, skin side down if skin is present, and leave them alone to cook undisturbed for 80–90 percent of the way through the cooking time, which typically takes 5–7 minutes per ½ inch of thickness. To finish cooking, turn off the heat and simply flip the fillets to allow the residual heat of the pan to gently cook through. Oftentimes I will remove the fish once it is almost cooked and make a sauce in the same pan. I then return the fish to the pan with the heat off, uncooked side down, in order to finish cooking it in the sauce.

Leaving the skin on the fillet allows the fat, which is located just under the skin, to melt, which crisps the skin evenly and decreases the chance of the fish sticking to the pan. The good, rendered fats and a lack of fiddling make it easy to turn the fillets so that they can finish cooking for just a minute or two before they are ready to serve.

I recommend employing a luxurious butter-basting technique, known as *poêle*, when sautéing fish. After the portion has been turned, add more butter, garlic, and fresh herbs to the pan. Once the butter has melted, constantly baste the fish with the browned butter solids. The scent of herbs and garlic permeates the flesh, and the resulting dish is very balanced—its richness undercut by the slight bitterness of the browned butter. Plus, you gain a wonderfully textured surface.

When removing sautéed seafood from the pan, use a slotted fish spatula to allow the excess fat to drip off the fish in the pan. Serve sautéed fish skin side up, if the skin is present, and flesh side up, if it is not.

PART THREE

BUTTERS, SAUCES, AND SPICE MIXES

BUTTERS

These combinations of butters are easy to make, and even better if they are made ahead of time, and so when dinner is served, all you have to do is place a pat on top of the cooked fish. Just about any cooking technique applied to any fish can be gracefully enhanced with any of the recipes that follow. I usually have several different variations of flavored butters in my freezer that I keep for up to 3 months. I can pull one out just a half hour before sitting down to the meal.

Anchovy Butter

MAKES ABOUT ½ CUP

6 tablespoons unsalted butter, softened

2 ounces anchovies in oil, minced

½ tablespoon sherry or red wine vinegar

Salt

Pinch cayenne pepper

Combine the butter, anchovies with their oil, and vinegar in a bowl and season with salt and cayenne pepper. Whisk vigorously until thoroughly combined. Shape the butter into a log, wrap it tightly in plastic, and refrigerate until ready to use, up to a week, or freeze for up to 3 months.

Anchovy-Almond Butter

MAKES ABOUT ½ CUP

6 tablespoons unsalted butter, softened

2 ounces anchovies in oil, minced

2 tablespoons slivered almonds, crushed nearly to a paste

1 tablespoon chopped fresh parsley

1 orange, zested and juiced

Salt

Black pepper

Combine the butter, anchovies with their oil, almonds, parsley, and orange zest and 1 tablespoon of the juice in a bowl, and season with salt and pepper. Whisk vigorously until thoroughly combined. Shape the butter into a log, wrap it tightly in plastic, and refrigerate until ready to use, up to a week, or freeze for up to 3 months.

Anchovy-Herb Butter

MAKES ABOUT ½ CUP

6 tablespoons unsalted butter, softened

2 ounces anchovies in oil, minced

1 lemon, zested and juiced

2 tablespoons chopped fresh herbs, such as chervil, chives, or tarragon

1 tablespoon grated Parmesan cheese

Salt

Black pepper

Combine the butter, anchovies with their oil, lemon zest and juice, herbs, and cheese in a bowl and season with salt and pepper. Whisk vigorously until thoroughly combined. Shape the butter into a log, wrap tightly in plastic, and refrigerate until ready to use, up to a week, or freeze for up to 3 months.

Anchovy-Horseradish Butter

MAKES ABOUT ½ CUP

6 tablespoons unsalted butter, softened

2 ounces anchovies in oil, minced

1 tablespoon prepared horseradish

Salt

Black pepper

Combine the butter, anchovies with their oil, and horseradish in a bowl and season with salt and pepper. Whisk vigorously until thoroughly combined. Shape the butter into a log, wrap tightly in plastic, and refrigerate until ready to use, up to a week, or freeze for up to 3 months.

Cilantro-Chile-Lime Butter

MAKES ABOUT ½ CUP

    6 tablespoons butter, softened

    3 tablespoons chopped fresh cilantro

    1 lime, zested and juiced

      Crushed red chile flakes

      Salt

Combine the butter, cilantro, lime juice and zest, and chile flakes in a bowl and season with salt. Whisk vigorously until thoroughly combined. Shape the butter into a log, wrap it tightly in plastic, and refrigerate until ready to use, up to a week, or freeze for up to 3 months.

Fennel Butter

MAKES ABOUT ½ CUP

    1 tablespoon fennel seeds, crushed

    6 tablespoons butter, softened, divided

    1 orange, zested

  1–2 teaspoons Pernod or Herbsaint (optional)

      Salt

      Crushed red chile flakes

In a small sauté pan over low heat, toast the fennel seeds in 2 tablespoons of the butter until they are highly aromatic. Let the mixture cool. In a bowl, combine the remaining 4 tablespoons of butter, orange zest and Pernod, if using. Season with salt and a pinch of chile flakes, and whisk vigorously. Shape the butter into a log, wrap it tightly in plastic, and refrigerate until ready to use, up to a week, or freeze for up to 3 months.

Garlic-Herb Butter

MAKES ABOUT ½ CUP

    6 tablespoons butter, softened

    2 garlic cloves, finely minced

    2 tablespoons chopped fresh herbs, such as chervil, chives, parsley, or tarragon

      Crushed red chile flakes

      Salt

Combine the butter, garlic, and herbs in a bowl and season with chile flakes and salt. Whisk vigorously until thoroughly combined. Shape the butter into a log, wrap it tightly in plastic, and refrigerate until ready to use, up to a week, or freeze for up to 3 months.

Horseradish Butter

MAKES ABOUT ½ CUP

    6 tablespoons butter, softened

    3 tablespoons prepared horseradish

    3 tablespoons chopped fresh herbs, such as chervil, chives, parsley, or tarragon

    1 lemon, zested and juiced

      Salt

Combine the butter, horseradish, herbs, and lemon juice and zest in a bowl and season with salt. Whisk vigorously until thoroughly combined. Shape the butter into a log, wrap it tightly in plastic, and refrigerate until ready to use, up to a week, or freeze for up to 3 months.

Lime-Dill Butter

MAKES ABOUT ½ CUP

> 6 tablespoons butter, softened
>
> 1 lime, zested and juiced
>
> 3 tablespoons chopped fresh dill
>
> Salt
>
> Black pepper

In a bowl, combine the butter, lime zest and juice, and dill, season with salt and pepper and whisk vigorously. Shape the butter into a log, wrap it tightly in plastic, and refrigerate until ready to use, up to a week, or freeze for up to 3 months.

Lime-Oregano Butter

MAKES ABOUT ½ CUP

> 6 tablespoons butter, softened
>
> 1 lime, zested and juiced
>
> 1½ tablespoons chopped fresh oregano (or 1 teaspoon dried oregano first soaked in the lime juice for 15 minutes)
>
> Salt
>
> Pinch cayenne pepper

Combine the butter, lime juice and zest, and oregano in a bowl and season with salt and cayenne pepper. Whisk vigorously until thoroughly combined. Shape the butter into a log, wrap it tightly in plastic, and refrigerate until ready to use, up to a week, or freeze for up to 3 months.

Meyer Lemon-Pepper Butter

MAKES ABOUT ½ CUP

> 6 tablespoons butter, softened
>
> 2 Meyer lemons, zested
>
> ½ teaspoon ground allspice
>
> Salt
>
> Black pepper

In a bowl, combine the butter, lemon zest, and allspice, season with salt and a generous amount of pepper, and whisk vigorously. Shape the butter into a log, wrap it tightly in plastic, and refrigerate until ready to use, up to a week, or freeze for up to 3 months.

Pine Nut Butter

MAKES ABOUT ½ CUP

> 2 tablespoons pine nuts, chopped
>
> 6 tablespoons butter, softened, divided
>
> 1 pinch ground sage
>
> 1 orange, zested
>
> Salt
>
> Black pepper

In a small sauté pan over low heat, toast the pine nuts in 2 tablespoons of the butter until they are golden brown. Turn off the heat, add the sage, and let the mixture cool. In a bowl, whisk the toasted pine nuts together with the remaining 4 tablespoons of butter and orange zest, and season with salt and pepper. Shape the butter into a log, wrap it tightly in plastic, and refrigerate until ready to use, up to a week, or freeze for up to 3 months.

Preserved Lemon-Mint Butter

MAKES ABOUT ½ CUP

    1 preserved lemon

    6 tablespoons butter, softened

    1 tablespoon chopped fresh mint

    1 shallot, finely diced

Prepare the preserved lemon by separating the inside of the lemon from the peel. Discard the bitter, white pith, but reserve ½ tablespoon of pulp. Mince the peel as finely as possible and combine it with the butter, pulp, mint, and shallot in a bowl. Whisk vigorously until thoroughly combined. Shape the butter into a log, wrap it tightly in plastic, and refrigerate until ready to use, up to a week, or freeze for up to 3 months.

Smoked Dulse Butter

MAKES ABOUT ½ CUP

    2 tablespoons smoked dulse flakes

    6 tablespoons butter, softened

    1 shallot, finely diced

    Worcestershire sauce

    Salt

In a small sauté pan gently toast the dulse until fragrant. Combine the dulse with the butter, shallot, and a dash of Worcestershire sauce in a bowl, and season with salt. Whisk vigorously until thoroughly combined. Shape the butter into a log, wrap it tightly in plastic, and refrigerate until ready to use, up to a week, or freeze for up to 3 months.

Sorrel Butter

MAKES ABOUT ½ CUP

    6 tablespoons butter, softened

    4 tablespoons finely chopped fresh sorrel

    Salt

Combine the butter and sorrel in a bowl and season with salt. Whisk vigorously until thoroughly combined. Shape the butter into a log, wrap it tightly in plastic, and refrigerate until ready to use, up to a week, or freeze for up to 3 months.

Sriracha Butter

MAKES ABOUT ½ CUP

    6 tablespoons unsalted butter, softened

    1½ tablespoons Sriracha sauce

    1 shallot, finely diced

Combine all ingredients and whisk vigorously. Shape the butter into a log, wrap it tightly in plastic, and refrigerate until ready to use, up to a week, or freeze for up to 3 months.

Sundried Tomato-Basil Butter

MAKES ABOUT ½ CUP

        6 tablespoons butter, softened

        4 sundried tomatoes, rehydrated in
           warm water, drained, patted dry, and
           finely chopped

        1 tablespoon finely chopped fresh basil

        Salt

Combine the butter, tomatoes, and basil, and season with salt. Whisk vigorously until thoroughly combined. Shape the butter into a log, wrap it tightly in plastic, and refrigerate until ready to use, up to a week, or freeze for up to 3 months.

Sweet Garlic Butter

MAKES ABOUT ½ CUP

10–15 garlic cloves

        Salt

        6 tablespoons butter, softened

        Cayenne pepper

Place the garlic in a small saucepan and barely cover the cloves with cold water. Bring the water to a simmer, remove the pan from the heat, and drain off the water. Repeat this process two more times, the last time adding salt to the water, and allowing the garlic to simmer for 5 minutes until it is very soft. Drain the pan and let the garlic cool. Mash the garlic with the butter, season with salt and a pinch of cayenne, and combine to make a smooth paste. Shape the butter into a log, wrap it tightly in plastic, and refrigerate until ready to use, up to a week, or freeze for up to 3 months.

SAUCES

In classic French cuisine, it was the sauce that made the fish tolerable (*La sauce fait passer le poisson*), or so the old saying goes. In modern cuisine, it's the fish that's the star of the plate. And with the influences of ethnic and regional cuisines we tend to favor a more ingredient-forward approach that complements the fish rather than the overpowers it. In these pages, you'll see the influences of elegant yet simple California cuisine, the rustic approach to the charismatic ingredients typical of Italian cooking, and the sophisticated and nuanced flavors that characterize sushi. But we will always love our cocktail and tartar sauces because they are delicious. Most of the sauces in this section are useful for any type of seafood regardless of method for preparation. They also work well with other proteins and vegetable dishes.

Basic Aioli

MAKES ABOUT 1 CUP

> 2 garlic cloves, grated
>
> 1 egg yolk
>
> 1 teaspoon sherry vinegar
>
> Salt
>
> 1 cup vegetable oil (or ¾ cup vegetable oil and ¼ cup olive oil for a stronger flavor)

Combine the garlic, egg yolk, vinegar, and salt using either a food processor or a hand whisk, and process into a fine paste. While the machine is running or you are whisking, slowly drizzle in the oil until the mixture is thickened. If it becomes too thick, add a couple of drops of water to thin.

VARIATIONS

- **Extra-Garlicky Aioli.** Add as much garlic as you like, if that's your thing.
- **Sweet Garlicky Aioli.** Replace raw garlic with garlic cloves that have simmered in salt water for 5 minutes to give the aioli a much softer flavor.
- **Herb Aioli.** Add 1 tablespoon chopped fresh herbs for every ½ cup aioli to make an herb aioli.
- **Smoky Aioli.** Add 2 teaspoons smoked sweet paprika.

Fake Aioli

This is a quick substitute for the real thing. Once mixed up, it can be used as a replacement for the aioli in any recipe.

MAKES ABOUT 1 CUP

If you don't have time to make aioli from scratch, you can fake it by mixing ½ cup mayonnaise with ½ cup Greek yogurt, a dash of sherry vinegar, and several cloves of grated garlic.

Chunky Almond Oil

MAKES ABOUT ¾ CUP

> ½ cup extra-virgin olive oil
>
> 4 ounces skinless slivered almonds

Combine the oil and almonds in a small pan. Cook over low heat, stirring occasionally, until the almonds have turned golden brown. Allow the mixture to cool to room temperature before using.

Cilantro-Pecan Pesto

MAKES ABOUT 1 CUP

> 2 garlic cloves, grated
>
> 1 bunch cilantro
>
> 1 lime, juiced
>
> Salt
>
> ½ cup vegetable oil
>
> ¼ cup pecans, toasted

Place the garlic, cilantro, lime juice, a pinch of salt, and the oil in a blender and process on high speed until you have a smooth paste. If needed, add more oil to get the mixture to the consistency of pancake batter. With the machine running, add the nuts and process until the pesto thickens. Season again with salt to taste.

Kelp-Walnut Pesto

MAKES ABOUT 1½ CUPS

    1 cup packed fresh or thawed frozen kelp,
        or ½ ounce dried kelp, rehydrated

    1 garlic clove

    ½ cup walnut pieces

    1 tablespoon lemon juice

    ½ cup vegetable oil

    Salt

In the bowl of a food processor, process the kelp and garlic until smooth. Add the walnuts, lemon juice, and oil. Process until blended. Add water, if necessary, to achieve the desired consistency. Season with salt.

Chermoula

This fragrant paste of fresh herbs and spices is found in North African cuisine.

MAKES ABOUT 1½ CUPS

    2 teaspoons smoked sweet paprika

    1 teaspoon ground coriander

    1 teaspoon ground cumin

    1 tablespoon fresh ginger, grated

    ¼ cup parsley leaves

    ¼ cup mint leaves

    ¼ cup cilantro leaves

    1 serrano or jalapeño pepper, seeded
        and chopped

    1 cup extra-virgin olive oil

    1 lemon, juiced

    Salt

Toast the paprika, coriander, and cumin in a dry sauté pan over medium heat until fragrant. Transfer the mixture to a food processor and add the ginger, parsley, mint, cilantro, chile pepper, olive oil, and lemon juice, and season with salt. Pulse the machine until the ingredients form a slightly chunky paste. Add more olive oil, if needed, if it is too thick.

Chimichurri

This garlicky herb and chile sauce is from Argentina.

MAKES ABOUT 1 CUP

    ½ cup parsley, chopped

    ½ cup cilantro, chopped

    2 shallots, finely diced

    1 jalapeño chile pepper, seeded and
        very finely diced

    1 Fresno chile pepper, seeded and
        very finely diced

    2 garlic cloves, grated

    3 tablespoons red wine vinegar

    Salt

    ½ cup extra-virgin olive oil

Combine the parsley, cilantro, shallots, chile peppers, garlic, vinegar, and a pinch of salt in a bowl and let the mixture sit for 20 minutes. Add the oil, mix well, and serve at room temperature.

Cocktail Sauce

MAKES ABOUT ¾ CUP

    ½ cup chili sauce

    1 tablespoon prepared horseradish

    2 teaspoons Worcestershire sauce

    2 teaspoons vinegar-based hot sauce,
        such as Crystal® brand

    1 tablespoon brandy

Whisk all the ingredients together in a bowl and serve chilled. Add extra brandy, if desired.

New Orleans Cocktail Sauce

This spicy sauce can be used anywhere you would use traditional cocktail sauce.

MAKES ABOUT 1 CUP

  ¾ cup extra-virgin olive oil

  2 tablespoons prepared horseradish

  1 lemon, juiced

  1 tablespoon or more of Crystal
    or Tabasco® hot sauce

Whisk all ingredients together. Serve at room temperature.

Crispy Mint and Caper Sauce

MAKES ABOUT 1¼ CUPS

  ¾ cup extra-virgin olive oil

  2 tablespoons capers, drained and
    pressed dry

  1 bunch fresh mint, leaves picked

  5 garlic cloves, sliced

  8 dried piri piri or Calabrian chiles (or
    1 tablespoon crushed red chile flakes)

Heat the oil in a small sauté pan over medium heat. Add the capers and cook until they begin to crisp, 5–7 minutes. Add the remaining ingredients to the pan and cook until the mint is crisp and the garlic slices are golden brown, about 5 minutes. Remove the pan from the heat and allow the sauce to cool; serve it at room temperature.

Dill Crème Fraîche

MAKES ABOUT 1 CUP

  ¾ cup crème fraîche or sour cream

  4 tablespoons fresh dill, chopped

    Salt

  1 lemon, juiced

Whisk together all the ingredients and let the mixture rest for at least 1 hour before serving it at room temperature.

Garlic-Parsley Oil

MAKES ABOUT 1¼ CUPS

   ¾ cup extra-virgin olive oil

10–15 garlic cloves, grated

   ½ cup fresh parsley, chopped

     Salt

In a small saucepan over low heat, gently warm the oil and cook the garlic until it is softened and just beginning to smell sweet, 7–10 minutes. Add the parsley and salt, and serve hot or at room temperature.

Green Goddess Dressing

MAKES ABOUT 1½ CUPS

1 cup Mayonnaise (page 29, or store-bought) or Greek yogurt

1 (2-ounce) tin anchovies in oil

1 bunch watercress, thick stems trimmed

1 bunch fresh tarragon, leaves picked

½ bunch parsley, leaves picked

1 lemon, juiced

Salt

Combine the anchovies and their oil with the watercress, tarragon, parsley, and lemon juice in a food processor and purée until the mixture is mostly smooth. Add the Mayonnaise or yogurt and pulse to combine. Season with salt to taste.

Gremolata

MAKES ABOUT ½ CUP

½ bunch parsley

2 lemons, zested

1 garlic clove

Salt

Ground mace

4 tablespoons extra-virgin olive oil

Chop together the parsley, lemon zest, garlic, and a pinch of salt until finely minced. Transfer the mixture to a bowl and stir in a pinch of mace and all of the oil and season with salt to taste. Serve at room temperature within a day.

Lemon-Chile-Soy Sauce

MAKES ABOUT ½ CUP

1 lemon, juiced

1 jalapeño or Serrano chile pepper, finely diced

1 shallot, finely diced

3 tablespoons soy sauce

3–4 scallions, thinly sliced on a bias

1 tablespoon balsamic vinegar or aji-mirin (sweet wine vinegar)

Combine the lemon juice with the pepper and shallot and let the mixture rest for 10 minutes. Add the remaining ingredients and serve the sauce at room temperature.

Mediterranean Yogurt Sauce

MAKES ¾ CUP

½ cup Labneh or Greek yogurt

¼ cup extra-virgin olive oil

Salt

1 pinch cayenne pepper

Whisk all the ingredients together, whipping it to add volume and give the sauce a silken texture. Bring it to room temperature just prior to serving.

Marinara Sauce

MAKES ABOUT 3 CUPS

    6 tablespoons extra-virgin olive oil

    4 garlic cloves, grated

    1 small onion, finely diced

    1 teaspoon dried oregano

    1 cup red or white wine

    1 (6-ounce) can tomato paste

    2 (14.5-ounce) cans fire-roasted diced tomatoes

    Salt

    Crushed red chile flakes (optional)

In a large saucepan over medium-low heat, warm the oil. Add the garlic and onion and cook until soft, about 5 minutes. Add the oregano and cook for 30 seconds. Add the wine, tomato paste, and diced tomatoes and season with salt. Add the chile flakes, if you are using them. Stir all the ingredients together and let the mixture simmer in the pan with the cover on, stirring every few minutes, for 30–40 minutes over medium-low heat.

Mayonnaise

MAKES 1½ CUPS

    2 egg yolks

    ½ teaspoon salt

    1 teaspoon dry mustard powder

    1 teaspoon sherry vinegar

    1¼ cups vegetable oil

    ¼ cup olive oil

Whisk together the egg yolks, salt, mustard, and vinegar. While whisking constantly, drizzle in the oils until the mixture has thickened. Mayonnaise can also be made quickly in a food processor.

Orange-Pistachio Piccata

MAKES ABOUT ½ CUP

    1 cup shelled raw pistachios

    2 tablespoons extra-virgin olive oil

    1 garlic clove, grated

    1 orange, zested

    Salt

In a dry sauté pan over medium heat, toast the pistachios until hot all the way through. Working quickly, roughly chop the pistachios (you want some to be powdery but others to be in larger chunks). While the nuts are still hot, stir them into the olive oil, garlic, and orange zest and season with a pinch of salt. Serve at room temperature. Do not refrigerate, as it will make the pistachios soggy.

Pickled Chiles

MAKES ABOUT ¾ CUP

    ¾ cup cider vinegar

    1 tablespoon brown sugar

    Salt

    1 stalk rosemary

    1 bay leaf

    Ground nutmeg

    3–4 hot chile peppers, such as Fresno, jalapeño, or serrano, sliced into (¼-inch) thick rings

In a small saucepan, over medium-high heat, warm the vinegar, brown sugar, a generous pinch of salt, rosemary, bay leaf, and a pinch of nutmeg and stir until the sugar is dissolved. Add the peppers and bring the mixture to a simmer. Remove the pan from the heat and let the mixture cool to room temperature. Let it sit for at least 2 hours and up to 2 days before serving at room temperature.

Pico de Gallo

MAKES ABOUT 1½ CUPS

1 small onion, finely diced

1–2 hot chile peppers, such as Fresno,
    jalapeño, or serrano, grated

1 lime, juiced

Salt

4 ripe plum tomatoes, diced

¼ cup chopped fresh cilantro

Combine the onion, peppers, lime juice, and salt
in a bowl, and let the mixture rest for 10 minutes.
Add the tomatoes and cilantro to the other
ingredients in the bowl and toss to combine.

Pine Nut Agrodolce

MAKES ABOUT ½ CUP

4 tablespoons extra-virgin olive oil

¼ cup pine nuts

2 garlic cloves, grated

2 tablespoons sherry vinegar

1 orange, juiced

2 tablespoons chopped herbs, such
    as parsley and tarragon

Salt

In a sauté pan over medium heat, cook the olive
oil and pine nuts until the nuts are golden brown.
Add the garlic and cook for 30 seconds. Add the
vinegar and orange juice and reduce the mixture
by two-thirds. Remove the pan from the heat,
stir in the herbs, and season with salt.

Pine Nut Piccata

MAKES ABOUT 1 CUP

¾ cup pine nuts

1 garlic clove, grated

4 tablespoons extra-virgin olive oil

1 lemon, zested

Salt

2 tablespoons chopped fresh herbs,
    such as parsley or tarragon

In a dry sauté pan over medium heat, toast the
pine nuts until they turn golden brown. While
still hot, roughly crush one-third of the nuts
with the broad side of a knife. Place all the pine
nuts into a bowl with the garlic, oil, and zest.
Stir the mixture to combine and let it cool to
room temperature before seasoning with salt,
and adding the herbs.

Modern Remoulade

MAKES ABOUT 1¼ CUPS

1 (7-ounce) container Greek yogurt

1 tablespoon Creole or whole grain mustard

1 garlic clove, grated

½ tablespoon Worcestershire sauce

4 scallions, thinly sliced

1 shallot, finely diced

1 celery stalk, finely diced

1 tablespoon chopped fresh parsley

Salt

Black pepper

In a medium bowl, whisk together all the
ingredients and let the mixture rest for 1 hour
before serving.

Traditional Remoulade Sauce

MAKES ABOUT ½ CUP

    4 tablespoons Mayonnaise (page 29, or
      store-bought)

    2 tablespoons gherkins or cornichons,
      finely diced

    1 shallot, finely diced

    2 tablespoons chopped fresh parsley

    1 tablespoon chopped fresh tarragon

    4 anchovy fillets, finely minced

Mix all the ingredients in a bowl and let the
mixture rest for 1 hour before serving.

Louisiana Remoulade

This vibrant version can be used interchangebly
with the traditional remoulade,

MAKES ABOUT 1 CUP

    2 tablespoons red wine vinegar

    1 teaspoon whole grain mustard

    ½ tin (2 ounces) anchovies with their
      oil, chopped

    ½ cup vegetable oil

    1 tablespoon prepared horseradish

    1 tablespoon smoked sweet paprika

    1 garlic clove, grated

    1 tablespoon chopped fresh parsley

    1 tablespoon chopped fresh tarragon

    2 scallions, thinly sliced

Combine the vinegar, mustard, anchovies,
vegetable oil, horseradish, paprika, and garlic in
a bowl, and let the mixture rest overnight in the
refrigerator. An hour or so before serving, stir
in the parsley, tarragon, and scallions. Serve the
remoulade at room temperature.

Romesco

MAKES ABOUT 3 CUPS

    1 red bell pepper, cut in half and
      seeds discarded

    8 plum tomatoes, cut in half lengthwise

    1 large onion, diced

    2 garlic cloves, smashed

    ½ cup almonds, sliced or slivered

    6 tablespoons extra-virgin olive oil, divided

    1 tablespoon smoked sweet paprika

    2 tablespoons sherry vinegar

    Salt

Preheat the broiler to high and place a rack in
the highest position. Toss the pepper, tomatoes,
onion, garlic, and almonds with 2 tablespoons
of the oil. Spread the mixture on a baking tray
and slide the tray under the broiler. Cook until
the pepper and tomato skins have blistered and
charred. Transfer the mixture to a bowl, cover
it with plastic wrap, and let it sit for 5 minutes.
Remove the skin from the pepper and the
tomatoes and discard. Place all the vegetables,
their juices, the paprika, vinegar, and a good
pinch of salt in a food processor. Process
the mixture until only small chunks remain.
With the machine running, slowly drizzle in
the remaining 4 tablespoons of oil until it is
incorporated and the purée is mostly smooth.
Let it sit at least 2 hours at room temperature
before serving.

Salsa Criolla

This is a spicy South American dish of pickled onion.

MAKES ABOUT ½ CUP

> 2 limes, juiced
>
> 1 tablespoon brown sugar
>
> ½ tablespoon kosher salt
>
> 1 tablespoon sherry vinegar
>
> 2 tablespoons extra-virgin olive oil
>
> 1 hot chile pepper, such as Fresno, jalapeño, or serrano, very thinly sliced
>
> 1 large red onion, thinly sliced, rinsed under cold running water, and patted dry

Combine the lime juice, brown sugar, salt, vinegar, olive oil, and chile peppers in a bowl. Stir the mixture to dissolve the sugar and salt. Add the onion and toss to combine. Let the salsa rest at room temperature for at least 30 minutes before serving.

Sicilian Herb Sauce

MAKES ABOUT ¾ CUP

> 2 shallots, diced
>
> 2 garlic cloves, grated
>
> 2 lemons, juiced
>
> 4 sprigs tarragon, leaves picked and chopped
>
> 2 sprigs fresh oregano, leaves picked and chopped, or 1 teaspoon dried oregano
>
> ½ cup chopped parsley leaves
>
> ⅓ cup olive oil
>
> Salt

Use a food processor or mortar and pestle to make a mostly smooth purée of the shallots, garlic, and lemon juice. Add the tarragon, oregano, parsley, and olive oil and process the mixture into a smooth purée. Add a bit of water if needed to achieve the right consistency. Season with salt.

VARIATION

+ Add 1 ounce anchovies, with their oil, to the food processor at the same time as you process the shallot mixture.

Tartar Sauce

MAKES ABOUT 1½ CUPS

> 1 cup Basic Aioli (page 25) or Mayonnaise (page 29, or store-bought)
>
> 1 tablespoon capers, rinsed and finely chopped
>
> 8 gherkins, finely diced
>
> ¼ cup grated Parmesan cheese
>
> 2 teaspoons Dijon mustard

Whisk together all the ingredients in a bowl and let the mixture rest for at least 1 hour before serving.

Teriyaki-Style Sauce

MAKES ABOUT ½ CUP

> ½ cup soy sauce
>
> ¼ cup aji-mirin (sweet wine vinegar)
>
> ¼ cup sugar
>
> 1 tablespoon rice wine vinegar
>
> 1 (1-inch) knob ginger, thinly sliced
>
> ½ lemon

Combine the soy sauce, mirin, sugar, vinegar, and ginger in a small saucepan. Simmer the mixture over low heat and add the lemon, cut side down. Cook the sauce until it reduces by half. Remove the pan from the heat, and discard the lemon and ginger before using.

SPICE MIXES

These potent pairings hail from different culinary cultures, but are all used to season seafood prior to cooking. Due to the short cooking times required for the seafood, these spices don't get the chance to burn like they might if they were rubbed into other proteins like chicken that take longer to cook. As the spices toast, their flavors bloom and perfume the fish.

Blackening Spice Mix

MAKES ABOUT ½ CUP

2 tablespoons kosher salt

1½ tablespoons smoked sweet paprika

1 tablespoon dried oregano

1 tablespoon garlic powder

1 tablespoon onion powder

2 teaspoons mustard powder

1 teaspoon chile powder

1 teaspoon ground allspice

Combine all ingredients.

Five Spice Mix

MAKES ABOUT 3 TABLESPOONS

2 teaspoons ground cinnamon

1 tablespoon fennel seeds, crushed

1 star anise pod, ground

1 tablespoon finely ground black pepper

½ teaspoon ground cloves

Combine all ingredients.

Herbes de Provence Mix

MAKES ABOUT 2 TABLESPOONS

1 teaspoon fennel seeds, crushed

½ teaspoon dried ground mint

½ teaspoon dried ground oregano

½ teaspoon dried ground marjoram

½ teaspoon dried ground thyme

¼ teaspoon dried ground rosemary

¼ teaspoon dried ground lavender

Combine all ingredients.

Jerk Seasoning Mix

MAKES ABOUT ¼ CUP

1 tablespoon ground allspice

1½ teaspoons dried thyme

1½ teaspoons smoked sweet paprika

1 teaspoon kosher salt

1½ teaspoons brown sugar

1 tablespoon black pepper

Pinch cayenne pepper

½ teaspoon ground mace

¼ teaspoon ground cinnamon

¼ teaspoon ground cloves

Combine all ingredients.

VINAIGRETTES AND MARINADES

Just as with the compound butters, a drizzle of vinaigrette over seafood, as soon as it comes straight out of the pan (or off the grill), is a surefire way to turn the pedestrian into something compelling. Vinaigrettes are also perfect partners for cooked seafood, served chilled, and do a marvelous job of reinvigorating the character of leftover cooked fish.

Although vinaigrettes do add richness through the oil, their main contribution is that of a bright, acidic component that enlivens anything it touches. Think back to how often seafood is served with nothing but a lemon wedge. That pairing is such a classic because it works so well. It's really the acid that makes the pairing shine, so think of a vinaigrette as Lemon 2.0. The recipes below are a bit more potent than those for a typical salad dressing, as they are designed for the heartier flavors of seafood.

Vinaigrettes can be made up to a day or two ahead of time, but they are best when made just before using.

Adobo Marinade

This spicy vinegar-based marinade can also be used as a punchy vinaigrette.

MAKES ABOUT 1½ CUPS

    3 garlic cloves, smashed
    1 cup water
    ½ cup sherry vinegar
    1 tablespoon dried oregano
    1 tablespoon smoked sweet paprika
    1 tablespoon kosher salt

Combine all the ingredients and stir to dissolve the salt.

Bay Leaf–Garlic Vinaigrette

MAKES ABOUT ½ CUP

¼ cup extra-virgin olive oil

¼ cup vegetable oil

15 bay leaves

5 garlic cloves, grated

2 tablespoons red or white wine vinegar

Salt

In a small saucepan over very low heat, warm the olive oil, vegetable oil, bay leaves, and garlic until the flavor of the bay leaves fully permeates the oil and the garlic is soft but not brown, about 30 minutes. Add the vinegar and salt and allow the mixture to cool to room temperature. Discard the bay leaves before using.

Charred Rosemary Vinaigrette

MAKES ABOUT ½ CUP

6 stalks fresh rosemary

1 garlic clove, grated

2 tablespoons red wine vinegar

1 tablespoon Dijon mustard

¼ cup extra-virgin olive oil

Salt

Toast the rosemary under a broiler until fragrant and crisp, about 5–7 minutes. Remove the leaves and mash them with the garlic, vinegar, and mustard to make a smooth paste. Whisk in the olive oil and season with salt.

Charred Tomato Vinaigrette

MAKES ABOUT 1–1½ CUPS

6 plum tomatoes, cut in half

4 sprigs thyme, leaves picked

Salt

½ cup extra-virgin olive oil

1½ tablespoons sherry vinegar

1 shallot, finely diced

4 scallions, thinly sliced

Toss the tomatoes with the thyme leaves, salt, and olive oil. Spread the mixture on a baking tray, slide the tray under the broiler, set the temperature to high, and cook until the tomatoes are charred and softened. Remove the tomato skins and discard them. Scrape the tomatoes and olive oil into a bowl, add the vinegar and shallot, and whisk vigorously to mash the tomatoes. Season again with salt, and stir in the scallions. Serve warm or at room temperature.

Cilantro-Yogurt Dressing

MAKES ABOUT ½ CUP

1 lemon, zested and juiced

2 tablespoons extra-virgin olive oil

3 tablespoons Greek yogurt

¼ cup chopped cilantro leaves

Salt

Place all ingredients in a bowl and stir to combine.

Creamy Lemon-Pecan Dressing

MAKES ABOUT ½ CUP

1 lemon, juiced

1 tablespoon Greek yogurt or sour cream

2 tablespoons extra-virgin olive oil

¼ cup pecans, chopped

½ teaspoon ground nutmeg

Salt

Black pepper

Mix the lemon juice, yogurt or sour cream, and olive oil. Whisk vigorously to combine. Fold in the pecans and nutmeg, and season with salt and pepper. Serve at room temperature.

Creamy Lime-Almond Dressing

MAKES ABOUT ½ CUP

3 tablespoons extra-virgin olive oil

2 tablespoons slivered almonds

1 lime, juiced

3 tablespoons Greek yogurt or sour cream

Salt

In a small sauté pan over medium heat, warm the olive oil, add the almonds, and toast them until they are golden brown, 3–5 minutes. Do not drain the almonds. Combine the almonds with the oil and lime juice in a bowl and let the mixture cool. Add the Greek yogurt and salt to the bowl and whisk to combine.

Lemon-Chile-Mint Dressing

MAKES ABOUT ½ CUP

1 Serrano chile pepper, thinly sliced

1 lemon, zested and juiced

4 tablespoons vegetable oil

Salt

5 sprigs fresh mint, leaves picked, thinly sliced

2 tablespoons chopped fresh parsley

Soak the chile pepper in the lemon juice, oil, and salt for 10 minutes. Add the mint and parsley to the dressing just before using.

Mint-Mustard Vinaigrette

MAKES ABOUT ½ CUP

2 tablespoons red or white wine vinegar

1 tablespoon Dijon mustard

½ tablespoon maple syrup or honey

¼ cup vegetable oil

1 shallot, finely diced

Salt

¼ cup fresh mint leaves, finely minced

Combine all the ingredients except the mint, and whisk until creamy. Add the mint just before serving.

Orange-Coriander Vinaigrette

MAKES ABOUT ½ CUP

    4 tablespoons extra-virgin olive oil

    1 orange, zested and juiced

    1 teaspoon ground coriander

    2 teaspoons ground fennel seeds

    Salt

Combine all the ingredients and whisk vigorously. Let the mixture rest for 10 minutes before using.

Orange-Walnut Vinaigrette

MAKES ABOUT ½ CUP

    2 tablespoons walnut oil

    ¼ cup vegetable oil

    1 orange, zested and juiced

    2 tablespoons sherry vinegar

    1 shallot, finely diced

    Salt

Combine all the ingredients and whisk vigorously.

Peruvian Marinade

MAKES ABOUT ½ CUP

    2 limes, juiced

    2 tablespoons white wine vinegar

    1 tablespoon kosher salt

    1 tablespoon sugar

    2 teaspoons extra-virgin olive oil

    1 teaspoon ground cumin

    2 teaspoons smoked sweet paprika

    2 teaspoons crushed red chile flakes

Combine all the ingredients and stir to dissolve the salt and sugar.

Red Wine–Shallot Vinaigrette

MAKES ABOUT ½ CUP

    2 tablespoons red wine vinegar

    1 shallot, finely diced

    6 sprigs thyme, leaves picked and chopped

    1 garlic clove, grated

    4 tablespoons extra-virgin olive oil

    Salt

    Black pepper

Combine all the ingredients and whisk vigorously.

Tarragon-Citrus Vinaigrette

MAKES ABOUT ½ CUP

    2 tablespoons chopped fresh tarragon

    2 tablespoons chopped fresh parsley or chives

    1 garlic clove, grated

    1 lemons or ½ orange, zested and juiced

    ½ tablespoon Pernod or Herbsaint (light rum is also good)

    Salt

    Black pepper

    ¼ cup extra-virgin olive oil

Place all the ingredients in a bowl and stir to combine.

PART FOUR

CHOWDERS, SOUPS, AND STEWS

Soups, stews, and chowders can be made from any form of seafood. They run the gamut from bright, refreshing quick simmers of summer-ripe ingredients to deeply satisfying, rich, wintertime braises that include the bold flavors of bacon, cream, and hearty spices such as cinnamon, allspice, and cloves.

The first (and basically only) rule for making seafood soups, stews, and chowders is this: start with great-quality ingredients. As mentioned, shopping for quality seafood is the most important step to ensuring the success of any recipe in this book.

One of the most appealing aspects of making any of the following recipes is that in seafood cookery one rarely has the opportunity to engage the delightful, slow, low-heat methods used to develop the rich flavors in meat-based braises and stews. It is a great skill and point of pride to coax a wide range of flavors into a complex and unified whole.

Most classic varieties of seafood soups, stews, and chowders come not from chefs but from fishermen. Often they are updated versions of simple, one-pot dishes that fishermen have cooked shore-side over the ages using whatever seafood they were able to catch. This was the food for the laborer.

Over time, these soups, stews, and chowders have found their way onto more elegant tables. Not only has our modern cookery evolved from these traditions and practices, so has our language. *Chaudière*, the French word for "stew pot," is thought to be the origin for the name of a dish we know well: chowder.

Traditionally recipes for soups, stews, and chowders have been built upon a base of plain water, but today we animate them with stocks, enrich them with cream, and spike them with brandy. While these adaptations may add flair and character, all flavors are gently guided into balance and unity in the process.

In the culinary world, great pride is built upon the execution of these classic dishes, although few people can agree on exactly which ingredients *should* be in a given preparation. For example, there is heated debate regarding which species *must* be included in Bouillabaisse, a dish that hails from the Mediterranean coast of France, in order for it to be a true version of the classic preparation. Given the profound regionalism of the debate, I do not claim any authority on such matters, so consequently the recipe for Bouillabaisse in this section is just a suggested version.

What makes recipes for stews, soups, and chowders really fun is that once you have practiced and mastered the art of simmering flavors into a harmonious concert, you will have the knowledge and skill to then choose your own adventure. Borrow a component from one dish to include in another, or make up an entirely new dish altogether. All stews, soups, and chowders develop an added depth of flavor when refrigerated overnight and gently reheated before serving.

As to the questions of which and how many varieties of seafood to use in any soup, stew, or chowder, my answer is: tell the fishmonger to give you "what's best today."

Buttermilk Salmon Chowder

SERVES 4–6

3 tablespoons butter

1 fennel bulb, finely diced

3 carrots, finely diced

1 onion, finely diced

1 celery stalk, finely diced

1 bay leaf

3 cups fish stock or water

1 (12-ounce) can of pink or red salmon, drained

1 cup buttermilk

1 cup Greek yogurt

2 tablespoons chopped fresh tarragon

Salt

Black pepper

Heat the butter in a large saucepan over medium-high heat. Add the fennel, carrots, onion, celery, and bay leaf. Cook until the vegetables have wilted but have not browned, about 5 minutes. Add the stock or water and simmer until the vegetables are tender. Reduce the heat to low, add the salmon, and cook until the mixture is heated through. Turn off the heat and stir in the buttermilk, yogurt, and tarragon, and season with salt. Discard the bay leaf and let the chowder rest for 30 minutes before reheating gently to serve. Garnish with pepper if desired.

Corn and Fish Chowder

SERVES 4–6

1½ pounds meaty dense fish (see page 65) skin off, cut into ½-inch pieces

Salt

6 ears of corn, shucked, kernels shaved from the cobs and cobs scraped with knife, reserved, and broken into thirds

4 tablespoons butter

1 onion, diced

Season the fish with salt and let it rest until needed. Place the cobs into a pot with 4–5 cups water and simmer for 30 minutes. Strain the stock, reserving the liquid and discarding the cobs. Use a blender to purée two-thirds of the corn kernels with 3 cups of the corn stock. Heat the butter in a large saucepan over medium heat, add the onion, and cook until soft but not browned, about 5 minutes. Add the puréed corn liquid, remaining kernels, and stock and bring to a boil. Reduce the heat to gently simmer. Cook it for 15 minutes, then add the fish. Gently simmer the mixture until the fish is cooked through. Break the fish into flakes, season with salt, and serve.

Conch Chowder

SERVES 4–6

 1 pound conch meat, finely chopped
  or ground

 2 cups white wine

 ¼ pound bacon, chopped

 1 tablespoon extra-virgin olive oil

 1 onion, finely diced

 3 celery stalks, finely diced

 1 red bell pepper, finely diced

 1 jalapeño pepper, thinly sliced

 ½ pound small red potatoes, cut in quarters

 1 (28-ounce) can crushed San Marzano
  tomatoes

 2 bay leaves

  Crushed red chile flakes

  Salt

In a medium saucepan over medium heat, simmer the conch meat in the white wine until the alcohol smell dissipates. Strain, reserving both liquid and meat. In a large saucepan over medium heat, cook the bacon in the olive oil until it is crisp. Add the onion, celery, bell pepper, and jalapeño. Cook until softened, about 5 minutes. Add the potatoes and tomatoes. Simmer the mixture over medium heat for 10 minutes. Add the reserved conch liquid and meat, 1 cup of water, the bay leaves, and a generous pinch of chile flakes, and season with salt. Reduce the heat to low and simmer until the potatoes are cooked through. Cool to room temperature and refrigerate the chowder overnight before reheating.

Salt Fish Chowder

SERVES 4–6

 1½ pounds flaky white fish (see page 64), skin
  off, cut into ½-inch pieces

 3 tablespoons kosher salt

 1 quart fish or vegetable stock

 2 tablespoons extra-virgin olive oil

 2 celery stalks, diced

 1 onion, diced

 4 tablespoons tomato paste

 1 star anise pod

 1 (1-inch) knob ginger, sliced

 1 pound red potatoes, diced

 2 (14-ounce) cans fire-roasted tomatoes

 ½ cup diced green olives

Salt the fish with the kosher salt and let it rest in the refrigerator overnight. Rinse the salt off the fish and soak it for 2 hours in cold water. In a saucepan over low heat, bring the stock to 170°F and slide the fish into the liquid. Poach the fish for 4–6 minutes per ½ inch of thickness. Remove the fish, flake it into large chunks, and reserve the poaching broth. Heat the olive oil in a large pot over medium-high heat. Add the celery and onion and cook until softened, about 5 minutes. Add the tomato paste, star anise, and ginger. Cook the mixture until the tomato paste changes to a deep rusty color. Add the potatoes, tomatoes, and reserved broth, and stir to combine. Simmer until the potatoes are soft. Remove the star anise and ginger. Add the pieces of cooked fish and olives, season with salt, and serve.

Manhattan (Long Island) Clam Chowder

MAKES 4–6 SERVINGS

24 large hard-shell clams (topneck or chowder size), scrubbed clean

½ pound salt pork or bacon, diced

2 cups diced celery

2 onions, diced

2 (14-ounce) cans fire-roasted tomatoes

Salt

Black pepper

Place the clams in a large pan with 3 cups of water. Cover the pan and cook over high heat until the clams open. Remove the clams from the pan with a slotted spoon. Remove the clams from their shells and cut the meat into ½-inch pieces. Strain the clam broth through a fine mesh strainer and reserve it. Cook the salt pork in a large pot over medium heat to render the fat, about 5 minutes. When the meat is crisp, add the celery and onions, and cook until the onions are translucent. Add the tomatoes, chopped clams, and reserved clam broth and bring the mixture to a simmer. Season it with salt. Cover the pot and continue to simmer the chowder over very low heat for 4–6 hours, stirring it occasionally. The chowder is best if it is cooled and then reheated prior to serving. Garnish with black pepper if desired.

VARIATION

+ **Spiced Manhattan Clam Chowder.** When cooking the celery and onions, add 1 cinnamon stick and ½ teaspoon ground mace. Remove the cinnamon stick before serving.

New England Clam Chowder

SERVES 4–6

24 large hard-shell clams (topneck or chowder size), scrubbed clean

¼ pound bacon or salt pork, diced

1 onion, diced

1 bay leaf

1 sprig fresh thyme

1 tablespoon butter

¾ pound new potatoes, cut into ½-inch cubes

2 cups light cream or half-and-half

Salt

Black pepper

Oyster crackers, for serving

Place the clams in a large pan with 3 cups of water. Cover the pan and cook over high heat until the clams open. Remove the clams from the pan with a slotted spoon. Remove the meat from the shells and cut it into ½-inch pieces. Strain the clam broth through a fine mesh strainer. Reserve both the clams and the broth. Cook the salt pork in a large pot over medium heat to render the fat, about 5 minutes. When the meat is crisp, add the onion, bay leaf, thyme, and butter. Cook until the onions are translucent, about 5 minutes. Add the potatoes, clams, reserved broth, and enough water to cover. Simmer the mixture until the potatoes are cooked, about 10–12 minutes. Add the cream and simmer for 5 more minutes. Season with pepper, and let it rest for at least 1 hour and optimally overnight before reheating. Serve with oyster crackers.

VARIATION

+ **New England Clam Chowder (Acidic Version).** Just before serving, add 1 tablespoon Worcestershire sauce and 2 tablespoons lemon juice.

Smoked Salmon Chowder

SERVES 4–6

>   12 ounces Hot-Smoked Salmon (page 341)
>
>   2 tablespoons butter
>
>   1 onion, diced
>
>   1 teaspoon ground coriander
>
>   ¾ pound russet or new potatoes, cut into ½-inch cubes
>
>   2 cups light cream or half-and-half
>
>   Salt
>
>   2 tablespoons chopped fresh herbs, such as chives or dill

Place the salmon in a large saucepan with 3 cups cold water and bring to a simmer over low heat. Cook until the salmon is softened and the water has taken on the flavor of the fish, about 10 minutes. Strain, reserving both the broth and the fish. Discard the skin if present. Heat the butter in a large saucepan over medium-high heat. Add the onion and coriander and cook until the onion is soft, about 5 minutes. Add the salmon broth and potatoes and simmer until the potatoes are cooked, about 10–15 minutes. Add the cream and use the back of a spoon to lightly mash some of the potatoes. Turn off the heat and flake the salmon into the mixture. Cover the pan and let it sit for 10 minutes. Season with salt, and garnish with the herbs.

Smoky White Fish and Tomato Chowder

SERVES 4–6

>   1½ pounds flaky fish (see page 64), skin off, cut into ½-inch pieces
>
>   Salt
>
>   4 tablespoons olive oil or butter
>
>   1 onion, diced
>
>   1 fennel bulb, diced
>
>   1 stick cinnamon
>
>   1 tablespoon smoked sweet paprika
>
>   1 (28-ounce) can peeled tomatoes
>
>   ½ pound red potatoes, cubed
>
>   3 cups fish stock or water
>
>   2 tablespoons chopped fresh herbs, such as chives or parsley

Season the fish with salt and let it rest for 15 minutes. Heat the oil or butter in a large pot over medium-high heat. Add the onion and fennel and cook until soft, about 5 minutes. Add the cinnamon and paprika and cook for 1 minute. Add the tomatoes and simmer for 5 minutes. Add the potatoes and stock and simmer until the potatoes are cooked, 10–15 minutes. Remove the cinnamon stick and discard it. Reduce the heat to low, add the fish, cover the pot, and simmer until the fish flakes, about 5–7 minutes. Season with salt, and garnish with the herbs.

Finnan Haddie Chowder

Finnan Haddie is a gently smoked haddock that is a staple of New England cuisine.

MAKES 4–6 SERVINGS

- 1 pound Finnan Haddie (see page 208), or use store-bought
- 2 tablespoons butter
- ¼ pound salt pork, diced
- 1 fennel bulb, diced
- 1 onion, diced
- 1 pound potatoes, diced
- Salt
- 2 cups light cream or half-and-half
- Smoked sweet paprika

Heat the butter and salt pork in a large pot over medium-high heat. Cook until the pork is crisp, about 5–7 minutes. Add the fennel and onion, and cook until the vegetables are soft, about 5 minutes. Add the Finnan Haddie and 3 cups water, cover, and simmer until the fish flakes. Remove the fish, discard the skin if present, flake it into bite-size pieces, and reserve. Add the potatoes to the pot and additional water to cover, if needed to fully submerge. Cook the potatoes until they are soft, about 10–15 minutes, then gently stir in the cream. Turn off the heat, add the reserved fish, and gently stir to incorporate. The flavors improve if allowed to chill overnight in the refrigerator. Reheat gently before serving garnished with paprika.

BLUSHING VARIATION

+ **Blushing Finnan Haddie Chowder.** Add 1 (14-ounce) can of fire-roasted tomatoes along with the potatoes. Reduce the amount of cream used to ½ cup. Follow instructions as above. Garnish with 2 tablespoons of fresh chopped tarragon.

White Fish Chowder

SERVES 4–6

- 1½ pounds flaky white fish (see page 64), skin off, cut into ½-inch pieces
- Salt
- 2 tablespoons butter
- ¼ pound bacon, diced
- 1 fennel bulb, diced
- 1 onion, diced
- ¾ pound potatoes, diced
- 3 cups stock or water
- 2 tablespoons Amontillado or cooking sherry
- 2 cups light cream or half-and-half
- Smoked sweet paprika

Season the fish with salt and let it rest for 15 minutes. Cook the butter and bacon in a large pot over medium-high heat. When the bacon is crisp, add the fennel and onion. Cook until the vegetables are soft, about 5 minutes. Add the potatoes and enough stock to cover the potatoes. Cook until the potatoes are soft, about 10–15 minutes. Add the sherry and white fish pieces to the pot and simmer for 5 minutes. Stir in the cream and gently heat through. Garnish with paprika and serve.

Cioppino

This West Coast seafood stew typically features Dungeness crab and crushed tomatoes.

SERVES 4–6

2 tablespoons olive oil

4 strips bacon, diced

1 onion, diced

2 fennel bulbs, diced

4 garlic cloves, sliced

4 sprigs thyme

2 sprigs fresh oregano or 1 teaspoon dried oregano

1 teaspoon crushed red chile flakes

2 tablespoons tomato paste

1 cup red wine

1 (28-ounce) can crushed tomatoes

3 (8-ounce) bottles clam juice or
   3 cups Basic Fish Stock (page 61)

1 bay leaf

2 Dungeness crabs, cooked and split

Salt

1 pound pounds flaky white fish (see page 64), skin off, cut into ½-inch pieces

1 dozen littleneck clams

1 pound mussels, cleaned and beards removed

1¼ pounds shell-on shrimp

½ cup chopped herbs, such as basil or parsley

Toasted bread rubbed with garlic, for serving

Heat the olive oil and bacon in a large pot over medium heat. Cook the bacon until crisp. Add the onion and fennel to the pan. Cook until the vegetables are translucent, about 5 minutes. Add the garlic, thyme, oregano, and chile flakes and cook for 2 minutes. Stir in the tomato paste and cook until the tomato paste has darkened in color and its aroma has softened, about 5 minutes. Add the wine and simmer until the alcohol smell dissipates. Add the crushed tomatoes, clam juice, and bay leaf and simmer for 30 minutes. Add the crab pieces and season with salt. Reduce the heat to medium-low, cover the pan, and simmer for about 20–25 minutes. Remove the pan from the heat and let the mixture rest at least 2 hours and preferably overnight in the refrigerator.

Return the pot to a simmer. Lightly season the fish with salt and set it aside. Add the clams and mussels to the pan. Cover the pan and cook until the shellfish open. Add the shrimp and fish. Let the mixture simmer gently until the fish and shrimp are just cooked through. Discard any clams and mussels that do not open. Stir in the herbs. Remove the pan from the heat and let it sit, covered, for 10–20 minutes. Serve the soup with toasted bread rubbed with garlic.

Crab Bisque

SERVES 6–8

   2 quarts Shellfish Stock (page 61)
   or Basic Fish Stock (page 61)
   or water

   10 allspice berries

   4 whole cloves

   1 bay leaf

   8 tablespoons butter

   4 carrots, sliced

   2 celery stalks, sliced

   2 onions, chopped

   ½ cup rice

   2 tablespoons tomato paste

   1 teaspoon ground mace

   2 cups white wine

   1 pound crabmeat, picked for cartilage

   ½ cup sour cream or heavy cream

   2 tablespoons Amontillado or
   cooking sherry

Combine the stock, allspice, cloves, and bay leaf in a large pot and bring to a simmer over medium heat. Simmer for 20 minutes. Pour the fortified stock through a fine mesh strainer into a large bowl. Reserve the stock.

Heat the butter in a large pot over medium-high heat. Add the carrots, celery, onions, and rice. Cook, stirring occasionally, until the onions are soft, about 5 minutes. Stir in in the tomato paste and mace. Cook until the tomato paste has darkened in color and its aroma has softened. Add the wine to the pot, bring the mixture to a boil, and cook until the alcohol smell dissipates. Add the reserved stock and season with salt. Reduce the heat to low, and simmer gently until the rice and carrots are fully cooked, about 30 minutes.

Reserve half of the crabmeat for garnish. Add the remaining meat to the stock and remove the pot from heat. Transfer the soup to a blender in batches, blending until the mixture is very smooth and silky, and then strain the soup mixture though a fine mesh strainer, pressing on the solids with the back of a ladle. Discard any solids that do not pass through the strainer. Gently reheat the bisque. Whisk in the sour cream and sherry. Serve immediately garnished with the reserved crabmeat.

Caldo Verde

This traditional Portuguese soup is thick with potatoes and kale. In this version, I substitute kelp for kale to add a nuanced ocean flavor.

SERVES 4–6

   2 tablespoons olive oil, plus more for garnish

   1 onion, diced

   1 garlic clove, minced

   1½ pounds potatoes, peeled and thinly sliced

   1 pound cooked linguiça sausage, cut into
   ½-inch rounds

   1 ounce dried kelp, crumbled into small pieces

   6 ounces smoked mussels

   Salt

   Black pepper

Heat two tablespoons of olive oil over medium heat in a large saucepan. Add the onion and garlic and cook until soft, about 5 minutes. Add the potatoes and sausage and cook until the potatoes begin to soften, about 5 minutes. Add 6 cups water and the kelp to the pan and bring the mixture to a simmer. Let it simmer for 15 minutes, or until the potatoes begin to fall apart. Mash the potatoes with the back of a spoon. Stimmer until tender, about 10 minutes. Turn off the heat, add the mussels, and season with salt. Let it rest 20 minutes before serving. Finish with a drizzle of olive oil and black pepper.

Crawfish Bisque

SERVES 6–8

> 2 quarts Shellfish Stock (page 61)
> or Basic Fish Stock (page 61)
>
> 4 tablespoons Blackening Spice Mix
> (page 33), divided
>
> 2½ pounds live crawfish
>
> 8 tablespoons unsalted butter
>
> 4 carrots, chopped
>
> 2 celery stalks, chopped
>
> 2 onions, chopped
>
> ½ cup rice
>
> 2 tablespoons tomato paste
>
> 2 (12-ounce) cans pilsner or lager style beer
>
> Salt
>
> ½ cup sour cream or heavy cream
>
> 2 tablespoons Herbsaint or Pernod

Combine the stock and 2 tablespoons of the Blackening Spice Mix in a large pot and bring it to a boil over high heat. Add the crawfish, cover the pot, and cook for 5 minutes. Remove the pot from the heat. Remove the crawfish to a bowl to cool, and reserve the stock. Working over the bowl to catch all the juices, crack the shells and remove the meat. Reserve the meat. Return the shells and juices to the pot with the stock and simmer gently for 20 minutes. Remove the pot from the heat and pour the fortified stock through a fine mesh strainer. Reserve the stock.

Heat the butter in a large pot over medium-high heat. Add the carrots, celery, onions, and rice. Cook, stirring occasionally, until the onions are soft. Stir in the tomato paste and remaining 2 tablespoons of the Blackening Spice Mix. Cook until the tomato paste has darkened in color and its aroma has softened. Add the beer, bring the mixture to a boil, and cook until the alcohol smell dissipates. Add the reserved stock and season with salt. Reduce the heat to low, and let the mixture simmer gently until the rice and carrots are fully cooked, about 30 minutes.

Reserve half of the crawfish meat for garnish. Add the remaining meat to the stock and remove the pot from the heat. Transfer the soup to a blender in batches, blending it until the mixture is very smooth and silky. Strain the soup though a fine mesh strainer, pressing on the solids with the back of a ladle. Discard any solids that do not pass through the strainer. Gently reheat the bisque. Whisk in the sour cream and Herbsaint or Pernod. Serve the soup immediately, garnished with the reserved crawfish meat.

Coconut Broth with Clams or Mussels

SERVES 4

> 24 littleneck clams, scrubbed, or 2 pounds
> mussels, cleaned and beards removed
>
> 3 (14-ounce) cans unsweetened coconut milk
>
> 1 lemongrass stalk, bruised with
> the back of a knife
>
> 2 star anise pods
>
> 1 lemon, zested in wide strips
>
> 1 bay leaf
>
> 1½ cups butternut squash, diced
>
> Salt
>
> ¾ cup cilantro, roughly chopped
>
> Crushed red chile flakes
>
> Almond oil
>
> 1 lime, cut in wedges

Place the shellfish and 1 cup of water in a large covered pot over medium-high heat until the shells open. Remove the shellfish with a slotted spoon and reserve. Strain the broth to remove grit and return it to the pan. Add the coconut milk, lemongrass, star anise, lemon zest, bay leaf, and squash, and season with salt. Simmer the mixture until the squash is tender. Add the reserved shellfish and cilantro. Sprinkle chile flakes on top and finish with drizzle of almond oil. Garnish each bowl with lime wedges.

Lobster Bisque

SERVES 6-8

- 2 quarts Shellfish Stock (page 61) or Basic Fish Stock (page 61)
- 10 allspice berries
- 4 cloves
- 1 bay leaf
- 2 (1¼ pound) lobsters, preferably new/soft shell
- 8 tablespoons butter
- 4 carrots, chopped
- 2 celery stalks, chopped
- 2 onions, chopped
- ½ cup rice
- 2 tablespoons tomato paste
- 1 teaspoon ground mace
- 2 cups white wine
- Salt
- ½ cup sour cream or heavy cream
- 2 tablespoons brandy

Combine the stock, allspice, cloves, and bay leaf in a large pot and bring it to a boil over high heat. Add the lobsters, cover the pot, and cook for 7 minutes. Remove the pot from the heat. Place the lobsters in a bowl to cool. Working over the bowl to catch all the juices, crack the shells and remove the meat. Reserve the meat. Return the shells and juices to the pot and simmer gently for 20 minutes. Remove the pot from the heat and pour the fortified stock through a fine mesh strainer. Reserve the stock.

Heat the butter in a large pot over medium-high heat. Add the carrots, celery, onions, and rice. Cook, stirring occasionally, until the onions are soft. Stir in the tomato paste and mace. Cook until the tomato paste has darkened in color and its aroma has softened. Add the wine, bring to a boil, and cook until the alcohol smell dissipates. Add the reserved stock and season with salt. Reduce the heat to low, and simmer gently until the rice and carrots are fully cooked, about 30 minutes.

Reserve half of the lobster meat for garnish. Add the remaining meat to the stock and remove the pot from the heat. Transfer the soup to a blender in batches, blending until the mixture is very smooth and silky. Strain the soup though a fine mesh strainer, pressing on the solids with the back of a ladle. Discard any solids that do not pass through the strainer. Gently reheat the bisque. Whisk in the sour cream and brandy. Season with salt, garnish with the reserved lobster meat, and serve immediately.

Miso Soup

SERVES 4-6

- 1 onion, thinly sliced
- 2 celery stalks cut into ½-inch pieces
- 2 ounces dried kelp
- 2 slices ginger
- ½ cup dried mushrooms, preferably shiitake
- ½ cup red miso paste
- Enoki mushrooms, sliced scallions, or diced tofu, as desired, for garnish

Combine 2 quarts of water, the onion, celery, kelp, ginger, and mushrooms in a large pot. Bring to a gentle boil. As soon as the stock comes to a boil, lower the heat and simmer for 20 minutes. Remove the pot from the heat and let the mixture steep for 1 hour. Strain the stock and pour it back into the pot. Whisk in the red miso paste and bring the soup to a simmer. Before serving, garnish the soup with enoki mushrooms, scallions, or diced tofu, as desired.

Gazpacho with Smoked Clams

SERVES 4–8

- 1 cucumber, peeled and roughly chopped
- 1 onion, roughly chopped
- 1 pound ripe tomatoes, roughly chopped
- 2 red bell peppers, roasted, peeled, and seeded, or 1 (7-ounce) jar roasted peppers, drained
- 1 garlic clove, peeled
- 2 tablespoons salt
- 2 tablespoons sherry vinegar
- ¼ cup extra-virgin olive oil
- 1 (7-ounce) can smoked clams

Place the cucumber, onion, tomatoes, peppers, garlic, salt, vinegar, and 1 scant cup of water in a blender. Purée the mixture and pass it through a fine mesh strainer, pressing on the solids with the back of a spoon. Discard the solids. Chill the soup for at least 1 hour and up to overnight. Just before serving, whisk in the olive oil. Garnish the soup with the smoked clams.

Savannah Crab Soup

SERVES 4

- 1 pound lump crabmeat
- 5 tablespoons butter, divided
- 1 onion, thinly sliced
- 2 stalks celery, sliced
- Cayenne pepper
- 4 cups shellfish, fish, or chicken stock
- 1 tablespoon flour
- ¼ cup crab roe
- 2 cups cream or half-and-half
- 2 teaspoons Worcestershire sauce
- ¼ cup Amontillado or cooking sherry, plus additional for serving
- 1 tablespoon chopped chives

Pick through the crabmeat, discard any bits of cartilage, and reserve. In a pot over medium heat, melt 4 tablespoons of the butter. Add the onion and celery and cook until soft. Add a pinch of cayenne pepper and the stock and bring to a boil. In a bowl, combine the remaining 2 tablespoons of butter and the flour, and whisk in ½ cup of the hot liquid until smooth. Pour the flour mixture into the pot. Add the crab roe and use a stick blender to process it until smooth. Add the cream, Worcestershire sauce, and sherry. Simmer for 15 minutes, turn off the heat, and add the crabmeat. When the crab is warmed through, serve the soup garnished with chopped chives and a splash of sherry.

Shellfish-Herb Soup

SERVES 4–6

3 cups Basic Fish Stock (page 61)
or Shellfish Stock (page 61)

1 (8-ounce) bottle clam juice

1 cup dry white vermouth

3 sprigs thyme

5 saffron threads

2 pieces orange peel

10 stems fresh parsley

1 bay leaf

4 tablespoons unsalted butter, divided

1 onion, diced

1 fennel bulb, diced

2 garlic cloves, sliced

24 littleneck clams, scrubbed

½ pound scallops

½ pound shrimp, peeled and deveined

2 plum tomatoes, diced

Salt

Baguette for serving

Combine the stock, clam juice, vermouth, thyme, saffron, orange peel, parsley, and bay leaf in a large pot over medium heat. Simmer for 30 minutes, strain, and reserve. Heat 2 tablespoons of the butter in the pot over medium-high heat. Add the onion, fennel, and garlic and cook until the onions are soft. Add the strained broth and simmer for 20 minutes. Add the clams, cover, and cook until they open. Discard any clams that do not open. Add the scallops, shrimp, and tomatoes. Season with salt and cook the soup until the shrimp are done, about 5 minutes. Garnish each bowl with a pat of the remaining butter.

Marseille-Style Fish Soup

SERVES 4–6

3 cups Basic Fish Stock (page 61)
or water

3 tablespoons olive oil

2 leeks, white part only, sliced and
rinsed well

2 garlic cloves, grated

1 fennel bulb, diced, fronds reserved

2 pounds small whole fish, such as
butterfish, whiting, or herring,
scaled and gutted

2 cups white wine

10 threads saffron

2 large tomatoes, diced

Salt

¼ pound orzo pasta

Black pepper

Parmesan cheese, grated, for garnish

2 tablespoons chopped fresh herbs, such as
chervil, parsley, or reserved fennel fronds

Heat the oil in a large heavy-bottomed pot over medium-high heat. Cook the leeks, garlic, and fennel until soft, about 5 minutes. Add the fish and cook 5 minutes. Add the wine and cook until the alcohol smell dissipates. Add the saffron and tomatoes, season with salt, and cook 5 minutes. Add the stock and bring the mixture to a simmer for 15 minutes. Transfer the soup to a blender in batches and blend until the mixture is very smooth and silky. Strain the soup though a fine mesh strainer, pressing on the solids with the back of a ladle. Discard any solids that do not pass through the strainer. Cook the pasta in the puréed broth according to the package instructions. Season with salt and black pepper. Serve the soup with Parmesan cheese and herbs.

Sweet Potato Soup with Cured Salmon Roe

SERVES 4–6

3 tablespoons extra-virgin olive oil, divided

1 onion, chopped

2 garlic cloves, sliced

1 tablespoon grated fresh ginger

1½ pounds sweet potato, peeled and chopped

Salt

4 ounces cream cheese

1 lime, juiced, divided

1 ounce salmon roe

1 ounce sparkling wine

Heat 2 tablespoons of the olive oil in a large pot over medium-high heat. Add the onion, garlic, and ginger. Cook until the onion is translucent, about 5 minutes. Add the sweet potatoes and 5 cups of water. Season generously with salt. Bring the mixture to a boil and reduce the heat to a simmer. Cook the mixture until the sweet potatoes are falling apart. Add the cream cheese and all but a few drops of the lime juice, reserving just a few drops. Transfer the soup to a blender in batches and blend until the mixture is very smooth and silky. Strain the soup through a fine mesh strainer, pressing on the solids with the back of a ladle. Discard any solids that do not pass through the strainer. Let the soup cool to room temperature.

Place the salmon roe in a bowl, cover it with cold water, and add a pinch of salt. Mix gently with your fingers to separate the eggs, and let the mixture rest for 10 minutes. Discard any broken or floating eggs, and pour off the water. Add the reserved lime juice, sparkling wine, and the remaining 1 tablespoon of olive oil, and stir gently.

Ladle the soup into bowls and place a spoonful of marinated salmon roe in the center of each. Serve immediately.

Shrimp Bisque

SERVES 6–8

    2 quarts Shellfish Stock (page 61)
        or Basic Fish Stock (page 61)

10 allspice berries

  4 cloves

  1 bay leaf

2½ pounds small shrimp, shell on

  8 tablespoons unsalted butter

  4 carrots, chopped

  2 stalks celery, chopped

  2 onions, chopped

  ½ cup rice

  2 tablespoons tomato paste

  1 teaspoon ground mace

  2 cups white wine

    Salt

  ½ cup sour cream

  2 tablespoons Amontillado or
        cooking sherry

Combine the stock, allspice, cloves, and bay leaf in a large pot and bring to a boil over high heat. Add the shrimp, cover the pot, and cook for 5 minutes. Remove the pot from the heat. Place the shrimp in a bowl to cool. Working over the bowl to catch all the juices, peel and clean the shrimp. Reserve the meat. Return the shells and juices to the pot and let the stock simmer gently for 20 minutes. Remove the pot from the heat and pour the fortified stock through a fine mesh strainer. Reserve the stock.

Heat the butter in a large pot over medium-high heat. Add the carrots, celery, onions, and rice. Cook the stock, stirring it occasionally, until the onions are soft. Stir in the tomato paste and mace. Cook until the tomato paste has darkened in color and its aroma has softened. Add the wine, bring to a boil, and cook until the alcohol smell dissipates. Add the reserved stock and season with salt. Reduce the heat to low, and simmer gently until the rice and carrots are fully cooked, about 40 minutes.

Reserve half of the shrimp meat for the garnish. Add the remaining meat to the stock and remove the pot from the heat. Transfer the soup to a blender in batches and blend until the mixture is very smooth and silky. Strain the soup though a fine mesh strainer, pressing on the solids with the back of a ladle. Discard any solids that do not pass through the strainer. Gently reheat the bisque. Whisk in the sour cream and sherry. Serve immediately, garnishing with the reserved shrimp meat.

STEWS

Bouillabaisse

This classic French dish consists of mixed seafood in a light broth.

SERVES 8

Basic Aioli (page 25)

2 quarts Basic Fish Stock (page 61) or Shellfish Stock (page 61)

6 tablespoons olive oil

3 tablespoons butter

4 celery stalks, finely diced

4 shallots, sliced

1 fennel bulb, finely diced

2 garlic cloves, smashed

1 bay leaf

4 tablespoons tomato paste

3 sprigs thyme

1 sprig fresh lavender or ½ teaspoon dried

1 tablespoon smoked sweet paprika

2 teaspoons crushed red chile flakes

2 cups white wine

1 pound red potatoes, cut into bite-size pieces

Salt

1 lemon, zested in wide strips

24 littleneck clams, scrubbed

1 pound mussels, cleaned and debearded

1 pound mixed fish fillets, skin off

¾ pound shrimp, head on, shelled

½ pound scallops

2 tablespoons Pernod or Herbsaint

Baguette, sliced

2 garlic cloves, sliced in half

Heat the olive oil and butter in a large stew pot over medium heat. Add the celery, shallots, fennel, garlic, and bay leaf. Cook until the shallots are softened. Stir in the tomato paste, thyme, lavender, paprika, and chile flakes. Cook until the tomato paste has darkened in color and its aroma has softened. Add the wine, bring to a boil, and cook until the alcohol smell dissipates. Add the stock and potatoes and season with salt. Bring the mixture to a boil, add the lemon and clams, cover the pot, and cook until the clams have opened. Add the mussels, cover the pot once again, and cook until the mussels have opened. Discard any shellfish that haven't opened. Reduce the heat to low and add the fish, shrimp, and scallops. Cover and simmer gently until the shrimp are cooked and the fish begins to flake apart, 5–8 minutes. Gently stir in the Pernod or Herbsaint, and remove the pot from the heat. Cover and let the mixture rest for 10–15 minutes. Serve the bouillabaisse in large bowls with baguette slices that have been rubbed with garlic and aioli on the side.

Creole Bouillabaisse

SERVES 6–8

4 cups Basic Fish Stock (page 61)

Blackening Spice Mix (page 33)

2 pounds snapper or striped bass, skin off, cut in 3-inch pieces

4 tablespoons butter, divided

1 onion, chopped

2 garlic cloves, minced

2 tablespoons flour

1 cup white wine

1 (14-ounce) can fire-roasted tomatoes

10 saffron threads

Salt

Black pepper

Season one side of the fish with Blackening Spice Mix and let it rest for 15 minutes. Heat 2 tablespoons of the butter in a large heavy-bottomed pot over high heat. Sauté the fish, spice side down until a dark crust forms. Do not flip. Remove the fish and reserve. Add the remaining 2 tablespoons of butter and the onion and garlic. Reduce heat to medium. Cook until the onion is soft. Add the flour and cook until it is golden brown. Add the wine, stock, tomatoes, and saffron. Cook for 15 minutes until the broth has thickened. Season with salt and pepper. Return the fish to the pot and simmer until cooked through.

Bourride

This is a mixed seafood and an aioli-fortified broth.

SERVES 6–8

1 recipe Basic Aioli (page 25)

2 quarts Basic Fish Stock (page 61)

2 pounds mixed white fish, skin off

Salt

½ cup olive oil

3 fennel bulbs, cut into wedges

1 onion, finely chopped

1 (½-inch) knob ginger, sliced

4 tablespoons butter

1 tablespoon smoked sweet paprika

10 saffron threads

2 cups white wine

¼ cup red wine vinegar

1 Fresno or serrano chile pepper, halved

1 pound mussels, cleaned and debearded

½ pound scallops

¾ pound shrimp, head on, shelled

2 tablespoons Amontillado or cooking sherry

2 tablespoons chopped chives

Toasted baguette slices for serving

Season the fish with salt and let it rest for 15 minutes. Heat the olive oil in a large, heavy pot over medium-high heat. Add the fennel, onion, and ginger. Cook until the onion softens. Add the butter, paprika, and saffron and cook 1 minute. Add the wine, bring the mixture to a boil, and cook until the alcohol smell dissipates. Add the stock, vinegar, chile pepper, and mussels. Simmer until the shells have opened. Reduce the heat to low; add the fish, scallops, and shrimp; and simmer until the seafood is just cooked through, 7–10 minutes. Remove the pot from the heat. Ladle most of the broth into a separate pan. Keep the fish covered and warm in the pot. Simmer the broth over low heat and whisk in the aioli. Cook until the broth thickens, whisking constantly. Remove the pan from the heat and stir in the sherry and chives. Divide the seafood mixture among bowls. Ladle the aioli-thickened broth over the seafood mixture. Serve with toasted baguette slices.

Burrida

This mixed-seafood dish has an almond-and-butter-thickened broth.

SERVES 6–8

> 6 cups Basic Fish Stock (page 61)
>
> 1 recipe Anchovy-Almond Butter (page 19), cut into pieces
>
> 4 tablespoons olive oil
>
> 4 celery stalks, diced
>
> 2 carrots, diced
>
> 1 fennel bulb, diced
>
> 1 leek, sliced
>
> 3 garlic cloves, sliced
>
> 2 pounds flaky white fish (see page 64), skin off, cut into pieces
>
> Salt
>
> 1 pound shrimp, head on, shelled
>
> 2 tablespoons Amontillado or cooking sherry
>
> Baguette for serving

Heat the olive oil in a large pot over high heat. Add the celery, carrots, fennel, leek, and garlic. Cook undisturbed for about 5 minutes until the vegetables are slightly browned. Season the fish with salt and let it rest for 15 minutes. Add the stock, sherry, and tomatoes to the vegetable mixture and bring to a simmer. Add the fish and shrimp, reduce the heat to low, and simmer until the shrimp are just cooked through, about 5–7 minutes. Season with salt to taste. Using a slotted spoon, transfer the fish and vegetables to large bowls. Bring the broth to a boil, add the Anchovy-Almond Butter, and whisk vigorously to combine. Boil until the broth is slightly thickened. Stir in the sherry. Ladle the broth over the seafood and vegetables and serve with slices of baguette.

Crawfish Étouffée

This is a Cajun or Creole dish of "smothered" shellfish cooked with a dark roux.

SERVES 4–6

> 4 cups Shellfish Stock (page 61) or water
>
> 8 tablespoons butter
>
> 2 tablespoons flour
>
> 1 onion, diced
>
> 4 scallions, sliced, reserve green for garnish
>
> 2 celery stalks, diced
>
> 2 garlic cloves, minced
>
> 1 green bell pepper, diced
>
> 2 ounces Amontillado or cooking sherry
>
> 2 (14-ounce) cans fire-roasted tomatoes
>
> Salt
>
> 2 pounds crawfish meat
>
> Cayenne pepper

Melt the butter in a large pot over medium heat and stir in the flour. Cook until the flour is dark brown. Add the onion, scallions, celery, garlic, and bell pepper and sauté until the vegetables are soft. Add the stock and tomatoes and bring to a boil. Reduce the heat to medium and simmer 10 minutes. Season with salt, add the crawfish meat, and simmer for 5 minutes. Remove it from the heat. Cover and let it sit for 20 minutes. Serve with the reserved scallion greens and cayenne pepper sprinkled over top.

Cotriade

This dish from northern France is flavored with earthy herbs like thyme and sage.

SERVES 6–8

- 6 cups Basic Fish Stock (page 61)
- 2 pounds flaky white fish (see page 64), skin off, cut into pieces
- Salt
- 1 pound mussels, cleaned and debearded
- 1 pound shrimp, head on, shelled
- 2 cups dry hard cider or white wine
- 8 tablespoons butter
- 3 sprigs fresh thyme
- 1 sprig fresh sage
- 1 lemon, zest removed in wide strips
- 10 saffron threads
- ½ cup flour
- 2 cups butternut squash, cut into 1-inch pieces
- 1 celery root, cut into 1-inch pieces
- 1 fennel bulb, diced
- 3 shallots, cut into thin wedges
- 1 leek sliced and rinsed
- 15 radishes, halved
- ½ cup chopped fresh herbs, such as parsley or tarragon

Season the fish with salt and let it rest for 15 minutes. Combine the fish, mussels, shrimp, stock, and cider or white wine in a large pot over medium heat. Bring the mixture to a simmer, and then cook until the mussels open and the fish begins to flake, about 6–8 minutes. Gently remove the seafood and set it aside. Strain the stock through a fine mesh sieve into a bowl and reserve.

Heat the butter in a large pot over medium heat. Add the thyme, sage, lemon zest, and saffron and cook until aromatic, about 2 minutes. Add the flour, whisking it into the mixture to ensure that no clumps form. Cook, stirring frequently, until the flour is golden brown. Add the reserved stock and whisk to combine. Add the squash, celery root, fennel, shallots, leek, and radishes. Cook until the squash is tender and the broth is lightly thickened. Discard the thyme and sage. Return the seafood to the broth and simmer gently until it is heated through. Adjust the seasoning, add the herbs, and serve.

Creole Gumbo

This is a highly flavored, slightly smoky version of a classic gumbo.

SERVES 6–8

- ¼ pound dried shrimp
- 8 tablespoons butter
- 2 tablespoons flour
- ½ pound bacon, diced
- 1 pound okra, cut into ½-inch pieces
- 1 onion, diced
- 1 green bell pepper, diced
- 4 celery stalks, thinly sliced
- 4 garlic cloves, minced
- 2 teaspoons crushed red chile flakes
- 2 teaspoons smoked sweet paprika
- 1 teaspoon dried thyme
- 2 bay leaves
- 1 tablespoon gumbo filé powder
- 1 pint lump crabmeat, cartilage removed
- 1 pint shucked oysters with their liquor
- Steamed white rice for serving

Place the shrimp in a large bowl, pour 1½ quarts of simmering water over them, and let them rest for 1 hour. Strain, reserving the shrimp and water separately. In a large, heavy pot, brown the butter over medium-high heat. Stir in the flour and cook until the flour is golden brown. Remove the flour mixture (roux) from the pot and reserve it.

Add the bacon to the pot and cook over medium heat until the fat is rendered and the bacon is crisp. Add the okra, onion, bell pepper, celery, and garlic. Cook for 10 minutes. Add the chile flakes, paprika, thyme, bay leaves, and gumbo filé. Cook for 2 minutes. Add the reserved roux and stir to combine. Whisk in the reserved shrimp broth and simmer for 45 minutes. Add the reserved shrimp, crabmeat, and oysters with their liquor. Simmer for 10 minutes. Let the mixture rest for at least 20 minutes before serving it over the rice.

Gumbo

SERVES 4–6

- 6 cups Basic Fish Stock (page 61), Shellfish Stock (page 61), or chicken stock
- 2 pounds skin-on, bone-in chicken thighs
- Salt
- 8 tablespoons butter, divided
- 1 pound sliced Andouille sausage
- 3 celery stalks, diced
- 1 onion, diced
- 1 green bell pepper, diced
- 1 fennel bulb, cut into eight wedges
- 3 garlic cloves, smashed
- 1 tablespoon crushed red chile flakes
- 1 bay leaf
- ½ cup flour
- 1 bottle dark beer
- 3 tablespoons Worcestershire sauce
- 1 pound okra, cut into ½-inch pieces
- 2 (14-ounce) cans diced fire-roasted tomatoes
- 2 lemons, cut in halves
- 1 pound shrimp, head on, shelled
- Steamed rice for serving

Season the chicken thighs with salt. Melt 2 tablespoons of the butter in a heavy-bottomed stew pot over high heat. Add the chicken and sear it, skin side down, until it is well browned. Reduce the heat to medium and add the sausage. Cook until it begins to color. Transfer the meats to a bowl and set them aside.

Add 2 tablespoons of the butter to the pan. Add the celery, onion, bell pepper, fennel, garlic, chile flakes, and bay leaf. Cook, stirring occasionally, until the vegetables have softened, about 5 minutes. Use a slotted spoon to transfer the vegetables to a bowl, leaving the fat in the pan. Add the remaining 4 tablespoons of butter and the flour. Stir to combine and cook over medium heat, stirring constantly, until the flour is golden brown. Add the beer and Worcestershire sauce, stirring until the mixture is smooth, and bring to a boil. Add all the remaining ingredients and the reserved meats. Bring the mixture to a boil, reduce the heat to low, cover, and simmer until thickened, about 1 hour. Remove the lemon halves and bay leaves. Check the seasoning and adjust it, if needed. Serve over steamed rice.

Seafood Pot Pie

SERVES 4–6

    1 frozen pie crust (or your own recipe)

    1 fennel bulb, cut into 1-inch pieces

    1 carrot, diced

    1 celery root, diced

    1 cup pearl onions, peeled

    ½ pound red potatoes, cut into
        1-inch pieces

    2 tablespoons extra-virgin olive oil

    2 sprigs fresh thyme

      Salt

    2 pounds flaky white fish (see page 64), skin
        off, cut into pieces

    2 tablespoons butter

    2 tablespoons flour

    ¼ teaspoon onion powder

    ¼ teaspoon garlic powder

    ⅛ teaspoon ground mace

    1 bay leaf

    2 cups milk

    2 ounces Amontillado or cooking sherry

    ¼ cup chopped fresh parsley

    1 tablespoon sweet smoked paprika

Slightly thaw the pie crust and remove it from its tin. Roll it flat on a parchment-lined baking sheet. Bake the crust at 400°F until it is golden brown. Remove the crust and parchment from the baking sheet and reserve. Toss the fennel, carrots, celery root, onions, and potatoes with the olive oil and thyme. Season with salt and roast on the baking sheet at 400°F until cooked through, about 20 minutes. Remove from the oven and reserve.

Season the fish with salt and let it rest for 15 minutes. Heat the butter in a large pot over medium-high heat. Stir in the flour and cook until it is golden brown. Add the onion and garlic powders, mace, and bay leaf. Whisk in the milk and reduce the heat to low. Cook the mixture until it has thickened, stirring constantly. Add the vegetables, fish, and sherry. Stir to combine. Cover and cook until the fish is done, about 10 minutes. Divide the mixture between serving bowls and sprinkle the top with the parsley and a pinch of paprika. Break the crust into large pieces over the top and serve.

STOCK

Making your own seafood stocks can be a hit-or-miss proposition. Since most cooks don't buy whole fish, they rarely have access to the freshest bones and trimmings from which good stocks are made. Using less-than-pristine-quality bones and trimmings will result in a stock that is not worth the trouble.

Seafood stocks can lose their clarity (visually and flavor-wise) if not cooked briefly and gently and handled with care. Any murky quality in a stock will carry through to the final preparation in which it is used.

So if you are going to make stock, you must be diligent throughout the entire process.

Now that I've scared you away from making stock, I must tell you that it's really easy to make a fabulous essence from all the best qualities of seafood. I use a method that precooks the mix of bones and trim (fins, flesh, heads), either simmering them in butter and their own juices or roasting them at a low temperature until they are cooked through and before adding the liquid in which it will simmer. This extra step gives the resulting stock greater sweetness and clarity. The main goal when making seafood stock is to gently and quickly extract just the subtle flavors of the fish. If the fish simmers too long, clarity will be sacrificed, though a stronger flavor is achieved.

Seafood stocks are different from meat-based stocks in that there is not as much gelatin to extract from fish bones to give weight to the texture of the liquid. But then some species of fish just swim against the tide of normal. Fish with cartilaginous skeletal structures, such as skate, shark, and sturgeon, can be used to make bright-tasting and voluptuous stocks that have a mouthfeel as rich as a beef or veal stock. These richer stocks are perfect for use in dishes like risotto or paella and give structure to tomato-based brothy soups. Monkfish in particular makes a very rich seafood stock. But it is not the body of the monkfish that enriches the stock. Rather, it is the head, which accounts for over 60 percent of the total weight of the monkfish, that makes all the difference. Monkfish heads are often cut off and discarded at sea, but if you happen across one of these grotesque creatures in its whole form, by all means snap it up and simmer it down into a versatile stock.

Basic Fish Stock

MAKES ABOUT 3 QUARTS

 4 tablespoons butter

 2 pounds fish trimmings (fins, flesh, heads) and bones from mild-flavored fish

 1 fennel bulb, sliced with fronds

 1 celery stalk, sliced

 2 cups white wine

 ½ cup red or white wine vinegar

 5 black peppercorns

 1 tablespoon kosher salt

In a large covered pot over low heat, warm the butter with the fish trimmings for 15 minutes without stirring. Add the remaining ingredients and bring to a simmer until the alcohol smell dissipates. Add 3 quarts of water to the pot, cover, and return to a low simmer for 15 minutes. Turn off the heat and let the mixture rest for 10 minutes. Ladle the liquid from the top, avoiding the solids. Let the stock rest for 20 minutes, pour off the clear liquid, and discard all solids and sediment.

VARIATION

+ **Simple Simmered Stock.** Omit the butter and combine all the ingredients and 3 quarts of water in a large pot over low heat. Bring to a gentle simmer and cook for 15–20 minutes. Turn off the heat and let the mixture rest for 10 minutes. Ladle the liquid from the top, avoiding the solids. Let the stock rest for 20 minutes, pour off the clear liquid, and discard all solids and sediment.

Shellfish Stock

MAKES 3½ QUARTS

 4 tablespoons vegetable oil

 6 lobster bodies or 3 cups shrimp shells and heads

 4 tablespoons butter

 1 onion, chopped

 1 leek, green part only, sliced

 3 carrots, chopped

 2 stalks celery, chopped

 2 bay leaves

 3 cups white wine

 4 tablespoons brandy

 1 tablespoon kosher salt

In a large pot, heat the oil over high heat. Add the shells and sear them for a few minutes, turning once, until they are lightly browned. Remove the shells and reserve. Reduce the heat to medium and add the butter. Add the onion, leek, carrots, celery, and bay leaves and cook them until the onion begins to soften. Add the shells, wine, and brandy and simmer until the alcohol smell dissipates. Add 3 quarts of water and the salt. Cover the pot and simmer over low heat for 20–30 minutes. The liquid should be clear and the flavor sweet. Turn off the heat. Let the stock rest for 20 minutes, pour off the clear liquid, and discard all solids and sediment.

VARIATION

+ **Red Seafood Stock.** Add 4 tablespoons of tomato paste along with the vegetables.

PART FIVE

RECIPES BY SPECIES

Culinary Categories

There are a great many species of fish in the sea, and each one is unique and wonderful in its own way. But you can easily categorize them into a half dozen buckets based on their general culinary attributes, such as texture, flavor, fat content, and color.

Within each of these culinary categories, you can use the species interchangeably in most recipes. This gives you the opportunity to buy whichever fish looks the freshest on any given day because, while you may not know that particular type of fish yet, you have known (and cooked using the recipes in this book) many others like it. You'll see that some species span two different categories, for example catfish can be either flaky and white or meaty and dense, depending on how the fish is treated in the recipe, which determines the outcome of the texture. This is by no means a precise categorization, but merely a reference for you to follow so that any of the recipes in this book can be used to prepare multiple types of species of seafood.

Not all seafood can be easily grouped with like seafood. Species such as clams, squid, or lobster are unique enough to stand alone as culinary categories.

Fillet Fish usually fit nicely into a large sauté pan. The flesh has a moderately high level of fat, and fillets are often cooked with their skin on, which helps the flesh retain its moisture when cooked. Generally, you can tell fillets are cooked when their flesh is uniformly opaque. When cooked, the fillets tend to have a snappy, slightly elastic texture and are pretty medium- to full-flavored.

Acadian Redfish, Barracuda, Barramundi, Bigeye, Black Bass, Bluefish, Bluegill, Boxfish, Branzino, Butterfish, Croaker, Cutlassfish, Dory, Drum Black/Red, Flying Fish, Freshwater Bass, Grouper, Grunt, Jack, Lionfish, Mackerel, Mullet, Pacific Rockfish, Parrotfish, Perch, Pike, Pompano, Porgy, Redfish, Salmon, Scup, Shad, Sheepshead, Skate (or Ray), Snapper, Splendid Alfonsino, Spot, Striped Bass (small), Tautog, Tilapia, Tilefish, Triggerfish, Tripletail, Trout, Walleye, Weakfish, Wolffish, Wrasse, Wreckfish, Yellowtail (aka Hiramasa/Hamachi)

Flaky White Fish, in general, have a lean texture and a large, curved flake when cooked. Their flavor is quite mild. You can usually tell a flaky white fish is fully cooked when it flakes under gentle pressure.

Acadian Redfish, Alaska Pollock, Barrelfish, Black Driftfish, Bowfin, Carp, Catfish, Cod, Cusk, Dab, Dogfish, Flatfish, Flounder, Grenadier, Haddock, Hake, Halibut, Lingcod, Lionfish, Lizardfish, Pacific Rockfish, Perch, Pollock, Remora, Sablefish, Scorpionfish, Sculpin, Sea Robin, Skate, Snakehead, Tilapia, Whitefish, Whiting, Wolffish

Meaty Dense Fish require long, slow cooking times because they typically have a high amount of connective tissue or have a texture akin to steak when raw. Their flavor is robust enough to hold up to these longer cooking times as well as hold their own when paired with strong flavors. When these fish are cooked, they feel springy to the touch.

Amberjack, Barrelfish, Black Driftfish, Blowfish, Bowfin, Carp, Catfish, Cobia, Cusk, Dogfish, Grouper, Lingcod, Lizardfish, Mahi Mahi, Marlin, Monkfish, Opah, Remora, Scorpionfish, Sea Robin, Sculpin, Shark, Snakehead, Striped Bass (large), Sturgeon, Swordfish, Tautog, Wreckfish, Wolffish, Yellowtail (aka Hiramasa/Hamachi)

Orange-Fleshed Fish comprise the salmon category of fish, where the pigment of their flesh gives away their direct connection. They have a medium-firm texture, most often coupled with a delicate flake. While widely recognized as being higher in (good) fats than other fish, the exact level of fat in each species within this category does vary. When cooked, the flesh is opaque but can be slightly rare toward the center. The flesh will flake with gentle pressure. Some species in this category are distinctly not orange; these are included here, as their general flake, fat content, and culinary character are similar to species easily identified by their orange color, and thus are interchangeable in recipes.

Arctic Char, Opah, Sablefish, Salmon varieties (King, Sockeye, Coho, Chum, Pink, and Atlantic), Steelhead Trout, Wolffish

Small Silver Fish are rich in flavor and healthy fats, and are most often eaten whole, bones and all. You usually find them cooked or cured in cans or jars, but if you find them fresh and cook them yourself, you know they are done when the skin is just starting to break apart and you can see the flesh is uniformly opaque.

Anchovies, Eulachon, Herring, Mackerel, Sardines, Smelt, Whiting

Steak Fish are large fish that are almost never sold whole but are cut into cross sections or steaks. They commonly have a full, rich flavor and a sturdy structure most often defined by concentric rings. These steaks can be cooked to doneness according to taste.

Mahi Mahi (sold as fillets), Marlin, Sharks, Sturgeon, Swordfish, Tuna (Albacore, Bonito, Blackfin, Bluefin, Yellowfin, Bigeye/Ahi), Wahoo

A NOTE TO INLAND SEAFOOD LOVERS

While there are certainly many celebrated species that swim in our inland waters, most still conform to the general culinary qualities of our coastal fish. I list some popular inland fish, and you can use this to reference applicable recipes. Some species, like carp and catfish, though, deserve their own entries.

ABALONE

The glossy patina lining an abalone's shell, when it's whittled into a mother-of-pearl caviar spoon, tends to attract more modern culinary attention than the mollusk's meat does. Abalone's mild flavor and interesting texture deserve both our attention and some time on the plate. But the meat should never spend more than 1 minute per side in a well-buttered sauté pan, as overcooking abalone renders it disappointingly tough.

Once the meat has been cut from the shell, the stomach must be removed from the side of the univalve (a one-shell mollusk) that was attached to the shell. The tough, edible portion, the foot, must be tenderized with a meat mallet before cooking and sliced thinly before eating. The dark mantle around the edges of the foot as well as the dark skin from the bottom of the foot must also be removed. These trimmings from fresh abalone are great minced and used in chowders and fritters just as you would use canned ones. I particularly like to smoke abalone steaks to intensify their flavor. As smoking reduces the water content significantly, smoked abalone must be shredded or powdered before being added to seafood pastas, risottos, and sauces.

The name is loosely translated from Greek to "sea ear," which aptly describes the mollusk's shape. Once abundant in the Pacific's intertidal and subtidal zones to depths of 200 feet, overfishing before and after World War II decimated the wild population. Most abalone on the market now come from farmed sources, and they are raising a consistently high-quality product.

Butter-Fried Abalone Steak with Sherry Herb Sauce

SERVES 4

- 4 abalone steaks, scored and pounded
- Salt
- Milk or water
- Flour
- 4 tablespoons butter
- 4 tablespoons sherry
- 2 tablespoon chopped fresh herbs, such as chervil or parsley

Season the abalone with salt and let it rest 10 minutes. Dip the steaks in milk and dredge in flour. In a sauté pan over medium-high heat, melt the butter and cook until golden brown. Add the coated steaks and cook each side until golden brown, about 1 minute. Remove the steaks from the pan, add the sherry and herbs, and stir to combine. Spoon the sauce over the steaks to serve.

Abalone en Saor (sweet-sour vinaigrette)

SERVES 4 AS AN APPETIZER

- 4 abalone steaks, scored and pounded
- Salt
- Milk or water
- Flour
- 4 tablespoons butter
- 2 tablespoons extra-virgin olive oil
- 1 small onion, sliced thin
- 2 tablespoons raisins
- 2 tablespoons pine nuts or slivered almonds
- 1½ cups white wine, such as Riesling or Sauvignon blanc
- 2 tablespoons sherry vinegar
- Black pepper

Season the abalone with salt and let it rest 10 minutes. Dip in milk and dredge in flour. In a sauté pan over medium-high heat, melt the butter and cook until golden brown. Add the coated steaks and cook each side until golden brown, about 1 minute. Remove the steaks from the pan. Reduce heat to medium. Add the olive oil, onion, raisins, and nuts to the pan. Cook until the onions are soft and the nuts are slightly toasted. Add the wine and vinegar and bring to a simmer. Reduce the liquid by one-half. Season with pepper. Smother the steaks with the onion-raisin-nut mixture and marinate for at least 1 hour. Serve at room temperature.

ACADIAN REDFISH
Flaky white fish, fillet fish

Acadian redfish and the closely related golden redfish are pretty unchallenging fish for most people's palates. Its sweet, lean, and very mild flavor is paired with a traditional fish texture and pearly white color, and redfish have gained popularity and appeal for being something like "snapper lite." Before 1950 it was one of the most often used fish for fish sticks and was thus overfished. But since populations made a rebound in this century, fillets, either skin on or skin off, are once again a popular fish to fry, sauté, or stew and can be used in any recipe that calls for mild white fish, such as haddock. These small, thin fillets can also stand in for species in the fillet fish category. They cook up fast and are best complemented by acidic ingredients like citrus and tomatoes. Overcooked, they lose charisma as their briny-sweet ocean flavor gives way to a cardboard-like aroma and coarse grain.

Acadian redfish, not to be confused with red drum, which is also called redfish, is sometimes sold under the name rosefish (because of its skin color) or ocean perch (because it has similar appeal to the freshwater perch). It is caught in the Gulf of Maine, and New Englanders sometimes call it "lobster bait," as its bodies and trim are fermented and used to trap the targeted shellfish. On the East Coast, Acadian redfish are often sold whole. Because they are caught at great depths, they often appear distended, with their eyes and air bladders bulging because of barotrauma, an effect of rapid change in pressure when they are hauled from fathoms below. This unattractive, bug-eyed presentation may hinder curb appeal, but it is not a representation of quality.

Broiled Acadian Redfish with Orange-Pistachio Piccata

SERVES 4

> 1 recipe Orange-Pistachio Piccata (page 29)
>
> 4 Acadian redfish portions, skin on and scored
>
> Salt
>
> Extra-virgin olive oil
>
> Black pepper

Season the fish with salt and let it rest for 15 minutes. Preheat the broiler to high and set the rack to the highest position. Place the fish skin side up on a baking tray. Coat with olive oil and sprinkle with black pepper. Slide the tray under the broiler and cook until the fish is done, 5–7 minutes, depending on thickness. Serve with Orange-Pistachio Piccata.

Roasted Acadian Redfish with Charred Tomato Vinaigrette

SERVES 4

> 1 recipe Charred Tomato Vinaigrette (page 35), room temperature
>
> 4 Acadian redfish portions, skin on and scored
>
> Salt
>
> Rice pilaf (for serving, suggested)

Season the fish with salt and let it rest for 15 minutes. Pour the vinaigrette into a baking dish just big enough to hold the fish in a single layer. Nestle the fish skin side down into the vinaigrette. Cover with foil and bake at 300°F until the fish is cooked through, about 15–20 minutes. Let it rest for 5 minutes before serving with rice pilaf.

Pan-Fried Acadian Redfish with Citrus and Herbs

SERVES 4

> 1 recipe Gremolata (page 28)
>
> 4 Acadian redfish portions, skin-on and scored
>
> Salt
>
> Flour
>
> 3 tablespoons butter

Season the fish with salt and let it rest for 15 minutes. Dredge the fillets in flour. In a sauté pan, melt the butter over medium heat. Add the fish skin side down and cook without flipping until almost done, then turn off the heat and flip to finish cooking. Serve with Gremolata.

Tempura-Fried Acadian Redfish

SERVES 4

1 recipe Pickled Chiles (page 29)

4 Acadian redfish portions, skin off

Salt

Vegetable or peanut oil

1 cup flour, sifted

2 tablespoons cornstarch, sifted

1½ cups seltzer water

Season the fish with salt and let it rest for 15 minutes. Pour 3–4 inches of oil into a high-sided pan. Place over medium-high heat and warm the oil to 375°F. Make a batter by combining the flour, cornstarch, seltzer water, and a pinch of salt. Whisk until smooth, and use within 10 minutes. Dip one piece of fish at a time into the batter, place it in the oil, and hold it there for 5 seconds before releasing it. Repeat the process, cooking the fillets two at a time. Turn with a slotted spoon to ensure that both sides crisp evenly. Remove the fillets as they finish, about 3–5 minutes, and place on paper towels to absorb the excess oil. Serve with Pickled Chiles.

Grilled Acadian Redfish Wrapped with Grape Leaves

SERVES 4

4 Acadian redfish portions, skin off

Salt

2 lemons, zested and halved

12–16 brined grape leaves, thick stems removed

Extra-virgin olive oil

Prepare a charcoal grill with a medium fire. Season the fish with salt and lemon zest and let it rest for 15 minutes. Arrange three grape leaves so they overlap and create a single flat sheet. Place one portion of fish in the center of the sheet and drizzle with olive oil. Fold the leaves over the fish to wrap it completely. Repeat the process with the other portions. Drizzle with olive oil, and place them seam side up and lemons cut side down on the grill. Cook for 4–5 minutes. Flip and cook until done, 1–2 minutes more. Serve the fish in grape leaves with the charred lemons, and drizzle with more olive oil.

NOTE *If using a gas grill, preheat all burners to medium and grill as described above.*

Acadian Redfish en Papillote (cooked in parchment)

SERVES 4

    1 recipe Cilantro-Chile-Lime Butter (page 20)

    4 Acadian redfish portions, skin on and scored

    Salt

    2 fennel bulbs, thinly sliced

    1 onion, thinly sliced

    1 cup white wine

    Butter, for greasing the parchment

    1 orange, thinly sliced

Season the fish with salt and let it rest for 15 minutes. In a shallow pan, place the fennel, onion, and wine. Season with salt and cook over medium heat until the vegetables are soft and the wine nearly reduced. Take four 18-inch squares of parchment paper and cut into heart shapes. Use butter to grease an 8-inch-square area in the middle of each. Evenly divide the vegetables and remaining liquid among parchments, cover each with two orange slices, place the fish skin side up on top, and top each fillet with 2 tablespoons of Cilantro-Chile-Lime Butter. Fold the paper over and crimp the edges tightly (empanada style) to form a pouch. Bake at 350°F for 10–12 minutes, depending on the thickness of the fillets. Serve in the pouch and slice open just prior to eating.

Poached Acadian Redfish with Dill Crème Fraîche

SERVES 4

    1 recipe Dill Crème Fraîche (page 27)

    4 Acadian redfish portions, skin on and scored

    Salt

    1 cup white wine

    2 tablespoons white wine vinegar

    1 small shallot, sliced

    1 small carrot, sliced

    10 black peppercorns

    1 bay leaf

Season the fish with salt and let it rest for 15 minutes. In a pan just wide enough to hold the fish in a single layer, combine 1 cup of water with the wine, vinegar, shallot, carrot, ½ tablespoon salt, peppercorns, and bay leaf. Simmer over low heat for 5 minutes. Bring the liquid to 170°F. Place the fish skin side down into the liquid so that it is barely submerged and cook until the fish is done, approximately 4–6 minutes per ½ inch of thickness. Transfer the fish to a plate and pat dry. Serve with Dill Crème Fraîche.

ANCHOVIES
Small silver fish

Though these little fish play an important role in many popular cuisines, they rarely get the credit they deserve. Most often they are unjustly maligned, likely due to poor-quality pizza toppers that have turned off too many an eater. But when added to sauces and vinaigrettes or perched atop salads and crostini, their zesty fillets accentuate the flavors of other ingredients more so than add their own.

What we consider the anchovy can be any one of twenty-plus species of fish legally marketed as such and packed in either salt or oil. Anchovies in oil are ready to use. Salt-packed anchovies are used just as oil-packed fillets, though they must first be soaked in cool water and deboned. This may take as long as 12 hours, depending on how salty you want them to be. After soaking, the fillets are easily removed from the bones by peeling them off from the tail toward the head. The bones can be deep-fried into a delicious and crunchy snack. The salt from the cans can be dried in a low oven and used as you would regular salt but with an added potent tang.

If you're lucky enough to find fresh anchovies, you might be surprised by their mild, light, briny flavor and fluffy texture. They can be broiled, pickled, fried, grilled, sautéed, or smoked. Treat them the same as you would smelt (page 379) or herring (page 222). Like those fish, they always pair well with fresh herbs, lemon juice, and olive oil.

It's best to first remove the head and viscera. The easiest way to do that is to use a pair of scissors to snip directly behind the head and through the backbone but not all the way through the fish. Then, holding the fish, leverage the head toward the belly and pull down and away. This motion will cleanly remove all the viscera. The scales do not need to be removed, though if you choose to do so, simply using your thumb to wash them off under running cold water is enough.

To fillet an anchovy, slice open the gutted belly cavity down to the tail. Place the fish belly down on a flat surface and, using your thumb, gently press down on the back of the fish to flatten and separate the fillets. Turn the fish over and peel out the backbone and, along with it, most of the small bones. Snip the backbone where it meets the tail and discard.

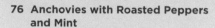

ANCHOVIES
Fresh

Grilled Fresh Anchovies

SERVES 4–6

1½ pounds fresh whole anchovies, headed and gutted

Salt

Black pepper

1 lemon, halved

Chopped fresh chives or parsley

Sliced baguette or rye bread and butter, for serving

Prepare a charcoal grill with a medium fire. Thread the fish onto skewers, season them with salt and black pepper, and let them rest for 15 minutes. Place the skewers on the grill directly over the coals and cook until singed, turning once. The fish will cook through in a matter of minutes. Remove skewers to a platter and squeeze with lemon juice and garnish with the herbs. Serve with sliced baguette or rye bread slathered with butter.

NOTE *If using a gas grill, preheat all burners to medium and grill as described above.*

Fresh Anchovies in Orange-Walnut Vinaigrette

SERVES 4–6 AS AN APPETIZER

> 1 recipe Orange-Walnut Vinaigrette (page 37)
>
> 1½ pounds fresh anchovies, headed and gutted
>
> Salt
>
> Extra-virgin olive oil
>
> Crusty bread, for serving

Season the fish with salt and let them rest for 15 minutes. Toss the fish with enough olive oil to coat them. Place a large sauté pan over high heat and let it get screaming hot. Add the fish and cook, turning once, until they are cooked through, 2–3 minutes. Transfer to a platter, cover with Orange-Walnut Vinaigrette, and let them rest in the refrigerator for 1–24 hours. Serve at room temperature with crusty bread.

Broiled Fresh Anchovies with Red Wine–Shallot Vinaigrette

SERVES 4–6 AS AN APPETIZER

> 1 recipe Red Wine–Shallot Vinaigrette (page 37), divided
>
> 1½ pounds fresh anchovies, headed and gutted

Toss the fish with half of the Red Wine–Shallot Vinaigrette and let them rest for 30 minutes. Preheat the broiler to high and place the rack in the position closest to the heat. Remove the fish from the marinade and discard the marinade. Arrange the fish in a single layer on a baking tray, slide the tray under the broiler, and cook until the skin crisps slightly, 4–5 minutes. Drizzle with the remaining marinade and serve.

Broiled Fresh Anchovies with Oregano and Lemon

SERVES 4–6

> 1½ pounds fresh whole anchovies, headed and gutted
>
> Salt
>
> Flour
>
> 4 tablespoons butter
>
> 1 lemon, thinly sliced
>
> 8 sprigs fresh oregano, leaves picked, or 1 tablespoon dried oregano

Season the anchovies with salt and let them rest for 15 minutes. Preheat the broiler to high and set the rack to the position closest to the heat. Dredge the anchovies in flour to coat. In a sauté pan over medium heat, melt the butter and cook until golden brown. Add the anchovies in a single layer and cook for 1 minute. Turn the fish, add the lemon slices, and season with salt and oregano. Place the pan under the broiler and cook 4–5 minutes until the fish become crispy and the lemons char.

ANCHOVIES
Canned

Anchovy-Parsley Spread

This Provençal dish is called *Anchoiade*.

MAKES ¾ CUP

> 1 (2-ounce) tin anchovies in oil
>
> 1 garlic clove
>
> 6 tablespoons extra-virgin olive oil
>
> 2 tablespoons white wine vinegar
>
> ⅓ cup parsley, chopped
>
> Crostini, for serving

In a food processor or using a mortar and pestle, purée the anchovies with their oil, garlic, olive oil, and vinegar until smooth. Add the parsley and pulse until the mixture is mostly smooth. If a smoother texture is desired, add more olive oil. Spread on crostini and bake, or use as a dip for raw sweet vegetables, such as snap peas, sweet peppers, and carrots.

Marinated Anchovies with Mint and Mace

SERVES 3–4 AS AN APPETIZER

> 2 (2-ounce) tins anchovies in oil
>
> 2 tablespoons extra-virgin olive oil
>
> Mace
>
> 5 sprigs mint, leaves picked and torn
>
> 1 lemon, cut into wedges
>
> Crostini for serving

On a serving platter, lay the anchovies with their oil in a single layer. Cover the anchovies with oil and a couple of pinches of mace. Let it rest for 1 hour. Scatter with torn mint and serve at room temperature with lemon wedges and crostini.

NOTE *This recipe can be easily increased in direct proportion to the amount needed.*

Marinated Anchovies with Clove Oil

SERVES 3–4 AS AN APPETIZER

> 2 (2-ounce) tins anchovies in oil
>
> 2 tablespoons extra-virgin olive oil
>
> 5 whole cloves
>
> Black pepper
>
> 1 lemon, cut into wedges
>
> Crostini for serving

Strain the oil from the anchovy tins into a small pan over low heat. Add the olive oil and cloves. When the oil just begins to simmer, turn off the heat and cool to room temperature. Lay the anchovies in a single layer on a serving platter. Strain the oil and discard the cloves. Drizzle the oil over the anchovies, and let it rest for 1 hour before serving at room temperature with black pepper, lemon wedges, and crostini.

NOTE *This recipe can be easily increased in direct proportion to the amount needed.*

Anchovy Bread and Butter with Crushed Red Chile Flakes

SERVES 3–4 AS AN APPETIZER

> Baguette, cut on the bias in ½-inch slices so that each piece is 3 inches long
>
> Unsalted butter, softened
>
> 1 (2-ounce) tin anchovies in oil
>
> Hot chile flakes, such as Aleppo, Calabrian, or Espelette, or crushed red chile flakes

Generously slather each slice of bread with butter. Place 1–2 anchovies on top of the butter and sprinkle with chile flakes.

NOTE *This recipe can be easily increased in direct proportion to the amount needed.*

Anchovies with Roasted Peppers and Mint

SERVES 4 AS AN APPETIZER

> 2–3 red or yellow bell peppers, roasted, peeled, deseeded, and sliced into ¾-inch strips
>
> 2 (2-ounce) tins anchovies in oil
>
> 1–2 tablespoons extra-virgin olive oil
>
> 5 sprigs mint, leaves torn into small pieces
>
> Mace
>
> Crostini for serving

Arrange the bell pepper strips on a serving platter and drizzle with the oil from the anchovy tins. Spread the anchovies evenly over the peppers. Drizzle with olive oil and mint and sprinkle with mace. Serve as is or with crostini.

VARIATION

+ **Anchovies with Pepper and Basil.** Replace mint with torn basil leaves.

Anchovy-Braised Greens

SERVES 4–6 AS A SIDE DISH

> ¼ cup extra-virgin olive oil
>
> 6 garlic cloves, thinly sliced
>
> 2 tablespoons fennel seeds
>
> 2 (2-ounce) tins anchovies in oil
>
> 1–2 teaspoons crushed red chile flakes
>
> 4 bunches Lacinato kale, leaves picked and roughly chopped
>
> 2 cups vegetable stock or water
>
> 1–2 tablespoons red wine vinegar (optional)
>
> Salt

In a large pan over medium heat, warm the olive oil and add the garlic and fennel seeds. Cook until the garlic begins to brown. Add the anchovies with their oil and chile flakes and cook until they have melted, about 2 minutes. Add the kale and toss to coat with oil. Add the stock, cover, and reduce the heat to low. Cook for 30–40 minutes, stirring occasionally, until the kale is completely wilted. Stir in the vinegar, if using, and season with salt before serving warm or at room temperature.

Anchovy Butter–Glazed Autumn Squash

SERVES 4–6 AS A SIDE DISH

1 recipe Anchovy Butter (page 19)

3 tablespoons extra-virgin olive oil

1 autumn squash, such as one medium butternut squash, peeled and cut into cubes, or two small acorn squash, sliced

Salt

2 tablespoons chopped fresh herbs, such as chervil, parsley, or tarragon

In a heavy sauté pan over high heat, warm the oil and add the squash. Season with salt and cook until lightly browned. Slide the pan into a 350°F oven and roast until the squash is tender. Remove the pan from the oven and transfer the squash to a serving platter. Place the pan over medium heat and add the Anchovy Butter and 3 tablespoons of water. Simmer, stirring constantly, until the sauce emulsifies. Stir in the herbs and pour the glaze over the squash.

Anchovy Butter–Glazed Zucchini and Summer Squash

SERVES 4–6 AS A SIDE DISH

1 recipe Anchovy-Almond Butter (page 19)

2 tablespoons extra-virgin olive oil

3–4 zucchini and/or summer squash, diced into 1-inch pieces

Salt

Black pepper

In a heavy sauté pan over medium-high heat, warm the oil. Add the zucchini and cook until lightly browned. Season with salt and pepper. Continue cooking until the squash is al dente in texture. Remove from the heat. Add the Anchovy-Almond Butter and toss until the butter is melted and the zucchini is evenly coated.

Anchovy-Tomato Sauce

MAKES ABOUT 3 CUPS

¼ cup extra-virgin olive oil

1 (2-ounce) tin anchovies in oil

4 garlic cloves, thinly sliced

1 (28-ounce) can whole, peeled San Marzano tomatoes

Salt

3 tablespoons chopped fresh herbs, such as basil or oregano (optional)

In a saucepan over medium-low heat, warm the olive oil and add the anchovies with their oil and garlic. Cook until the anchovies have melted and the garlic has softened, about 3 minutes. Add the tomatoes and crush with the back of a spoon. Season with salt and add the herbs, if using. Cover and simmer over low heat for 1 hour, stirring occasionally.

Anchovy-Garlic Bread

SERVES 4–6 AS A SIDE DISH

1 recipe Anchovy-Herb Butter (page 19)

½ baguette, sliced lengthwise as if for a sandwich

Grated Parmesan cheese

Cayenne pepper (optional)

Preheat the broiler to medium and place the rack in the position closest to the heat. Spread the Anchovy-Herb Butter on the sliced baguette and place on a baking sheet. Sprinkle each with Parmesan cheese and cayenne pepper, if using. Slide the tray under the broiler and cook until the edges are browned.

Anchovy Bloody Mary Mix

MAKES ONE SERVING

3–4 anchovy fillets in oil

¾ cup tomato or V8® juice

1 lime, juiced

1 generous tablespoon prepared horseradish

1 tablespoon Worcestershire sauce

1 tablespoon sherry or red wine vinegar

1 teaspoon ground celery seeds

Hot sauce

Salt

1–2 shots vodka or gin

Garnishes, such as pickled green beans, celery stalks, and/or crisp bacon slices

In a blender, combine the anchovies, tomato or V8 juice, lime juice, horseradish, Worcestershire sauce, vinegar, celery seeds, and hot sauce to taste. Blend until smooth, season with salt, and serve over ice with your choice of booze and garnishes.

Roasted Tomatoes with Anchovy, Garlic, and Thyme

SERVES 4–6 AS A SIDE DISH

1 (2-ounce) tin anchovies in oil

2 garlic cloves, minced

¼ cup extra-virgin olive oil

6 sprigs thyme, leaves picked

2 pounds plum tomatoes, halved lengthwise

Salt

Black pepper

In a large bowl, mash the anchovies with their oil, garlic, olive oil, and thyme. Add the tomatoes, season with salt, and toss. Spread the tomatoes cut side up in a single layer on a baking sheet, drizzle with any remaining oil, and season with black pepper. Roast in the oven at 275°F until the tomatoes have shriveled but are not fully dry, about 2–4 hours. Serve as a garnish to salads, as part of a vegetable platter, or chopped as a salsa.

Anchovy Flatbread

SERVES 4–6

2 (2-ounce) tins anchovies in oil

3 tablespoons extra-virgin olive oil

3 pounds onions, thinly sliced

1 sprig fresh rosemary

Salt

1 pound pizza dough, store-bought or homemade

Crushed red chile flakes

3 tablespoons minced, cured black olives, such as Kalamata

In a sauté pan over medium heat, warm the oil from the anchovies and the olive oil. Add the onions and rosemary and stir to coat. Season with salt and cook, stirring occasionally, until the onions are caramelized, 30–40 minutes. Roll out the pizza dough into a thin rectangle shape and place it on a sheet pan. Mash the onions into a thick paste and spread over the dough. Place the anchovy fillets evenly across the dough and sprinkle with the chile flakes and olives. Slide the pan into a 450°F oven and cook until the dough is cooked and the edges crisped, about 15–20 minutes.

Anchovy-Herb Sauce for Vegetables

This is an Italian version of Bagna Càuda.

MAKES ABOUT ¾ CUP

¼ cup extra-virgin olive oil

3–6 garlic cloves, grated

2 (2-ounce) tins anchovies in oil

⅓ cup white wine

8 tablespoons cold butter, cut into tablespoon-size pieces

Black pepper

2 tablespoons finely chopped fresh herbs, such as chervil, parsley, or tarragon

In a saucepan over medium heat, warm the olive oil. Add the garlic and the anchovies with their oil and cook until the anchovies have melted and the garlic has softened, 2–3 minutes. Add the wine and simmer until the alcohol smell dissipates. Remove from the heat and whisk in the butter 1 tablespoon at a time. Season with black pepper and stir in the herbs. Serve warm as a dip for raw vegetables or as a sauce drizzled over roasted vegetables, fish, or chicken.

Bitter Greens with Anchovy Vinaigrette and Parmesan

SERVES 4–6 AS A SIDE DISH

1 pound mixed young bitter greens, such as puntarelle, dandelion greens, and/or radicchio, stems trimmed and leaves cut into bite-size pieces

Salt

2 garlic cloves, grated

1 (2-ounce) tin anchovies in oil

½ cup extra-virgin olive oil

3 tablespoons red wine vinegar

Black pepper

Shaved Parmesan cheese

Place the salad greens in salted ice water for 1 hour before draining and drying thoroughly. In a bowl, mash the garlic with the anchovies and their oil. Add the olive oil, vinegar, and a pinch of salt and whisk until smooth. Drizzle half of the vinaigrette over the greens and toss to combine. Drizzle the remaining vinaigrette over the top and garnish with a generous amount of pepper and cheese.

Broiled Broccoli with Anchovies

SERVES 4–6 AS A SIDE DISH

2 garlic cloves, grated

1 (2-ounce) tin anchovies in oil

⅓ cup extra-virgin olive oil, divided

2 tablespoons red wine vinegar

Salt

2 heads broccoli, cut into large florets, blanched in boiling salted water, and drained

Crushed red chile flakes (optional)

In a bowl, mash the garlic with the anchovies and their oil. Add ¼ cup of the olive oil, vinegar, and a pinch of salt and whisk until smooth. Preheat the broiler to high and place the rack in the position closest to the heat. Spread the blanched broccoli in a single layer on a baking tray. Drizzle with the remaining ¼ cup olive oil and slide under the broiler. Cook until the broccoli is crisp and charred, about 6–8 minutes. Garnish with chile flakes, if using.

Broiled Kale Salad with Pecan-Anchovy Dressing

SERVES 4–6

4 tablespoons extra-virgin olive oil, divided

3–6 garlic cloves, grated

2 (2-ounce) tins anchovies in oil

½ cup pecan pieces

2 lemons, juiced

2 teaspoons crushed red chile flakes

2 large bunches kale, leaves picked and roughly chopped

In a saucepan over medium heat, warm 2 tablespoons of the olive oil. Add the garlic, anchovies with their oil, and pecan pieces. Cook until the anchovies have melted and the garlic has softened, 2–3 minutes. Add the lemon juice and chile flakes and stir to combine. Toss the kale with the remaining 2 tablespoons of olive oil to coat the leaves, spread them out on a sheet pan, and roast at 375°F until crisp, 20–30 minutes. Put the kale on a serving platter and drizzle with the warm pecan dressing.

Creamy Butter Beans with Anchovies

SERVES 4–6 AS A SIDE DISH

3 tablespoons extra-virgin olive oil

1 onion, finely diced

5 garlic cloves, smashed

1 (2-ounce) tin anchovies in oil

Crushed red chile flakes

2 (14-ounce) cans butter beans, drained with half of the liquid reserved

1½ cups stock or water

¼ cup chopped fresh chives, parsley, and/or tarragon

In a sauté pan over medium heat, warm the oil. Add the onion and garlic and cook until the onions are transparent. Add the anchovies with their oil and a pinch of chile flakes. Cook until the anchovies have melted, 2–3 minutes. Add the beans, reserved liquid, and stock. Simmer for 20 minutes, stirring regularly, until creamy. Stir in the herbs. Serve warm or at room temperature.

Linguine with Anchovy, Almond, and Tarragon

SERVES 4–6

  1 pound linguine, cooked al dente in salted water, drained, with 1 cup of cooking liquid reserved

  2 tablespoons extra-virgin olive oil

  ½ cup crushed almonds

  1 (2-ounce) tin anchovies in oil

  4 tablespoons butter

  3 tablespoons chopped fresh tarragon

In a large sauté pan over medium heat, warm the olive oil. Add the almonds and cook until fragrant. Add the anchovies with their oil. Cook until the anchovies have melted, 2–3 minutes. Add the pasta, reserved liquid, and butter. Simmer until the pasta has absorbed most of the liquid and the sauce coats the pasta. Stir in the tarragon and serve.

Marinated Boquerones

These are Spanish pickled anchovies.

SERVES 2–4 AS AN APPETIZER

  1 (4-ounce) package boquerones, drained

  1 small red onion, thinly sliced, rinsed under cold running water, and patted dry

  ½ cup mint, leaves picked and torn

  ½ cup parsley leaves

  2 tablespoons extra-virgin olive oil

  1 lemon, juiced

  Salt

  Black pepper or crushed red chile flakes

  Crostini or endive for serving

Arrange the boquerones on a serving platter. In a bowl combine the onion, mint, parsley, olive oil, and lemon juice. Season with salt and pepper. Scatter the onion-herb mixture over the fish. Serve at room temperature with crostini or endive.

VARIATION

+ **Boquerones with Mint and Mace.** Place the boquerones on a platter and cover with olive oil, red wine vinegar, torn mint, and a sprinkling of ground mace. Marinate 1 hour to 2 days. Serve at room temperature.

Spice-Cured Anchovies

MAKES ABOUT 1 POUND CURED ANCHOVIES

  15 almonds

  3 bay leaves

  10 allspice berries

  6 tablespoons kosher salt

  6 tablespoons sugar

  2 pounds fresh anchovies, headed and gutted

Use a mortar and pestle to make a paste of the almonds, bay leaves, and allspice. Add the salt and sugar. Place the fish in a baking dish just large enough to hold them in a single layer. Sprinkle the cure mixture evenly over the fish and cover tightly. Keep chilled. The fish will be cured in 5 days but will keep refrigerated up to 6 months. These are best when washed, filleted, and marinated in extra-virgin olive oil.

Spaghetti with Anchovies and Escarole

SERVES 4

> 1 pound spaghetti, cooked al dente in salted water, drained, with 1 cup of cooking liquid reserved
>
> 2 tablespoons butter
>
> 1 cup fresh bread crumbs
>
> ¼ cup extra-virgin olive oil
>
> 2 (2-ounce) tins anchovies in oil
>
> 4 garlic cloves, sliced
>
> 1 tablespoon crushed red chile flakes
>
> 1 head escarole, cut into 1-inch pieces

In a large sauté pan over medium heat, melt the butter. Add the bread crumbs and toast until crispy and brown. Transfer to a plate and wipe the pan clean. Return the pan to medium heat and add the olive oil, anchovies with their oil, and garlic. Cook until the anchovies have melted and the garlic has softened, 2–3 minutes. Add the chile flakes and escarole, toss to combine, and cook until wilted. Add ½ cup of the reserved pasta water and simmer until the liquid evaporates. Add the pasta and remaining pasta water and simmer until pasta is warmed and the liquid coats the pasta. Sprinkle the bread crumbs over the top.

Traditional Tapenade

This spiced black olive spread can be used as spread for sandwiches or on crostini, or to coat baked fish, chicken, or lamb.

MAKES ABOUT 1½ CUPS

> ¾ cup dry-cured pitted black olives, such as Kalamata
>
> ¼ cup sliced almonds
>
> 1 (2-ounce) tin anchovies in oil
>
> ½ cup extra-virgin olive oil or melted butter, divided
>
> 2 tablespoons capers, rinsed
>
> 2 garlic cloves, grated
>
> 1 orange, zested and juiced

Soak the olives in hot water for 10 minutes and then drain, reserving the liquid for another use, such as adding to pasta cooking water. Place the olives in a food processor with the almonds, anchovies with their oil, ¼ cup of the olive oil, capers, garlic, and orange zest and juice. Pulse until finely chopped. Transfer to a bowl and whisk in the remaining ¼ cup of olive oil. Serve at room temperature.

Non-traditional Tapenade

This spiced black olive–fig spread can be used as a spread for sandwiches or on crostini, or to coat baked fish, chicken, or lamb.

MAKES ABOUT 2½ CUPS

> ¾ cup dry-cured pitted black olives, such as Kalamata
>
> 6 dried figs
>
> 1 garlic clove, grated
>
> 1 fennel bulb, roughly chopped
>
> ¼ cup sliced almonds
>
> ¾ cup extra-virgin olive oil or butter, divided
>
> 1 (2-ounce) tin anchovies in oil
>
> 4 sprigs thyme, leaves picked
>
> 1 orange, zested and juiced
>
> 1 lemon, zested and juiced
>
> 1 generous pinch of crushed red chile flakes

Soak the olives and figs in hot water for 10 minutes and then drain, reserving the liquid for another use, such as adding to pasta cooking water. Place the olives and figs in a food processor with the garlic, fennel, almonds, ¼ cup of the olive oil, anchovies with their oil, thyme leaves, orange and lemon zest and juice, and chile flakes. Pulse until finely chopped. Transfer to a bowl and whisk in the remaining ½ cup olive oil. Serve at room temperature as a spread for sandwiches or on crostini, or use as a crust for baked fish, chicken, or lamb.

Txalaparta Bread Dip

This is a delicious dip for bread or vegetables that I had at the Basque restaurant Txalaparta.

MAKES ABOUT 2½ CUPS

> ¾ cup extra-virgin olive oil
>
> 6 garlic cloves, grated
>
> 1 (2-ounce) tin anchovies in oil
>
> Crushed red chile flakes
>
> ½ cup chopped parsley
>
> Baguette for serving

In a saucepan over medium heat, warm the olive oil. Add the garlic and anchovies with their oil. Cook until the anchovies have melted and the garlic has softened, 2–3 minutes. Remove from the heat and add a generous amount of chile flakes and parsley. Serve warm with a baguette for dipping.

BARRACUDA
Fillet fish

As delicious as a barracuda is when it's sitting on a plate, it is equally as menacing to its prey while lurking in Atlantic and Pacific waters. These intimidatingly toothed fish live relatively dormant lives until they snap into high gear—bursting up to 27 miles per hour—to capture their prey. Weighing between 1½ and 6 pounds, these fish, sometimes called sea pike, possess a unique, bold taste; dull gray or pinkish flesh; large, soft flake; and luscious fat content. Widely consumed up until the 1970s, barracuda is now a rare find at fish markets. But if you do come across steak, fillet, or whole barracuda, grill, smoke, or slow roast it and pair it with acidic sauces and flavors, such as thyme, basil, or oranges.

Barracuda Ceviche
SERVES 4

1 pound barracuda fillets, skin off, diced into ½-inch pieces

Salt

¾ cup lemon juice

1 orange, zested and juiced

1–2 hot chiles, such as Fresno or serrano, thinly sliced

1 red onion, thinly sliced, rinsed under cold running water, and patted dry

¼ cup extra-virgin olive oil

1 cup parsley, leaves picked

Keep this dish cold at all times during preparation. Season the fish with salt and let it rest for 5 minutes. Combine the fish with the lemon juice, orange zest and juice, and chiles and let it rest for 45 minutes. Add the onion and let it rest for another 10 minutes. Add the olive oil and parsley and toss well.

Slow-Roasted Barracuda with Sorrel Butter
SERVES 4

1 recipe Sorrel Butter (page 22)

4 barracuda portions, skin on and scored

Salt

Extra-virgin olive oil

Season the fish with salt and let it rest for 20 minutes. Lightly oil a baking dish and place the fish skin side up. Bake at 275°F for 20–25 minutes until cooked through. Once it is cooked, remove the skin and any dark muscle tissue from each portion. Serve with Sorrel Butter.

Grilled Barracuda with Red Wine–Shallot Vinaigrette

SERVES 4

> 1 recipe Red Wine–Shallot Vinaigrette (page 37), divided
>
> 4 barracuda portions, skin on and scored

Combine the fish with ½ of the Red Wine–Shallot Vinaigrette and let it rest for 4–6 hours. Prepare a charcoal grill with a medium fire, concentrating the hot coals on one side of the kettle. Remove the fish from the marinade and place it skin side down directly over the coals. Cook until the skin begins to crisp, 3–4 minutes. Lift the entire grill grate and rotate it so the fish rests opposite the hot coals. Cover the grill and continue to cook over indirect heat until the fish is done. Serve with the remaining vinaigrette.

NOTE *If using a gas grill, preheat all burners to high. Place the barracuda on one side of the hot grates. Once it begins to char around the edges, turn off the burner directly under the fish and cover the grill to finish cooking. Serve with the remaining vinaigrette*

Plank-Grilled Barracuda with Cilantro-Pecan Pesto

SERVES 4

> 1 recipe Cilantro-Pecan Pesto (page 25)
>
> 4 barracuda portions, skin on and scored
>
> Salt
>
> Extra-virgin olive oil

Season the fish with salt and let it rest for 20 minutes. Prepare a charcoal grill with a medium fire. Lightly oil the fish, place on a cedar plank, put the plank on the grill, and cover the grill. Cook for 8–12 minutes, or until done. Serve with Cilantro-Pecan Pesto.

NOTE *If using a gas grill, preheat all burners to medium and follow the grilling instructions above.*

VARIATION

+ Simply grill as per previous recipe and serve with Cilantro-Almond Pesto.

Sautéed Barracuda with Brown Butter and Orange

SERVES 4

> 4 barracuda portions, skin on and scored
>
> Salt
>
> 6 tablespoons butter, divided
>
> 2 garlic cloves, finely minced
>
> 2 oranges, segmented

Season the fish with salt and let it rest for 20 minutes. In a sauté pan over medium heat, melt 2 tablespoons of the butter and cook until golden brown. Place the fish in the pan, skin side down. Cook without flipping until almost done and then remove the fish and wipe the pan clean. Add the remaining 4 tablespoons of butter and the garlic. Cook until butter is dark brown. Add the orange segments and season with salt. Stir gently to combine. Turn off the heat and return the fish to the pan, uncooked side down, to finish cooking.

BARRAMUNDI
Fillet fish

This fish is native to Australia and Southeast Asia. According to aboriginal folktales, barramundi has special aphrodisiac qualities and is sometimes called passion fish. Recently, farmed barramundi has become widely available in the American market, typically sold as frozen fillets. Barramundi has a sweet, buttery flavor overall, with larger fish having a stronger taste profile than smaller ones. The dense meat has large, firm flakes, and the fish has few bones, which are removed easily. The flesh's moderate-to-high fat content helps keep it moist while cooking, lending itself to myriad preparations including sautéing, broiling, frying, grilling, and steaming. Barramundi is a good substitute in recipes that call for grouper, snapper, or halibut.

Citrus-Coated Barramundi with Pine Nut Piccata

SERVES 4

> 1 recipe Pine Nut Piccata (page 30)
>
> 4 portions barramundi, skin off, cut into 2-inch strips
>
> Salt
>
> Vegetable or peanut oil
>
> ¼ cup citrus juice
>
> Flour
>
> Panko

Season the fish with salt and let it rest for 15 minutes. Pour 3–4 inches of oil into a high-sided pan. Place over medium-high heat and warm the oil to 375°F. Dip pieces of the fish into the juice, then into flour to coat both sides, then into the juice again, and finally into the panko to coat both sides. Place the breaded piece into the oil and hold it for 5 seconds before releasing it. Repeat the process, cooking the fish a few pieces at a time. Turn with a slotted spoon to ensure that both sides crisp evenly. Remove the pieces as they finish and place on paper towels to absorb the excess oil. Serve drizzled with Pine Nut Piccata.

Broiled Barramundi with Grapes

SERVES 4

> 4 barramundi portions, skin on and scored
>
> Salt
>
> 6 tablespoons butter
>
> 1 cup seedless grapes
>
> 2 tablespoons chopped fresh herbs, such as parsley or tarragon
>
> 1 lemon, cut into wedges

Season the fish with salt and let it rest for 15 minutes. Preheat the broiler to medium-high. In a sauté pan over medium heat, melt the butter and cook until it is dark brown. Place the fish skin side down in the pan. Spoon the brown butter over the fish and arrange the grapes among the fish. Place the pan under the broiler and cook until the grapes have blistered and released some juice and the fish is cooked through. Garnish with herbs and lemon wedges.

Sautéed Barramundi with Pico de Gallo

SERVES 4

> 1 recipe Pico de Gallo (page 30)
>
> 4 barramundi portions, skin on and scored
>
> Salt
>
> 3 tablespoons butter or olive oil

Season the fish with salt and let it rest for 15 minutes. In a sauté pan over medium heat, melt the butter. Place the fish in the pan skin side down. Cook until almost done, then flip to finish cooking. Serve with Pico de Gallo.

BLACK BASS
Fillet fish

These handsome fish have long been highly esteemed by both anglers and diners. Historically and into the present day they're among the few fish sold live, as they are resilient fish and, especially in the era before refrigeration, they are able to be kept in live tanks, thus ensuring quality. While black bass, sometimes called black sea bass, provide fabulous eating all year round, it is in the late fall and winter that their flavor and fat are most luxurious. They are great fish for whole presentations and possess an uncommonly elegant flavor in a lithe and thin-skinned fillet. The flesh is firm and, because they feed primarily on shrimp, crabs, and clams, also rich and silky.

Whole fish lend themselves to poached, steamed, or baked preparations. Pair with ginger whenever possible, as it draws out the sweeter, more floral character of the fish. The roe, milt, and liver are all worth fighting over. These parts I will simply sauté in butter with thyme and serve on toast. The roe and milt are ideal when beaten with warmed butter, then cooled to form a smooth paste for use as compound butter melted over fillets. The heads and bones make a rich stock. And if that isn't enough to ask of one fish, black bass is one of the most delicious fish served cold: its nuanced flavor persists, charismatic, full, and perfect flaked over salad or as garnish to gazpacho.

Whole Fried Black Bass with Pine Nut Agrodolce

SERVES 2–4

1 recipe Pine Nut Agrodolce (page 30)

2 (1- to 2- pound) whole black bass, scaled, gutted, gills removed, and skin scored

Salt

1 lemon, juiced

Vegetable or peanut oil

½ cup flour, sifted

½ cup cornstarch, sifted

Season the fish with salt and lemon juice and let it rest for 20 minutes. Pour 2–3 inches of vegetable oil into a high-sided pan big enough to hold one fish. Place over medium-high heat and warm the oil to 350°F. Combine the flour and cornstarch in a large bowl and dredge one fish in the mixture, coating both sides. Slide the fish into the hot oil. Cook until golden and crispy on one side, and then gently flip the fish to cook the other side, 6–8 minutes per side. Remove the fish from the oil and place on paper towels to absorb the excess oil. Repeat the process with the second fish. Top each fish with Pine Nut Agrodolce.

VARIATION

+ **Spicy Fried Whole Black Bass.** Substitute Lemon-Chile-Soy Sauce (page 28) or Pickled Chiles (page 29) for Pine Nut Agrodolce.

Poached Black Bass with White Wine and Ginger

SERVES 4

4 black bass portions, skin on and scored

½ tablespoon kosher salt

1 cup white wine

1 (1-inch) knob of ginger, thinly sliced

1 star anise pod

4 tablespoons cold butter, cut into pieces

2 tablespoons chopped fresh herbs, such as chervil or tarragon

Season the fish with salt and let it rest for 15 minutes. In a pan just wide enough to hold the fish in a single layer, combine 1 cup of water with the wine, ginger, salt, and star anise. Simmer over low heat for 5 minutes. Bring the liquid to 170°F. Add the fish skin side down so that it is barely submerged, and cook until it is opaque and flakes under gentle pressure, 4–6 minutes per ½ inch of thickness. Transfer the fish to a plate and keep warm. Strain 1 cup of the poaching liquid into a saucepan, place over high heat, and reduce to 3 tablespoons. Turn off the heat, add the butter, and swirl the sauce in the pan to incorporate the butter. Add the herbs, season with salt, and spoon over the fish.

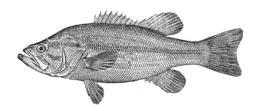

Sautéed Black Bass with Rosemary and Orange

SERVES 4

> 4 black bass portions, skin on and scored
>
> Salt
>
> 6 tablespoons butter, divided
>
> 2 garlic cloves, finely minced
>
> 2 sprigs fresh rosemary, leaves picked
>
> 1 orange, zested and juiced

Season the fish with salt and let it rest for 15 minutes. In a sauté pan over medium heat, melt 2 tablespoons of the butter and cook until golden brown. Place the fish in the pan skin side down. Cook until almost done and then remove the fish and wipe the pan clean. Add the remaining 4 tablespoons of butter, garlic, rosemary, and orange zest. Cook until the garlic is browned and the rosemary is crisp. Add the orange juice and season with salt. Stir to combine. Turn off the heat and return the fish to the pan skin side up to finish cooking.

Sautéed Black Bass with Black Butter and Pecans

SERVES 4

> 4 black bass portions, skin on and scored
>
> Salt
>
> 6 tablespoons butter, divided
>
> ½ cup chopped pecans
>
> 1 lemon, juiced

Season the fish with salt and let it rest for 15 minutes. In a sauté pan over medium heat, melt 2 tablespoons of the butter and cook until golden brown. Place the fish in the pan skin side down. Cook without flipping until almost done and then remove the fish and wipe the pan clean. Add the remaining 4 tablespoons of butter and cook until the butter is nearly black. Add the pecans and cook 30 seconds. Add the lemon juice and season with salt. Stir to combine. Turn off the heat and return the fish to the pan skin side up to finish cooking.

Steamed Black Bass with Lemongrass and Citrus

SERVES 4

> 4 black bass portions, skin on and scored
>
> Salt
>
> 3 lemongrass stalks, sliced in half and bruised with the back of a knife
>
> 1 orange, thinly sliced
>
> 1 lemon, thinly sliced
>
> ½ cup white wine
>
> 4 tablespoons butter, melted, or 2 tablespoons nut oil, such as almond or roasted peanut

Season the fish with salt and let it rest for 15 minutes. In a wide, shallow pot over medium-low heat, place the lemongrass and orange and lemon slices to create a raft for the fish. Add the wine and enough water to cover the bottom of the pot. Bring to a simmer. Place the fish skin side down on top of the aromatics, cover, and cook until done, 7–8 minutes. Remove the fish. Serve each portion with 1 tablespoon of butter or ½ tablespoon of oil and a spoonful of the remaining cooking liquid drizzled over it.

VARIATIONS

+ **Holiday-Scented Black Bass.** Substitute a cinnamon stick for the lemongrass.

+ **Fennel and Orange–Scented Black Bass.** Use orange slices, sprigs of fresh thyme, and thinly sliced fennel as a raft.

+ **Rosemary-Lemon Scented Black Bass.** Use 2 stalks of rosemary, lemon slices, and sliced onion as a raft.

Chilled Poached Black Bass with Vinaigrette

SERVES 4

> 4 black bass portions, skin on and scored
> Salt
> 1 cup white wine
> 3 tablespoons white wine vinegar, divided
> 1 small shallot, sliced
> 1 small carrot, sliced
> 10 black peppercorns
> 1 bay leaf
> 2 teaspoons whole grain mustard
> 3 tablespoons extra-virgin olive oil

Season the fish with salt and let it rest for 15 minutes. In a pan just wide enough to hold the fish in a single layer, combine 1 cup of water with the wine, 2 tablespoons vinegar, shallot, carrot, peppercorns, and bay leaf. Simmer over low heat for 5 minutes. Season the broth with salt and bring it to 170°F. Add the fish skin side down so that it is barely submerged and cook until it is opaque and flakes under gentle presure, 4–6 minutes per ½ inch of thickness. Remove the pan from the heat and cool the fish in the poaching liquid to room temperature and then in the refrigerator overnight. Transfer the fish to a serving plate and pat dry. Strain 1 cup of the poaching liquid into a saucepan, place over high heat, and reduce to 3 tablespoons. Turn off the heat and whisk in the mustard, olive oil, and rest of the vinegar. Spoon the vinaigrette over the fish and serve at room temperature.

Salt-Roasted Whole Black Bass with Orange and Thyme

SERVES 2–4

> 2 pounds kosher salt
> 1 (2- to 2½-pound) whole black bass, scaled, gutted, gills removed, and skin scored
> 2 oranges, thinly sliced
> 12 sprigs thyme
> 2 tablespoons extra-virgin olive oil
> 4 tablespoons butter, melted, or additional olive oil

Season the fish with salt and let it rest for 20 minutes. Combine 2 pounds of salt with enough water that the mixture resembles wet sand. Place a thin layer of the salt mixture on a baking sheet and top with half of the orange slices and half of the thyme. Place the fish on top and then place the remaining oranges and thyme on top of the fish. Drizzle the olive oil over the fish and pack on the remaining salt mixture to completely encase the fish. Bake at 375°F for 25–30 minutes. Remove the fish from the oven and let it rest for 5 minutes. Crack the salt crust and discard. To serve, discard the oranges and thyme and peel off the skin before transferring the top fillet to a platter. Remove and discard the backbone, and transfer the bottom fillet without its skin to a platter. Drizzle the fish with the melted butter.

BLOWFISH
Meaty dense fish

Blowfish are members of the pufferfish family, and these two names are often interchangeable. As a group these creatures are distinguished from other fish by their effective but comical defense mechanism. They are covered in sharp spines and can rapidly inflate their bodies into a balloon shape. Some are poisonous (less comical). This combination makes most predators wary, but humans are strange animals and not so easily deterred.

Great care must be taken when handling these fish, as some of them have toxins usually contained in the organs and sometimes present in the flesh. Some species are less dangerous than others, which can lead you to think you should prepare these yourself using a YouTube video as a guide. Please don't. Leave it to a professional. Proper preparation is, of course, essential, but much of the risk comes from misidentification of the fish, as more than a dozen species swim in our coastal waters. Don't eat puffers unless they come from a known, trusted, and experienced provider.

Only the small tails are eaten, and if you can find them, they will have been cleaned before coming to market and resemble large skinless chicken drumsticks. Blowfish is some of the most delicate seafood in the world's oceans. It is at once creamy and custard-like in richness and has an engaging elasticity to the bite. The texture is often described as akin to that of frog legs. As a more relatable example, I think that they are like the best chicken wings you could possibly imagine. Maybe that is why blowfish is sometimes referred to as sea squab.

Broiled Marinated Blowfish Tails

SERVES 4

> 1 recipe Red Wine–Shallot Vinaigrette (page 37), divided
>
> 2 pounds bone-in blowfish tails, cleaned

Marinate the blowfish tails in half the vinaigrette for 1–8 hours, reserving the other half to finish. Preheat the broiler to medium and set the rack in the position closest to the heat. Remove the tails from the marinade and place them on a baking tray. Slide the tray under the broiler and cook until slightly charred. 7–10 minutes, depending on the thickness. Drizzle with the remaining vinaigrette.

Grilled Blowfish Tails with Sicilian Herb Sauce

SERVES 4

> 1 recipe Sicilian Herb Sauce (page 32), divided
>
> 2 pounds bone-in blowfish tails, cleaned

Marinate the blowfish tails in half of the Sicilian Herb Sauce for 4–8 hours, reserving the other half of the sauce for serving. Prepare a charcoal grill with a medium fire. Place the tails on the grill directly over the coals and spoon the marinade over the top. Cook, turning just once, until the marinade has charred and the fish is cooked through, 5–7 minutes. Serve with the reserved sauce.

NOTE *If using a gas grill, preheat all the burners to medium and proceed with the grilling directions above.*

Blowfish Tails en Saor (sweet-sour vinaigrette)

SERVES 4

> 2 pounds bone-in blowfish tails, cleaned
>
> Salt
>
> ¾ cup extra-virgin olive oil, divided
>
> 3 tablespoons pine nuts or slivered almonds
>
> 2 tablespoons raisins
>
> 1 small onion, thinly sliced
>
> 1 red bell pepper, finely diced
>
> 1 small eggplant, ½-inch dice, about 2 cups
>
> ¼ cup red wine vinegar
>
> 1 tablespoon brown sugar
>
> Baguette for serving

Season the fish tails with salt and let them rest for 15 minutes. In a sauté pan over medium heat, warm ¼ cup of the olive oil. Place the fish in the pan and cook, turning once when slightly brown, until done, about 8 minutes. Remove the fish from the pan. Add the remaining ½ cup of olive oil over medium-high heat, the pine nuts (or almonds), and raisins, and cook until the pine nuts are golden brown and the raisins plump. Add the onion and red bell pepper and cook until the pepper begins to soften. Add the eggplant and cook until it has softened and has absorbed much of the oil. Stir in the vinegar and brown sugar and season with salt. Turn off the heat and nestle the cooked fish into the sauce. The flavors improve if allowed to chill overnight in the refrigerator and then brought to room temperature before serving. At a minimum, let it sit at least 1 hour before serving at room temperature with slices of baguette.

BLUEFISH
Fillet fish

Bluefish's popularity has been up and down in the history of American seafood cuisine. For two centuries it was considered among the most important, most appreciated, and most valued of all fish, keeping company with mackerel and pompano in the highest culinary echelon. In more recent times, bluefish has become known more for its popularity among recreational anglers. But though it is fun to catch, it is largely ignored at the table. I'd like to see a change in the tide of this culinary trend.

For my money, the late-summer fat blues are lusty and bright in flavor. Smaller fish, those weighing between 1 and 3 pounds, offer a milder flavor than their bigger brethren and are more versatile in the kitchen. They take particularly well to the grill and smoked preparations. They are also well flattered by curing, roasting, and sautéing.

For a bluefish to reflect its full flavor potential, once caught it must be immediately bled, eviscerated, and iced. Most often found at the market as fresh fillets (it does not freeze well), bluefish has gunmetal- to beige-colored flesh. Its thick bloodline—the highly flavored, dark red tissue just under the skin—can easily be removed after cooking. Fresh bluefish has an animated aroma and an energetic flavor that's sharp, not strong. Its excellent taste is well balanced with notes of herb, citrus, and brine. It is also somewhat gamey, like sockeye salmon, and is punctuated by a slight sourness. The brine flavor fades into a lingering malty or creamy aftertaste that is tart with a touch of natural smokiness. Blues are best paired with tangy ingredients, such as vinegar, citrus, mustard, or tart fruit like sour apples. It is a fish that can cross the boundaries of ethnic cuisines with ease and is a good canvas for spices. But its best friend in the world is fresh basil.

Braised Bluefish with Spiced Coconut Broth

SERVES 4

4 bluefish portions, skin off, bloodline sliced away and discarded

Salt

3 tablespoons peanut oil, divided

1 lime, cut into quarters

1 red onion, cut into wedges

1 (1-inch) knob ginger, sliced

1 garlic clove, sliced

¼ cup slivered almonds

¼ pound shiitake mushrooms, sliced

1 pound carrots, cut into 1-inch pieces

2 (14-ounce) cans unsweetened coconut milk

1 sprig fresh basil

2 scallions, sliced on the bias

Rice for serving (optional)

Season the fish with salt and let it rest for 20 minutes. In a large sauté pan over high heat, warm 1 tablespoon of the oil. Add the lime and onion and cook undisturbed until the onion gets a good char, almost burned, 3–5 minutes. Remove the onion and lime from the pan and reserve separately. Reduce the heat to medium and add the remaining 2 tablespoons of oil, ginger, garlic, almonds, mushrooms, and carrots. Sauté until the almonds are toasted and the carrots just softened. Nestle the onion and fish into the vegetables. Add the coconut milk and basil. Cover, turn the heat to low, and cook until the fish is done, 7–10 minutes, depending on thickness. Discard the basil and ginger slices. Garnish with scallions and seared limes. Serve with rice.

Broiled Bluefish with Oregano and Raisin Flambé

SERVES 4

4 bluefish portions, skin on

Salt

1 lemon, zested and juiced

10 sprigs fresh oregano

3 tablespoons raisins

2 tablespoons slivered almonds

4 tablespoons butter

1½ ounces dark rum

Season the fish with salt and the lemon juice and zest and let it rest for 20 minutes. Preheat the broiler to medium and set the rack in the position closest to the heat. In the bottom of an ovenproof dish, arrange the oregano and place the fish on top, skin side up. Scatter the raisins and almonds around the fish. Place 1 tablespoon of butter on top of each portion, slide the dish under the broiler, and cook until done, about 7–10 minutes, depending on thickness. Remove from the broiler, add the dark rum, and flambé by lighting it with a match. Allow the alcohol to burn off before serving.

Broiled Bluefish with Sorrel Butter

SERVES 4

> 1 recipe Sorrel Butter (page 22)
>
> 4 bluefish portions, skin on
>
> Salt
>
> Extra-virgin olive oil

Season the fish with salt and let it rest for 20 minutes. Preheat the broiler to medium and set a rack in the position closest to the heat. Place the fish skin side up on a baking tray. Drizzle with a bit of olive oil and slide the tray under the broiler. Cook until done, 7–10 minutes, depending on thickness. Top with Sorrel Butter.

VARIATION

+ **Broiled Bluefish wiht Sundried Tomato Butter.** Use Sundried Tomato and Basil Butter (page 21) instead of Sorrel Butter.

Broiled Bluefish with Rosemary Flambé

SERVES 4

> 4 bluefish portions, skin on
>
> Salt
>
> 1 lemon, zested and juiced
>
> 10 sprigs fresh rosemary
>
> 4 tablespoons butter
>
> 1½ ounces Herbsaint or Pernod

Season the fish with salt and the lemon zest and let it rest for 20 minutes. Preheat the broiler and juice to medium and set the rack in the position closest to the heat. In the bottom of an ovenproof dish, arrange the rosemary and place the fish on top, skin side up. Place 1 tablespoon of butter on top of each portion, slide the dish under the broiler, and cook until done, 7–10 minutes, depending on thickness. Remove from the broiler and discard the rosemary. Add Herbsaint and lemon juice and flambé by lighting it with a match. Allow the alcohol to burn off before serving.

Broiled Bluefish with Ginger and Pernod

SERVES 4

> 3 tablespoons Mayonnaise (page 29, or store-bought)
>
> 4 bluefish portions, skin off, bloodline sliced away and discarded
>
> Salt
>
> 1 tablespoon Pernod or Herbsaint
>
> 1 tablespoon grated fresh ginger
>
> 2 garlic cloves, grated
>
> 1 lemon, juiced
>
> ¼ cup chopped fresh herbs, such as chervil, parsley, or tarragon

Season the fish with salt and let it rest for 20 minutes. Preheat the broiler to medium and set the rack in the position closest to the heat. Whisk together the remaining ingredients. Place the fish on a baking tray. Spread the mayonnaise mixture evenly over the top of the fish. Slide the tray under the broiler. Cook until the top has browned and the fish is done, 7–10 minutes, depending on thickness.

Grilled Bluefish with Basil

SERVES 4

    4 bluefish portions, skin on and scored
    Salt
 20 fresh basil leaves
    Extra-virgin olive oil
    Black pepper
  1 lemon, cut into wedges

Lightly season the fish with salt and cover with the basil. Wrap the fish in plastic wrap. Place a light weight on top of the fish to press the basil into the flesh and let it rest for 2 hours. Prepare a charcoal grill with a medium fire, concentrating the coals on one side of the kettle. Remove the plastic wrap and basil from the fish and discard. Drizzle the fish with olive oil and season with a small amount of black pepper. Place the fish skin side down directly over the coals. Cook until the skin begins to crisp, 3–4 minutes. Lift the entire grill grate and rotate it so the fish rests opposite the hot coals. Cover the grill and continue to cook over indirect heat until the fish is done. Drizzle with olive oil and serve with lemon wedges.

NOTE *If using a gas grill, preheat all burners to medium. Place the bluefish on one side of the hot grates. Once it begins to char around the edges, turn off the burner directly under the fish and cover the grill to finish cooking.*

Grilled Bluefish with Cilantro and Frisée Salad

SERVES 4

  4 bluefish portions, skin on
    Salt
  2 tablespoons extra-virgin olive oil
  2 cups cilantro, leaves picked from the stems
  2 heads frisée lettuce, washed and trimmed
  1 medium red onion, thinly sliced, rinsed under cold running water, and patted dry
    Black pepper

Season the fish with salt and let it rest for 20 minutes. Prepare a charcoal grill with a medium fire, concentrating the hot coals on one side of the kettle. Brush the fish with olive oil. Place the fish skin side down directly over the coals. Cook until the skin begins to crisp, 3–4 minutes. Lift the entire grill grate and rotate it so the fish rests opposite the hot coals. Cover the grill and continue to cook over this indirect heat until the fish is done. Combine the cilantro, frisée, and onion in a bowl and dress with olive oil, salt, and pepper. Serve on top of the fish.

NOTE *If using a gas grill, preheat all burners to medium. Place the bluefish on one side of the hot grates. Once it begins to char around the edges, turn off the burner directly under the fish and cover the grill to finish cooking.*

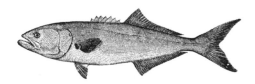

Bluefish Gravlax with Dill

SERVES 8 AS AN APPETIZER

    ¾ cup kosher salt

    ¾ cup packed brown sugar

    2 teaspoons ground mace

    2 teaspoons onion powder

    2 similarly shaped (1- to 1½-pound)
        bluefish fillets, skin on and scored

    10–15 sprigs fresh dill

Mix the salt, sugar, mace, and onion powder.
Rub the flesh of each fillet with one-third of
the salt mixture. In a glass or ceramic dish lined
with plastic wrap, sprinkle a thin layer of the salt
mixture and place one fillet skin side down on it.
Cover the fillet with the dill and place the second
fillet, flesh to flesh, on top of the first one. Sprinkle
the remaining salt mixture over the skin of the
top fillet. Tightly wrap the fish with plastic wrap,
place a dish of a similar size and shape as the fish
on top of it, and set a couple of heavy cans on the
plate to weight it down. Refrigerate for 12 hours.
Flip the fish and refrigerate, still weighed down,
for another 12 hours. Remove the weight, unwrap
the fish, pour off any liquid that has collected in
the dish, cover loosely with plastic, and let it rest
for another 24 hours, flipping once. Rinse the
fillets with cold water to remove excess salt and
brine and pat dry. Discard the dill. Wrap each
fillet individually in plastic wrap and store in the
refrigerator for up to 1 week. To serve, thinly slice
the fillet on the bias, starting at the thicker end
of the fillet and working toward the thinner side.
These slices can be laid out as carpaccio, with olive
oil and lemon juice drizzled over the top, draped
over salads, or served on bagels.

VARIATION

+ **Bluefish Gravlax with Tarragon and Orange.**
  Replace the dill with an equal amount of
  fresh tarragon and add a couple of orange
slices between the fillets, layering the tarragon
beneath and on top of them so that the citrus
does not directly touch the flesh.

Grilled Bluefish with Sicilian Herb Sauce

SERVES 4

    1 recipe Sicilian Herb Sauce (page 32),
        divided

    4 bluefish portions, skin on

    2 lemons, halved

Marinate the fish with half of the Sicilian Herb
Sauce for 4 hours, reserving the other half of the
sauce for serving. Prepare a charcoal grill with a
medium fire, concentrating the hot coals on one
side of the kettle. Place the fish skin side down on
the grill directly over the coals. Cook until the skin
begins to crisp, 3–4 minutes. Lift the entire grill
grate and rotate it so the fish rests opposite the
hot coals. Place the lemons on the grill, cut side
down, directly over the hot coals. Cover the grill
and continue to cook over this indirect heat until
the fish is done and the lemons are charred. Serve
with grilled lemons and the remaining sauce.

NOTE *If using a gas grill, preheat all burners to
medium. Place the bluefish on one side of the hot
grates. Once it begins to char around the edges,
turn off the burner directly under the fish. Place
the lemons on the hot side of the grill cut side down
directly over the coals. Cover the grill and continue
to cook until the fish is done and the lemons
are charred. Serve with grilled lemons and the
remaining sauce.*

Grilled Bluefish with Orange-Coriander Vinaigrette

SERVES 4

> 1 recipe Orange-Coriander Vinaigrette (page 37), divided
>
> 4 bluefish portions, skin on

Marinate the fish with half of the Orange-Coriander Vinaigrette for 1–8 hours, reserving the other half for serving. Prepare a charcoal grill with a medium fire, concentrating the hot coals on one side of the kettle. Remove the fish from the marinade and place it skin side down on the grill directly over the coals. Cook until the skin begins to crisp, 3–4 minutes. Lift the entire grill grate and rotate it so the fish rests opposite the hot coals. Cover the grill and continue to cook over this indirect heat until the fish is done. Serve with the reserved vinaigrette drizzled over the top.

NOTE *If using a gas grill, preheat all burners to medium. Place the bluefish on one side of the hot grates. Once it begins to char around the edges, turn off the burner directly under the fish and cover the grill to finish cooking. Serve with the reserved vinaigrette drizzled over the top.*

Pinecone-Grilled Bluefish with Citrus and Herbs

SERVES 4

> 1 recipe Gremolata (page 28)
>
> 4 bluefish portions, skin on
>
> Salt
>
> 1 tablespoon extra-virgin olive oil
>
> 3–4 large pinecones

Season the fish with salt and let it rest for 20 minutes. Prepare a charcoal grill with a medium fire, concentrating the hot coals on one side of the kettle. Brush the fish with olive oil and place it skin side down on the grill directly over the coals. Cook until the skin begins to crisp, 3–4 minutes. Lift the entire grill grate and rotate it so the fish rests opposite the hot coals. Add the pinecones to the fire. When they begin to smolder, cover the grill and continue to cook over this indirect heat until the fish is done. Serve with Gremolata.

NOTE *If using a gas grill, preheat all burners to medium. Place the bluefish on one side of the hot grates. Once it begins to char around the edges, turn off the burner directly under the fish. Add the pinecones to the burner with the flame still lit. When they begin to smolder, cover the grill to finish cooking.*

Sautéed Bluefish au Poivre Flambé

SERVES 4

> 4 bluefish portions, skin off, bloodline sliced away and discarded
>
> Salt
>
> 1½ tablespoons black peppercorns, coarsely ground
>
> 1½ tablespoons fennel seeds, crushed
>
> 4 tablespoons butter
>
> 1½ ounces cognac or brandy

Season the fish with salt on both sides and on one side with pepper and fennel. Press the seasonings into the flesh and let it rest for 20 minutes. In a sauté pan over medium heat, melt the butter and cook until golden brown. Place the fish pepper side down in the pan. Cook without flipping until almost done and then flip to finish cooking. Turn off the heat. Add the cognac or brandy and flambé by lighting with a match. Allow the alcohol to burn off before serving.

Hot-Smoked Bluefish

SERVES 6–8 AS AN APPETIZER

1 (2-pound) bluefish fillet, skin on

⅓ cup kosher salt

⅓ cup packed brown sugar

1 orange, juiced

10 juniper berries

1 tablespoon fennel seeds

1 cinnamon stick

4 tablespoons Pernod or other anise-flavored liqueur, divided

In a saucepan over medium heat, simmer 1 cup of water with the salt, brown sugar, orange juice, juniper berries, fennel seeds, and cinnamon for 5 minutes. Turn off the heat, add 3 cups of cold water and 2 tablespoons of the Pernod to the brine, and stir to dissolve the salt and sugar. Place the fish in a glass or ceramic baking dish, pour the brine over it, and refrigerate for 2 hours. Remove the fish from the liquid, pat it dry, and brush with the remaining 2 tablespoons of Pernod. Refrigerate the fish uncovered on a wire rack overnight. Using a smoker, smoke the fish skin side down for 1–2 hours at as low a temperature as possible (below 100°F). Increase the temperature to 150°F and smoke for another 2 hours. Remove from the smoker and cool to room temperature. Tightly wrap the fillet in plastic and refrigerate overnight before using. This will keep for up to 5 days.

VARIATIONS

+ **Allspice-Scented Smoked Bluefish.** To the smoking wood, add 2 tablespoons allspice berries.

+ **Basil-Infused Smoked Bluefish.** When removing the bluefish from smoker, immediately cover with fresh basil or mint leaves before wrapping to gently perfume the fish. Remove the leaves prior to serving.

Smoked Bluefish Dip

SERVES 6–8 AS AN APPETIZER

8 ounces Hot-Smoked Bluefish (at left), or store-bought, skin removed

¼ cup sour cream

1 tablespoon extra-virgin olive oil

1 lemon, zested and juiced

Black pepper

Crostini or endive leaves for serving

Flake the fish into a bowl with ½ cup of warm water and let it rest for 20 minutes. Strain, reserving both fish and liquid. Whisk ¼ cup of the reserved liquid with the sour cream, olive oil, and lemon zest and juice. Fold in the fish and stir vigorously until just a few flakes remain. Chill overnight and serve at room temperature with black pepper and crostini or endive leaves.

Chilled Poached Bluefish with Creamy Lemon-Pecan Dressing

SERVES 4

1 recipe Creamy Lemon-Pecan Dressing (page 36)

4 bluefish portions, skin off, bloodline sliced away and discarded

Salt

1 cup white wine

2 tablespoons white wine vinegar

1 shallot, sliced

1 teaspoon ground mace

30 black peppercorns

1 bay leaf

Season the fish with salt and let it rest for 20 minutes. In a pan just wide enough to hold the fish in a single layer, combine 1 cup of water with the wine, vinegar, shallot, mace, peppercorns, and bay leaf. Simmer over low heat for 5 minutes. Season the broth with salt and bring it to 170°F. Place the fish into the pan so that it is barely submerged, adding more wine if needed, and cook until just done, about 4 minutes per ½ inch of thickness. Remove the pan from the heat; cool the fish in the poaching liquid to room temperature, remove the fish from the liquid, and pat dry. Transfer the fish to a plate and serve with Creamy Lemon-Pecan Dressing.

Pickled Bluefish Herring Style

SERVES 4–6 AS AN APPETIZER

1¼ pounds bluefish fillet, skin on, cut into 1-inch cubes

2 tablespoons kosher salt

1 tablespoon sugar

1½ cups red or white wine vinegar

2 medium-size crisp apples, such as Honeycrisp, diced

1 large onion, thinly sliced

20 black peppercorns

5–6 juniper berries

1 tablespoon fennel seeds

¼ cup slivered almonds

4 bay leaves

Soak the fish in enough cold water to barely cover it and kosher salt for 12 hours. Drain from the brine and discard the brine. Mix the sugar and vinegar and stir to dissolve the sugar. Place the fillets in a porcelain or glass dish in a single layer. Add layers of apples, onion, peppercorns, juniper berries, fennel seeds, almonds, and bay leaves, repeating until all the ingredients have been added. Pour the vinegar mixture over the layers to cover. Cover the container and place it in the refrigerator. The fish will be ready to use after

24 hours; if a firmer texture is desired, wait 48 hours. The fish will keep up to 4 days in the refrigerator.

Pickled Bluefish with Radish and Raisins

SERVES 4–6 AS AN APPETIZER

1¼ pounds bluefish fillets, skin on, cut into 1-inch slices

2 tablespoons kosher salt

¼ cup red wine vinegar

¼ cup Pernod or vermouth

2 large shallots, thinly sliced

10 radishes, sliced into ¼-inch slices

2 tablespoons raisins

Soak the fish in enough cold water to barely cover it and kosher salt for 12 hours. Drain from the brine and discard the brine. Place the vinegar, Pernod or vermouth, shallots, radishes, and raisins in a saucepan over medium heat and bring to a simmer. Cook until the shallots have just barely softened, about 1 minute. Allow the pickling liquid to cool. Remove the vegetables from the pickling liquid and layer in a jar with the bluefish, alternating layers. Pour the pickling liquid over the fish and vegetables, and refrigerate. The fish will be ready to use after 24 hours; if a firmer texture is desired, wait 48 hours. The fish will keep up to 4 days in the refrigerator.

BRANZINO
Fillet fish

Branzino, or European sea bass, is both fished in the Mediterranean Sea and farmed commercially around the world. It has an iconic place in Mediterranean cuisine and is becoming very popular elsewhere due to its delicate white flesh and a mild, almost sweet flavor and culinary versatility. Branzino typically ranges in size between 1 and 3 pounds. Because of its size and the fact that it has relatively few and relatively small bones, this fish is easy to fillet or to prepare whole for an impressive table presentation. Branzino can be prepared by nearly any method, but it is best when braised, grilled, poached, or roasted.

Branzino en Papillote (cooked in parchment)

SERVES 4

> 1 recipe Anchovy-Almond Butter (page 19)
>
> 4 branzino portions, skin on and scored
>
> Salt
>
> 4 stalks celery, sliced
>
> 2 fennel bulbs, thinly sliced
>
> 1 small red onion, sliced, rinsed under cold running water, and patted dry
>
> 1 cup white wine
>
> Butter, for greasing the parchment
>
> 1 orange, cut into segments

Season the fish with salt and let it rest for 15 minutes. In a shallow pan, place the celery, fennel, onion, and wine. Season with salt and cook until the vegetables are soft and the wine nearly reduced. Take four 18-inch squares of parchment paper and cut them into heart shapes. Use butter to grease an 8-inch square area in middle of each. Evenly divide the vegetables and remaining liquid among the parchments, place the fish on top, and add a couple of orange segments and 2 tablespoons of Anchovy-Almond Butter to each. Fold the paper over, then crimp the edges tightly (empanada-style) to form a pouch. Bake at 350°F for 10–12 minutes, depending on the thickness of the fillets. Serve in the pouch and slice open just prior to eating

Salt-Roasted Branzino with Lemon and Tarragon

SERVES 2

> 3 pounds kosher salt
>
> 1 (1½- to 2½-pound) whole branzino, scaled, gutted, gills removed, and skin scored
>
> 2 lemons, thinly sliced
>
> 8 sprigs tarragon
>
> 4 tablespoons butter, melted

Combine the salt with enough water so that it resembles wet sand. Place a thin layer on a baking sheet and top with half of the lemon slices and half of the tarragon. Place the fish on top of the tarragon. Place the remaining lemon slices and tarragon on top of the fish. Pack on the remaining salt mixture to completely encase the fish. Bake at 375°F for 20–25 minutes. Remove the fish from the oven and let it rest for 5 minutes. Crack the salt crust and discard. To serve, discard the lemons and tarragon and peel off the skin before carefully transferring the top fillet to a platter. Remove and discard the backbone and transfer the bottom fillet without its skin to the platter. Drizzle the fish with melted butter.

Broiled Branzino with Charred Tomato Vinaigrette

SERVES 4

>   1 recipe Charred Tomato Vinaigrette
>   (page 35)
>
>   4 branzino portions, skin on, scored
>
>   Salt
>
>   Extra-virgin olive oil
>
>   Crusty bread for serving

Season the fish with salt and let it rest for 15 minutes. Preheat the broiler to medium and set the rack in the position closest to the heat. Pour the vinaigrette into a baking dish just large enough to hold the fish. Nestle the fish skin side up into the vinaigrette and drizzle the top with olive oil. Place the dish under the broiler, and cook until the fish is slightly singed and the sauce is bubbling. Remove and let it rest for 5 minutes before serving with crusty bread.

Grilled Branzino with Anchovy-Herb Butter

SERVES 4

>   1 recipe Anchovy-Herb Butter (pages 19)
>
>   4 branzino portions, skin on and scored
>
>   Salt
>
>   Extra-virgin olive oil

Season the fish with salt and let it rest for 15 minutes. Prepare a charcoal grill with a medium fire, concentrating the hot coals on one side of the kettle. Brush the fish with oil and place the fish skin side down on the grill directly over the coals. Cook until the edges of the fish begin to char, about 3 minutes. Lift the entire grill grate and rotate it so the fish rests opposite the hot coals. Cover the grill and continue to cook over this indirect heat until the fish is done, 4–6 minutes. Serve topped with Anchovy-Herb Butter.

NOTE *If using a gas grill, preheat all burners to medium. Place the branzino on one side of the hot grates. Once it begins to char around the edges, turn off the burner directly under the fish and cover the grill to finish cooking.*

Whole Grilled Branzino with Lime-Oregano Butter

SERVES 2–4

>   1 recipe Lime-Oregano Butter (page 21)
>
>   2 (1½-pound) whole branzino, scaled,
>   gutted, gills removed, and skin scored
>
>   Salt

Season the fish with salt and let it rest for 20 minutes. Prepare a charcoal grill with a medium fire, concentrating the hot coals on one side of the kettle. Place the fish on the grill directly over the coals. Cook until the skin begins to char, about 3–4 minutes. Gently flip the fish and cook for 3 more minutes. Lift the entire grill grate and rotate it so the fish rest opposite the hot coals. Cover the grill and continue to cook over this indirect heat until the fish is done, 4–6 minutes. Serve topped with Lime-Oregano Butter.

NOTE *If using a gas grill, preheat all burners to medium. Place the branzino on one side of the hot grates. Cook until the skin begins to char, about 3–4 minutes. Gently flip the fish and cook for 3 more minutes. Turn off the burner directly under the fish and cover the grill to finish cooking.*

BUTTERFISH
Fillet fish

Butterfish have long been a summertime favorite of the mid-Atlantic and New England regions in whose waters they swim from late spring through the fall. All along these coasts these 6- or 7-inch-long and very thin fish answer to many different names. They are dollar fish in Maine, pumpkinseeds in Massachusetts, and harvest fish in the mid-Atlantic.

Butterfish have microscaled skin with a dull mirrored-silver color. They are almost always served with the skin on, as removing it decreases the edible yield to unrewarding levels. The skin, which need not be scaled, and the fins crisp beautifully and give a wonderful textural contrast to the melt-in-your-mouth meat. The flesh is a grayish color when raw and light beige when cooked. Its flavor is born of the crustaceans and mollusks on which it feeds, though it also exhibits a dairy-like sweetness. The fat content is high enough that the fish self-baste when broiled, grilled, or sautéed. I believe they are best smoked. In addition to its buttery flavor, butterfish was bestowed its name by fishermen because, according to dockside legend, these slippery fish would regularly escape their grasp.

Most any recipe for mackerel is also well suited to butterfish.

Crispy Fried Butterfish with Herbs and Garlic

SERVES 4

 1 recipe Gremolata (page 28)
 2 pounds whole butterfish, headed, gutted, and skin scored
 Salt
 Vegetable or peanut oil
 1 cup flour, sifted
 2 tablespoons cornstarch, sifted
 1 teaspoon garlic powder
 1 teaspoon onion powder
 1½ cups seltzer water

Season the fish with salt and let them rest for 15 minutes. Pour 3–4 inches of oil into a high-sided pan. Place over medium-high heat and warm the oil to 375°F. Make a batter by combining the flour, cornstarch, garlic powder, onion powder, seltzer water, and salt to taste. Whisk until smooth and use within 10 minutes. Dip one fish at a time into the batter and place it in the oil, holding it for 5 seconds before releasing. Repeat the process, cooking the fish in small batches. Turn with a slotted spoon to ensure that both sides crisp evenly. Remove the pieces as they finish and place on paper towels to absorb excess oil. Serve sprinkled with the Gremolata.

Citrusy Fried Butterfish with Herbs

SERVES 4

 1 recipe Peruvian Marinade (page 37)

 4 portions butterfish fillets, skin on and scored

 Vegetable or peanut oil

 Flour

 2 eggs, beaten

 ¼ cup chopped fresh mint and parsley

 Crushed red chile flakes

Combine the fish with the Peruvian Marinade and let them rest for 30 minutes. Pour 3–4 inches of oil into a high-sided pan. Place over medium-high heat and warm the oil to 375°F. Working with one piece at a time, dredge the fillet in flour, then dip it into the beaten eggs, and then dredge it again in flour, making sure to completely coat the fish. Place the coated fillets in the oil, holding them for 5 seconds before releasing. Repeat the process, cooking the fish in small batches. Turn with a slotted spoon to ensure that both sides crisp evenly. Remove the fillets as they finish and place on paper towels to absorb excess oil. While still hot, toss the fried fillets with the herbs and chile flakes.

Sautéed Butterfish Almondine

SERVES 4

 4 portions butterfish fillets, skin on and scored

 Salt

 6 tablespoons butter, divided

 ½ cup sliced almonds

 2 lemons, juiced

Season the fish with salt and let it rest for 15 minutes. In a sauté pan over high heat, melt 2 tablespoons of the butter and cook until golden brown. Place the fillets in the pan skin side down. Cook without flipping until almost done and then remove the fish and wipe the pan clean. Reduce the heat to medium and add the remaining 4 tablespoons of butter and cook until golden brown. Add the almonds and cook until they are browned. Add the lemon juice and season with salt. Stir to combine. Turn off the heat and return the fish to the pan uncooked side down to finish cooking.

Sautéed Butterfish Provençal

SERVES 4

 4 portions butterfish fillets, skin on and scored

 Salt

 6 tablespoons extra-virgin olive oil

 1 garlic clove, finely minced

 1 (14-ounce) can fire-roasted diced tomatoes, drained, or 1¾ cups large diced fresh tomatoes

 2 tablespoons chopped green or black olives

 1 tablespoon red or white wine vinegar

Season the fish with salt and let them rest for 15 minutes. In a sauté pan over medium heat, warm the olive oil and place the fish in the pan skin side down. Cook without flipping until almost done and then remove the fish. Add the garlic and cook for 1 minute. Add the tomatoes, olives, and vinegar. Season with salt and simmer for 5 minutes. Turn off the heat and nestle the fish skin side up into the sauce to finish cooking. Serve hot or at room temperature.

CARP
Flaky white fish, meaty dense fish

These freshwater fish are native to Asia and have been farmed successfully since 500 BCE. They play a prominent role in Jewish cooking worldwide as a principal ingredient in gefilte fish. Once introduced to America in the 1870s, they had propagated so wildly by the early 1990s that the US government was actively creating markets for these fish to help control their population levels. Carp is still very popular in the Midwest.

Carp can have a natural musty flavor, but that can be tempered if the head and tail are cut off at capture. Sometimes carp are sold live, so you can control that process yourself. Smaller fish—those weighing between 2 and 3 pounds—caught in the winter are considered the best-quality carp.

The skin, though edible, holds beneath it a layer of fat that can be dingy tasting, so it is best to remove both before cooking. To do that, parboil the fish for 30 seconds, slough off the skin, and scrape away the underlying fat. A thick red muscle runs along the fillet, and this chewy, strongly flavored band should also be removed.

The flesh of a well-cleaned carp is firm, pearly white, and mildly flavored.

If you are not game for dealing with a live carp, you can often find it sold as skinless fillets. Soaking the fillets in milk and lemon juice or salting them for 6–24 hours prior to use will brighten the personality of the fish.

Carp takes well to braising, even pairing well with strong flavors such as red wine (page 108). My preferred preparations are hot-smoking it (page 110) after it's been sitting in a brine heavily laden with bay leaves, or beer-battering it and frying it crisp (page 109).

Sautéed Carp with Cider–Brown Butter Sauce

SERVES 4

- 1 tablespoon kosher salt
- ½ tablespoon sugar
- 2 lemons, juiced
- 4 carp portions, skin off, dark tissue trimmed
- 5 tablespoons butter, divided
- 2 garlic cloves, finely minced
- ½ cup apple cider or hard cider

In a small saucepan over low heat, warm ½ cup of water with the salt and sugar, and stir to dissolve. Remove from the heat and add 1 cup ice water and half of the lemon juice. Refrigerate the brine until cold. Place the fish in a baking dish, cover with the brine, and let it rest for 1 hour. Remove the fish from the brine and pat dry.

In a sauté pan over medium heat, melt 2 tablespoons of the butter and cook until golden brown. Place the fish in the pan. Cook without flipping until almost done and then remove the fish. Add the remaining 4 tablespoons of butter and the garlic and cook until golden brown. Add the remaining lemon juice and cider, reduce until the sauce is emulsified, and season with salt. Turn off the heat and return the fish to the pan uncooked side down to finish cooking.

Braised Carp with Cider

SERVES 4

- 1 tablespoon kosher salt
- ½ tablespoon sugar
- 1½ cups white wine, divided
- 4 carp portions, skin off, dark tissue trimmed
- Flour
- 3 tablespoons peanut or vegetable oil
- 1 cup apple cider
- 1 bay leaf
- 2 sprigs fresh thyme
- ½ tablespoon prepared horseradish
- 4 tablespoons cold butter, cut into pieces
- 3 tablespoons chopped fresh herbs, such as chervil, chives, parsley, or tarragon

In a small saucepan over low heat, warm ½ cup of water with the salt and sugar and stir to dissolve. Remove from the heat and add 1 cup ice water and ½ cup of the wine. Refrigerate the brine until cold. Place the fish in a baking dish, cover with the brine, and let it rest for 1 hour. Remove the fish from the brine and pat dry.

Roll the fish in flour. In a sauté pan over high heat, warm the oil. Place the fish in the pan and cook for 1 minute on each side. Remove the fish and wipe the oil from the pan. Add the remaining 1 cup of wine, cider, bay leaf, and thyme. Bring to a boil over medium heat and cook for 5 minutes. Turn the heat to low and nestle the fish into the sauce. Simmer until the fish is cooked through and easily flakes apart, 10–15 minutes. Remove the fish and reduce the sauce to ¼ cup. Turn off the heat. Add the horseradish, butter, and herbs. Stir to incorporate and spoon the sauce over the fish.

Braised Carp with Spiced Red Wine

SERVES 4

- 1 tablespoon kosher salt
- ½ tablespoon sugar
- 1½ cups fruity red wine, such as Beaujolais, divided
- 4 carp portions, skin off, dark tissue trimmed
- 1 orange, zested and juiced
- 4 sprigs fresh thyme
- 1 bay leaf
- 10 black peppercorns
- 5 whole cloves
- 5 tablespoons butter, divided
- 1 onion, sliced
- 1 fennel bulb, sliced
- 1 (2-ounce) tin anchovies in oil
- 1 tablespoon prepared horseradish
- 3 tablespoons chopped fresh herbs, such as chervil, parsley, tarragon, or any combination

In a small saucepan over low heat, warm ½ cup of water with the salt and sugar and stir to dissolve. Remove from the heat and add 1 cup of ice water and ½ cup of the wine. Refrigerate the brine until cold. Place the fish in a baking dish, cover with the brine, and let it rest for 1 hour. Remove the fish from the brine and pat dry.

In a saucepan over medium heat, combine 1 cup of water and the remaining 1 cup of wine with the orange juice, thyme, bay leaf, peppercorns, and cloves. Simmer for 15 minutes. Strain, reserving the liquid and discarding the solids. In a sauté pan over high heat, warm 2 tablespoons of the butter. Add the onion and fennel and cook without stirring until they begin to brown. Reduce the heat to medium and add the anchovies with their oil and the orange zest. Cook until the anchovies have melted. Place the fish on top of the vegetables. Add the reserved spiced wine, season with salt, cover with foil, and cook in the oven at 300°F for 20 minutes. Remove the foil, increase the oven temperature to 350°F, and continue to cook, basting regularly until the fish is cooked through and easily flakes apart, 10–15 minutes. Transfer the fish and vegetables to a platter. Bring the cooking liquid to a simmer and reduce to ¼ cup. Turn off the heat. Add the remaining 4 tablespoons of butter, horseradish, and herbs. Swirl to incorporate the butter, and spoon the sauce over the fish.

Teriyaki-Glazed Carp

SERVES 4

1 recipe Teriyaki-Style Sauce (page 32)

1 tablespoon kosher salt

½ tablespoon sugar

1 lemon, juiced

4 carp portions, skin off, dark tissue trimmed

2 teaspoons Worcestershire sauce

1 tablespoon sesame oil

¼ cup sliced scallions for garnish

In a small saucepan over low heat, warm ½ cup of water with the salt and sugar and stir to dissolve. Remove from the heat and add 1 cup ice water and the lemon juice. Refrigerate the brine until cold. Place the fish in a baking dish, cover with the brine, and let it rest for 1 hour. Remove the fish from the brine and pat dry. Preheat the broiler to medium and set the rack in the position closest to the heat. Combine the Teriyaki-Style Sauce and the Worcestershire sauce. Brush a baking dish with the sesame oil. Place the fish in the dish, coat with half of the sauce, and slide the dish under the broiler. Cook, basting with the remaining sauce every 2 minutes until done, 7–10 minutes, depending on the thickness. Garnish with sliced scallions.

Beer-Battered Carp

SERVES 4

1 recipe Louisiana Remoulade (page 31), Traditional Remoulade Sauce (page 31), or Modern Remoulade (page 30)

4 carp portions, skin off, dark tissue trimmed, cut into 2-inch pieces

Salt

1 lemon, juiced

2 tablespoons vegetable or peanut oil

¾ cup flour, sifted

¾ cup cornstarch, sifted

¾ cup pilsner beer

2 tablespoons vegetable oil

1 egg, separated

Malt vinegar

Season the fish with salt and lemon juice and let it rest for 30 minutes. Pour 3–4 inches of oil into a high-sided pan. Place over medium-high heat and warm the oil to 375°F. Make a batter by combining the flour, cornstarch, beer, vegetable oil, egg yolk, and ½ tablespoon of salt. Beat the egg white to soft peaks and fold into the batter. Dip one piece of fish at a time into the batter, place it in the oil, and hold it there for 5 seconds before releasing it. Repeat the process, cooking the fish in small batches. Turn with a slotted spoon to evenly render both sides golden and crispy. Remove pieces as they finish and place on paper towels to absorb excess oil. Serve with Remoulade Sauce and malt vinegar.

Pan-Fried Carp in Bacon Drippings

SERVES 4

1 tablespoon kosher salt

1 tablespoon sugar

2 lemons, 1 juiced, 1 cut into wedges

4 carp portions, skin off, dark tissue trimmed

Flour

Black pepper

6 tablespoons bacon drippings or combination drippings and butter

In a small saucepan over low heat, warm ½ cup of water with the salt and sugar and stir to dissolve. Remove from the heat and add 1 cup ice water and the lemon juice. Refrigerate the brine until cold. Place the fish in a baking dish, cover with the brine, and let it rest for 1 hour. Remove the fish from the brine and pat dry.

Roll the fish in flour to coat and then season one side with pepper, gently pressing the pepper into the flesh. In a sauté pan over medium heat, warm the bacon drippings. Place the fish in the pan peppered side down and cook until almost done, then flip to finish cooking. Serve with lemon wedges.

Hot-Smoked Carp

SERVES 4–8

1 cup apple cider vinegar

2 tablespoons kosher salt

2 tablespoons sugar

1½ pounds carp fillets, skin off, dark tissue trimmed

2 tablespoons Pernod or rum

1 lemon, zested and juiced

Combine 3 cups of water with the vinegar, salt, and sugar and stir to dissolve. Add the fish and let it rest for 6 hours. Remove the fish from the brine and pat dry. Mix the Pernod and lemon juice and zest and brush it onto the fish. Refrigerate the fish uncovered on a wire rack overnight. Using a smoker, cold-smoke the fish for 1–2 hours at as low a temperature as possible (below 100°F). Increase the temperature to 150°F and smoke for an additional 2 hours. Remove from the smoker and allow to cool to room temperature. Tightly wrap the fillet in plastic and refrigerate overnight before using. Serve flaked over salads, in place of the bluefish in Smoked Bluefish Dip (page 100), or as part of a chowder.

VARIATIONS

+ **Mint-Scented Hot-Smoked Carp.** When removing the fish from the smoker, immediately cover with fresh mint or sage leaves before wrapping and let cool to gently perfume the fish. Remove the leaves prior to serving.

+ **Hot-Smoked Carp au Poivre.** After brushing the brined fish with the Pernod and lemon juice and zest, heavily season with coarse ground black pepper and crushed fennel seeds.

Stir-Fried Carp with Onion and Ginger

SERVES 4

4 carp portions, skin off, dark tissue trimmed, each cut into ½-inch slices on the bias

Salt

1 lemon, juiced

4 tablespoons peanut or vegetable oil, divided

1 onion, thinly sliced

2 garlic cloves, thinly sliced

1 tablespoon grated fresh ginger

4 stalks celery, sliced thin on the bias

2 tablespoons brown sugar

3 tablespoons soy sauce

3 tablespoons white wine

Cornstarch

NOTE *If possible, flavor the fish with cold smoke for a few minutes before starting the preparation.*

Season the fish with salt and lemon juice and let it rest for 30 minutes. In a sauté pan over high heat, warm 1 tablespoon of the oil. Add the onion, garlic, ginger, and celery. Cook over high heat, stirring occasionally, until the onion begins to singe and the celery is al dente. Mix the brown sugar with the soy sauce and white wine. Add the liquid to the pan and toss vigorously for 30 seconds before removing the glazed vegetables from the pan. Wipe out the pan and heat the remaining 3 tablespoons of oil over medium heat. Toss the fish in cornstarch to coat and add to the pan. Cook without turning until almost cooked through, flipping for the last 30 seconds to cook the other side. Remove from the pan and cover with the vegetables.

CATFISH
Flaky white fish, meaty dense fish

Catfish is one of America's most familiar seafoods. It's been a part of our fishing and culinary folklore in nearly every region, both north of the Mason-Dixon Line—where in early Philadelphia, catfish and waffles was a particularly popular dish—and south of the line, where catfish has always been part of traditional Southern cooking. Though not highly pedigreed, it often seems to fit the bill, whether it's a fried catfish po'boy, smoked catfish chowder, or blackened catfish tacos.

Numerous species of catfish swim wild or are farmed in America's fresh, brackish, and salt waters. Catfish take on the characteristics of the water in which they swim, so that's where the species has picked up its muddy-tasting reputation. But when properly farmed or caught wild in clean water and skillfully prepared, catfish exhibits a very delicate, charming, and elegant flavor that pairs well with bold seasonings and subtle accompaniments.

Catfish skin is thick, chewy, and not appropriate for eating. Raw fillets have a translucent quality; when cooked, they become pearly white and opaque. The flesh has a dense and meaty flake and a snappy texture that doesn't fall apart during cooking, making catfish a great option for chowders, gumbos, and fried preparations.

Pan-Fried Catfish in Bacon Drippings

SERVES 4

>   4 catfish portions, skin off
>
>   Salt
>
>   Flour
>
>   Black pepper
>
>   6 tablespoons bacon drippings or combination drippings and butter
>
>   1 lemon, cut into wedges

Season the fish with salt and let it rest for 15 minutes. Roll the fish in flour to coat and then season one side with cracked pepper, gently pressing the pepper into the flesh. In a sauté pan over medium heat, warm the bacon drippings. Place the fish in the pan peppered side down and cook until almost done, then flip to finish cooking. Serve with lemon wedges.

Stewed Catfish with Romesco

SERVES 4

>   1 recipe Romesco (page 31)
>
>   4 catfish portions, skin off
>
>   Salt
>
>   Rice for serving (optional)

Season the fish with salt and let it rest for 15 minutes. Pour the Romesco into a pan just big enough to comfortably fit the fish in a single layer. Nestle the fish into the sauce, cover, and place over low heat. Cook until the fish is flaky, 12–15 minutes. Remove from the heat and let it rest for 5 minutes. Check the sauce for seasoning. Serve over rice.

Stewed Catfish with Marinara

SERVES 4

>   1 recipe Marinara Sauce (page 29)
>
>   4 catfish portions, skin off
>
>   Salt
>
>   Rice (optional) for serving

Season the fish with salt and let it rest for 15 minutes. Pour the Marinara Sauce into a pan just big enough to comfortably fit the fish in a single layer. Nestle the fish into the sauce, cover, and place over low heat. Cook until the fish is flaky, 12–15 minutes. Remove from the heat and let it rest for 5 minutes. Check the sauce for seasoning. Serve over rice.

Broiled Catfish with Ginger, Garlic, and Scallions

SERVES 4

>   3 tablespoons Mayonnaise (page 29, or store-bought)
>
>   4 catfish portions, skin off
>
>   Salt
>
>   2 garlic cloves, grated
>
>   1 tablespoon grated fresh ginger
>
>   1 lime, juiced
>
>   Dash of hot sauce
>
>   Dash of soy sauce
>
>   ¼ cup sliced scallions

Season the fish with salt and let it rest for 15 minutes. Preheat the broiler to medium and set the rack in the position closest to the heat. Whisk the Mayonnaise with the remaining ingredients. Place the fish on a baking tray. Spread the mayonnaise mixture evenly over the fish. Slide the tray under the broiler. Cook until the mayonnaise has browned and is bubbling and the fish is done, 7–10 minutes, depending on thickness.

Broiled Catfish with Crunchy Ritz® Cracker Topping

SERVES 4

> 3 tablespoons Mayonnaise (page 29, or store-bought)
>
> 4 catfish portions, skin off
>
> Salt
>
> 8 tablespoons crushed Ritz Crackers
>
> 1 lemon, zested and cut into wedges

Season the fish with salt and let it rest for 15 minutes. Preheat the broiler to medium and set the rack in the middle position. Stir together the Mayonnaise, crushed crackers, and lemon zest. Place the fish on a baking tray. Spread the mayonnaise mixture evenly over the fish. Slide the tray under the broiler. Broil until the fish is done and the topping is browned, about 7–10 minutes, depending on thickness. Serve with lemon wedges.

Pickle-Brined Fried Catfish

SERVES 4

> 4 catfish portions, skin off, each cut into 2-inch pieces
>
> 2 cups pickle juice
>
> Vegetable or peanut oil
>
> Flour
>
> 1 cup buttermilk

Combine the fish and pickle juice, and let it rest for 30 minutes. Remove the fish from the brine and pat dry. Pour 3–4 inches of oil into a high-sided pan. Place over medium-high heat and warm the oil to 375°F. Roll the fillets in the flour, dip them in the buttermilk, and then roll them

again in the flour, making sure to completely and evenly coat the fish. Place one piece of coated fish at a time into the oil and hold it for 5 seconds before releasing it. Repeat the process, cooking a couple of pieces at a time. Turn with a slotted spoon to ensure that both sides crisp evenly. Remove the fillets as they finish and place on paper towels to absorb excess oil.

Grilled Catfish Kebabs with Mint-Mustard Vinaigrette

SERVES 4

> 1 recipe Mint-Mustard Vinaigrette (page 36)
>
> 4 catfish portions, skin off, cut into 1½-inch pieces

Marinate the catfish in half the vinaigrette for 1 hour, reserving the other half for serving. Thread the fish onto skewers. Prepare a charcoal grill with a medium fire, concentrating the hot coals on one side of the kettle. Place the skewers on the grill directly over the hot coals. Cook until the edges of the fish begin to char, about 2 minutes. Turn the kebabs, placing them away from the hot coals. Cover and continue to cook over this indirect heat until the fish is done, 2–3 minutes. Serve with the remaining vinaigrette drizzled on top.

NOTE *If using a gas grill, preheat all burners to medium. Place the kebabs on one side of the hot grates and cook until the edges of the fish begin to char, about 2 minutes. Turn the kebabs, turn off the burner directly under the fish, and cover the grill to finish cooking, 2–3 minutes*

Blackened Catfish

SERVES 4

- 1 recipe Blackening Spice Mix (page 33)
- 4 catfish portions, skin off
- Salt
- 4 tablespoons butter, melted, divided
- ¼ cup vegetable or peanut oil
- 1 lemon, cut into wedges

Lightly season the fish with salt and let it rest for 15 minutes. Heat a cast iron skillet or heavy-bottomed sauté pan over high heat until it is screaming hot. Combine 2 tablespoons of the butter and all of the oil in a bowl and brush each portion of the fish so it glistens all over. Dredge one side of each portion in Blackening Spice Mix, coating evenly. Place the fish in the pan spice side down and drizzle half of the remaining butter-and-oil mixture over the top. Reduce the heat to medium-low and cook without flipping until a dark crust forms, then flip to cook through. Drizzle with the remaining butter and serve with lemon wedges.

Sautéed Catfish Almondine

SERVES 4

- 4 catfish portions, skin off
- Salt
- 6 tablespoons butter, divided
- 2 garlic cloves, finely minced
- ¼ cup sliced almonds
- 1 lemon, juiced

Season the fish with salt and let it rest for 15 minutes. In a sauté pan over medium heat, melt 2 tablespoons of the butter and cook until golden brown. Place the fish in the pan. Cook without flipping until almost done, then remove the fish and wipe the pan clean. Add the remaining 4 tablespoons of butter, garlic, and almonds. Cook until the almonds are browned. Add the lemon juice and season with salt. Stir to combine. Turn off the heat and return the fish to the pan uncooked side down to finish cooking.

Sautéed Catfish with Brown Butter and Thyme

SERVES 4

- 4 catfish portions, skin off
- Salt
- 6 tablespoons butter, divided
- 2 garlic cloves, minced
- 8 sprigs thyme, leaves picked
- 1 lemon, zested and juiced

Season the fish with salt and let it rest for 15 minutes. In a sauté pan over medium heat, melt 2 tablespoons of the butter and cook until golden brown. Place the fish in the pan. Cook without flipping until almost done, then remove the fish and wipe the pan clean. Add the remaining 4 tablespoons of butter, garlic, and thyme. Cook until the garlic is brown. Add the lemon zest and juice, and season with salt. Stir to combine. Turn off the heat and return the fish to the pan uncooked side down to finish cooking.

Sautéed Prosciutto-Wrapped Catfish

SERVES 4

- 4 catfish portions, skin off
- Salt
- 2 tablespoons chopped fresh parsley or tarragon
- 1 lemon, zested and juiced
- 2 pinches ground mace
- 2 tablespoons white wine
- 8 thinly sliced pieces prosciutto
- 4 tablespoons butter

Season the fish with salt and let it rest for 15 minutes. Mix the herbs, lemon zest and juice, mace, and wine. Marinate the fish in the mixture for 2 hours. Wrap each portion in two slices of prosciutto and secure with a toothpick. In a sauté pan over medium heat, melt the butter and cook until golden brown. Add the fish to the pan. Cook until the prosciutto is crisp and the fish is almost done, then flip to finish cooking. Serve drizzled with butter from the pan.

Sautéed Catfish with Black-Eyed Peas and Tarragon

SERVES 4

- 4 catfish portions, skin off
- Salt
- 6 tablespoons butter, divided
- 1 small red bell pepper, diced
- 3 stalks celery, diced
- 1 small onion, diced
- 1 (14-ounce) can black eyed peas, drained with liquid reserved
- 2 tablespoons chopped tarragon

Season the fish with salt and let it rest for 15 minutes. In a sauté pan over medium heat, melt 2 tablespoons of the butter and cook until golden brown. Place the fish in the pan. Cook without flipping until almost done, then remove the fish and wipe the pan clean. Add the remaining 4 tablespoons butter, bell pepper, celery, and onion, and cook until just softened. Add the black-eyed peas and tarragon and stir to combine. Cook until the beans are heated through. Nestle the fish uncooked side down into the mixture. Add 3 tablespoons of the reserved liquid and cover the pan to finish cooking the fish.

Stir-Fried Catfish with Onion and Ginger

SERVES 4

4 catfish portions, cut into ½-inch slices on the bias

Salt

4 tablespoons peanut or vegetable oil, divided

1 onion, thinly sliced

2 garlic cloves, thinly sliced

1 tablespoon grated fresh ginger

4 stalks celery, sliced thin on the bias

2 tablespoons brown sugar

3 tablespoons soy sauce

3 tablespoons white wine

Cornstarch

NOTE *If possible, flavor the fish with cold smoke for just a few minutes before starting the preparation.*

Season the fish with salt and let it rest for 15 minutes. In a sauté pan over high heat, warm 1 tablespoon of the oil. Add the onion, garlic, ginger, and celery. Cook over high heat, stirring occasionally, until the onions begin to singe and the celery is al dente. Mix the brown sugar with the soy sauce and white wine. Add the liquid to the pan and toss vigorously for 30 seconds before removing the glazed vegetables from the pan. Wipe the pan clean and heat the remaining 3 tablespoons of oil over medium heat. Toss the fish in cornstarch to coat, and add it to the pan. Cook without turning until almost cooked through, flipping for the last 30 seconds to cook other side. Remove from the pan and cover with the vegetables.

Catfish Tacos

SERVES 4

1 recipe Orange-Coriander Vinaigrette (page 37) or Lemon-Chile-Mint Dressing (page 36)

1 recipe Pico de Gallo (page 30) or store-bought salsa

1 pound catfish fillets, skin off

Salt

Sour cream

2 avocados, sliced

½ cup cilantro, leaves picked

¼ head cabbage, shaved, or coleslaw

16 corn tortillas

Season the fish with salt and let it rest for 15 minutes. Grill, bake, broil, or poach the fish until cooked. Flake the fish into bite-size pieces and toss with the vinaigrette. Set out bowls of Pico de Gallo, sour cream, avocado, cilantro, and shredded cabbage. Place the tortillas in a dry heavy-bottomed pan over medium heat and cook until toasted yet pliable. Keep them warm in a kitchen towel. For each taco, stack two tortillas together. Let everyone build their own tacos just the way they like.

CLAMS

America's love affair with clams is centuries old. They are most often sold alive in their shells, but they also can be found shucked in cans, breaded and frozen, smoked, and pickled. Their liquor is bottled straight from the shell as clam "juice," slightly diluted as "broth," and reduced as "nectar."

Clams are best distinguished based on the shape and strength of their shells. The majority of the live clams at market are hard-shell varieties, because they have a longer shelf life than soft-shell clams. Also known as quahogs, hard-shell clams are available year-round. Live hard-shell clams should be tightly closed, an indicator that the clam is still fresh.

Quahogs are sold by size. East Coast littlenecks weigh in at 6–10 per pound. These and West Coast butter clams are best for eating raw, because their texture is crunchy and their flavor is mild. The next size up are cherrystones, weighing in at 4–6 per pound. Topneck or countneck are next, at 4 per pound. Chowders are the largest, with 3 or fewer per pound. Their meat is chewy, and they are best in braises, ground in fritters, or long-cooked into chowders.

Soft-shell clams were long considered a New England regional specialty until Howard Johnson introduced "sweet as a nut" fried clams on the menu of his restaurants. Coinciding with the dawn of America's interstate highways, Howard Johnson's® restaurants proliferated across the country, bringing the breaded and fried soft clam to national attention. The regional name of soft-shell clams, "steamers,"

comes from another common preparation in which they are steamed with a bit of water and served piping hot with lemon, drawn butter, and a cup of steaming clam broth.

A very different form of clam, of which multiple species are found along both coasts, is the razor clam. They range in size and shape according to geography, but they share culinary characteristics. Their long, thin, narrow shells are shaped like old, straight razors, have beige-colored meats that fill their shells, and are usually too chewy to be eaten raw. They are excellent when steamed and served with butter, used in fritters, fried, or griddled and covered with a garlic, herb, and olive oil vinaigrette. Razor clams can be substituted in nearly any recipe calling for hard-shell clams.

Clam Broth Pick-Me-Up

MAKES ABOUT 4 CUPS

12 large hard-shell clams, scrubbed

2 cups white wine

1 stalk celery, roughly chopped

1 small onion or shallot, roughly chopped

2 teaspoons fennel seeds

4 tablespoons butter, cut into pieces

1 tablespoon chopped fresh tarragon

Cayenne pepper (optional)

In a pot over medium-high heat, combine 1 cup of water with the clams, wine, celery, onion or shallot, and fennel seeds. Cover the pot and bring to a boil, cooking until the clams open. Remove the clams and reserve for another use. Strain the broth into a clear container, discard the solids, and wipe out the pot. Let the broth sit undisturbed for 5 minutes. Slowly decant the broth back into the pot and leave any grit in the bottom of the container. Serve the clam broth piping hot in mugs and garnish with pats of butter, chopped tarragon, and cayenne pepper if using.

Bloody Mary Clam Shooters

MAKES 4 SHOOTERS

⅓ cup V8 vegetable juice

2 tablespoons bottled clam juice

2 teaspoons prepared horseradish

1 teaspoon Worcestershire sauce

6 ounces vodka or gin

2 limes, 1 juiced and 1 cut into wedges

2 teaspoons Old Bay® seasoning

4 littleneck clams, shucked

In a cocktail shaker, combine the vegetable juice, clam juice, horseradish, Worcestershire sauce, vodka, and lime juice. Use a lime wedge to moisten the rims of four shooter glasses and press the rims into Old Bay to coat. Shake the Bloody Mary mix with ice, strain into the glasses, and top each with a shucked clam.

Mezcal-Lime Clam Shooters

MAKES 4 SHOOTERS

1 tablespoon kosher salt

½ tablespoon onion powder

1 teaspoon smoked sweet paprika

1 teaspoon sugar

½ teaspoon ground oregano

1 lime, cut into wedges

4 shots mezcal

4 littleneck clams, shucked

Combine the salt, onion powder, paprika, sugar, and oregano. Moisten the rims of four shooter glasses with the lime wedges, then roll the rims in the spice mixture to coat. Pour the mezcal into the shooter glasses and garnish with a lime wedge and a clam.

Clam and Pepper Salad

SERVES 4

   12 large hard-shell clams, scrubbed

    1 cup white wine

    2 teaspoons fennel seeds

    1 tablespoon whole grain mustard

    2 tablespoons red or white wine vinegar

    6 tablespoons extra-virgin olive oil

    1 red bell pepper, diced small

    1 green bell pepper, diced small

    1 large red onion, thinly sliced, rinsed in cold water, and patted dry

    1 head celery, sliced thinly on the bias

   ½ cup chopped fresh herbs such as chervil, tarragon, and parsley

    Salt

    Black pepper

In a saucepan over medium-high heat, place the clams, wine, fennel seeds, and ½ cup of water. Cover the pot, bring to a boil, and cook until the clams open. Remove the clams from the pot, pull the meat from the shells, strain the broth into a measuring cup, and rinse the pot. Let the broth sit undisturbed for 5 minutes. Slowly decant the broth back into the pot and leave any grit in the bottom of the measuring cup. Place the pot back over medium-high heat and reduce the broth to ¼ cup. In a bowl, whisk the reduced broth, mustard, vinegar, and olive oil. Cut the clams into nickel-size pieces and add to the vinaigrette to marinate for 30 minutes. Combine the peppers, onion, celery, and herbs. Toss with the marinated clams and vinaigrette and season with salt and black pepper.

Clam Risotto

SERVES 4–6

   12 large hard-shell clams, scrubbed

    2 cups white wine

    1 stalk celery, cut into pieces

    2 teaspoons fennel seeds

    6 tablespoons butter, divided

    1 onion, diced small

    1 fennel bulb, diced small

    2 cups Arborio rice

   ¼ cup Pernod or dry white vermouth

    3 tablespoons chopped fresh tarragon or chives

In a pot over medium-high heat, combine 1 cup of water with the clams, wine, celery, and fennel seeds. Cover the pot and bring to a boil, cooking until the clams open. Remove the clams from their shells and reserve. Strain the broth into a clear container, discard the solids, and wipe out the pot. Let the broth sit undisturbed for 5 minutes. Slowly decant the broth back into the pot and leave any grit in the bottom of the container. You should have 3–4 cups of broth in total; add enough water to make 5 cups. Place the pot over low heat to keep the broth warm. Remove the clam meat from the clam shells, cut the clams into nickel-size pieces, and set aside. In a second pot over medium heat, melt 2 tablespoons of the butter and sauté the onion and fennel until translucent. Add the rice and toss to coat. Add the Pernod or vermouth and cook until dry. Add 2 cups of clam broth and stir until the rice has absorbed all of the liquid. Repeat with another 2 cups of broth. To finish, stir in the remaining 1 cup of broth and the clam pieces, the remaining 4 tablespoons of butter, and herbs. Bring to a simmer. Remove from the heat, cover, and let sit until the liquid is absorbed and the rice is creamy.

Clams and Mussels en Escabeche

The cooked shellfish is marinated in vinegar and spices.

SERVES 4–6 AS AN APPETIZER

 24 littleneck clams, scrubbed

 1 cup white wine

 2 pounds mussels, rinsed and beards removed

 1 cup extra-virgin olive oil

 2 carrots, sliced into thin rounds

 2 shallots, sliced into rings

 4 garlic cloves, smashed

 1 tablespoon smoked sweet paprika

 1 teaspoon ground coriander

 6 sprigs thyme and/or 3 stalks rosemary

 1 orange, zested in wide strips

 1 tablespoon sherry vinegar

 2 tablespoons chopped fresh herbs, such as chives, parsley or tarragon

 Sliced baguette for serving

In a pot over medium-high heat, combine the clams with the wine. Cover the pot and bring to a boil, cooking until the clams open. Remove the clams and reserve. Repeat with mussels using the same broth. Once the mussels are cooked, strain the broth into a clear container, discard the solids, and wipe out the pot. Let the broth sit undisturbed for 5 minutes. Slowly decant the broth back into the pot and leave any grit in the bottom of the container. Place the pot over medium-high heat and reduce to ½ cup and reserve. Remove the meats from the shells.*

In a sauté pan over medium heat, warm the olive oil. Add the carrots, shallots, and garlic and cook until the carrots begin to soften. Add the paprika, coriander, thyme, and orange zest and cook for 2 minutes, until the aromas bloom. Add the reserved broth and sherry vinegar, season with salt, and simmer for 5 minutes. Add the chopped fresh herbs. Stir to combine and pour over the cooked shellfish. Cool to room temperature. Wait at least 1 hour before serving. The flavors improve if the dish is allowed to chill overnight in the refrigerator before returning it to room temperature. Serve with a sliced baguette or with meats in their shells.

 * Reserve one shell per meat if you intend to serve in the shell.

Clams with Spicy Red Wine–Tomato Sauce

SERVES 4–6

   1 pound linguine, cooked al dente in salted water, drained, with 1 cup of cooking liquid reserved

36 littleneck clams, scrubbed

   2 cups fruity red wine, divided

¼ cup extra-virgin olive oil, plus extra for garnish

   6 garlic cloves, sliced

   1 small onion, thinly sliced

   1 dry chipotle pepper, seeds and stem discarded, or 5–6 Calabrian or de árbol chiles

   1 (28-ounce) can crushed San Marzano tomatoes

   Salt

   1 orange, zested

   1 lemon, zested and juiced

In a pot over medium-high heat, add the clams and 1 cup of the wine. Cover the pot and bring to a boil, cooking until the clams open. Remove the clams from their shells and reserve. Strain the broth into a clear container, discard the solids, and wipe out the pot. Let the broth sit undisturbed for 5 minutes. Slowly decant the broth back into the pot and leave any grit in the bottom of the container. In a large sauté pan over medium-high heat, warm the olive oil, then add the garlic and onion. Cook until slightly browned and add the chipotle. Toast the pepper until fragrant, 1–2 minutes. Add the clam broth and remaining 1 cup of wine and bring to a boil. Reduce by half. Add the tomatoes and season with salt and orange zest. Cover and reduce the heat to low. Simmer for 30–40 minutes, until the tomatoes no longer taste raw, and mash the chipotle into the sauce. Add the clams and toss with the sauce. Add the lemon juice and zest, and drizzle with olive oil. Add the pasta and remaining pasta water, and simmer until the pasta is warmed and the liquid coats the pasta.

Clams Casino

MAKES 12 MEDIUM CLAMS AS AN APPETIZER

   4 strips bacon

   4 tablespoons butter

   1 red bell pepper, finely diced

   2 shallots, diced

   3 garlic cloves, minced

   1 teaspoon ground dry oregano

12 littleneck clams, shucked, top shell discarded, liquor reserved

½ cup Amontillado or cooking sherry or white wine

   2 tablespoons grated Parmesan

   2 tablespoons chopped fresh parsley

   6 tablespoons bread crumbs

   1 lemon, cut into wedges

In a skillet over medium heat, cook the bacon until crisp. Transfer the bacon to a paper towel and leave the rendered fat in the pan. Add the butter, bell pepper, shallots, garlic, and oregano and cook until the pepper begins to soften. Add the reserved clam liquor and sherry and simmer until the alcohol smell dissipates. Remove from the heat and cool to room temperature. Stir in the Parmesan and parsley. Place the clams in their shell on a baking sheet and evenly distribute the vegetable mixture in a mound atop each clam. Sprinkle bread crumbs and crumble bacon over each clam. Bake in a 475°F oven until the clams are bubbling and the topping is slightly charred. Serve with lemon wedges.

Clams with Mustard and Scallions

SERVES 4–6 AS AN APPETIZER

¼ cup extra-virgin olive oil

4 garlic cloves, smashed

36 littleneck clams, scrubbed

1 cup white wine

¼ cup whole grain mustard

1 bunch scallions, thinly sliced

4 tablespoons butter, cut into pieces

Baguette for serving

In a wide skillet over high heat, warm the olive oil. Add the garlic and cook until it begins to brown. Add the clams, wine, and mustard. Cover the pot and cook until the clams open. Transfer the clams to a serving bowl and add the scallions and butter to the sauce, swirling to incorporate them completely. Pour the sauce over the clams and serve with a baguette.

Raw Clams with Lime and Ginger

SERVES 4–6 AS AN APPETIZER

24 littleneck clams, scrubbed, shucked, and liquor reserved

1 (1-inch) knob ginger, sliced

½ cup lime juice

2 tablespoons almond, walnut, or roasted peanut oil

Crushed red chile flakes

Remove the clams from their shells and rub the inside of each shell with ginger, then discard the ginger. Mix the clams with the lime juice, oil, and a generous pinch of chile flakes, and marinate for 15–30 minutes. Spoon the clams back into the shells and garnish with a dash of the marinade.

Raw Clams with Sizzling Andouille Sausage

SERVES 4–6 AS AN APPETIZER

½ pound Andouille sausage

24 littleneck clams, shucked, top shell discarded

1 lemon, cut into wedges

Cook the sausage until sizzling hot. Slice and serve immediately alongside ice-cold clams and lemon wedges.

VARIATION

+ Substitute chorizo for Andouille sausage.

Grilled Clams with Lime-Oregano Butter

SERVES 4–6 AS AN APPETIZER

2 recipes Lime-Oregano Butter (page 21)

24 littleneck clams, shucked, top shell discarded, liquor reserved

Black pepper

Prepare a charcoal grill with a medium fire. Place a dollop of the Lime-Oregano Butter on each shucked clam and season with pepper. Place the clams on the grill shell side down and cook until they are heated through and the butter is bubbling around them.

NOTE *If using a gas grill, preheat all burners to medium.*

VARIATIONS

+ **Grilled Clams with Anchovy-Horseradish Butter.** Prepare the clams as above, replacing the butter with 2 recipes Anchovy-Horseradish Butter (page 19).

+ **Grilled Clams with Garlic-Herb Butter.** Prepare the clams as above replacing the butter with 2 recipes Garlic-Herb Butter (page 20).

Braised Clams with Coconut and Spice

SERVES 4

   36 littleneck clams, scrubbed

   1 (14-ounce) can unsweetened coconut milk

   1 (2-inch) knob ginger, thinly sliced

   2 star anise pods

   1 bay leaf

   2 large sweet potatoes, cut into 1-inch cubes

   Salt

   4 plum tomatoes, diced

   ¼ cup chopped fresh cilantro

   1 lime, zested and cut into wedges

   Crushed red chile flakes

In a pot over medium-high heat, add the clams and ½ cup of water. Cover the pot and bring to a boil, cooking until the clams open. Remove the clams from the pot and reserve. Strain the broth into a clear container, discard the solids, and wipe out the pot. Let the broth sit undisturbed for 5 minutes. Slowly decant the broth back into the pot and leave any grit in the bottom of the container. Combine the broth with the coconut milk, ginger, star anise pods, and bay leaf and simmer over the lowest heat for 5 minutes. Strain the milk mixture and discard the solids. Cook the sweet potatoes in salted boiling water until tender and drain them. In a large pot, combine spiced coconut milk, sweet potatoes, tomatoes, cilantro, lime zest, a generous pinch of chile flakes, and clams, and simmer gently until warmed through. Serve hot with lime wedges.

Geoduck Clams with Lime and Ginger

Geoducks are very large clams found in the Pacific Northwest

SERVES 4–6 AS AN APPETIZER

   1 geoduck clam

   1 (1-inch) knob of ginger, sliced

   2 tablespoons almond, walnut, or roasted peanut oil

   ¼ cup fresh lime juice

   Crushed red chile flakes

   Salt

Blanch the geoduck for 45 seconds in salted boiling water, then shock it in ice water. Remove the viscera and cut off the siphon, reserving the rest of the clam for other uses. Peel and discard the rough outer skin from the siphon, slice the siphon lengthwise, and wash to remove grit. Rub the serving plate(s) with slices of fresh ginger to impart a flavor that will perfume the clam, then discard the ginger. Thinly slice the meat on the bias and lay it on plates as you would carpaccio. Mix the oil, lime juice, and a pinch of chile flakes. Drizzle the lime mixture over the clam slices, season with salt, and serve cold.

Potato Salad with Bacon and Clam Vinaigrette

SERVES 4–6 AS A SIDE DISH

12 large hard-shell clams, scrubbed

1 cup white wine

¼ cup extra-virgin olive oil

8 strips bacon, chopped

1 fennel bulb, finely diced

1 small onion, finely diced

¼ cup apple cider vinegar

1½ pounds fingerling or small red potatoes

Salt

¼ cup chopped fresh herbs, such as chervil, chives, or tarragon

In a pot over medium-high heat, add the clams and the wine. Cover the pot and bring to a boil, cooking until the clams open. Remove the clams from their shells and reserve. Strain the broth into a clear container, discard the solids, and wipe out the pot. Let the broth sit undisturbed for 5 minutes. Slowly decant the broth back into the pot and leave any grit in the bottom of the container. You should have about 2 cups of broth.

In a sauté pan over medium heat, warm the olive oil. Add the bacon and cook until it is crisp and the fat has rendered. Add the fennel and onion and cook until they begin to soften. Add the vinegar and strained clam broth. Bring the mixture to a boil and reduce by half. In a large pot over high heat, boil the potatoes in salted water until tender. Strain, return to the pot, and pour the vinaigrette over the potatoes. Gently crush about half of the potatoes. Add the clams and herbs and stir to combine. Serve warm or at room temperature.

Linguine with Clam Sauce

SERVES 4

- 1 pound linguine, cooked according to package instructions, ½ cup cooking liquid reserved
- 12 large hard-shell clams, scrubbed
- 2 cups white wine
- 6 tablespoons butter
- ¼ cup flour
  Worcestershire sauce
- 1 bay leaf
  Ground mace
- 1½ ounces Amontillado or cooking sherry or Rainwater Madeira
- 2 egg yolks
- 2 tablespoons chopped fresh herbs, such as chervil, chives, or tarragon

In a pot over medium-high heat, add the clams and the wine. Cover the pot and bring to a boil, cooking until the clams open. Remove the clams from their shells, cut into dime-size pieces, and reserve. Strain the broth into a clear container, discard the solids, and wipe out the pot. Let the broth sit undisturbed for 5 minutes. Slowly decant the broth back into the pot and leave any grit in the bottom of the container. You should have about 3 cups of broth. Add water to equal 3 cups, if needed.

In a wide skillet over medium heat, melt the butter. Whisk in the flour until it forms a loose paste. Add the clam broth, a couple of dashes of Worcestershire sauce, the bay leaf, a pinch of mace, and the sherry. Simmer, stirring constantly, until it is slightly thickened. In a separate bowl, beat the egg yolks and whisk in ¼ cup of the clam sauce. Add the yolk mixture to the pot with the clam sauce and simmer over very low heat, stirring constantly, until the sauce is thickened, 2–4 minutes.

Add the pasta, remaining pasta water, clam pieces, and herbs and simmer until the pasta is warmed and the liquid coats the pasta.

VARIATION

- Use chopped clams instead of fresh. Strain 2 cups of chopped clams, reserving their liquor. Add as much white wine or water as needed to the clam liquor to equal 3 cups and proceed with the recipe.

New England–Style Steamer Clams

SERVES 2 AS AN ENTRÉE, 4 AS AN APPETIZER

- 2 pounds steamer clams, scrubbed
- 1 cup white wine
- 1 small onion, thinly sliced
- ½ pound linguiça sausage, sliced into ½-inch rounds
  Crushed red chile flakes
- 2 lemons, 1 halved, 1 cut into wedges
- 1 cup butter, melted

Place the clams in a pot with the wine, onion, sausage, a generous pinch of chile flakes, and lemon halves. Cover the pot and bring to a boil, cooking until the clams open. Remove the sausage and the clams in their shells and reserve. Strain the broth into a clear container, discard the solids, and wipe out the pot. Let the broth sit undisturbed for 5 minutes. Slowly decant the broth back into the pot and leave any grit in the bottom of the container. Serve the clams and sausage with a bowl of broth, the lemon wedges, and a ramekin of melted butter alongside.

Stuffed Clams

SERVES 4–6 AS AN APPETIZER

    16 littleneck clams, scrubbed

    2 cups white wine

    8 tablespoons butter

    6 garlic cloves, grated

    1 tablespoon smoked sweet paprika

    ½ tablespoon crushed red chile flakes

    1 teaspoon ground mace

    1 cup Amontillado or cooking sherry

    2 cups crumbled Ritz or saltine crackers

    3 lemons, 1 zested and juiced, 2 cut into wedges

    ½ cup chopped fresh herbs, such as parsley, chives, and tarragon

In a pot over medium-high heat, add the clams and the wine. Cover the pot and bring to a boil, cooking until the clams open. Remove the clams in their shells and reserve. Strain the broth into a clear container, discard the solids, and wipe out the pot. Let the broth sit undisturbed for 5 minutes. Slowly decant the broth back into the pot and leave any grit in the bottom of the container. You should have about 3 cups of broth. Add water to equal 3 cups, if needed. Remove the meats from the shells and cut the clams into dime-size pieces.

In a sauté pan over medium heat, melt the butter and cook the garlic until fragrant. Add the paprika, chile flakes, and mace and cook for 30 seconds. Combine the spiced butter and clams in a bowl and add the sherry, reserved clam broth, crackers, lemon zest and juice, and chopped herbs. Stuff the clam shells with this mixture and bake at 350°F for 20–25 minutes until they are browned on top and hot through. Serve with lemon wedges.

Griddled Razor Clams

SERVES 4–6 AS AN APPETIZER

    1 recipe Garlic-Parsley Oil (page 27)

    24 razor clams, scrubbed

    Baguette for serving

Cook the clams on a hot griddle until the meats set and the shells are fully open. Douse with Garlic-Parsley Oil and serve with a baguette.

COBIA
Meaty dense fish

Cobia is a unique species of fish. Its dense, round body with long tapered snout and forked tail makes it an attractive fish. Its varying colors go from dark green on its back to lighter shades on its sides, and stripes extend from head to tail. These stripes have earned it the name sergeant fish, as they resemble military epaulettes. Because cobia's favorite food is crabs, it also carries the nickname crab-eater. Other monikers include lemonfish, black kingfish, black salmon, black bonito, blob, and prodigal son. Just as it has many names, it has many uses in the kitchen.

Its texture is firm but flaky, with just a hint of squeak. It is well suited to frying, broiling, steaming, and especially to grilling, when its texture evolves into a chewy bite equal to swordfish. When raw, it is juicy and flavorful in sushi and sashimi, and it makes for a wonderful ceviche fish. Thick fillet portions are great for grilling and broiling, belly fillets for steaming and sautéing, and thin bias-cut "sheets" perfect for a quick pan-fried dish. Despite all of the uses for which cobia is outstanding, making stock from its bones is not one of them. The resulting broth, though sweet and aromatic, also has an undesirable muddy quality.

Cobia swim near to shore off Maryland and Virginia, where a commercial fishery supports local consumption, and in the Gulf of Mexico, where they're fished recreationally. They have a growing fan base and have become an important species in aquaculture, for which it is particularly well suited, given its rapid growth rate, value, and fitness for thriving in farming conditions. I find the farmed product superior to the wild, as it is consistently of a higher quality and the flavor is more refined than the oftentimes brassy flavor of the wild product.

Braised Cobia with Red Wine

SERVES 4

½ cup Basic Fish Stock (page 61) or vegetable stock or water

4 cobia portions, skin off

Salt

6 tablespoons butter, divided

1 carrot, shredded

4 shallots, sliced

2 garlic cloves, sliced

1 cup fruity red wine, such as Beaujolais

2 sprigs fresh thyme

2 tablespoons chopped fresh parsley or tarragon

Season the fish with salt and let it rest for 20 minutes. In a large pot over medium-high heat, melt 2 tablespoons of butter. Add the carrot, shallots, and garlic and cook until the shallots are wilted. Add the wine, bring to a boil, and cook until the alcohol smell dissipates. Add the fish stock and thyme. Season with salt, reduce the heat to low, and nestle the fish into the sauce. Cover and cook the fish through, about 12–15 minutes. Remove the fish and reduce the liquid over high heat to ¼ cup. Add the remaining 4 tablespoons of butter and herbs and stir to incorporate.

Broiled Cobia Kebabs en Adobo

SERVES 4

1 recipe Adobo Marinade (page 34)

4 cobia portions, skin off, cut into 1-inch pieces

Marinate the fish in the Adobo for 6–8 hours. Preheat the broiler to high and set the rack in the position closest to the heat. Remove the fish from the marinade, pat dry, thread onto skewers, and place on a baking tray. Slide the tray under the broiler and cook without turning until done, 5–7 minutes.

Cobia Crudo with Orange and Chile

SERVES 4 AS AN APPETIZER

1 pound cobia fillet, skin off, sliced on the bias into ¼-inch-thick ribbons, avoiding any dark tissue

Smoked salt or sea salt

Crushed red chile flakes, such as Aleppo or Espelette

1 orange, zested

Extra-virgin olive oil (fruity is best)

Slice the fish and lay the slices directly onto serving plates. Season the fish with salt, chile, and zest and let it rest for 10 minutes. Drizzle with olive oil and serve cold.

Grilled Cobia Wrapped with Grape Leaves

SERVES 4

> 1 recipe Mediterranean Yogurt Sauce (page 28) or Dill Crème Fraîche (page 27)
>
> 4 cobia portions, skin off
>
> Salt
>
> 1 lemon, zested
>
> 12–16 brined grape leaves, thick stems removed
>
> Extra-virgin olive oil

Season the fish with salt and lemon zest and let it rest for 20 minutes. Prepare a charcoal grill with a medium fire. Arrange 3–4 grape leaves so they overlap and create a single flat sheet. Place one portion of fish in the center of the sheet and fold the leaves over the fish to wrap it completely. Repeat the process with the other portions. Drizzle with olive oil and place the wrapped fish seam side up on the grill directly over the coals. Cook for 4–5 minutes. Flip the bundled fish and cook until done, 3–4 minutes more. Serve the fish in the grape leaves with a drizzle of olive oil and the Mediterranean Yogurt Sauce or Dill Crème Fraîche.

NOTE *If using a gas grill, preheat all burners to medium, and follow the directions as above.*

Grilled Cobia with Sweet Garlic Butter

SERVES 4

> 1 recipe Sweet Garlic Butter (page 23)
>
> 4 cobia portions, skin off
>
> Salt
>
> Extra-virgin olive oil

Season the fish with salt and let it rest for 20 minutes. Prepare a charcoal grill with a medium fire, concentrating the hot coals on one side of the kettle. Brush the fish with oil and place it on the grill directly over the hot coals. Cook until the edges of the fish begin to char, about 3 minutes. Lift the entire grill grate and rotate it so the fish rests opposite the hot coals. Cover the grill and continue to cook over this indirect heat until the fish is done, 4–6 minutes. Serve topped with Sweet Garlic Butter.

NOTE *If using a gas grill, preheat all burners to medium. Place the cobia on one side of the hot grates. Once it begins to char around the edges, turn off the burner directly under the fish and cover the grill to finish cooking.*

Sautéed Cobia with Lemon and Pepper

SERVES 4

4 cobia portions, skin off

Salt

2 lemons, zested and juiced

3 tablespoons black pepper, coarsely ground

6 tablespoons butter, divided

Season the fish all over with salt and on one side with lemon zest and pepper, gently pressing the zest and pepper into the flesh, and let it rest for 20 minutes. In a sauté pan over medium heat, melt 2 tablespoons of the butter. Place the fish lemon-pepper side down in the pan and cook without flipping until almost done, then remove the fish and wipe the pan clean. Add the remaining 4 tablespoons of butter and cook until golden brown. Add the lemon juice and season with salt. Turn off the heat and return the fish to the pan uncooked side down to finish cooking.

Steamed Cobia with Tarragon-Citrus Vinaigrette

SERVES 4

1 recipe Tarragon-Citrus Vinaigrette (page 37)

4 cobia portions, skin off

Salt

3–4 stalks celery

2 lemons, sliced

15 black peppercorns

½ cup white wine

Season the fish with salt and let it rest for 20 minutes. Place the celery stalks, lemon slices, and peppercorns in a pot to form a raft that will hold the fish. Add the wine and enough water to cover the bottom of the pot, and place the pot over medium-low heat. Bring to a simmer. Place the fish on top of the raft, cover, and cook until done, 8–9 minutes. Serve the fish with a drizzle of vinaigrette.

Cobia Tacos

SERVES 4

1 recipe Orange-Coriander Vinaigrette (page 37) or Lemon-Chile-Mint Dressing (page 36)

1 recipe Pico de Gallo (page 30) or store-bought salsa

1 pound cobia fillets, skin off

Salt

Sour cream

2 avocados, sliced

1 bunch cilantro, leaves picked

¼ head cabbage, shaved, or coleslaw

16 corn tortillas

Season the fish with salt and let it rest for 20 minutes. Grill, bake, broil, or poach the fish until cooked. Flake the fish into bite-size pieces and toss with the vinaigrette. Set out bowls of Pico de Gallo, sour cream, avocado, cilantro, and shredded cabbage or coleslaw. Place the tortillas in a dry heavy-bottomed pan over medium heat and cook until toasted yet pliable. Keep them warm in a kitchen towel. For each taco, stack two tortillas together. Let everyone build their own tacos just the way they like.

COD
Flaky white fish

Cod has a unique place in American history. Before European explorers came looking for new lands to discover for their sovereigns, they came looking for cod. Atlantic cod is the fish upon whose back America built its first independent economy, as it was once incredibly plentiful in the cold New England waters. While it is only one of several species caught in New England's storied fisheries, it is by far the most well known. But there is a relative and culinary twin that swims off the other coast, the Pacific cod. For the purposes of this book, both species are discussed as one.

Cod—like the other flaky white fish that share its culinary category—are sedentary; most of their fat is stored in their liver rather than in the muscles, so their flesh is very lean. When cooked, cod has a dense texture and a large flake, which allows it to hold on to its moisture a bit better than smaller flaked white fish, like haddock. In terms of flavor, cod is mild with a slightly sour note.

Sometimes you can get your hands on a whole fish (be sure to cook the head, if you do), but most often you'll find cod fillets. The loin, sometimes called the captain's cut, is the thickest part of the fillet and considered the best part of the fish. The mate's cut is the tail end of the fillet. Both cuts benefit from a sprinkling of kosher salt 20 minutes before cooking to help bring out the cod's nuanced flavors and firm up its flesh for cooking. Regardless of the cut, cod can be broiled, fried, poached, roasted, smoked, steamed, or stewed. Cod cheeks and tongues are a real treat if you can find them. They render a gelatinous sauce when sautéed with butter or olive oil, parsley, and sherry (page 140) and are a fantastic addition to stews (pages 54–59).

Spanish-Style Braised Cod

SERVES 4

>4 cod portions, skin off
>
>Salt
>
>½ cup extra-virgin olive oil, divided
>
>10 garlic cloves, sliced
>
>Crushed red chile flakes
>
>½ cup white wine
>
>1 lemon, juiced
>
>2 tablespoons chopped fresh parsley or tarragon

Season the fish lightly with salt and let it rest overnight. Wash the salt off the cod under cold running water and pat dry. In a large pot over low heat, warm ¼ cup of the olive oil. Add the fish and garlic. Cook the fish without flipping until almost done, then flip to finish cooking. Remove the fish and add the chile flakes, wine, and lemon juice to the pot. Increase the heat to medium and simmer until the liquid is reduced to 2 tablespoons. Turn off the heat and slowly drizzle in the remaining ¼ cup of olive oil, whisking vigorously to emulsify the sauce. Add the herbs and spoon the sauce over the fish.

Braised Cod Puttanesca

The cod is braised in a lively tomato sauce with capers and olives.

SERVES 4

>4 cod portions, skin off
>
>Salt
>
>6 tablespoons extra-virgin olive oil, divided
>
>1 (2-ounce) tin anchovies in oil
>
>4 garlic cloves, sliced
>
>4 dried árbol chiles, or ½ tablespoon crushed red chile flakes
>
>2 (14-ounce) cans fire-roasted diced tomatoes
>
>½ cup white wine
>
>2 tablespoons capers, rinsed and patted dry
>
>¼ cup pitted cured black olives
>
>6 basil leaves, torn, for garnish

Season the fish with salt and let it rest for 20 minutes. In an ovenproof sauté pan over medium-high heat, warm 3 tablespoons of the olive oil, anchovies with their oil, garlic, and chiles, and cook until the anchovies melt. Add the tomatoes, wine, capers, and olives. Bring to a simmer and cook for 10 minutes. Nestle the fish into the sauce and drizzle with the remaining 3 tablespoons of olive oil. Cover the pan and place it in a 275°F oven for 30 minutes. Remove and let it rest for 10 minutes before serving with scattered, torn basil leaves.

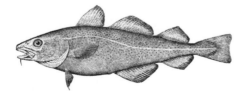

Curried Cod

SERVES 4

  2 cups Basic Fish Stock (page 61) or
    vegetable stock

  4 cod portions, skin off

  Salt

  6 tablespoons butter, divided

  1 onion, minced

  1 apple, diced into ½-inch pieces

  ½ pound potatoes, cut into ½-inch cubes

  1 tablespoon curry powder

  Crushed red chile flakes

  2 tablespoons flour

  ½ cup full-fat Greek-style yogurt or cream

  ¼ cup fresh cilantro leaves

  1 Fresno or serrano pepper, thinly sliced

  1 lime, cut into wedges

Season the fish with salt and let it rest for
20 minutes. In a large pot over high heat, melt
2 tablespoons of the butter. Add the onion,
apple, and potatoes. Sauté until the apples are
lightly browned. Remove the vegetables, add
the remaining 4 tablespoons of butter, and cook for
1 minute. Add the flour and cook another minute,
stirring to incorporate the flour with the butter.
Add the vegetables, whisk in the stock, and simmer
until the sauce thickens. Add the fish, season with
salt, cover, and simmer 12–14 minutes over low
heat. Turn off the heat, add the yogurt, and stir to
incorporate. Let it rest for 20 minutes. Garnish
with the cilantro and hot peppers and serve with
lime wedges.

Braised Cod à la Grecque

The cod is braised and marinated in a flavorful
Mediterranean broth.

SERVES 4

  4 cod portions, skin off

  Salt

  ½ cup extra-virgin olive oil

  ½ cup white wine

  3 tablespoons white wine vinegar

  ½ tablespoon ground coriander

  1 tablespoon fennel seeds

  6 sprigs fresh thyme

  3 bay leaves

  ½ pound carrots, cut into ½-inch rounds

  2 onions, cut into 1-inch wedges

  ½ pound small mushrooms, cut in half

  Crusty bread for serving

Season the fish with salt and let it rest for
20 minutes. In a large pot over medium heat,
combine ½ cup of water with the olive oil, white
wine, vinegar, coriander seeds, fennel seeds,
thyme, bay leaves, and a good pinch of salt.
Simmer for 5 minutes, then add the carrots,
onions, and mushrooms. Cover and simmer
until the carrots are just tender. Nestle the fish
into the sauce. Cover and cook over very low
heat until the cod is cooked through, about
12–14 minutes. Remove from the heat, cool to
room temperature, and serve with crusty bread.

NOTE *The flavors improve if the fish is chilled
overnight and brought back to room temperature
before serving.*

Stewed Cod with Chickpeas and Garlic Toast

SERVES 4

1 cup Basic Fish Stock (page 61) or vegetable stock

4 cod portions, skin off

Salt

2 tablespoons extra-virgin olive oil

3 onions, sliced

2 (14-ounce) cans chickpeas, drained and liquid reserved, divided

1 teaspoon nutmeg

¼ cup chopped parsley

Baguette, sliced

2 garlic cloves, sliced

Season the fish with salt and let it rest for 20 minutes. In a large pot over medium-high heat, warm the olive oil. Add the onions and cook until caramelized, about 20–30 minutes. Mash ½ cup of the chickpeas into a paste and add them, the remaining chickpeas, nutmeg, reserved liquid, and stock to the pot. Season with salt, bring to a simmer, and cook until slightly thickened. Add the cod, cover, and reduce the heat to low. Cook until the fish is done, about 12–14 minutes. Remove from the heat and stir in the parsley. Serve with baguette slices that have been rubbed with garlic.

Teriyaki-Glazed Cod

SERVES 4

1 recipe Teriyaki-Style Sauce (page 32)

4 cod portions, skin off

Salt

2 teaspoons Worcestershire sauce

1 tablespoon sesame oil

¼ cup sliced scallions

Season the fish lightly with salt and let it rest for 20 minutes. Preheat the broiler to medium and set the rack in the position closest to the heat. Combine the Teriyaki-Style Sauce and the Worcestershire sauce. Brush a baking dish with the sesame oil. Place the fish in the dish, coat with half of the sauce, and slide the dish under the broiler. Cook, basting with the remaining sauce every 2 minutes until done. Garnish with sliced scallions.

Braised Cod with Bacon and Root Vegetables

SERVES 4

4 cod portions, skin off

Salt

2 cups white wine

2 tablespoons butter

1 (2-ounce) tin anchovies in oil

½ pound thick-cut bacon, diced small

1½ pounds root vegetables, such as butternut squash, parsnip, potato, rutabaga, or turnip, cut into 1-inch pieces

6 garlic cloves, crushed

Crushed red chile flakes

3 tablespoons chopped fresh herbs, such as chives, parsley, and tarragon

Season the fish with salt and let it rest overnight. Wash the salt off the cod under cold running water and pat dry. Soak the fish in the wine for 1 hour. In a large pot over medium heat, melt the butter and add the oil from the anchovies. Add the bacon and cook until the fat is rendered and the meat is crispy. Remove the bacon, leaving the fat in the pan, and add the root vegetables, anchovies, and garlic. Cook until the anchovies have melted. Remove the cod from the wine and pour the wine and 1 cup water into the pot with the vegetables. Season the vegetables with salt, bring to a boil, cover, and cook until the vegetables are tender, 8–10 minutes. Reduce the heat to low, nestle the fish into the pot, cover, and cook until the fish is done, about 15 minutes. Divide the vegetables and fish among warm bowls. Place the pot over high heat, reduce the cooking liquid to a glaze, add the herbs, and spoon over the fish and vegetables.

Cod Cakes

SERVES 4

¾ pound cod fillets, skin off

Salt

1 fennel bulb, finely diced

2 bay leaves

¾ pound potatoes, peeled and cut into 1-inch pieces

1½ cups light cream or milk

4 tablespoons butter

1 lemon, cut into wedges

Season the fish with salt and let it rest for 20 minutes. In a covered sauté pan over medium heat, place the fish, fennel, bay leaves, and just enough water to cover. Simmer for 6–8 minutes. Strain the poaching liquid into a separate pot, reserving the fennel and cod. Flake the cod into large pieces. Add the potatoes to the poaching liquid and additional water to cover. Season generously with salt and boil until the potatoes are easily pierced with a fork. Drain the potatoes and mash them with cream. Add the cod and fennel and gently stir to combine without mashing the fish too much. Shape into patties. In a sauté pan over medium heat, melt the butter and cook until golden brown. Add the fish cakes and cook until browned on both sides. Serve with lemon wedges.

Beer-Battered Cod

SERVES 4

1 recipe Traditional Remoulade
Sauce (page 31; optional)

4 cod portions, skin off, cut into 2-inch pieces

Salt

1 lemon, juiced

2 tablespoons vegetable or peanut oil

¾ cup flour, sifted

¾ cup cornstarch, sifted

¾ cup beer

2 tablespoons vegetable oil

1 egg, separated

Malt vinegar for serving

Season the fish with salt and the lemon juice and let it rest for 20 minutes. Pour 3–4 inches of oil into a high-sided pan. Place over medium-high heat and warm the oil to 375°F. Make a batter by combining the flour, cornstarch, beer, vegetable or peanut oil, egg yolk, and ½ tablespoon salt. Beat the egg white to soft peaks and fold it into the batter. Dip one piece of fish at a time into the batter, place it into the hot oil, and hold it there for 5 seconds before releasing it. Repeat the process, cooking only a couple of fillets at a time. Turn with a slotted spoon to ensure that both sides crisp evenly. Remove the pieces as they finish, and place on paper towels to absorb excess oil. Serve with Remoulade Sauce and malt vinegar.

VARIATIONS

+ **Curried Beer-Battered Cod.** Add 2 teaspoons of curry powder to the salt and lemon juice when seasoning.

+ **Vinegar-Spiked Beer-Battered Cod.** Marinate the fish in Adobo (page 34) for 2 hours, drain, and pat the fish dry before coating the fish with batter.

+ **Alternate Dipping Sauces.** Use Green Goddess Dressing (page 28), Basic Aioli, (page 25) Tartar Sauce (page 32), or Dill Crème Fraîche (page 27) instead of the Traditional Remoulade Sauce.

+ **Beer-Battered Cod Sandwich.** Assemble fried fish sandwiches by topping a potato bun with a piece of fried fish, Tartar Sauce, coleslaw, a slice of American or cheddar cheese, and sliced tomatoes.

Cod with Citrus and Herb Crust

SERVES 4

4 cod portions, skin off

Salt

½ cup panko

2 tablespoons chopped parsley

1 tablespoon chopped fresh thyme leaves

1 orange, zested

1 lemon, zested

6 tablespoons butter, melted

Season the fish with salt and let it rest for 20 minutes. Preheat the broiler to low and set the rack in the position closest to the heat. Combine the panko, parsley, thyme, zests, and butter to make a paste. Place the fish on a baking dish and cover with the bread-crumb mixture, patting it down gently. Place under the broiler and cook until the fish is done and the crust is lightly browned, about 7–10 minutes, depending on thickness.

Holiday-Scented Poached Cod with Drawn Butter

SERVES 4

4 cod portions, skin off

Salt

2 cups red wine

¼ cup red wine vinegar

2 shallots, sliced

2 teaspoons ground mace

20 black peppercorns

1 bay leaf

1 cinnamon stick

1 handful needles from your backyard tree or Christmas tree, making sure the tree wasn't sprayed with chemical treatment

4 tablespoons butter, melted

Black pepper

Season the fish with salt and let it rest for 20 minutes. In a pan just wide enough to hold the fish in a single layer, combine 1 cup of water with the wine, vinegar, shallots, mace, peppercorns, bay leaf, cinnamon stick, and tree needles. Simmer over low heat for 5 minutes. Season with salt and bring it to 170°F. Lower the fish into the liquid so that it is fully submerged. Poach over low heat until it flakes under gentle pressure, about 4–6 minutes per inch of thickness. Transfer to a plate and serve with melted butter and pepper.

Poached Cod with Rosemary and Orange

SERVES 4

1 recipe Gremolata (page 28)

4 cod portions, skin off

Salt

2 cups red wine

¼ cup red wine vinegar

2 shallots, sliced

2 teaspoons ground mace

20 black peppercorns

1 bay leaf

1 orange, zested and juiced

2 stalks fresh rosemary

4 tablespoons butter, melted

Season the fish with salt and let it rest for 20 minutes. In a deep pan just wide enough to hold the fish in a single layer, combine 1 cup of water with the wine, vinegar, shallots, mace, peppercorns, bay leaf, orange zest and juice, and rosemary. Simmer over low heat for 5 minutes. Season with salt and bring it to 170°F. Lower the fish into the liquid so that it is fully submerged. Poach over low heat until it flakes under gentle pressure, about 4–6 minutes per inch of thickness. Transfer to a plate and serve with Gremolata and melted butter.

Roasted Cod Head with Lemon Vinaigrette

SERVES 4–6

> 2 whole cod heads, collars still attached, about 5 pounds total
>
> 5 lemons, zested and juiced
>
> ½ cup extra-virgin olive oil
>
> ¼ cup prepared horseradish
>
> 2 tablespoons salt
>
> 4 teaspoons ground mace or nutmeg
>
> 2 fennel bulbs, thinly sliced
>
> 2 onions, thinly sliced
>
> ¼ cup dry vermouth
>
> 5 tablespoons butter, divided
>
> Crusty bread for serving

Remove the gills from the fish heads, wash the heads with cold water, and pat dry. Make a marinade with the juice of four lemons, lemon zest, olive oil, horseradish, salt, and mace. Combine the marinade with the heads in large plastic zipper bags and let them rest for 4–8 hours. In a pot of boiling salted water, blanch the fennel and onions until tender. Drain the vegetables and use them to line the bottom of a baking dish big enough to hold both heads. Remove the heads from the vinaigrette and place them as they would swim, with collars spread like wings, on top of the vegetables. Pour the vermouth over the heads and place 1 tablespoon of the butter on each head. Place the pan in a 375°F oven and roast for 45 minutes, basting the heads with pan juices every 15 minutes. Remove from the oven. Drain the pan juices and whisk with the remaining 4 tablespoons of butter and the juice of one lemon to make a sauce. Serve heads with the sauce, vegetables, crusty bread, and the instructions that if it's not a bone, it's edible.

Roasted Cod with Anchovy-Herb Butter

SERVES 4

> 4 tablespoons Anchovy-Herb Butter (page 19)
>
> 4 cod portions, skin off
>
> Salt
>
> 2 carrots, thinly sliced
>
> 1 fennel bulb, thinly sliced
>
> 1 onion, thinly sliced

Season the fish with salt and let it rest for 20 minutes. In a pot of boiling salted water, blanch the carrots, fennel, and onion until tender. Drain the vegetables and use them to line the bottom of a baking dish big enough to hold the fish. Place the fish on the vegetables and top each with 1 tablespoon of Anchovy-Herb Butter. Bake in a 300°F oven until cooked through, 12–14 minutes.

Sautéed Cod Cheeks and Tongues with Sherry

SERVES 4–6 AS AN APPETIZER

 1 pound cod cheeks and tongues
 Salt
 6 tablespoons extra-virgin olive oil
 4 garlic cloves, thinly sliced
 ½ cup Amontillado or cooking sherry
 2 tablespoons chopped fresh parsley
 Baguette for serving

Season the cheeks and tongues with salt and let them rest for 15 minutes. In a sauté pan over medium heat, warm the olive oil. Place the cheeks and tongues and garlic in the pan and cook until the garlic is soft. Add the sherry and parsley. Simmer until the alcohol smell dissipates, cover the pan, and cook until the sauce thickens, about 4–5 minutes. Serve with a baguette.

VARIATION

+ **Sautéed Cod Cheeks with Anchovy-Horseradish Butter.** When adding the sherry and parsley, also add 4 tablespoons of Anchovy-Horseradish Butter (page 19).

Sautéed Cod with Brown Butter, Garlic, and Rosemary

SERVES 4

 4 cod portions, skin off
 Salt
 6 tablespoons butter, divided
 2 sprigs rosemary, leaves picked
 2 garlic cloves, minced
 1 orange, zested and juiced

Season the fish with salt and let it rest for 20 minutes. In a sauté pan over medium heat, melt 2 tablespoons of the butter and cook until golden brown. Place the fish in the pan. Cook without flipping until almost done, then remove the fish and wipe the pan clean. Add the remaining 4 tablespoons of butter, rosemary, and garlic. Cook over medium heat until the butter is dark brown and the rosemary is crisp. Add the orange zest and juice, season with salt, and stir to combine. Turn off the heat and return the fish to the pan uncooked side down to finish cooking.

Blackened Cod

SERVES 4

 1 recipe Blackening Spice Mix (page 33)
 4 cod portions, skin off
 Salt
 4 tablespoons butter, melted, divided
 ¼ cup vegetable oil
 1 lemon, cut into wedges

Lightly season the fish with salt and let it rest for 15 minutes. Heat a cast iron skillet or heavy-bottomed sauté pan over high heat until it is screaming hot. Combine 2 tablespoons of the butter and all of the oil in a bowl and use to brush each portion so the fish glistens all over. Dredge one side of each portion in Blackening Spice Mix, coating evenly. Place the fish in the pan spice side down and drizzle half of the remaining butter-and-oil mixture over the top. Reduce the heat to medium-low and cook without flipping until a dark crust forms, then flip to cook through. Drizzle with the remaining butter and serve with lemon wedges.

Sautéed Prosciutto-Wrapped Cod

SERVES 4

> 4 cod portions, skin off
>
> Salt
>
> 1 lemon, zested and juiced
>
> 2 tablespoons white wine
>
> 2 tablespoons chopped fresh parsley or tarragon
>
> 2 pinches ground mace
>
> 8 thin slices prosciutto
>
> 4 tablespoons butter

Season the fish with salt. Mix the lemon zest and juice, wine, herbs, and mace. Marinate the fish in the mixture for 2 hours. Remove the fish from the marinade and pat dry. Wrap each portion of fish in two slices of prosciutto and secure with a toothpick. In a sauté pan over medium heat, melt the butter and cook until golden brown. Add the fish to the pan. Cook until the prosciutto is crisp and the fish is almost done, then flip to finish cooking, about 7–8 minutes total. Serve drizzled with butter from the pan.

Cod Tacos

SERVES 4

> Orange-Coriander Vinaigrette (page 37) or Lemon-Chile-Mint Dressing (page 36)
>
> 1 recipe Pico de Gallo (page 30) or store-bought salsa
>
> 1 pound cod fillets, skin off
>
> Salt
>
> Sour cream
>
> 2 avocados, sliced
>
> ½ cup cilantro, leaves picked
>
> ¼ head cabbage, shaved, or coleslaw
>
> 16 corn tortillas

Season the fish with salt and let it rest for 20 minutes. Grill, bake, broil, or poach the fish until cooked. Flake the fish into bite-size pieces and toss with the vinaigrette. Set out bowls of Pico de Gallo, sour cream, avocado, cilantro, and shredded cabbage. Place the tortillas in a dry heavy-bottomed pan over medium heat and cook until toasted yet pliable. Keep them warm in a kitchen towel. For each taco, stack two tortillas together. Let everyone build their own tacos just the way they like.

COD, SALT COD

The history of cod in worldwide cuisine features salted cod in greater measure than fresh cod. Because cod cures well, it was the fish that was most often salted and hung to dry, thus providing a durable food for long voyages at sea and a safe and affordable protein source before the advent of refrigeration. Judging by the number of languages in which salt cod is named—from the Spanish *bacalao salado* and the French *cabillaud* to the East African *makayabu* and the Scandinavian *klippfisk*—salt cod has an international legacy.

The traditional method of salting cod entails splitting the whole fish, salting it, and leaving it to cure in the open air on racks called flakes. There are several different styles of cure that depend on the type of salt used and the length of the cure and air-drying, all of which determined the character of the final product.

These days, salted cod can most often be found in two forms. You can purchase whole, bone-in, skin-on sides ranging from 1 to 5 pounds either online or in specialty Italian and Portuguese groceries. Pricier packaged and refrigerated boneless, skinless fillets are more widely available in supermarkets. Any salt cod you're buying should have whitish flesh with no spots or discoloration, and smell mildly of the sea.

Preparing salt cod first requires soaking it in a succession of freshwater baths. Once desalinated and moistened to near its original texture, the fillets can be used in chowders and stews (pages 54–59), shredded and used in cakes, topped with butter and broiled, or sliced very thinly and layered on a platter to be served in carpaccio style, drizzled with olive oil and a sprinkling of mace and fresh chopped mint (page 146).

Soaking or Refreshing Salt Cod and Other Salt Fish

Wash the fish under cold, running water to remove the salt from the outside. Place the fish in a dish and completely submerge it in room-temperature water. Let it rest in the fridge, changing the water every 6–12 hours. The total soaking time will range between 12 and 48 hours, depending on the intended use for the fish. To calculate the proper amount of salt fish to buy, consider that the dried fish will be about 20 percent heavier after soaking.

Soaking for 12 hours is best for dishes where there is a lot of liquid, like chowder, where the fish will season the whole dish while continuing to rehydrate.

Soaking for 24 hours is best for preparations in which the fish is simmered in a moderate amount of liquid as part of a dish like a thicker stew, where it will rehydrate the fish somewhat and the salt will help season the dish.

Soaking for 36 hours is best for preparations such as pickling, carpaccio, and ceviche in which a little salt is advantageous but the texture needs to be close to a fresh cod.

Soaking for 48 hours is best for dishes in which the fish will be cooked with no liquid, such as broiled and topped with butter, quickly sautéed with pan sauce, or grilled. The absence of liquid in the preparation requires the fish to be desalted to a properly seasoned level.

A mixture of equal parts water and wine can be used in the final soaking to give the fish a brighter flavor and to add nuance to a final dish. This is best for preparations such as ceviche, carpaccio, broiling, and sautéing.

Salt Cod Brandade

SERVES 4–6 AS AN APPETIZER

½ pound salt cod, cut into 1-inch pieces and soaked in cold water for 24 hours

2 bay leaves

10 peppercorns

5 allspice berries

¾ pound potatoes, peeled and cut into 1-inch dice

2 cups cream

1 garlic clove, grated

1 lemon, zested and juiced

Pinch cayenne pepper

1 baguette, sliced on the bias

Extra-virgin olive oil or melted butter

In a saucepan over low heat, combine the soaked salt cod, bay leaves, peppercorns, and allspice and barely cover with water. Poach for 5 minutes. Cool the fish in the poaching liquid. Remove the fish and strain the poaching liquid into a separate pot. Add potatoes to the cod liquid and additional water if needed to cover. Boil the potatoes until they are easily pierced with a fork, drain, and set aside. Place the cod in the pot and add the cream, garlic, and lemon zest. Place over medium-low heat and simmer for 5 minutes. In a bowl, vigorously whisk the salt cod mixture and potatoes into a slightly chunky purée. Stir in the cayenne and lemon juice. Slather the brandade on baguette slices, drizzle with olive oil or melted butter, slide under the broiler set to high, and cook until the tops begin to char.

Slow-Roasted Salt Cod with Mint-Mustard Vinaigrette

SERVES 4

1 recipe Mint-Mustard Vinaigrette (page 36)

1 pound salt cod, cut into 4 portions

¼ cup extra-virgin olive oil

2 plum tomatoes, chopped

10 radishes, thinly sliced

1 small red onion, thinly sliced and washed under cold running water, patted dry

1 fennel bulb, thinly sliced

¼ cup parsley, leaves picked

¼ cup mint, leaves picked

Salt

Black pepper

Soak the salt cod for 36 hours in several changes of water. Remove from the liquid and pat dry. Place the fish in a baking dish, drizzle with the olive oil, and roast in a 250°F oven for 25 minutes. Remove the fish from the oven and flake it into bite-size pieces. Toss the cod with its cooking oil and half of the vinaigrette and let it rest for at least 30 minutes at room temperature. In a second bowl, toss the tomatoes, radishes, onion, fennel, parsley, and mint with the remaining vinaigrette and season with salt and pepper. Portion the salad and place the flaked fish over the top.

Roasted Salt Cod with Marinara

SERVES 4

> 1 recipe Marinara Sauce (page 29)
> 1 pound salt cod, cut into 4 portions
> ¼ cup extra-virgin olive oil
> Crusty bread for serving

Soak the salt cod for 36–48 hours in several changes of water. Remove from the soaking liquid and pat dry. Warm the Marinara Sauce and pour it into a baking dish just large enough to hold the fish. Nestle the fish into the sauce and drizzle with olive oil. Cover the dish with foil and slide into a 275°F oven for 25 minutes. Remove and let it rest for 10 minutes before serving with crusty bread.

Braised Salt Cod with Fennel

SERVES 4

> 1 pound salt cod, cut into 4 portions
> 6 tablespoons butter, divided
> 2 fennel bulbs, cut into ½-inch wedges
> 2 oranges, juiced
> 1 cup white wine
> Salt
> 2 tablespoons chopped fresh chives
> or parsley

Soak the salt cod for 36–48 hours in several changes of water. Remove from the soaking liquid and pat dry. In a large pot over medium-high heat, melt 3 tablespoons of the butter. Add the fennel and cook until it begins to brown. Reduce the heat to medium, add the orange juice and wine, and season with salt. Cover and simmer until the fennel is barely softened, 7–8 minutes. Place the salt cod on top of the fennel and reduce the heat to low. Cover and cook for 12–14 minutes. Remove the salt cod and fennel. Reduce the remaining liquid to a syrup and whisk in the remaining 3 tablespoons of butter and the herbs. Drizzle the sauce over the fish and fennel, and serve warm or at room temperature.

Braised Salt Cod à la Barigoule

The cod and vegetables are braised and marinated in a spiced broth.

SERVES 4

1 recipe Basic Aioli (page 25), made with oil skimmed from the cooked dish

1 pound salt cod, cut into 4 portions

3 stalks celery, chopped

2 carrots, sliced

4 ounces mushrooms, cut in quarters

2 garlic cloves, thinly sliced

5 sprigs thyme

1 teaspoon ground coriander seeds

1½ cups white wine

Salt

1 (14-ounce) can halved artichoke hearts in oil

½ lemon, thinly sliced

1 cup extra-virgin olive oil

Crushed red chile flakes (optional)

Crusty bread for serving

Soak the salt cod for 36 hours in several changes of water. In a large pot over medium heat, combine the celery, carrots, mushrooms, garlic, thyme, coriander, wine, and ½ cup of water. Season lightly with salt and simmer until the alcohol smell dissipates. Add the artichoke hearts with their oil, lemon slices, and olive oil. Reduce the heat to low. Nestle the fish into the pot so it is barely submerged. If desired, add chile flakes to taste. Cover and cook the fish for 15–20 minutes. Remove the pot from the heat and cool to room temperature. The flavors improve if the dish is allowed to chill overnight. Use a ladle to skim off the olive oil, and use it when making Basic Aioli. Serve at room temperature with crusty bread and the aioli.

Salt Cod Carpaccio with Celery, Mint, and Mace

SERVES 4 AS AN APPETIZER

¾ pound salt cod

2 stalks celery, thinly sliced on the bias

¼ cup torn fresh mint leaves

Ground mace

Black pepper

1 teaspoon crushed red chile flakes

¼ cup extra-virgin olive oil

1 lemon, juiced

Soak the salt cod for 36 hours in several changes of water. Working from the tail toward the head, thinly slice the fish on the bias into sheets. Lay the sheets on a serving platter as you slice. Garnish the fish with the celery, mint, a pinch of mace, black pepper, chile flakes, and olive oil. Let it rest for 10–15 minutes. Drizzle with the lemon juice and serve at room temperature.

Salt Cod Simmered with Molasses

SERVES 4

> 1 pound salt cod
>
> 1 cup white wine
>
> ½ cup molasses
>
> 2 lemons, 1 juiced and 1 cut into wedges
>
> 1 pound red potatoes
>
> 4 tablespoons butter, melted

Soak the salt cod for 24 hours in several changes of water. Drain the fish and place in a large pot. Whisk together 2 cups of hot water with the wine, molasses, and lemon juice. Pour the mixture over the fish. Cover, place in a 250°F oven, and cook for 6–8 hours. Remove the fish from the pot and boil the potatoes in the same liquid until tender. Drain the potatoes and serve them on a platter with the fish. Drizzle with melted butter and serve with lemon wedges.

VARIATION

+ **Smoky Salt Cod Simmered with Molasses.** For a smoky version, prepare this dish in a Dutch oven nestled into a fire in a fireplace, and cook uncovered until the liquid absorbs a smoky flavor. Cover the pot and place in an oven to continue cooking as above.

Salt Cod Poached with Potatoes, Olives, and Aioli

SERVES 4

> 1 recipe Basic Aioli (page 25)
>
> 1 pound salt cod, cut into 4 portions
>
> 1 pound Yukon Gold or red potatoes, cut into ½-inch slices
>
> ¼ cup pitted and sliced cured black olives, such as Kalamata
>
> 2 tablespoons extra-virgin olive oil

Soak the salt cod in water for 36 hours in several changes of water. In a pan just wide enough to hold the fish in a single layer, add the potatoes, salt cod, and just enough water to barely cover. Place over low heat, cover, and simmer until the potatoes are barely cooked. Remove from the heat and let it rest for 5 minutes. Transfer the fish and potatoes to a platter, add the olives, drizzle with olive oil, and serve with Basic Aioli.

CONCH AND WHELK

Americans likely know this species of gastropods more by their shells than by their presence on the plate. The queen conch, native to Florida, has beautiful, large, high-spired, pastel-colored shells. Conch shells have been used for everything from ear trumpets to doorstops and mantelpiece fixtures to bathroom candleholders. Conch and their whelk cousins are essentially large sea snails that live inside these shells.

Conchs are vegetarians, easy to catch, and subject to overfishing. The majority of conch on the market is farmed in the Caribbean. Whelks dine carnivorously on bivalves and get pulled out of the sea off the New England coast as by-catch in lobster traps between April and November. The flavor of both is briny, with a nutty, mushroom-like aroma. Whelks have an additional layer of flavor, slightly more complex and reminiscent of oysters.

Much of the meat on the market is frozen whole or chopped and canned. If you find a fresh animal, you must free the meat from the shell. This can be done most invasively by drilling a hole at the top, using a paring knife to cut the thin bone-like disc that covers the meat at the opening of the shell, and pulling the meat from its shell. The hammer method, an obvious technique, works well too. You can drop the whole shell in boiling, salted water for just a few minutes until the meat releases its grip and can be plucked out of the shell. For every pound of in-shell conch/whelk you will get about ¼ pound of meat.

The meat is similar to squid in that it should be either cooked very quickly or braised for long periods of time. When quickly boiled and dipped in garlic and herb-infused butter, they are springy and pleasantly chewy, but I prefer to braise them slowly in a flavorful broth. The meat can be ground and made into burgers or sliced and featured in a ceviche-style dish. Most people's first experience with conch or whelk has been in Bahamian-style conch fritters.

Conch Ceviche with Tomatoes

SERVES 4 AS AN APPETIZER

¾ pound cooked conch or whelk meat, trimmed, peeled, and diced into ¼-inch pieces

Salt

1 cup lime juice or ½ cup key lime juice and ½ cup lime juice

2 stalks celery, grated on a box grater

¼ cup extra-virgin olive oil

1 red onion, thinly sliced, rinsed under cold running water, and patted dry

1 serrano or jalapeño chile, thinly sliced

3 plum tomatoes, diced into ¼-inch pieces

¼ cup chopped fresh cilantro

Combine the conch with a pinch of salt, lime juice, celery, and olive oil and let it rest for 30–90 minutes. Add the onion, chile, tomatoes, and cilantro and toss well. Serve chilled.

Braised Conch or Whelk

SERVES 4–6

6 pounds live conch or whelk

Salt

8 tablespoons butter, divided

1 onion, thinly sliced

1 green bell pepper, diced

1 serrano or jalapeño chile, finely diced

¼ cup slivered almonds

4 garlic cloves, sliced

1 bay leaf

1 cup white wine

1 cup stock or water

2 ounces Amontillado or cooking sherry

4 plum tomatoes, seeded and diced

¼ cup chopped fresh parsley or tarragon

Cooked rice for serving

In a pot over high heat, boil the live conchs/whelks for 4 minutes in enough salted water to cover. Remove the meat from the shells and discard the hard disk at the base of each. Peel and trim the meat and cut it into large slices. In a wide sauté pan over medium heat, melt 4 tablespoons of the butter. Add the onion, bell pepper, chile, almonds, and garlic and cook until the pepper has softened. Add the bay leaf, wine, and stock and bring to a boil. Add the meat and reduce the heat to low. Cover and simmer for 1½ hours, until the meat is tender. Strain the liquid into a second pot and reduce by half. Add the sherry, remaining 4 tablespoons of butter, tomatoes, and parsley. Whisk to combine and add back to the pot of meat. Serve with rice.

Conch Salad with Fennel and Radishes

SERVES 4 AS AN APPETIZER

- ¾ pound cooked conch or whelk meat, trimmed, peeled, and thinly sliced
- 1 orange, zested and juiced
- 2 limes, juiced
- ⅓ cup extra-virgin olive oil
- ¼ cup chopped fresh parsley
- Salt
- Black pepper
- ½ teaspoon ground allspice
- 1 fennel bulb, thinly sliced
- 1 head celery with leaves, thinly sliced
- ½ pound radishes, thinly sliced
- 2 Fresno or serrano chiles, thinly sliced

Combine the sliced conch, orange juice and zest, lime juice, olive oil, and parsley. Season with salt, black pepper, and allspice and let marinate for 30–60 minutes. Add the fennel, celery, and radishes and toss to combine. Garnish with chiles.

Conch/Whelk Fritters

SERVES 4–6 AS AN APPETIZER

- 1 recipe Louisiana Remoulade Sauce (page 31) or Basic Aioli (page 25)
- ¾ pounds cooked conch or whelk meat
- 1½ cups flour
- 3 eggs, separated
- 1 shallot, finely diced
- 1–2 Fresno or serrano chiles, finely diced
- 3 stalks celery, grated on a box grater
- Black pepper
- 1 teaspoon garlic salt
- ¾ bottle pilsner-style beer
- 2 teaspoons baking powder
- Vegetable oil
- Lime wedges

Peel and trim the meat and chop it into small pieces. In a bowl, whisk together the flour, egg yolks, shallot, chiles, celery, black pepper, garlic salt, beer, and baking powder. Stir in the chopped meat. Beat the egg whites until stiff, and gently fold them into the batter. Pour 3–4 inches of oil into a high-sided pan. Place over medium-high heat and warm the oil to 350°F. Drop 1 tablespoon of batter per fritter into the hot oil and cook, turning once, so both sides are brown and crisp. Serve with Louisiana Remoulade Sauce or Basic Aioli.

Grilled Whelks

SERVES 4

- 6 pounds live whelks
- 8 tablespoons butter
- 4 garlic cloves, grated
- 1 lemon, juiced
- 1–2 tablespoons finely chopped herbs, such as parsley or tarragon

Wash the whelks thoroughly under cold running water. Prepare a charcoal grill for a medium fire. In a mesh basket, grill the whelks over high heat for 5–7 minutes. In a saucepan over low heat, melt the butter. Add the garlic and cook until fragrant. Turn off the heat and add the lemon juice and herbs. To eat, remove the meat with a toothpick, discard the hard disk at the bottom, and dip in the garlic butter.

NOTE *If using a gas grill, preheat all burners to medium.*

Whelks with Garlic Butter

SERVES 4

- 6 pounds live whelks
- Salt
- 8 tablespoons butter
- 4 garlic cloves, grated
- 2 tablespoons finely chopped herbs, such as parsley or tarragon

Wash the whelks thoroughly under cold running water. Cook the whelks in heavily salted boiling water for 4–5 minutes. In a saucepan over low heat, melt the better. Add the garlic and cook until fragrant. Add the herbs. To eat, remove the meat with a toothpick, discard the hard disk at the bottom, and dip in the garlic butter.

CRAB

The sweet meat of any crab defies the species' generally cantankerous demeanor. Fortunately, most eaters only deal with them in their more tranquil states, either boiled whole or conveniently picked apart by someone else and folded into a salad or crab cake.

There are essentially four types of crab consumed on a regular basis in the United States: blue crab, Dungeness crab, king crab, and Jonah crab. Other regionally popular species are found throughout the States but are generally limited to smaller markets. There is also widespread availability of imitation crabmeat, also called surimi. This product is made of fish, either Alaska pollock or Pacific whiting, that is processed and turned into a gel and flavored to taste like crab.

Blue crab, the king of the Chesapeake, boiled with lager and Old Bay seasoning, is what a lot of my youth tasted like. While these crabs have only a 15 percent edible yield, that comprises several types of meat. The best and sweetest is the jumbo lump and lump. Backfin and special meat are briny and buttery, claw meat is gamey, and the paste, extracted from all other edible parts, is robust and should be used sparingly. One of the best parts of the crab, often discarded, is the soft yellow or brown fat scraped from the corners inside the shell. Another is the liver, a creamy yellow substance from the middle. It's acidic and adds great complexity to any seafood dish to which it is added.

With the blue crab there is a period of seasonal availability of what's known as a soft-shell crab. These are available generally between May and September, when they have sloughed off their hard shells in order to grow larger ones. Soft-shell crabs are sold live, must be shipped quickly to market, and command a high price. They are typically eaten whole but for the face, gills, and tail flap, all of which must be removed before the crab is either sautéed or fried.

More recently in northern New England, a growing concern over invasive green crabs decimating the soft-shell clam population has enterprising locals there trying to create a market for both hard- and soft-shell green crabs.

Born of cold, deep West Coast waters, from Alaska down through Southern California, Dungeness crab boasts an incredibly intricate flavor and entertaining eating, since your crab-picking effort is rewarded by a generous yield. The super-sweet meat is particularly good with lemon and pickling spices.

King crab legs are a delicacy that may or may not be worth the potentially deadliest trip out to catch them, but they are certainly worth a short trip to the store where they are almost always marketed as frozen and precooked. These leg segments are boiled and frozen before being sent to market and therefore need only be warmed through before eating. They are wonderful reheated in water that has been spiked with jalapeños and beer.

Jonah, or peekytoe, and various species of rock crab are so similar as to be indiscernible to the amateur and are nearly always sold intermixed. These more modestly flavored crabs are not widely available live outside of New England and Southern California, where they are caught. However, their picked meat can be found nationwide. The shells of these crabs are very sturdy, but the meat is finer in texture and slightly stringy, and it has a sweet, briny flavor and a recognizable flakiness. These are particularly good cooked with seaweed in seawater and benefit from a little bit of a spicy kick in the mix. The meat is also great for cakes or as part of a seafood stuffing mix.

The crab most commonly found is cooked and picked crabmeat. It is available fresh, frozen, and canned. It is ready to eat and can be added to salads, stirred into soups, or cooked into a dish. All crabmeat should be gently picked through to remove any remaining bits of shell or cartilage that might have been missed in the packing process.

Crab Boil

In a pot twice as big as the volume of crabs, fill halfway with seasoned water. Add vegetables such as corn, garlic, onions, potatoes, and even artichokes. When the liquid is at a rapid boil, add a few beers to it and then put in the crab. Return to a boil, then kill the heat and let the crab steep to cook fully and absorb the flavorful spicy juices. Drain and serve over newspaper.

+ **Blue crab.** Add lager and Old Bay seasoning to the water. Cook for 10 to 15 minutes.

+ **Dungeness crab.** Add lemon and pickling spices to the water. Cook 1½- to 2½-pound crabs for 15–18 minutes; 3-pound for about 20 minutes.

+ **King crab legs.** Add jalapeños and beer to the water. Boil for 5–7 minutes to warm through.

+ **Jonah/peekytoe crab.** Add sea salt, seaweed, and lemons to a pot of seawater. Boil for 12–15 minutes.

Crab Remoulade

SERVES 4

> 1 recipe Louisiana Remoulade (page 31)
> 1 pound jumbo lump or lump crabmeat
> 1 head iceberg lettuce, thinly sliced

Pick through the crabmeat and discard any bits of cartilage. Gently mix the crab with the Remoulade and let sit for 1–24 hours. Serve over lettuce.

Crab Cakes

SERVES 4

- 6 tablespoons Mayonnaise (page 29, or store-bought)
- 1 pound crabmeat (Dungeness or blue crab)
- ¼ cup brioche bread crumbs, panko, or Ritz Cracker crumbs
- 1 tablespoon Potlatch Seasoning (if using Dungeness) or Old Bay seasoning (if using blue crab)
- 4 tablespoons butter
- 1 lemon, cut into wedges

Pick through the crabmeat and discard any bits of cartilage. Mix the bread crumbs, seasoning, and Mayonnaise together. Gently fold in the crabmeat, keeping the pieces as intact as possible. Shape into four patties and chill for 1 hour.

In a sauté pan over high heat, melt the butter. When the butter has lightly browned, add the crab cakes and reduce the heat to medium. Cook until the edges begin to crisp. Gently flip the cakes and place the entire pan in 350°F oven. Cook until heated through, 7–10 minutes. Serve with lemon wedges.

Baltimore-Style Crab Cakes

SERVES 4

- ½ cup Mayonnaise (page 29, or store-bought)
- 1 pound jumbo lump crabmeat
- 1 large egg, beaten
- 1 tablespoon Dijon mustard
- 2 tablespoons Worcestershire sauce
- 1 teaspoon Tabasco sauce
- 1 cup crushed saltines (about 20 crackers)
- 4 tablespoons butter, cut into pieces

Pick through the crabmeat and discard any bits of cartilage. Gently mix all ingredients except the crabmeat and butter. Gently fold in the crabmeat, keeping the pieces as intact as possible. Shape into four patties, place them on a baking tray, and chill for 1 hour. Place 1 tablespoon of butter on each cake. Preheat the broiler to high and position the rack in the middle position. Slide the tray under the broiler and cook until golden brown and heated through.

Crab in Aioli with Bitter Lettuce

SERVES 4

- 1 recipe Basic Aioli (page 25)
- 1 pound crabmeat
- 2 tablespoons chopped fresh chives
- 2 tablespoons chopped fresh tarragon
- 2 heads Belgian endive, thinly sliced
- 2 bunches watercress, thick stems trimmed
- 1 red onion, thinly sliced and washed under cold running water, patted dry
- 1 lemon, juiced
- 2 tablespoons extra-virgin olive oil
- Salt
- ½ tablespoon smoked sweet paprika

Pick through the crabmeat and discard any bits of cartilage. Combine the Basic Aioli, chives, and tarragon in a bowl. Fold in the crab. Toss the endive, watercress, and onion with the lemon juice and olive oil and season with salt. Plate the greens and top with the dressed crab. Sprinkle with paprika.

Crab-Stuffed Avocados

SERVES 4 AS AN APPETIZER

>   3 tablespoons Mayonnaise (page 29, or store-bought) or Basic Aioli (page 25)
>
>   1 pound lump crabmeat
>
>   2 limes, juiced
>
>   2 tablespoons chopped fresh dill
>
>   4 avocados, halved with pit removed
>
>   Salt
>
>   Crushed red chile flakes
>
>   ¼ cup extra-virgin olive oil or melted butter
>
>   Hot sauce

Pick through the crabmeat and discard any bits of cartilage. Gently mix the crab with the lime juice, Mayonnaise, and dill. Preheat the broiler to low and place the rack in the position closest to the heat. Cut the avocado halves in their skins by making several slices in a checkerboard fashion. Season the avocados with salt and chile flakes and slide under the broiler to warm through. Remove from the broiler. Divide the crab mixture among the avocados and drizzle each with ½ tablespoon of olive oil. Increase the broiler heat to high, slide the stuffed avocadoes under the broiler, and cook until they have browned slightly and the crab is heated through. Serve with hot sauce.

Marinated King Crab

SERVES 4 AS AN APPETIZER

>   1 pound shelled king crabmeat, cut on the bias into ½-inch-thick slices
>
>   1 Fresno or serrano chile, thinly sliced
>
>   2 limes, juiced
>
>   10 radishes, thinly sliced
>
>   1 red onion, thinly sliced, rinsed under cold running water, and patted dry

>   ¼ cup torn fresh mint leaves
>
>   ¼ cup extra-virgin olive oil
>
>   Black pepper
>
>   Tortilla chips or spicy greens for serving

Toss the crab with chiles and lime juice and let it rest for 30 minutes. Toss the crab mixture with the radishes, onion, mint, olive oil, and black pepper. Serve as you would a ceviche with tortilla chips or on top of a salad of spicy greens.

VARIATION

+ **Surimi Substitute.** Substitute imitation crabmeat for the king crab.

King Crab Cobb Salad

SERVES 4

>   1 recipe Marinated King Crab (at left)
>
>   6 plum tomatoes, cut into quarters
>
>   Salt
>
>   1 large head escarole or romaine lettuce, chopped
>
>   2 bunches watercress, thick stems trimmed
>
>   2 avocados, thinly sliced
>
>   4 hard-boiled eggs, sliced
>
>   Black pepper

Season the tomatoes with salt and let sit for 10 minutes. Divide the escarole, watercress, avocados, Marinated King Crab Meat, salted tomatoes, and eggs among four plates. Drizzle the remaining vinaigrette from the king crab over the salads and season with salt and black pepper.

Grilled King Crab or Imitation Crab Skewers

SERVES 4 AS AN APPETIZER

> 1 recipe Garlic-Parsley Oil (pg 27)
>
> 2 pounds king crab legs in the shell or imitation crabmeat, threaded onto skewers
>
> 1 tablespoon vegetable oil

Toss the crab with the vegetable oil to lightly coat. Prepare a medium charcoal fire and place the crab directly over the coals. Cook until the shells/edges are beginning to char. Remove to a cooler part of the grill, cover, and let cook until warmed through. Serve with the Garlic-Parsley Oil for dipping.

NOTE *If using a gas grill, preheat all burners to medium-high. Place the crab legs on one side of the hot grates. Once they begin to char around the edges, turn off the burner directly under the crabs and cover the grill to finish cooking.*

Crab and Toasted Garlic Pasta

SERVES 4

> 1 pound crabmeat
>
> 6 tablespoons butter
>
> 4 garlic cloves, minced
>
> 2 teaspoons grated fresh ginger
>
> ¼ cup Herbsaint or Pernod
>
> 1 pound spaghetti, cooked according to package instructions, reserving 1 cup of cooking liquid
>
> 1 lemon, zest and juice
>
> 3 tablespoons chopped fresh herbs, such as chives or parsley
>
> Black pepper

Pick through the crabmeat, discard any bits of cartilage, and reserve. In a large sauté pan over low heat, melt the butter. Add the garlic and ginger and cook until the garlic is slightly brown. Remove the pan from the heat and add the Herbsaint or Pernod. Use a match to light the alcohol and let it burn. Add the pasta and reserved liquid to the garlic butter and bring to a boil. Simmer until the pasta is fully cooked and the water is mostly absorbed. Add the crabmeat, lemon zest and juice, herbs, and black pepper and gently toss to combine.

Pan-Roasted Dungeness Crabs

SERVES 4

> 4 cooked Dungeness crabs
>
> 6 garlic cloves, grated
>
> 5 tablespoons crushed fennel seeds
>
> 1 tablespoon crushed red chile flakes
>
> 4 stalks rosemary, leaves picked
>
> 1 cup chopped parsley
>
> 2 tablespoons salt
>
> 1 cup extra-virgin olive oil
>
> 4 lemons, halved
>
> Crusty bread for serving

Prepare the crabs by removing the shells and scooping out the soft innards and grayish gills. Crack the claws, but do not separate. Cut the crab bodies in quarters, and place all pieces in a large baking dish. Combine the garlic, fennel seeds, chile flakes, rosemary, parsley, salt, and olive oil. Pour the vinaigrette over the crabs, add the lemons, and toss to combine. Roast the crabs in a 425°F oven until they are crisped and golden brown. Serve with crusty bread.

Soft-Shell Crabs with Corn Relish

SERVES 4

- 1 cup fine-ground cornmeal
- 1 tablespoon Old Bay seasoning (optional)
- 4 large (or 8 small) soft-shell blue crabs, gills, face, and tail flap removed
- 7 tablespoons butter
- 2 tablespoons vegetable oil
- 1 garlic clove, minced
- 1 lemon, zested and juiced
- 1 lime, juiced
- 4 large ears corn, shucked and kernels cut off the cob
- Salt
- 1 large cucumber, peeled and seeded, finely diced
- 2 plum tomatoes, seeds discard, finely diced

Combine the cornmeal and Old Bay seasoning, if using, in a shallow bowl. Dredge each crab in the coating. In a heavy-bottomed sauté pan big enough to hold all the crabs in a single layer, heat 2 tablespoons of butter and vegetable oil over medium-high heat. When the butter is foaming, add the crabs, shell side down. Reduce the heat to medium and cook until the coating is crisp, about 5 minutes. Turn the crabs over and add 2 more tablespoons butter. Cook for another 5 minutes. Remove the crabs from the pan and pat off any excess oil with paper towels.

In a large sauté pan over medium heat, melt the remaining 3 tablespoons butter. Add the garlic and lemon zest and cook for 1 minute. Add the corn kernels, season with salt, and toss to combine. Cook for a few minutes, until the corn begins to soften. Remove from the heat, add the lemon and lime juice, and let cool. Toss the corn with the cucumber and tomato and season with salt. Serve the crabs with the corn relish spooned over the top.

Pasta with Imitation Crabmeat and Fennel Cream Sauce

SERVES 4

- 1 pound linguine, cooked according to package instructions, reserve 1 cup of cooking liquid
- 6 tablespoons butter, divided
- 4 garlic cloves, sliced
- 1 fennel bulb, thinly sliced
- 1 pound imitation crabmeat
- ¼ cup Pernod or Herbsaint
- ½ cup cream
- Black pepper, to taste
- 2 tablespoons chopped fresh tarragon or parsley

In a sauté pan over medium heat, melt 4 tablespoons of the butter. Add the garlic and fennel and cook until softened. Add the imitation crabmeat and remove the pan from the heat. Add the Pernod or Herbsaint. Use a match to light the alcohol and let it burn. Add the pasta, reserved liquid, cream, and remaining 2 tablespoons butter to the imitation crabmeat sauce and bring to a boil. Simmer until the sauce is thick and the pasta is fully cooked. Stir in the black pepper and tarragon.

CRAWFISH

The Atchafalaya Basin, the country's largest wetland, is also its largest source of wild crawfish. Beaux Bridge, Louisiana, sits in the center of that swamp and is the self-proclaimed crawfish capital of the world. A crawfish boil there comprises large pots of water seasoned with "boil spice," be it Zatarain's® or Rex®, handfuls of garlic, lemons, lots of cayenne pepper, wine or beer, and whatever else the cook deems appropriate. It is recommended that each guest place their face over the pot and take in ten deep breaths through the nose to cleanse their spirits.

While crawfish are caught in many regions from Oregon to Maine and called crayfish or crawdads, depending on where you are, it is in Louisiana that Creole charm seduces the best character from these "mudbugs." The season for catching wild crawfish begins in early winter when they first emerge from the mud, hungry after hibernation and so lean that it can take up to thirty of them to make a pound. The season continues through Mardi Gras and into early summer. It's just around Mardi Gras that I, and many others, think wild crawfish are at their peak. Fattened up from feeding on rice stalks and lily pad roots, their size has increased to thirteen to eighteen per pound. Their bodies are full of rich sienna-colored fat or butter, tucked between the tail and head, and females are heavily laden with colorful roe. But 90 percent of the crawfish on the market today is farmed, so you can get these plump crayfish year-round. Like all shellfish, they molt and are caught as soft-shell, which can be eaten whole.

Depending on the source and specific variety, live crawfish vary in color from yellow or beige to deep maroon, red, and black, though all are sold simply as crawfish and all shells become a familiar red once cooked. But the way we most often encounter crawfish is as cooked-and-picked tail meat. This is often frozen and is ready to use in many dishes like étouffée, sherry-spiked bisques, and creamy pastas.

Crawfish with Garlic Butter

SERVES 4

6 tablespoons butter, divided

4 garlic cloves, sliced

1 pound picked crawfish meat

¼ cup Amontillado or cooking sherry or white wine

Black pepper, to taste

2 tablespoons chopped fresh tarragon

Rice, pasta, or Texas toast for serving

In a sauté pan over medium-high heat, melt 4 tablespoons of the butter. Add the garlic and cook until softened. Add the crawfish meat and toss to combine. Add the remaining 2 tablespoons of butter, sherry, black pepper, and tarragon. Simmer until the sauce thickens. Serve over rice, pasta, or Texas toast.

Crawfish Boil

SERVES 2–4

 3 beers

 ½ cup salt

 1 cup Cajun spice, such as Rex or Zatarain's

 15 pounds crawfish

 1 onion, sliced into rings

 3 lemons, quartered

 2 pounds small red potatoes, halved

 1–3 jalapeño peppers (depending on your preference), halved lengthwise

In a large stockpot over high heat, combine 2 gallons of water with the beer, salt, and seasoning and bring to a boil. Place the crawfish, onion, lemons, potatoes, and jalapeños into a strainer basket, lower it into the pot, and return to a boil. Cover and boil for 15 minutes, then turn off the heat and allow the crawfish to continue to soak for an additional 15 minutes. Remove the strainer basket, pour the crawfish and vegetables onto a serving platter, and eat while hot.

NOTE *The quantities can be increased easily to serve more people.*

Pasta with Crawfish and Fennel Cream Sauce

SERVES 4

 1 pound linguine, cooked according to package instructions, reserve 1 cup of cooking liquid

 6 tablespoons butter, divided

 4 garlic cloves, sliced

 1 fennel bulb, thinly sliced

 1 pound cooked crawfish meat

 ¼ cup Pernod or Herbsaint

 ½ cup cream

 Black pepper, to taste

 2 tablespoons chopped fresh tarragon or parsley

In a sauté pan over medium heat, melt 4 tablespoons of the butter. Add the garlic and fennel and cook until softened. Add the crawfish meat and remove the pan from the heat. Add the Pernod or Herbsaint and use a match to light the alcohol and let it burn. Add the pasta (reserving the liquid), cream, and remaining 2 tablespoons butter to the crawfish sauce and bring to a boil. Simmer until the sauce is thick and the pasta is fully cooked. Stir in the black pepper and tarragon.

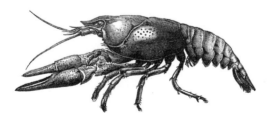

CROAKER
Fillet fish

Croaker is easy to like and easy to use. A member of the drum family, these fish swim on both of America's coasts and distinguish themselves from their cousins by the plaintive moaning sounds they make. Croakers croak, and drums drum.

While there are croakers with names like southern king, old wife, herring, and Catalina croaker, the most common is the Atlantic croaker, which swims along the Atlantic coast, reaching into Texan waters. They flood near-shore waters in the spring to spawn and remain there through the fall, when they reach prime quality, having fattened and grown sweet during the summer's feeding.

Croakers are typically caught weighing 1–2 pounds and are most often sold pan-dressed, making them perfect for pan frying, the most common way to cook them. But croakers are also great for grilling whole, as the thin skin crisps up well. If you find croaker fillets, they are best sautéed.

I think this is the perfect white fish: it's mild but with a slight tang, the texture yields a slightly elastic bite, and the moderate fat content makes them easy to cook. Croakers are pleasant for fish beginners and interesting for seafood lovers.

Whole Fried Croaker with Orange-Pistachio Piccata

SERVES 2–4

> 1 recipe Orange-Pistachio Piccata (page 29)
>
> 2 (1½- to 2-pound) whole croakers, scaled, gutted, and skin scored
>
> Salt
>
> 1 lemon, juiced
>
> Vegetable or peanut oil
>
> ¾ cup flour, sifted
>
> ¾ cup cornstarch, sifted

Season the fish with salt and lemon juice and let it rest for 20 minutes. Pour 2–3 inches of vegetable oil into a high-sided pan big enough to hold one fish. Place over medium-high heat and warm the oil to 350°F. Combine the flour and cornstarch on a large plate and dredge one fish in the mixture, coating both sides. Slide the fish into the hot oil. Cook until golden crispy on one side, then gently flip the fish to cook the other side, about 8–10 minutes total. Remove the fish from the oil and place it on paper towels to absorb excess oil. Repeat the process with the second fish. Serve with Orange-Pistachio Piccata scattered over the fish.

Grilled Croaker with Five Spice Rub

SERVES 4

1 recipe Five Spice Mix (page 33)

4 croaker portions, skin on and scored

Salt

2 tablespoons extra-virgin olive oil

2 lemons, halved

Season the fish with salt and Five Spice Mix and let it rest for 15 minutes. Prepare a charcoal grill with a medium fire, concentrating the hot coals on one side of the kettle. Lightly brush the fish with olive oil and place it skin side down on the grill directly over the coals. Cook until the skin begins to crisp, about 3 minutes. Lift the entire grill grate and rotate it so the fish rests opposite the hot coals. Place the lemons cut side down on the grill directly over the hot coals, cover, and continue to cook until the fish is done and the lemon halves are charred, 3–4 minutes.

NOTE *If using a gas grill, preheat all burners to medium. Place the croaker on one side of the hot grates. Once it begins to char around the edges, turn off the burner directly under the fish, place the lemons cut side down on the grill directly over the heat, and cover the grill to finish cooking.*

Whole Grilled Croaker with Salsa Criolla

SERVES 2-4

1 recipe Salsa Criolla (page 32)

2 (1½- to 2-pound) whole croaker, gutted, scaled, and scored

Salt

Season the fish with salt and let it rest for 20 minutes Prepare a charcoal grill with a medium fire, concentrating the hot coals on one side of the kettle. Place the fish on the grill directly over the coals. Cook until the skin begins to char, about 3–4 minutes. Gently flip the fish and cook for 3 more minutes. Lift the entire grill grate and rotate it so the fish rest opposite the hot coals. Cover the grill and continue to cook over this indirect heat until the fish is done, 4–6 minutes. Serve with Salsa Criolla.

NOTE *If using a gas grill, preheat all burners to medium. Place the croaker on one side of the hot grates. Once it begins to char around the edges, turn off the burner directly under the fish and cover the grill to finish cooking.*

Sautéed Croaker with Brown Butter and Orange

SERVES 4

4 croaker portions, skin on and scored

Salt

Black pepper

6 tablespoons butter, divided

½ orange, cut into quarters and sliced thinly

Season the fish with salt and pepper and let it rest for 15 minutes. In a sauté pan over medium heat, melt 2 tablespoons of the butter and cook until golden brown. Place the fish skin side down in the pan. Reduce the heat to medium. Cook without flipping until almost done, then remove the fish. Add the remaining 4 tablespoons of butter and the orange, and cook until the orange slices are slightly caramelized. Season with salt and turn off the heat. Return the fish to the pan skin side up and finish cooking.

CUSK
Flaky white fish, meaty dense fish

Cusk is a deep water–dwelling cousin of cod that is not very often found outside of the fishing communities where it is caught as bycatch of other groundfish fisheries. Cusk looks like a cod crossed with an eel, and its culinary qualities are rather well explained by that crossing.

The head is very unattractive and so large that it must be removed at sea to conserve space in the ship's hold. The flesh, almost always sold as skinless fillets, has a generous, large flake like cod with a pleasant firmness like monkfish. Fillets should be pearly white, moist, and glistening, with no hint of yellowing around the edges, which is a sign of age.

Cusk has a row of pin bones that runs nearly three-quarters of the way down the length of the fillet. The bones are easily removed by slicing on either side and removing the entire strip. But this leaves a difficult-to-portion fillet. One workaround is to cut it into chunks for kebabs, stew, or chowder, as it holds its texture well. Like most cod kin, its flavor is somewhat muted and needs the tang of citrus or vinegar in a vinaigrette or sauce to bring its character to the fore.

Cusk is one of the very best fish to eat as leftovers, as its flavor, once the fish is cooked, matures and gets better if left overnight. Lightly dressed with a vinaigrette and placed atop bitter greens, it makes for a great meal.

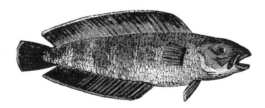

Broiled Cusk with Crunchy Ritz Cracker Topping

SERVES 4

> 6 tablespoons Mayonnaise (page 29, or store-bought)
>
> 4 cusk portions, skin off
>
> Salt
>
> 6 tablespoons crushed Ritz Crackers
>
> 1 lemon, zested and cut into wedges

Season the fish with salt and let it rest for 15 minutes. Preheat the broiler to medium and set the rack in the middle position. Stir together the Mayonnaise, crushed crackers, and lemon zest. Place the fish on a baking tray. Spread the mayonnaise mixture evenly over the fish. Slide the tray under the broiler. Broil until the fish is done and the topping is browned, about 7–10 minutes, depending on thickness. Serve with lemon wedges.

Poached Cusk and Celery Salad

SERVES 4

> 3 tablespoons Mayonnaise (page 29, or store-bought)
>
> 4 cusk portions, skin off
>
> Salt
>
> 1 cup white wine
>
> 2 tablespoons white wine vinegar
>
> 3 stalks celery
>
> 1 shallot, sliced
>
> 2 small carrots, cut in half lengthwise
>
> 10 black peppercorns
>
> 1 bay leaf
>
> Crushed red chile flakes

Season the fish with salt and let it rest for 15 minutes. In a pan just big enough to hold the fish in a single layer, combine 1 cup of water with the wine, vinegar, celery, shallot, carrots, peppercorns, and bay leaf. Simmer over low heat for 5 minutes. Season the broth with salt and bring it to 170°F. Add the fish and cook until it is opaque and flakes under gentle pressure, about 5 minutes per ½ inch of thickness. Remove the pan from the heat and cool the fish in the poaching liquid to room temperature. Transfer the fish to a plate, pat dry, and flake it into bite-size pieces. Remove the celery and carrots from the liquid and thinly slice. In a small bowl gently combine the Mayonnaise, chile flakes, fish, and celery. Use as you would tuna salad or place atop dressed greens.

Blackened Cusk

SERVES 4

> 1 recipe Blackening Spice Mix (page 33)
>
> 4 cusk fillets, skin off
>
> Salt
>
> 4 tablespoons butter, melted, divided
>
> ¼ cup vegetable oil
>
> 1 lemon, cut into wedges

Lightly season the fish with salt and let it rest for 15 minutes. Heat a cast iron skillet or heavy-bottomed sauté pan over high heat until it is screaming hot. Combine 2 tablespoons of the butter and all of the oil in a bowl and brush each portion so the fish glistens all over. Dredge one side of each portion in Blackening Spice Mix, coating evenly. Place the fish in the pan spice side down and drizzle half of the remaining butter-and-oil mixture over the top. Reduce the heat to medium-low and cook without flipping until a dark crust forms, then flip to cook through. Drizzle with the remaining butter and serve with lemon wedges.

Sautéed Cusk with Brown Butter and Thyme

SERVES 4

> 4 cusk portions, skin off
>
> Salt
>
> 1 orange, zested and juiced
>
> 6 tablespoons butter, divided
>
> 2 garlic cloves, finely minced
>
> 10 sprigs thyme, leaves picked

Season the fish with salt and the zest and let it rest for 15 minutes. In a sauté pan over medium heat, melt 2 tablespoons of the butter and cook until golden brown. Place the fish in the pan. Cook without flipping until almost done, then remove the fish and wipe the pan clean. Add the remaining 4 tablespoons of butter, garlic, and thyme. Cook until the butter is dark brown. Add the orange juice and season with salt. Stir to combine. Turn off the heat and return the fish to the pan uncooked side down to finish cooking.

Stir-Fried Cusk with Onion and Ginger

SERVES 4

> 4 cusk portions, skin off, each cut into ½-inch slices on the bias
>
> Salt
>
> 1 lemon, juiced
>
> 4 tablespoons peanut or vegetable oil, divided
>
> 4 stalks celery, sliced thin on the bias
>
> 1 onion, thinly sliced
>
> 2 garlic cloves, thinly sliced
>
> 1 tablespoon grated fresh ginger
>
> 2 tablespoons brown sugar
>
> 3 tablespoons soy sauce
>
> 3 tablespoons white wine
>
> Cornstarch

Season the fish with salt and let it rest for 15 minutes. In a sauté pan over high heat, warm 1 tablespoon of the oil. Add the celery, onion, garlic, and ginger. Cook over high heat, stirring occasionally, until the onion begins to singe and the celery is al dente. Mix the brown sugar with the soy sauce and wine. Add the liquid to the pan and toss vigorously for 30 seconds before removing the glazed vegetables from the pan. Wipe the pan and heat the remaining 3 tablespoons of oil over medium-high heat. Toss the fish in the cornstarch to coat and add to the pan. Cook without turning until almost cooked through, flipping for last 30 seconds to cook the other side. Remove from the pan and cover with vegetables.

CUTLASSFISH
Fillet fish

Cutlassfish have a long, thin, tapered body that has an iridescent steel-blue hue. Its name—as well as its aliases saberfish and scabbardfish—conveys this sword-like physique. Fishermen have long resented these fish for their razor-sharp teeth that slice through nets.

They swim along both US coasts. In winter, they gather in large schools off the coast of Florida, but because there is no culinary tradition or market for the fish, they remain underutilized. Instead of scales, their bodies are sheathed in a thin silver membrane that sloughs off with handling. Cutlassfish flesh is soft and bruises easily, so when buying a whole fish, look for those with unblemished skin. These fish grow up to 4 feet but are so lean as to weigh little more than 3 pounds.

To prepare the fish, eviscerate it and remove its head. The belly cavity is one-third of the length of the fish; thus, the belly flaps should be removed, as they are thin and hard to cook. The thinness of the fish can make portioning a challenge. I generally discard the last few inches of the tail section, where it becomes more bone than flesh, and use it for other purposes such as stock.

When raw, the flesh is soft, but the texture tightens when cooked, resulting in a small flake with notable firmness and a pleasant mouthfeel. The flavor is delicate; I describe it as tidal with a baked potato aroma. Whole fish or large sections are great when marinated and grilled or broiled. The thin skin singes, and the meat pairs well with the slight burnt taste. Once cut, cutlassfish portions are well suited to stir-frying, paired with onion, ginger, and peanuts to lend texture and flavor. The sections can also be simply breaded and fried. When filleted, the cuts are too thin to effectively sauté but can be rolled and poached.

Fried Cutlassfish with Mint and Pepper

SERVES 4

> 4 cutlassfish portions, skin on, cut into cross sections or fillets
>
> Salt
>
> Vegetable or peanut oil
>
> Rice flour or cornstarch
>
> ¼ cup mint, leaves picked and torn
>
> 1 shallot, thinly sliced
>
> Black pepper
>
> Thai fish sauce

Season the fish with salt and let it rest for 15 minutes. Pour 3–4 inches of oil into a high-sided pan. Place over medium-high heat and warm the oil to 375°F. Dredge one piece of fish in rice flour or cornstarch, place it into the oil, and hold it for 5 seconds before releasing it. Repeat the process, cooking the pieces a few at a time. Turn with a slotted spoon to ensure both sides crisp evenly. Remove the pieces as they finish and place them on paper towels to absorb excess oil. Season with salt. Scatter the fish with the mint, shallot, black pepper, and a few splashes of fish sauce.

Grilled Cutlassfish with Chimichurri

SERVES 4

> 1 recipe Chimichurri (page 26)
>
> 4 cutlassfish portions, skin on and scored, cut into cross-sections
>
> Salt
>
> Extra-virgin olive oil

Prepare a charcoal grill with a medium fire. Season the fish with salt and let it rest for 15 minutes. Lightly brush the fish with oil and place it on the grill over the hot coals. Cook until the edges begin to crisp, about 3 minutes. Flip the fish and cook another 3 minutes until done. Remove from the grill and drizzle with Chimichurri. These are best eaten with your fingers.

NOTE *If using a gas grill, preheat all burners to medium.*

Sautéed Cutlassfish Almondine

SERVES 4

    4 cutlassfish portions, skin on and scored
    Salt
    6 tablespoons butter, divided
    2 garlic cloves, finely minced
    ¼ cup sliced almonds
    1 lemon, juiced

Season the fish with salt and let it rest for 15 minutes. In a sauté pan over medium heat, melt 2 tablespoons of the butter and cook until golden brown. Place the fish in the pan and cook without flipping until almost done, then flip to finish cooking. Remove the fish and wipe the pan clean. Add the remaining 4 tablespoons of butter, garlic, and almonds. Cook until the almonds are browned. Add the lemon juice and season with salt. Stir to combine. Turn off the heat and return the fish to the pan skin side up to finish cooking.

Sautéed Cutlassfish with Rosemary

SERVES 4

    4 cutlassfish portions, skin on and scored
    Salt
    4 tablespoons butter
    4 sprigs rosemary
    1 lemon, cut into wedges

Season the fish with salt and let it rest for 15 minutes. In a sauté pan over medium heat, melt the butter. Place the fish and rosemary in the pan. Cook without flipping until almost done, then flip to finish cooking. Serve with lemon wedges and crumbled, crisp rosemary leaves.

Cutlassfish en Saor (sweet-sour vinaigrette)

SERVES 4

    2 pounds bone-in cutlassfish, skin on and scored, cut into cross-section portions
    Salt
    ¾ cup extra-virgin olive oil, divided
    3 tablespoons pine nuts or slivered almonds
    2 tablespoons raisins
    1 small onion, thinly sliced
    1 red bell pepper, finely diced
    1 small eggplant, ½-inch dice, about 2 cups
    ¼ cup red wine vinegar
    1 tablespoon brown sugar
    Baguette, sliced, for serving

Season the fish with salt and let them rest for 15 minutes. In a sauté pan over medium heat, warm ¼ cup of the olive oil. Place the fish in the pan and cook, turning once when almost brown, until done, about 8 minutes. Remove the fish and wipe the pan clean. Heat the remaining ½ cup of olive oil over medium-high heat, add the pine nuts (or almonds) and raisins, and cook until the pine nuts are golden brown and the raisins plump. Add the onion and bell pepper and cook until the pepper begins to soften. Add the eggplant and cook until it has softened and has absorbed much of the oil. Stir in the vinegar and brown sugar and season with salt. Turn off the heat and nestle the cooked fish into the sauce. The flavors improve if allowed to chill overnight in the refrigerator and then brought to room temperature before serving. At a minimum, let it sit at least 1 hour before serving at room temperature with slices of baguette.

DOGFISH
Flaky white fish, meaty dense fish

Dogfish gets a bad rap. Yes, fishermen on both coasts loathe it because this shark tends to hunt in packs, scaring other, more fetching fish from their nets. And yes, eaters have traditionally shied so far away from it, even though stocks are abundant, that the government has attempted to market it as Japanese halibut, ocean white fish, and mustel so eaters might find it more appealing.

But I think, if it is prepared properly, that it is a fine food fish that can be treated in any number of ways in the kitchen, just as you'd treat cod, flounder, or halibut for a fraction of the price. The firm and meaty flesh of dogfish is forgiving in cooking, as it maintains its moisture well. It has a rich flavor, more savory-briny than sweet, and is basically a better version of halibut.

The skin is inedible, and underneath it lies a thin membrane. Both are almost always removed before dogfish is in the fish case. Its long, thin body makes for fillets that are, on average, about the diameter of a half dollar at the thickest part before tapering significantly toward the tail. This can make it a little more challenging to cook, given the range of thickness. My favorite way to prepare dogfish is to poach it, let it cool in the poaching liquid, and then serve it chilled with a sauce made from the liquid. But like monkfish, cutting it into chunks for grilled or broiled kebabs or for chowders and stews works well, too. Its semisoft, cartilaginous skeleton makes for a delightfully aromatic yet richly textured broth and, in stews especially, adds a gelatinous depth of body and structure without an overwhelming flavor.

Curried Dogfish with Raisins

SERVES 4

    4 dogfish portions, skin off, cut into
       1-inch pieces

    Salt

    4 tablespoons butter

    3 tablespoons slivered almonds

    2 tablespoons raisins

    2 garlic cloves, sliced

    2 teaspoons curry powder

    1 cup fish or vegetable stock or coconut
       water

    ½ cup sour cream

    3 tablespoons chopped fresh herbs, such
       as cilantro or parsley, for garnish

    Lime, cut into wedges, for garnish

Season the fish with salt and let it rest for 20 minutes. In a large pan over high heat, melt the butter. Add the fish and sear until lightly colored. Remove the fish from the pan. Add the almonds, raisins, and garlic. Cook until the raisins begin to plump. Add the curry powder and stir to toast the spices for 30 seconds. Add the stock and sour cream and stir to combine. Add the fish, season with salt, bring to a very low simmer, and cook until done, about 10–12 minutes. Garnish with the herbs and lime.

Stewed Dogfish in Romesco

SERVES 4

    1 recipe Romesco (page 31)

    4 dogfish portions, skin off

    Salt

    Rice, for serving

Season the fish with salt and let it rest for 20 minutes. Pour the Romesco in a pan wide enough to comfortably fit the fish in a single layer. Nestle the fish into the sauce, cover, and place over low heat. Cook until the fish is flaky, about 12 minutes. Check the sauce for seasoning. Serve over rice.

Braised Dogfish in Madeira

SERVES 4

    ½ cup Basic Fish Stock (page 61) or water

    4 dogfish portions, skin off

    Salt

    6 tablespoons butter, divided

    2 shallots, sliced

    ¼ cup walnuts, crushed

    3 tablespoons raisins

    4 garlic cloves, sliced

    ½ cup Madeira, a drier style such as Sercial
       or Verdelho

    2 tablespoons chopped fresh tarragon

Season the fish with salt and let it rest for 20 minutes. In a sauté pan over high heat, melt 2 tablespoons of the butter. Add the fish to the pan, sear on one side, and remove. Reduce the heat to medium, add 2 tablespoons of the butter, shallots, walnuts, raisins, and garlic. Cook until the raisins begin to plump and the walnuts have toasted. Add the Madeira and stock and bring to a simmer. Season with salt. Add the fish, cover, and simmer on low heat until the fish is cooked through, about 8–10 minutes. Remove the fish and bring the sauce to a boil over high heat. Stir in the remaining 2 tablespoons of butter and the tarragon and pour over the fish.

Braised Dogfish Puttanesca

The fish is braised in a lively tomato sauce with capers and olives.

SERVES 4

>   4 dogfish portions, skin off
>   Salt
>   4 tablespoons extra-virgin olive oil, divided
>   1 (2-ounce) tin anchovies in oil
>   4 garlic cloves, sliced
>   4 dried árbol chiles or ½ tablespoon crushed red chile flakes
>   2 (14-ounce) cans fire-roasted diced tomatoes
>   ¾ cup white wine
>   2 tablespoons capers, rinsed and patted dry
>   ¼ cup pitted cured black olives
>   6 basil leaves, torn, for garnish

Season the fish with salt and let it rest for 20 minutes. In an ovenproof sauté pan over medium-high heat, warm 3 tablespoons of the olive oil, anchovies with their oil, garlic, and chiles, and cook until the anchovies melt. Add the tomatoes, wine, capers, and olives. Bring to a simmer and cook for 10 minutes. Nestle the fish into the sauce and drizzle with the remaining 3 tablespoons of olive oil. Cover the pan and place in a 275°F oven for 30 minutes. Remove and let it rest for 10 minutes before serving with torn basil leaves.

Braised Dogfish à la Barigoule

The dogfish and vegetables are braised and marinated in a spiced broth.

SERVES 4

>   1 recipe Basic Aioli (page 25), made with oil skimmed from the cooked dish
>   4 dogfish portions, skin off
>   Salt
>   3 stalks celery, chopped
>   2 carrots, sliced
>   4 ounces mushrooms, cut in quarters
>   2 garlic cloves, thinly sliced
>   5 sprigs thyme
>   1 teaspoon ground coriander seeds
>   1½ cups white wine
>   1 (14-ounce) can halved artichoke hearts in oil
>   ½ lemon, thinly sliced
>   1 cup extra-virgin olive oil
>   Crushed red chile flakes (optional)
>   Crusty bread for serving

Season the fish with salt and let it rest for 20 minutes. In a large pot over medium heat, combine the celery, carrots, mushrooms, garlic, thyme, coriander, wine, and ½ cup of water. Season lightly with salt and simmer until the alcohol smell dissipates, about 5 minutes. Add the artichoke hearts with their oil, lemon slices, and olive oil. Reduce the heat to low. Nestle the fish into the pot so it is barely submerged. If desired, add the chile flakes. Cover and cook for 15–20 minutes. Remove the pot from the heat and cool to room temperature. The flavors improve if allowed to chill overnight in the refrigerator. Use a ladle to skim off the olive oil and use it to make Basic Aioli. Serve at room temperature with crusty bread and Basic Aioli.

Beer-Battered Dogfish

SERVES 4

 4 dogfish portions, skin off, cut into
    2-inch pieces

 Salt

 Vegetable or peanut oil

 ¾ cup flour, sifted

 ¾ cup cornstarch, sifted

 ¾ cup lager or pilsner-style beer

 2 tablespoons vegetable oil

 1 egg, separated

Season the fish with salt and let it rest for
20 minutes. Pour 3–4 inches of oil into a
high-sided pan. Place over medium-high heat
and warm the oil to 375°F. Make a batter
by combining the flour, cornstarch, beer,
2 tablespoons of vegetable oil, and egg yolk. Beat
the egg white to soft peaks and fold into the
batter. Season with salt to taste. Dip one piece
of fish at a time into the batter, place it in the oil,
and hold it there for 5 seconds before releasing
it. Repeat the process, cooking the pieces a few
at a time. Turn with a slotted spoon if necessary
to ensure both sides become golden and crispy.
Remove the fillets as they finish and place on
paper towels to absorb excess oil.

Fried Dogfish en Adobo

SERVES 4

 1 recipe Adobo Marinade (page 36)

 4 dogfish portions, skin off, cut into
    2-inch pieces

 Vegetable or peanut oil

 Fine ground cornmeal

 Salt

 ½ cup parsley leaves

 ½ cup mint leaves

 Fresno or serrano chiles, thinly sliced

Marinate the fish in Adobo for 6–24 hours.
Pour 3–4 inches of oil into a high-sided pan.
Place over medium-high heat and warm the oil
to 375°F. Remove the fish from the vinaigrette
and pat dry. Working with one piece at a time,
roll the fish in the cornmeal, making sure to
completely and evenly coat. Place the fish in hot
oil and hold it for 5 seconds before releasing it.
Repeat the process, cooking the pieces a few at
a time. Turn with a slotted spoon if necessary
to ensure both sides become golden and crispy.
Remove the fillets as they finish cooking and
place on paper towels to absorb excess oil.
Transfer the fish to a large platter. Scatter the
parsley, mint, and chile slices over the top.

Chilled Poached Dogfish in Vinaigrette

SERVES 4

4 dogfish portions, skin off

Salt

2 cups white wine

3 tablespoons white wine vinegar, divided

3 shallots, 2 sliced, 1 minced

2 small carrots, cut in half lengthwise

20 black peppercorns

2 bay leaves

1 teaspoon mustard powder

¼ cup extra-virgin olive oil

2 tablespoons chopped fresh herbs, such as chervil or tarragon

2 apples, cored and thinly sliced

3 heads Belgian endive, cut into ½-inch strips

Season the fish with salt and let it rest for 20 minutes. In a deep pan just wide enough to hold the fish in a single layer, combine 1 cup of water with the wine, 2 tablespoons of the vinegar, sliced shallots, carrots, peppercorns, bay leaves, and 1 tablespoon of salt. Simmer over low heat for 5 minutes. Season the broth with salt and bring it to 170°F. Add the fish and cook until it is opaque and flakes under gentle pressure, about 5 minutes per ½ inch of thickness. Remove the pan from the heat and cool the fish in the poaching liquid overnight. Transfer the fish to a serving plate and flake into bite-size pieces. Remove carrots and slice, adding them to the fish. Strain 1 cup of the poaching liquid into a small pan, reduce over high heat to 2 tablespoons, and whisk in the mustard, remaining 1 tablespoon of vinegar, olive oil, minced shallot, and herbs. Toss the apples and endive with half of the vinaigrette. Coat the fish and carrots with the remaining vinaigrette and serve on top of the salad.

Sautéed Dogfish with Brown Butter and Rosemary

SERVES 4

4 dogfish portions, skin off

Salt

6 tablespoons butter, divided

2 garlic cloves, finely minced

2 stalks rosemary, leaves picked

1 lemon, zested and juiced

Season the fish with salt and let it rest for 20 minutes. In a sauté pan over medium heat, melt 2 tablespoons of the butter and cook until golden brown. Place the fish in the pan. Cook without flipping until almost done, then remove the fish and wipe the pan clean. Add the remaining 4 tablespoons of butter, garlic, and rosemary. Cook until the butter is dark brown and rosemary is crisp. Add the zest and juice, season with salt, and stir to combine. Turn off the heat and return the fish to the pan uncooked side down to finish cooking.

Sautéed Dogfish au Poivre Flambé

SERVES 4

    4 dogfish portions, skin off
    Salt
    1 tablespoon black peppercorns, coarsely
        ground
    1 tablespoon fennel seeds, crushed
    4 tablespoons butter
    1½ ounces cognac or bourbon

Season the fish with salt on both sides and on one side with the pepper and fennel seeds. Press the seasonings into the flesh and let it rest for 20 minutes. In a sauté pan over medium heat, melt the butter and cook until golden brown. Place the fish pepper side down in the pan. Cook without flipping until almost done, then flip to finish cooking. Turn off the heat. Add the cognac and flambé by lighting with a match. Allow the alcohol to burn off before serving.

Sautéed Dogfish with Brown Butter and Grapes

SERVES 4

    4 dogfish portions, skin off
    Salt
    6 tablespoons butter
    1 cup seedless grapes
    2 tablespoons chopped fresh herbs,
        such as parsley or tarragon
    1 lemon, juiced

Season the fish with salt and let it rest for 20 minutes. Set the broiler to medium-high. In a sauté pan over medium heat, melt the butter and cook until dark brown. Place the fish in the pan. Spoon the brown butter over the fish and arrange the grapes among the portions. Place the pan under the broiler and cook until the grapes have blistered and released some juice and the fish is cooked through. Scatter the herbs over the top and drizzle with lemon juice.

DORY
Fillet fish

Dory, aka John Dory, is a fish of great culinary quality. It is revered in Europe for its taste and mythical connections to Zeus. But since there is not much commercial demand for it in the United States, fishermen here don't tend to target it as a species. So if you are fortunate enough to see Dory in a fish case, buy it.

Dory is a unique-looking fish. It has paper-thin, leathery, scaleless, gray skin; a big head for a fish of its size; a face that is mostly mouth; and a dark black spot behind its gill plate. It is further distinguished by having three distinct sections of each fillet that naturally separate when cooked. It has a moderate, sweet flavor; good briny finish; and firm yet smooth texture. Dory's very thin fillets resemble flounder and have an off-white color that brightens when cooked.

Dory is sometimes sold whole, and the yield on the average 12- to 18-inch, 2- to 4-pound fish is relatively low, only about 35–40 percent. Prior to cooking, you must score the skin to prevent the fillet from curling away from the heat. The skin is delicious and has a gelatinous richness. Though the skin can be crisped beautifully, the amount of heat required to do so can diminish the nuance and character of the meat, and so I prefer methods such as poaching, slow roasting, and—my favorite—slowly sautéing it in a small amount of fat, cooking it through from the skin side up. This method allows the skin's flavor to permeate the meat while preserving the moisture in the fillet. The skin can easily be removed after cooking, and the distinct pieces of the fillets can be stacked in an interesting presentation.

The moderately lean and subtle flavor of Dory is flattered by bright fresh herbs like tarragon and sharp vinegar or citrus accents. Dory is well suited for soups and stews, evidenced by its starring role in traditional bouillabaisse. A whole Dory smokes nicely but needs a lengthy soak in a mild brine before smoking for many hours over a low, sweet orchard wood fire.

Grilled Dory with Five Spice Rub

SERVES 4

    1 recipe Five Spice Mix (page 33)

    4 Dory portions, skin on and scored

    Salt

    Extra-virgin olive oil

    2 lemons, halved

Season the fish with salt and Five Spice Mix and let it rest for 15 minutes. Prepare a charcoal grill with a medium fire, concentrating the hot coals on one side of the kettle. Lightly brush the fish with oil and place it skin side down on the grill over the hottest part of the fire. Cook until the skin begins to crisp, about 2 minutes. Lift the entire grill grate and rotate it so the fish rests opposite the hot coals. Place the lemons cut side down on the grill over the hot coals, cover, and continue to cook until the fish is done and the lemon halves are charred.

NOTE *If using a gas grill, preheat all burners to medium. Place the Dory on one side of the hot grates. Once it begins to char around the edges, turn off the burner directly under the fish and cover the grill to finish cooking.*

Dory en Papilotte (cooked in parchment)

SERVES 4

    1 recipe Anchovy-Almond Butter (page 19)

    4 Dory portions, skin off

    Salt

    4 stalks celery, sliced

    2 fennel bulbs, thinly sliced

    1 small red onion, sliced, rinsed under cold running water, and patted dry

    1 cup white wine

    Butter, for greasing the parchment

    1 orange, cut into segments

Season the fish with salt and let it rest for 15 minutes. In a shallow pan, place the celery, fennel, onion, and wine. Season with salt and cook until the vegetables are soft and the wine nearly reduced. Take four (18-inch) squares of parchment paper and cut into heart shapes. Use butter to grease an 8-inch square area in middle of each. Evenly divide the vegetables and remaining liquid among the parchment hearts, place the fish on top, and add a couple of orange segments and 2 tablespoons of Anchovy-Almond Butter. Fold the paper over, then crimp the edges tightly (empanada-style) to form a pouch. Roast at 350°F for 10–12 minutes, depending on the thickness of the fillets. Serve in the pouch and slice open just prior to eating

Poached Dory with Tomatoes and Herbs

SERVES 4

4 Dory portions, skin off

Salt

1 cup white or red wine

1 carrot, diced

1 shallot, sliced

2 sprigs thyme

1 lemon, zest removed in wide strips

4 whole cloves

4 tablespoons cold butter, cut into pieces

2 plum tomatoes, finely diced

2 tablespoons chopped fresh herbs, such as chives or tarragon

Season the fish with salt and let it rest for 15 minutes. In a pan just wide enough to hold the fish in a single layer, combine 1 cup of water with the wine, carrot, shallot, thyme, lemon zest, and cloves. Season the broth with salt and bring it to 170°F. Add the fish and cook until it is opaque and flakes under gentle pressure, about 7–8 minutes. Transfer the fish to a plate. Strain 1 cup of the poaching liquid into a small pan and reduce over high heat to 2 tablespoons. Remove from the heat and whisk in the butter. Add the tomatoes and herbs and season with salt.

Poached Dory with Jellied Herb Aioli

SERVES 4

1 recipe Basic Aioli (page 25)

4 Dory portions, skin off

Salt

1 cup white wine

2 tablespoons white wine vinegar

1 shallot, sliced

1 small carrot, sliced

10 black peppercorns

1 bay leaf

2 teaspoons powdered gelatin

2 tablespoons finely chopped fresh tarragon

Lightly dressed spicy greens for serving

Season the fish with salt and let it rest for 15 minutes. In a pan just wide enough to hold the fish in a single layer, combine 1 cup of water with the wine, vinegar, shallot, carrot, ½ tablespoon salt, peppercorns, and bay leaf. Simmer over low heat for 5 minutes. Bring the liquid to 170°F. Place the fish into the pan so that it is barely submerged and cook until done, 7–8 minutes. Transfer the fish to a plate. Dissolve the gelatin in ¼ cup of the warm poaching liquid and combine with the Basic Aioli and tarragon. Cover the fish with a thin layer of the aioli mixture and chill to set overnight. Remove from the refrigerator and serve at room temperature with greens.

Salt-Roasted Dory with Lemon and Tarragon

SERVES 2

3–4 pounds kosher salt

1 (2½–3½ pound) whole Dory, gutted

2 lemons, thinly sliced

8 sprigs tarragon

4 tablespoons butter, melted

Combine the salt with enough water so that it resembles wet sand. Place a thin layer on a baking sheet and top with half of the lemon slices and half of the tarragon. Place the fish on top of the tarragon. Place the remaining lemon slices and tarragon on top of the fish. Pack on the remaining salt mixture to completely encase the fish. Bake at 375°F for 20–30 minutes. Remove the fish from the oven and let it rest for 5 minutes. Crack the salt crust and discard. To serve, remove the lemons and tarragon and peel off the skin before carefully transferring the top fillet to a platter. Remove and discard the backbone and transfer the bottom fillet without its skin to the platter. Drizzle the fish with melted butter.

Butter-Basted Dory with Chile and Mint

SERVES 4

4 Dory portions, skin on and scored

Salt

6 tablespoons butter, divided

1 garlic clove, minced

2 dried chiles, such as árbol or Calabrian

20 mint leaves

1 lemon, cut into wedges

Season the fish with salt and let it rest for 15 minutes. In a sauté pan over medium-high heat, melt 2 tablespoons of the butter and cook until golden brown. Place the fish in the pan skin side down, cook until the skin begins to crisp around the edges, about 2 minutes, and then flip the fish. Add the remaining 3 tablespoons of butter, garlic, chiles, and mint. Cook until the butter is frothy, then angle the pan toward you and use a spoon to continuously baste the fish with the butter until it is cooked through. Remove the fish from the pan. Discard the chiles and strain the butter, reserving the crisped garlic and mint to scatter over the fish. Serve with lemon wedges.

DRUM, BLACK/RED
Fillet fish

The drum family of fish is so named because of the percussive-like sound they make by flexing a muscle in their throat, a soft noise that is then amplified by their air bladders. You can hear just one fish drumming from shore, so the chorus generated by a whole school of drums seems otherworldly. This family of fish comprises both the red drum of New Orleans culinary fame and its lesser known but interchangeable sibling, the black drum.

Red drum, also commonly called redfish, gained international acclaim when chef Paul Prudhomme first presented it under a thick layer of blackening spice (page 182) in his Louisiana restaurant in the 1980s. That dish gained global fame and replication, and soon the wild populations were decimated. While these wild stocks are recovering, it is now available as a farmed product. Though red drum is rightly famous, black drum is its culinary twin for most intents and purposes. Grilling unscaled drum fillets is another classic Southern preparation known as "on the half shell" (page 181). The scales protect the meat from the fire and add a unique perfume to the flesh as they char.

Though delicious, and with abiding popularity in the South, they don't possess a particularly unique flavor. They are a fine food fish, at peak in the late fall when full of meaty flavor. The meat has a soft texture but firm flake. The bloodline is compact and should not be removed, as its mild flavor complements the fillet. The beautifully patterned skin can be somewhat thick, especially on fish larger than 10 pounds, and tough unless cooked properly, but overall it crisps well. A layer of subcutaneous fat sitting between the skin and flesh bastes the former and moistens the latter when the fish is broiled, grilled, roasted, or sautéed. The layer of fat that lies along the dorsal ridge is a true delicacy and should be left on when filleting. The head and shoulders of drum make a fantastic dish in themselves when split, seasoned, and broiled until crisp.

The bones of all drums make good stock. The roe, especially that of black drum, is worth getting your hands on. It is delicious both fresh and sautéed, as you would cook shad roe.

Braised Drum à la Barigoule

In this recipe, the drum and vegetables are braised and marinated in spiced broth.

SERVES 4

- 1 recipe Basic Aioli (page 25), made with oil skimmed from the cooked dish
- 4 drum portions, skin off
- Salt
- 3 stalks celery, chopped
- 2 carrots, sliced
- 4 ounces mushrooms, cut in quarters
- 2 garlic cloves, thinly sliced
- 5 sprigs thyme
- 1 teaspoon ground coriander
- 1½ cups white wine
- 1 (14-ounce) can halved artichoke hearts in oil
- ½ lemon, thinly sliced
- 1 cup extra-virgin olive oil
- Crushed red chile flakes (optional)
- Crusty bread for serving

Season the fish with salt and let it rest for 20 minutes. In a large pot over medium heat, combine the celery, carrots, mushrooms, garlic, thyme, coriander, wine, and ½ cup of water. Season lightly with salt and simmer until the alcohol smell dissipates, about 5 minutes. Add the artichoke hearts with their oil, lemon slices, and olive oil. Reduce the heat to low. Nestle the fish into the pot so it is barely submerged. If desired, add the chile flakes. Cover and cook for 15–20 minutes. Remove the pot from the heat and cool to room temperature. The flavors improve if allowed to chill overnight in the refrigerator. Use a ladle to skim off the olive oil and use it in making the Basic Aioli. Serve at room temperature with crusty bread and aioli.

Broiled Drum with Orange, Rosemary, and Rum Flambé

SERVES 4

- 4 drum portions, skin on, scored
- Salt
- 1 orange, zested
- 4 stalks rosemary
- 4 tablespoons butter, cut into pieces
- 2 ounces dark rum

Season the fish with salt and zest, and let it rest for 20 minutes. Preheat the broiler to medium and set the rack to the position closest to the heat. In the bottom of an ovenproof dish, arrange the rosemary in a single layer and place the fish on top, skin side up. Put a pat of butter on top of each serving. Cook until done, about 7–10 minutes. Remove from the broiler. Add the rum and flambé by lighting it with a match. Allow the alcohol to burn off before serving.

Broiled Drum with Parmesan and Chile

SERVES 4

4 tablespoons Mayonnaise (page 29, or store-bought)

4 drum portions, skin off

Salt

2 tablespoons grated Parmesan cheese

2 garlic cloves, grated

Worcestershire sauce

Crushed red chile flakes

1 lemon, juiced

Lightly season the fish with salt and let it rest for 20 minutes. Preheat the broiler to medium and set the rack in the middle. Whisk together the Mayonnaise, cheese, garlic, 2–3 dashes of Worcestershire sauce, a pinch of chile flakes, and lemon juice. Place the fish on a baking tray. Spread the mayonnaise mixture evenly over the fish. Slide the tray under the broiler. Broil until the fish is done and the topping is browned, about 7–10 minutes, depending on thickness.

Teriyaki-Glazed Drum

SERVES 4

1 recipe Teriyaki-Style Sauce (page 32)

4 drum portions, skin on and scored

Salt

2 teaspoons Worcestershire sauce

1 tablespoon sesame oil

¼ cup sliced scallions for garnish

Season the fish lightly with salt and let it rest for 20 minutes. Preheat the broiler to medium and set the rack in the position closest to the heat. Combine the Teriyaki-Style Sauce and the Worcestershire sauce. Brush a baking dish with the sesame oil. Place the fish in the dish skin side up, coat with half of the sauce, and slide the dish under the broiler. Cook, basting with the remaining sauce every 2 minutes until done, about 7–10 minutes, depending on thickness. Garnish with sliced scallions.

Grilled Drum with Red Wine–Shallot Vinaigrette

SERVES 4

>1 recipe Red Wine–Shallot Vinaigrette (page 37)
>
>4 drum portions, skin on and scored

Reserve half of the Red Wine–Shallot Vinaigrette for serving. Coat the fish with the remaining vinaigrette and let it marinate for 4–8 hours. Prepare a charcoal grill with a medium fire, concentrating the hot coals on one side of the kettle. Remove the fish from the marinade and pat dry. Place the fish skin side down on the grill over the hottest part of the fire. Cook until it begins to crisp, about 3 minutes. Lift the entire grill grate and rotate it so the fish rests opposite the hot coals. Cover the grill and continue to cook over this indirect heat until the fish is done. Serve with the reserved vinaigrette.

NOTE *If using a gas grill, preheat all burners to medium. Place the drum on one side of the hot grates. Once it begins to char around the edges, turn off the burner directly under the fish and cover the grill to finish cooking.*

Grilled Drum on the Half Shell

SERVES 4

>1 recipe compound butter of your choice (pages 18–23)
>
>1 (2-pound) drum fillet with scales and skin intact
>
>Salt
>
>Black pepper
>
>2 tablespoons butter, melted
>
>1 cup picked fresh herbs, such as chervil, parsley, tarragon, and/or mint

Prepare a charcoal grill with a medium fire. Season the fish with salt and pepper and let it rest for 20 minutes. Place the fish skin side down directly over the hot coals. Baste the fillets with the melted butter, cover the grill, and cook until done. Transfer to a serving platter, slather with compound butter, top with herbs, and serve with instructions to eaters to spoon the fish off the skin, leaving the skin and scales on the platter.

NOTE *If using a gas grill, preheat all burners to medium.*

Blackened Drum

SERVES 4

    1 recipe Blackening Spice Mix (page 33)

    4 drum portions, skin off

    Salt

    4 tablespoons butter, melted, divided

    ¼ cup vegetable oil

    1 lemon, cut into wedges

Lightly season the fish with salt and let it rest for 20 minutes. Heat a cast iron skillet or heavy-bottomed sauté pan over high heat until it is screaming hot. Combine 2 tablespoons of the butter and all of the oil in a bowl and brush each portion so the fish glistens all over. Dredge one side of each portion in Blackening Spice Mix, coating evenly. Place the fish in the pan spice side down and drizzle the remaining butter-and-oil mixture over the top. Reduce the heat to medium-low and cook without flipping until a dark crust forms, then flip to cook through. Drizzle with the remaining butter and serve with lemon wedges.

Sautéed Drum with Brown Butter, Walnuts, and Raisins

SERVES 4

    4 drum portions, skin on and scored

    Salt

    6 tablespoons butter, divided

    ¼ cup chopped walnuts

    2 garlic cloves, finely minced

    2 tablespoons raisins

    1 lemon, juiced

Season the fish with salt and let it rest for 20 minutes. In a sauté pan over medium heat, melt 2 tablespoons of the butter and cook until golden brown. Place the fish in the pan skin side down. Cook without flipping until almost done, then remove the fish and wipe the pan clean. Add the remaining 4 tablespoons of butter, walnuts, garlic, and raisins. Cook until the walnuts are toasted, the raisins are plump, and the butter is dark brown. Add the lemon juice and season with salt. Stir to combine. Turn off the heat and return the fish to the pan skin side up to finish cooking.

Drum en Escabeche

In this recipe, the cooked drum is marinated in vinegar and spices.

SERVES 4

- 1½ pounds drum, skin off, cut into 2-inch sections
- Salt
- 1 cup plus 2 tablespoons extra-virgin olive oil, divided
- Flour
- 2 carrots, sliced into thin rounds
- 2 shallots, sliced into rings
- 4 garlic cloves, smashed
- 1 tablespoon smoked sweet paprika
- 1 teaspoon ground coriander
- 6 sprigs thyme and/or 3 stalks rosemary
- 1 orange, zest removed in wide strips
- ½ cup white wine
- 1 tablespoon sherry vinegar
- ¼ cup chopped fresh herbs, such as chives, parsley, or tarragon
- Sliced baguette for serving

Season the fish pieces with salt and let them rest for 20 minutes. Roll in flour to coat. In a sauté pan over medium heat, warm 2 tablespoons of the olive oil. Place the fish into the pan and cook without flipping until almost done, then flip to finish cooking and wipe the pan clean. Transfer the cooked fish to a baking dish. Heat the remaining 1 cup of olive oil. Add the carrots, shallots, and garlic and cook until the carrots begin to soften. Add the paprika, coriander, thyme and/or rosemary, and orange zest, and cook for 2 minutes, until the aromas bloom. Add the wine and vinegar, season with salt, and simmer until the liquid is reduced by half. Add the herbs. Stir to combine and pour over the cooked fish. Cool to room temperature. Wait at least 1 hour before serving. The flavors improve if allowed to chill overnight in the refrigerator before returning it to room temperature. Serve with a sliced baguette.

FLOUNDER/FLATFISH
(DAB, PLAICE, SOLE)
Flaky white fish

Sole, flounder, turbot, dab, plaice, and halibut all are characterized scientifically as flatfish. They all undergo one of the oddest transitions to emerge as the fish we recognize on our plates. When young, they are of orthodox fish shape—swimming upright, belly down, facing forward. But as they resolve themselves to their bottom-dwelling adulthood, one eye migrates across their body to the other side of their head. The fish changes its orientation from vertical to horizontal, eyes on top. The top side of a flatfish is colored to camouflage itself from predators looking down. The bottom side is generally white, so that if the fish is seen from below, it's backlit and seems to disappear into the light.

This category counts within it many families, some with several dozen species swimming in American waters. The fish range in shape from the oval true soles of the Atlantic to the more oblong and diamond-shaped flounders and flukes to the elliptical-shaped so-called soles on the Pacific coast (they are actually flounders).

Halibut is the largest flatfish, but given its size, it cooks different from its relations. But other than halibut, it is generally true that flatfish of commercial and culinary value have similar flavor qualities. Across the board, the flavor of flatfish is elegant, though by no means strong. Their flavors tend to be flat (pun intended), with a mineral and herbal character, but various species have different personalities. Though all species have distinguishing aspects, the shared similarities mean they can be recommended more as equals. As such, they present a versatile canvas for other flavors and are ideally suited to be sautéed, broiled, baked, or poached and then paired with bright sauces. The biggest differences among the group are in the textures. Some are very soft-fleshed, whereas others have a pleasant tautness. The texture determines whether a particular method of preparation is suitable or not for a species. When a recipe specifically calls for flounder (regardless of the types, which include fish called fluke, summer flounder, winter flounder, blackback flounder, and yellowtail flounder) or another species to be used, that means that the fish is best suited for the preparation because of its texture. If the recipe just says "flatfish," that means that any of the flaky white fish can be used.

The skin has tiny scales that must be removed if you choose to serve it skin on, but mostly these are prepared without skin. The fillets from the top side of the fish are roughly 30 percent thicker than those from the underside. All flatfish fillets benefit from being salted lightly for up to 45 minutes before cooking. This firms the flesh, making it easier to handle, and focuses the flavor. The roe, milt, and liver of all flatfish are delicious and can be used in a variety of ways. In spring, pale orange flounder roe and the snow-white roe of soles can weigh up to a quarter of the weight of the whole fish. The liver is best dusted in flour,

fried in butter, and finished with a squeeze of lemon or a dash of sherry. But it can also be mashed into butter to mount into sauces or stir into fish soups or stews.

Braised Whole Flounder with Madeira, Orange, and Rosemary

SERVES 2–4

1 cup Basic Fish Stock (page 61) or hot water

1 (2- to 3-pound) flounder, headed, gutted, and skin scaled (trim tail if needed to fit in pan)

6 tablespoons butter, divided

1 onion, thinly sliced

1 fennel bulb, thinly sliced

4 orange slices

2 stalks rosemary

½ cup Madeira, a drier style such as Sercial or Verdelho

Salt

2 tablespoons chopped fresh herbs, such as chives, parsley, or tarragon

In a large sauté pan over high heat, melt 4 tablespoons of the butter. Add the onion, fennel, orange slices, and rosemary. Cook until the vegetables are slightly browned. Place the fish in the pan and add the stock, Madeira, and a pinch of salt. Bring to a simmer, cover, and reduce the heat to low. Cook until the fish is firm to the touch, about 25 minutes. Carefully remove the fish from the liquid, increase the heat to high, and reduce the remaining liquid to a glaze. Add the remaining 2 tablespoons of butter and the herbs. Stir to combine. Peel back the skin and discard. Transfer the top fillets to a platter and remove and discard the backbone. Lift the lower fillet off the skin and transfer to a platter. Discard the skin and rosemary. Serve with the vegetables and sauce.

Flounder Ceviche

SERVES 4

> 1 pound flounder fillets, skin off, diced into ½-inch pieces
>
> Salt
>
> 3 tablespoons raisins or currants
>
> 1 cup lime juice
>
> 2 tablespoons sherry vinegar
>
> 1–2 Fresno or serrano chiles, thinly sliced
>
> 1 red onion, thinly sliced, rinsed under cold running water, and patted dry
>
> ¼ cup slivered almonds or whole pine nuts, toasted
>
> ¼ cup extra-virgin olive oil
>
> 1 cup chervil or parsley, leaves picked
>
> 1 teaspoon ground mace or nutmeg

Keep this dish cold at all times during preparation. Season the fish with salt and let it rest for 5 minutes. Combine the fish with the raisins or currants, lime juice, vinegar, and chiles and let it rest for 20 minutes. Add the onion and nuts and let it rest for another 10 minutes. Add the olive oil and chervil or parsley, and toss well. Garnish with mace or nutmeg.

Fluke Crudo with Mint and Lemon

Fluke is a large flounder with a firm texture.

SERVES 4 AS AN APPETIZER

> 1 pound fluke fillets, skin off, sliced thinly on the bias into ½-inch-thick ribbons
>
> Salt
>
> Extra-virgin olive oil, fruity is best
>
> 4 sprigs mint, leaves picked and thinly sliced
>
> 1 lemon, zested and juiced
>
> Crushed red chile flakes

Keep this dish cold at all times during preparation. Season the sliced fish with salt and let it rest for 10 minutes. Drizzle the fish with oil and garnish with the mint, lemon zest and a few drops of juice, and chile flakes.

Fried Cornmeal-Crusted Flatfish

SERVES 4

> 4 flatfish portions, skin off, cut into 2-inch pieces
>
> Salt
>
> Vegetable or peanut oil
>
> Flour
>
> 1 cup buttermilk or milk
>
> Fine cornmeal

Season the fish with salt and let it rest for 15 minutes. Pour 3–4 inches of oil into a high-sided pan. Place over medium-high heat and warm the oil to 375°F. Dip one piece in buttermilk, roll the fish in flour, dip it in buttermilk again, and then roll in the cornmeal to coat both sides. Place the fish in oil and hold for 5 seconds before releasing. Repeat the process, cooking the pieces a few at a time. Turn with a slotted spoon to ensure that both sides crisp evenly. Remove the pieces as they finish, and place on paper towels to absorb excess oil.

Citrus-Coated Fried Flatfish

SERVES 4

> 4 flatfish portions, skin off, cut into
> 2-inch pieces
>
> Salt
>
> Vegetable or peanut oil
>
> ¼ cup citrus juice
>
> Flour
>
> Panko

Season the fish with salt and let it rest for
15 minutes. Pour 3–4 inches of oil into a high-sided pan. Place over medium-high heat and
warm the oil to 375°F. Dip one piece in juice, roll
in flour, dip in juice again, and then roll in panko
to coat both sides. Place the fish in the oil and
hold for 5 seconds before releasing. Repeat the
process, cooking a few pieces at a time. Turn with
a slotted spoon to ensure that both sides crisp
evenly. Remove the pieces as they finish, and
place on paper towels to absorb excess oil.

VARIATIONS

+ Serve with Pine Nut Agrodolce (page 30)
  or Lemon-Chile-Soy Sauce (page 28).

Grilled Whole Flounder with Charred Tomato Vinaigrette

SERVES 2–4

> 1 recipe Charred Tomato Vinaigrette
> (page 35)
>
> 2 stalks rosemary, leaves picked and bruised
> with the back of a knife
>
> 1 whole (2- to 3-pound) flounder, headed,
> gutted, scaled, and scored, tail cut off

Place the fish in a baking dish. Reserve three-quarters of the Charred Tomato Vinaigrette
in a bowl. Combine the remainder with the
rosemary and pour the mixture over the fish.
Marinate for 1–8 hours. Prepare a charcoal grill
with a medium fire, concentrating the hot coals
on one side of the kettle. Remove the fish from
the vinaigrette and place the fish colored side
down on the grill over the hottest part of the fire.
Cook until the edges begin to crisp, about 4–5
minutes. Carefully flip the fish and brush it with
the remaining used vinaigrette. Lift the entire
grill grate and rotate it so the fish rests opposite
the hot coals. Cover the grill and continue to
cook over this indirect heat until the fish is done,
another 6–8 minutes per pound. Drizzle the
cooked fish with the reserved vinaigrette.

NOTE *If using a gas grill, preheat all burners to
medium-high. Place the flounder on one side of the
hot grates. Once it begins to char around the edges,
turn off the burner directly under the fish and
cover the grill to finish cooking.*

Flatfish en Papilotte (cooked in parchment)

SERVES 4

  1 recipe Anchovy-Almond Butter (page 19)

  4 flatfish portions, skin off

    Salt

  4 stalks celery, sliced

  2 fennel bulbs, thinly sliced

  1 small red onion, sliced, rinsed under cold running water, and patted dry

  1 cup white wine

    Butter, for greasing the parchment

  1 orange, cut into segments

  ¼ cup mint, leaves torn

Season the fish with salt and let it rest for 15 minutes. In a shallow pan, place the celery, fennel, onion, and wine. Season with salt and cook over medium heat until the vegetables are soft and the wine nearly reduced. Take four (18-inch) squares of parchment paper and cut into heart shapes. Use the butter to grease an 8-inch square area in the middle of each. Evenly divide the vegetables and remaining liquid among the parchment hearts, place the fish on top, and add a couple of orange segments and 2 tablespoons of Anchovy-Almond Butter. Sprinkle with mint. Fold the paper over, then crimp the edges tightly (empanada-style) to form a pouch. Roast at 350°F for 10–12 minutes, depending on the thickness of the fillets. Serve in the pouch and slice open just prior to eating.

Poached Flatfish with Tomatoes and Herbs

SERVES 4

  4 flatfish portions, skin off

    Salt

  1 cup white wine

  1 shallot, sliced

  2 sprigs thyme

  1 lemon, zest peeled in wide strips

  4 whole cloves

  4 tablespoons cold butter, cut into pieces

  2 plum tomatoes, seeded and finely diced

  2 tablespoons chopped fresh herbs, such as chives or tarragon

Season the fish with salt and let it rest for 15 minutes. In a pan just wide enough to hold the fish in a single layer, combine ½ cup of water with the wine, shallot, thyme, zest, and cloves. Simmer over low heat for 5 minutes. Season the broth with salt and bring it to 170°F. Add the fish and cook until it is opaque and flakes under gentle pressure, 4–5 minutes per ½ inch of thickness. Transfer the fish to a plate. Strain 1 cup of the poaching liquid into a small pan and reduce over high heat to 2 tablespoons. Remove from the heat and whisk in the butter. Add the tomatoes and herbs and season with salt.

Poached Flatfish Veronique

In this recipe, the fish is prepared with a white wine and grape sauce.

SERVES 4

  4 flatfish portions, skin off

    Salt

  1 cup white wine

  2 tablespoons white wine vinegar

1 shallot, sliced

10 black peppercorns

1 bay leaf

1 tablespoon butter

½ tablespoon flour

20 grapes, peeled and halved

Season the fish with salt and let it rest for 15 minutes. In a pan just wide enough to hold the fish in a single layer, combine 1 cup of water with the wine, vinegar, shallot, peppercorns, and bay leaf. Simmer over low heat for 5 minutes. Season the broth with salt and bring it to 170°F. Add the fish and cook until it is opaque and flakes under gentle pressure, about 4–5 minutes per ½ inch of thickness. Transfer the fish to a baking dish. Set the broiler to high, and position the rack in the position closest to the heat. In a small saucepan over medium heat, melt the butter. Add the flour and cook for 1 minute. Add ½ cup of the strained poaching liquid, whisk to combine, and simmer to thicken. Add the grapes. Spoon the sauce over the fish, season with salt, and place under the broiler until slightly browned, about 1–2 minutes.

Sautéed Flatfish Almondine

SERVES 4

4 flatfish portions, skin off

Salt

Flour

6 tablespoons butter, divided

2 garlic cloves, finely minced

¼ cup sliced almonds

1 lemon, juiced

Season the fish with salt and let it rest for 15 minutes. Roll the fish in flour to lightly coat. In a sauté pan over medium heat, melt 2 tablespoons of the butter and cook until golden brown. Place the fish in the pan. Cook without flipping until almost done, flip to finish, about 30 seconds. Remove the fish and wipe the pan clean. Add the remaining 4 tablespoons of butter, garlic, and almonds. Cook until the almonds are browned. Add the lemon juice and season with salt. Stir to combine.

Sautéed Flatfish with Brown Butter, Raisins, and Tarragon

SERVES 4

4 flatfish portions, skin off

Salt

Flour

6 tablespoons butter, divided

2 garlic cloves, finely minced

2 tablespoons raisins

1 tablespoon chopped fresh tarragon

1 tablespoon white wine vinegar

Season the fish with salt and let it rest for 15 minutes. Roll the fish in flour to lightly coat it. In a sauté pan over medium heat, melt 2 tablespoons of the butter and cook until golden brown. Place the fish in the pan. Cook without flipping until almost done, then flip to finish, about 30 seconds. Remove the fish and wipe the pan clean. Add the remaining 4 tablespoons of butter, garlic, and raisins. Cook until the butter is very dark. Add the tarragon and vinegar and season with salt. Stir to combine.

Braised Flatfish Puttanesca

In this recipe, the fish is braised in a lively tomato sauce with capers and olives.

SERVES 4

    4 flatfish portions, skin off
    Salt
    4 tablespoons extra-virgin olive oil, divided
    1 (2-ounce) tin anchovies in oil
    2 garlic cloves, sliced
    4 dried árbol chiles, or ½ tablespoon crushed red chile flakes
    2 (14-ounce) cans fire-roasted diced tomatoes
    ½ cup white wine
    2 tablespoons capers, rinsed and patted dry
    ¼ cup pitted cured black olives
    6 basil leaves, torn, for garnish

Season the fish with salt and let it rest for 15 minutes. In an ovenproof sauté pan over medium-high heat, warm 3 tablespoons of the olive oil, flatfish with their oil, garlic, and chiles until the anchovies melt. Add the tomatoes, wine, capers, and olives. Bring to a simmer and cook for 10 minutes. Nestle the fish into the sauce and drizzle with the remaining 3 tablespoons of olive oil. Cover the pan and place it in a 275°F oven for 20 minutes. Remove and let it rest for 10 minutes before serving scattered with torn basil leaves.

Sautéed Flatfish with Dill, Anchovies, and Cream

SERVES 4

    4 flatfish portions, skin off
    Salt
    Flour
    5 tablespoons butter, divided
    4 anchovy fillets, minced
    1 lemon, zested and juiced
    2 tablespoons cream
    3 tablespoons chopped fresh dill

Season the fish with salt and let it rest for 15 minutes. Roll the fish in flour to lightly coat it. In a sauté pan over medium heat, melt 2 tablespoons of the butter and cook until golden brown. Place the fish in the pan. Cook without flipping until almost done, then flip to finish, about 30 seconds. Remove the fish and wipe the pan clean. Add the remaining 3 tablespoons of butter, anchovies, and zest to the pan and cook, stirring, until the anchovies have melted. Add the lemon juice and cream. Season with salt and simmer until the sauce emulsifies and thickens. Turn off the heat, stir in the dill, and serve.

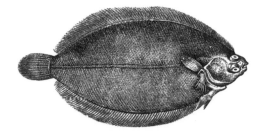

Sautéed Flatfish Provençal

SERVES 4

    4 flatfish portions, skin off

    Salt

    Flour

    6 tablespoons extra-virgin olive oil, divided

    4 garlic cloves, finely minced

    1 (14-ounce) can fire-roasted, diced tomatoes, drained or 1 cup large diced tomatoes

    2 tablespoons chopped green or black olives

    1 tablespoon red or white wine vinegar

Season the fish with salt and let it rest for 15 minutes. In a sauté pan over medium heat, warm 2 tablespoons olive oil and place the fish in the pan. Cook without flipping until almost done, then flip to finish, about 30 seconds. Remove the fish and wipe the pan clean. Add the remaining 4 tablespoons olive oil and garlic and cook for 1 minute. Add the tomatoes, olives, and vinegar. Season with salt, cover, and simmer for 7–10 minutes. Turn off the heat and nestle the fish into the sauce. Cover and let it rest 5 minutes. Serve hot or at room temperature.

Flatfish en Escabeche

In this recipe, the cooked flatfish is marinated in vinegar and spices

SERVES 4

    1½ pounds flatfish fillets, skin off, cut into 3-inch sections

    Salt

    Flour

    1 cup plus 2 tablespoons extra-virgin olive oil, divided

    2 carrots, sliced into thin rounds

    2 shallots, sliced into rings

    4 garlic cloves, smashed

    1 tablespoon smoked sweet paprika

    1 teaspoon ground coriander

    6 sprigs thyme and/or 3 stalks rosemary

    1 orange, zest peeled in wide strips

    ½ cup fruity white wine

    1 tablespoon sherry vinegar

    ¼ cup chopped fresh herbs such as parsley, tarragon, and chives

    Sliced baguette, for serving

Season the fish pieces with salt and let them rest for 15 minutes. Roll the fish in flour. In a sauté pan over medium heat, warm 2 tablespoons of the olive oil. Place the fish into the pan and cook without flipping until almost done, then flip to finish cooking. Transfer the cooked fish to a baking dish. Heat the remaining 1 cup of olive oil. Add the carrots, shallots, and garlic and cook until the carrots begin to soften. Add the paprika, coriander, thyme, and orange zest and cook for 2 minutes, until the aromas bloom. Add the wine and vinegar, season with salt, and simmer until the liquid is reduced by half. Add the chopped fresh herbs. Stir to combine and pour over the cooked fish. Cool to room temperature. Wait at least 1 hour before serving. The flavors improve if allowed to chill overnight in the refrigerator before returning the dish to room temperature. Serve with a sliced baguette.

Sautéed Flatfish with Lemon Slices

SERVES 4

    4 flatfish portions, skin off
    Salt
    6 tablespoons butter
    1 lemon, quartered and thinly sliced
    Flour

Season the fish with salt and let it rest for 15 minutes. In a sauté pan over medium heat, melt the butter. Add the lemon slices and cook until slightly softened. Dredge the fish in flour. Place the fish in the pan with lemons. Cook the fish until almost done, flip, and continue to cook until done, about 30 seconds.

Steamed Flatfish with Lemongrass and Bay Leaf

SERVES 4

    4 flatfish portions, skin off
    Salt
    3 lemongrass stalks, halved, and bruised with the back of a knife
    1 bay leaf
    ½ cup white wine
    4 tablespoons butter, melted

Season the fish with salt and let it rest for 15 minutes. In the bottom of a wide, shallow pot over low heat, place the lemongrass and bay leaf to create an aromatic raft. Add the wine and enough water to cover the bottom of the pot. Bring to a simmer. Place the fish on top of the aromatics, cover, and cook until done, about 7–8 minutes. Serve each portion with 1 tablespoon of butter and a spoonful of the remaining cooking liquid drizzled over it.

Steamed Flatfish with Orange and Star Anise

SERVES 4

    4 flatfish portions, skin off
    Salt
    1 orange, thinly sliced
    2 star anise pods
    ½ cup wine
    4 tablespoons butter, melted

Season the fish with salt and let it rest for 15 minutes. In the bottom of a wide, shallow pot over low heat, place the orange slices and star anise to create an aromatic raft. Add the wine and ½ cup of water to cover the bottom of the pot. Bring to a simmer. Place the fish on top of the aromatics, cover, and cook until done, about 7–8 minutes. Serve each portion with 1 tablespoon of butter and a spoonful of the remaining cooking liquid drizzled over it.

FLYING FISH
Fillet fish

In every family there's at least one relative who's just a little different. In the fish family, it's the flying fish. These schooling fish have wings and employ gymnastics as means to escape predators by launching themselves above the waterline. Though they are not usually found in markets, they are common in our waters from Massachusetts throughout the Gulf of Mexico and along the Pacific coast and are worth seeking out for the table.

The fish's flesh ranges from white to light pink in color, its texture sports nice, firm flakes, its flavor is delicious and unique, and it has a slightly cured taste with a somewhat sour, citrus aroma. Flying fish is not as oily as mackerel, but it is richer than a typical flaky white fish. Given the strength and structure needed for flight, these fish are bony, but they can be filleted and the bones sliced out with relative ease. Flying fish take well to any preparation you would use for a small, oily fish like herring or sardines, but they are especially good when marinated with citrus and fresh herbs and are perfectly delicious when simply grilled over the smoke of a charcoal fire.

Broiled Flying Fish with Fennel and Madeira Flambé

SERVES 4

4 flying fish fillets, skin on

Salt

1 lemon, zested and juiced

1 large onion, thinly sliced

1 fennel bulb, thinly sliced

4 tablespoons butter, cut into pieces

1½ ounces Madeira, a drier style such as Sercial or Verdelho

1½ ounces rum

Season the fish with salt and lemon zest and let it rest for 15 minutes. Preheat the broiler to medium and set the rack in the position closest to the heat. Blanch the onion and fennel in salted water until barely tender, and drain. In the bottom of an ovenproof dish, arrange the vegetables in a single layer and place the fish on top, skin side up. Put a pat of butter on the top of each fillet, slide the dish under the broiler, and cook until done, 7–10 minutes, depending on thickness. Remove from the broiler. Add the Madeira and rum, and flambé by lighting it with a match. Allow the alcohol to burn off before serving. Sprinkle lemon juice over the top and serve.

Broiled Flying Fish with Orange-Coriander Vinaigrette

SERVES 4

> 1 recipe Orange-Coriander Vinaigrette (page 37)
>
> 4 flying fish portions, skin on
>
> Black pepper

Reserve half of the Orange-Coriander Vinaigrette. Combine the remaining vinaigrette with the fish and marinate for 2–8 hours. Preheat the broiler to medium and set the rack in the position closest to the heat. Remove the fish from the vinaigrette, pat dry, and place it on a baking tray, and sprinkle with black pepper. Slide the tray under the broiler and cook until done, 5–7 minutes, depending on thickness. Pour the reserved vinaigrette over the top.

Flying Fish en Escabeche

In this recipe, the cooked fish is marinated in vinegar and spices

SERVES 4

> 4 flying fish portions, skin on
>
> Salt
>
> Flour
>
> 1 cup plus 2 tablespoons extra-virgin olive oil, divided
>
> 2 carrots, sliced into thin rounds
>
> 2 shallots, sliced into rings
>
> 4 garlic cloves, smashed
>
> 1 tablespoon smoked sweet paprika
>
> 1 teaspoon ground coriander
>
> 6 sprigs thyme and/or 3 stalks rosemary
>
> 1 orange, zest peeled in wide strips
>
> ½ cup fruity white wine
>
> 1 tablespoon sherry vinegar
>
> ¼ cup chopped fresh herbs, such as chives, parsley, and tarragon
>
> Sliced baguette for serving

Season the fish with salt and let it rest for 15 minutes. Roll the fish in flour. In a sauté pan over medium heat, warm 2 tablespoons of the olive oil. Place the fish into the pan and cook without flipping until almost done, then flip to finish cooking. Alternatively, the fish can be broiled. Transfer the cooked fish to a baking dish. Add the remaining 1 cup of olive oil, carrots, shallots, and garlic and cook until the carrots begin to soften. Add the paprika, coriander, thyme or rosemary, and orange zest and cook for 2 minutes, until the aromas bloom. Add the wine and vinegar, season with salt, and simmer until reduced by half. Add the herbs. Stir to combine and pour over the cooked fish. Cool to room temperature. Wait at least 1 hour before serving. The flavors improve if allowed to chill overnight in the refrigerator before returning the dish to room temperature. Serve with slices of baguette.

GRENADIER
Flaky white fish

Grenadier is a relative of cod that deserves special attention because, well, we simply should be eating more of it. Grenadier are among the most abundant of all fish in the Pacific Ocean and swim in the Atlantic as well. The West Coast grenadier fishery didn't begin until the early 1990s, as these very deep water–dwelling species had previously been beyond the reach of fishermen and conventional gear. Decline in other fisheries forced fishermen to target new species and develop new gear to harvest them. Grenadier landings peaked in that decade, with only 3 percent of the peak catch being landed more recently. Despite the lack of grenadier in the market, chefs have started to take note of the quality and low price and are putting it on their menus more often.

Grenadier is nightmarish to see. It's got a huge head with eyes so oversized that one of its nicknames is onion eye. The other is rattail, because the fish's body flares just behind the head and tapers into a whisper-thin tail. Its scales are thick and dense and require mechanical removal. The fish's physique means it yields just 20 percent edible meat. But that flesh is fine-grained with a natural intensity, iodine tang, and a shrimp-like sweetness, given their steady diet of shrimp and crustaceans. Since grenadier are legion, tasty, and cheap, this fish could soon overshadow its famous cousin and become a household name because it can be cooked in any way cod can.

Grenadier in Charred Tomato Vinaigrette

SERVES 4

1 recipe Charred Tomato Vinaigrette (page 35)

4 grenadier portions, skin off

Salt

Extra-virgin olive oil

Crusty bread for serving

Season the fish with salt and let it rest for 15 minutes. Preheat the broiler to medium and set the rack in the position closest to the heat. Pour the vinaigrette into a baking dish just large enough to hold the fish. Nestle the fish skin side up into the vinaigrette and drizzle the top with olive oil. Place the dish under the broiler, and cook until the fish is slightly singed and the sauce is bubbling, 7–10 minutes, depending on thickness. Remove and let it rest for 5 minutes before serving with crusty bread.

Chilled Poached Grenadier with Mint-Mustard Vinaigrette and Tomato Salad

SERVES 4

> 1 recipe Mint-Mustard Vinaigrette (page 36)
>
> 4 grenadier portions, skin off
>
> Salt
>
> 2 cups white wine
>
> 10 black peppercorns
>
> 10 star anise pods
>
> Crushed red chile flakes
>
> Tomatoes, sliced
>
> Radishes, thinly sliced

Season the fish with salt and let it rest for 15 minutes. In a pan just wide enough to hold the fish in a single layer, combine 1 cup of water with the wine, peppercorns, star anise, and a pinch of chile flakes. Simmer over low heat for 5 minutes. Season the broth with salt and bring it to 170°F. Add the fish and cook until it is opaque and flakes under gentle pressure, about 4 minutes per ½ inch of thickness. Remove the pan from the heat and cool the fish in the poaching liquid. Transfer the fish to a serving plate and flake it into bite-size pieces. Strain 1 cup of the poaching liquid into a saucepan, place over high heat, and reduce to 2 tablespoons. Turn off the heat and whisk in the Mint-Mustard Vinaigrette. Toss the flaked fish with the sauce and serve over tomatoes and radishes.

Grenadier with Brown Butter, Coriander, and Orange

SERVES 4

> 4 grenadier portions, skin off
>
> Salt
>
> 1½ tablespoons coriander seeds, crushed
>
> 6 tablespoons butter, divided
>
> 2 garlic cloves, finely minced
>
> 1 orange, zested and juiced
>
> Black pepper

Season the fish with salt on both sides and on one side with coriander. Press the seasonings into the flesh and let it rest for 15 minutes. In a sauté pan over medium heat, melt 2 tablespoons butter and cook until golden brown. Place the fish coriander side down in the pan. Cook without flipping until almost done, then remove the fish and wipe the pan clean. Add the remaining 4 tablespoons butter and garlic and cook until dark brown. Add the zest, season with black pepper, and cook for 30 seconds. Add the orange juice and season with salt. Turn off the heat and return the fish to the pan uncooked side down to finish cooking.

GROUPER
Fillet fish, meaty dense fish

As a species, grouper serve as an all-purpose fish because the pearly white meat cooperates with just about any flavor profile and most cooking methods. Their troupe has a cast of characters ranging from the 700-plus-pound Goliath grouper to the pan-size Coney. Groupers exhibit incredible intelligence and are characteristically plump in shape, often loners, sometimes hermaphrodites, and somewhat expert at camouflage.

The vast majority is caught in the Gulf of Mexico, though there are significant fisheries throughout the Southeast. Pacific fisheries are relatively low volume, except in Hawaii, where grouper are important in the traditional cuisine. Grouper populations have been badly depleted in the past, but fisheries management programs have allowed most to recover. That said, some are still depleted, so check a sustainability guide before buying.

There is nothing challenging about grouper's flavor, color, or bones. They are easy to fillet. Their skin, though, is oftentimes very bitter and should be removed before cooking, as it can influence the flavor of the flesh. The meat tends to be lean and exceptionally firm and has a snappy texture. When fresh, grouper have a mild ocean-breeze aroma with a moderate flavor that is initially sweet-briny followed by a sharp and sometimes sour tang and a lingering flavor similar to clams. Their bones and heads make for a particularly resonant and well-flavored stock that adds fullness to chowders or stews.

Scamp is considered the very best grouper, the standard to which all other groupers are held. Averaging 3–5 pounds, scamp are the best tasting, as the flavor is a bit more pronounced, with greater sweetness and an uncommon vibrancy. Unlike many other groupers, the crab-like flavor and texture of the scamp is of equal quality at any size fish. Some of the smallest groupers are the coney, sand perch, and graysby. Usually less than 1 foot in length, these all make excellent panfish. My favorite preparation is to braise them whole in a white wine broth seasoned with woodsy thyme and lemon. Unlike other groupers, the skin of these small ones is neutral tasting and thin enough to serve. Red grouper, which average about 18 inches long, are most common and account most US landings. You're likely find the fish both whole and filleted at the fish counter.

Although grouper is versatile and can be cooked using many methods, it is prone to drying out and becoming coarse when cooked over high heat. Neither is it particularly well suited for salt preserving or smoking. Better preparations include pan-roasting, deep-frying, poaching, and gentle sautéing. Grouper is particularly good in chowders, soups, stews, and braises. If you can't find grouper, suitable substitutions are barramundi, cobia, jack, sablefish, tautog, and tilapia.

(continued)

Braised Grouper à la Barigoule

In this recipe, the grouper and vegetables are braised and marinated in spiced broth.

SERVES 4

  1 recipe Basic Aioli (page 25), made with oil skimmed from the cooked dish

  4 grouper portions, skin off

  Salt

  3 stalks celery, chopped

  2 carrots, sliced

  4 ounces mushrooms, cut in quarters

  2 garlic cloves, thinly sliced

  5 sprigs thyme

  1 teaspoon ground coriander

1½ cups white wine

  1 (14-ounce) can halved artichoke hearts in oil

  ½ lemon, thinly sliced

  1 cup extra-virgin olive oil

  Crushed red chile flakes (optional)

  Crusty bread for serving

Season the fish with salt and let it rest for 20 minutes. In a large pot over medium heat, combine the celery, carrots, mushrooms, garlic, thyme, coriander, wine, and ½ cup of water. Season lightly with salt and simmer until the alcohol smell dissipates, about 5 minutes. Add the artichoke hearts with their oil, lemon slices, and olive oil. Reduce the heat to low. Nestle the fish into the pot so it is barely submerged. If desired, add a pinch of chile flakes. Cover and cook the fish for 12–15 minutes. Remove the pot from the heat and cool to room temperature. The flavors improve if allowed to chill overnight in the refrigerator. Use a ladle to skim off the olive oil, and use it to make Basic Aioli. Serve at room temperature with crusty bread and aioli.

Braised Grouper with Madeira, Rosemary, and Cranberries

SERVES 4

4 grouper portions, skin off

Salt

6 tablespoons butter, divided

2 tablespoons dried cranberries, unsweetened or low sugar

1 onion, thinly sliced

1 fennel bulb, thinly sliced

2 stalks rosemary

1 cup stock or water

½ cup Madeira, a drier style such as Sercial or Verdelho

2 tablespoons chopped fresh chives or parsley

Season the fish with salt and let sit 20 minutes. In a sauté pan over high heat, melt 3 tablespoons of butter. Add the cranberries and cook until they begin to plump. Add the onion, fennel, and rosemary, and season with salt. Cook until the vegetables are slightly browned. Place the fish in the pan and add the stock, Madeira, and a pinch of salt. Bring to a simmer, cover, and reduce the heat to low. Cook until the fish is firm to the touch, about 15 minutes. Remove the fish from the pot, increase the heat to high, and reduce the remaining liquid to a glaze. Add the remaining 3 tablespoons butter, chives or parsley, and black pepper to taste. Stir to combine. Discard the rosemary and serve the fish over the glazed vegetables.

Broiled Grouper with Oregano Flambé

SERVES 4

4 grouper portions, skin off

Salt

1 lemon, zested and juiced

10 sprigs fresh oregano

4 tablespoons butter, cut into pieces

1½ ounces Herbsaint or Pernod

Season the fish with salt and zest and let it rest for 20 minutes. Preheat the broiler to medium and set the rack in the position closest to the heat. In the bottom of an ovenproof dish, arrange the oregano and place the fish on top. Place 1 tablespoon of the butter on top of each portion, slide the dish under the broiler, and cook until done, 7–10 minutes, depending on thickness. Remove from the broiler. Discard the oregano. Add the Herbsaint or Pernod and flambé by lighting it with a match. Sprinkle lemon juice over the fish.

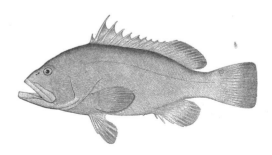

Grouper Ceviche with Sweet Onion

SERVES 4 AS AN APPETIZER

  1 pound grouper fillets, skin off, diced into ½-inch pieces

  Salt

  1 cup lime juice

  2 tablespoons Champagne or sherry vinegar

  1–2 Fresno or serrano chiles, thinly sliced

  1 sweet onion, thinly sliced, rinsed under cold running water, and patted dry

  ¼ cup extra-virgin olive oil

  1 cup cilantro, leaves picked

  Black pepper

  ½ teaspoon ground allspice for garnish

Keep this dish cold at all times during preparation. Season the fish with salt and let it rest for 5 minutes. Combine the fish with the lime juice, vinegar, and chiles and let it rest for 30–40 minutes. Add the onion, olive oil, and cilantro and toss well. Let it rest another 5 minutes, season with black pepper, and garnish with allspice.

Chilled Poached Grouper with Sweet Onion and Herb Salad

SERVES 4

  4 grouper portions, skin off

  Salt

  1 cup white wine

  5 black peppercorns

  5 star anise pods

  Crushed red chile flakes

  1 teaspoon mustard powder

  1 tablespoon sherry vinegar

  ¼ cup extra-virgin olive oil

  1 shallot, minced

  2 cups chervil, leaves picked, and 2 tablespoons chopped chervil or parsley

  1 large sweet onion, thinly sliced, rinsed under cold running water, and patted dry

  10 radishes, thinly sliced

Season the fish with salt and let it rest for 20 minutes. In a pan just wide enough to hold the fish in a single layer, combine 1 cup of water with the wine, peppercorns, star anise, and a pinch of chile flakes. Simmer over low heat for 5 minutes. Season the broth with salt and bring it to 170°F. Add the fish and cook until it is opaque and flakes under gentle pressure, about 5–7 minutes per ½ inch of thickness. Remove the pan from the heat, and cool the fish in the poaching liquid to room temperature. Transfer the fish to a serving plate and flake it into bite-size pieces. Strain 1 cup of the poaching liquid into a small pan and reduce over high heat to 3 tablespoons. Turn off the heat and whisk in the mustard, vinegar, olive oil, shallot, and chopped chervil. Coat the flaked fish with the sauce. Combine the onion, radishes, and chervil leaves. Serve the dressed fish over the salad.

Grouper en Escabeche

In this recipe, the cooked grouper is marinated in vinegar and spices.

SERVES 4–6

1½ pounds grouper, skin off, cut into 3-inch sections

Salt

Flour

1 cup plus 2 tablespoons extra-virgin olive oil, divided

2 carrots, sliced into thin rounds

2 shallots, sliced into rings

4 garlic cloves, smashed

1 tablespoon smoked sweet paprika

1 teaspoon ground coriander

6 sprigs thyme and/or 3 stalks rosemary

1 orange, zest peeled in wide strips

½ cup fruity white wine

1 tablespoon sherry vinegar

¼ cup chopped fresh herbs such as parsley, tarragon, and chives

Baguette for serving

Season the fish with salt and let it rest for 20 minutes. Roll the fish in flour. In a sauté pan over medium heat, warm 2 tablespoons of the olive oil. Place the fish into the pan and cook without flipping until almost done, then flip to finish cooking. Alternatively, the fish can be broiled. Transfer the cooked fish to a baking dish. Heat the remaining 1 cup of olive oil. Add the carrots, shallots, and garlic and cook until the carrots begin to soften. Add the paprika, coriander, thyme, and orange zest and cook for 2 minutes, until the aromas bloom. Add the wine and vinegar, season with salt, and simmer until reduced by half. Add the chopped fresh herbs. Stir to combine and pour over the cooked fish. Cool to room temperature. Wait at least 1 hour before serving. The flavors improve if allowed to chill overnight in the refrigerator before returning the dish to room temperature. Serve with a sliced baguette.

Grouper in Black Pepper Broth

SERVES 4

4 grouper portions, skin off

Salt

2 cups white wine

30 black peppercorns

5 star anise pods

Crushed red chile flakes

4 tablespoons cold butter, cut into pieces

3 tablespoons finely chopped chives, tarragon, or parsley

Season the fish with salt and let it rest for 20 minutes. In a deep pan just wide enough to hold the fish in a single layer, combine 1 cup of water with the wine, peppercorns, star anise, and a pinch of chile flakes. Simmer over low heat for 5 minutes. Season the broth with salt and bring it to 170°F. Add the fish and cook until it is opaque and flakes under gentle pressure, about 5–7 minutes per ½ inch of thickness. Transfer the fish to a warm plate. Strain the poaching liquid and reduce to about ⅓ cup. Whisk the butter into the liquid, stir in the chives, and season with salt.

Grilled Grouper Kebabs with Peruvian Marinade

SERVES 4

1 recipe Peruvian Marinade (page 37)

4 grouper portions, skin off, cut into
   1-inch pieces

Thread 3–4 pieces of fish onto each of four skewers. Place the skewers in a nonreactive baking dish. Reserve one-quarter of the Peruvian Marinade for serving. Pour the remaining marinade over the fish and let it rest for 2–8 hours. Prepare a charcoal grill with a medium fire, concentrating the hot coals on one side of the kettle. Remove the skewers from the marinade and place them on the grill directly over the coals. Cook until the edges of the fish begin to char, about 2 minutes. Lift the entire grill grate and rotate it so the fish rests opposite the hot coals. Cover the grill and continue to cook over the indirect heat until the fish is done, 2–3 minutes. Serve with the reserved marinade.

NOTE *If using a gas grill, preheat all burners to medium. Place the kebabs on one side of the grill and cook until the fish edges begin to char. Turn the kebabs and shut off the burner directly below them. Brush the kebabs with marinade, cover the grill, and continue to cook over the indirect heat until the fish is done, 2–3 minutes.*

Broiled Jerk Grouper Flambé

SERVES 4

1 recipe Jerk Seasoning Mix (page 33)

4 grouper portions, skin off

   Salt

5 tablespoons butter, divided

1½ ounces dark rum

Season the fish with salt all over and the Jerk Seasoning Mix on one side, and let it rest for 20 minutes. Preheat the broiler to medium and set the rack in the position closest to the heat. Coat a baking sheet lightly with 1 tablespoon of the butter, place the fish on it, spice side up, and top each portion with 1 tablespoon of the remaining butter. Slide the tray under the broiler and cook until done, 7–10 minutes, depending on thickness. Remove from the broiler. Add the rum, and flambé by lighting it with a match.

Blackened Grouper

SERVES 4

1 recipe Blackening Spice Mix (page 33)

4 grouper portions, skin off

   Salt

4 tablespoons butter, melted, divided

¼ cup vegetable oil

1 lemon, cut into wedges

Lightly season the fish with salt and let it rest for 20 minutes. Heat a cast iron skillet or heavy-bottomed sauté pan over high heat until it is screaming hot. Combine 2 tablespoons of the butter and all of the oil in a bowl and brush each portion so the fish glistens all over. Dredge one side of each portion in Blackening Spice Mix, coating evenly. Place the fish in the pan spice side down and drizzle the remaining butter-and-oil mixture over the top. Reduce the heat to medium-low and cook without flipping until a dark crust forms, then flip to cook through. Drizzle with the remaining butter and serve with lemon wedges.

Pan-Roasted Grouper with Caramelized Pearl Onions Flambé

SERVES 4

 4 grouper portions, skin off

 Salt

 Black pepper

 5 tablespoons butter, divided

 2 garlic cloves, finely minced

 1½ cups boiled pearl onions, red, white, or mixed, halved

 1½ ounces brandy

 2 tablespoons chopped fresh herbs, such as parsley or tarragon

Season the fish with salt and pepper and let it rest for 20 minutes. In a sauté pan over medium-high heat, melt 2 tablespoons of the butter and cook until golden brown. Place the garlic and the onions in the pan cut side down and cook until they slightly color. Nestle the fish between the onions and reduce the heat to medium-low. Cook without flipping until the fish is almost done, then flip to finish cooking. Remove the fish. Add the remaining 3 tablespoons of butter and ¼ cup of water to deglaze the pan; cook until the water is boiled off. Turn off the heat. Add the brandy and flambé by lighting it with a match. Sprinkle with herbs and swirl to incorporate.

Butter-Basted Grouper with Lime and Ginger

SERVES 4

 4 portions grouper, skin off

 Salt

 6 tablespoons butter, divided

 ¼ cup sliced scallions

 1 garlic clove, minced

 1 tablespoon finely grated fresh ginger

 1 lime, cut into wedges

Season the fish with salt and let it rest for 20 minutes. In a sauté pan over high heat, melt 2 tablespoons of the butter. Place the fish in the pan and sear until colored. Reduce the heat to medium and flip. Add the remaining 4 tablespoons of butter, scallions, garlic, and ginger. Cook until the butter is frothy. Angle the pan toward you and use a spoon to continuously baste the fish with the butter until cooked through. Remove the fish from the pan, strain the butter, and reserve the crisped garlic, ginger, and scallions to scatter over the fish. Serve with lime wedges.

Grouper with Sicilian Herb Sauce

SERVES 4

> 1 recipe Sicilian Herb Sauce (page 32)
>
> 4 grouper portions, skin off
>
> Salt
>
> 2 tablespoons butter

Season the fish with salt and let it rest for 20 minutes. In a sauté pan over medium-low heat, melt the butter. Place the fish in the pan and cook without flipping until almost done, then flip to finish cooking. Serve with Sicilian Herb Sauce.

Sautéed Grouper with Butter, Garlic, Thyme, and Lime

SERVES 4

> 4 grouper portions, skin off
>
> Salt
>
> 4 tablespoons butter
>
> 6 garlic cloves, crushed
>
> 8 sprigs thyme, leaves picked
>
> 2 limes, juiced

Season the fish with salt and let it rest for 20 minutes. In a sauté pan over medium-low heat, melt the butter. Add the garlic and thyme and place the fish in the pan. Cook without flipping until almost done, then flip to finish cooking. Remove the fish, garlic, and thyme. Turn off the heat. Add the lime juice and swirl to combine. Pour the sauce over the fish and garnish with crispy thyme leaves and garlic cloves.

Grouper with Peppers and Mint

SERVES 4

> 4 grouper portions, skin off
>
> Salt
>
> 6 tablespoons extra-virgin olive oil or butter, divided
>
> 1 red bell pepper, seeded and cut into ½-inch strips
>
> 1 yellow bell pepper, seeded and cut into ½-inch strips
>
> 1 Fresno or serrano chile, minced (optional)
>
> 2 garlic cloves, minced
>
> 1 tablespoon sherry vinegar
>
> ½ teaspoon ground mace
>
> 2 tablespoons chopped fresh mint

Season the fish with salt and let it rest for 20 minutes. In sauté pan over medium-low heat, warm 4 tablespoons of the oil or butter. Place the fish in the pan. Cook without flipping until almost done and remove the fish. Add the remaining 2 tablespoons of oil or butter, bell pepper, chile, and garlic, and cook until the pepper softens. Season with salt, vinegar, and mace, and stir. Nestle the fish into the pepper uncooked side down and cook until done. Sprinkle with mint and serve hot or at room temperature.

HADDOCK
Flaky white fish

A staple of northern cuisine, this fish is similar to mild, lean cod. Haddock are generally smaller than cod, averaging only 3–5 pounds. You will find haddock fillets in either the fresh or frozen fish cases. Haddock has a sweeter taste and a smaller flake than cod. Any recipe that calls for cod will be just as good when made with haddock.

Haddock takes to brining very well. Brining is always done to skin-on fillets to make the most iconic preparation of haddock: Finnan Haddie (page 208). Once the brined haddock fillets are air-dried, they then are cold-smoked. The result is better than bacon, especially in seafood chowders.

FRESH

FRESH SMOKED (FINNAN HADDIE)

HADDOCK
Fresh

Sautéed Haddock with Brown Butter and Thyme

SERVES 4

4 haddock fillets, skin off

Salt

1 orange, zested and juiced

6 tablespoons butter, divided

2 garlic cloves, finely minced

10 sprigs thyme, leaves picked

Season the fish with salt and the zest and let it rest for 15 minutes. In a sauté pan over medium heat, melt 2 tablespoons of the butter and cook until golden brown. Place the fish in the pan. Cook without flipping until almost done, then remove the fish and wipe the pan clean. Add the remaining 4 tablespoons of butter, garlic, and thyme. Cook until the butter is dark brown. Add the orange juice and season with salt. Stir to combine. Turn off the heat, and return the fish to the pan uncooked side down to finish cooking.

Fried Haddock en Adobo

SERVES 4

 1 recipe Adobo Marinade (page 34)

 4 haddock portions, skin on, cut into 2-inch pieces

 Vegetable or peanut oil

 Fine ground cornmeal

 Salt

 ½ cup parsley leaves

 ½ cup mint leaves

 Fresno or serrano chiles, thinly sliced

In advance, marinate the fish in the Adobo for 1–4 hours. Then pour 3–4 inches of oil into a high-sided pan. Place over medium-high heat and warm the oil to 375°F. Remove the fish from the vinaigrette and pat it dry. Working with one piece at a time, roll the fish in the cornmeal, making sure to coat it completely and evenly. Place the fish in hot oil and hold it for 5 seconds before releasing it. Repeat the process, cooking the pieces a few at a time. Turn with a slotted spoon if necessary to ensure that both sides become golden and crispy. Remove the fillets as they finish cooking and place them on paper towels to absorb any excess oil. Transfer the fish to a large platter. Scatter the parsley, mint, and chile slices over the top.

Broiled Haddock with Spinach-Parmesan Crust

SERVES 4

 4 haddock portions, skin off

 Salt

 4 tablespoons Mayonnaise (page 29, or store-bought)

 3 tablespoons cooked, drained, and chopped spinach

 2 tablespoons grated Parmesan cheese

 2 garlic cloves, grated

 1 lemon, juiced

Season the fish with salt and let it rest for 15 minutes. Preheat the broiler to high and set the rack in the position closest to the heat. Whisk together the Mayonnaise, spinach, cheese, garlic, and lemon juice. Place the fish on a baking tray. Spread the mayonnaise mixture evenly over the fish. Slide the tray under the broiler. Broil until the fish is done and the topping is browned, about 7–10 minutes, depending on thickness.

Stewed Haddock with Marinara

SERVES 4

 1 recipe Marinara Sauce (page 29)

 4 haddock portions, skin off

 Salt

 Rice for serving (optional)

Season the fish with salt and let it rest for 15 minutes. Pour the Marinara Sauce into a pan just big enough to comfortably fit the fish in a single layer. Nestle the fish into the sauce, cover, and place over low heat. Cook until the fish is flaky, 12–15 minutes. Check the sauce for seasoning. Serve over rice.

Broiled Haddock with Crunchy Ritz Cracker Topping

SERVES 4

> 4 tablespoons Mayonnaise (page 29, or store-bought)
>
> 4 haddock portions, skin off
>
> Salt
>
> 8 tablespoons crushed Ritz Crackers
>
> 1 lemon, zested and cut into wedges

Season the fish with salt and let it rest for 15 minutes. Preheat the broiler to high and set the rack in the middle position. Mix the Mayonnaise, crushed crackers, and lemon zest. Place the fish on a baking tray. Spread the mayonnaise mixture evenly over the fish. Slide the tray under the broiler. Broil until the fish is done and the topping browned, 7–10 minutes, depending on thickness. Serve with lemon wedges.

Pinecone-Grilled Haddock with Citrus and Herbs

SERVES 4

> 1 recipe Gremolata (page 28)
>
> 4 haddock portions, skin on
>
> Salt
>
> Extra-virgin olive oil
>
> 3 pinecones

Season the fish with salt and let it rest for 15 minutes. Prepare a charcoal grill with a medium fire, concentrating the hot coals on one side of the kettle. Lightly brush the fish with oil and place it skin side down on the grill directly over the coals. Cook until the fish begins to char, about 3 minutes. Lift the entire grill grate and rotate it so the fish rests opposite the hot coals. Add 2 or 3 pinecones to the fire, cover the grill, and continue to cook over smoky indirect heat until the fish is done, 4–5 minutes. Serve with Gremolata.

NOTE *If using a gas grill, preheat all burners to medium. Place the haddock on one side of the hot grates. Once it begins to char around the edges, turn off the burner directly under the fish and cover the grill to finish cooking.*

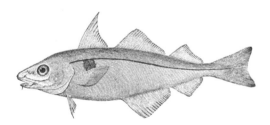

Braised Smoked Haddock in Tomato Sauce

SERVES 4–6

- 1½ pounds Finnan Haddie (at left, or purchased)
- ¾ cup extra-virgin olive oil
- 6 garlic cloves, crushed
- 1 onion, diced
- 2 (14-ounce) cans fire-roasted tomatoes
- 1 lemon, zested and juiced
- 2 bay leaves
-   Crushed red chile flakes, to taste
-   Salt
-   Crusty bread, for serving

In a large pot over medium heat, warm the olive oil. Add the garlic and onion and cook until soft. Add the tomatoes, lemon zest and juice, bay leaves, and chile flakes. Season with salt, cover, and simmer rapidly for 20 minutes. Nestle the Finnan Haddie into the sauce. Cover and cook over low heat until the fish is very tender, about 15 minutes. Remove from the heat and cool to room temperature, then gently rewarm and serve with crusty bread.

VARIATION

+ When cooling the cooked dish, use a ladle to skim off the olive oil and refrigerate it until cold. Use the oil to make Basic Aioli (page 25), and serve it alongside.

Finnan Haddie (cold-smoked haddock)

MAKES ABOUT 1½ POUNDS

- ⅓ cup kosher salt
- ¼ cup sugar
- 5 peppercorns
- 5 allspice or juniper berries
- 1 bay leaf
- 1½ pounds haddock fillets, skin on

Bring 1 cup of water to a boil in a small saucepan over high heat. Add the salt, sugar, peppercorns, allspice berries, and bay leaf and stir until the salt and sugar dissolve. Remove from the heat and add 3 cups cold water to the brine. Refrigerate the brine until it is cold.

Lay the haddock fillets in a nonreactive baking dish in a single layer. Pour the chilled brine over the fish to completely submerge them. Refrigerate for 1½ hours. Remove the fillets from the brine, pat dry, and lay them on a wire rack. Let the haddock dry, uncovered, in the refrigerator for 1–12 hours.

Using a smoker, smoke the fish over the lowest heat possible (under 100°F). Avoid using mesquite or hickory woods, as these have a strong flavor that can overpower the fish. Smoke for 1–2 hours, depending on the intensity of smoke flavor desired.

Remove the fish from the smoker and refrigerate it, uncovered, for 1–24 hours. The Finnan Haddie can be used at this point or wrapped tightly in multiple layers of plastic wrap and frozen until needed, up to 1 month.

Marinated Smoked Haddock

SERVES 4–6

1½ pounds Finnan Haddie (page 208, or purchased)

2 shallots, thinly sliced

¼ cup extra-virgin olive oil

2 tablespoons red or white wine vinegar

¼ cup chopped flat-leaf parsley

2 tablespoons chopped chives or tarragon

1 cup white wine

Combine the shallots, olive oil, vinegar, parsley, and chives in a bowl. In a saucepan over low heat, combine 2 cups of water and the wine. Add the fish and simmer until the fish flakes, 7–8 minutes. Drain the fish and discard the liquid. While the fish is still warm, break it into flakes and place it in the vinaigrette and cover. Chill 12–24 hours before serving at room temperature over sliced heirloom tomatoes or a salad of bitter greens.

Creamed Chipped Smoked Haddock on Toast

SERVES 4–6

1½ pounds Finnan Haddie (page 208, or purchased)

1 bay leaf

3½ cups whole milk, plus additional, if needed

4 tablespoons butter

⅓ cup flour

4 slices Texas toast or sourdough bread

2 tablespoons chopped chives

Crushed red chile flakes

In a saucepan over low heat, simmer the Finnan Haddie and bay leaf in the milk for 10 minutes. Discard the bay leaf. Remove the fish from the liquid and flake it into bite-size pieces. Reserve the poaching liquid. In a sauté pan over medium heat, melt the butter. Add the flour and cook, stirring constantly, for 2 minutes. Whisk in the poaching liquid and cook until thickened, about 10 minutes. Add the flaked fish and gently stir to combine. Add a bit more milk if the sauce is too thick. Serve hot over Texas toast topped with chopped chives and chile flakes.

Smoked Haddock Quiche

SERVES 4

1 (9-inch-wide and 2-inch-deep) pie crust, pre-baked according to instructions on the package

1 pound Finnan Haddie (page 208, or purchased)

3 cups half-and-half

6 large eggs, beaten

3 tablespoons chopped fresh tarragon or 1 tablespoon dried tarragon

1 lemon, zested

Salt

In a pan over low heat, combine the Finnan Haddie and half-and-half and simmer for 10 minutes. Turn off the heat and cool to room temperature. Remove the fish, reserving the poaching liquid, and flake it into bite-size pieces into the pie shell set on a baking tray. Whisk the eggs, poaching liquid, tarragon, lemon zest, and salt. Pour the batter into the shell, slide the tray into a 375°F oven, and bake until set, 30–45 minutes. Cool to room temperature and serve with a salad of spicy greens.

HAKE
Flaky white fish

Hake is a storied New England species with familial ties to cod and practical ties to beer. Aboard the schooners fishing the abundant waters when America was young, the cooks' duties included removing the sounds (air bladders) from hake and preserving them in salt until they could be sold and processed into isinglass, a gelatinous clarifying agent used in the production of ale. In addition to hake's contribution to the beer industry, its flesh has long been a fisherman's favorite for flavor as well. When at peak quality, hake's bright, briny clam-and-cucumber aroma and sweet flavor are balanced with just a hint of sweet and sour. On the other hand, hake does not age well, as it develops a spent-dishrag smell when it's past its prime.

The two most important species of hake in the northern fishery are the white hake and red hake, also known as the squirrel hake. Additional species of hake range throughout the southern Atlantic and Gulf of Mexico, but only Gulf hake grows large enough and is abundant enough to potentially support a fishery.

Hake fillets are almost always cooked with the skin removed because of its small and firmly attached scales. The fillets have a characteristic off-white or beige "stitching" running down their centerline, as though someone had hemmed it neatly. A row of pin bones extends about three-fifths of the fillet's length and causes some loss in yield. Hake has a very small flake and therefore requires a delicate hand when cooking by just about any technique. Hake benefits from a process known as green salting or slack salting, in which the fish is coated with salt for a day or two, not to preserve it, but to firm the texture and punctuate the flavor while maintaining the fresh, or "green," character of the flesh. Once the fish has been green-cured, you simply rinse off the salt, pat the flesh dry, and proceed to cooking it as you choose.

Broiled Hake with Citrus Herb Crust

SERVES 4

> 4 hake portions, skin off
> Salt
> ½ cup panko
> 2 tablespoons chopped parsley
> 1 tablespoon chopped fresh thyme leaves
> 1 orange, zested
> 1 lemon, zested
> 6 tablespoons butter, melted

Season the fish with salt and let it rest for 20 minutes. Preheat the broiler to low and set the rack in the position closest to the heat. Combine the panko, parsley, thyme, orange and lemon zest, and butter. Place the fish on a baking dish and cover with the bread-crumb mixture, patting it down. Slide the dish under the broiler and cook until the fish is done and the crust is lightly browned, 7–10 minutes, depending on thickness.

Broiled Spiced Hake

SERVES 4

> 1 recipe Garlic-Herb Butter (page 20)
> 1 onion, grated
> 2 tablespoons brown sugar
> 2 teaspoons grated fresh ginger
> 1 teaspoon ground mace
> 1 teaspoon ground allspice
> 4 hake portions, skin off
> Salt

Combine the onion, brown sugar, ginger, mace, and allspice. Season the fish with salt, coat with the spice mixture, and marinate 2–8 hours. Scrape off the vinaigrette and discard. Preheat the broiler to medium and set the rack in the position closest to the heat. Place a cast iron skillet over high heat. Place four pats of Garlic-Herb Butter into the pan and place a portion of fish on top of each one. Slide the skillet under the broiler and cook until the fish is done, 7–10 minutes, depending on thickness. Top the fish with the remaining butter.

Hake with Ginger, Garlic, and Scallions

SERVES 4

> 4 tablespoons Mayonnaise (page 29, or store-bought)
> 4 hake portions, skin off
> Salt
> 2 garlic cloves, grated
> 1 tablespoon grated fresh ginger
> ¼ cup minced scallions
> 1 lime, juiced
> Dash hot sauce
> Dash soy sauce

Season the fish with salt and let it rest for 20 minutes. Preheat the broiler to medium and set the rack in the position closest to the heat. Whisk together the Mayonnaise, garlic, ginger, scallions, lime juice, hot sauce, and soy sauce. Place the fish on a baking tray. Spread the mayonnaise mixture evenly over the fish. Slide the tray under the broiler and broil until done and the coating has browned, 7–10 minutes, depending on thickness.

Teriyaki-Glazed Hake

SERVES 4

> 1 recipe Teriyaki-Style Sauce (page 32)
>
> 2 teaspoons Worcestershire sauce
>
> 4 hake portions, skin off
>
> 1 tablespoon sesame oil
>
> ¼ cup sliced scallions for garnish

Combine the Teriyaki-Style Sauce and the Worcestershire sauce. Marinate the hake with ½ of the sauce and let it rest for 20 minutes. Preheat the broiler to medium and set the rack in the position closest to the heat. Brush a baking dish with the sesame oil. Place the fish with the marinade in the dish, and slide the dish under the broiler. Cook, basting with the remaining sauce every 2 minutes until done, 7–10 minutes, depending on thickness. Garnish with sliced scallions.

Chilled Poached Hake with Aioli

SERVES 4

> 1 recipe Basic Aioli (page 25)
>
> 4 hake portions, skin off
>
> Salt
>
> 2 cups white wine
>
> 10 black peppercorns
>
> 10 star anise pods
>
> Crushed red chile flakes
>
> 2 shallots, thinly sliced
>
> ½ cup mint leaves, torn
>
> 1 cup parsley leaves
>
> 1 lemon, juiced

Season the fish with salt and let it rest for 20 minutes. In a pan just wide enough to hold the fish in a single layer, combine 1 cup of water with the wine, peppercorns, star anise, and a pinch of chile flakes. Simmer over low heat for 5 minutes. Season the broth with salt and bring it to 170°F. Add the fish and cook until it is opaque and flakes under gentle pressure, about 4–5 minutes per ½ inch of thickness. Remove the pan from the heat, and cool the fish in the poaching liquid to room temperature. Combine the shallots, mint, and parsley, and sprinkle with lemon juice. Transfer the fish to a serving platter. Serve with Basic Aioli and the salad.

Poached Hake with Sundried Tomato Butter Sauce

YIELD SERVES 4

> 4 hake portions, skin off
>
> Salt
>
> 1 cup white wine
>
> 2 shallots, finely diced
>
> 4 sprigs thyme
>
> 1 orange, zested and juiced
>
> ¼ cup shredded sundried tomatoes, divided
>
> 4 tablespoons cold butter, cut into pieces
>
> 2 tablespoons chopped chives or tarragon

Season the fish with salt and let it rest for 20 minutes. In a pan just wide enough to hold the fish in a single layer, combine 1 cup of water with the wine, shallots, thyme, zest, and juice. Simmer for 5 minutes. Place the fish in the pan so that it is barely submerged, add the sundried tomatoes, and cook until the fish is done, 4–5 minutes per ½ inch of thickness. Transfer the fish to a warm plate and discard the thyme. Strain the poaching liquid, reserving the solids and 1 cup liquid. Reduce the liquid to ¼ cup. Whisk in the butter and simmer until the butter is incorporated. Season with salt and add the chives and reserved sundried tomatoes.

Sautéed Hake with Dill, Anchovies, and Cream

SERVES 4

4 hake portions, skin off

Salt

4 tablespoons butter

4 anchovy fillets

1 lemon, zested and juiced

3 tablespoons cream

¼ cup chopped fresh dill

Season the fish with salt and let it rest for 20 minutes. In a sauté pan over medium heat, melt the butter and cook until frothy. Place the hake in the pan. Cook without flipping until almost done, then remove the hake. Add the anchovies and zest to the pan and cook, stirring, until the anchovies have melted. Add the lemon juice and cream. Season with salt and simmer until the sauce emulsifies and thickens. Turn off the heat, stir in the dill, and return the fish to the pan uncooked side down to finish cooking.

Sautéed Hake with Brown Butter, Almonds, and Parsley

SERVES 4

4 hake portions, skin off

Salt

6 tablespoons butter, divided

2 garlic cloves, finely minced

¼ cup sliced almonds

1 lemon, zested and juiced

2 tablespoons chopped fresh parsley

Season the fish with salt and let it rest for 20 minutes. In a large sauté pan over medium heat, melt 2 tablespoons of the butter and cook until golden brown. Place the fish in the pan. Reduce the heat to medium. Cook without flipping until almost done, then remove the fish and wipe the pan clean. Add the remaining 4 tablespoons butter, garlic, almonds, and zest. Cook until the almonds are golden brown. Add the lemon juice and parsley and season with salt. Stir to combine. Turn off the heat and return the fish to the pan uncooked side down to finish cooking.

HALIBUT
Flaky white fish

Halibut, the largest of the flatfish in both the Atlantic and the Pacific Oceans that can weigh as much as 700 pounds, feed on a wide variety of fish, lobster, and crabs, giving them a nuanced culinary character. The flavor is mild with a somewhat delicate sea-brine aroma that is punctuated with a fresh, bright, herbal smell. Its personality fades and becomes stale pretty quickly. Halibut needs the addition of both sweet and sour flavor components to bring its personality into full focus.

Halibut is fun to work with because its super-thick fillets cook slowly and can be infused with great depth of flavor, whether through a long, slow poach or a slow-roast method. The snowy-white flesh has beautiful, big flakes once cooked and presents beautifully.

Harvested halibut typically weigh between 30 and 80 pounds and can be cut in many ways, as they have four long fillets, two each on top and bottom. Very large fish are cut into four sections and then again into long, 4-inch-wide strips called fletches. Smaller fish can be cut crosswise into steaks or into thick blocks. The skin is edible, though the heat needed to crisp it sufficiently will sacrifice quality of the flesh. When poaching or steaming, it's best to leave the skin on, as it infuses flavor into the flesh and adds body to the poaching liquid.

Female halibut grow larger than the males and are considered to be overall better food fish. The great benefit of finding female halibut is the roe, which is as good as roe gets. It can be cured and smoked or sautéed in butter and herbs. Halibut cheeks are wonderfully different from its fillets, as these sometimes softball-size muscles have a sinewy texture that, when braised, becomes quite elegant. The halibut liver is large, has a milder flavor than those of most white fish, and can be sliced and pan-seared like foie gras. The fatty fins are excellent brined and slowly smoked; the fat and collagen remain in the tissue, yielding a dish that is a slightly crisp, somewhat greasy, and pleasantly smoky offering akin to bacon.

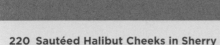
Braised Halibut Puttanesca

In this recipe, the fish is braised in a lively tomato sauce with capers and olives.

SERVES 4

4 halibut portions, skin off

Salt

6 tablespoons extra-virgin olive oil, divided

1 (2-ounce) tin anchovies in oil

4 garlic cloves, sliced

4 dried árbol chiles or ½ tablespoon crushed red chile flakes

2 (14-ounce) cans fire-roasted diced tomatoes

¾ cup white wine

2 tablespoons capers, rinsed and patted dry

¼ cup pitted cured black olives

6 basil leaves, torn, for garnish

Season the fish with salt and let it rest for 20 minutes. In an ovenproof sauté pan over medium-high heat, warm 3 tablespoons of the olive oil, anchovies with their oil, garlic, and chiles, and cook until the anchovies melt. Add the tomatoes, wine, capers, and olives. Bring to a simmer and cook

for 10 minutes. Nestle the fish into the sauce and drizzle with the remaining 3 tablespoons of olive oil. Cover the pan and place in a 275°F oven for 30 minutes. Remove and let it rest for 10 minutes before serving scattered with torn basil leaves.

Braised Halibut in Spiced Coconut Broth

SERVES 4

4 halibut portions, skin off

Salt

3 tablespoons peanut oil, divided

1 lime, cut into quarters

1 red onion, cut into wedges

1 (1-inch) knob ginger, sliced

1 garlic clove, sliced

¼ pound shiitake mushrooms, sliced

¼ cup slivered almonds

½ pound carrots, cut into 1-inch pieces

2 (14-ounce) cans unsweetened coconut milk

1 sprig fresh basil

2 scallions, sliced on the bias

Seared limes for garnish

Rice for serving (optional)

Season the fish with salt and let it rest for 20 minutes. In a large sauté pan over high heat, warm 1 tablespoon of the oil. Add the lime and onion and cook undisturbed until the onion gets a nice char, almost burned, about 3–5 minutes. Remove the onion and lime from the pan. Reduce the heat to medium and add the remaining 2 tablespoons of oil, ginger, garlic, mushrooms, almonds, and carrots. Sauté until the almonds are toasted. Nestle the onion and fish into the pan. Add coconut milk and basil. Cover, turn the heat to low, and cook until the fish is done, about 10 minutes. Discard the basil and ginger slices. Garnish with the scallions and seared limes. Serve with rice.

Broiled Halibut Cheeks with Charred Rosemary Vinaigrette

SERVES 4

> 1 recipe Charred Rosemary Vinaigrette (page 35)
>
> 4 portions halibut cheeks or fillet, skin off
>
> Salt

Toss the cheeks with half of the Charred Rosemary Vinaigrette and marinate 30 minutes to 2 hours. Preheat the broiler to medium and set the rack in the position closest to the heat. Place the cheeks in a baking dish, slide under the broiler, and cook until done, 7–10 minutes, depending on thickness. Serve with the remaining vinaigrette.

Broiled Halibut with Blistered Tomatoes

SERVES 4

> 4 halibut portions, skin off
>
> Salt
>
> ¼ cup extra-virgin olive oil
>
> 4 garlic cloves, sliced
>
> 2 pints cherry tomatoes
>
> 1 stalk rosemary

Season the fish with salt and let it rest for 20 minutes. Preheat the broiler to medium and set the rack in the position closest to the heat. In an ovenproof pan over medium heat, warm the olive oil. Add the garlic and cook until golden brown. Add the tomatoes and rosemary. When the tomatoes begin to blister, season with salt. Nestle the fish into the tomatoes, slide the skillet under the broiler, and cook until the fish is done, 7–10 minutes, depending on thickness. Discard the rosemary.

Broiled Halibut with Caramelized Onions

SERVES 4

> 4 halibut portions, skin off
>
> Salt
>
> 4 large onions, thinly sliced
>
> 4 tablespoons butter
>
> 1 bay leaf
>
> 1 tablespoon red wine or Champagne vinegar
>
> Black pepper

Season the fish with salt and let it rest for 20 minutes. Place a cast iron skillet over high heat. When the pan is very hot, add the onions to the dry pan and cook until slightly charred. Reduce the heat to medium-high and add the butter, bay leaf, and 3 tablespoons water. Season with salt. Cook until the water is evaporated and the onions deepen in color. Repeat as necessary until the onions are deeply browned and very soft. Preheat the broiler to low and place the rack in the position closest to the heat. Nestle the halibut into the onions and slide the pan under the broiler. Cook until done, 7–10 minutes, depending on thickness. Sprinkle the dish with the vinegar and season with fresh cracked pepper.

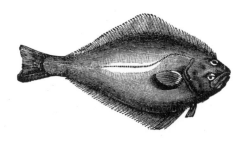

Halibut Gravlax with Dill

SERVES 8 AS AN APPETIZER

> 2 similarly shaped (1- to 1½-pound) halibut fillets, skin on and scored
>
> ¾ cup salt
>
> ¾ cup brown sugar
>
> 2 teaspoons ground mace
>
> 2 teaspoons onion powder
>
> 10–15 sprigs fresh dill

Mix the salt, sugar, mace, and onion powder. Rub the flesh side of each fillet with one-third of the salt mixture. In a glass or ceramic dish lined with plastic wrap, sprinkle a thin layer of the salt mixture and place one fillet skin side down on it. Cover the fillet with dill and place the second fillet, flesh to flesh, on top of the first one. Sprinkle the remaining salt mixture over the skin of the top fillet. Tightly wrap the fish with plastic wrap, place a dish of a similar size and shape as the fish on top of it, and set a couple of cans on the plate to weigh it down. Refrigerate for 12 hours. Flip the fish and refrigerate, still weighed down, for another 12 hours. Remove the weight, unwrap the fish, pour off any liquid that has collected in the dish, cover loosely with plastic, and let it rest for another 24 hours, flipping once. Rinse the fillets with cold water to remove excess salt and brine. Discard the dill. Wrap each fillet individually in plastic wrap and store in the refrigerator for up to 1 week. To serve, thinly slice the fillet on the bias, starting at the thicker end of the fillet and working toward the thinner end. These slices can be laid out as carpaccio, with olive oil and lemon juice drizzled over the top, draped over salads, or served on bagels.

NOTE: *For thinner fillets, decrease the curing time by 12 hours total.*

VARIATION

+ **Balsam Fir– and Orange-Scented Gravlax.** Replace the dill with balsam fir boughs. Add orange slices to cure, but use a layer of fir below and on top of them so that the citrus does not directly touch the flesh.

Broiled Halibut with Parmesan and Chile

SERVES 4

> 4 tablespoons Mayonnaise (page 29, or store-bought)
>
> 4 halibut portions, skin off
>
> Salt
>
> 2 tablespoons grated Parmesan cheese
>
> 2 garlic cloves, grated
>
> 3 dashes Worcestershire sauce
>
> Crushed red chile flakes
>
> 1 lemon, juiced

Season the fish with salt and let it rest for 20 minutes. Preheat the broiler to high and set the rack in the position closest to the heat. Whisk together the Mayonnaise, cheese, garlic, Worcestershire sauce, a pinch of chile flakes, and lemon juice. Place the fish on a baking tray. Spread the mayonnaise mixture evenly over the fish. Slide the tray under the broiler. Cook until the top has browned and the fish is done, 7–10 minutes, depending on thickness.

Teriyaki-Glazed Halibut

SERVES 4

>   1 recipe Teriyaki-Style Sauce (page 32)
>   Salt
>   2 teaspoons Worcestershire sauce
>   4 halibut portions, skin off
>   1 tablespoon sesame oil
>   ¼ cup sliced scallions for garnish

Combine the Teriyaki-Style Sauce and the Worcestershire sauce. Marinate the halibut with ½ of the sauce and let it rest for 20 minutes. Preheat the broiler to medium and set the rack in the position closest to the heat. Brush a baking dish with the sesame oil. Place the fish with the marinade in the dish, and slide the dish under the broiler. Cook, basting with the remaining sauce every 2 minutes until done, 7–10 minutes, depending on thickness. Garnish with sliced scallions.

Citrus-Crusted Fried Halibut

SERVES 4

>   4 halibut portions, skin off, cut into 2-inch pieces
>   Salt
>   Vegetable or peanut oil
>   ½ cup citrus juice
>   Flour
>   Panko

Season the fish with salt and let it rest for 20 minutes. Pour 3–4 inches of oil into a high-sided pan. Place over medium-high heat and warm the oil to 375°F. Dip the fish into the juice, then into flour to coat both sides, then into juice again, and finally into the panko to coat both sides. Place a breaded piece in oil and hold it for 5 seconds before releasing. Repeat the process, cooking the fish a few pieces at a time. Turn with a slotted spoon to ensure that both sides crisp evenly. Remove the fillets as they finish and place on paper towels to absorb excess oil.

Halibut en Papillote (cooked in parchment)

SERVES 4

>   4 halibut portions, skin off
>   Salt
>   4 stalks celery, thinly sliced
>   1 small fennel bulb, thinly sliced
>   1 small onion, thinly sliced
>   1 cup white wine
>   1 bay leaf
>   4 tablespoons butter, plus additional for greasing the parchment, cut into pieces
>   2 tablespoons sherry vinegar

Season the fish with salt and let it rest for 20 minutes. In a shallow pan, place the celery, fennel, onion, wine, and bay leaf, season with salt, and cook until the vegetables are soft and the wine is nearly reduced. Discard the bay leaf. Take four (18-inch) squares of parchment paper, cut into heart shapes. Use butter to grease an 8-inch square area in the middle of each. Evenly divide the vegetables and remaining liquid among parchments, place the fish on top, and add 1 tablespoon of butter to each fillet. Sprinkle each portion with ½ tablespoon of the vinegar. Fold the paper over, then crimp the edges tightly (empanada style) to form a pouch. Bake at 350°F for 10–12 minutes, depending on the thickness of the fillets. Serve in the pouch and slice open just prior to eating.

Poached Halibut with Green Goddess Dressing

SERVES 4

    1 recipe Green Goddess Dressing (page 28)

    4 halibut portions, skin off

    Salt

    2 cups white wine

    ¼ cup white wine vinegar

    1 orange, zest peeled in wide strips and juiced

    10 whole cloves

    10 juniper berries

    2 bay leaves

Season the fish with salt and let it rest for 20 minutes. In a deep pan just wide enough to hold the fish in a single layer, combine 2 cups of water with the wine, vinegar, orange zest and juice, cloves, juniper, bay leaves, and 1 tablespoon of salt. Simmer over low heat for 5 minutes. Season the broth with salt and bring it to 170°F. Add the fish and cook until it is opaque and flakes under gentle pressure, about 5–7 minutes per ½ inch of thickness. Transfer the fish to a warm plate and serve with Green Goddess Dressing.

Roasted Halibut Heads with Apple and Fennel

SERVES 4

    1 or 2 whole halibut heads, collars still attached (4–6 pounds, total)

    Salt

    3 lemons, zested and juiced, divided

    4 teaspoons ground mace or nutmeg

    8 sprigs thyme, leaves picked

    ½ cup extra-virgin olive oil

    10 stalks celery, thinly sliced

    2 onions, thinly sliced

    4 tart apples, cored and cut into wedges

    4 tablespoons Amontillado or cooking sherry, divided

    6 tablespoons cold butter, divided

    Crusty bread for serving

Remove the gills, wash the heads with cold water, and pat dry. Combine the lemon zest, juice of 2 lemons, mace or nutmeg, thyme leaves, olive oil, and 2 tablespoons of salt. Pour the vinaigrette over the heads and let them sit for at least 1 hour and as long as overnight. In a pot of boiling salted water, blanch the celery and onions for 30 seconds. Drain and spread the vegetables and apple wedges in the bottom of a roasting pan large enough to hold the fish heads. Remove the heads from the vinaigrette and place them, eyes upward and collars spread like wings, on top of the vegetables. Pour the sherry over each head and place 2 tablespoons of butter on each head. Place the pan in a 375°F oven and roast for 45 minutes, basting the heads every 15 minutes. Remove from the oven. Whisk the pan juices with the remaining 2 tablespoons of cold butter and the juice of 1 lemon. Serve with crusty bread, the sauce, vegetables, apples, and instructions that if it's not a bone, it's edible.

Slow-Roasted Halibut with Lime-Oregano Butter

SERVES 4

    1 recipe Lime-Oregano Butter (page 21)

    4 halibut portions, skin off

    Salt

    Oil

Season the fish with salt and let it rest for 20 minutes. Lightly oil a baking dish and place the fish into the dish. Place 1 tablespoon of Lime-Oregano Butter on top of each portion. Roast at 275°F for 20–25 minutes per inch of thickness. Serve with the remaining butter on top.

Pan-Roasted Halibut with Caramelized Pearl Onions Flambé

SERVES 4

  4 halibut portions, skin off

  Salt

  Black pepper

  5 tablespoons butter, divided

  1½ cups boiled pearl onions, red, white, or mixed, halved

  1½ ounces brandy

  2 tablespoons chopped parsley or tarragon

Season the fish with salt and pepper and let it rest for 20 minutes. In a sauté pan over medium-high heat, melt 2 tablespoons of the butter and cook until golden brown. Place the onions in the pan cut side down and cook until they slightly color. Nestle the fish between the onions and reduce heat to medium-low. Cook without flipping until the fish is almost done, then flip to finish cooking. Remove the fish. Add the remaining 3 tablespoons water and ¼ cup of water to deglaze the pan, and cook until the water is boiled off. Turn off the heat. Add the brandy and flambé by lighting it with a match. Sprinkle with herbs and swirl to incorporate.

Sautéed Halibut Cheeks in Sherry Pan Sauce

SERVES 4

  1 pound halibut cheeks

  Salt

  6 tablespoons extra-virgin olive oil

  4 garlic cloves, thinly sliced

  ½ cup Amontillado or Palo Cortado sherry

  2 tablespoons chopped fresh parsley

  Baguette for serving

Season the cheeks with salt and let them rest for 20 minutes. In a sauté pan over medium heat, warm the olive oil. Place the cheeks and tongues and garlic in the pan and cook until the garlic is soft. Add the sherry and parsley. Simmer until the alcohol smell dissipates and the sauce thickens. Serve with a baguette.

Pan-Roasted Halibut with Lemon, Olives, and Rosemary

SERVES 4

  4 halibut portions, skin on and scored

  Salt

  6 tablespoons butter, divided

  1 lemon, thinly sliced

  ⅓ cup cured green or black olives

  4 stalks rosemary

Season the fish with salt and let it rest for 20 minutes. In a sauté pan over medium heat, melt 3 tablespoons of the butter. Add the lemon slices, olives, and rosemary. Cook until the lemon slices begin to soften. Add the fish to the pan skin side down. Cook undisturbed until the fish is almost done. Flip the fish to finish cooking. Top each fillet with pieces of the remaining butter. Serve with lemon slices, olives, and crispy rosemary leaves.

Butter-Basted Halibut

SERVES 4

    4 halibut portions, skin on and scored
    Salt
    6 tablespoons butter, divided
    2 garlic cloves, minced
    1 shallot, minced
    2 stalks rosemary, leaves picked
    1 lemon, cut into wedges

Season the fish with salt and let it rest for 20 minutes. In a sauté pan over medium heat, melt 2 tablespoons of the butter. Place the fish in the pan skin side down and cook until the edges begin to crisp. Flip the fish. Add the remaining 4 tablespoons of butter, garlic, shallot, and rosemary. Heat until the butter is frothy, angle the pan toward you, and use a spoon to continuously baste the fish with butter until cooked through. Remove the fish from the pan. Strain the butter; reserve the crisped garlic, shallot, and rosemary; and scatter them over the fish. Serve with lemon wedges.

Sautéed Halibut with Brown Butter and Lemon

SERVES 4

    4 halibut portions, skin off
    Salt
    6 tablespoons butter, divided
    2 garlic cloves, finely minced
    2 lemons, cut into segments

Season the fish with salt and let it rest for 20 minutes. In a sauté pan over medium heat, melt 2 tablespoons of the butter and cook until golden brown. Place the fish in the pan. Cook without flipping until almost done, then remove the fish and wipe the pan clean. Add the remaining 4 tablespoons of butter and cook until dark brown. Add the garlic and lemon segments and season with salt. Stir to combine. Turn off the heat and return the fish to the pan uncooked side down to finish cooking.

Steamed Halibut with Orange and Star Anise

SERVES 4

    4 halibut portions, skin off
    Salt
    1 orange, thinly sliced
    4 fennel fronds or celery stalks
    2 star anise pods
    ½ cup white wine
    ½ tablespoon white wine vinegar
    4 tablespoons butter, melted

Season the fish with salt and let it rest for 20 minutes. In a wide, shallow pot over low heat, place the orange slices, fennel, and star anise to create a raft for the fish. Add the wine, vinegar, and enough water to cover the bottom of the pot. Bring to a simmer. Place the fish on top of the aromatics, cover, and cook until done, about 10–12 minutes. Remove the fish. Serve each portion with 1 tablespoon of butter and a spoonful of the remaining cooking liquid drizzled over it.

HERRING
Small silver fish

It's astonishing that these small, delicious fish barely register on modern American culinary radar. American eaters are missing the boat, because these small fish offer very dynamic culinary possibilities. When herring are fresh, the flavor is similar to perch, with a distinctly malty, spicy, and acidic character. They are at their very best just prior to spawning, when their fat content can reach as high as 20 percent. Because of this richness, herring can also go rancid pretty quickly, so it's best to cook or cure them very quickly after acquiring them.

Herring have deciduous scales, so named as they slough off as easily as leaves from an October tree. Their flesh is quite tender in texture, and special care needs to be taken with whole fish so as not to rip the delicate belly or scrape the skin off the fillets. I like to firm the texture by conditioning the meat under a thin coating of salt for up to 30 minutes before cooking. Or, if the recipe is amenable, I will paint the fillets with lemon juice and a light seasoning of salt. Either way, the salt does not need to be washed off prior to preparation.

The high fat content of the fish means it can handle high-heat cooking methods like broiling, frying, and grilling. The extreme heat renders the fat, which bastes the skin as it crisps and chars, while the meat inside remains moist and rich in flavor. After removing them from the heat, I'll then marinate them with lots of chopped herbs mixed with a scant bit of olive oil and a bit of sherry vinegar to highlight the fish's natural flavors.

Broiled Herring with Almond and Mace

SERVES 4

 4 herring portions, whole and dressed, or fillets, skin on

 Salt

 6 tablespoons butter, softened

 ¼ cup almonds, finely chopped

 ½ teaspoon mace

 1 lemon, cut into wedges

Season the fish with salt and let it rest for 20 minutes. Preheat the broiler to high and set the rack in the position closest to the heat. Combine the butter, almonds, and mace. Place the fish on a baking tray and coat with the almond mixture. Slide the tray under the broiler and cook until done, about 7 minutes for dressed or 3–5 minutes for fillets. Serve with lemon wedges.

Whole Grilled Herring with Mint

SERVES 4

> 1 recipe Mint-Mustard Vinaigrette (page 36)
>
> 4 stalks rosemary, leaves picked and bruised with the back of a knife
>
> 2 pounds herring, whole and dressed
>
> 2 apples, quartered and thinly sliced
>
> 10 radishes, thinly sliced

Mix the Mint-Mustard Vinaigrette with the rosemary leaves. Reserve half of the vinaigrette to use as sauce, and pour half over the fish and let marinate at least 1 hour and as long as overnight. Prepare a charcoal grill with a medium fire, concentrating the hot coals on one side of the kettle. Remove the fish from the vinaigrette and place them on the grill over the hot coals. Cook until the skin begins to crisp, about 2–3 minutes. Flip the fish and brush with any remaining marinade. Lift the entire grill grate and rotate it so the fish rest opposite the hot coals. Cover the grill and continue to cook over this indirect heat until the fish are done, another 3–5 minutes. Toss the apples and radish with the remaining vinaigrette. Remove the fish from the grill and scatter the apples over the top. Drizzle with any remaining vinaigrette.

NOTE *If using a gas grill, preheat all burners to medium-high. Place the herring on one side of the hot grates. Once they begin to char around the edges, turn off the burner directly under the fish and cover the grill to finish cooking.*

Pickled Herring

SERVES 4–6 AS AN APPETIZER

> 1 pound herring fillets, skin on
>
> 2 tablespoons kosher salt
>
> 1 tablespoon sugar
>
> 1½ cups red or white wine vinegar
>
> 2 medium-size crisp apples, such as Honeycrisp, chopped fine
>
> 1 large onion, thinly sliced
>
> 20 peppercorns
>
> 1 tablespoon fennel seeds
>
> ¼ cup slivered almonds
>
> 4 bay leaves

Soak the herring in cold water and kosher salt for 12 hours. Remove the fish from the brine and fillet. Discard the brine. Mix the sugar and vinegar. Combine all other ingredients in a bowl. Place the fish in a jar or small porcelain dish in a single layer. Then place the apple-and-onion mixture on top of the fish. Pour the vinegar mixture over the layers to cover. Cover the container and refrigerate. The herring will be ready to use after 24 hours (or after 48 hours if a firmer texture is desired). The herring will keep up to 4 days in the refrigerator.

VARIATIONS

+ **Spicy Pickled Herring.** Add several dried chiles to the pickle mix.

+ **Dill Pickled Herring.** Add ¼ cup chopped fresh dill to the pickle mix.

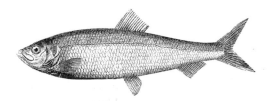

Broiled Whole Herring with Lemon and Herbs

SERVES 4

> 2 pounds herring, whole and dressed
>
> Salt
>
> 5 stalks rosemary
>
> 5 sprigs thyme
>
> 1 lemon, thinly sliced
>
> 4 tablespoons butter, melted

Season the fish with salt and let it rest for 20 minutes. Preheat the broiler to high and set the rack in the position closest to the heat. Line a baking dish with the rosemary and thyme and top with the lemon slices. Place the fish on top of the lemons, drizzle with butter, and slide the tray under the broiler. Broil until the skin is charred, and then gently flip the fish and cook another couple of minutes, about 7–8 minutes total.

Pickled Herring in Sour Cream

SERVES 4 AS AN APPETIZER

> 1 recipe Pickled Herring (page 223) or store-bought
>
> 1 onion, thinly sliced
>
> 1 fennel bulb, thinly sliced
>
> Salt
>
> 1 cup sour cream
>
> 1 tablespoon Dijon mustard
>
> 2 tablespoons chopped fresh tarragon, chives, or parsley
>
> 1 lemon, juiced

Slice the pickled herring into 1-inch segments. Quickly blanch the onion and fennel in salted water until just beginning to soften. Drain and cool. Combine the vegetables with the sour cream, mustard, tarragon, and lemon juice. Season with salt and mix with the herring pieces.

Let it rest for 4 hours and up to overnight. Serve over salads or on rye toast with fresh herbs and a drizzle of olive oil.

Herring en Saor (sweet-sour vinaigrette)

SERVES 4 AS AN APPETIZER

> 2 pounds herring, whole and dressed, or 1 pound fillets, skin on and scored
>
> Salt
>
> ¾ cup extra-virgin olive oil, divided
>
> 3 tablespoons pine nuts or slivered almonds
>
> 2 tablespoons raisins
>
> 1 small onion, thinly sliced
>
> 1 red bell pepper, finely diced
>
> 1 small eggplant, ½-inch dice, about 2 cups
>
> ¼ cup red wine vinegar
>
> 1 tablespoon brown sugar
>
> Baguette for serving

Season the fish with salt and let them rest for 20 minutes. In a sauté pan over medium heat, warm ¼ cup of the olive oil. Place the fish in the pan skin side down and cook without flipping until almost done, then flip and finish cooking. Remove the fish from the pan. Add the remaining ½ cup of olive oil over high heat. Add the pine nuts and raisins and cook until the pine nuts are golden brown and the raisins plump. Add the onion and red bell pepper and cook until the peppers begin to soften. Add the eggplant and cook until it has softened and has absorbed much of the oil. Stir in vinegar and brown sugar, and season with salt. Turn off the heat and nestle the fish into the sauce. This dish is best if allowed to marinate overnight in the refrigerator and then brought to room temperature before serving. At a minimum, let it sit at least 1 hour before serving at room temperature with slices of baguette.

JACKS
Fillet fish, meaty dense fish (some species)

Jacks can be found in temperate waters all over the world and are generally considered to be a fabulous fish to eat. Identifying the species of the extended jack family can feel like a shell game. Individual species have many names, and many have nearly fraternal twins swimming in another ocean that are so similar in culinary characteristics that they are rarely distinguished in spite of being different species. These rich fish often pick up another name if they are farmed because they can be raised with even more fat in their fillets.

The pompano (page 314) is the most renowned of the family, considered by many to be a benchmark of quality by which other fish are measured. Pompano is unique enough in this category to warrant a separate section. Outside of this fish, there are some generalities that can be made about the other members of the jack family like amberjack, almaco jack, hamachi, Hawaiian yellowtail, hiramasa, jack mackerel, kingfish, and scad. All jack share a texture that sports a tight flake and a greasy richness. The flesh is generally creamy white with tan undertones, sometimes having a marked orange tint.

They all have a thin layer of red muscle tissue underneath the skin that on larger fish should be removed, as its texture is distinct and its flavor distracting. All members of this family are flattered when salted 1 hour or so before cooking, giving the dense flesh time to become evenly seasoned.

Larger wild-caught jacks like the greater amberjack, mostly caught for sport on both coasts, are extremely susceptible to parasites. They are usually sold as fillets so as to guarantee market appeal. These larger fish should not be eaten raw. A quick sear for texture and color followed by a slow finish in a low-temperature oven yields a succulent but chewy texture, almost like that of good heritage pork. The meat's coarse texture makes it particularly well suited for vinaigrettes, as it absorbs flavors well. When cooked, it exudes a subtle stone fruit aroma, and its flavor is pleasantly sour, balanced by a vaguely sweet finish. The amberjack responds differently to various cooking fats. When cooked in butter, it develops a strong mace- or nutmeg-like flavor. When cooked in olive oil, the fish's acidic profile is blurred and its flavor loses much of its allure.

Smaller jacks, both farmed and wild, are popular in sashimi, crudo, and ceviche preparations. They are also great when seared and served rare. Because its defining characteristic is its richness, these smaller jacks are particularly well suited to broiling and grilling, especially over a live fire.

(continued)

Broiled Jack with Mint-Mustard Vinaigrette

SERVES 4

> 1 recipe Mint-Mustard Vinaigrette (page 36)
>
> 4 jack portions, skin off
>
> 1 orange, sliced thinly
>
> Black pepper

Combine half of the Mint-Mustard Vinaigrette with fish and let it rest for 2–8 hours. Reserve the other half of the vinaigrette for serving. Preheat the broiler to medium and set the rack in the position closest to the heat. Remove the fish from the vinaigrette. Place the orange slices on a baking tray and arrange the fish on the top. Season with black pepper. Slide the tray under the broiler and cook until done, 5–7 minutes, depending on thickness. Pour the remaining vinaigrette over the top.

Broiled Jack with Salsa Criolla

SERVES 4

> 1 recipe Salsa Criolla (page 32)
>
> 4 jack portions, skin off
>
> Salt
>
> 3 tablespoons butter, divided

Season the fish with salt and let it rest for 15 minutes. Preheat the broiler to medium and set the rack in the position closest to the heat. Grease a baking tray with 1 tablespoon of the butter and place the fish on the tray. Place a ½ tablespoon of the remaining butter on each portion and slide the tray under the broiler and cook until done, 5–7 minutes, depending on thickness. Serve with Salsa Criolla.

Jack Ceviche

SERVES 4 AS AN APPETIZER

> 1 pound jack fillets from smaller fish, skin off, diced into ½-inch pieces, avoiding any dark tissue
>
> Salt
>
> 1 cup lime juice
>
> ½ red bell pepper, finely diced
>
> 1 small red onion, finely diced, rinsed under cold running water, and patted dry
>
> 1 tablespoon nut oil, such as almond, pistachio, walnut, or roasted peanut
>
> 1 tablespoon chopped fresh cilantro
>
> 1–2 Fresno or serrano chiles, thinly sliced

Keep this dish cold at all times during preparation. Season the fish with salt and let it rest for 5 minutes. Combine the fish with the lime juice and let it rest for 20 minutes. Add the red bell pepper and onion and let it rest for another 10 minutes. Add the oil and cilantro and toss well. Garnish with the chiles.

Jack Crudo with Pickled Ginger and Mint

SERVES 4 AS AN APPETIZER

> 1 pound jack fillets from smaller fish, skin off, sliced on the bias into ½-inch-thick ribbons, avoiding any dark tissue
>
> Salt
>
> 1 tablespoon finely shredded pickled ginger
>
> 5–6 mint leaves, torn
>
> Almond, peanut, or sesame oil

Slice the fish and lay it directly onto serving plates. Season the fish with salt, ginger, and mint and let it rest for 10 minutes. Drizzle with a few drops of the oil and serve cold.

Grilled Jack Sandwich

SERVES 4

> 1 recipe Tartar Sauce (page 32)
>
> 1 cup coleslaw
>
> 4 jack portions, skin off
>
> Salt
>
> Vegetable oil
>
> 4 potato buns
>
> Sliced tomatoes

Prepare a charcoal grill with a medium fire, concentrating the hot coals on one side of the kettle. Season the fish with salt and let it rest for 15 minutes. Drizzle with oil. Place the fish over the hottest part of the fire. Cook until the edges begin to crisp, about 2 minutes. Lift the entire grill grate and rotate it so the fish rests opposite the hot coals. Cover the grill and continue to cook over the indirect heat until the fish is done. Assemble the sandwiches by topping each bun with a piece of grilled fish, Tartar Sauce, coleslaw, and sliced tomatoes.

NOTE *If using a gas grill, preheat all burners to medium. Place the jack on one side of the hot grates. Once it begins to char around the edges, turn off the burner directly under the fish and cover the grill to finish cooking.*

Grilled Jack with Bay Leaf–Garlic Vinaigrette

SERVES 4

> 1 recipe Bay Leaf–Garlic Vinaigrette (page 35)
>
> 4 jack portions, skin off and scored

Reserve half of the vinaigrette for serving. Combine the other half with the fish and let it rest for 2–8 hours. Prepare a charcoal grill with a medium fire, concentrating the hot coals on one side of the kettle. Remove the fish from the vinaigrette and place it directly over the hot coals. Cook until the edges of the fish begin to crisp, about 2 minutes. Lift the entire grill grate and rotate it so the fish rests opposite the hot coals. Cover the grill and continue to cook over the indirect heat until the fish is done. Serve with the reserved vinaigrette.

NOTE *If using a gas grill, preheat all burners to medium. Place the jack on one side of the hot grates. Once it begins to char around the edges, turn off the burner directly under the fish and cover the grill to finish cooking.*

Grilled Jack with Orange-Pistachio Piccata

SERVES 4

> 1 recipe Orange-Pistachio Piccata (page 29)
>
> 4 jack portions, skin off
>
> Salt
>
> Vegetable oil

Season the fish with salt and let it rest for 15 minutes. Prepare a charcoal grill with a medium fire, concentrating the hot coals on one side of the kettle. Drizzle the fish with oil and place directly over the coals. Cook until the edges of the fish begin to char, 3–4 minutes.

Lift the entire grill grate and rotate it so the fish rests opposite the hot coals. Cover the grill and continue to cook over this indirect heat until the fish is done. Serve with Orange-Pistachio Piccata.

NOTE *If using a gas grill, preheat all burners to medium. Place the jack on one side of the hot grates. Once it begins to char around the edges, turn off the burner directly under the fish and cover the grill to finish cooking.*

Jack en Papillote (cooked in parchment) with Fennel, Mint, and Pernod

SERVES 4

> 4 jack portions, skin off
>
> Salt
>
> 2 fennel bulbs, thinly sliced
>
> 1 small red onion, thinly sliced, rinsed under cold running water, and patted dry
>
> 1 cup white wine
>
> 5 tablespoons butter, plus additional for greasing the parchment, cut into pieces
>
> ½ cup mint leaves, thinly sliced
>
> 2 tablespoons Pernod

Season the fish with salt and let it rest for 15 minutes. In a shallow pan, place the fennel, onion, and wine. Season with salt and cook over medium heat until the vegetables are soft and the wine nearly reduced. Take four (18-inch) squares of parchment paper and cut into heart shapes. Use 1 tablespoon butter to grease an 8-inch square area in the middle of each. Evenly divide the fennel, onion, and mint among the parchment hearts, place the fish on top, and add a tablespoon of butter to each fillet. Sprinkle with Pernod. Fold the paper over, then crimp the edges tightly (empanada style) to form a pouch. Roast at 350°F for 10–12 minutes, depending on the thickness of the fillets. Serve in the pouch and slice open just prior to eating.

Poached Jack with White Wine and Basil Sauce

SERVES 4

> 4 jack portions, skin off
>
> Salt
>
> 2 cups white wine
>
> 8 sprigs basil, reserve and thinly slice 4 large basil leaves
>
> 4 tablespoons butter, cut into pieces

Season the fish with salt and let it rest for 15 minutes. In a wide, deep pan, combine 2 cups of water with the wine and basil sprigs. Simmer over low heat for 5 minutes. Season the broth with salt and bring it to 170°F. Add the fish and cook until it is opaque and flakes under gentle pressure, 4–6 minutes per ½ inch of thickness. Transfer the fish to a warm plate and discard the basil. Strain 1 cup of the poaching liquid into a saucepan, place over high heat, and reduce to 3 tablespoons. Turn off the heat, add the butter, and swirl the sauce in the pan to incorporate. Add the sliced basil leaves, season with salt, and spoon over the fish.

Slow-Sautéed Jack with Cinnamon and Black Pepper

SERVES 4

> 4 jack portions, skin off
>
> Salt
>
> 5 tablespoons butter, divided
>
> 1 cinnamon stick
>
> 10 black peppercorns
>
> ¼ cup white wine
>
> 1 lemon, juiced
>
> 1 tablespoon chopped chives or tarragon

Season the fish with salt and let it rest for 15 minutes. In a sauté pan over medium-low heat, melt 2 tablespoons of the butter. Add the cinnamon and peppercorns. Place the fish in the pan and reduce heat to low. Cook without flipping until almost done, then flip to finish cooking. Remove the fish and discard the cinnamon and peppercorns. Add the wine and lemon juice. Raise the heat to medium-high and boil until reduced to a syrup. Turn off the heat, add the remaining 3 tablespoons butter and the herbs, and swirl to combine. Season with salt.

Sautéed Jack with Brown Butter, Garlic, and Thyme

SERVES 4

> 4 jack portions, skin off
>
> Salt
>
> 6 tablespoons butter, divided
>
> 8 thyme sprigs
>
> 2 garlic cloves, finely minced
>
> 1 orange, zested and juiced

Season the fish with salt and let it rest for 15 minutes. In a sauté pan over medium heat, melt 2 tablespoons of the butter and cook until golden brown. Place the fish in the pan. Cook without flipping until almost done, then remove the fish. Add the remaining 4 tablespoons of butter, thyme, and garlic. Cook until the garlic is browned and the thyme has crisped. Add the orange zest and juice and season with salt. Stir to combine. Turn off the heat and return the fish to the pan uncooked side down to finish cooking.

Sautéed Jack with Brown Butter and Walnuts

SERVES 4

    4 jack portions, skin off

    Salt

    6 tablespoons butter, divided

    ¼ cup chopped walnuts

    2 garlic cloves, finely minced

    1 lemon, juiced

Season the fish with salt and let it rest for 15 minutes. In a sauté pan over medium heat, melt 2 tablespoons of the butter and cook until golden brown. Place the fish in the pan. Cook without flipping until almost done, then remove the fish and wipe the pan clean. Add the remaining 4 tablespoons of butter, walnuts, and garlic. Cook until the walnuts are toasted and the butter is dark brown. Add the lemon juice and season with salt. Stir to combine. Turn off the heat and return the fish to the pan uncooked side down to finish cooking.

Sautéed Jack with Mushroom Sauce

SERVES 4

    4 jack portions, skin off

    Salt

    6 tablespoons butter, divided

    2 garlic cloves, finely minced

    1 shallot, thinly sliced

    1 cup finely chopped mushrooms

    ⅔ cup white wine

Season the fish with salt and let it rest for 15 minutes. In a sauté pan over medium heat, melt 2 tablespoons of the butter and cook until golden brown. Place the fish in the pan. Cook without flipping until almost done, then remove the fish. Add the remaining 4 tablespoons of butter, garlic, shallot, and mushrooms. Cook until the shallot wilts, about 3 minutes. Add the wine and simmer until reduced and the sauce is thick. Turn off the heat and return the fish to the pan uncooked side down to finish cooking.

Sautéed Jack with Charred Tomato Vinaigrette

SERVES 4

    1 recipe Charred Tomato Vinaigrette (page 35)

    4 jack portions, skin off

    Salt

    2 tablespoons butter

Season the fish with salt and let it rest for 15 minutes. In a sauté pan over medium heat, melt the butter. Place the fish in the pan and cook without flipping until almost done, then flip to finish cooking. Serve with Charred Tomato Vinaigrette.

Sautéed Jack with Herbes de Provence

YIELD SERVES 4

    1 recipe Herbes de Provence Mix (page 33)

    4 jack portions, skin off

    Salt

    3 tablespoons butter

    1 lemon, cut into wedges

Season the fish with salt all over and on one side with the Herbes de Provence. Press the spices into the flesh and let it rest for 15 minutes. In a sauté pan over medium heat, melt the butter. Place the fish in the pan spice side down and cook without flipping until almost done, then flip to finish cooking. Serve with lemon wedges.

JELLYFISH

Though we have no taste for them in America, jellyfish are in significant demand in Asia, and there is a developing fishery in the southeastern United States to supply them. They have a very subtle flavor but add great texture to a dish. As jellyfish are mostly water and spoil very rapidly, they must be salted and pressed for 2–10 days until dry, at which point they are shelf-stable. Jellyfish are not particularly nutritious but are loaded with collagen and calcium, which earns some credit with health food fans. Dried jellyfish must be soaked overnight in a mixture of water and flavored liquids. Once rehydrated and pliable, they are blanched and used in stir-fries, salads, and fish stews.

Mediterranean Jellyfish Salad

SERVES 4 AS APPETIZER

½ pound dried jellyfish

Salt

2 cups cider or wine vinegar

1 fennel bulb, thinly sliced

4 stalks celery, thinly sliced

2 Fresno or serrano chiles, thinly sliced

¼ cup mint, leaves picked and torn

1 lemon, juiced

4 tablespoons extra-virgin olive oil

Soak the dried jellyfish overnight in enough water to cover. In a pot over high heat, combine 6 cups of lightly salted water and the vinegar to a boil. Blanch the jellyfish for 2 minutes. Drain, slice thinly, and toss with the fennel, celery, chiles, and mint. Dress with the lemon juice and olive oil.

LIMPETS

The limpet is notable for its incredible strength and obstinacy in clinging to rocks. There's not much of a commercial demand for them, if any, because they are so challenging to harvest. But if you have the fortitude to harvest them, limpets that are 2 inches or more can be treated like abalone: the meat removed from the shell and pounded or rolled into thin steaks, then breaded and fried. Their taste and texture are as fine-grained and smooth as the rare and expensive abalone.

To prepare any species of limpet, start by soaking them in fresh seawater or salted water to ensure that any grit loosens and falls away. The most common preparation is simply steaming or boiling them. A 2-inch-diameter limpet needs only 8–10 minutes in the pot to become tender and cooked through. A benefit of this preparation is that limpets exude a delicious and fortifying broth that I serve steaming in a mug with a swirl of butter on top. My favorite way to cook limpets is to place them in a hot cast iron pan with dried fennel stalks and set them aflame (page 233). The residual smolder is a perfect measure of heat to cook the limpets through while perfuming them with a charred and seductive aroma.

Steamed Limpets

SERVES 4 AS AN APPETIZER

> 1 cup Basic Fish Stock (page 61) or water
>
> 1 cup white wine
>
> 4 pounds (2-inch diameter) limpets, washed, dried
>
> 4 tablespoons butter, melted

In a large pot over high heat, boil the wine and stock. Add the limpets. Cover and steam for 8–10 minutes. Remove the limpets and strain the stock. Divide the stock among 4 mugs and add 1 small pat of butter to each serving. Serve the limpets separately with toothpicks and the remaining butter on the side.

Limpets Cooked in Fennel

SERVES 4

4 pounds limpets, washed, dried

Dried fennel stalks

4 tablespoons butter, melted, or
extra-virgin olive oil

Place the limpets shell side down in a hot cast
iron pan and cover them with dried fennel
stalks. Turn on your exhaust fan to high and
set the stalks aflame with a torch or under the
broiler. Cook the limpets for 10 minutes in the
residual heat of the smoldering stalks. Serve with
toothpicks and the melted butter or olive oil.

Broiled Limpets with Garlic Butter

SERVES 4

4 pounds limpets, washed, dried

2 garlic cloves, grated

8 tablespoons butter

2 lemons, 1 zested and juiced, 1 cut
into wedges

Preheat the broiler to high and set the rack in
the position closest to the heat. Place the limpets
shell side down on a broiler pan. Mash together
the garlic, butter, zest, and juice. Evenly distribute
the garlic butter among the limpets. Slide the
dish under the broiler and cook just until the
butter begins to sizzle, 4–8 minutes. They are
done when the meat separates frm the shell Serve
with toothpicks and lemon wedges.

LINGCOD
Flaky white fish, meaty dense fish

Lingcod is a relative of neither cod nor ling. It is actually the most popular member of the greenling family, a diverse, colorful clan of fish that swim mostly in the Pacific Northwest and Alaska. Some greenlings swim on the bottom of the sea, where the lingcod does, while others take refuge in the kelp forests closer to the surface. Historically favored by First Nations people and later by Italian and Portuguese immigrants, these fish, from a cook's perspective, are very similar to Pacific rockfish or cod with dense white flesh that renders large flakes.

Lingcod has a Greek name that loosely translates to describe a long snake with teeth, which exactly depicts its shape. Its large head and bones make a very rich, delicious stock. The heads of larger fish poached or roasted over thyme make an interesting meal, as they contain many different bits and textures of meat, including the well-developed cheeks, tongues, chins, collars, and the thin strips of fatty flesh that run along the top of the head between the eyes (see Roasted Cod Head with Lemon Vinaigrette, page 139).

The very large flake of its flesh makes it good for fish and chips, and its firm texture is well suited to grilling and broiling. Larger fish are often cut into steaks. Lightly salting the flesh for 1 hour and then washing and drying it before any preparation focuses its flavor and makes its texture more uniform for even cooking.

Braised Lingcod à la Barigoule

In this recipe, the lingcod and vegetables are braised and marinated in a spice broth.

SERVES 4

> 1 recipe Basic Aioli (page 25), made with oil skimmed from the cooked dish
>
> 4 lingcod portions, skin off
>
> Salt
>
> 3 stalks celery, chopped
>
> 2 carrots, sliced
>
> 4 ounces mushrooms, cut in quarters
>
> 2 garlic cloves, thinly sliced
>
> 5 sprigs thyme
>
> 1 teaspoon ground coriander seeds
>
> 1½ cups white wine
>
> 1 (14-ounce) can halved artichoke hearts in oil
>
> ½ lemon, thinly sliced
>
> 1 cup extra-virgin olive oil
>
> Crushed red chile flakes (optional)
>
> Crusty bread for serving

Season the fish with salt and let it rest for 20 minutes. In a large pot over medium heat, combine the celery, carrots, mushrooms, garlic, thyme, coriander, wine, and ½ cup of water. Season lightly with salt and simmer until the alcohol smell dissipates, about 5 minutes. Add the artichoke hearts with their oil, lemon slices, and olive oil. Reduce the heat to low. Nestle the fish into the pot so it is barely submerged. If desired, add chile flakes. Cover and cook for 20–25 minutes. Remove the pot from the heat and cool to room temperature. The flavors improve if allowed to chill overnight in the refrigerator. Use a ladle to skim off olive oil and use it to make Basic Aioli. Serve at room temperature with crusty bread and the aioli.

Broiled Lingcod with Charred Rosemary Vinaigrette

SERVES 4

> 1 recipe Charred Rosemary Vinaigrette (page 35)
>
> 4 lingcod portions, skin off

Combine half of the Charred Rosemary Vinaigrette with the fish and marinate for 2–8 hours, reserving the other half of the vinaigrette for serving. Preheat the broiler to medium and set the rack in the position closest to the heat. Remove the fish from the vinaigrette and place on a baking tray. Slide the tray under the broiler and cook until done, 7–10 minutes, depending on thickness. Serve with the remaining vinaigrette.

Sautéed Lingcod with Fennel and Garlic

SERVES 4

> 4 lingcod portions, skin off
>
> Salt
>
> 6 tablespoons butter, divided
>
> 2 garlic cloves, thinly sliced
>
> 1 fennel bulb, chopped
>
> 1 lemon, juiced

Season the fish with salt and let it rest for 20 minutes. In a sauté pan over medium heat, melt 2 tablespoons of the butter. Place the fish in the pan and cook without flipping until almost done, then remove the fish. Add the remaining 4 tablespoons of butter, garlic, and fennel. Cook until the fennel is softened, about 5 minutes. Stir in the lemon juice and season with salt. Turn off the heat and return the fish to the pan uncooked side down to finish cooking.

Marinated Beer-Battered Lingcod

SERVES 4

1 recipe Basic Aioli (page 25)

1 tablespoon red wine vinegar

2 teaspoons onion powder

1 teaspoon garlic powder

Kosher salt

4 lingcod portions, skin off, cut into 2-inch-wide pieces

Vegetable or peanut oil

¾ cup flour, sifted

¾ cup cornstarch, sifted

⅔ cup beer

1 egg, separated

Combine the vinegar, onion powder, garlic powder, and ½ tablespoon of salt. Add the fish and let it rest for 30 minutes. Remove the fish from the vinaigrette. Pour 3–4 inches of oil into a high-sided pan. Place over medium-high heat and warm the oil to 375°F. Make a batter by combining the flour, cornstarch, beer, 2 tablespoons of vegetable oil, and the egg yolk. Beat the egg white to soft peaks and fold it into the batter. Season with salt to taste. Dip one piece of fish at a time into the batter, place it in the oil, and hold it there for 5 seconds before releasing it. Repeat the process, cooking the fish in small batches. Turn with a slotted spoon to evenly render both sides golden and crispy. Remove the pieces as they finish and place on paper towels to absorb excess oil. Serve with Basic Aioli.

Lingcod Poached with White Wine, Shallots, and Pistachios

SERVES 4

4 lingcod portions, skin off

Salt

2 cups white wine

2 shallots, sliced

½ cup toasted pistachios

4 tablespoons butter, cut into pieces

Season the fish with salt and let it rest for 20 minutes. In a pan just wide enough to hold the fish in a single layer, combine 2 cups of water with the wine, shallots, and ½ tablespoon of salt. Simmer over low heat for 5 minutes. Season the broth with salt and bring it to 170°F. Add the fish and cook until it is opaque and flakes under gentle pressure, 5–7 minutes per ½ inch of thickness. Transfer the fish to a warm plate. Strain 1 cup of the poaching liquid into a small pan over high heat, add the pistachios, and reduce the liquid by three-quarters. Turn off the heat, add the butter, swirl the pan to incorporate it, and season with salt.

LIONFISH
Flaky white fish, fillet fish

Lionfish have long-spined fins that drape from its body like willow branches, creating a constellation of crystalline orange-and-black threads and camouflaged webbing. As stunning as lionfish are, this particular member of the mail-cheeked fish family (which is identified by the species' telltale bony face and gill covers) does not belong in any American waters. Though the real story is less entertaining, urban legend has it that during Hurricane Andrew in 1992, just a few specimens of this species were set free from the home aquariums of drug lords living in Miami.

Carnivorous lionfish are decimating juvenile populations of reef-dwelling fish, including such important market fish as snapper, grouper, and parrotfish. As they have with many invasive species, management authorities have established initiatives to eradicate lionfish from their new habitats by creating a market for them. Steps to reduce the number of lionfish in US waters are working mainly because these malicious creatures have a texture that is a perfect cross between meaty monkfish and taut, firm grouper and their flavor has all the sweetness of snapper. It also behaves like flaky white fish in many applications.

Lionfish braise well and are excellent fried as finger-size portions or as part of a fritto misto. Their fillets tend to be quite small and are best when brined in a weak solution before cooking. This step helps maintain the integrity of the flesh and accentuates its sweetness. Adding a little vinegar to the brine enlivens the fish's flavor, especially for preparations in which it is to be deep-fried or breaded and baked.

Stewed Lionfish in Romesco

SERVES 4

    1 recipe Romesco (page 31),
      room temperature

    4 lionfish portions, skin off

    Salt

    Rice (optional)

Season the fish with salt and let it rest for 15 minutes. Pour the Romesco in a pan just big enough to comfortably fit the fish in a single layer. Nestle the fish into the sauce, cover, and place over low heat. Cook until the fish is flaky, 12–15 minutes. Remove from the heat and let it rest for 5 minutes. Check the sauce for seasoning. Serve over rice.

Tempura Lionfish

SERVES 4

> 1 recipe Pickled Chiles (page 29)
>
> 4 lionfish portions, skin off and cut into 2-inch pieces
>
> Salt
>
> Vegetable or peanut oil
>
> 1 cup flour, sifted
>
> 2 tablespoons cornstarch, sifted
>
> 1½ cups seltzer water

Season the fish with salt and let it rest for 15 minutes. Pour 3–4 inches of oil into a high-sided pan. Place over medium-high heat and warm the oil to 375°F. Make a batter by combining the flour, cornstarch, seltzer water, and salt to taste. Whisk until smooth, and use within 10 minutes. Dip one piece of fish at a time into the batter, place it in the oil, and hold it there for 5 seconds before releasing it. Repeat the process, cooking only a couple of pieces at a time. Turn with a slotted spoon to ensure that both sides crisp evenly. Remove the fillets as they finish and place on paper towels to absorb excess oil. Serve with Pickled Chiles.

Lionfish Ceviche

SERVES 4 AS AN APPETIZER

> 1 pound lionfish fillets, skin off, diced into ¼-inch pieces
>
> Salt
>
> 1 cup lime juice
>
> 2 shallots, thinly sliced
>
> ¼ cup toasted pecan pieces
>
> ¼ cup extra-virgin olive oil
>
> 2 tablespoons chopped fresh mint
>
> 1 tablespoon chopped fresh cilantro
>
> 1–2 Fresno or serrano chiles, thinly sliced

Keep this dish cold at all times during preparation. Season the fish with salt and let it rest for 5 minutes. Combine the fish with the lime juice and let it rest for 20 minutes. Add the shallots and nuts and let it rest for another 10 minutes. Add the olive oil, mint, and cilantro and toss well. Garnish with chiles.

LOBSTER

More Americans propose to their beloved over a dinner of lobster than any other food. But America's love affair with the bright red crustaceans was not always a matter of bliss. Native Americans historically understood the value of lobster as available sustenance. But early European settlers only ate them if there was nothing else. It wasn't until the mid-1800s, when lobster canning operations in Maine and continental railroad connections made shipping processed meat and whole lobsters westward possible, that they started appearing widely on restaurant menus and in cookbooks.

Modern refrigeration, cheap air freight, and advanced processing techniques collectively enable cooks to buy lobster in nearly all locations. Given past overfishing and present warming water, most lobsters sold in the United States come from Maine and Canada, where it comprises one of the largest fisheries in North America. The Maine industry has taken great pains to manage this natural resource well.

Cold-water lobsters are available in two seasons: hard-shell lobsters, which are what most Americans outside New England find in markets, are available year-round; and new-shell lobsters, which are newly molted, are available only in the warmer months. Their meat is sweeter, though the edible yield is lower, and traditionally these haven't been shipped out of New England. But if you find yourself in New England in summertime, seek them out.

Whole lobsters should always be purchased and kept alive and kicking until cooked. Be wary of the precooked whole ones sitting in the fish case in a grocery store, because you can't be sure when and under what water conditions they were dropped into the pot. Lobster meat, though, is a different story. It is processed from fresh-cooked or raw just-out-of-the-water lobsters and can be a very high-quality product.

Lobsters should always travel to your kitchen in cold and damp condition, ideally surrounded with rockweed you can use to season the water you'll cook the shellfish in. Dry seaweed will do if rockweed is unavailable.

Boiled or steamed lobster is straightforward summertime fare, but lobster is a versatile ingredient. Grilling is a most rewarding way to cook and enjoy lobster. The work of cracking open the lobster is done ahead of time, making this a much less messy and labor-intensive way to serve it. Lobster pairs well with lemon and butter, but it can also hold its own when served with nontraditional ingredients like linguiça sausage, lots of limes, and spicy dried chiles.

The shells make great stock for the base of soups and sauces. The roe, the dark green jelly on the body that turns coral when cooked, makes a tasty flavored butter you can use to top other grilled seafood. Don't use the light green liver, though; it's full of toxins and should be discarded.

(continued)

Preparing the Lobster

To treat the lobster with respect, it is best to first pierce the head with a knife to kill the lobster before dropping it into the pot. Carefully place the tip of a large knife just behind its eyes. Hold the lobster firmly with your hand at a safe distance, and press down through the shell and rotate the knife handle down to complete the cut. The lobster dies instantly.

Grilled Lobster

SERVES 4

> 8 tablespoons butter, melted, divided
>
> 1 teaspoon ground mace
>
> ½ teaspoon vanilla extract
>
> 1 lemon, zested and juiced
>
> 4 (1¼-pound) lobsters or 4 spiny lobster tails, split (if using spiny lobsters, skip to page 248)

Combine 4 tablespoons of the butter, mace, vanilla, lemon juice, and lemon zest in a small bowl. Keep at room temperature. In a large pot, bring 6 cups of salted water to a boil. Lower the lobsters headfirst into the pot and tightly cover it. Cook for 4 minutes. Remove from the water and cool. Halve the lobsters lengthwise and remove the sand sack just behind the head and the vein running down the tail. Crack the claws with the back of a knife, but do not remove the meat. Prepare a large, hot fire with the coals in the center of the grill. Brush the cut side of the lobsters with the remaining 4 tablespoons of butter and place the lobster bodies, two halves at a time, directly over the coals, cut side down. Grill for about 3 minutes, then use a spatula to flip and place them on the outer part of the grill shell side down. Slather each grilled half lobster with the spiced butter and repeat with the remaining lobsters.

NOTE *If using a gas grill, preheat half of the burners to low and half to high. Place the lobsters cut side down over the high heat and cook for 3 minutes. Flip the lobsters and move them to the medium heat side of the grill to finish cooking.*

Lobster with Zucchini and Aioli

SERVES 4

1 cup Basic Aioli (page 25)

¼ cup extra-virgin olive oil

1 (1-inch) knob ginger, grated

2 garlic cloves, minced

2 pounds zucchini, cut into 1-inch pieces

Salt

2 fennel bulbs, thinly sliced

4 (1¼-pound) lobsters

10 sprigs mint, leaves torn

2 lemons, juiced

In a sauté pan over high heat, warm the oil. Add the ginger and garlic and cook for 1 minute. Add the zucchini and cook until brown, then season with salt and cook until the juices release. Add the fennel and toss. Turn off the heat and let it rest. In a large pot, bring 6 cups of salted water to a boil. Lower the lobsters headfirst into the pot and tightly cover the pot. Cook for 7–9 minutes. Remove the lobsters from the pot and chill. Pick and chop the meat into 1-inch pieces. Dress the lobster meat with Basic Aioli. Toss the zucchini mixture with the mint and lemon juice. Plate and top with the lobster.

Lobster Boil

SERVES 4

8 tablespoons butter, melted, or 1 recipe Basic Aioli (page 25)

1½ pounds small red-skin potatoes

1 pound pearl onions

2 jalapeño peppers

Salt

4 (1¼-pound) lobsters

8 ears of corn, shucked and halved

1 cup fresh herbs, such as basil and mint

In a large boiling pot, place the potatoes, onions, and jalapeños. Cover with 2 inches of water, season generously with salt, and bring to a boil. Cook until the potatoes are almost done, about 8–10 minutes. Lower the lobsters headfirst into the pot and place the corn around the lobsters, submerging the ears as much as possible. Lay the herbs over the top, return to a boil, cover, and cook for 7–9 minutes. Turn off the heat and let it rest for 3 minutes. Strain off the water and dump the whole pot onto a table generously covered with newspaper. Serve with melted butter or Basic Aioli.

Broiled Lobster with Cilantro-Chile-Lime Butter

SERVES 4

1 recipe Cilantro-Chile-Lime Butter (page 20), softened

4 (1½-pound) lobsters

In a large pot, bring 6 cups of salted water to a boil. Lower the lobsters headfirst into the pot and tightly cover the pot. Cook for 5–7 minutes. Remove the lobsters. Once the lobsters are cool, remove the meat from the claws and discard the shells. Use scissors to cut the tail down the center along the top shell. Crack the tail open and remove the meat. Save the empty tail shell. Dice the meat from the lobster tail and claws into ¾-inch pieces and return to the shells. Cover with generous dollops of Cilantro-Lime Butter. Preheat the broiler to high. Place the lobsters meat side up on a tray and broil until just bubbling.

VARIATION

+ Try another compound butter, such as Fennel Butter (page 20) or Sweet Garlic Butter (page 23).

Lobster Mac and Cheese

SERVES 4

4 (1¼-pound) lobsters

1 pound macaroni

6 tablespoons butter

6 tablespoons flour

1 teaspoon ground mace

2 cups milk

12 ounces shredded cheddar cheese, divided

1 cup crushed Ritz Crackers

In a large pot, bring 6 cups of water to a boil. Lower the lobsters headfirst into the pot and tightly cover the pot. Cook for 5–7 minutes. Remove the lobsters and reserve the cooking liquid. Cook the pasta in the lobster liquid according to package instructions. Strain and reserve 1 cup of the liquid. Once the lobsters are cool, remove and chop the meat into ¾-inch pieces and set it aside. Heat the butter in a small saucepan over medium-high heat. Add the flour and cook, whisking constantly, until it is smooth and a light roux forms, about 6 minutes. Reduce the heat to medium and continue to cook the roux, stirring regularly, until it is a deep caramel color. Stir in the mace and cook until lightly toasted, about 30 seconds. Add the milk, whisking constantly to incorporate and break up any lumps. Reduce the heat to medium-low and simmer, stirring constantly, until the sauce has thickened and coats the back of a spoon, about 10 minutes. Add the reserved pasta water to thin as needed. Remove from the heat, add 8 ounces of the cheese, and stir to combine. Add the lobster and macaroni and stir until it is evenly coated. Spread the mac and cheese into a serving dish. Combine the cracker crumbs with the remaining 2 ounces of cheese and spread on top. Brown under the broiler.

Lobster Newburg

SERVES 4

4 (1¼-pound) lobsters

2 tablespoons butter

2 tablespoons flour

¼ cup Amontillado or cooking sherry

2 teaspoons tomato paste

1 leek, finely chopped

1 carrot, finely chopped

½ cup half-and-half

1 egg yolk

   Salt

2 tablespoons chopped tarragon

In a large pot, bring 6 cups of salted water to a boil. Lower the lobsters headfirst into the pot and tightly cover the pot. Cook for 5–7 minutes. Remove the lobsters and reserve 1 cup of the cooking liquid. Once the lobsters are cool, remove and chop the meat into ¾-inch pieces and set it aside. Melt the butter in a saucepan over medium heat. Whisk in the flour and cook for 2–3 minutes to create a blond roux. Do not brown. Whisk in the sherry and tomato paste until smooth. Add the lobster cooking liquid and whisk until fully incorporated. Add the leek and carrot and cook until just tender, about 4 minutes. Stir in the half-and-half and bring to a boil. Reduce the heat and cook until sauce thickens, 5–6 minutes. Remove from the heat and stir in the lobster meat.

In a separate bowl, whisk the egg yolk with ½ cup of the liquid. Add the yolk mixture to the lobster mixture and stir to combine. Season with salt and tarragon. Divide mixture into four (6-ounce) ramekins. Place the ramekins into a large roasting pan and place in 350°F oven. Fill roasting pan with 1 inch of boiling water. Cook for 20–25 minutes, until it is bubbling hot and the sauce is lightly set.

Lobster Paella

SERVES 4-6

> 1 recipe Basic Aioli (page 25)
>
> 10 saffron threads
>
> 7 cups shellfish (lobster) stock (page 61) or chicken stock, divided
>
> 1 bay leaf
>
> ½ pound chorizo, raw, sliced
>
> 2 (1¼-pound) lobsters
>
> ⅓ cup extra-virgin olive oil
>
> ¼ cup slivered almonds
>
> 3 garlic cloves, sliced
>
> 2 tablespoons smoked sweet paprika
>
> 2 tablespoons tomato paste
>
> 1½ cups Arborio rice
>
> Salt
>
> ½ cup peas, blanched
>
> 1 beefsteak tomato, cut into wedges

Toast the saffron in a dry stock pot for 30 seconds until aromatic. Add 4 cups of the stock and the bay leaf and bring to a simmer. Poach the chorizo in the stock for 5 minutes; reserve. Bring the water to a boil over high heat and lower the lobsters headfirst into the pot and tightly cover. Cook for 5–7 minutes. Remove the lobsters and let them cool. Reserve the liquid. Working over a bowl in order to catch all juices, remove the meat from the lobsters. Reserve the meat and strain the collected juices back into the pot. In a paella pan over medium heat, warm the olive oil. Add the almonds, garlic, and paprika, and cook until the garlic is aromatic and the almonds are toasted, about 3–5 minutes.

Reduce the heat to low, add the tomato paste, and cook for 5 minutes. Add the reserved lobster cooking stock to the paella pan. Bring to a boil. Add the rice, stir to submerge, and season with salt. Boil the rice for 10 minutes or until it has absorbed most of the stock. Add the remaining stock and arrange the sausage, lobster, peas, and tomatoes around the paella pan. Cook another 7–10 minutes until the rice is al dente. Remove from the heat, cover, and let it rest for 5 minutes. Serve with generous spoonfuls of Basic Aioli.

Maine Lobster Roll

SERVES 4

> ¼ cup Mayonnaise (page 29, or store-bought)
>
> 4 (1¼-pound) lobsters
>
> Salt
>
> Butter
>
> 4 split-top potato hot dog buns
>
> 1 lemon, cut into wedges

In a large pot, bring 6 cups of salted water to a boil. Lower the lobsters headfirst into the pot and tightly cover the pot. Cook for 7–9 minutes. Remove the lobsters and cool. Remove the meat from the shells and roughly chop into ¾-inch pieces. Mix the meat with the Mayonnaise and season with salt. Butter and toast the buns. Divide the lobster mixture among the buns. Serve with lemon wedges.

Connecticut-Style Lobster Roll

SERVES 4

- 4 (1¼-pound) lobsters
- 4 tablespoons butter, plus more for toasting the buns
- 1 tablespoon chives, chopped
- Butter
- 4 split-top hot dog buns

In a large pot, bring 6 cups of salted water to a boil. Lower the lobsters headfirst into the pot and tightly cover the pot. Cook for 7–9 minutes. Remove the lobsters and let cool. Remove the meat and roughly chop into ¾-inch pieces. Melt 4 tablespoons of butter in a sauté pan over low heat. Add the lobster meat, cook until heated through, and stir in the chives. Season with salt. Butter and toast the buns. Divide the lobster mixture among the buns.

Lobster Rossejat

SERVES 4–6

- 1 recipe Basic Aioli (page 25)
- 1 pound spaghetti
- 3½ tablespoons extra-virgin olive oil, divided
- 2 (1¼-pound) lobsters
- 5–10 garlic cloves, chopped
- 1 tablespoon smoked sweet paprika
- ¼ cup chopped herbs, such as chervil or tarragon
- 1 lemon, cut into wedges

Break the spaghetti into roughly 1-inch pieces and place on a baking sheet. Drizzle with 1½ teaspoons of the olive oil and toss to coat. Bake in a 325°F oven, tossing every few minutes, until deep brown all over, 10–12 minutes. In a large pot, bring 6 cups of lightly salted water to a boil. Lower the lobsters headfirst into the pot and tightly cover the pot. Cook for 7–9 minutes. Remove from the heat, transfer the lobsters to a bowl, and reserve the cooking water. Working over the bowl to catch all juices, remove the meat from the lobsters, cut the lobster tails into small medallions, and halve the claws. Strain the collected juices back into the cooking water. Bring to a gentle simmer.

In a paella or wide enameled pan over medium heat, warm the remaining 2 tablespoons of olive oil. Add the garlic and cook until it begins to brown. Add the paprika and cook, stirring, for 30 seconds. Add the toasted noodles and toss to coat with oil. Add the hot lobster broth, 3 cups at a time, allowing it to come to a full boil and absorb into the noodles between additions. Heat the broiler to high. Slide the entire pan directly under the hot broiler. Cook until the noodles are dry and curl up with crispy ends, 5–7 minutes.

Remove the pan from the broiler. Neatly arrange the lobster meat around the pan. Place a very large dollop of Basic Aioli in the center of the dish and scatter the herbs over top. Serve with the remaining aioli and lemon wedges.

Lobster Thermidor

SERVES 4

    4 (1¼-pound) lobsters
    4 tablespoons butter
    ¼ pound trimmed and sliced mushrooms
    1 teaspoon smoked sweet paprika
    Salt
    ½ cup half-and-half, scalded
    1 tablespoon Amontillado or cooking sherry
    2 egg yolks

In a large pot, bring 6 cups of salted water to a boil. Lower the lobsters into the pot headfirst and tightly cover the pot. Cook for 5–7 minutes. Remove the lobsters and reserve ½ cup of the cooking liquid and keep it warm. Once the lobsters are cool, remove the meat from the claws, discard the shells, separate the body from the tail, and discard the body. Using scissors, cut the tail in half and remove the meat. Rinse and reserve the empty tail shell halves. Chop all of the lobster meat into ¾-inch pieces.

In a saucepan over medium-low heat, melt the butter. Sauté the mushrooms in the butter until browned. Add the paprika and season with salt. Add the half-and-half and sherry and cook an additional 5 minutes. In a separate bowl, whisk the egg yolks with ½ cup of the reserved lobster cooking liquid. Add the yolk mixture and lobster meat to the mushroom mixture and stir to combine. Spoon the mixture into the reserved shells. Preheat the broiler to high. Place the lobsters meat side up on a tray and broil until just bubbling, about 4–5 minutes. Spoon any remaining sauce over the top before serving.

Lobster Waldorf Salad

SERVES 4

    ½ cup Basic Aioli (page 25) or Mayonnaise (page 29, or store-bought)
    4 (1¼-pound) lobsters
    1 celery heart, thinly sliced
    1 cup grapes, quartered
    ¾ cup walnut pieces, toasted
    2 tablespoons chopped tarragon
    Mixed greens for serving

In a large pot, bring 6 cups of salted water to a boil. Lower the lobsters headfirst into the pot and tightly cover the pot. Cook for 7–9 minutes. Remove the lobsters from the water and cool. Pick the lobster meat, chop the tails and knuckle meat into ¾-inch pieces, and leave the claws whole. Combine the chopped meat with the celery heart, grapes, walnuts, and tarragon. Toss with the Basic Aioli or Mayonnaise. Plate with the mixed greens and top with the reserved claws.

Thanksgiving Stuffed Lobster

SERVES 4

- 4 (1¼-pound) lobsters
- 4 tablespoons butter
- ⅓ cup finely diced dried apricots
- 2 tablespoons pine nuts
- 1½ cups diced celery
- 1½ cups diced onion
- 1½ cups diced fennel
- ¼ cup chopped parsley
- Crushed red chile flakes
- 10 ounces brioche, cubed and toasted
- Salt
- Black pepper
- 8–16 stalks rosemary

In a large pot, bring 6 cups of salted water to a boil. Lower the lobsters headfirst into the pot and tightly cover the pot. Cook for 7 minutes. Remove the lobsters and reserve the cooking liquid. Once the lobsters are cool, working over a bowl to catch all the juices, remove the meat from the claws and discard the shells. Separate the head from the tail and remove the insides of the body, leaving just the outer shell. Using scissors, cut the tail in half and remove the meat. Rinse and reserve the empty tail shell halves. Chop the lobster tail meat into ¾-inch pieces.

In a large sauté pan over medium-high heat, melt the butter. Add the apricots and pine nuts and cook until the apricots have darkened and the pine nuts have toasted to a deep brown color. Add the celery, onion, and fennel and cook until the celery is softened, 3–5 minutes. Add the parsley and a pinch of chile flakes. Season with salt and pepper. Add the brioche and toss to combine. Add the reserved lobster juices from the bowl and 3 cups of the reserved cooking liquid, and cook over low heat until the bread has absorbed all of the liquid, 3–5 minutes.

Toss the diced meat into the stuffing. Position the tail and body shells together on a sheet tray. Divide the stuffing among the shells. Place rosemary stalks under the shells to help stabilize them. Set the broiler to medium-high and slide the tray under it. Cook until the stuffing is crisped and golden brown, 7–10 minutes. Top each lobster half with a reserved claw. Cook for 30 seconds more to warm through. Serve immediately.

Ember-Roasted Lobster Tails

SERVES 4

> 4 (6-ounce) lobster tails (either Maine or spiny)
>
> 2 lemons, halved
>
> Salted butter, melted

Prepare a charcoal grill with all of the coals on one side. When the coals have burned down to embers, place the lobster tails directly on the hot coals, hard-shell side down. Place the lemons cut side down on the grill grate. Cover the grill and cook for 6–10 minutes, until the shells are bright red and the meat turns opaque. A little charring is preferred. The lemons will be charred at this point, too. Serve the tails with the grilled lemons and melted butter.

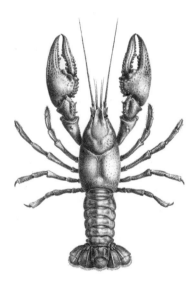

Lobster and Linguine with Chive and Tomato

SERVES 4

> 4 (1¼-pound) lobsters
>
> 4 tablespoons extra-virgin olive oil
>
> 1 onion, diced
>
> 4 garlic cloves, sliced
>
> 6 plum tomatoes, chopped
>
> 1 pound linguine
>
> Salt
>
> Chopped fresh chives

In a large pot, bring 6 cups of salted water to a boil. Lower the lobsters headfirst into the pot and tightly cover the pot. Cook for 7–9 minutes. Remove the lobsters from the pot and reserve the cooking water. Working over a bowl to catch all juices, pick the lobster meat from the tail and cut it into ½-inch dice. Remove the claw meat from the shell and reserve. Strain and reserve the lobster juices.

In a saucepan over medium heat, heat the olive oil and sauté the onion and garlic until aromatic, about 2 minutes. Add the tomatoes, reserved juices, and 1 cup of the reserved cooking water. Reduce the heat to a simmer and cook until the tomatoes begin to break down and the onion softens, about 5 minutes. Remove from the heat. Add a good amount of salt to the remaining lobster cooking water and cook the pasta according to the package instructions. When the pasta is al dente, strain off all but ½ cup of the cooking water. Add the pasta and reserved water to the tomato sauce and continue to cook the pasta for another minute, until it has absorbed most of the liquid. Remove from the heat and toss in the chopped meat. Place the claws on top of the pasta and garnish with chives.

LOBSTER, SPINY

The Caribbean spiny lobster that lives in the Gulf and the California spiny lobster in the Pacific comprise fairly significant fisheries in those parts of the country. But they weigh in at just a fraction of the Maine lobster haul. These species have a recognizable elongated lobster shape but no claws. The tail is the only edible part of the spiny lobster worth the effort of eating, and it presents beautifully, as the shell can be split along the back by scissors and the meat removed and splayed within the shell, brushed with seasoned butter, and broiled. These tails have a much firmer, more muscular texture than Maine lobster tails once cooked. They are almost always sold as frozen tails and should be thawed just prior to cooking.

Broiled Spiny Lobster with Warm Grapefruit Vinaigrette

SERVES 4

    4 (6-ounce) spiny lobster tails, halved
        lengthwise
    Salt
    2 tablespoons butter
    3 garlic cloves
    1 shallot, diced
    1 grapefruit, zested and flesh cut into
        small segments
    ½ cup extra-virgin olive oil
    2 tablespoons chopped tarragon
    1 tablespoon balsamic vinegar

Season the cut side of the tails with salt. Mix together the butter, garlic, shallot, zest, and olive oil. Slather half of the mixture on the tails. Warm the remaining mixture over low heat and add the grapefruit segments, tarragon, and vinegar. Set the broiler to medium-high, arrange the tails on a baking tray cut side up, and slide the tray under the broiler. Cook the tails until the meat is opaque and the butter is bubbling, 6–8 minutes. Drizzle the tails with the vinaigrette and serve hot or at room temperature.

Grilled Spiny Lobster with Anchovy-Almond Butter

SERVES 4

> 1 recipe Anchovy-Almond Butter (page 19)
>
> 4 (6-ounce) spiny lobster tails, halved lengthwise
>
> Salt
>
> 1 tablespoon vegetable oil
>
> 1 lime, cut into wedges

Season the lobster tails with salt. Prepare a large, hot fire with the coals in the center of the grill. Brush the cut side of the lobsters with oil and place the lobster tails directly over the coals, cut side down. Grill for about 3 minutes until the meat is set, then use a spatula to flip and place them on the outer part of the grill and spread Anchovy-Almond Butter on the meat. Cook until the butter sizzles, 4–6 minutes. Serve with lime wedges.

NOTE *If using a gas grill, preheat half of the burners to medium and half to high. Place the lobster tails cut side down over the high heat and cook for 3 minutes. Flip the lobsters and move them to the medium heat side of the grill. Spread Anchovy-Almond Butter on the meat. Cook until the butter sizzles, 4–6 minutes. Serve with lime wedges.*

Poached Spiny Lobster with Tarragon Aioli

SERVES 4

> 1 recipe Basic Aioli (page 25)
>
> 15 sprigs tarragon, leaves removed and chopped, stems reserved
>
> 2 cups white wine
>
> 1 small onion, thinly sliced
>
> 1 fennel bulb, thinly sliced
>
> 2 bay leaves
>
> Salt
>
> 4 (6-ounce) spiny lobster tails, split

Combine the Basic Aioli with the chopped tarragon and reserve. In a saucepan, combine the tarragon stems, wine, onion, fennel, and bay leaves with 6 cups of water and season with salt. Simmer for 10 minutes, until the fennel begins to soften. Bring the liquid to 170°F. Add the lobster tails to the liquid and cook over low heat until the meat is cooked through, 8–10 minutes. Remove the tails from the water, set them on a rack cut side down, and cool to room temperature. Strain the cooking liquid and discard the tarragon stems and bay leaves. Cool the onion-and-fennel mixture to room temperature. Toss the fennel and onion with enough Basic Aioli to barely coat. Remove the lobster meat from the shells, slice it, and return it to the shells. Top the tails with the aioli and serve with vegetables.

MACKEREL
Fillet fish, small silver fish

The culinary history of mackerel in America has been a tale of boom and bust, periods of immense popularity followed by disdain. While our current tastes and modern cuisine do not revere mackerel's confident flavor and firm flesh, it continues to present one of the greatest seafood opportunities to cooks.

They are among the prettiest of fish. Their bright, smooth silver skin magnifies their colorful spots, stripes, and oily sheen. Mackerel swim in almost every ocean in the world. But the ones readily accessible to Americans—the Spanish mackerel with its yellow spots and Boston and chub mackerels with their tiger stripes—are found along all US coasts. Mackerel are available year-round, but they are at peak flavor in fall, after they've spawned in spring and fattened up by predatory eating habits all summer but before they head out to deeper waters for the winter. I don't cook the larger king mackerel very often, though the recipes that follow can be adopted for that fish.

Mackerel meat is equally good served hot or cold. One of my favorite methods is marinating pan-fried fillets in a potent mix of aromatic vegetables and vinegar in the style of Mackerel en Escabeche (page 261). Smoke is one of the best matches to mackerel, as the oily, rich flesh absorbs the flavor and rewards the eater with a moist and meaty bite. It must be hot-smoked so that the flesh is fully cooked. When grilling whole or filleted, it is best to keep the skin on to keep the flesh from drying out. It can easily be peeled off before serving. All mackerel are flattered by acidic ingredients like lime juice, vinegar, or wine. And it is a fish that pairs particularly well with freshly ground black pepper. Among the herbs that complement mackerel are fennel, mint, and rosemary.

Mackerel milt and, even more so, their beautiful orange, cashew-shaped roe makes for fabulous eating. The roe are traditionally cooked like shad roe (page 361) but can be salted and air-dried as bottarga (page 466).

MACKEREL
Fresh

Broiled Mackerel with Rosemary Flambé

SERVES 4

> 4 mackerel portions, skin on
>
> Salt
>
> 1 lemon, zested
>
> 8 stalks rosemary
>
> 4 tablespoons butter, cut into pieces
>
> 1½ ounces Pernod or Herbsaint

Season the fish with salt and zest and let it rest for 15 minutes. Preheat the broiler to medium and set the rack in the position closest to the heat. In bottom of an ovenproof dish, arrange the rosemary in a single layer and place the fish on top. Put 1 tablespoon of butter on top of each serving, slide the dish under the broiler, and cook until done, 5–7 minutes, depending on thickness. Remove from the broiler. Add the Pernod and flambé by lighting it with a match. Allow the alcohol to burn off before serving.

Roasted Whole Mackerel with Citrus and Herbs

SERVES 4

> 1 recipe Gremolata (page 28)
>
> 2 (1½- to 2-pound) whole mackerel, gutted and skin scored
>
> Salt
>
> 4 sprigs thyme or stalks rosemary
>
> 1 lemon, thinly sliced
>
> 1½ ounces Herbsaint or Pernod
>
> 2 fennel bulbs, thinly sliced
>
> Extra-virgin olive oil

Season the fish inside and out with salt and stuff the belly cavity with the thyme and lemon slices. Pour the Herbsaint over the fish and let it rest for 30 minutes to 2 hours. In a pot of boiling salted water, blanch the fennel for 30 seconds. Drain and spread the fennel in the bottom of a roasting pan large enough to hold both fish. Place the fish on top of the fennel, drizzle with olive oil, and roast in a 375°F oven until done, 15–20 minutes. Serve with Gremolata.

Broiled Mackerel with Sorrel Butter

SERVES 4

> 1 recipe Sorrel Butter (page 22)
>
> 4 mackerel portions, skin on
>
> Salt
>
> Extra-virgin olive oil
>
> Black pepper

Season the fish with salt and let it rest for 15 minutes. Preheat the broiler to high and set the rack in the position closest to the heat. Place the fish skin side up on a baking tray. Brush with olive oil. Sprinkle with black pepper. Slide the tray under the broiler and cook until the fish is done, 5–7 minutes, depending on thickness. Remove from the broiler and slather with Sorrel Butter.

Mackerel Ceviche

SERVES 4 AS AN APPETIZER

> 1 pound mackerel fillets, skin off, diced into ½-inch pieces, avoiding any dark tissue
>
> Salt
>
> ¾ cup lemon juice
>
> 1 orange, zested and juiced
>
> 2 tablespoons golden raisins
>
> 1–2 Fresno or serrano chiles, thinly sliced
>
> 1 red onion, thinly sliced, rinsed under cold running water, and patted dry
>
> ¼ cup extra-virgin olive oil
>
> ½ cup parsley, leaves picked
>
> Black pepper

Keep this dish cold at all times during preparation. Season the fish with salt and let it rest for 5 minutes. Combine the fish with the lemon juice, orange zest and juice, raisins, and chiles and let it rest for 20 minutes. Add the onion and let it rest for another 10 minutes. Add the olive oil and parsley and toss well. Season with black pepper.

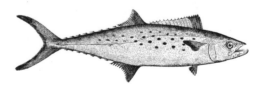

Mackerel Crudo with Raisins and Almonds

SERVES 4 AS AN APPETIZER

1 pound mackerel fillets, skin on, sliced on the bias into ½-inch-thick ribbons

Salt

2 tablespoons golden raisins

1 lemon, juiced

Extra-virgin olive oil, fruity is best

2 tablespoons crushed almonds

When slicing the fish, lay the pieces directly onto serving plates. Season the fish with salt and let it rest for 10 minutes. Rehydrate the raisins with lemon juice and 2 tablespoons of hot water until plump. Scatter the raisins and any remaining juice over the fish. Drizzle with the olive oil and garnish with the almonds.

Japanese-Style Cured Mackerel with Citrus and Herbs

SERVES 4 AS AN APPETIZER

1 recipe Gremolata (page 28)

4 mackerel fillet portions, skin on

2 tablespoons sugar

Salt

½ cup red or white wine vinegar

Sprinkle the fish with the sugar and let it rest for 20 minutes. Wash the fish in cold water and pat it dry. Season the fish with salt and let it rest for 25 minutes. Combine the vinegar with 2 cups of water and use half the liquid to wash away the salt. Place the fish in a dish large enough to hold it without overlap, pour the remaining vinegar/water mixture over the fish, and let it rest for 20 minutes. Remove the fish from the dish, pat it dry, and refrigerate for at least 4 hours and up to 2 days. To serve, position the fish skin side up and slice in ½-inch-wide strips. Serve sashimi-style with Gremolata.

Deep-Fried Whole Mackerel

SERVES 2–4

2 (1-pound) whole mackerel, gutted, gills removed, and skin scored

2 tablespoons kosher salt

1½ tablespoons sugar

2 stalks rosemary

Vegetable or peanut oil

Flour

Cornstarch

Heat 1 cup of water in a small saucepan until it is steaming. Add the salt and sugar, stirring to dissolve. Remove the pan from the heat, add the rosemary and 2 cups of cold water, and chill. Place the fish in the chilled brine and let it rest for 2 hours. Remove the fish and pat dry. Pour 2–3 inches of oil into a high-sided skillet big enough to hold one fish. Place over medium-high heat and warm the oil to 350°F. Combine equal parts of flour and cornstarch on a large plate and dredge one fish in the mixture, coating both sides. Slide the fish into the hot oil. Cook until golden and crispy on one side, then flip to finish cooking, 8–10 minutes total. Remove the fish from the oil and place it on paper towels to drain excess oil. Season with salt. Repeat the process with the second fish.

Grilled Mackerel with Spicy Onion Salad

SERVES 4

> 4 mackerel portions, skin on and scored
>
> Salt
>
> Extra-virgin olive oil
>
> 1 red onion, thinly sliced and rinsed under cold water, patted dry
>
> ½ cup picked parsley leaves
>
> ¼ cup picked mint leaves
>
> 2 teaspoons sherry vinegar
>
> Crushed red chile flakes

Prepare a charcoal grill with a medium fire, concentrating the hot coals on one side of the kettle. Season the fish with salt and let it rest for 15 minutes. Drizzle the fish with olive oil and place it skin side down on the grill over the hot coals. Cook until the skin begins to crisp, about 2 minutes. Lift the entire grill grate and rotate it so the fish rests opposite the hot coals. Cover the grill and continue to cook over this indirect heat until the fish is done. In a bowl, combine the onion, parsley, and mint leaves and toss with 2 teaspoons of olive oil, vinegar, and chile flakes. Season with salt and serve with the fish.

NOTE *If using a gas grill, preheat all the burners to medium. Place the mackerel on one side of the hot grates. Once it begins to char around the edges, turn off the burner directly under the fish and cover the grill to finish cooking.*

Grilled Butterflied Mackerel with Bay Leaf–Garlic Vinaigrette

SERVES 2–4

> 1 recipe Bay Leaf–Garlic Vinaigrette (page 35)
>
> 2 (1-pound) whole mackerel, gutted, butterflied, and skin scored
>
> 1 cup chopped herbs, such as chives, parsley, or tarragon
>
> 1 lemon or lime, cut into wedges

Coat the fish inside and out with half of the vinaigrette and let it marinate for 2–8 hours. Prepare a charcoal grill with a medium fire, concentrating the hot coals on one side of the kettle. Fold the fish back to its original shape and place it on the grill over the hot coals. Cook until the skin begins to crisp, about 2–3 minutes. Gently flip the fish and brush it with the remaining marinade. Lift the entire grill grate and rotate it so the fish rests opposite the hot coals. Cover the grill and continue to cook over this indirect heat until the fish is done. Drizzle with the remaining vinaigrette and herbs, and serve with lemon or lime wedges.

NOTE *If using a gas grill, preheat all burners to medium. Place the mackerel on one side of the hot grates. Once it begins to char around the edges, turn off the burner directly under the fish, gently flip the fish, brush with marinade, and cover the grill to finish cooking.*

Grilled Mackerel over Fennel Stalks with Orange-Pistachio Piccata

SERVES 4

1 recipe Orange-Pistachio Piccata (page 29)

4 mackerel portions, skin on and scored

Salt

Extra-virgin olive oil

8–10 fennel stalks

Season the fish with salt and let it rest for 15 minutes. Prepare a charcoal grill with a medium fire. Drizzle the fish with olive oil. Arrange a thick layer of fennel stalks on the grill over the hot coals. Place the fish skin side down on top of the fennel. Cover the grill and cook until the fish is done. Remove the fish from the grill and discard the fennel stalks. Serve with Orange-Pistachio Piccata.

NOTE *If using a gas grill, preheat burners to medium-high.*

Pickled Mackerel

SERVES 4

1 pound mackerel fillets, skin on, cut into 1-inch pieces

2 tablespoons kosher salt

1 tablespoon sugar

1½ cups red or white wine vinegar

2 medium crisp apples, like Honeycrisp, finely chopped

1 large onion, thinly sliced

20 black peppercorns

1 tablespoon fennel seeds

¼ cup slivered almonds

4 bay leaves

Soak the fish in 2 cups of cold water and the kosher salt for 2–8 hours. Discard the brine. Mix the sugar and vinegar. Combine the remaining ingredients in a bowl. Place some pieces of fish in jar or small porcelain dish in a single layer. Then place a layer of the apple-and-onion mixture on top of the fish, repeating this process until all ingredients have been added. Pour the vinegar mixture over the stacked layers. Cover the container and refrigerate. The mackerel will be ready to use after 24–48 hours, depending on how firm you desire the fish to be. The mackerel will keep up to 4 days in the refrigerator.

VARIATIONS

+ **Spicy Pickled Mackerel.** Add several dried chiles to the pickle mix.
+ **Dill Pickled Mackerel.** Add ¼ cup of chopped fresh dill or tarragon to the pickle mix.

Chilled Poached Mackerel with Green Goddess Dressing

SERVES 4

  1 recipe Green Goddess Dressing (page 28)

  4 mackerel portions, skin on

   Salt

  1 cup white wine

  2 tablespoons white wine vinegar

  1 small shallot, sliced

  1 small carrot, sliced

  10 whole black peppercorns

  1 bay leaf

   Peppery greens such as arugula or watercress for serving

Season the fish with salt and let it rest for 15 minutes. In a pan just wide enough to hold the fish in a single layer, combine 1 cup of water with the wine, vinegar, shallot, carrot, peppercorns, and bay leaf. Simmer over low heat for 5 minutes. Season the broth with salt and bring it to 170°F. Add the fish and cook until it is opaque and flakes under gentle pressure, 4–6 minutes per ½ inch of thickness. Remove the pan from the heat and cool the fish in the poaching liquid. Remove the fish from the liquid and pat dry. Transfer the fish to a plate with skin facing up. Serve chilled or at room temperature with Green Goddess Dressing and peppery greens.

Mackerel and White Bean Crostini

SERVES 4–8 AS AN APPETIZER

  1 pound mackerel fillets, skin on

   Salt

  1 cup white wine

  2 tablespoons white wine vinegar

  3 small shallots, 1 sliced, 2 finely minced

  1 small carrot, sliced

  10 whole black peppercorns

  1 bay leaf

  1 (14-ounce) can cannellini beans, drained

  1 tablespoon red wine vinegar

  2 tablespoons chopped parsley

   Baguette, sliced

   Extra-virgin olive oil

Season the fish with salt and let it rest for 15 minutes. In a pan just wide enough to hold the fish in a single layer, combine 1 cup of water with the wine, white wine vinegar, sliced shallots, carrot, peppercorns, and bay leaf. Simmer over low heat for 5 minutes. Season the broth with salt and bring it to 170°F. Add the fish skin side down and cook until it is opaque and flakes under gentle pressure, 4–6 minutes per ½ inch of thickness. Remove the pan from the heat and cool the fish in the poaching liquid to room temperature.

Remove the fish from the liquid, remove the skin, and break the fish into 1-inch pieces. Strain 1 cup of the poaching liquid into a small pan over high heat and reduce to ½ cup. Combine the reduction with the beans, red wine vinegar, minced shallots, and parsley. Use a spoon to crush the beans into a chunky paste. Arrange the baguette slices on a baking sheet, drizzle with olive oil, and bake in a 350°F oven until slightly browned. Remove from the oven and cool. Gently fold the flaked fish into the bean mixture and spoon atop the baguette slices.

New England-Style
Milk-Poached Mackerel

SERVES 4

    4 mackerel portions, skin on

    Salt

    Ground mace

    1 cup whole milk

    ¼ cup cream or half-and-half

    2 egg yolks

    Black pepper

    2 tablespoons chopped chervil or tarragon

Season the fish with salt and a dash of mace and let it rest for 15 minutes. Arrange the fish in a single layer in a wide pan and cover with the milk and cream. Over the lowest heat possible, simmer until the fish is cooked, 4–6 minutes per ½ inch of thickness. Remove the fish from the liquid and peel off the skin and discard. Keep the fish warm. In a small bowl, whisk the egg yolks with ¼ cup of the poaching liquid. Add the tempered egg mixture to the pan and simmer gently, whisking constantly, until the sauce thickens. Season the sauce with salt and pepper, stir in the herbs, and coat the fish with sauce.

Mackerel en Saor
(sweet-sour vinaigrette)

SERVES 4–8

    1½ pounds mackerel fillets, skin-on, or small whole headed and gutted fish

    Salt

    ¾ cup extra-virgin olive oil

    3 tablespoons pine nuts or slivered almonds

    2 tablespoons raisins

    1 small onion, thinly sliced

    1 red bell pepper, finely diced

    1 small eggplant, ½-inch dice, about 2 cups

    ¼ cup red wine vinegar

    1 tablespoon brown sugar

    Baguette for serving

Season the fish with salt and let it rest for 15 minutes. In a sauté pan over medium heat, warm ¼ cup of the olive oil. Place the fish in the pan skin side down and cook without flipping until almost done, then flip to finish cooking. Remove the fish from the pan. Add the remaining ½ cup of olive oil over high heat, add the pine nuts (or slivered almonds) and raisins, and cook until the nuts are golden brown and the raisins plump. Add the onion and red bell pepper and cook until the pepper begins to soften. Add the eggplant and cook until it has softened and absorbed much of the oil. Stir in the vinegar and brown sugar and season with salt. Turn off the heat and nestle the cooked fish into the sauce. The flavors improve if allowed to chill overnight in the refrigerator and then brought to room temperature before serving. At a minimum, let it sit at least 1 hour before serving at room temperature with slices of baguette.

Sautéed Mackerel with Grapes

SERVES 4

> 4 mackerel portions, skin on
>
> Salt
>
> 6 tablespoons butter
>
> 1 cup seedless grapes
>
> 2 tablespoons chopped fresh herbs, such as parsley or tarragon
>
> 1 lemon, juiced

Season the fish with salt and let it rest for 15 minutes. Set the broiler to medium-high. In an oven-safe sauté pan over medium heat, melt the butter and cook until golden brown. Place the fish skin side down in the pan. Spoon the brown butter over the fish and arrange the grapes among the fish. Place the pan under the broiler and cook until the grapes have blistered and released some juice and the fish is cooked through, about 5–7 minutes. Garnish with the herbs and lemon juice.

Sautéed Mackerel with Mint

SERVES 4

> 4 mackerel portions, skin on
>
> Salt
>
> 20–30 mint leaves
>
> ¼ cup extra-virgin olive oil

Season the fish with salt, cover completely with fresh mint leaves, and let it rest for 45 minutes. In a sauté pan over medium heat, warm the olive oil. Remove the mint leaves and discard. Place the fish in the pan skin side down, cook without flipping until almost done, and then flip to finish cooking.

Sautéed Mackerel with Garlic and Rosemary

SERVES 4

> 4 mackerel portions, skin on
>
> Salt
>
> 4 tablespoons butter
>
> 2 garlic cloves, smashed
>
> 2 stalks rosemary
>
> 1 lemon, cut into wedges

Season the fish with salt and let it rest for 15 minutes. In a sauté pan over medium heat, melt the butter and cook until golden brown. Place the fish in the pan skin side down. Add the garlic and rosemary. Cook without flipping until almost done, then flip to finish cooking. Serve the fish with crumbled crisped rosemary leaves, bits of smashed garlic, and lemon wedges.

Sautéed Mackerel with Pickled Chiles

SERVES 4

1 recipe Pickled Chiles (page 29)

4 mackerel portions, skin on

Salt

2 tablespoons extra-virgin olive oil

Season the fish with salt and let it rest for 15 minutes. In a sauté pan over medium heat, warm the olive oil. Place the fish in the pan skin side down, cook without flipping until almost done, and then flip to finish cooking. Serve with Pickled Chiles.

Sautéed Mackerel with Peppers and Mint

SERVES 4

4 mackerel portions, skin on

Salt

6 tablespoons extra-virgin olive oil or butter, divided

1 red bell pepper, seeded and cut into ½-inch strips

1 yellow bell pepper, seeded and cut into ½-inch strips

1 Fresno or serrano chile, minced (optional)

1 tablespoon sherry vinegar

2 garlic cloves, minced

½ teaspoon ground mace

2 tablespoons chopped fresh mint

Season the fish with salt and let it rest for 15 minutes. In sauté pan over medium-low heat, warm 4 tablespoons of the oil or butter. Place the fish in the pan skin side down. Cook without flipping until almost done, then remove the fish. Add the remaining 2 tablespoons of oil or butter, bell pepper, chile, and garlic, and cook until the pepper softens. Season with salt, vinegar, and mace and stir. Nestle the fish into the pepper uncooked side down and cook until done. Sprinkle with mint and serve hot or at room temperature.

Sautéed Spiced Mackerel

SERVES 4

4 mackerel portions, skin on

Salt

½ teaspoon onion powder

½ teaspoon garlic powder

⅛ teaspoon ground coriander

⅛ teaspoon ground oregano

⅛ teaspoon black pepper

2 tablespoons cider vinegar

4 tablespoons extra-virgin olive oil or butter

Season the flesh side of the fish with salt, onion powder, garlic powder, coriander, oregano, and black pepper. Massage the spices into the fish and sprinkle the cider vinegar over it. Cover and let it rest in the refrigerator for 6 hours. In a sauté pan over medium heat, warm the olive oil. Place the fish in the pan skin spiced side down and cook for 45 seconds. Flip the fish and cook until done.

Sautéed New England Mackerel Breakfast

SERVES 4

> 4 mackerel portions, skin on
>
> Salt
>
> ¼ cup bacon drippings
>
> Biscuits for serving
>
> Butter for serving
>
> 1 lemon, juiced

Season the flesh with salt and let it rest for 15 minutes. In a sauté pan over medium heat, warm the bacon drippings. Place the fish in the pan skin side down, cook without flipping until almost done, and then flip to finish cooking. Serve over buttered biscuits and drizzled with lemon juice.

Sautéed Mackerel au Poivre Flambé

SERVES 4

> 4 mackerel portions, skin on
>
> Salt
>
> 1½ tablespoons black peppercorns, coarsely ground
>
> 1½ tablespoon fennel seeds, crushed
>
> 4 tablespoons butter
>
> 1½ ounces cognac or bourbon

Season the fish with salt on both sides and on the flesh side with the pepper and fennel seeds. Press the seasonings into the flesh and let it rest for 15 minutes. In a sauté pan over medium heat, melt the butter and cook until golden brown. Place the fish seasoned side down in the pan. Cook without flipping until almost done, then flip to finish cooking. Turn off the heat. Add the cognac or bourbon, and flambé by lighting with a match. Allow the alcohol to burn off before serving.

Hot-Smoked Pepper Mackerel

MAKES ABOUT 1¼ POUNDS

> 2 cups milk or water
>
> ½ cup white wine
>
> 1 tablespoon kosher salt
>
> 1½ pounds mackerel fillets, skin on
>
> 2 tablespoons Pernod or rum
>
> 1 lemon, zested and juiced
>
> 2 tablespoons crushed black peppercorns
>
> 2 tablespoons crushed fennel seeds

Combine the milk, wine, and salt in a baking dish. Stir to dissolve the salt. Add the fish and let it rest for 4–6 hours. Remove the fish from the brine and pat it dry. Brush with Pernod and lemon juice mixed with zest. Season the flesh side with the peppercorns and fennel seeds, gently massaging them into the flesh. Refrigerate the fish uncovered on a wire rack overnight. Cold-smoke the fish skin side down for 1–2 hours at as low a temperature as possible (below 100°F). Increase the temperature to 150°F and smoke for 1 additional hour. Remove from the smoker and allow to cool to room temperature. Tightly wrap the fish in plastic and refrigerate overnight before using. Serve flaked over salads, as part of a smoked fish dip (see Smoked Bluefish Dip, page 100), or as part of a chowder.

VARIATIONS

+ **Holiday-Scented Smoked Mackerel.** To the smoking wood, add allspice wood or berries or pine cones.

+ **Mint- or Sage-Scented Smoked Mackerel.** When removing the fish from the smoker, immediately cover with fresh sage or mint leaves and let cool to gently perfume the fish. Remove leaves prior to serving.

Hot-Smoked Mackerel Cobb Salad

SERVES 4

> 1 recipe Tarragon-Citrus Vinaigrette (page 37)
>
> 6 plum tomatoes, cut into quarters
>
> 1 pound flaked Hot-Smoked Pepper Mackerel (page 260, or store-bought)
>
> 1 large head endive, chopped
>
> 1–2 bunches watercress, thick stems trimmed
>
> 2 avocados, thinly sliced
>
> 4 hard-boiled eggs, sliced
>
> Salt
>
> Black pepper

Toss the tomatoes and smoked mackerel with half of the vinaigrette and let it sit 20 minutes. Set up four plates with equal portions of endive, watercress, avocados, smoked fish, tomatoes, and hard-boiled eggs. Drizzle the remaining vinaigrette over the salads and season with salt and pepper.

Mackerel en Escabeche

The cooked mackerel is marnated in vinegar and spices.

SERVES 4

> 1½ pounds mackerel, skin on, cut into 2-inch sections
>
> Salt
>
> Flour
>
> 1 cup plus 2 tablespoons extra-virgin olive oil, divided
>
> 2 carrots, sliced into thin rounds
>
> 2 shallots, sliced into rings
>
> 4 garlic cloves, smashed
>
> 1 tablespoon smoked sweet paprika
>
> 1 teaspoon ground coriander
>
> 6 sprigs thyme and/or 3 stalks rosemary
>
> 1 orange, zest removed in wide strips
>
> ½ cup white wine
>
> 1 tablespoon sherry vinegar
>
> ¼ cup chopped fresh herbs, such as chives, parsley, or tarragon
>
> Sliced baguette for serving

Season the fish sections with salt and let them rest for 30 minutes. Roll in flour to coat. In a sauté pan over medium heat, warm 2 tablespoons of the olive oil. Place the fish into the pan and cook without flipping until almost done, then flip to finish cooking and wipe the pan clean. Transfer the cooked fish to a baking dish. Heat the remaining 1 cup of olive oil. Add the carrots, shallots, and garlic and cook until the carrots begin to soften. Add the paprika, coriander, thyme and/or rosemary, and orange zest, and cook for 2 minutes, until the aromas bloom. Add the wine and vinegar, season with salt, and simmer until the liquid is reduced by half. Add the herbs. Stir to combine, and pour the mixture over the cooked fish. Cool to room temperature. Wait at least 1 hour before serving. For best results, allow the fish to marinate overnight in the refrigerator before returning it to room temperature. Serve with a sliced baguette.

Mackerel Melt

SERVES 4

⅓ cup Mayonnaise (page 29, or store-bought)

2 (7-ounce) tins mackerel, drained

1 teaspoon celery salt

4 slices pumpernickel bread

Sliced cheddar or Monterey Jack cheese

Preheat the broiler to medium and set the rack in the middle position to the heat. Flake the fish into a bowl. Add the Mayonnaise and celery salt. Gently stir to combine. Divide the fish among the slices of bread and cover each with slices of cheese. Place the melts on a tray, slide the tray under the broiler, and cook until the fish is warmed through and the cheese is melted, 4–6 minutes.

Smoked Mackerel with Carrot, Radish, and Celery Salad

SERVES 4

1 recipe Orange-Walnut Vinaigrette (page 37)

2 (7-ounce) tins smoked mackerel in oil

½ pound young carrots, shaved into long, thin ribbons

½ pound radishes, thinly sliced

1 fennel bulb, thinly sliced

6 stalks celery, thinly sliced

1 small red onion, thinly sliced, washed under cold running water, and patted dry

Combine the Orange-Walnut Vinaigrette with oil from the canned fish. Flake the fish into bite-size pieces and gently toss with half of the vinaigrette. Toss the vegetables with the remaining vinaigrette and spread the fish over the top.

MAHI MAHI
Meaty dense fish, steak fish

One important fact a cook needs to know about mahi mahi is that it is not dolphin. Its other names are dorado and dolphinfish, but mahi mahi is absolutely unrelated to the mammal we know and love as Flipper. This one-of-a-kind fish, which ranges between 5 and 85 pounds, has a bullet-shaped body and a flat head. It swims on both American coasts and is common in the waters around Hawaii, where it's a revered seafood in native cuisine. When mahi mahi is pulled from the water, its thick, inedible skin shimmers in a rainbow of colors.

Mahi mahi has guiltlessly rich flesh; a firm texture with large, angular flakes; and a clear, bright flavor that carries a briny, sweet finish. When fresh, raw mahi mahi fillets are pinkish-white in color with a compact, bright red bloodline. Mahi mahi shows sign of age quickly, so pass on fillets that look washed out and gray.

Mahi mahi is often widely available in the summertime, so grilling is a great option for cooking it, and its sweet and meaty flavor is nicely complemented by the smokiness of the fire. Grilled mahi mahi is often paired with fruit. The combination of stone fruit, citrus, and chile really does wonders for mahi mahi's character. It also is a good fish to hot-smoke, using both a wet brine to firm the flesh and assertive woods like spicy oak and hickory to flavor it.

The orange/yellow-colored mahi mahi roe can weigh up to 5 pounds and be prepared like shad roe (page 361), simply sautéed in bacon grease or butter until medium rare. Or, put to its best use, the roe can be cured and dried to make bottarga (page 466). While curing, it can be sliced very thinly for a meltingly tender and explosively flavored taste experience. Once the roe has cured, it can be grated on top of any dish to add a rich, umami-like accent.

Braised Mahi Mahi à la Grecque

In this dish, the fish is braised and marinated in a flavorful Mediterranean broth.

SERVES 4

>   4 mahi mahi portions, skin off
>   Salt
>   ½ cup extra-virgin olive oil
>   ½ cup white wine
>   3 tablespoons white wine vinegar
>   ½ tablespoon ground coriander
>   1 tablespoon fennel seeds
>   6 sprigs fresh thyme
>   3 bay leaves
>   ½ pound carrots, cut into ½-inch rounds
>   2 onions, cut into 1-inch wedges
>   ½ pound small mushrooms
>   Crusty bread for serving

Season the fish with salt and let it rest for 20 minutes. In a large pot over medium heat, combine ½ cup of water with the olive oil, white wine, vinegar, coriander, fennel seeds, thyme, bay leaves, and a good pinch of salt. Simmer for 5 minutes, then add the carrots, onions, and mushrooms. Cover and simmer until the carrots are just tender. Nestle the fish into the sauce. Cover and cook over very low heat until the fish is cooked through, 12–14 minutes. Remove from the heat and cool to room temperature. Serve with crusty bread.

NOTE *The flavors improve if chilled overnight in the refrigerator and brought back to room temperature before serving.*

Broiled Mahi Mahi with Orange Flambé

SERVES 4

>   1 recipe Lemon-Chile-Mint Dressing (page 36)
>   4 mahi mahi portions, skin off
>   1 orange, cut into segments
>   4 tablespoons cold butter, cut into pieces
>   Black pepper
>   1½ ounces dark rum

Combine the Lemon-Chile-Mint Dressing with the fish and let it rest for 2–8 hours. Preheat the broiler to medium and set the rack in the position closest to the heat. Remove the fish from the vinaigrette, place it on a baking tray, and top with the orange segments, butter, and a sprinkling of black pepper. Slide the tray under the broiler and cook until done, 7–10 minutes, depending on thickness. Remove from the broiler. Add the rum and flambé by lighting it with a match. Allow the alcohol to burn off before serving.

Broiled Marinated Mahi Mahi with Cilantro-Pecan Pesto

SERVES 4

>   1 recipe Cilantro-Pecan Pesto (page 25)
>   4 mahi mahi portions, skin off
>   1 lemon, cut into wedges

Marinate the fish in one-half of the pesto for 2–8 hours, reserving the other half for serving. Preheat the broiler to medium and set the rack in the position closest to the heat. Place the fish on a baking tray. Slide the tray under the broiler and cook until done, 7–10 minutes, depending on thickness. Serve with the remaining pesto and lemon wedges.

Grilled Mahi Mahi with Sundried Tomato-Basil Butter

SERVES 4

  1 recipe Sundried Tomato-Basil Butter (page 23)

  4 mahi mahi portions, skin off

  Salt

  Extra-virgin olive oil

Prepare a charcoal grill with a medium fire, concentrating the hot coals on one side of the kettle. Season the fish with salt and let it rest for 20 minutes. Drizzle the fish with olive oil and place on the grill over the hot coals. Cook until the edges of the fish begin to crisp, about 2 minutes. Lift the entire grill grate and rotate it so the fish rests opposite the hot coals. Cover the grill and continue to cook over this indirect heat until the fish is done. Serve with Sundried Tomato-Basil Butter.

NOTE *If using a gas grill, preheat all burners to medium. Place the mahi mahi on one side of the hot grates. Once it begins to char around the edges, turn off the burner directly under the fish and cover the grill to finish cooking.*

VARIATION

+ **Pico de Gallo Mahi Mahi.** Replace the Sundried Tomato-Basil Butter with 1 recipe Pico de Gallo (page 30).

Chilled Spice-Marinated Mahi Mahi

SERVES 4

  4 mahi mahi portions, skin off

  Salt

  2 cup white wine

 10 black peppercorns

 10 star anise pods

  ¾ cup extra-virgin olive oil

  1 orange, zest removed in wide strips

  2 stalks rosemary

  ½ tablespoon black peppercorns, cracked

  ½ tablespoon fennel seeds, crushed

2–3 dried chiles, such as de árbol or Calabrian

  2 tablespoons chopped parsley or tarragon

  Toast points for serving

Season the fish with salt and let it rest for 20 minutes. In a deep pan just wide enough to hold the fish in a single layer, combine 2 cups of water with the wine, peppercorns, and star anise. Simmer over low heat for 5 minutes. Season the broth with salt and bring it to 170°F. Add the fish and cook until it is opaque and flakes under gentle pressure, 5–7 minutes per ½ inch of thickness. Remove the pan from the heat and cool the fish in the poaching liquid to room temperature. In a small pan over low heat, warm the olive oil. Add the zest, rosemary, peppercorns, fennel seeds, and chiles. When the oil is aromatic, remove the pan from the heat and cool to room temperature. Remove the fish from the poaching liquid and pat it dry. Flake the fish into a dish. Pour the oil over the poached fish, add herbs, and marinate for 1–3 days. Serve the fish on toast points dipped in marinade oil.

Blackened Mahi Mahi

SERVES 4

    1 recipe Blackening Spice Mix (page 33)
    4 mahi mahi portions, skin off
     Salt
    4 tablespoons butter, melted, divided
    ¼ cup extra-virgin olive oil
    1 lemon, cut into wedges

Lightly season the fish with salt and let it rest for 20 minutes. Heat a cast iron skillet or heavy-bottomed sauté pan over high heat until it is screaming hot. Combine 2 tablespoons of the butter and all of the oil in a bowl and brush each portion so the fish glistens all over. Dredge one side of each portion in Blackening Spice Mix, coating evenly. Place the fish in the pan spice side down and drizzle half of the remaining butter-and-oil mixture over the top. Reduce the heat to medium-low and cook without flipping until a dark crust forms, then flip to cook through. Drizzle with the remaining butter and serve with lemon wedges.

VARIATION

+ **Blackened Mahi Mahi Sandwich.** Serve the blackened mahi mahi on a soft baguette, topped with Mayonnaise (page 29, or store-bought), tomato, and shredded cabbage or coleslaw.

Sautéed Mahi Mahi with Brown Butter, Grapes, and Rosemary

SERVES 4

    4 mahi mahi portions, skin off
     Salt
    5 tablespoons butter
    1 cup seedless grapes
    ½ tablespoon chopped fresh rosemary
    1 lemon, juiced

Season the fish with salt and let it rest for 20 minutes. Set the broiler to medium-high. In an oven-safe sauté pan over medium heat, melt the butter and cook until golden brown. Place the fish in the pan and arrange the grapes among the fish. Add the rosemary. Spoon the brown butter over the fish and grapes, and place the pan under the broiler. Cook until the grapes have blistered and released some juice and the fish has cooked through, about 7–10 minutes, depending on thickness. Sprinkle with lemon juice.

Sautéed Mahi Mahi with Brown Butter, Coriander, and Orange

SERVES 4

> 4 mahi mahi portions, skin off
>
> Salt
>
> 1½ tablespoons coriander seeds, crushed
>
> 6 tablespoons butter
>
> 2 garlic cloves, finely minced
>
> 1 orange, zested and juiced
>
> Black pepper

Season each fish portion with salt all over and with coriander on one side only, and let it rest for 20 minutes. In a sauté pan over medium heat, melt 2 tablespoons of the butter and cook until golden brown. Place the fish in the pan coriander side down. Cook without flipping until almost done, then remove the fish and wipe the pan clean. Add the remaining 4 tablespoons of butter and the garlic and cook until dark brown. Add the zest, season with black pepper, and cook for 30 seconds. Add the orange juice and season with salt. Turn the heat off. Return the fish to the pan skin side down to finish cooking.

Mahi Mahi Tacos

SERVES 4

> 1 recipe Orange-Coriander Vinaigrette (page 37) or Lemon-Chile-Mint Dressing (page 36)
>
> 1 recipe Pico de Gallo (page 30) or store-bought salsa
>
> 1 pound mahi mahi fillets, skin off
>
> Salt
>
> Sour cream
>
> 2 avocados, sliced
>
> ½ cup cilantro, leaves picked
>
> ¼ head cabbage, shaved, or coleslaw
>
> 16 corn tortillas

Season the fish with salt and let it rest for 20 minutes. Grill, roast, broil, or poach the fish until cooked. Flake the fish into bite-size pieces and toss with the vinaigrette. Set out bowls of Pico de Gallo, sour cream, avocado, cilantro, and shredded cabbage. Warm the tortillas in a dry heavy-bottomed pan over medium heat until crisped yet pliable. Keep them warm in a kitchen towel. For each taco, stack two tortillas together. Let everyone build their own tacos just the way they like.

MARLIN
Meaty dense fish, steak fish

Americans recognize marlin more from the pages of Hemingway's *The Old Man and the Sea* than from the pages of restaurant menus. It's a billfish, one of the few of the large spearheaded species besides swordfish to be landed as seafood. While a swordfish's bill is flat and pointed like a true sword, the marlin's is more round, like a spear, and the fish uses it to slash through schools of fish to injure them for easy eating.

Though marlin have a delicate, subtly sweet flavor with hints of sour and nuttiness, mainland commercial fisheries never expanded beyond a cottage industry because most marlin swim far from shore, requiring a great deal of labor and danger to catch. The American marlin catch is limited to Hawaii, where it is mostly caught as part of the swordfish fishery. As marlin can grow to 16 feet in length, they are cut into sectioned loins for easier transport.

Marlin steaks can be prepared using the same methods used to cook swordfish (page 408). It is generally a bit leaner and therefore less forgiving when overcooked. Applying moderate heat and ample attention are good techniques to avoid having overdone fish. Another trick is to constantly baste the fish with butter or oil as it cooks, helping it to retain moisture. Marinating marlin in a mild salt brine heavily spiked with vinegar and herbs for up to 3 days gives the fish an intense flavor while tenderizing the meat, making it perfect for slow-roasting large chunks over a charcoal or wood fire. Marlin also takes well to smoke.

If you are adventurous, ask for the collars, the bony plate just behind the gills. These long curved bones have a steak-like chop of meat attached that is tasty when marinated and grilled or broiled, offering a variety of textures and a perfectly Flintstonian presentation.

Broiled Marlin with Rosemary and Lemon Flambé

SERVES 4

> 4 marlin portions, skin off
>
> Salt
>
> 1 lemon, zested
>
> 10 stalks rosemary
>
> 4 tablespoons butter, cut into pieces
>
> 1½ ounces Herbsaint or Pernod

Season the fish with salt and lemon zest and let it rest for 20 minutes. Preheat the broiler to medium and set the rack in the position closest to the heat. In bottom of an ovenproof dish, arrange the rosemary and place the fish on top. Place pats of butter on top of each portion, slide the dish under the broiler, and cook until done, 7–10 minutes, depending on thickness. Remove from the broiler. Add the Herbsaint or Pernod, and flambé by lighting it with a match. Allow the alcohol to burn off before serving.

Sautéed Marlin Provençal

SERVES 4

> 4 marlin portions, skin off
>
> Salt
>
> 6 tablespoons extra-virgin olive oil
>
> 1 garlic clove, finely minced
>
> 1 (14-ounce) can fire-roasted, diced tomatoes, drained, or ¾ cup large diced tomatoes
>
> 2 tablespoons chopped green or black olives
>
> 1 tablespoon red or white wine vinegar

Season the fish with salt and let it rest for 20 minutes. In a sauté pan over medium heat, warm the olive oil and place the fish in the pan. Cook without flipping until almost done, then remove the fish. Add the garlic and cook for

1 minute. Add the tomatoes, olives, and vinegar. Season with salt and simmer for 5 minutes. Turn off the heat and nestle the fish cooked side up into the sauce to finish cooking. Serve hot or at room temperature.

Grilled Marlin en Adobo

SERVES 4

> 1 recipe Adobo Marinade (page 34)
>
> 4 marlin portions, skin off
>
> ½ cup parsley leaves
>
> ¼ cup torn mint leaves
>
> 1 Fresno or serrano chile, sliced

Marinate the fish in Adobo for 2–24 hours. Prepare a charcoal grill with a medium fire, concentrating the hot coals on one side of the kettle. Remove the fish from the marinade and place the fish on the grill over the hot coals. Cook until the edges of the fish begin to char, about 2 minutes. Lift the entire grill grate and rotate it so the fish rests opposite the hot coals. Cover the grill and continue to cook over this indirect heat until the fish is done. Remove the fish; scatter the parsley, mint, and chile over the fish; and serve.

NOTE *If using a gas grill, preheat all burners to medium. Place the marlin on one side of the hot grates. Once it begins to char around the edges, turn off the burner directly under the fish and cover the grill to finish cooking.*

Grilled Marlin with Peruvian Marinade

SERVES 4

    1 recipe Peruvian Marinade (page 37)

    4 marlin portions, skin off

    ½ cup parsley leaves

    ¼ cup torn mint leaves

    1 Fresno or serrano chile, sliced

Reserve one-third of the Peruvian Marinade for serving. Combine the remaining marinade with the fish and let it rest for 4–8 hours. Prepare a charcoal grill with a medium fire, concentrating the hot coals on one side of the kettle. Remove the fish from the marinade and place it on the grill over the hottest part of the fire. Cook until the edges begin to char, about 2 minutes. Lift the entire grill grate and rotate it so the fish rests opposite the hot coals. Cover the grill, baste the fish with any remaining used marinade, and continue to cook over this indirect heat until the fish is done. Drizzle the remaining marinade and scatter the parsley, mint, and chiles over the fish, and serve.

NOTE *If using a gas grill, preheat all burners to medium. Place the marlin on one side of the hot grates. Once it begins to char around the edges, turn off the burner directly under the fish and cover the grill to finish cooking.*

Sautéed Marlin au Poivre Flambé

SERVES 4

    4 marlin portions, skin off

    Salt

    1½ tablespoons black peppercorns, coarsely ground

    1½ tablespoons fennel seeds

    4 tablespoons butter

    1½ ounces cognac or bourbon

Season the fish with salt on all sides and on one side with the peppercorns and fennel seeds. Gently press the seasonings into the flesh and let it rest for 20 minutes. In a sauté pan over medium heat, melt the butter and cook until golden brown. Place the fish pepper side down in the pan. Cook without flipping until almost done, then flip to finish cooking. Turn off the heat. Add the cognac or bourbon and flambé by lighting with a match. Allow the alcohol to burn off before serving.

Sautéed Marlin with Brown Butter and Sherry

SERVES 4

    4 marlin portions, skin off

    Salt

    6 tablespoons butter, divided

    1 lemon, zested and juiced

    2 tablespoons Amontillado or cooking sherry

Season the fish with salt and let it rest for 20 minutes. In a sauté pan over medium heat, melt 2 tablespoons of the butter. Place the fish in the pan. Cook without flipping until almost done and then remove the fish, and wipe the pan clean. Add the remaining 4 tablespoons of butter. Cook over medium heat until dark brown. Add the lemon zest and juice and sherry and season with salt. Stir to combine. Turn off the heat and return the fish to the pan uncooked side down to finish cooking.

MONKFISH
Meaty dense fish

Monkfish are so ugly it's almost charming. This voracious predator has a head comprising half its weight and a third of its length. It lurks at the bottom of cold New England waters, luring prey to the vicinity of its long, jagged-toothed jaws with a thread hanging off its dorsal fin.

Monkfish had long been considered a nuisance by fishermen because they were too often pulled up in nets with more marketable fish, and not many Americans were known to eat it. Then along came Julia Child, who pushed the species as a cheap delicacy to be used in her classic French recipes. Costing just a fraction of what more popular fish cost in the 1970s, monkfish was dubbed poor man's lobster because its sweet taste and snappy texture resembled the meat of lobster tail. Americans' taste for it peaked by the early 1990s, as supplies of it tanked even as its price rose to the level of lobster. Conservation efforts have since brought stocks back up to sustainable levels.

Monkfish is most often sold in loins, of which there are two per fish, and they can be easily sliced into medallions. It can be grilled, broiled, butterflied and sautéed, or simply roasted, but it's best braised. Its rich flavor and springy texture make it a good pairing for the heartier ingredients typical of cold-weather cooking. It is equally comfortable bathed in red or white wine and takes well to deeply scented herbs, like rosemary and bay leaf, and seductive spices, like mace and allspice.

Whole monkfish tail also makes its way to market on occasion. It is covered in a thin purplish skin that should be removed, as it will curl during cooking, and contains a single cartilaginous spine running down its center. When cooked and served on the bone, monkfish tail mimics meat in the form of an osso buco.

Monkfish bones yield weighty stock that has a sweet and sour taste redolent of clams and lobster. Its cheeks render a gelatinous sauce when sautéed with butter or olive oil, parsley, and sherry. Monkfish livers are large and are similar to goose and duck liver in texture but have a decidedly marine taste. They can be cured, cooked into pâtés, mashed into compound butters, or puréed and added to finish soups or sauces. They can also be sliced thickly and sautéed with sweet apples and finished with vinegar, which is why it is referred to as the foie gras of the sea.

Braised Monkfish à la Barigoule

The monkfish and vegetables are braised and
marinated in spiced broth.

SERVES 4

1 recipe Basic Aioli (page 25), made with oil
skimmed from the cooked dish

4 monkfish portions, skin off

Salt

3 stalks celery, chopped

2 carrots, sliced

4 ounces mushrooms, cut in quarters

2 garlic cloves, thinly sliced

5 sprigs thyme

1 teaspoon ground coriander seeds

1½ cups white wine

1 (14-ounce) can halved artichoke
hearts in oil

½ lemon, thinly sliced

1 cup extra-virgin olive oil

Crushed red chile flakes (optional)

Crusty bread for serving

Season the fish with salt and let it rest for
20 minutes. In a large pot over medium heat,
combine the celery, carrots, mushrooms, garlic,
thyme, coriander, wine, and ½ cup of water.
Season lightly with salt and simmer until the
alcohol smell dissipates, about 5 minutes. Add
the artichoke hearts with their oil, lemon slices,
and olive oil. Reduce the heat to low. Nestle the
fish into the pot so it is barely submerged. If
desired, add chile flakes. Cover and cook the fish
for 25–30 minutes. Remove the pot from the
heat and cool to room temperature. The flavors
improve if allowed to chill overnight in the
refrigerator. Use a ladle to skim off the olive oil
and use it as part of making Basic Aioli.
Serve at room temperature with crusty bread
and the aioli.

Monkfish in Tomato Sauce

SERVES 4

1 recipe Basic Aioli (page 25), made with
skimmed oil from the stew

4 monkfish portions, sliced on the bias into
½-inch medallions

Salt

1 cup extra-virgin olive oil

6 garlic cloves, crushed

1 onion, diced

Crushed red chile flakes

1 orange, zested and juiced

2 bay leaves

2 (14-ounce) tins fire-roasted diced
tomatoes

Crusty bread for serving

Season the fish with salt and let it rest for
20 minutes. In a large pot over medium heat,
warm the oil. Add the garlic and cook until it
is soft and lightly browned. Add the onion and
a good pinch of chile flakes and cook until the
onion begins to soften. Add the orange zest
and juice, bay leaves, and tomatoes. Season
with salt and simmer for 10 minutes. Nestle
the fish into the sauce, reduce the heat to low,
and cover. Cook until the fish is very tender,
1–1½ hours. Remove from the heat and cool to
room temperature. Use a ladle to skim off the
olive oil and refrigerate the stew until cold. Use
the skimmed oil to make Basic Aioli. Gently
rewarm the fish in the sauce and serve with
crusty bread and the aioli.

Fried Monkfish en Adobo

SERVES 4

> 1 recipe Basic Aioli (page 25)
>
> 1 recipe Adobo Marinade (page 34)
>
> 4 monkfish portions, cut into 2-inch pieces
>
> Vegetable or peanut oil
>
> Cornmeal
>
> Salt
>
> ½ cup parsley leaves
>
> ½ cup mint leaves
>
> Fresno or serrano chiles, thinly sliced

Marinate the fish in Adobo for 12–48 hours in the refrigerator. Pour 3–4 inches of oil into a high-sided pan. Place over medium-high heat and warm the oil to 375°F. Remove the fish from the marinade. Working with one piece of fish at a time, roll the fish in cornmeal, making sure to completely and evenly coat. Place a battered piece of fish in the hot oil and hold it for 5 seconds before releasing it. Repeat the process, cooking the fish in small batches. Turn with a slotted spoon to ensure both sides crisp evenly. Remove pieces as they finish and place on paper towels to absorb excess oil. Season with salt. Transfer the fish to a large platter and scatter with parsley, mint, and chiles. Serve with Basic Aioli.

Grilled Monkfish with Bay Leaf–Garlic Vinaigrette

SERVES 4

> 1 recipe Bay Leaf–Garlic Vinaigrette (page 35)
>
> 4 monkfish portions, sliced on the bias into 1-inch-thick medallions

Reserve half of the vinaigrette for serving. Toss the other half with the fish and let it rest for 4–8 hours. Prepare a charcoal grill with a medium fire, concentrating the hot coals on one side of the kettle. Remove the fish from the vinaigrette and place it on the grill over the hottest part of the fire. Cook until the edges of the fish begin to crisp, about 2 minutes. Lift the entire grill grate and rotate it so the fish rests opposite the hot coals. Cover the grill and continue to cook over this indirect heat until the fish is done. Serve with the reserved vinaigrette.

NOTE *If using a gas grill, preheat all burners to medium. Place the monkfish on one side of the hot grates. Once it begins to char around the edges, turn off the burner directly under the fish and cover the grill to finish cooking.*

Poached Monkfish with Sundried Tomatoes

SERVES 4

- 4 monkfish loin portions, sliced into ½-inch-thick medallions
- Salt
- 2 shallots, finely diced
- 4 thyme sprigs
- 3 whole cloves
- 1 orange, zested and juiced
- ¼ cup shredded sundried tomatoes
- ½ cup white or red wine
- 4 tablespoons butter, cut into pieces
- 3 tablespoons fresh chopped chives or tarragon
- Crusty bread for serving

Season the fish with salt and let it rest for 20 minutes. In a large sauté pan over medium heat, combine the shallots, thyme, cloves, orange zest and juice, sundried tomatoes, wine, and 1 cup of water. Simmer over low heat for 5 minutes. Season the broth with salt and bring it to 170°F. Add the fish and cook until it is opaque and cooked through, 5–6 minutes. Transfer the fish to a warm plate. Discard the thyme and cloves. Reduce the liquid to ½ cup. Whisk in the butter, add the chives or tarragon, and season with salt. Return the fish to the pan and stir to coat. Serve with crusty bread.

Poached Monkfish with Sherry and Tomatoes

SERVES 4

- 4 monkfish portions, sliced on the bias into ½-inch-thick medallions
- Salt
- ⅔ cup Amontillado or cooking sherry
- 1 stalk celery, finely diced
- 1 carrot, finely diced
- 1 shallot, finely diced
- 4 sprigs thyme
- 1 lemon, zest removed in wide strips and juiced
- 6 tablespoons butter, cut into pieces
- 1 plum tomato, seeded and finely diced
- Black pepper for garnish

Season the fish with salt and let it rest for 20 minutes. In a pan just wide enough to hold the fish in a single layer, combine ⅔ cup of water with the sherry, celery, carrot, shallot, thyme, and lemon zest and juice. Simmer over low heat for 5 minutes. Season the broth with salt and bring it to 170°F. Add the fish and cook until it is opaque and flakes under gentle pressure, 6–8 minutes. Remove the fish and discard the zest and thyme. Strain the poaching liquid into a pan, reserving the vegetables, and over high heat reduce the liquid to ½ cup. Whisk in the butter and tomato, simmer the sauce until the butter is incorporated, and season with salt. Return the fish and vegetables to the pan to warm through. Garnish with fresh cracked pepper.

Butter-Basted Monkfish

SERVES 4

  4 monkfish portions, sliced on the bias into
  1-inch-thick medallions

  Salt

  6 tablespoons butter, divided

  3 garlic cloves, smashed

  4 sprigs thyme, leaves picked

  1 lemon, cut into wedges

Season the fish with salt and let it rest for
20 minutes. In a sauté pan over medium heat,
melt 2 tablespoons of the butter. Place the fish
in the pan and sear until it is golden brown. Flip
the fish. Add the remaining butter, garlic, and
thyme. Heat until the butter is frothy, angle the
pan toward you, and use a spoon to continuously
baste the fish with butter until cooked through.
Remove the fish from the pan. Strain the butter,
reserve the crisped thyme and garlic, and scatter
them over the fish. Serve with lemon wedges.

Slow-Sautéed Monkfish with Herbs

SERVES 4

  4 monkfish portions, sliced on the bias into
  1-inch-thick medallions

  Salt

  5 tablespoons butter

  1 lemon, juiced

  ¼ cup chopped herbs, such as chervil, chives,
  or parsley

Season the fish with salt and let it rest for
20 minutes. In a sauté pan over medium-low
heat, melt 2 tablespoons of butter. Place the fish
in the pan. Reduce the heat to low. Cook without
flipping until almost done, then flip to finish
cooking. Add the remaining 3 tablespoons butter,
lemon juice, and herbs. Swirl to combine. Pour
the sauce over the fish.

MULLET
Fillet fish

When schools of mullet converge as they migrate from their freshwater summer digs to colder brackish homes along the southeastern coast in the fall, they jump out of the water and splash back in, creating a sound like distant rolling thunder. As the fish enter colder waters, their gray, muddy-tasting flesh becomes white, firm, admirably fatty, and most delicious.

The striped mullet is the largest mullet in size, growing up to 4 feet long, and supports the largest commercial mullet fishery. Mullet has a dense texture with a medium flake and a silken fattiness. Their flavor is mild and nutty but varies depending on where they are caught. Those hauled from the sandy bottoms on the west coast of Florida have a cleaner, brighter flavor than those caught to the west, where the Mississippi is a greater influence and the bottoms are muddier. This dull flavor can be eliminated through several soakings in salted and acidulated water. The fish have a bloodline that comprises one-third of the fillet, and it can add a bold iodine flavor.

Mullet are mainly sold whole. Their fillets represent a 50 percent yield on the fish and are best pan-fried or grilled, as they self-baste in their own fat. They are even better dry-salted for 1 hour and then washed clean, brushed with lemon juice, and rubbed with olive oil before grilling. This green salting technique augments the quality of the meat, regardless of the intended preparation.

Because of its high fat content, mullet is one of the very best smoking fish. It can be cured using various methods and is traditionally smoked over sweet bay, hickory, oak, pecan, or eucalyptus woods, though it is at its zenith when smoked over dried palmetto roots. Smoked mullet is called Biloxi bacon because of its past prevalence on the breakfast table in coastal Mississippi.

The bonus of buying whole mullet is its gizzards, liver, and roe. The gizzards are easily removed from the fish's throat and can be preserved in salt and added to hearty stews. When fresh, they can be ground for use in chowders or sautéed in butter and garnished with herbs for a unique snack. Lightly salted and flavored with smoke before sautéing or broiling with butter, the liver is similar in consistency to foie gras but has a richness of flavor like chicken liver. The roe can be brined for days and then dried and pressed under boards, or it can be heavily salted for several days and then dried for up to a week in the open air. Grated as a seasoning or sliced as part of a salad, the cured bottarga (see page 466) adds a fermented, intensely salty punctuation mark to a dish.

Broiled Mullet with Ginger, Garlic, and Scallions

SERVES 4

    4 tablespoons Mayonnaise (page 29, or
        store-bought)

    4 mullet portions, skin off

    Salt

    2 garlic cloves, grated

    1 tablespoon grated fresh ginger

    1 lime, juiced

    Hot sauce

    Soy sauce

    ¼ cup minced scallions

Season the fish with salt and let it rest for 15 minutes. Preheat the broiler to medium and set the rack in the position closest to the heat. Whisk together the Mayonnaise, garlic, ginger, lime juice, a dash of hot sauce, and a dash of soy sauce. Fold in the scallions. Place the fish on a baking tray, spread the mayonnaise mixture evenly over the fish, and slide the tray under the broiler. Broil until done, 7–10 minutes, depending on thickness.

Broiled Marinated Mullet with Lemon-Chile-Mint Dressing

SERVES 4

    1 recipe Lemon-Chile-Mint Dressing
        (page 36)

    4 mullet portions, skin off

    3 tablespoons butter

Combine the Lemon-Chile-Mint Dressing with the fish and marinate for 1–8 hours. Preheat the broiler to medium and set the rack in the position closest to the heat. Remove the fish from the marinade and place on a baking tray. Slide the tray under the broiler and cook until

done, 7–10 minutes, depending on thickness. Pour the used marinade into a small saucepan. Over high heat, bring it to a rolling boil. Remove from the heat, add the butter, and swirl the pan to combine. Serve the sauce over the fish.

Pickled Mullet with Apples and Fennel

SERVES 4

    4 mullet portions, skin on, sliced into
        1-inch-thick ribbons

    2 tablespoons kosher salt

    1 tablespoon sugar

    1½ cups red or white wine vinegar

    2 medium-size crisp apples, such as
        Honeycrisp, chopped fine

    1 large onion, thinly sliced

    ¼ cup slivered almonds

    20 peppercorns

    1 tablespoon fennel seeds

    4 bay leaves

Combine the kosher salt with 2 cups of cold water. Soak the fish in the salted water for 2–8 hours. Drain and discard the brine. Mix the sugar and vinegar. Combine the remaining ingredients in a bowl. Place about ⅓ of the fish in a jar or small porcelain dish in a single layer. Then place a layer of apple-and-onion mixture on top of the fish, repeating until all ingredients have been added. Pour the vinegar mixture over the layers to cover. Cover the container and refrigerate. The fish will be ready to use after 24 hours—after 48 hours if a firmer texture is desired. It will keep up to 4 days in the refrigerator.

Salt-Roasted Mullet with Lemon and Bay

SERVES 2

>   3 pounds kosher salt
>
>   2 lemons, thinly sliced
>
> 12 bay leaves
>
>   1 (1½- to 2½-pound) mullet, scaled, gutted, and scored
>
>   4 tablespoons butter, melted, or extra-virgin olive oil

Combine the salt with enough water so that it resembles wet sand. Place a thin layer on a baking sheet and top with half of the lemon slices and half of the bay leaves. Place the fish on top of the bay leaves. Place the remaining lemon slices and bay leaves on top of the fish. Pack on the remaining salt mixture to completely encase the fish. Roast at 375°F for 20–30 minutes. Remove the fish from the oven and let it rest for 5 minutes. Crack the salt crust and discard. Serve whole, or remove the lemon and bay leaves and peel off the skin before carefully transferring the top fillet to a platter. Remove and discard the backbone and transfer the bottom fillet without its skin to the platter. Drizzle the fish with melted butter.

Slow-Sautéed Mullet with Lemon-Chile-Soy Sauce

SERVES 4

>   1 recipe Lemon-Chile-Soy Sauce (page 28)
>
>   4 mullet portions, skin on and scored
>
>   Salt
>
>   4 tablespoons butter

Season the fish lightly with salt and let it rest for 15 minutes. In a sauté pan over medium-low heat, melt the butter. Place the fish in the pan skin side down. Reduce the heat to low. Cook without flipping until almost done, then flip to finish cooking. Serve with Lemon-Chile-Soy Sauce.

Grill-Smoked Mullet

SERVES 4

    1½ pounds mullet fillet, skin on

    1 cup white wine

    ⅓ cup kosher salt

    3 tablespoons sugar

    4 tablespoons butter, melted, divided

    1 lemon, zested and juiced

    Chopped chives

In a small saucepan over low heat, warm the wine, salt, and sugar and stir to dissolve. Add 1 cup of ice water and chill. Place the fish in a baking dish, cover with the brine, and let it rest 30 minutes. Remove the fish from the brine and pat dry. Prepare a medium fire with all coals positioned one side of grill and add wood chips to it. Place the fish skin side down directly over the hot coals and cook for 3 minutes. Rotate the grill grate so the fish sit opposite the coals, adding more chips to maintain moderate smoke. Cover the grill and cook for 5–7 minutes before brushing the fish with 1 tablespoon of the butter and lemon zest. Cover and cook until the fish is firm and cooked through. Remove from the grill and baste with the remaining 3 tablespoons of butter and lemon juice. Garnish with chopped chives.

NOTE *If using a gas grill, preheat all burners to medium. Put a handful of wood chips in an insert or on a makeshift foil pouch and place over the flame. Position the fish on one side of the hot grates, and cook for 3 minutes. Turn off the burner directly under the fish. Follow the directions as above to finish cooking.*

Steamed Mullet with Orange and Star Anise

SERVES 4

    4 mullet portions, skin off

    Salt

    1 orange, thinly sliced

    2 star anise pods

    ½ cup wine

    4 tablespoons butter, melted

Season the fish with salt and let it rest for 15 minutes. In a wide shallow pot over low heat, place the orange slices and star anise to create a raft for the fish. Add the wine and enough water to cover the bottom of the pot. Bring to a simmer. Place the fish on top of the aromatics, cover, and cook until done, 7–8 minutes. Remove the fish. Strain the liquid and reserve. Serve each portion with 1 tablespoon of butter and a spoonful of the remaining cooking liquid drizzled over it.

MUSSELS

Mussels are cheap, quick, delicious, healthy, and sustainable. We should all eat more of them.

Most mussels on the market today are farmed. They grow attached to ropes suspended from rafts at the top of the water column. There they are flushed with the tides, provided with lots of food, and kept away from naturally provided particles and sediment that can make wild mussels gritty. Farmed mussels can be harvested throughout the year with consistent quality.

The dark blue, near-black, ear-shaped shells open to tender meat that is versatile in the kitchen. All species of mussels cook similarly and are best steamed, smoked, or added to seafood stew. There are few ingredients that don't go with mussels. If a savory flavor combination of ingredients sounds good to you, then it's likely to be paired well with mussels. But each species has a slightly different flavor. If the dish is mussels steamed with wine, garlic, cream, and butter, then the type of mussel is of no concern. But in more nuanced dishes, it is worth considering the personality of the particular mussel. Atlantic blues farmed in Maine and the Canadian Maritimes are typically the smallest and have firm gray-orange meats and aromatic liquor. The Mediterranean mussels are farmed in the Pacific. They are similar to their East Coast cousins, but they sport a broader shell and their liquor has a cucumber-like fresh aroma. The California mussel is the largest species and tends to have orange-colored meats, a sweet flavor, and a soft, buttery texture.

When buying live mussels, look for moist ones, with no broken or gaping shells. Store them in the refrigerator, in a casserole dish, covered with several layers of wet paper towels. Before cooking, rinse them well under cold running water to remove any grit. Gently tap any that are open against a hard surface—if they close right away, they are fine to use. If they close lethargically or not at all, discard them. If a mussel has a beard attached (that's the hairy thread it uses to hold on to things), use your thumb and forefinger to grasp and pull it away from the shell.

Mussels hold a rich, briny liquor that infuses anything cooked with them. Add just enough aromatic liquid to wet the bottom of the pan, as too much liquid can dilute the final sauce. I often roast mussels over aromatic components like wood chips, pine boughs, or hearty herbs. This gives them a unique flavor, a drier texture, and an interesting presentation. If they're roasted over a fire, the liquor is lost, but the mussels pick up the scent of the flames and, when paired with a fatty sauce, such as Basic Aioli or a good vinaigrette, they are amazing.

FRESH

MUSSELS
Fresh

Mussels and Clams en Escabeche

The shellfish are marinated in vinegar and spices.

(see page 121)

Steamed Mussels with Pale Ale and Roasted Garlic

SERVES 4

4 stalks rosemary

4 pounds mussels, scrubbed and debearded

2 heads roasted garlic, halved

½ bottle IPA beer

6 tablespoons butter, cut into pieces

Salt

Crusty bread, for serving

Heat a large heavy pot over high heat. Add the rosemary and toast for 1 minute. Add the mussels and roasted garlic. Cook until the mussels begin to crack open, about 1 minute. Add the beer. Cover the pot and cook until the mussels have opened completely, 5–7 minutes. Discard any mussels that have not opened. Add the butter and season with salt. Stir to combine. Turn off the heat, cover and let sit for 2 minutes. Serve with crusty bread.

Steamed Mussels with Lemon and Thyme

SERVES 4

6 tablespoons butter, divided

10 sprigs thyme

2 lemons, zested

4 pounds mussels, scrubbed and debearded

1 cup white wine or hard cider

2 tablespoons chopped fresh herbs, such as chives or parsley

Salt

Crusty bread for serving

In a large heavy pot over high heat, melt 2 tablespoons of the butter. Add the thyme, lemon zest, and mussels. Cook until the mussels begin to crack open, about 1 minute. Add the wine, cover the pot, and cook until the mussels have opened completely, 5–7 minutes. Discard any mussels that have not opened. Add the remaining 4 tablespoons of butter and the herbs and season with salt. Stir to combine. Turn off the heat, cover and let sit for 2 minutes. Serve with crusty bread.

Steamed Mussels with White Wine, Cream, and Leeks

SERVES 4

6 tablespoons butter, divided

1 large leek, trimmed and cut into 1-inch matchsticks

2 lemons, zested

1 cup white wine

½ cup cream

4 pounds mussels, scrubbed and debearded

2 tablespoons chopped fresh herbs, such as chives or parsley

Salt

Crusty bread for serving

In a large heavy pot over high heat, melt 3 tablespoons of the butter. Add the leek and lemon zest and sauté until wilted. Add the wine and cream and bring to a boil. Add the mussels, cover the pot, and cook until the mussels have opened completely, 5–7 minutes. Discard any mussels that have not opened. Add the remaining 3 tablespoons of butter and the herbs, and season with salt. Stir to combine. Turn off the heat, cover, and let sit for 2 minutes. Serve with crusty bread.

Steamed Mussels with Red Wine, Tomato, and Mint

SERVES 4

6 tablespoons butter, divided

2 shallots, finely diced

10 sprigs thyme

6 plum tomatoes, seeded and diced

1 cup red wine

4 pounds mussels, scrubbed and debearded

6 sprigs mint, leaves torn

Salt

Crusty bread for serving

In a large heavy pot over high heat, melt 2 tablespoons of the butter. Add the shallots and thyme and sauté until crisp. Add the tomatoes and wine and bring to a boil. Add the mussels, cover the pot, and cook until the mussels have opened completely, 5–7 minutes. Discard any mussels that have not opened. Add the remaining 4 tablespoons of butter and mint and season with salt. Stir to combine. Turn off the heat, cover, and let it sit for 2 minutes. Serve with crusty bread.

Cold Poached Mussels with Dijon-Dill Sauce

SERVES 4

1 cup white wine

4 pounds mussels, scrubbed and debearded

4 tablespoons butter

1 tablespoon powdered mustard

½ cup sour cream

3 tablespoons chopped fresh dill

Boil the wine in a large heavy pot. Add the mussels, cover the pot, and cook until the mussels have opened completely, 5–7 minutes. Discard any mussels that have not opened. Remove the mussels and strain the broth through a fine mesh strainer or cheesecloth, discarding all solids. Let the broth rest undisturbed for 5 minutes so that any grit may settle out. In a small pan, heat the butter and mustard. Slowly decant the broth, leaving any grit behind. Add the broth to the pan, bring to a boil, and reduce to ½ cup. Turn off the heat and whisk in the sour cream and dill. Remove the mussels from their shells, reserving the top shell of each, and toss the meats with the warm sauce. Cool to room temperature. Serve immediately, or marinate them overnight. Place each mussel back into a cleaned shell to serve.

Pine Bough–Grilled Mussels

SERVES 4

> 1 recipe Basic Aioli (page 25)
>
> 3 tablespoons chopped tarragon
>
> 4 pounds mussels, scrubbed and debearded

Combine the Basic Aioli and tarragon and set aside. Prepare a charcoal grill with a large fire and cover the grill grate with fresh, untreated pine boughs. As soon as the pine begins to sizzle and release wisps of steam and smoke, scatter the mussels over the boughs and cover the grill. Uncover the grill and check the mussels after 4–5 minutes. Remove mussels that have opened and continue to cook those that haven't opened for another 5 minutes. Discard any that remain closed. Serve with the aioli.

NOTE *If using a gas grill, preheat all burners to high. Follow the recipe as above.*

Coconut Broth with Mussels

SERVES 4

> 4 pounds mussels, scrubbed and debearded
>
> 1 cup white wine
>
> 2 (14-ounce) cans unsweetened coconut milk
>
> 1 stalk lemongrass, bruised
>
> 2 strips lime or lemon zest
>
> 2 star anise pods
>
> 1 bay leaf
>
> 2 cups diced butternut squash, 1-inch pieces
>
> 2 plum tomatoes, diced
>
> ½ cup chopped cilantro
>
> Crushed red chile flakes
>
> Almond or roasted peanut oil
>
> 1 lime, cut into wedges

Boil the wine in a large heavy pot. Add the mussels, cover the pot, and cook until the mussels have opened completely, 5–7 minutes. Discard any mussels that have not opened. Remove the mussels and strain the broth through a fine mesh strainer or cheesecloth, discarding all solids. Let the broth rest undisturbed for 5 minutes so that any grit may settle out. Return the broth to the pan and add the coconut milk, 1 cup of water, lemongrass, lime zest, star anise, and bay leaf. Bring to a simmer over medium heat and cook for 5 minutes. Pluck out the lemongrass, lime zest, star anise, and bay leaf and discard. Add the butternut squash and simmer until tender, 8–10 minutes. Remove the mussels from their shells and reserve the meat. Add the tomatoes, cilantro, a pinch of chile flakes, and the reserved mussel meat and simmer gently until warmed through. Season with salt if needed. Divide the soup among four bowls, drizzle each with almond or peanut oil, and serve with the lime wedges.

Steamed Spiced Mussels with Chorizo

SERVES 4

½ cup vegetable oil

6 garlic cloves

1 small onion, chopped

1 tablespoon sweet smoked paprika

1 tablespoon fennel seeds

2 teaspoons ground coriander

4 pounds mussels, scrubbed and debearded

¾ cup white wine

Salt

4 tablespoons butter, cut into pieces

4 ounces dried Spanish chorizo, thinly sliced

Crusty bread for serving

In a blender or food processor, purée the oil, garlic, onion, paprika, fennel seeds, and coriander. Add more oil if necessary to make a mostly smooth paste. In a large sauté pan, cook the paste over high heat for 3 minutes until it no longer smells of raw garlic. Add the mussels and cook for a few minutes. As soon as the mussels begin to open, add the wine and season with salt. Cover the pan and allow the mussels to steam open, about 5–7 minutes. When the mussels have opened, uncover the pot and add the butter and chorizo. Reduce the heat to medium, cook until the butter is incorporated, then toss to coat the mussels in the sauce. Discard any mussels that haven't opened by this point. Divide the mussels among four shallow bowls, and serve with bread.

Smoke-Roasted Mussels

SERVES 4

10 sprigs fresh oregano

1 cup wood chips for smoking

4 pounds mussels, scrubbed and debearded

2 lemons, cut into wedges

1 cup white wine

Salt

4 tablespoons butter, melted

Heat a wide cast iron pan until screaming hot. Cover the bottom of the pan with the oregano and wood chips. As soon as the wood begins to smolder, add the mussels and lemon wedges. Cover the pan and continue to cook over high heat until the mussels begin to hiss. Add the wine and season generously with salt. Cover and boil over high heat until the mussels are cooked, 5–7 minutes. Discard any mussels that have not opened. Serve with melted butter.

Portuguese-Style Mussels

SERVES 4

2 cups Basic Fish Stock (page 61) or water

½ cup vegetable oil

6 garlic cloves

1 small onion, chopped

1 tablespoon sweet smoked paprika

1 tablespoon fennel seeds

2 teaspoons ground coriander

½ pound sliced linguiça or chorizo sausage

1 bunch kale, stemmed and chopped

4 pounds mussels, scrubbed and debearded

1 cup red or white wine

6 tablespoons butter, cut into pieces

Black pepper

Bread, toasted, for serving

In a blender or food processor, purée the oil, garlic, onion, paprika, fennel seeds, and coriander. Add more oil if necessary to make a mostly smooth paste. In a large pot over medium heat, sear the sausage until crisp, about 5 minutes. Stir in the spice paste and cook until the color changes slightly and the raw garlic aroma has dissipated, about 3 minutes. Stir in the kale and cook until just wilted. Stir in the mussels, fish stock, and wine. Increase the heat to high and bring the mixture to a boil. Stir once more and cover tightly. Cook until all the mussels have opened, 5–7 minutes. Discard any mussels that do not open. Using a slotted spoon, divide the mussels and kale among four large soup bowls. Whisk the butter into the broth and season with black pepper. Ladle the broth into each of the bowls and serve with toast.

MUSSELS
Canned

Canned Smoked Mussels with Carrot, Radish, and Celery Salad

SERVES 4

1 recipe Orange-Coriander Vinaigrette (page 37)

10–12 ounces canned smoked mussels in oil

½ pound carrots, shaved into long, thin ribbons

1 fennel bulb, thinly sliced

½ pound radishes, thinly sliced

6 stalks celery, thinly sliced

1 small red onion, thinly sliced, washed under cold running water, and patted dry

Combine half of the Orange-Coriander Vinaigrette with the mussels and their oil. Toss the carrots, fennel, radishes, celery, and onion with the remaining vinaigrette and scatter the mussels over the top.

OCTOPUS

The success of any octopus dish lies in its tenderness. Tenderizing techniques for these leggy, bottom-dwelling creatures range from dashing them on rocks to rubbing their flesh with daikon radish and salt. The best method, in my opinion, calls for dipping raw octopus into a pot of boiling, well-seasoned cooking liquid for 3–5 seconds, then removing it and allowing it to chill slightly. This process should be repeated three to five times, as it slowly softens the proteins rather than suddenly shocks them, thus preserving tenderness. The broth, if not seasoned too highly, becomes a stock worth keeping. It is full-flavored and slightly gelatinous, a perfect addition to heartier stews like Bouillabaisse (page 54) or Cioppino (page 46). Be warned, though: its deep purple color and rich flavor can dominate more timid seafood.

Octopus meat is highly perishable, and the vast majority of the market is for frozen, cleaned product. Fortunately, freezing does not diminish the product but has a tenderizing effect.

Its flavor, regardless of the species of octopus, is almost universally the same: nuanced and subtle, buttery like scallops, and somewhat sweet with a crab-like aftertaste due to its crab-heavy diet.

Octopus can be served hot or cold and can be cooked using many techniques, oftentimes a combination of two different ones. If octopuses are small, they can be cooked straightaway. Larger 3- to 6- pounds must be boiled or roasted prior to undergoing finishing preparation. When roasting octopus, lay it on a bed of aromatic herbs and vegetables and roast it covered in a moderate oven for a couple of hours so the meat releases its juices. The octopus will be done when the juices have reduced to a thick syrup, which, when thinned with olive oil, makes a great sauce.

Octopus can be boiled, simmered, or braised in red wine with hearty spices like peppercorns and bay leaf. It is best chilled in its cooking liquid, as this allows it to reabsorb moisture and establish its own flavor. Octopus is also good friends with smoke in nearly any form, from that of a searing-hot charcoal grill to a dusting of smoked paprika over a finished dish. As good in ceviche as it is in sushi, octopus deserves to find greater value on the American table than it currently enjoys.

OCTOPUS
Fresh

Red Wine–Braised Octopus

SERVES 4

> 1 recipe Gremolata (page 28)
>
> 1 (3- to 6-pound) frozen skin-on octopus, thawed
>
> 1 bottle (750 milliliters) red wine
>
> Salt
>
> 2 stalks celery, chopped
>
> 1 onion, chopped
>
> 15 black peppercorns, tied in a sachet

In a large pot, combine the octopus with the wine and enough water to submerge it completely. Season generously with salt. Add the celery, onion, and peppercorns. Weigh the octopus down with a plate, place the pot over medium-high heat, and simmer until the meat is tender to the touch, 45–60 minutes. Remove the pot from the heat and cool the octopus in the poaching liquid to room temperature. Remove the octopus from the liquid, pat dry, slice thinly, and serve with Gremolata.

NOTE *Octopus prepared with this basic recipe can be used for nearly any preparation in this section.*

Garlic and Rosemary Marinated Octopus

SERVES 4

> 1 recipe Red Wine–Braised Octopus (see above)
>
> 4 garlic cloves, minced
>
> 2 stalks rosemary, leaves picked and finely chopped

> 2 shallots, finely diced
>
> 6 tablespoons extra-virgin olive oil
>
> ¼ cup red wine vinegar
>
> Salt

Cut the braised octopus into 3-inch segments, leaving as much skin intact as possible. In a bowl, combine the remaining ingredients and season with salt to taste. Add the octopus, toss to coat, and marinate in the refrigerator for at least 24 hours. Serve at room temperature.

Roasted Octopus

SERVES 4

> 1 onion, sliced
>
> 1 fennel bulb, thinly sliced
>
> 2 stalks rosemary, leaves picked and finely chopped
>
> 2–3 bay leaves
>
> 1 (3- to 6-pound) frozen skin-on octopus, thawed
>
> ¼ cup extra-virgin olive oil
>
> Salt

Spread the onion, fennel, rosemary, and bay leaves in the bottom of a baking dish large enough to hold the octopus. Place the octopus on top, season with salt, and cover with foil. Roast in a 350°F oven for 1 hour. Reduce the heat to 300°F, uncover, and continue to cook until tender, 1–2 more hours. Remove from the oven and let cool until it can be handled. Thinly slice the octopus. Discard the bay leaves. Combine the vegetables and cooking juices from the baking dish with the olive oil and season with salt to taste. Spoon the mixture over the sliced octopus.

Octopus à la Gallega

Famous in northern Spain, this dish is fortified with boiled potatoes and smoked paprika.

SERVES 4

>   1 recipe Red Wine–Braised Octopus (page 287)
>
>   1 recipe Basic Aioli (page 25)
>
>   ¾ pound new potatoes
>
>   Salt
>
>   1–2 tablespoons red wine or sherry vinegar
>
>   1 tablespoon sweet smoked paprika

In a saucepan over high heat, boil the potatoes in salted water until tender. Drain and slice the potatoes into ½-inch-thick rounds and pile in the middle of a serving platter. Slice the braised octopus into ½-inch-thick rings and place around the potatoes. Sprinkle the entire dish with the vinegar and paprika, and serve with Basic Aioli.

Chile-Lime Octopus

SERVES 4

>   1 recipe Red Wine–Braised Octopus (page 287)
>
>   2 Fresno or serrano chiles, thinly sliced
>
>   2 shallots, thinly sliced, rinsed under cold running water, and patted dry
>
>   3 limes, juiced
>
>   ¼ cup extra-virgin olive oil
>
>   ½ cup mint leaves, torn
>
>   ½ cup parsley leaves
>
>   Spicy greens, such as arugula or mesclun mix

Cut the braised octopus into 3-inch segments, leaving as much skin intact as possible. In a bowl, combine the chiles, shallots, lime juice, and oil. Add the octopus, toss to coat, and marinate in the refrigerator for 1–12 hours. Bring the octopus to room temperature. Toss the mint, parsley, and greens with the marinade from the octopus and serve alongside.

OCTOPUS
Canned

Canned Octopus in Creamy Lime-Almond Dressing

SERVES 2–4

>   1 recipe Creamy Lime-Almond Dressing (page 36)
>
>   2 (4-ounce) tins octopus in oil
>
>   Toast rubbed with garlic, or cooked pasta

Toss the octopus and its oil with the dressing and marinate for 15–30 minutes. Serve over toast rubbed with garlic or tossed with cooked pasta.

OPAH

Orange-fleshed fish, meaty dense fish

Opah, most of which is caught by Hawaiian swordfish and tuna fishermen, is also called moonfish because its round, flat body mimics a full moon and its crescent tail evokes a waning or waxing moon. These large fish are at their peak of fat and flavor in spring and summer. And they are as colorful as they are delicious, boasting bright red fins and blue-gray-green skin iridescent with rosy, purple, and gold tones.

The fillets naturally separate into three distinct sections.

The top loin, running from head to tail, is thick and salmon colored, with a texture like tuna. This cut is great sliced thin and served raw or cut into large sections as you would a pork roast and cooked in a similar fashion. Below the spine is the belly loin, again salmon in color and with streaks of fat running between the musculature. The top and belly loins are both flattered by pickling or smoking, as the fat absorbs the rustic flavor. They also sear very well, forming a crunchy exterior as they self-baste, but they should not be cooked to more than medium for the best texture and flavor.

Farther forward on the lower portion of the fish is a circular cut of meat called the breast, a deep iron-red cut resembling beef liver more than fish. There is also liver-red meat on the underside of the jaw called chin jowl meat. And there are small bits of cheek muscle just under the eyes. The breast, chin, and cheeks are tougher and are ideal for braising with warm spices like cinnamon and allspice balanced with the bite of chiles, ginger, or garlic.

Regardless of the cut, opah's meat is very dense, noticeably oily, and flaky. During cooking, it releases a lot of fat. When cooked in butter, the flesh absorbs its sweet buttermilk and cracker-like scent, and the flesh gives off a floral aroma. The skin is quite thick, but if scored and cooked slowly it can be made crispy, as when rendering the skin of a duck.

Braised Opah with Sundried Tomatoes

SERVES 4

> 4 opah portions, skin off
>
> Salt
>
> 2 shallots, finely diced
>
> 4 sprigs thyme
>
> 3 whole cloves
>
> 1 orange, zested and juiced
>
> ¼ cup shredded sundried tomatoes
>
> ½ cup white or red wine
>
> 4 tablespoons butter, cut into pieces
>
> 3 tablespoons fresh chopped chives or tarragon
>
> Crusty bread

Season the fish with salt and let it rest for 20 minutes. In a large skillet over medium heat, combine the shallots, thyme, cloves, orange zest and juice, sundried tomatoes, wine, and ½ cup of water. Simmer for 5 minutes. Add the fish, cover, and simmer until cooked through, about 12–15 minutes. Transfer the fish to a warm plate. Discard the thyme and cloves. Increase the heat to high and reduce the sauce to ½ cup. Whisk in the butter, add the chives or tarragon, and season with salt. Return the fish to the pan and stir to coat. Serve with crusty bread.

Broiled Opah with Anchovy-Almond Butter

SERVES 4

> 1 recipe Anchovy-Almond Butter (page 19)
>
> 4 opah portions, skin off
>
> Salt
>
> 1 lemon, zested
>
> 1½ ounces Amontillado or cooking sherry

Season the fish with salt and the lemon zest and let it rest for 20 minutes. Preheat the broiler to medium and set the rack in the middle position to the heat. Place the fish on a baking tray and top each portion with 1 tablespoon of Anchovy-Almond Butter. Drizzle each portion with sherry. Slide the tray under the broiler and cook until done, 7–10 minutes, depending on thickness. Remove from the broiler and top with remaining Anchovy-Almond Butter.

Grilled Opah Kebabs with Tarragon-Citrus Vinaigrette

SERVES 4

> 1 recipe Tarragon-Citrus Vinaigrette (page 37)
>
> 4 opah portions, skin off and cut into 1-inch pieces
>
> Salt

Thread 3–4 pieces of fish onto each skewer. Place the skewers in a baking dish and season with salt. Set half of the vinaigrette aside for serving. Pour the other half over the fish and let it marinate for 1–8 hours. Prepare a charcoal grill with a medium fire, concentrating the hot coals on one side of the kettle. Remove the skewers from the marinade and place over the hot coals. Cook until the edges of the fish begin to crisp, about 2 minutes. Lift the entire grill grate and rotate it so the fish rests opposite the hot coals. Brush the kebabs with any remaining marinade, cover the grill, and continue to cook over this indirect heat until the fish is done, 3–4 minutes. Serve with the reserved marinade.

NOTE *If using a gas grill, preheat all burners to medium-high. Place the kebabs on one side of the grill and cook until the edges of the fish begin to crisp. Turn the kebabs, and turn off the burner directly below them. Brush the kebabs with marinade, cover the grill, and continue to cook over this indirect heat until the fish is done, 2–3 minutes.*

Grilled Opah with Peruvian Marinade

SERVES 4

> 1 recipe Peruvian Marinade (page 37)
>
> 4 opah portions, skin off

Reserve one-third of the Peruvian Marinade for serving. Combine the remaining marinade with the fish and let it rest for 4–8 hours. Prepare a charcoal grill with a medium fire, concentrating the hot coals on one side of the kettle. Remove the fish from the marinade and place it on the grill over the hottest part of the fire. Cook until the edges begin to char, about 2 minutes. Lift the entire grill grate and rotate it so the fish rests opposite the hot coals. Cover the grill, baste the fish with any remaining used marinade, and continue to cook over this indirect heat until the fish is done. Serve with the reserved marinade drizzled over.

NOTE *If using a gas grill, preheat all burners to medium-high. Place the opah on one side of the hot grates. Once it begins to char around the edges, turn off the burner directly under the fish and cover the grill to finish cooking.*

Opah au Poivre Flambé

SERVES 4

> 4 opah portions, skin off
>
> Salt
>
> 1½ tablespoons black peppercorns, coarsely ground
>
> 1½ tablespoons fennel seeds, crushed
>
> 4 tablespoons butter
>
> 1½ ounces cognac or brandy

Season the fish on all sides with salt and on one side with the pepper and fennel. Press the seasonings into the flesh and let it rest for 20 minutes. In a sauté pan over medium heat, melt the butter and cook until golden brown. Place the fish pepper side down in the pan. Cook without flipping until almost done, then flip to finish cooking. Turn off the heat. Add the cognac or brandy, and flambé by lighting with a match. Allow the alcohol to burn off before serving.

Slow-Sautéed Opah with Herbes de Provence

SERVES 4

> 1 recipe Herbes de Provence Mix (page 33)
>
> 4 opah portions, skin off
>
> Salt
>
> 3 tablespoons butter
>
> 1 lemon, cut into wedges

Season the fish with salt on both sides and on one side with the herb mixture. Press the seasonings into the flesh and let it rest for 20 minutes. In a sauté pan over medium-low heat, melt the butter. Place the fish herbed side down in the pan. Cook without flipping until almost done, then flip to finish cooking. Serve with lemon wedges.

OYSTERS

Every oyster is a reflection of its origin and is celebrated for that provenance. The salinity and brackishness of the water, the quantity of nutrients, the strength of the tides, and the depth of the water are all details of any oyster's tale. That said, there are some regional commonalities that apply when shopping for oysters, which you can do year-round. The old adage that warned against eating oysters in months without the letter *r* no longer holds true, because of refrigeration.

Almost all East Coast oysters are farmed now and are of the same species, *Crassostrea virginica*. Eastern oysters tend to be quite briny, increasingly so the farther north they grow. They may also exhibit strong minerality, crisp acidity, or hints of butter, melon, and coriander, to name just a few tastes. Oyster aquaculture is considered very sustainable, as these filter feeders clean up to 50 gallons of water a day as they eat, help repopulate the wild oyster supplies decimated by Americans' hunger for them, and provide a great opportunity for watermen to make a living year-round, an economic boost that keeps coastal communities thriving.

There are multiple West Coast wild and farmed species including the Pacific, Kumamoto, and Olympia. These oysters tend to exhibit more intense flavors than their East Coast counterparts. They have a notable sweetness and common notes of cucumber, melon, copper, and seaweed.

The European flat oyster has a distinct copper-iron flavor and a tangy personality. While grown on both coasts here, they are native to France, where they are known as Belon.

Southern oysters raised south of the Chesapeake Bay and throughout the Gulf of Mexico tend to have a softer texture and less brine than their more northern counterparts. The warmer waters make the oysters grow rapidly, so they tend to be bigger than cold-water ones. The South has a rich culinary tradition of serving these oysters roasted, broiled, grilled, and fried, as well as shucked raw. These are the best oysters for Oysters Rockefeller (page 298).

Raw shellfish has a long list of classic accompaniments, including cocktail sauce, lemon juice, horseradish, and the French sauce known as mignonette, a mixture of vinegar and water flavored with freshly diced shallots and peppercorn that particularly enlivens a briny oyster.

For oysters destined to be fried for traditional Po Boys or newly popular tacos, it's best to poach them first for only 15 seconds in an acid-spiked court bouillon. This removes some of their slippery, viscous liquor and sets the meat, allowing an easier and more even coating of bread or cracker crumbs.

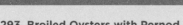

Broiled Oysters with Pernod

SERVES 4

>   2 tablespoons Mayonnaise (page 29, or store-bought)
>   Rock salt
>   24 oysters, shucked, liquor and bottom shells reserved
>   3 tablespoons chopped parsley
>   1 garlic clove, grated
>   2 tablespoons lemon juice
>   2 tablespoons Pernod or dry vermouth
>   4 tablespoons butter, softened
>   3 tablespoons panko
>   ½ teaspoon grated nutmeg

Line a baking tray with rock salt or folded aluminum foil. Preheat the broiler to medium and set the rack in the position closest to the heat. Arrange the oysters in their shells on the lined tray. Combine the parsley, garlic, lemon juice, Pernod or dry vermouth, butter, panko, Mayonnaise, nutmeg, and up to 3 tablespoons of the reserved oyster liquor in a small bowl and mix well. Place a generous dollop on each oyster. Slide the tray under the broiler and cook until the topping is browned and bubbling hot and the edges of the oysters have curled in their shells, 4–5 minutes.

Bloody Mary Shooters

MAKES 4 SHOOTERS

>   ⅓ cup V8 vegetable juice
>   2 tablespoons bottled clam juice
>   2 teaspoons prepared horseradish
>   1 teaspoon Worcestershire sauce
>   6 ounces vodka or gin
>   2 limes, 1 juiced and 1 cut into wedges
>   2 teaspoons Old Bay seasoning
>   4 oysters, shucked on the half shell

In a cocktail shaker, combine the vegetable juice, clam juice, horseradish, Worcestershire sauce, vodka, and lime juice. Use a lime wedge to moisten the rim of four shooter glasses and press the rims into the Old Bay to coat. Shake the Bloody Mary mix with ice, strain into the glasses, and top each with a shucked oyster.

Raw Oysters with Sizzling Sausage

SERVES 4

½ pound merguez or linguiça sausage

24 oysters, shucked, top shell discarded

1 lemon, cut into wedges

Cook the sausage until sizzling hot. Slice and serve immediately alongside ice-cold oysters and lemon wedges.

Broiled Oysters with Anchovy-Herb Butter

SERVES 4

2 recipes Anchovy-Herb Butter (page 19), softened

Rock salt

24 oysters, shucked, liquor and bottom shells reserved

½ cup almonds, finely chopped

2 tablespoons chopped parsley

1 orange, zested

Line a baking tray with rock salt or folded aluminum foil. Preheat the broiler to medium and set the rack in the position closest to the heat. Arrange the oysters in their shells on the lined tray. Combine the Anchovy-Herb Butter, almonds, parsley, zest, and up to 3 tablespoons of the reserved oyster liquor in a small bowl and mix well. Place a generous dollop on each oyster. Slide the tray under the broiler and cook until the topping is bubbling hot and the edges of the oysters have curled in their shells.

New Orleans–Style Sizzling Oysters

SERVES 4

24 oysters, shucked, liquor and bottom shells reserved

2 teaspoons ground fennel seeds

2 lemons, zested and juiced

Black pepper

16 tablespoons butter

4 garlic cloves, grated

1 tablespoon smoked sweet paprika

Rock salt

Combine the oysters in a bowl with the fennel seeds, lemon zest, and pepper. In a saucepan over medium heat, melt the butter. Add the garlic and smoked paprika and cook for 1 minute. Add the lemon juice and keep warm. Line a baking tray with rock salt or folded aluminum foil and arrange the empty oyster shells on top. Put the tray in a 425°F oven and cook until the shells are very hot, about 20 minutes. While the shells are screaming hot, place a generous dollop of seasoned butter into each and top with an oyster. Serve immediately.

Hangtown Fry

This classic recipe is for an omelet made with fried oysters.

SERVES 4

1 tablespoon white or red wine vinegar

24 oysters, shucked, liquor reserved

1 cup flour

10 eggs, beaten

2 cups Ritz Cracker crumbs

8 tablespoons butter

Salt

¼ cup chopped chives

Caviar (optional)

In a pot bring 2 cups of water and the vinegar to 170°F. Drop the oysters into the water, stir for 15 seconds, and then drain, reserving the oysters. Pat the oysters dry. Combine the reserved oyster liquor with the beaten eggs. Roll the oysters in flour, and then dredge them in the beaten egg and coat with cracker crumbs. In a sauté pan over medium-high heat, melt the butter. Add the oysters and cook until crisp on all sides. Remove the oysters. Pour in the remaining egg mixture, season with salt, and cook as you would an omelet. Garnish with the fried oysters, chopped chives, and caviar, if using.

Brown Butter–Seared Oysters Flambé

SERVES 4 AS AN APPETIZER

8 tablespoons butter

24 oysters, shucked and drained, liquor reserved

1 tablespoon Worcestershire sauce

2 ounces brandy

2 tablespoons chopped fresh herbs, such as chives or tarragon

Crusty bread for serving

In a sauté pan over medium-high heat, melt the butter and cook until dark brown. Add the oysters and sear until the edges begin to curl. Add the Worcestershire sauce and reserved liquor and bring to a boil. Turn off the heat and add the brandy. Flambé by lighting it with a match. Allow the alcohol to burn off before stirring in the herbs. Serve with crusty bread.

Oyster Roast

SERVES 4-8

1 recipe Basic Aioli (page 25)

1 recipe Traditional Remoulade Sauce (page 31)

1 recipe Cocktail Sauce (page 26)

1 bushel (about 100 oysters) large Southern oysters, cleaned

2 cans beer

Tabasco

2 lemons, cut into wedges

Butter, melted

Prepare a large wood fire in a fire pit. Place cinderblocks on either side of the fire and lay a thick sheet of metal or two layers heavy-duty chicken wire over the flame. If using a metal sheet, wait for it to get hot. If using chicken wire, place a couple more cinderblocks on top to hold it in place. Throw the oysters onto the metal sheet or wire. Wait 1 minute, then pour the beer directly over the oysters. When the oysters begin to open, remove them from the heat. Serve with the sauces, lemon wedges, and butter.

Oysters Kirkpatrick

In this recipe, the broiled oysters are seasoned with butter and bacon.

SERVES 4

> Rock salt
>
> 24 oysters, shucked, liquor and bottom shells reserved
>
> 1 cup Heinz® Chili Sauce
>
> 2 tablespoons Worcestershire sauce
>
> 8 tablespoons butter, melted
>
> 8 strips bacon, cut into three pieces each

Line a baking tray with rock salt or folded aluminum foil. Preheat the broiler to medium and set the rack in the position closest to the heat. Arrange the oysters in their shells on the lined tray. Combine the reserved liquor, chili sauce, Worcestershire sauce, and butter in a small bowl. Add a spoonful of sauce to each oyster and top each with a piece of bacon. Slide the tray under the broiler and cook until the bacon is crisped and the edges of the oysters have begun to curl.

Classic Mignonette for Raw Oysters

MAKES ENOUGH FOR 1–2 DOZEN OYSTERS

> 2 tablespoons shallots, minced and rinsed in cold water, patted dry
>
> Black pepper
>
> Salt
>
> 3 tablespoons red wine vinegar

Combine the shallots, a few turns of cracked pepper, a pinch of salt, and the red wine vinegar in a small bowl. Let it rest for at least 10 minutes.

Add up to 2 tablespoons of water to balance the acidity of the sauce. Serve alongside freshly shucked oysters, and spoon it over them just prior to eating.

Spicy West Coast Mignonette for Raw Oysters

MAKES ENOUGH FOR 1–2 DOZEN OYSTERS

> 2 tablespoons shallots, minced and rinsed in cold water, patted dry
>
> 1 Fresno or serrano pepper, finely minced
>
> 1 teaspoon grated fresh ginger
>
> Black pepper
>
> Salt
>
> 1 lime, juiced
>
> 2 tablespoons white wine vinegar
>
> 1 tablespoon finely chopped cilantro
>
> 1½ teaspoons finely chopped tarragon

Combine the shallots, chiles, ginger, black pepper, a pinch of salt, lime juice, and vinegar. Allow the mixture to sit for at least 10 minutes. Add the cilantro and tarragon and up to a tablespoon of water to balance the acidity of the sauce. Serve alongside freshly shucked oysters, and spoon it over them just prior to eating.

Oyster Stew, Modern Method

SERVES 4

    1 garlic clove, smashed

    4 cups whole milk

  24 large oysters, shucked, liquor reserved

    4 tablespoons butter

    2 ounces Amontillado or dry sherry

      Salt

      Smoked sweet paprika or black pepper

      Crusty bread or oyster crackers

Rub the garlic clove all over the inside of a medium saucepan. Discard the garlic. Add the milk to the pan, place it over low heat, and bring it to 170°F. Add the oysters and their liquor and simmer until the edges of the oysters begin to curl, 5–7 minutes. Add the butter and sherry and season with salt. Garnish with paprika or black pepper and serve with bread or crackers.

Oyster Stew, Old-Fashioned Method

SERVES 4

  24 oysters, shucked and liquor reserved

    2 ounces dry vermouth

  10 egg yolks

    2 cups cream or half-and-half

    2 cups whole milk

    1 teaspoon ground mace

      Cayenne pepper

      Crusty bread for serving

Using a mortar and pestle, grind the oysters, their liquor, vermouth, and egg yolks into a smooth paste. In a saucepan over low heat, warm the cream, milk, mace, and a pinch of cayenne.

Whisk the oyster mixture into the sauce and cook slowly, stirring constantly until thickened. Serve with crusty bread.

Oyster Stew, Another Old-Fashioned Method

SERVES 4

    8 tablespoons butter

    2 shallots, finely minced

    2 stalks celery, finely minced

    1 (2-ounce) tin anchovies in oil

    1 tablespoon Dijon mustard

    2 cups cream or half-and-half

    2 cups whole milk

    1 teaspoon ground mace

      Cayenne pepper

  24 oysters, shucked and liquor reserved

    2 ounces Amontillado or cooking sherry

      Crusty bread for serving

In a saucepan over medium-low heat, melt the butter, add the shallots and celery, and cook until softened, about 5 minutes. Add the anchovies with their oil and cook until the anchovies have melted. Add the mustard, cream, milk, mace, and cayenne and bring to a simmer. Add the oysters, their liquor, and the sherry and cook until the edges of the oysters begin to curl, 5–7 minutes. Serve with crusty bread.

Oysters Rockefeller

In this classic dish, the broiled oysters are topped with a rich sauce of herbs and spices

SERVES 4

>   Rock salt
>
> 24 oysters, shucked, liquor and bottom shells reserved
>
> 16 tablespoons butter, cut into pieces, divided
>
> 2 teaspoons smoked sweet paprika
>
> 1 teaspoon ground mace
>
> 2 bunches watercress, trimmed, blanched and minced
>
> 1 bunch scallions, blanched and minced
>
> ¼ cup flat-leaf parsley, blanched and minced
>
>   Salt
>
> 1 cup heavy cream
>
> 2 tablespoons Herbsaint, Pernod, or pastís
>
> 2 tablespoons Worcestershire sauce
>
>   Panko
>
>   Crusty bread, sliced
>
> 1 lemon, cut into wedges

Line an ovenproof tray with rock salt or folded aluminum foil. Arrange the oysters in their shells on the tray. In a sauté pan over medium heat, melt 8 tablespoons of the butter. Add the paprika and mace, stir, and cook for 1 minute. Add the watercress, scallions, and parsley and season with salt. Cook for 3 minutes, then increase the heat to high. Add the cream, Herbsaint, and Worcestershire sauce and cook until the liquid has begun to thicken, about 5 minutes. Remove the sauce from the heat, and whisk in the remaining butter, 1 tablespoon at a time, until the sauce is thick and emulsified. Cool to room temperature. Preheat the broiler to medium and set the rack in the position closest to the heat. Divide the sauce evenly among the oysters and sprinkle panko over each oyster. Slide the tray under the broiler and cook until the edges of the oysters have begun to curl, 3–4 minutes. Serve with bread and lemon wedges.

Texas BBQ Oysters

SERVES 4

> 16 tablespoons butter, softened
>
> 2 Fresno or jalapeño chiles, finely diced
>
> ½ cup chopped parsley
>
> ¼ cup tarragon, chopped
>
> 8 ounces Pecorino Romano cheese, grated
>
> 24 oysters, scrubbed
>
>   Saltines
>
>   Hot sauce

Combine the butter, chiles, parsley, tarragon, and cheese in a small bowl. Prepare a charcoal grill with a large fire. Place 6–8 oysters cupped shell side down on the grill directly over the coals. Cook until the oysters begin to steam in their shells, about 2–4 minutes. Cover your hand with a thick towel, take one hot oyster, and use tongs or an oyster knife to separate the top and bottom shells. Discard the top shell and place the bottom shell holding the oyster back on the grill. Top with a spoonful of the seasoned butter. Repeat until all oysters have been popped and buttered. Cook until bubbling hot and the edges of the oysters begin to curl. Remove from the heat and serve with saltines and hot sauce.

NOTE *If using a gas grill, preheat all burners to high.*

Grilled Oysters with Apricot Butter

SERVES 4

16 tablespoons butter, softened

4 ripe apricots, finely chopped

1 tablespoon smoked sweet paprika

Salt

24 oysters, scrubbed clean

Combine the butter, apricots, paprika, and a pinch of salt and stir until smooth. Prepare a charcoal grill with a large fire. Place 6–8 oysters cupped shell side down on the grill directly over the coals. Cook until the oysters begin to steam in their shells, about 2 minutes. Cover your hand with a thick towel, take one hot oyster, and use tongs or an oyster knife to separate the top and bottom shells. Discard the top shell and place the bottom shell holding the oyster back on the grill. Top each oyster with a generous dollop of the butter. Repeat until all the oysters have been popped and buttered. Cook until bubbling hot and the edges of the oysters have curled in their shells.

NOTE *If using a gas grill, set burners to high.*

Smoked Oyster Stuffing

MAKES ABOUT 6 CUPS

1 (1-pound) loaf brioche bread, cut into 1-inch cubes

8 tablespoons butter

4 stalks celery, thinly sliced

1 medium onion, finely diced

1 garlic clove, thinly sliced

4 fresh sage leaves, chopped

Chicken broth or water

1 (4-ounce) can smoked oysters, drained, liquor reserved in a measuring cup

Salt

Spread the bread cubes on a baking tray, place in 350°F oven, and toast until they are dried out and crunchy, about 15–20 minutes. In a large sauté pan over medium heat, melt the butter. Add the celery, onion, and garlic and cook until the onion is translucent, about 5 minutes. Add the sage and toasted bread cubes and stir to coat. Add enough chicken broth to the measuring cup holding the oyster liquid to total 1 cup. Add the liquid and oysters to the pan, stir to combine, and season to taste with salt. Transfer to a baking dish and bake until hot throughout, about 30 minutes. Or, if using this to stuff a bird, pack it into the cavity as instructed in your turkey recipe.

Basic Fried Oysters

SERVES 4

1 tablespoon white or red wine vinegar

24 oysters, shucked, liquor reserved

1 cup flour

2 eggs, beaten

2 cups Ritz Cracker crumbs

In a pot, bring 2 cups of water and the vinegar to 170°F. Drop the oysters into the water, stir for 15 seconds, and then drain, reserving the oysters. Pour 2–3 inches of oil into a high-sided pan. Place over medium-high heat and warm the oil to 350°F. Pat the oysters dry and roll them in flour. Combine the reserved oyster liquor with the beaten eggs. Dredge the oysters in the beaten egg and coat with cracker crumbs. Drop the oysters one at a time into the hot oil. Cook until golden and crispy, about 2–4 minutes. Remove the oysters from the oil and place on paper towels to absorb excess oil. Repeat the process with the remaining oysters.

PACIFIC ROCKFISH
Flaky white fish, fillet fish

There are more than seventy species in this branch of the *Sebastes* family of fish that swim in the Pacific from the Bering Sea to Baja California. They are a slow-growing lot, which makes them susceptible to overfishing. They are, however, well-managed and the fish has rebounded.

Known for their affordability and year-round availability on the West Coast, most Pacific rockfish are landed between 2 and 5 pounds and sold whole and as skin-on and skin-off fillets. The deeper they swim, down to 300 fathoms, the brighter their skin. Many get their nicknames from their skin color—green, brown, dusky, blue, black, copper, olive, and red—but they are often marketed as rock cod or Pacific red snapper. While Pacific rockfish is really no relation to either cod or snapper, any one of the three would be a fine substitute in a recipe that calls for another one of them.

Pacific rockfish flesh is lean and meaty with a dense yet flaky structure and a moderate, briny flavor that plays well with most other ingredients. Though some are better suited to moist cooking, as in chowders or stews, while others perform better in sautéed, broiled, or grilled preparations, these species are mostly interchangeable, so it's best to buy whichever one appears to be freshest.

Stewed Pacific Rockfish with Chickpeas and Garlic Toast

SERVES 4

> 1 cup Basic Fish Stock (page 61) or vegetable stock
>
> 4 Pacific rockfish portions, skin off
>
> Salt
>
> 2 tablespoons extra-virgin olive oil
>
> 3 onions, sliced
>
> 2 (14-ounce) cans chickpeas with their liquid
>
> 1 teaspoon nutmeg
>
> ¼ cup parsley, chopped
>
> Baguette, sliced
>
> 2 garlic cloves, sliced

Season the fish with salt and let it rest for 15 minutes. In a large pot over medium heat, warm the olive oil. Add the onions and cook until caramelized, about 20 minutes. Mash ½ cup of the chickpeas with their liquid into a paste and add it with the remaining chickpeas, nutmeg, and stock. Season with salt, bring to a simmer, and cook until slightly thickened. Add the fish, cover, and reduce the heat to low. Cook until the fish is done, about 6–8 minutes. Remove from the heat and stir in the parsley. Serve with the sliced baguette rubbed with sliced garlic.

Broiled Pacific Rockfish with Pine Nut Agrodolce

SERVES 4

> 1 recipe Pine Nut Agrodolce (page 30)
>
> 4 Pacific rockfish portions, skin on
>
> Extra-virgin olive oil

Season the fish with salt and let it rest for 15 minutes. Preheat the broiler to medium and set the rack in the position closest to the heat. Place the fish skin side up on a baking tray and drizzle each portion with olive oil. Slide the tray under the broiler and cook until done, 5–8 minutes, depending on thickness. Remove from the broiler and top with Pine Nut Agrodolce.

Broiled Pacific Rockfish with Orange-Coriander Vinaigrette

SERVES 4

> 1 recipe Orange-Coriander Vinaigrette (page 37), divided
>
> 4 Pacific rockfish portions, skin off

Marinate the fish in half of the vinaigrette for 1–8 hours. Preheat the broiler to medium and set the rack in the position closest to the heat. Remove the fish from the marinade, place it on a baking tray, slide the tray under the broiler, and cook the fish until done, about 5–8 minutes, depending on thickness. Serve with the remaining vinaigrette.

Pacific Rockfish en Papillote (cooked in parchment) with Bay Leaf, Juniper, and Sherry Vinegar

SERVES 4

4 Pacific rockfish portions, skin off

Salt

4 stalks celery, thinly sliced

2 fennel bulbs, thinly sliced

1 small onion, thinly sliced

1 cup white wine

4 juniper berries

1 bay leaf

4 tablespoons butter, cut into pieces, plus additional for greasing the parchment

2 tablespoons sherry vinegar

Season the fish with salt and let it rest for 15 minutes. In a shallow pan, combine the celery, fennel, onion, wine, juniper berries, and bay leaf and season with salt. Cook until the vegetables are soft and the wine is nearly evaporated. Remove the bay leaf and juniper berries. Take four (18-inch) squares of parchment paper and cut into heart shapes. Use plain butter to grease an 8-inch-square area in the middle of each. Evenly divide the vegetables and remaining liquid among the parchment hearts, place the fish on top, and add 1 tablespoon of butter to each fillet. Sprinkle with the vinegar. Fold the paper over, then crimp the edges tightly (empanada style) to form a pouch. Roast at 350°F for 12–15 minutes, depending on the thickness of the fillets. Serve in the pouch and slice open just prior to eating.

Butter-Basted Pacific Rockfish with Garlic, Shallot, and Rosemary

SERVES 4

4 Pacific rockfish portions, skin on

Salt

6 tablespoons butter, divided

2 garlic cloves, minced

1 shallot, diced

2 stalks rosemary, leaves picked

1 lemon, cut into wedges

Season the fish with salt and let it rest for 15 minutes. In a sauté pan over medium-high heat, melt 2 tablespoons of the butter. Place the fish in the pan skin side down and sear until it begins to brown. Flip the fish. Add the remaining 4 tablespoons of butter, garlic, shallot, and rosemary. Heat until the butter is frothy, angle the pan toward you, and use a spoon to continuously baste the fish with the butter until cooked through. Remove the fish from the pan. Strain the butter; reserve the crisped garlic, shallot, and rosemary; and scatter them over the fish. Serve with lemon wedges.

Chilled Poached Pacific Rockfish with Citrus Vinaigrette

SERVES 4

    4 Pacific rockfish portions, skin off
      Salt
    1 cup white wine
    2 tablespoons white wine vinegar
    2 shallots, 1 sliced, 1 minced
    1 small carrot, sliced
   10 black peppercorns
    1 bay leaf
    1 orange, zest removed in wide strips
      and juiced
    1 stalk fresh rosemary
    2 teaspoons grainy mustard
    2 tablespoons lemon juice
   ¼ cup extra-virgin olive oil
    2 tablespoons chopped chives or tarragon
    2 apples, cored and thinly sliced
    3 heads Belgian endive, cut into
      ½-inch strips

Season the fish with salt and let it rest for 15 minutes. In a pan just wide enough to hold the fish in a single layer, combine 1 cup of water with the wine, vinegar, sliced shallots, carrot, peppercorns, bay leaf, orange juice and zest, and rosemary. Simmer over low heat for 5 minutes. Season the broth with salt and bring it to 170°F. Add the fish and cook until it is opaque and flakes under gentle pressure, 4 minutes per ½ inch of thickness. Remove the pan from the heat and cool the fish in the poaching liquid. Transfer the fish to a serving plate and flake it into bite-size pieces. Strain the poaching liquid into a pan; reduce over high heat to 4 tablespoons. Turn off the heat and whisk in the diced shallots, mustard, lemon juice, olive oil, and chives. Toss the apples and endive with the vinaigrette and serve with the fish.

Braised Pacific Rockfish Puttanesca

This fish is braised in a lively tomato sauce with capers and olives.

SERVES 4

- 4 Pacific rockfish portions, skin off
- Salt
- 6 tablespoons extra-virgin olive oil, divided
- 1 (2-ounce) tin anchovies in oil
- 4 garlic cloves, sliced
- 4 dried árbol chiles or ½ tablespoon crushed red chile flakes
- 2 (14-ounce) cans fire-roasted diced tomatoes
- ¾ cup white wine
- 2 tablespoons capers, rinsed and patted dry
- ¼ cup pitted cured black olives
- 6 basil leaves, torn, for garnish

Season the fish with salt and let it rest for 15 minutes. In an ovenproof sauté pan over medium-high heat, warm 3 tablespoons of the olive oil, anchovies with their oil, garlic, and chiles, and cook until the anchovies melt. Add the tomatoes, wine, capers, and olives. Bring to a simmer and cook for 10 minutes. Nestle the fish into the sauce, and drizzle with the remaining 3 tablespoons of olive oil. Cover the pan and place in a 275°F oven for 30 minutes. Remove and let it rest for 10 minutes before serving scattered with torn basil leaves.

Sautéed Prosciutto-Wrapped Pacific Rockfish

SERVES 4

- 4 Pacific rockfish portions, skin off
- Salt
- 2 tablespoons chopped fresh parsley or tarragon
- 1 lemon, zested and juiced
- 2 pinches ground mace
- 2 tablespoons white wine
- 8 thin slices prosciutto
- 4 tablespoons butter

Season the fish with salt, then mix with the parsley, lemon zest and juice, mace, and wine. Marinate for 1 hour. Wrap each portion in two slices of prosciutto and secure with a toothpick. In a sauté pan over medium heat, melt the butter and cook until golden brown. Add the fish to the pan. Cook until the prosciutto is crisp and the fish is almost done, then flip to finish cooking. Serve drizzled with butter from the pan.

Sautéed Pacific Rockfish with Brown Butter and Grapes

SERVES 4

4 Pacific rockfish portions, skin off

Salt

6 tablespoons butter

1 cup grapes

2 tablespoons chopped fresh parsley or tarragon

1 lemon, juiced

Season the fish with salt and let it rest for 15 minutes. Set the broiler to medium. In an ovenproof pan over medium heat, melt the butter and cook until dark brown. Place the fish in the pan. Arrange the grapes among the fillets. Spoon the brown butter over the fish and grapes, and place the pan under the broiler. Cook until the grapes have blistered and released some juice and the fish is cooked through, 5–8 minutes, depending on thickness. Scatter the parsley and squeeze lemon juice over the top.

Steamed Pacific Rockfish with Ginger and Lime

SERVES 4

4 Pacific rockfish portions, skin off

Salt

1 (1-inch) knob of ginger, peeled and thinly sliced

2 whole cloves

2 limes, sliced

½ cup white wine or sake

4 tablespoons butter, melted

Season the fish with salt and let it rest for 15 minutes. In the bottom of a wide, shallow pot over low heat, place the ginger, cloves, and lime slices to create a raft. Add the wine or sake and enough water to cover the bottom of the pot. Bring to a simmer. Place the fish on top of the aromatics, cover, and cook until done, 7–8 minutes. Serve each portion with 1 tablespoon butter and a spoonful of the remaining cooking liquid drizzled over it.

Pacific Rockfish Tacos

SERVES 4

1 recipe Orange-Coriander Vinaigrette (page 37) or Lemon-Chile-Mint Dressing (page 36)

1 recipe Pico de Gallo (page 30) or store-bought salsa

1 pound Pacific rockfish fillets, skin off

Salt

Sour cream

2 avocados, sliced

½ cup cilantro, leaves picked

¼ head cabbage, shaved, or coleslaw

16 corn tortillas

Season the fish with salt and let it rest for 15 minutes. Grill, roast, broil, or poach the fish until cooked. Flake the fish into bite-size pieces and toss with the vinaigrette. Set out bowls of Pico de Gallo, sour cream, avocado, cilantro, and shredded cabbage or coleslaw. Warm the tortillas in a dry heavy-bottomed pan over medium heat until crisped yet pliable. Keep them warm in a kitchen towel. For each taco, stack two tortillas together. Let everyone build their own tacos just the way they like.

Corned Pacific Rockfish

SERVES 4

> 4 Pacific rockfish portions, skin off
>
> Salt
>
> 4 tablespoons butter
>
> 2 garlic cloves, grated
>
> 1 cup white wine
>
> 2 bay leaves
>
> 1 lemon, juiced

Season the fish with salt and let it rest for 8–12 hours. In a small saucepan over medium heat, melt the butter and add the garlic. Keep it warm. In a deep pan wide enough to hold the fish in a single layer, combine 1 cup of water with the wine and bay leaves. Simmer over low heat for 5 minutes. Season the broth with salt and bring it to 170°F. Add the fish and cook until it is opaque and flakes under gentle pressure, 4–6 minutes per ½ inch of thickness. Transfer the fish to a serving plate, add the lemon juice to the reserved garlic butter, and spoon the sauce over the fish to serve.

PARROTFISH
Fillet fish

Parrotfish are flamboyant. Their natural costume is a mash-up of puffy paint, tie-dye, and the pages of a child's coloring book. Smaller species are sold as aquarium fish, but larger ones with names like midnight, blue, rainbow, queen, redtail, and stoplight parrotfishes are food fish. Though they are found in reef ecosystems along all of our coasts, they are not widely appreciated in the kitchen outside of Hawaii, where they are known as *uhu*.

Their scales are thick and large, and removing them is a messy task. What lies beneath are thick fillets of tender white flesh encased in a thin, colorful skin that crisps nicely. The flavor of the flesh is predictably mild and moderately sweet. While parrotfish doesn't possess much overt charm, its elegance is revealed when paired with aromatic ingredients like lemongrass, ginger, herbs, and citrus. The nuttiness of butter accentuates the fish's sweetness and highlights its briny and floral flavors. But paring it with olive oil does the fish no favors, as the combination amplifies the taste and aroma of the algae these fish dine on.

Braised Parrotfish Puttanesca

The fish is braised in a lively tomato sauce with capers and olives.

SERVES 4

4 parrotfish portions, skin off

Salt

6 tablespoons butter, divided

1 (2-ounce) tin anchovies in oil

4 garlic cloves, sliced

4 dried árbol chiles or ½ tablespoon crushed red chile flakes

2 (14-ounce) cans fire-roasted diced tomatoes

¾ cup white wine

2 tablespoons capers, rinsed and patted dry

¼ cup pitted cured black olives

6 basil leaves, torn, for garnish

Season the fish with salt and let it rest for 15 minutes. In an ovenproof sauté pan over medium-high heat, warm the butter, anchovies with their oil, garlic, and chiles, and cook until the anchovies melt. Add the tomatoes, wine, capers, and olives. Bring to a simmer and cook for 10 minutes. Nestle the fish into the sauce, cover the pan, and place in a 275°F oven for 30 minutes. Remove and let it rest for 10 minutes before serving scattered with torn basil leaves.

Parrotfish Ceviche with Tomatoes

SERVES 4

1 pound parrotfish fillets, skin off and diced into ½-inch pieces

Salt

1 cup lime juice

1 orange, zested and juiced

1–2 Fresno or serrano chiles, thinly sliced

1 small red onion, finely diced, rinsed in cold running water and patted dry

2 tablespoons almond or avocado oil

2 plum tomatoes, diced into ¼-inch pieces

1 tablespoon chopped fresh cilantro

Black pepper

Keep this dish cold at all times during preparation. Season the fish with salt and let it rest for 5 minutes. Combine the fish with the lime juice, orange zest and juice, and chiles and let it rest for 20 minutes. Add the onion and let it rest another 10 minutes. Add the oil, tomatoes, and cilantro and toss. Season with black pepper.

Parrotfish Crudo with Cinnamon and Orange

SERVES 4 AS AN APPETIZER

1 pound parrotfish fillets, skin off, sliced on the bias into ¼-inch-thick ribbons, avoiding any dark tissue

Salt

Ground cinnamon

1 orange, zested

Almond or avocado oil

Slice the fish and lay it directly onto serving plates. Season the fish with salt, a scant pinch of cinnamon, and the zest and let it rest for 10 minutes. Drizzle with oil and serve cold.

Grilled Parrotfish on the Half Shell with Red Wine–Shallot Vinaigrette

SERVES 4

> 1 recipe Red Wine–Shallot Vinaigrette (page 37)
>
> 1 (3- to 5-pound) whole parrotfish, gutted and filleted, but scales and skin intact

Reserve half of the Red Wine–Shallot Vinaigrette for serving. Combine the remaining half of the vinaigrette with the fish and let it marinate for 4–8 hours. Prepare a charcoal grill with a medium fire, concentrating the hot coals on one side of the kettle. Remove the fish from the vinaigrette and place it skin side down on the grill over the hot coals. Cook until the edges begin to char, about 6 minutes. Lift the entire grill grate and rotate it so the fish rests opposite the hot coals. Cover the grill and continue to cook over this indirect heat until the fish is done. Scoop the flesh from the skin and discard the skin and scales. Serve with the reserved vinaigrette.

NOTE *If using a gas grill, preheat all burners to medium-high. Place the parrotfish on one side of the hot grates. Once it begins to char around the edges, turn off the burner directly under the fish and cover the grill to finish cooking.*

Sautéed Sesame-Crusted Parrotfish with Brown Butter

SERVES 4

> 4 parrotfish portions, skin off
>
> Salt
>
> ⅓ cup sesame seeds
>
> 6 tablespoons butter, divided
>
> 1 orange, juiced

Season the fish with salt and let it rest for 15 minutes. Dredge one side of the fish in sesame seeds and press them firmly into the flesh. In a sauté pan over medium-low heat, melt 4 tablespoons of the butter and cook until golden brown. Place the fish in the pan sesame seed side down. Cook without flipping until the fish is almost done and sesame seeds are crisp and brown, then flip to finish cooking. Remove the fish from the pan. Add the remaining 2 tablespoons of butter and the orange juice. Swirl to incorporate and season with salt.

PERCH
Fillet fish, flaky white fish

Most often caught in the mid-Atlantic region and widely distributed through the Midwest, white perch are much loved in those places even if they are maligned as fertilizer in the South. They are a perfect pan size with a very mild flavor, thin skin, and a delicate texture. Their small fillets are quite firm in flake and grayish-white in color. Their skin is considered by some to take on a bitter quality in the summer months, but many of us prefer to remove the skin any time of year.

Rarely growing larger than 12 inches, these dense, round fish take well to roasting, grilling, or frying whole. They pair well with fresh herbs, especially chervil and parsley. Their fillets can also hold their own when stewed in a mixture of sherry and wine flavored with nutmeg, anchovy, and parsley. As the culinary qualities of white perch and its unrelated freshwater yellow perch are similar, recipes for either work equally well for both.

Perch Braised in Sherry

SERVES 4

>   4 perch portions, skin off
>   Salt
>   4 tablespoons butter, divided
>   1 (2-ounce) tin anchovies in oil
>   ½ teaspoon ground nutmeg
>   ½ cup Amontillado or cooking sherry
>   1 cup white wine or water
>   2 tablespoons chopped parsley or tarragon
>   Crusty bread for serving

Season the fish with salt and let it rest for 15 minutes. In a large skillet over medium-high heat, add 2 tablespoons butter, anchovies with their oil, and nutmeg. Cook until the anchovies melt. Add the sherry and wine and bring to a simmer. Reduce the heat to low and add the fish. Cover and cook until done, 8–10 minutes. Remove the fish and reduce the sauce to ⅓ cup. Stir in the remaining 2 tablespoons butter and parsley, season with salt, and serve warm with crusty bread.

Pan-Fried Cornmeal-Crusted Perch

SERVES 4

>   4 perch portions, skin off
>   Salt
>   Cornmeal
>   6 tablespoons bacon drippings or a combination of bacon drippings and butter
>   1 lemon, cut into wedges

Season the fish with salt and let it rest for 15 minutes. Then dredge one side in cornmeal. In a sauté pan over medium heat, melt the bacon drippings. Place the fish in the pan cornmeal side down. Cook until almost done, then flip to finish cooking. Serve with lemon wedges.

Whole Fried Perch with Lemon-Chile-Soy Sauce

SERVES 2-4

> 1 recipe Lemon-Chile-Soy Sauce (page 28)
>
> 2 (1- to 2-pound) whole perch, scaled, gutted, and skin scored
>
> Salt
>
> 1 lemon, juiced
>
> Vegetable or peanut oil
>
> 1 cup flour, sifted
>
> 1 cup cornstarch, sifted

Season the fish with salt and the lemon juice and let it rest for 20 minutes. Pour 2–3 inches of oil into a high-sided pan big enough to hold one fish, place over medium-high heat, and warm the oil to 350°F. Combine the flour and cornstarch in a large bowl and dredge one fish at a time in the mixture, coating both sides. Slide the fish into the hot oil. Cook until golden and crispy on one side, then gently flip the fish to cook other side, 4–6 minutes per side. Remove the fish from the oil and place on paper towels to absorb excess oil. Repeat the process with the other fish. Serve the fish with Lemon-Chile-Soy Sauce.

Whole Grilled Perch with Red Wine–Shallot Vinaigrette and Rosemary

SERVES 2-4

> 1 recipe Red Wine–Shallot Vinaigrette (page 37)
>
> 2 stalks rosemary, leaves picked and bruised with the back of a knife
>
> 2 (1- to 2-pound) whole perch, scaled, gutted, and skin scored

Place the fish in a baking dish. Reserve half of the Red Wine–Shallot Vinaigrette. Combine the remainder with the rosemary leaves and pour the mixture over the fish. Marinate for 1–8 hours. Prepare a charcoal grill with a medium fire, concentrating the hot coals on one side of the kettle. Remove the fish from the vinaigrette and place on the grill over the hot coals. Cook until the skin begins to char, 4–5 minutes. Flip the fish and brush with any remaining marinade. Lift the entire grill grate and rotate it so the fish rest opposite the hot coals. Cover the grill and continue to cook over this indirect heat until the fish is done, another 8–10 minutes per pound. Serve drizzled with the reserved vinaigrette.

NOTE *If using a gas grill, preheat all the burners to medium. Place the perch on one side of the hot grates. Once it begins to char around the edges, turn off the burner directly under the fish. Flip the fish, brush with vinaigrette, and cover the grill to finish cooking*

Butter-Basted Perch with Garlic and Thyme

SERVES 4

> 4 perch portions, skin on and scored
>
> Salt
>
> 6 tablespoons butter, divided
>
> 3 garlic cloves, smashed
>
> 4 sprigs thyme, leaves picked
>
> 1 lemon, cut into wedges

Season the fish with salt and let it rest for 15 minutes. In a sauté pan over medium heat, melt 2 tablespoons of the butter. Place the fish in the pan skin side down and sear until it begins to brown. Flip the fish. Add the remaining 4 tablespoons of butter, garlic, and thyme. Heat until the butter is frothy. Angle the pan toward you, and use a spoon to continuously baste the fish with the butter until cooked through. Remove the fish from the pan. Strain the butter, reserve the crisped thyme and garlic, and scatter them over the fish. Serve with lemon wedges.

PERIWINKLES

Periwinkles offer much more of a seaside experience than a market one, as they are the ultimate expression of tide-pool cuisine. These small conical shellfish, usually about ½ inch long, blanket the rocks of the coast and are accessible in profusion at low tide. They are a treat but do not provide any substantial sustenance. While available year-round, they are at their best in July and August, when they have grown full after a summer of feeding.

Periwinkles should only be cooked from the live state, which can be tested by their reaction when the opening of the shell is gently touched. If it doesn't flinch or close tightly, don't bother cooking it. Prior to cooking, soak live periwinkles in seawater or salted water for about 30 minutes, then rinse well in cold water before draining and cooking.

Their texture once cooked is springy, chewy, and almost scallop-like. Periwinkles are commonly simmered in seawater or a flavored broth. The liquid can be augmented with heavy seasoning, such as bay leaves, rosemary, or black peppercorns, but adding wine or beer dilutes their natural briny flavor. They can also be roasted over a bed of herbs, and are great grilled using a fine mesh grill basket. Cooking time by any method is always just about 5–7 minutes. Doneness is tested when the thin disc at the bottom of the shell, the operculum, is easily flicked off using just a toothpick, which is the only utensil you need to pull them from their shells and pop them into your mouth.

Broiled Periwinkles with Garlic Butter

SERVES 4–8 AS AN APPETIZER

- 4 pounds periwinkles, washed and dried
- 6 tablespoons butter melted
- 4 garlic cloves, grated
- 2 lemons, 1 zested and juiced, 1 cut into wedges

Preheat the broiler to high, and set the rack in the position closest to the heat. Toss the periwinkles with salt, butter, garlic, zest, and juice, and place them in a broiling pan. Slide the dish under the broiler and cook until done, 3–4 minutes. Serve with toothpicks and lemon wedges.

Roasted Periwinkles

SERVES 4–8 AS AN APPETIZER

- 1 recipe Basic Aioli (page 25) or melted butter
- 10–15 thyme sprigs or rosemary stalks
- 4 pounds periwinkles, washed and dried

Heat a cast iron pan until it is very hot. Add a thick layer of thyme sprigs and place the periwinkles on the top. Slide the pan into a 450°F oven and cook for 5 minutes. Serve the cooked periwinkles with toothpicks and Basic Aioli.

POLLOCK AND ALASKA POLLOCK
Flaky white fish

Atlantic pollock is the cod kin with the firmest texture and the most assertive flavor, which is both pleasantly sour and clean with hints of a sweet, gamey character. The raw light pinkish-gray fillets cook up pearly white. Its dense flesh has a toothsome bite and a higher fat content than cod, making it more resilient to cooking. For all these reasons, I think pollock is among the most interesting eating fish in the flaky white fish culinary category.

Alaska pollock swims plentifully in the Pacific, and it is increasingly available to consumers, mostly as high-quality frozen fillets. It is also a fish that many of us are quite familiar with, as it goes into making many frozen, breaded products, and is the fish in McDonald's Filet-O-Fish® sandwich. It is also processed into Surimi, better known in the United States as imitation crabmeat. Alaska pollock is starting to make its way into the market as both skin-on and skin-off fillets, giving us access to a versatile and affordable dinner option that stands in for any other flaky white fish variety.

Roasted Pollock with Sundried Tomato-Basil Butter

SERVES 4

    1 recipe Sundried Tomato-Basil Butter
    (page 23), divided

    4 pollock portions, skin off

    Salt

    1 lemon, cut into wedges

    Rice for serving (optional)

Season the fish with salt and let it rest for 15 minutes. In a sauté pan over medium-high heat, melt the Sundried Tomato-Basil Butter. Add the fish to the pan, and spoon some of the melted butter over the top. Place the pan in a 325°F oven, and cook until the fish is cooked through, about 7–9 minutes. Serve with lemon wedges and rice, if desired.

Sautéed Pollock with Brown Butter and Capers

SERVES 4

    4 pollock portions, skin on or off

    Salt

    6 tablespoons butter, divided

    3 tablespoons capers, rinsed and patted dry

    1 lemon, zested and juiced

Season the fish with salt and let it rest for 15 minutes. In a sauté pan over medium heat, melt 2 tablespoons of the butter and cook until golden brown. Place the fish in the pan skin side down, if using. Cook without flipping until almost done, then remove the fish. Add the remaining 4 tablespoons of butter and capers, and cook until the butter is brown and the capers are crispy. Add the lemon zest and juice and season with salt. Stir gently to combine. Turn off the heat and return the fish to the pan uncooked side down to finish cooking.

Roasted Spiced Whole Pollock

SERVES 4–6

>   1 (3- to 4-pound) whole pollock, gutted
>   and scaled
>   3 lemons, thinly sliced
>   10 sprigs thyme
>   4 tablespoons butter
>   Salt
>   1 teaspoon ground allspice
>   1 teaspoon black pepper
>   1 tablespoon crushed fennel seeds

Score the fish with several ½-inch-deep gashes
on both sides. Stuff the belly cavity with half
of the lemon slices and all the thyme. Rub the
butter all over the fish and into the gashes.
Season generously with salt, allspice, pepper,
and fennel seed. Line a baking tray with the
remaining lemon slices and place the fish on top
as if it were swimming. Slide the baking tray into
a 325°F oven and roast until the fish is done,
25–40 minutes.

Chilled Poached Pollock with Citrus Vinaigrette

SERVES 4

>   4 pollock portions, skin off
>   Salt
>   1 cup white wine
>   2 tablespoons white wine vinegar
>   2 shallots, 1 sliced and 1 minced
>   1 orange, zested in wide strips and juiced
>   10 black peppercorns
>   1 bay leaf
>   1 sprig fresh rosemary
>   ¼ cup extra-virgin olive oil
>   2 teaspoons grainy mustard
>   2 tablespoons lemon juice
>   2 tablespoons chopped tarragon or chives
>   2 apples, cored and thinly sliced
>   3 heads Belgian endive, cut into ½-inch
>   strips

Season the fish with salt and let it rest for
15 minutes. In a pan just wide enough to hold
the fish in a single layer, combine 1 cup of
water with the wine, vinegar, sliced shallots,
orange juice and zest, peppercorns, bay leaf, and
rosemary. Simmer over low heat for 5 minutes.
Season the broth with salt and bring it to 170°F.
Add the fish and cook until it is opaque and
flakes under gentle pressure, about 4 minutes
per ½ inch of thickness. Remove the pan from
the heat and cool the fish in the poaching liquid.
Transfer the fish to a serving plate and flake it
into bite-size pieces. Strain 1 cup of the poaching
liquid into a pan, reduce over high heat to
2 tablespoons, and whisk in the minced shallot,
olive oil, mustard, lemon juice, and tarragon.
Toss with the apples and endive and serve
with the fish.

POMPANO
Fillet fish

Pompano are built to swim fast. These sleek blue-green fish with yellow bellies can skim across the surface of the water like a flat stone skipped by a child. They also perform very well on the plate.

Pompano has been, from very early American seafood cuisine, a favorite against which other fish are measured. Pompano is wonderfully balanced, as its fatty and rich mouthfeel flatter the small but silky flake of the fillet. Its flavor is reminiscent of sweet crab, and its distinct ocean brine needs very little embellishment to accentuate the beauty of this fish—just a few herbs, aromatic vegetables, and a splash of wine or flavored spirits such as Pernod are enough to enliven any dish. Pompano range from the south shore of Cape Cod down to Florida and into the Gulf of Mexico, the vast majority of the catch coming from North Carolina and points south during fall and winter. Their average market weight is 1½–2 pounds. The profusion of bones in these fishes' relatively small bodies is the only downside to this fish. That said, the bones are easy to remove.

Pompano can be broiled, grilled, sautéed, or stewed. It is also the fish featured in the American fine dining classic Pompano en Papillote (page 316). The delicate fish is laid on a sheet of parchment paper and layered with aromatic vegetables, a splash of wine, and butter, then wrapped in the paper to form a half-moon shape with an airtight seal. When roasted, this packet puffs like a balloon and is served tableside. The pageantry is completed at the table with quite a show when the parchment is cut open and it releases a cloud of sensuously aromatic steam.

Though butter is certainly a fine medium, olive oil enhances the fish's flavor, making it more robust. Pairing pompano with mint and ginger elevates its flavors with a slight spice and comforting aroma. Given pompano's high oil content, it is well suited to smoking, either for cooking through or as a mild treatment for flavoring prior to cooking.

315 Pompano Crudo with Chile and Orange

315 Whole Grilled Pompano with Peruvian Marinade

316 Pompano en Papillote (cooked in parchment)

316 Chilled Pompano with Chermoula

317 Pan-Fried Pompano with Sage and Orange

317 Sautéed Pompano with Brown Butter and Orange

Pompano Crudo with Chile and Orange

SERVES 4 AS AN APPETIZER

> 1 pound pompano fillets, skin off, sliced on the bias into ¼-inch-thick ribbons, avoiding any dark tissue
>
> Salt
>
> Crushed red chile flakes
>
> 1 orange, zested
>
> Chunky Almond Oil (page 25) or Garlic-Parsley Oil (page 27)

Slice the fish and lay the pieces directly onto serving plates. Season the fish with salt, chile flakes, and zest and let it rest for 10 minutes. Drizzle with oil and serve.

Whole Grilled Pompano with Peruvian Marinade

SERVES 4

> 1 recipe Peruvian Marinade (page 37)
>
> 2 whole pompano, gutted, scaled, skin on and scored

Reserve one third of the Peruvian Marinade for serving. Combine the remaining marinade with the fish and let it rest for 4–8 hours. Prepare a charcoal grill with a medium fire, concentrating the hot coals on one side of the kettle. Remove the fish from the marinade and place it skin side down on the grill over the hottest part of the fire. Cook until the skin begins to char, about 2 minutes. Lift the entire grill grate and rotate it so the fish rests opposite the hot coals. Cover the grill, baste the fish with any remaining used marinade and continue to cook over this indirect heat until the fish is done, another 8–10 minutes per pound. Serve with the reserved marinade drizzled over the fish.

NOTE *If using a gas grill, preheat all burners to medium-high. Place the pompano on one side of the hot grates. Once it begins to char around the edges, turn off the burner directly under the fish and cover the grill to finish cooking.*

Pompano en Papillote (cooked in parchment)

SERVES 4

> 1 recipe Horseradish Butter (page 20)
>
> 4 pompano portions, skin off
>
> Salt
>
> 4 stalks celery, sliced
>
> 2 fennel bulbs, thinly sliced
>
> 1 small onion, sliced, rinsed under cold running water and patted dry
>
> 1 cup white wine
>
> Butter
>
> 1 orange, cut into segments

Season the fish with salt and let it rest for 15 minutes. In a shallow pan, combine the celery, fennel, onion, and wine and season with salt. Cook until the vegetables are soft and the wine is nearly evaporated. Take four 18-inch squares of parchment paper and cut them into heart shapes. Use plain butter to grease an 8-inch square area in the middle of each. Evenly divide the vegetables and remaining liquid among the parchment hearts, place the fish on top, and add a couple of orange segments and 2 tablespoons of Horseradish Butter to each fillet. Fold the paper over, then crimp the edges tightly (empanada style) to form a pouch. Roast at 350°F for 10–12 minutes, depending on the thickness of the fillets. Serve in the pouch and slice open just prior to eating.

Chilled Pompano with Chermoula

SERVES 4

> 1 recipe Chermoula (page 26)
>
> 4 pompano portions, skin off
>
> Salt
>
> 1 cup white wine
>
> 10 black peppercorns
>
> 10 star anise pods

Season the fish with salt and let it rest for 15 minutes. In a pan just wide enough to hold the fish in a single layer, combine 1 cup of water with the wine, peppercorns, and star anise. Simmer over low heat for 5 minutes. Season the broth with salt and bring it to 170°F. Add the fish and cook until it is opaque and flakes under gentle pressure, 4–6 minutes per ½ inch of thickness. Remove the pan from the heat and cool the fish in the poaching liquid to room temperature. Remove the fish from the liquid and pat dry. Serve at room temperature with Chermoula.

Pan-Fried Pompano with Sage and Orange

SERVES 4–6

1½ pounds pompano fillets, skin off, cut into 2-inch sections

Salt

1 orange, zest removed in large strips and juiced

1¼ cups extra-virgin olive oil, divided

2 tablespoons raisins

3 sprigs fresh sage, leaves picked

6 garlic cloves, smashed

2 onions, thinly sliced, top to bottom

1 cup white wine vinegars or ½ cup sherry vinegar

Flour

Crusty bread for serving

Season the fish with salt and the orange juice and let it rest for 15 minutes. In a large pot over medium heat, combine 1 cup of the olive oil, orange zest, raisins, sage, and garlic and cook until the raisins begin to plump and the sage crisps. Add the onions, season generously with salt, and cook until the onions are wilted, about 5 minutes. Add orange juice, vinegar, and ¾ cup of water and simmer for 15 minutes. Roll the fish in flour. In a sauté pan over medium heat, warm the remaining ¼ cup of oil. Add the fish and fry until one side is brown and crisp, then flip to finish cooking. Transfer the fish to a baking dish and pour the onion marinade over it. Cool to room temperature. Cover and refrigerate for at least a couple of hours and up to 3 days. Serve at room temperature with crusty bread.

Sautéed Pompano with Brown Butter and Orange

SERVES 4

4 pompano portions, skin off

Salt

6 tablespoons butter, divided

2 garlic cloves, finely minced

1 orange, zested and juiced

Black pepper

Season the fish with salt and let it rest for 15 minutes. In a sauté pan over medium heat, melt 2 tablespoons of the butter and cook until golden brown. Place the fish in the pan. Cook without flipping until almost done, then remove the fish, and wipe the pan clean. Add the remaining 4 tablespoons of butter and the garlic and cook until golden brown. Add the zest, season with black pepper, and cook for 30 seconds. Add the orange juice and season with salt. Turn the heat off. Return the fish to the pan skin side down to finish cooking.

PORGY
Fillet fish

The Narragansett name for this abundant small, round fish that played a big part in earlier American life is *mishcuppaug*. The fact that the nomenclature morphed into scup on northern East Coast shores, and paugy and then porgy in the Carolinas, proves the fish's consistent role in the cuisines of the East Coast.

These fish can grow to be 5 pounds and be sold as fillets, but most porgies landed are quite small, weighing just about 1 pound, and are generally sold whole. The smaller fish are best grilled, roasted, or pan-fried whole. All porgies have thick skin that holds fast to their scales, which must be removed quickly after capture. If the scales are allowed to dry even slightly, they become very hard to remove.

Porgies of all sizes are fine food fish and share similar culinary characteristics: They are mild and aromatic with a sweet cucumber brininess to them. Their flesh is flaky and firm. Their skin is prone to curling significantly when cooked, so scoring it is necessary before cooking.

Larger fish are certainly easier to work with, as the bones are more easily removed than those of smaller fish and they have a more developed and nuanced flavor. On larger fish, the collar can be a wonderful cut to serve on its own; the meat is more firm, and the bone itself adds dramatic appeal, especially when simmered into soups or stews. Or gather several collars from smaller fish; marinate them in vinegar, chiles, and salt; deep-fry them; and serve them like chicken wings. Another unique quality of this fish is that the flanks of meat covering the belly are quite thick—fatty and wonderfully flavored—and every effort should be taken to make use of them.

Broiled Porgy in Charred Tomato Vinaigrette

SERVES 4

>1 recipe Charred Tomato Vinaigrette (page 35)
>
>4 porgy portions, skin on, scored
>
>Extra-virgin olive oil
>
>Crusty bread for serving

Preheat the broiler to medium and set the rack in the position closest to the heat. Pour the vinaigrette into a baking dish just large enough to hold the fish. Nestle the fish skin side up into the vinaigrette and drizzle the top of the fish with olive oil. Slide the dish under the broiler and cook until the skin is slightly singed and the sauce is bubbling. Remove and let it rest for 5 minutes before serving with crusty bread.

VARIATION

+ **Rosemary Porgy.** Replace the Charred Tomato Vinaigrette with Charred Rosemary Vinaigrette (page 35).

Sautéed Prosciutto-Wrapped Porgy

SERVES 4

>4 porgy portions, skin off
>
>Salt
>
>2 tablespoons chopped fresh parsley or tarragon
>
>1 lemon, zested and juiced
>
>2 pinches ground mace
>
>2 tablespoons white wine
>
>8 thin slices prosciutto
>
>4 tablespoons butter

Season the fish with salt, then mix with the parsley or tarragon, lemon zest and juice, mace, and white wine. Marinate for 2 hours. Wrap each portion in two slices of prosciutto and secure with a toothpick. In a sauté pan over medium heat, melt the butter and cook until golden brown. Add the fish to the pan. Cook until the prosciutto is crisp and the fish is almost done, then flip to finish cooking. Serve drizzled with butter from the pan.

Sautéed Porgy with Brown Butter, Coriander, and Orange

SERVES 4

>4 porgy portions, skin off
>
>Salt
>
>1½ tablespoons coriander seeds, crushed
>
>6 tablespoons butter, divided
>
>2 garlic cloves, finely minced
>
>1 orange, zested and juiced
>
>Black pepper

Season the fish all over with salt and on one side with coriander, and let it rest for 15 minutes. In a sauté pan over medium-low heat, melt 2 tablespoons of the butter and cook until golden brown. Place the fish in the pan coriander side down. Cook without flipping until almost done, then remove the fish, and wipe the pan clean. Add the remaining 4 tablespoons of butter and the garlic and cook until golden brown. Add the zest, season with black pepper, and cook for 30 seconds. Add the orange juice and season with salt. Turn the heat off. Return the fish to the pan uncooked side down to finish cooking.

Sautéed Porgy with Brown Butter and Grapes

SERVES 4

> 4 porgy portions, skin on and scored
>
> Salt
>
> 6 tablespoons butter
>
> 1 cup grapes
>
> 2 tablespoons chopped fresh parsley or tarragon
>
> 1 lemon, juiced

Season the fish with salt and let it rest for 15 minutes. Set the broiler to medium-high. In an oven-safe sauté pan over medium heat, melt the butter and cook until golden brown. Place the fish skin side down in the pan. Arrange the grapes among the fillets. Spoon the brown butter over the fish and grapes and place the pan under a medium-hot broiler. Cook until the grapes have blistered and released some juice and the fish is cooked through, 4–5 minutes. Scatter the herbs and drizzle the lemon juice on top.

Porgy Grilled on the Half Shell

SERVES 4

> 1 recipe Preserved Lemon-Mint Butter (page 22)
>
> 4 portions porgy fillets, with scales and skin intact, bones removed
>
> Salt
>
> Black pepper
>
> 1 cup picked fresh herbs, such as chervil, parsley, tarragon, and/or mint

Prepare a charcoal grill with a medium fire. Season the fish with salt and pepper and let it rest for 15 minutes. Place the fish skin side down directly over the hot coals. Baste the fillets with the melted butter, cover, and cook until done. Transfer to a serving platter, slather with Preserved Lemon-Mint Butter, top with the herbs, and serve with instructions to eaters to spoon the fish off the skin, leaving the skin and scales on the platter.

NOTE *If using a gas grill, preheat all burners to medium-high.*

VARIATION

+ **Porgy with Meyer Lemon.** Substitute Meyer Lemon-Pepper Butter (page 21) for the Preserved Lemon-Mint Butter.

Porgy Roasted on Bacon and Vegetables

SERVES 4

    1 recipe Horseradish Butter (page 20)

    3 stalks celery, diced

    1 fennel bulb, diced

    ½ cup diced carrots

    ¼ pound bacon, diced

    4 porgy portions, skin off

    Salt

    2 sprigs thyme, leaves picked

In a saucepan over medium heat, combine 2 cups of lightly salted water with the celery, fennel, carrots, and bacon. Simmer for 5 minutes. Strain the liquid from the vegetables, reserving both. Chill the vegetable mixture. In a saucepan over medium-high heat, reduce the liquid to ½ cup. Season the fish with salt and let it rest for 15 minutes. Scatter the chilled vegetable mixture in the bottom of a baking dish, place the fish on top, scatter the thyme over the fish, and drizzle the reduced liquid around the edges of the pan. Place 2 tablespoons Horseradish Butter on top of each portion. Roast the fish in a 350°F oven until done, about 8–10 minutes.

Poached and Marinated Porgy

SERVES 4

    4 porgy portions, skin off

    Salt

    2 cups white wine

    10 black peppercorns

    10 star anise pods

    Crushed red chile flakes

    1 cup extra-virgin olive oil

    1 orange, zest removed in wide strips

    2 stalks rosemary

    ½ tablespoon coarse ground black pepper

    ½ tablespoon crushed fennel seeds

    2–3 dried chiles, such as de árbol or Calabrian

    1 tablespoon sherry vinegar

    ¼ cup chopped herbs, such as chives or parsley

    Toast points

Season the fish with salt and let it rest for 15 minutes. In a deep pan just wide enough to hold the fish in a single layer, combine 2 cups of water with the wine, peppercorns, star anise, and a pinch of chile flakes. Simmer over low heat for 5 minutes. Season the broth with salt and bring it to 170°F. Add the fish and cook until it is opaque and flakes under gentle pressure, 4–6 minutes per ½ inch of thickness. Remove the pan from the heat and cool the fish in the poaching liquid to room temperature. In a small pan over low heat, warm the olive oil. Add the zest, rosemary, ground pepper, fennel seeds, and dried chiles. When the oil is highly aromatic, about 3 minutes, remove the pan from the heat and cool to room temperature. Remove the fish from the liquid and pat dry. Pour the oil over poached fish, add the vinegar and herbs, and marinate for 1–3 days. Serve the fish at room temperature on toast dipped in the marinade.

REMORA
Flaky white fish, meaty dense fish

Remoras are suckers—truly, I mean no disrespect.

They have a hard, scratchy plate on the top of their heads that they use to grasp on to the sides and underbellies of sharks and whales. They tend to be named after the fish they stick to: sharksucker, marlinsucker, and so forth. Only remoras that reach 2 feet in length or more are worth any culinary effort. They have no scales and range in color from a sooty, mottled black to a sporty striped look.

The yield is quite low because even though remoras have small rib cages, pin bones run back in the fillet nearly half the fish's length. Their smoky-pink flesh has very dense muscle ribboned with fat. Its texture is a cross between sablefish and mahi mahi, missing the tiny flake of the former and the meatiness of the latter. Its taste is savory and salty, with hints of a green seaweed–type aroma and a flavor and aftertaste very rich in umami. Its oily mouthfeel is ameliorated if it is cooked slowly so that its fat renders out. Because of the streaky fat in its fillets, it takes the flavors of smoke very well. Both the shape and size of the fillets make for an awkward presentation, so mixing remoras into stews and chowders is a good idea.

Gently poaching the fish prior to moving on to a secondary preparation both adds flavor and helps render out some of the fat. From there, remora is suitable for just about any cooking technique. It's unique among fish in that it can be at its best when cooked twice, as its texture becomes wonderfully soft and yielding, though it maintains its resiliency.

Curried Remora with Raisins

SERVES 4

> 1 cup Basic Fish Stock (page 61) or vegetable stock or coconut water
>
> 4 remora portions, skin off and cut into 1-inch pieces
>
> Salt
>
> 4 tablespoons butter
>
> 2 tablespoons raisins
>
> 3 tablespoons slivered almonds
>
> 2 garlic cloves, sliced
>
> 2 teaspoons curry powder
>
> ½ cup sour cream
>
> 3 tablespoons chopped fresh herbs, such as cilantro or parsley

Season the fish with salt and let it rest for 20 minutes. In a large pot over high heat, melt the butter. Add the fish and sear until lightly colored. Remove from the pan. Reduce the heat to medium and add the raisins, almonds, and garlic. Cook until the raisins begin to plump. Add the curry powder and stir to toast the spices for 30 seconds Add the stock and sour cream and stir to combine. Add the fish, cover, and bring to a very low simmer, and cook until done, 10–12 minutes. Garnish with herbs.

Broiled Remora with Creamy Lemon-Pecan Dressing

SERVES 4

> 1 recipe Creamy Lemon-Pecan Dressing (page 36)
>
> 4 remora portions, skin off
>
> Salt

Season the fish with salt and let it rest for 20 minutes. Preheat the broiler to medium and set the rack in the position closest to the heat. Place the fish on a baking tray and slide the tray under the broiler. Cook until done, about 8 minutes. Serve with Creamy Lemon-Pecan Dressing.

Remora with Almond Brown Butter

SERVES 4

> 4 remora portions, skin off
>
> Salt
>
> 6 tablespoons butter, divided
>
> ½ cup sliced almonds
>
> Ground cinnamon
>
> 2 lemons, juiced

Season the fish with salt and let it rest for 20 minutes. In a sauté pan over medium heat, melt 2 tablespoons of the butter and cook until golden brown. Place the fish in the pan. Cook without flipping until almost done, then remove the fish, and wipe the pan clean. Reduce the heat to medium and add the remaining 4 tablespoons of butter, almonds, and a pinch of cinnamon. Cook until the almonds are browned. Add the lemon juice and season with salt. Stir to combine. Turn off the heat and return the fish to the pan uncooked side down to finish cooking.

SABLEFISH
Flaky white fish, orange-fleshed fish

This incredibly svelte queen of the cold northern Pacific is about as elegant as seafood gets. Its name is a reflection of its silken flesh, which some say is as luxurious as the fur of a sable. More than two-thirds of the domestic sablefish landed is taken in Alaska, where they often grow to roughly 5 pounds or greater. Sablefish freezes really well, enabling its largely remote fisheries to deliver high-quality product year-round to the lower forty-eight states. But it can be expensive, so make a celebration of it.

Sablefish's culinary characteristics resemble those of the popular Chilean sea bass: bright white-fleshed fillets with exceptional richness. The flavor is complex and savory, with a shellfish-like sweetness, and it takes on a caramelized pecan nutty finish when cooked, especially over high heat. A quick dry cure in salt and sugar for about 1 hour accentuates its flavor and tenses its texture.

When raw, sablefish has an elastic texture that is easy to work with. The bones are not easily pulled out of the raw fillet, but they can be removed by making shallow incisions on either side of the bones, known as a V-cut, to remove the entire strip. Once the fish is cooked, the bones can be removed easily with tweezers or fingers. The spine and ribs are relatively soft, and those from smaller fish can be soaked in a heavy brine and then deep-fried until crisp or barbecued over a wood fire for a crunchy snack. Sablefish collars, while hard to find, as the fish is usually sold in fillet form, also make a delightful nibble, as the bone holds a very tasty chunk of meat.

The elasticity of the raw fish yields to a beautiful flake once it's broiled, fried, poached, roasted, sautéed, or smoked. The skin, which must be scaled before cooking, crisps well and adds a nice counterpoint to the fish's texture, though the flesh is equally good with the skin off.

Sablefish is a good candidate for both cold- and hot-smoking. It is best when paired with hearty but not overpowering woods, such as pecan, oak, or maple. When serving smoked sablefish, grilled lemons or an acidic vinaigrette is a welcome balance to the rich fish.

Broiled Sablefish with Herbes de Provence

SERVES 4

1 recipe Herbes de Provence Mix (page 33)

4 sablefish portions, skin off

Salt

Extra-virgin olive oil or melted butter

1 lemon, cut into wedges

Season the fish all over with salt and on one side with the Herbes de Provence Mix and let it rest for 15 minutes. Preheat the broiler to medium and set the rack in the position farthest from the heat. Place the fish on a baking tray herbed side up and drizzle it with olive oil. Slide the tray under the broiler and cook until done, 7–10 minutes, depending on thickness. Serve with lemon wedges.

Broiled Sablefish with Orange, Rosemary, and Crunchy Ritz Cracker Topping

SERVES 4

3 tablespoons Mayonnaise (page 29, or store-bought)

4 sablefish portions, skin off

Salt

4 tablespoons crushed Ritz Crackers

1 teaspoon minced rosemary leaves

1 orange, zested and cut into wedges

Season the fish with salt and let it rest for 15 minutes. Preheat the broiler to medium and set the rack in the middle position. Stir together the Mayonnaise, crushed crackers, rosemary, and orange zest. Place the fish on the baking tray. Spread the mayonnaise mixture evenly on top of the fish. Slide the tray under the broiler. Broil until the fish is done and the topping is browned, 7–10 minutes, depending on thickness. Serve with orange wedges.

Poached Sablefish

SERVES 4

4 sablefish portions, skin off

Salt

1 cup white wine

3 tablespoons red or white wine vinegar

5 black peppercorns

1 bay leaf

1 lemon, zest removed in wide strips and juiced

4 tablespoons butter, melted

Season the fish with salt and let it rest for 15 minutes. In a deep pan just wide enough to hold the fish in a single layer, combine 2 cups of water with the wine, vinegar, peppercorns, bay leaf and zest. Simmer over low heat for 5 minutes. Season the broth with salt and bring it to 170°F. Add the fish and cook until it is opaque and flakes under gentle pressure, 4–6 minutes per ½ inch of thickness. Transfer the fish to a serving platter. Spoon melted butter over the fish and finish with lemon juice.

Sautéed Sablefish with Brown Butter and Thyme

SERVES 4

> 4 sablefish portions, skin off
>
> Salt
>
> 5 tablespoons butter, divided
>
> 2 garlic cloves, minced
>
> 8 sprigs thyme, leaves picked
>
> 1 lemon, zested and juiced

Season the fish with salt and let it rest for 15 minutes. In a sauté pan over medium heat, melt 2 tablespoons of the butter and cook until golden brown. Place the fish in the pan. Cook without flipping until almost done, then remove the fish, and wipe the pan clean. Add the remaining 3 tablespoons of butter, garlic, and thyme. Cook until the garlic is brown. Add the lemon zest and juice and season with salt. Stir to combine. Turn off the heat and return the fish to the pan uncooked side down to finish cooking.

Sautéed Sablefish au Poivre Flambé

SERVES 4

> 4 sablefish portions, skin off
>
> Salt
>
> 1½ tablespoons black peppercorns, coarsely ground
>
> 1½ tablespoons fennel seeds, crushed
>
> 4 tablespoons butter
>
> 1½ ounces cognac or bourbon

Season the fish with salt on both sides and on one side with the pepper and fennel seeds. Press the seasonings into the flesh and let it rest for 15 minutes. In a sauté pan over medium heat, melt the butter and cook until golden brown.

Place the fish pepper side down in the pan. Cook without flipping until almost done, then flip to finish cooking. Turn off the heat. Add the cognac or bourbon and flambé by lighting with a match. Allow the alcohol to burn off before serving.

Prosciutto-Wrapped Sablefish

SERVES 4

> 4 sablefish portions, skin off
>
> Salt
>
> 2 tablespoons chopped fresh parsley or tarragon
>
> 1 lemon, zested and juiced
>
> 2 pinches ground mace
>
> 2 tablespoons white wine
>
> 8 thinly sliced pieces prosciutto
>
> 4 tablespoons butter

Season the fish with salt and then mix with the parsley or tarragon, lemon zest and juice, mace, and white wine. Marinate for 2 hours. Wrap each portion in two slices of prosciutto and secure with a toothpick. In a sauté pan over medium heat, melt the butter and cook until golden brown. Add the fish to the pan. Cook until the prosciutto is crisp and the fish is almost done, then flip to finish cooking. Serve drizzled with butter from the pan.

Sautéed Sablefish with Rosemary and Madeira

SERVES 4

> 4 sablefish portions, skin on or off
>
> Salt
>
> 5 tablespoons butter, divided
>
> 2 stalks rosemary
>
> ½ cup Madeira, a drier style such as Sercial or Verdelho

Season the fish with salt and let it rest for 15 minutes. In a sauté pan over medium heat, melt 2 tablespoons of the butter and cook until golden brown. Place the fish (skin side down, if using) in the pan. Add the rosemary. Cook without flipping until almost done, then remove the fish, and wipe the pan clean. Discard the rosemary. Add the Madeira and cook until it has reduced to about 2 tablespoons. Turn off the heat and add the remaining 3 tablespoons of butter, and swirl gently to combine. Return the fish to the pan uncooked side down to finish cooking.

Sautéed Sablefish with Brown Butter, Ginger, and Orange

SERVES 4

    4 sablefish portions, skin on or off
    Salt
    6 tablespoons butter, divided
    1 teaspoon grated ginger
    1 orange, segmented

Season the fish with salt and let it rest for 15 minutes. In a sauté pan over medium heat, melt 2 tablespoons of the butter and cook until golden brown. Place the fish (skin side down if using) in the pan. Cook without flipping until almost done, then remove the fish, and wipe the pan clean. Add the remaining 4 tablespoons of butter and cook until the butter is dark brown. Add the ginger and cook for 30 seconds. Add the orange segments and season with salt. Stir gently to combine. Turn the heat off. Return the fish to the pan uncooked side down to finish cooking.

Hot-Smoked Sablefish

MAKES ABOUT 1½ POUNDS

    ⅓ cup kosher salt
    ⅓ cup packed brown sugar
    1 orange, juiced
    10 juniper berries
    1 tablespoon fennel seeds
    1 cinnamon stick
    ¼ cup Pernod or other anise-flavored liqueur, divided
    1 (1½-pound) sablefish fillet, skin on

In a saucepan over medium heat, simmer 1 cup of water with the salt, brown sugar, orange juice, juniper berries, fennel seeds, and cinnamon for 5 minutes. Add 3 cups of cold water and 2 tablespoons of the Pernod to the brine and stir. Place the fish in a glass or ceramic baking dish, pour the brine over it, and refrigerate for 2 hours. Remove the fish from the liquid, pat dry, and brush with the remaining 2 tablespoons of Pernod. Refrigerate the fish uncovered on a wire rack overnight. Cold-smoke the fish skin side down for 1–2 hours at as low a temperature as possible (below 100°F). Increase the temperature to 150°F and smoke for another 2 hours. Remove from the smoker and cool to room temperature. Tightly wrap the fillet in plastic and refrigerate overnight before using.

VARIATIONS

+ **Allspice-Smoked Sablefish.** Periodically add a couple of allspice berries to the smoke source.

+ **Herb-Scented Smoked Sablefish.** When removing the sablefish from the smoker, immediately cover the fish with fresh basil or mint leaves to gently perfume it. Remove the leaves prior to serving.

SALMON
Orange-fleshed fish, fillet fish

Salmon has become ubiquitous, and I think many cooks now overlook how dynamic an ingredient it is. It has a rich texture and a unique flavor that makes it a crowd-pleaser at home and a restaurant staple from the temples of haute cuisine to the neighborhood diner.

When cooked, salmon have a somewhat nutty, buttery taste and the faint aroma of baked potato. When raw, fresh salmon has a cucumber scent and a very mild and nuanced flavor. The flavor of salmon intensifies as it cooks, much the way lamb does, not reaching its potential until cooked at least to medium doneness.

Farmed Salmon: All commercial wild Atlantic salmon fisheries in the United States were closed by 1948. Atlantic salmon is now farmed all over the world in oceans far from the Atlantic and even on land. It has rapidly become one of the most important globally traded seafoods and has had an impressive impact in increasing the seafood intake of Americans. This darling of the culinary world, because of its consistent availability and affable personality, is an easy fish to prepare. It's often considered a "gateway" fish, since it is a great vehicle on which to learn common cooking methods, from slow roasting to grilling to smoking that can be applied to less-available species. There is a wide spectrum of quality in farmed salmon: some are incredibly rich and flavorful, whereas others are leaner and milder in flavor. Salmon farming suffers from a bad environmental reputation, but as the industry matures, some companies are now farming the fish with admirable success in terms of environmental sustainability and flavor.

Wild Salmon: There are five major species of wild salmon from the West Coast. Each offers a twist on the standard salmon flavor profile. **Chum**, while not as common as other species, has the same texture and light flavor as farmed Atlantic salmon, with a nuanced taste and fat that is well integrated into the meat. **Coho** has a wonderful balance of sweet flavor and robust, oily richness. **King** is the richest and most expensive of the salmons. Worth every penny, it has a robust, haunting flavor that ranks in the top tier of culinary delights. King sears well, though it is best finished by cooking slowly, such as when grilled over direct heat then cooked through away from the fire. **Pink** is the leanest, most delicate, and cleanest in flavor in the family. While typically canned, when well cared for, the fresh (and most often fresh-frozen) product is a fine candidate for hot-smoking. **Sockeye** is the gamiest in taste of all the salmon species. It has a brilliant sunset orange hue and a darker, more mineral flavor. It should be cooked over low heat to retain moisture and its fat.

All salmon is marketed in many forms: sold whole, filleted, and as cross-cut steaks; the latter is the best way to enjoy all the nuances of flavor and texture in one dish, from its skin, which crisps without curling, to the firm fillet and around the buttery soft belly meat.

Salmon are also over 90 percent edible, with everything except the gallbladder, gills, and contents of the stomach having culinary merit. The liver makes for a great breakfast when sautéed with bacon and served with a good squeeze of lemon juice. Salmon roe is most often cured in a mixture of salt and sugar and sold in much the same way as caviar. Immature skeins and milt can be sautéed in butter with hard herbs like rosemary or thyme. It's best to coat the softer milt in flour before sautéing. Salmon heads make a full-flavored and hearty stock that must be simmered over the lowest heat to avoid becoming murky and overpoweringly strong.

Smoked Salmon: There are two basic types of smoked salmon: cold and hot. Cold-smoked salmon, the kind you typically see sliced and served with bagels, has been cured in salt and/or sugar and flavored with smoke but not actually cooked. Hot-smoked salmon, more typically seen flaked atop salads, has been gently cooked in a warm, smoky environment that both flavors it and cooks it through.

Salmon of all varieties are among the best fish to eat when cooked and then served chilled.

(continued)

SALMON
Fresh

Broiled Salmon with Blistered Cherry Tomatoes

SERVES 4

    4 salmon portions, skin on

    Salt

    ½ cup extra-virgin olive oil

    4 garlic cloves, sliced

    2 pints cherry tomatoes

    1 stalk rosemary

Season the fish with salt and let it rest for 20 minutes. Preheat the broiler to medium and set the rack in the middle position. In an ovenproof pan over high heat, warm the olive oil and garlic and cook until the garlic is golden brown. Add the tomatoes and rosemary. When the tomatoes begin to blister, season with salt. Nestle the fish skin side up into the tomatoes, and spoon a bit of the olive oil over the skin. Slide the skillet under the broiler, and cook until the fish is done, 7–10 minutes, depending on thickness. Discard the rosemary before serving.

Broiled Salmon with Mayonnaise, Sour Cream, and Dill

SERVES 4

    3 tablespoons Mayonnaise (page 29, or
    store-bought)

    4 salmon portions, skin off

    Salt

    3 tablespoons sour cream

    2 tablespoons Amontillado or cooking sherry

    2 tablespoons chopped fresh dill

Season the fish with salt and let it rest for 20 minutes. Preheat the broiler to medium and set the rack in the middle position. Whisk together the Mayonnaise, sour cream, sherry, and dill. Place the fish on a baking tray. Spread the mayonnaise mixture evenly over the top of the fish. Slide the tray under the broiler. Broil until done, 7–10 minutes, depending on thickness.

Teriyaki-Glazed Salmon

SERVES 4

    1 recipe Teriyaki-Style Sauce (page 32)

    4 salmon portions, skin on

    Salt

    2 teaspoons Worcestershire sauce

    1 tablespoon sesame oil

    ¼ cup sliced scallions

Season the fish lightly with salt and let it rest for 20 minutes. Preheat the broiler to medium and set the rack in the middle position. Combine the Teriyaki-Style Sauce and the Worcestershire sauce. Brush the fish with the sesame oil. Place the fish skin side up in a baking dish, coat with half of the sauce, and slide the dish under the broiler. Cook, basting with the remaining sauce every 2 minutes until done, 7–10 minutes, depending on thickness. Garnish with sliced scallions.

Broiled Salmon with Green Goddess Dressing

SERVES 4

    1 recipe Green Goddess Dressing (page 28)

    2 tablespoons dry vermouth

    4 salmon portions, skin on

Season the fish with salt, sprinkle with the vermouth, and let it rest for 20 minutes. Preheat the broiler to medium and set the rack in the middle position. Place the fish on a baking tray, slide the tray under the broiler, and cook until done, 7–10 minutes, depending on thickness. Serve with Green Goddess Dressing.

Broiled Salmon with Sorrel Butter

SERVES 4

    1 recipe Sorrel Butter (page 22)

    4 salmon portions, skin on

    Salt

    Extra-virgin olive oil

    Black pepper

Season the fish with salt and let it rest for 20 minutes. Preheat the broiler to medium and set the rack in the middle position. Place the fish skin side up on a baking tray. Drizzle with olive oil and season with black pepper. Slide the tray under the broiler and cook until the fish is done, 7–10 minutes, depending on thickness. Top each portion with Sorrel Butter.

Salmon Ceviche with Dill

SERVES 4 AS AN APPETIZER

    1 pound previously frozen wild salmon fillets or fresh farmed salmon fillets, skin off, diced into ½-inch pieces

    Salt

    1 cup lime juice

    2 tablespoons sherry vinegar

1–2 thinly sliced Fresno or serrano chiles

    1 teaspoon dried oregano

    1 large red onion, thinly sliced, rinsed under cold running water, and patted dry

    ¼ cup extra-virgin olive oil

    ¼ cup chopped dill

    Ground nutmeg for garnish

Keep this dish cold at all times during preparation. Season the fish with salt and let it rest for 5 minutes. Combine the fish with the lime juice, vinegar, chiles, and oregano and let it rest for 30 minutes. Add the onion and let it rest another 10 minutes. Add the olive oil and dill and toss well. Garnish with nutmeg.

Salmon Gravlax

MAKES ABOUT 1½ POUNDS

¾ cup kosher salt

¾ cup brown sugar

2 teaspoons ground mace

2 teaspoons onion powder

2 (1-pound) similarly shaped salmon fillets, skin on and scored

15 sprigs fresh dill

Mix the salt, sugar, mace, and onion powder. Rub the flesh of each fillet with one-third of the salt mixture. In a glass or ceramic dish lined with plastic wrap, sprinkle a thin layer of the salt mixture and place one fillet skin side down on it. Cover the fillet with the dill and place the second fillet, flesh to flesh, on top of the first one. Sprinkle the remaining salt mixture over the skin of the top fillet. Tightly wrap the fish with plastic wrap, place a dish of a similar size and shape as the fish on top of it, and set a couple of soup cans on the plate to weigh it down. Refrigerate for 12 hours. Flip the fish and refrigerate, still weighed down, for another 12 hours. Remove the weight, unwrap the fish, pour off any liquid that has collected in the dish, cover loosely with plastic, and let it rest another 24 hours, flipping once. Rinse the fillets with cold water to remove excess salt and brine. Discard the dill. Pat dry and wrap each fillet individually in plastic and store in the refrigerator for up to 1 week. To serve, thinly slice the fillet on the bias, starting at the thicker end of the fillet and working toward the thinner side. These slices can be laid out as carpaccio, with olive oil and lemon juice drizzled over the top, draped over salads, or served on bagels.

NOTE *For thinner fillets, decrease the overall curing time by 12 hours.*

VARIATION

+ **Pine-Scented Gravlax.** Replace the dill with young untreated pine boughs and place thin slices of orange between the fish and the pine.

Salmon Gravlax with Pastrami Spices

MAKES ABOUT 1½ POUNDS

1 recipe Salmon Gravlax (at left) or 1½ pounds purchased

⅓ cup molasses

4 bay leaves

Crushed red chile flakes

2 tablespoons fennel seeds, crushed

1 tablespoon caraway seeds, crushed

1 tablespoon coriander seeds, crushed

1 tablespoon smoked sweet paprika

1 tablespoon black pepper, coarsely ground

In a saucepan over low heat, warm the molasses with the spices. Let cool to just above room temperature. Remove the bay leaves from the molasses and use a brush to evenly coat the cured salmon flesh with the barely warm molasses and spices. Refrigerate uncovered for 12–48 hours before serving.

VARIATION

+ **Beet-Horseradish Gravlax.** Replace the molasses and spices with a mixture of 1 pound of finely grated raw beets; ¼ cup brandy, Pernod, or rum; and 5 tablespoons of prepared horseradish.

Salmon Gravlax Carpaccio with Herbs and Nuts

SERVES 4–6 AS AN APPETIZER

> 1 fillet Salmon Gravlax (page 332, or purchased)
>
> Extra-virgin olive oil, hazelnut oil, or almond oil
>
> 4 shallots, thinly sliced, rinsed under cold running water, and patted dry
>
> 1 cup picked parsley, chervil, and/or mint
>
> 1 lemon, juiced
>
> Salt
>
> Freshly cracked black pepper or crushed red chile flakes
>
> ¼ cup chopped toasted nuts

Slice the salmon gravlax and lay it on serving plates in a single layer. Drizzle each serving with oil. Combine the shallots and parsley and lightly dress with lemon juice and season with salt. Scatter the salad over the salmon. Season with black pepper or chile flakes and finish with a sprinkling of toasted chopped nuts.

Grilled Salmon with Louisiana Remoulade

SERVES 4

> 1 recipe Louisiana Remoulade (page 31)
>
> 4 salmon portions, skin on
>
> Salt
>
> Extra-virgin olive oil

Season the fish with salt and let it rest for 20 minutes. Prepare a charcoal grill with a medium fire, concentrating the hot coals on one side of the kettle. Lightly drizzle the fish with olive oil. Place the fish skin side down on the grill over the hot coals. Cook until the edges of the fish begin to crisp, about 3–4 minutes.

Lift the entire grill grate and rotate it so the fish rests opposite the hot coals. Cover the grill and continue to cook over this indirect heat until the fish is done. Serve with Louisiana Remoulade.

NOTE *If using a gas grill, preheat all burners to medium-high. Place the salmon on one side of the hot grates. Once it begins to char around the edges, turn off the burner directly under the fish and cover the grill to finish cooking.*

Pine-Grilled Salmon with Chunky Almond Oil

SERVES 4

> 1 recipe Chunky Almond Oil (page 25)
>
> 4 salmon portions, skin on
>
> Salt
>
> Extra-virgin olive oil
>
> Pine boughs

Season the fish with salt and let it rest for 20 minutes. Prepare a charcoal grill with a medium fire, concentrating the hot coals on one side of the kettle. Place the pine boughs on the grill above the hot coals. Lightly drizzle the fish with oil and place it skin side down on the pine boughs. Cook until the pine begins to smolder, about 3–4 minutes. Lift the entire grill grate and rotate it so the fish rests opposite the hot coals. Cover the grill, and continue to cook over this indirect heat until the fish is done. Peel off and discard the skin. Serve with Chunky Almond Oil.

NOTE *If using a gas grill, preheat all burners to medium-high. Place the pine boughs on one side of the grill. Lightly drizzle the salmon with oil and place it skin side down on the pine boughs. Cook until the pine begins to smolder, about 3–4 minutes. Turn off the burner directly under the fish and cover the grill to finish cooking.*

Plank-Grilled Salmon with Dill Crème Fraîche

SERVES 4

> 1 recipe Dill Crème Fraîche (page 27)
>
> 4 salmon portions, skin off
>
> Salt
>
> Extra-virgin olive oil

Season the fish with salt and let it rest for 20 minutes. Prepare a charcoal grill with a medium fire. Lightly oil the fish, place it on a cedar plank, put the plank on the grill above the coals, and cover the grill. Cook for 8–12 minutes, or until done. Serve with Dill Crème Fraîche.

NOTE *If using a gas grill, preheat all the burners to medium.*

Grilled Salmon with Pernod and Herbs

SERVES 4

> ¼ cup Pernod or dry vermouth
>
> 1 shallot, finely diced
>
> 3 tablespoons extra-virgin olive oil
>
> ¼ cup chopped fresh tarragon and/or parsley
>
> 1 tablespoon kosher salt
>
> 4 salmon portions, skin on
>
> 1 lemon, cut into wedges

Combine the Pernod, shallot, olive oil, tarragon or parsley, and salt. Pour the mixture over the salmon and let it rest for 1–4 hours. Prepare a charcoal grill with a medium fire, concentrating the hot coals on one side of the kettle. Remove the fish from the marinade and place it skin side down on the grill over the hot coals. Cook until the skin begins to char, about 3–4 minutes. Lift the entire grill grate and rotate it so the fish

rests opposite the hot coals. Pour any remaining marinade over the fish. Cover the grill and continue to cook over this indirect heat until the fish is done. Serve with lemon wedges.

NOTE *If using a gas grill, preheat all burners to medium. Place the salmon on one side of the hot grates. Once it begins to char around the edges, turn off the burner directly under the fish. Pour any remaining marinade over the fish and cover the grill to finish cooking.*

Creamed Chipped Smoked Salmon

SERVES 4

> 1 pound Hot-Smoked Salmon (page 341, or purchased)
>
> 3½ cups whole milk, plus more as needed
>
> 1 bay leaf
>
> 4 tablespoons butter
>
> ¼ cup flour
>
> 4 slices Texas toast, sourdough bread, or rye toast for serving
>
> 2 tablespoons chopped fresh parsley
>
> Crushed red chile flakes

In a saucepan over low heat, combine the salmon, milk, and bay leaf. Simmer gently for 7 minutes. Remove the fish from the milk and flake into bite-size pieces. Discard the bay leaf. In a sauté pan over medium heat, melt the butter. Add the flour and cook, stirring constantly, for 2 minutes. Whisk in the warm milk and cook, stirring constantly until thickened, about 10 minutes. Add the flaked fish and stir to combine. Add a bit more milk if the sauce is too thick. Serve hot over Texas toast, sourdough, or rye toast, and top with chopped parsley and chile flakes

Marinated Salmon Roe

SERVES 4–6 AS AN APPETIZER

    4 ounces cured salmon roe

    ½ tablespoon kosher salt

    2 tablespoons extra-virgin olive oil

    ¼ cup sparkling wine

    1 tablespoon chopped fresh chives or tarragon

    Toast points for serving

Soak the roe in 1 cup room-temperature water seasoned with the salt for 10 minutes. Discard any broken eggs that float to the surface. Drain and allow to air-dry a few minutes. Toss the roe with the olive oil, wine, and chives. Serve with toast or as a garnish to salads.

Smoked Salmon Quiche

SERVES 4–8

    1 (9-inch-wide and 2-inch-deep) pie crust, pre-baked according to instructions on the package

    1 pound Hot-Smoked Salmon (page 341, or purchased)

    3 cups half-and-half

    6 large eggs, beaten

    3 tablespoons chopped fresh tarragon or 1 tablespoon dried tarragon

    1 lemon, zested

    Salt

    Spicy greens for serving

Set the pie shell on a baking tray. In a pan over low heat, combine the salmon and half-and-half and simmer for 5 minutes. Turn off the heat and cool to room temperature. Remove the fish and flake it into bite-size pieces into the pie shell. Whisk together the eggs, poaching liquid, tarragon, lemon zest, and salt to taste. Pour the batter into the shell, slide the tray into a 375°F oven, and bake until set, 30–45 minutes. Cool to room temperature and serve with a salad of spicy greens.

Pickled Salmon

SERVES 6–8 AS AN APPETIZER

    1¼ pounds salmon, skin off, cut into 1-inch cubes

    2 tablespoons kosher salt

    1 tablespoon sugar

    1½ cups red or white wine vinegar

    2 medium-size crisp apples, such as Honeycrisp, peeled and finely chopped

    1 large onion, thinly sliced

    20 peppercorns

    5–6 juniper berries

    1 tablespoon fennel seeds

    ¼ cup slivered almonds

    4 bay leaves

Soak the fish in 2 cups cold water and kosher salt for 12 hours. Drain from the brine and discard the brine. Mix the sugar and vinegar. Place some fish in the bottom of a jar or small porcelain dish in a single layer. Then place layers of apples, onion, peppercorns, juniper berries, fennel seeds, almonds, and bay leaves, repeating until all the ingredients have been added. Pour the vinegar mixture over the layers to cover. Cover the container and place it in the refrigerator. The fish will be ready to use after 24 hours—48 hours if a firmer texture is desired. The pickled salmon will keep up to 4 days in the refrigerator.

Chilled Salmon with Horseradish and Walnuts

SERVES 4

4 salmon portions, skin on

Salt

1 cup white wine

2 tablespoons white wine vinegar

1 shallot, sliced

1 small carrot, sliced

10 black peppercorns

1 bay leaf

¼ cup walnuts, very finely chopped

½ cup sour cream or Greek yogurt

2 tablespoons prepared horseradish

1 teaspoon brown sugar

1 lemon, zest and juice

Season the fish with salt and let it rest for 20 minutes. In a pan just wide enough to hold the fish in a single layer, combine 2 cups of water with the wine, vinegar, shallot, carrot, ½ tablespoon kosher salt, peppercorns, and bay leaf. Simmer over low heat for 5 minutes. Season the broth with salt and bring it to 170°F. Add the fish and cook until it flakes under gentle pressure, 4–6 minutes per ½ inch of thickness. Remove the pan from the heat and cool the fish in the poaching liquid to room temperature. Combine the walnuts, sour cream, horseradish, brown sugar, and lemon zest and juice, and stir to form a thick sauce. Remove the fish from the liquid, and pat dry. Remove the skin from the fish and discard. Serve the fish with the sauce.

Chilled Poached Salmon with Star Anise and Herb Salad

SERVES 4

4 salmon portions, skin on

Salt

1 cup white wine

5 black peppercorns

5 star anise pods

Crushed red chile flakes

¼ cup mint, leaves picked

½ cup parsley, leaves picked

1 shallot, thinly sliced

1 lemon, juiced

2 tablespoons extra-virgin olive oil

Season the fish with salt and let it rest for 20 minutes. In a pan just wide enough to hold the fish in a single layer, combine 2 cups of water with the wine, peppercorns, star anise, and chile flakes. Simmer over low heat for 5 minutes. Season the broth with salt and bring it to 170°F. Add the fish skin side down and cook until it flakes under gentle pressure, 4–6 minutes per ½ inch of thickness. Remove the pan from the heat and cool the fish in the poaching liquid to room temperature. Remove the fish from the poaching liquid, remove and discard the skin, and pat dry. Combine the mint, parsley, and shallot and toss with the lemon juice and olive oil and season with salt. Serve the fish topped with the herb salad.

Chilled Poached Salmon with Citrus-Tarragon Vinaigrette

SERVES 4

> 4 salmon portions, skin on
>
> Salt
>
> 1 cup white wine
>
> 2 tablespoons white wine vinegar
>
> 2 shallots, 1 sliced, 1 minced
>
> 1 small carrot, sliced
>
> 10 black peppercorns
>
> 1 bay leaf
>
> 1 orange, zested in wide strips and juiced
>
> 1 sprig fresh rosemary
>
> 2 teaspoons whole grain mustard
>
> 2 tablespoons lemon juice
>
> ¼ cup extra-virgin olive oil
>
> 2 tablespoons chopped tarragon or chives
>
> 2 apples, cored and thinly sliced
>
> 3 heads Belgian endive, cut into
> ½-inch strips

Season the fish with salt and let it rest for 20 minutes. In a pan just wide enough to hold the fish in a single layer, combine 1 cup of water with the wine, vinegar, sliced shallot, carrot, salt, peppercorns, bay leaf, orange juice and zest, and rosemary. Simmer over low heat for 5 minutes. Season the broth with salt and bring it to 170°F. Add the fish and cook until it flakes under gentle pressure, 4–6 minutes per ½ inch of thickness. Remove the pan from the heat and cool the fish in the poaching liquid to room temperature. Remove the fish from the poaching liquid, remove and discard the skin, and pat dry. Transfer to a serving plate and flake the fish into bite-size pieces. Strain 1 cup of the poaching liquid into a pan, and reduce over medium heat until about 2 tablespoons remain. Turn off the heat and whisk in the minced shallot, mustard, lemon juice, olive oil, and tarragon or chives. Toss the apples and endive with the vinaigrette and serve with the fish.

Poached Salmon with Orange-Pistachio Piccata

SERVES 4

> 1 recipe Orange-Pistachio Piccata
> (page 29)
>
> 4 salmon portions, skin on
>
> Salt
>
> 1 cup white wine
>
> 2 tablespoons white wine vinegar
>
> 1 shallot, sliced
>
> 1 small carrot, sliced
>
> 10 whole black peppercorns
>
> 1 bay leaf

Season the fish with salt and let it rest for 20 minutes. In a pan just wide enough to hold the fish in a single layer, combine 2 cups of water with the wine, vinegar, shallot, carrot, peppercorns, and bay leaf. Simmer over low heat for 5 minutes. Season the broth with salt and bring it to 170°F. Add the fish skin side down and cook until it flakes under gentle pressure, 4–6 minutes per ½ inch of thickness. Remove the fish from the liquid and pat it dry. Remove the skin and discard. Serve the fish with Orange-Pistachio Piccata.

Chilled Poached Salmon with Shredded Carrot and Currant Salad and Almond Aioli

SERVES 4

    1 recipe Basic Aioli (page 25)

    4 salmon portions, skin on

    1 cup white wine

    5 sprigs parsley

    5 sprigs thyme

    1 shallot, thinly sliced

    2 garlic cloves, crushed

    1 teaspoon ground mace

    Kosher salt

    ¼ cup currants

    3 lemons, 2 juiced, 1 cut in half

    2 pounds carrots, shredded on a box grater

    2 tablespoons extra-virgin olive oil

    15 mint leaves, finely sliced

    ¼ cup crushed toasted almonds

In a pan just wide enough to hold the fish in a single layer, combine 2 cups of water with the wine, parsley, thyme, shallot, garlic, and mace. Simmer over low heat for 5 minutes. Season the broth with salt and bring it to 170°F. Add the fish skin side down and cook until it flakes under gentle pressure, about 4–6 minutes per ½ inch of thickness. Remove the pan from the heat and cool the fish in the poaching liquid to room temperature. Mix the currants and lemon juice, let them rest for 30 minutes, then mix with the carrots, olive oil, and mint, and season with salt. Remove the fish from the poaching liquid, remove and discard the skin, and pat it dry. Mix the Basic Aioli with the almonds. Serve the fish with the salad and aioli.

Slow-Roasted Whole Pink Salmon with Dill and Potatoes

SERVES 4–6

    1 (3-pound) whole pink salmon, gutted and scored

    1 garlic clove, thinly sliced

    Salt

    20 sprigs dill

    1 lemon, thinly sliced

    1 pound fingerling potatoes, washed

    Extra-virgin olive oil

Wedge the garlic slices into the cuts on the sides of the fish and season with salt. Lay 5 sprigs of the dill and half of the lemon slices down on a sheet pan big enough to hold the fish. Place the fish on top. Stuff the fish's belly with 5 sprigs of dill. Arrange the remaining lemon slices on top of the fish and cover it completely with the remaining dill. Place the pan into a 275°F oven and roast until almost done, about 40–50 minutes. Check doneness by inserting a knife into the thickest part and revealing the flesh. It is cooked when it is evenly colored and opaque throughout. Remove the fish from the oven. Put the potatoes in a pot over medium-high heat and cover with cold water. Season generously with salt and bring to a boil. Cook until the potatoes are tender. Drain the potatoes and toss with olive oil. Set the broiler to medium-high and place the rack in the middle position. Arrange the cooked potatoes around the fish, drizzle the fish with olive oil, and slide the pan under the broiler. Cook until the dill begins to burn and the potatoes get crispy, about 5 minutes. To serve, remove the dill and gently flake the fish away from the bones.

Roasted Salmon Head with Chile, Garlic, and White Wine

SERVES 4

2–3 whole salmon heads, collars still attached (4–5 pounds, total)

2 tablespoons kosher salt

1 cup white wine

4 garlic cloves, grated

4 teaspoons mace or nutmeg

4 teaspoons crushed red chile flakes

½ cup extra-virgin olive oil

6 stalks celery

1 fennel bulb, thinly sliced

2 onions, thinly sliced

¼ cup dry vermouth

6 tablespoons butter, cut into pieces, divided

1 lemon, juiced

Crusty bread for serving

Remove the gills from the heads, wash the heads with cold water, and pat dry. Combine the kosher salt with the wine, garlic, mace, chile flakes, and olive oil. Pour the marinade over the heads and let them rest for 4–8 hours. In a pot of boiling salted water, blanch the celery, fennel, and onions until tender. Drain the vegetables and use them to line the bottom of a baking dish big enough to hold the heads. Remove the heads from the marinade and place them, eyes upward and collars spread like wings, on top of the vegetables. Pour the vermouth over the heads and place 1 tablespoon of butter on each head. Place the pan in a 375°F oven and roast for 45 minutes, basting the heads with the pan juices every 15 minutes. Remove from the oven. Drain the pan juices and whisk with the remaining 3–4 tablespoons of butter and the lemon juice to emulsify. Serve the heads with the sauce, vegetables, crusty bread, and instructions that if the meat comes off the bones, it's edible.

Pan-Roasted Salmon with Garlic and Thyme

SERVES 4

4 salmon portions, skin on or off

Salt

4 tablespoons butter

4 garlic cloves, smashed

10 sprigs thyme

1 lemon, cut into wedges

Season the fish with salt and let it rest for 20 minutes. In a sauté pan over medium-low heat, melt the butter. Place the fish in the pan skin side down, if using, add garlic and thyme, and cook without flipping until the fish is almost done. Flip the fish to finish cooking. Serve with pieces of garlic, crisped thyme leaves, lemon wedges, and butter from the pan drizzled over the top.

Sautéed Salmon with Kimchi

SERVES 4

4 salmon portions, skin on

Salt

6 tablespoons butter, divided

¼ cup chopped kimchi

1 lime, juiced

Season the fish with salt and let it rest for 20 minutes. In a sauté pan over medium heat, melt 2 tablespoons of the butter. Place the fish skin side down in the pan and cook without flipping until the fish is almost done. Remove the fish from the pan, and wipe the pan clean. Add the remaining 4 tablespoons of butter and cook until foamy. Add the kimchi and cook until it has browned slightly. Add the lime juice and stir to combine. Turn off the heat and place the fish uncooked side down in the pan to finish cooking.

Sautéed Salmon with Brown Butter, Capers, and Rosemary

SERVES 4

4 salmon portions, skin on or off

Salt

6 tablespoons butter, divided

2 stalks rosemary, leaves picked

3 tablespoons capers, rinsed and patted dry

1 lemon, zested and juiced

Season the fish with salt and let it rest for 20 minutes. In a sauté pan over medium heat, melt 2 tablespoons of the butter and cook until golden brown. Place the fish in the pan, skin side down if using. Cook without flipping until almost done, then remove the fish, and wipe the pan clean. Add the remaining 4 tablespoons of butter, rosemary, and capers. Cook until the butter is brown and the capers are crisp. Remove the rosemary and reserve. Add the lemon zest and juice to the pan and season with salt. Stir gently to combine. Turn off the heat and return the fish to the pan uncooked side down to finish cooking. Garnish with crumbled rosemary leaves.

Sautéed Salmon with Red Wine Butter Sauce

SERVES 4

4 salmon portions, skin on

Salt

6 tablespoons butter, cut into pieces, divided

2 tablespoons minced shallots

1 cup red wine

Season the fish with salt and let it rest for 20 minutes. In a sauté pan over medium heat, melt 2 tablespoons of the butter. Place the fish skin side down in the pan and cook without

flipping until the fish is almost done. Flip the fish to finish cooking. Remove the fish and wipe the pan clean. Add the shallots and red wine to the pan, increase the heat to high, and reduce until about 2 tablespoons remain. Turn off the heat and whisk in the remaining 4 tablespoons of butter, 1 tablespoon at a time. Season with salt.

Sautéed Salmon Livers

SERVES 4

8 salmon livers, washed, bile sacs and arteries removed

Salt

Flour

8 tablespoons butter, divided

2 onions, sliced

2 garlic cloves, minced

1 lemon, juiced

Toast for serving

Season the livers with salt and let them rest for 20 minutes. In a sauté pan over high heat, melt 3 tablespoons of the butter. Dredge the livers in flour and place them in the pan. Cook for 1–2 minutes on each side to medium doneness. Remove the livers, and wipe the pan clean. Add the remaining 5 tablespoons of butter, onions, and garlic and cook until slightly browned and softened. Turn off the heat and add the lemon juice and livers to the pan to warm through. Serve over toast.

Cold-Smoked Salmon
MAKES ABOUT 2 POUNDS

1½ cups kosher salt

¾ cup brown sugar

2 tablespoons onion powder

2 tablespoons garlic powder

1 tablespoon ground allspice

1 tablespoon mace

1 (2-pound) salmon fillet, skin on

Pernod, Herbsaint, gin, or brandy

Combine the salt, brown sugar, onion powder, garlic powder, allspice, and mace. Line a dish with plastic wrap and lightly sprinkle the wrap with the salt mixture. Place the fish skin side down on the salt. Cover the flesh side of the fish with the remaining salt mixture. Wrap the fish very tightly in the plastic wrap and refrigerate for 24 hours, turning once halfway through the curing time. Remove the fish from the plastic, rinse off the cure mix in cold water, and pat dry. Brush the fish with your choice of alcohol and refrigerate it uncovered on a wire rack overnight. Cold-smoke the fish at as low a temperature as possible (under 100°F) for 3–5 hours, depending on the desired intensity of smoke flavor. Cool the smoked fish to room temperature, wrap tightly in plastic wrap, and let it rest in the refrigerator for 24 hours to allow the smoke flavors to mature. To serve, thinly slice on the bias, starting at the thick end slicing toward the thin end.

Hot-Smoked Salmon
MAKES ABOUT 1¾ POUNDS

⅓ cup kosher salt

⅓ cup brown sugar

1 orange, juiced

10 juniper berries

1 tablespoon fennel seeds

1 cinnamon stick

¼ cup Pernod or other anise-flavored liqueur, divided

1 (2-pound) salmon fillet, skin on

In a saucepan over medium heat, simmer 1 cup of water with the salt, brown sugar, orange juice, juniper, fennel seeds, and cinnamon for 5 minutes. Add 3 cups of cold water and 2 tablespoons of the Pernod to the brine. Place the fish in a glass or ceramic baking dish, add the brine to completely submerge it, and refrigerate for 3 hours. Remove the fish from the liquid, pat dry, and brush with the remaining 2 tablespoons of Pernod. Refrigerate the fish uncovered on a wire rack overnight. Cold-smoke the fish skin side down for 1–2 hours at as low a temperature as possible (below 100°F). Increase the temperature to 150°F and smoke for another 2–3 hours. Remove from the smoker and cool to room temperature. Tightly wrap the fillet in plastic and refrigerate overnight before using.

VARIATIONS

+ **Allspice Hot-Smoked Salmon.** Add 2 tablespoons of allspice berries to the smoking wood.

+ **Herb-Scented Hot-Smoked Salmon.** When removing the salmon from the smoker, immediately cover with fresh basil or mint leaves before wrapping to gently perfume the fish. Remove the leaves prior to serving.

Hot-Smoked Salmon Cobb Salad

SERVES 4

- 1 pound Hot-Smoked Salmon (page 341, or store-bought) flaked into bite-size pieces
- 1 recipe Red Wine–Shallot Vinaigrette (page 37)
- 6 plum tomatoes, cut into quarters
- 1 large head endive, chopped
- 1 or 2 bunches watercress, thick stems trimmed
- 2 avocados, thinly sliced
- 4 hard-boiled eggs, sliced
- Salt
- Black pepper

Toss the tomatoes and salmon with half of the vinaigrette and let it rest for 20 minutes. Set up four plates with equal portions of endive, watercress, avocados, and hard-boiled eggs. Drizzle the remaining vinaigrette over the salads and season with salt and pepper. Top each salad with marinated tomatoes and salmon.

Hot-Smoked Salmon with Roasted Apples and Watercress

SERVES 4

- 1 recipe Mint-Mustard Vinaigrette (page 36)
- 1 pound Hot-Smoked Salmon (page 341, or store-bought) flaked into bite-size pieces
- 3 apples, cored and cut into wedges
- 2 tablespoons honey
- ¼ cup extra-virgin olive oil, divided
- 2 bunches watercress, thick stalks discarded
- ¾ cup parsley, leaves picked
- ¾ cup chervil, leaves picked
- 1 lemon, zested and juiced
- Salt

Toss the salmon with half of the Mint-Mustard Vinaigrette. Toss the apples with the honey and 2 tablespoons of the olive oil and spread on a baking sheet. Set the broiler to high and place the rack in the position closest to the heat. Slide the sheet under the broiler and cook until the apples are brown and nearly tender, 7–10 minutes, depending on thickness. Toss the watercress, parsley, and chervil with the remaining vinaigrette, lemon juice and zest, and the remaining 2 tablespoons of olive oil and season with salt. Plate the salad, and top with the warm apples and marinated fish.

Pink or Sockeye Salmon Melt

SERVES 4

⅓ cup Mayonnaise (page 29, or
store-bought)

2 (7-ounce) tins pink or sockeye salmon,
drained

1 teaspoon celery salt

4 slices pumpernickel bread

Cheddar or Monterey jack cheese, sliced

Preheat the broiler to medium and set the rack
in the middle position. Flake the fish into a bowl.
Add the Mayonnaise and celery salt. Gently stir
to combine. Place the bread slices on a baking
tray. Divide the fish salad among the slices of
bread and cover each with slices of cheese. Slide
the tray under the broiler and cook until the
salmon is warmed through and the cheese is
melted, about 5–7 minutes.

Pink or Sockeye Salmon Cakes

SERVES 4

4 tablespoons Mayonnaise (page 29, or
store-bought)

¼ cup panko bread crumbs

1 tablespoon chopped dill

2 teaspoons whole grain mustard

1 pinch mace

1 (14¾-ounce) tin pink or sockeye salmon,
drained

4 tablespoons butter

1 lemon, cut into wedges

Preheat the oven to 400°F. Combine the bread
crumbs, dill, Mayonnaise, mustard, and mace
in a bowl. Add the salmon and gently combine.
Form the mixture into four patties and let them
rest for 5 minutes. In an ovenproof sauté pan
over medium heat, melt the butter and cook
until it is foaming. Add the cakes and cook for
5 minutes. After the edges turn golden brown,
flip the cakes, place the pan into the oven, and
cook until the cakes are warmed through. Serve
with lemon wedges.

Salmon Salad Sandwich

SERVES 4

¼ cup Mayonnaise (page 29, or
store-bought)

1 teaspoon celery salt

1 lime, juiced

1 (14¾-ounce) tin pink or sockeye salmon,
drained, or leftover cooked salmon

1 tablespoon prepared horseradish

8 slices whole wheat bread or rye bread
for serving

Sliced tomatoes (optional)

Arugula (optional)

In a bowl, mix the Mayonnaise, celery salt, and
lime juice. Flake the salmon and gently fold it
into the mayonnaise mixture. Serve either open-
faced on toast or as a traditional sandwich with
tomato and arugula.

SARDINES
Small silver fish

Sardines are likely to be found in most pantries in America, yet no one seems to really like them.

Sardines are widely available in tins, but if you're lucky, you can find them fresh. Call your fish market few days ahead and let the monger know you're looking for them. Buy fresh sardines with clean, unbruised, and unbroken skin, as they're delicate and often get damaged in transport. Fresh sardines should be bright and shiny and smell sweetly of the sea.

Fresh sardines can be filleted or cooked whole and range from very full-flavored to very mild and clean, despite their high fat content. These delicious, roughly 6-inch-long silver-skinned fish are briny, sweet, and packed with ocean flavor. They can be scaled easily by scraping the skin with your thumbnail from the tail to the head under cold running water. The belly cavity is simple to remove with a paring knife. My preferred way to treat these little guys is to salt-cure them. But they also do very well on the grill. Like many well-flavored fish, sardines are well suited to a few cracks of fresh pepper, grilled citrus, or an acidic dressing to tame the richness of the fish.

Canned sardines are among the most economical seafood available, offering both flavor and versatility. Canned sardines seem to be making a comeback. The legendary canneries of Monterey Bay are long gone, but there are lots of new brands attempting to elevate this forgotten favorite to new heights

of deliciousness. They come in a variety of preparations, including smoked, bathed in mustard, or packed in tomato sauce. I prefer the tiny two-layer tins of smoked fish packed in oil, as they are easy to eat and make a simple meal with the addition of a little Tabasco.

Canned sardines are also available salt-packed and these are best used like anchovies, but first they must be soaked in cool water for up to 12 hours. After soaking, the fillets are easily removed from the bones by peeling them off from the tail toward the head. The bones can be deep-fried into a delicious and crunchy snack. The salt from the cans can be dried in a low oven and used as you would regular salt but with an added potent tang.

FRESH

CANNED

SARDINES
Fresh

Broiled Sardines with Orange-Pistachio Piccata

SERVES 4

    1 recipe Orange-Pistachio Piccata (page 29)

    2 pounds whole sardines, scaled and gutted

    Salt

    Extra-virgin olive oil

    Cracked black pepper

Season the fish with salt and let them rest for 15 minutes. Preheat the broiler to high and set the rack in the position closest to the heat. Place the fish on a baking tray. Drizzle the fish with olive oil and sprinkle with cracked black pepper. Slide the tray under the broiler and cook until the fish is done, flipping once, about 5–7 minutes. Serve with Orange-Pistachio Piccata.

Cured Sardines with Lemon and Herbs

SERVES 4–8 AS AN APPETIZER

    2 pounds whole fresh sardines

    4 tablespoons kosher salt

    3 tablespoons sugar

    1 lemon, zested and juiced

10–15 sprigs thyme

    2 tablespoons chopped chives or parsley

    Ground mace

    Extra-virgin olive oil

Separate the fillets by cutting just beneath the head and remove the bones by pulling the head toward the tail.

Combine the salt, sugar, and lemon zest. Season the flesh with half of the salt mixture. Spread a thin layer of the salt mixture in the bottom of a baking dish large enough to hold half of the fish in a single layer. Lay half of the fish splayed and skin side down on top of the salt. Cover the fish with thyme. Place the remaining fillets splayed and skin side up on top of the thyme. Cover with the remaining salt mixture. Cover the dish with plastic wrap and refrigerate for 8–12 hours. Gently wash the fillets and pat dry. Wrap the cured fish tightly and refrigerate for up to a week. To serve, sprinkle the cured sardines with lemon juice, herbs, and a pinch of ground mace, and drizzle with olive oil. Serve at room temperature with toast or on top of a salad.

VARIATION

+ **Sardines and Butter on Rye.** Serve the cured sardines with slices of rye bread with a thick slather of soft butter and crushed red chile flakes.

Grilled Whole Sardines with Charred Rosemary Vinaigrette

SERVES 4

> 1 recipe Charred Rosemary Vinaigrette (page 35)
>
> 2 pounds whole sardines, scaled and gutted
>
> ¼ cup chopped herbs, such as chervil, parsley or tarragon
>
> 1 lemon, cut into wedges

Pour half of the vinaigrette over the fish and let them marinate for 1–8 hours. Prepare a charcoal grill with a medium fire, concentrating the hot coals on one side of the kettle. Working in batches, remove half of the fish from the marinade and place them on the grill over the hot coals. Cook until the edges of the fish begin to crisp, about 2–3 minutes. Gently flip the fish and brush with any remaining marinade. Lift the entire grill grate and rotate it so the fish rest opposite the hot coals. Cover the grill and continue to cook over this indirect heat until the fish are done, another 2–3 minutes. Repeat with the remaining fish. Serve the fish drizzled with the remaining vinaigrette, chopped herbs, and lemon wedges.

VARIATION

+ **Grilled Sardine Skewers.** Scale and fillet the fish and remove any pin bones. Skewer the fillets by piercing them through the skin side of the tail end and again at the head end so that the majority of the skewer is on the flesh side. Marinate the skewered fish for 1–2 hours and grill skin side down without flipping until done, 3–4 minutes.

NOTE *If using a gas grill, preheat all burners to medium-high. Place the sardines on one side of the hot grates. Once they begin to char around the edges, turn off the burner directly under the fish and cover the grill to finish cooking.*

Sardines en Saor (sweet-sour vinaigrette)

SERVES 4

> 2 pounds whole fresh sardines, scaled, headed, and gutted
>
> Salt
>
> ¾ cup extra-virgin olive oil, divided
>
> 3 tablespoons pine nuts or slivered almonds
>
> 2 tablespoons raisins
>
> 1 small onion, thinly sliced
>
> 1 red bell pepper, finely diced
>
> 1 small eggplant, ½-inch dice, about 2 cups
>
> ¼ cup red wine vinegar
>
> 1 tablespoon brown sugar
>
> Baguette for serving

Season the fish with salt and let them rest for 15 minutes. In a sauté pan over medium heat, warm ¼ cup of the olive oil. Place the fish in the pan and cook without flipping until almost done, about 4–5 minutes, then flip to finish cooking. Alternatively, the fish can be grilled. Remove the fish from the pan. Add the remaining ½ cup of olive oil over high heat, add the pine nuts and raisins, and cook until the pine nuts are golden brown and the raisins plump. Add the onion and bell pepper and cook until the pepper begins to soften. Add the eggplant and cook until it has softened and has absorbed most of the oil. Stir in the vinegar and brown sugar and season with salt. Turn off the heat and nestle the cooked fish into the sauce. This dish is best if allowed to marinate overnight and then brought to room temperature before serving. But at a minimum, let it sit at least 1 hour before serving at room temperature with slices of baguette.

Sardines en Escabeche

In this recipe, the cooked sardines are marinated in vinegar and spices.

SERVES 4–8

> 2 pounds whole fresh sardines, scaled, headed and gutted
>
> Salt
>
> Flour
>
> 1 cup plus 2 tablespoons extra-virgin olive oil
>
> 2 carrots, sliced into thin rounds
>
> 2 shallots, sliced into rings
>
> 4 garlic cloves, smashed
>
> 1 tablespoon smoked sweet paprika
>
> 1 teaspoon ground coriander
>
> 6 sprigs thyme or 3 stalks rosemary
>
> 1 orange, zest removed in wide strips
>
> ½ cup fruity white wine
>
> 1 tablespoon sherry vinegar
>
> ¼ cup chopped fresh herbs, such as chives, parsley, or tarragon
>
> Baguette for serving

Season the fish with salt and let them rest for 15 minutes. Roll the fish in flour. In a sauté pan over medium heat, warm 2 tablespoons of the olive oil. Place the fish into the pan and cook without flipping until almost done, about 4–5 minutes, then flip to finish cooking. Alternatively, the fish can be broiled. Transfer the cooked fish to a baking dish. In the pan over medium heat, warm the remaining 1 cup of olive oil. Add the carrots, shallots, and garlic and cook until the carrots begin to soften. Add the paprika, coriander, thyme, and orange zest and cook 2 minutes, until the aromas bloom. Add the wine and vinegar, season with salt, and simmer until reduced by half. Add the chopped fresh herbs. Stir to combine and pour over the cooked fish. Cool to room temperature.

Wait at least 1 hour before serving. For best results, allow the fish to marinate overnight in the refrigerator before returning the dish to room temperature. Serve with sliced baguette.

Pickled Sardines

SERVES 4–8 AS AN APPETIZER

> 2 bay leaves
>
> 1 cup red or white wine vinegar
>
> 6 black peppercorns
>
> 1 teaspoon kosher salt
>
> ½ teaspoon sugar
>
> 1 small orange, zest removed in wide strips
>
> 2 pounds whole fresh sardines, scaled and gutted
>
> Extra-virgin olive oil
>
> 1 shallot, sliced

Combine the bay leaves, vinegar, peppercorns, salt, sugar, and ¼ cup of water in a small pot and bring to a boil. Once the brine has boiled, turn off the heat and add the orange zest. Cool to room temperature. To fillet each sardine, press gently down on the backbone in the direction of the belly. Separate the fillets by cutting the backbone just beneath the head, and remove the bones by pulling the head toward the tail. Grease a baking dish with just enough olive oil to prevent the fish from sticking. Pour ½ inch of water into a medium pot, heavily season with salt, and bring the water to a gentle simmer over medium heat. Add the sardines a few at a time, cook for 30 seconds, very gently remove the fish, and place them in a single layer skin side down in the prepared dish. Cool the sardines to room temperature. Pour the pickle brine over the sardines. Cover and let sit at least 2 days in the refrigerator before using. These will keep up to 5 days in the refrigerator.

Smoked Sardines with Carrot, Radish, and Celery Salad

SERVES 4

> 1 recipe Lemon-Chile-Mint Dressing (page 36)
>
> 2 (4-ounce) tins smoked sardines in oil
>
> ½ pound carrots, shaved into long, thin ribbons
>
> 1 fennel bulb, thinly sliced
>
> ½ pound radishes, thinly sliced
>
> 6 stalks celery, thinly sliced
>
> 1 small red onion, thinly sliced, washed under cold running water, and patted dry
>
> Salt

Combine the dressing with the oil from the canned fish. Flake the fish into bite-size pieces and gently toss with half of the vinaigrette. Toss the vegetables with the remaining dressing and season with salt. Serve the salad with the fish scattered over top.

Smoked Sardines with Chickpeas and Hot Sauce

SERVES 2

> 2 (4-ounce) tins smoked sardines in oil
>
> 1 (14-ounce) can chickpeas, drained, with ¼ cup liquid reserved
>
> 1 lemon, zested and juiced
>
> 2 tablespoons extra-virgin olive oil
>
> Hot sauce

In a bowl, combine the sardines in their oil, chickpeas, reserved liquid, and lemon zest and juice. Toss to gently flake the fish. Add the olive oil and hot sauce to taste.

Smoked Sardines with Heirloom Tomato Salad

SERVES 4

> 3 pounds heirloom tomatoes, thickly sliced
>
> Salt
>
> Freshly cracked black pepper
>
> 2 (4-ounce) tins smoked sardines in oil
>
> 2 shallots, thinly sliced, rinsed under cold water, and patted dry
>
> 4 ounces arugula
>
> ¼ cup fresh mint, leaves picked and torn
>
> ½ cup parsley, leaves picked
>
> 1 lemon, zested and juiced, or 2 tablespoons red wine vinegar
>
> 2 tablespoons extra-virgin olive oil

Arrange the tomatoes on plates and season with salt and black pepper. Open the sardine tins and pour the oil over the tomatoes. Flake the sardines into bite-size pieces and scatter them over the tomatoes. In a large bowl, toss the shallots, arugula, mint, and parsley with the zest and juice and olive oil. Season with salt and serve on top of the tomatoes.

SCALLOPS

Sea scallops are among the most popular shellfish on the market because of their rich, sweet flavor. The vast majority of them are caught using dredges that are dragged behind a boat. But there is a very small market for ultra-high-end scallops collected by scuba divers, choosing only the largest ones by hand between December and February. For obvious reasons, these fetch a higher price. But since the introduction of the term "diver scallop" it has largely come to mean any scallop large enough so that ten or fewer (U10s) of them together weigh 1 pound, whether they've been brought to market by dredge or hand.

Because of their larger size and ease of handling, U10s are the best scallops for searing and raw dishes such as a carpaccio of raw scallops. Medium-size scallops, called U20s because it takes under 20 to make a pound, are perfect for kebabs or as part of a seafood stew or chowder. The very smallest bay scallops, weighing in at about 70+ per pound, are best when quickly sautéed and stirred into pasta dishes (page 351) or used as part of a ceviche.

The only part of the scallop that we eat is the adductor muscle that the animal uses to open and close its shell. As such, scallops are almost always shucked at sea. Fishermen and wholesalers have historically been allowed to soak or treat scallops in sodium-based brines that act as water-retention agents, causing the meat to absorb excess moisture. Not only do treated scallops have a lingering chemical taste, but as they cook, swollen cell walls rupture to release the added liquid, making caramelization difficult. Scallops that have been treated must by law be labeled as such and are called "wet pack" or simply "treated" scallops. Though they are a little more expensive I always buy "dry-packed" or "untreated" scallops. Also, scallops will naturally have subtle variations in the color of the meats, from glowing pearly white to rust-colored orange meats, called blushing scallops. The variation doesn't represent any significant difference in taste or quality.

Roasted Scallops with Charred Tomato Vinaigrette

SERVES 4

> 1 recipe Charred Tomato Vinaigrette (page 35)
>
> 4 portions scallops
>
> Salt
>
> Rice pilaf

Season the scallops with salt and let them rest for 20 minutes. Pour the vinaigrette into a baking dish just big enough to hold the scallops in a single layer. Nestle the scallops into the vinaigrette. Cover with foil and roast at 300°F until the scallops are cooked through. Let them rest for 5 minutes before serving with rice pilaf.

Scallop Ceviche with Fennel and Mint

SERVES 4–6 AS AN APPETIZER

> 1 pound whole bay scallops or small sea scallops, halved
>
> Salt
>
> 1 cup lime juice
>
> 1 Fresno or serrano chile, thinly sliced
>
> 3 stalks celery, thinly sliced
>
> 1 red onion, thinly sliced, rinsed under cold running water and patted dry
>
> 1 fennel bulb, thinly sliced
>
> ¼ cup extra-virgin olive oil
>
> ¼ cup mint leaves, torn
>
> 1 teaspoon grated mace for garnish

Keep this dish cold at all times during preparation. Season the scallops with salt and let them rest for 5 minutes. Combine the scallops with the lime juice and chile and let them rest for 20 minutes. Add the celery, onion, and fennel and let it rest another 10 minutes. Add the olive oil and mint and toss well. Garnish with mace.

Bay Scallops Marinated with Meyer Lemon

SERVES 4–8 AS AN APPETIZER

> 2 Meyer lemons, zested and juiced
>
> ¼ cup extra-virgin olive oil
>
> ¼ cup mint leaves, torn
>
> 1 shallot, finely diced
>
> Salt
>
> Crushed red chile flakes
>
> 1 pound bay scallops
>
> 1 cup white wine

In a medium bowl, combine the lemon zest and juice, olive oil, mint, shallot, salt, and chile flakes to taste. Season the scallops with salt and let them rest for 10 minutes. In a saucepan over medium-high heat, combine the wine with 3 cups of salted water and bring to a simmer. Add the scallops, cook for 30 seconds, and drain. Toss the warm scallops with the lemon vinaigrette, let them sit for at least 1 hour and up to 1 day. Serve at room temperature with toothpicks or scattered over a salad of spicy greens.

Linguine with Bay Scallops, Butternut Squash, and Walnuts

SERVES 4

½ pound bay scallops

Salt

1 pound linguine, cooked al dente according to package instructions, reserving 1 cup of cooking liquid

8 tablespoons butter, divided

1 small butternut squash, peeled and diced into ½-inch pieces

½ cup walnut pieces, toasted

¼ cup chopped herbs, such as chervil, parsley, or tarragon

Season the scallops with salt and let them rest for 20 minutes. In a sauté pan over medium heat, melt 4 tablespoons of the butter and cook until it is golden brown. Add the butternut squash and cook until it is barely soft, about 5 minutes. Add the walnut pieces and toss to combine. Remove the squash and nuts from the pan. Increase the heat to high and add 2 tablespoons of the remaining butter. Place the scallops in the pan and cook without moving them until they are barely firm, 2–3 minutes. Remove the scallops from the pan. Add the squash, walnuts, drained pasta, and reserved water to the pan and simmer for 2 minutes until the liquid is absorbed. Add the remaining 2 tablespoons of butter, chopped herbs, and scallops. Toss to combine.

Pan-Fried Scallops Marinated with Sage and Lemon

SERVES 4–8

1½ pounds medium scallops, cut in half across the middle

Salt

1 orange, zest removed in large strips and juiced

1¼ cups extra-virgin olive oil, divided

2 tablespoons raisins

3 sprigs fresh sage, leaves picked

6 garlic cloves, smashed

2 onions, thinly sliced top to bottom

1 cup white wine vinegar or ½ cup sherry vinegar

Crusty bread for serving

Season the scallops with salt and lemon juice and let them rest for 20 minutes. In a large pot over medium heat, combine 1 cup of the olive oil, orange zest, raisins, sage, and garlic and cook until the raisins begin to plump and the sage crisps. Add the onions, season generously with salt, and cook until the onions are wilted, about 5 minutes. Add the orange juice, vinegar and ¾ cup of water and simmer for 15 minutes. In a sauté pan over high heat, warm the remaining ¼ cup of oil. Add the scallops and fry until one side is brown and crisp, then flip to finish cooking. Transfer the scallops to a baking dish and pour the onion marinade over them. Cool to room temperature. Cover and refrigerate for at least a couple of hours and up to 3 days. Serve at room temperature with crusty bread.

Sautéed Scallops with Brown Butter, Raisins, and Tarragon

SERVES 4

4 portions large scallops

Salt

6 tablespoons butter, divided

2 tablespoons raisins

1 lemon, juiced

1 tablespoon chopped fresh tarragon

Season the scallops with salt and let them rest for 20 minutes. In a sauté pan over medium-high heat, melt 2 tablespoons of the butter and cook until golden brown. Place the scallops in the pan. Cook without flipping until almost done, then remove the scallops. Reduce the heat to medium and add the remaining 4 tablespoons of butter and the raisins. Cook until the butter is very dark. Add the lemon juice and tarragon and season with salt. Stir to combine. Turn off the heat and return the scallops to the pan uncooked side down to finish cooking.

Sautéed Scallops with Cider–Brown Butter

SERVES 4

4 portions large scallops

Salt

6 tablespoons butter

1½ cups apple cider

Season the scallops with salt and let them rest for 20 minutes. In a sauté pan over medium-high heat, melt 2 tablespoons of the butter and cook until golden brown. Place the scallops in the pan.

Cook without flipping until almost done, then flip and continue to cook until done. Remove the scallops and keep warm. Add 3 tablespoons of butter, and reduce the heat to medium. Cook until the butter is dark brown. Add the cider and reduce until it is thick. Turn off the heat and swirl in the remaining tablespoon of butter to finish the sauce.

Sautéed Scallops au Poivre Flambé

SERVES 4

4 portions large scallops

Salt

1½ tablespoons black peppercorns, coarsely ground

1½ tablespoons fennel seeds, crushed

4 tablespoons butter

1½ ounces cognac or brandy

Season the scallops all over with salt and on one side with the pepper and fennel, pressing seasonings into the flesh. Let them rest for 20 minutes. In a sauté pan over medium heat, melt the butter and cook until golden brown. Place the scallops pepper side down in the pan. Cook without flipping until almost done, then flip to finish cooking. Turn off the heat. Add the cognac or brandy and flambé by lighting with a match. Allow the alcohol to burn off before serving.

Scallops with Sherry and Apple

SERVES 4

    4 portions large scallops
    Salt
    6 tablespoons butter, divided
    ¼ cup peeled and diced apple
    2 ounces Amontillado or cooking sherry
    1 tablespoon chopped fresh tarragon

Season the scallops with salt and let them rest for 20 minutes. In a sauté pan over medium-high heat, melt 2 tablespoons of the butter and cook until golden brown. Place the scallops in the pan. Cook without flipping until almost done, then remove from the pan. Add the remaining 4 tablespoons of butter and the apples. Cook until the butter is dark brown and the apples have softened. Add the sherry and tarragon and season with salt. Stir to combine. Turn off the heat and return the scallops to the pan uncooked side down to finish cooking.

Sautéed Scallop Peanut Satay

SERVES 4

    4 portions medium scallops
    Salt
    2 tablespoons smooth peanut butter
    2 tablespoons rice vinegar, divided
    1 tablespoon soy sauce
    1 tablespoon aji mirin or white wine
    ½ tablespoon grated fresh ginger
    1 garlic clove, grated
    ¼ cup peanut oil
    Bamboo skewers

Season the scallops with salt and let them rest for 20 minutes. Whisk together the peanut butter, 1 tablespoon of the rice vinegar, soy sauce, mirin, ginger, and garlic. Set aside half of the peanut marinade and pour the other half over the scallops. Toss gently to coat the scallops. Thread 3–4 scallops onto each bamboo skewer and return to the marinade. Marinate at least 20 minutes or up to 8 hours. Heat the oil in a large sauté pan over medium-high heat. Add the scallop skewers and cook, without moving, until the scallops develop a dark caramelized crust. Turn off the heat, flip the skewers, and leave in the pan until cooked through. Whisk the remaining 1 tablespoon of vinegar into the reserved marinade and drizzle over the scallops.

Butter-Basted Scallops with Garlic and Thyme

SERVES 4

    4 portions large scallops
    Salt
    6 tablespoons butter, divided
    3 garlic cloves, minced
    4 sprigs thyme, leaves picked
    1 lemon, cut into wedges

Season the scallops with salt and let them rest for 20 minutes. In a sauté pan over medium-high heat, melt 2 tablespoons of the butter and cook until golden brown. Place the scallops in the pan and sear until they begin to brown. Reduce the heat to medium and flip the scallops. Add the remaining 4 tablespoons of butter, garlic, and thyme. Cook until the butter is frothy, angle the pan toward you, and use a spoon to continuously baste the scallops with butter until they are cooked through. Remove the scallops from the pan, strain the butter, and reserve the crispy garlic and thyme to scatter over the scallops. Serve with lemon wedges.

Hot-Smoked Scallops

MAKES ABOUT 1 POUND

>   1 cup white wine
>   ⅓ cup kosher salt
>   ⅓ cup brown sugar
>   1 tablespoon onion powder
>   1 tablespoon garlic powder
>   1¼ pounds scallops
>   2 tablespoons Pernod or Herbsaint

In a saucepan over medium heat, warm the wine with salt, sugar, onion powder, and garlic powder and stir to dissolve. Add 3 cups of cold water to the brine and chill. Put the scallops in a baking dish, cover them with the brine, and soak for 40 minutes for large scallops and 20 minutes for small ones. Remove the scallops from the brine and pat dry. Toss the scallops with the Pernod or Herbsaint and refrigerate uncovered on a wire rack overnight. Cold-smoke the scallops at as low a temperature as possible (below 100°F) for 1–2 hours. Increase the temperature to 160°F and smoke for 1 hour more until they are firm and cooked. Cool the scallops to room temperature. Use thinly sliced on top of salads or drizzled with vinaigrette, or serve whole, warmed through and paired with melted butter and lemon.

Smoked Scallops with Orange Fennel Salad

SERVES 4

>   1 pound Hot-Smoked Scallops (at left), thinly sliced
>   2 large fennel bulbs, thinly sliced
>   ⅓ cup extra-virgin olive oil
>   4 oranges, zested and segmented
>   2 tablespoons sherry vinegar
>   ½ cup mint leaves, torn
>   Salt
>   Freshly cracked black pepper for garnish

Gently toss the fennel, olive oil, orange zest and segments, sherry vinegar, and mint. Season with salt. Drape the scallop slices over the salad and garnish with freshly cracked black pepper.

SCORPIONFISH/SEA ROBIN/SCULPIN
Flaky white fish, meaty dense fish

Scorpionfish and the closely related sea robins are bottom-dwelling loners. They are sometimes called rockfish or stonefish because their skin is camouflaged to match the rocks and reefs in which they lie in wait for their prey with their poisonous spines and big mouths, ready to pounce. Of the many similar species that swim in all American waters, they are all related to and closely resemble their European counterparts that serve as the linchpin ingredient in classic bouillabaisse. Formally their names are California scorpionfish, stone scorpionfish, and rainbow scorpionfish, but these fish, which average in length between 18 and 24 inches, are often sold as sculpin because they share many of the same culinary attributes. They have heavy scales, thick skin, and firm, coarse-textured flesh. A common solution to dealing with a scorpionfish's many bones is to roast the fish whole, which allows the meat to be easily flaked away. Their poisonous spines can be removed easily with kitchen shears, although cooking denatures the venom as a matter of course. Their flaky flesh cooks up firm and mostly white with just a thin coat of slightly darker flesh in some areas just under the skin. The taste is mild and sweet. Some compare it to cooked lobster meat. The flesh holds together well but flakes apart easily enough on the plate. The skin curls significantly when heat is applied, so it is best to remove it before sautéing, steaming, or poaching the fillets, and to score it well if grilling the fish.

Scorpionfish in Dashi Broth

SERVES 4

> 4 scorpionfish portions, skin off
>
> Salt
>
> 1 cup white wine
>
> 1 star anise pod
>
> 1 lemon, half sliced, half zest removed in wide strips
>
> 1 slice fresh ginger
>
> ¼ ounce dried kelp
>
> 4 tablespoons bonito flakes
>
> Sliced scallions
>
> Crushed red chile flakes

Season the fish with salt and let it rest for 15 minutes. Combine the wine, star anise, lemon zest, and ginger in a small pot over high heat. Boil until the alcohol smell dissipates. Add 3 cups of water and the kelp. Reduce the heat to medium-low and simmer for 20 minutes. Add the bonito flakes and remove the pan from the heat and let rest for 5 minutes. Strain the broth and discard the solids. Season the broth with salt and bring it to 170°F. Add the fish and cook until it is opaque and flakes under gentle pressure, about 4–5 minutes per ½ inch of thickness. Transfer the fish to four bowls. Divide the broth between the bowls and garnish each with scallions and a pinch of chile flakes. Arrange lemon slices on top of the fish and serve immediately.

Grilled Scorpionfish with Bay Leaves and Charred Lemons

SERVES 4

> 4 scorpionfish portions, skin on and scored
>
> Salt
>
> 4 bay leaves
>
> 2 lemons, halved

Season the fish with salt and push one bay leaf onto the flesh side of each portion. Let rest for 15 minutes. Prepare a charcoal grill with a medium fire, concentrating the hot coals on one side of the kettle. Place the fish skin side down on the grill over the hot coals. Cook until the skin begins to char, about 2 minutes. Lift the entire grill grate and rotate it so the fish rests opposite the hot coals. Place the lemons cut side down over the hot coals. Cover the grill and cook until the fish is done and the lemons are charred. Discard the bay leaves and serve.

NOTE *If using a gas grill, preheat all burners to medium-high. Place the scorpionfish on one side of the hot grates. Once it begins to char around the edges, turn off the burner directly under the fish, place the lemons cut side down over the live burner, and cover the grill to finish cooking.*

Sautéed Scorpionfish with Herbes de Provence

SERVES 4

> 1 recipe Herbes de Provence Mix (page 33)
>
> 4 scorpionfish portions, skin off
>
> Salt
>
> 3 tablespoons extra-virgin olive oil
>
> 1 lemon, cut into wedges

Season the fish with salt all over and on one side with Herbes de Provence Mix. Press the spices into the flesh and let it rest for 15 minutes. In a sauté pan over medium-low heat, warm the olive oil. Place the fish in the pan spice side down. Cook without flipping until almost done, then flip and continue to cook until done. Serve with the cooking oil drizzled over the top and lemon wedges.

Sautéed Prosciutto-Wrapped Scorpionfish

SERVES 4

4 scorpionfish portions, skin off

Salt

2 tablespoons chopped fresh parsley
or tarragon

1 lemon, zested and juiced

Ground mace

2 tablespoons white wine

8 thinly sliced pieces of prosciutto

4 tablespoons butter

Season the fish with salt, then mix with the parsley, lemon zest and juice, a couple of pinches of mace, and white wine. Marinate for 2–4 hours. Wrap each portion in two slices of prosciutto and secure with a toothpick. In a sauté pan over medium heat, melt the butter and cook until golden brown. Add the fish to the pan. Cook until the prosciutto is crisp and the fish is almost done, then flip to finish cooking. Serve drizzled with butter from the pan.

Sautéed Sesame-Crusted Scorpionfish

SERVES 4

4 scorpionfish portions, skin off

Salt

½ cup sesame seeds

6 tablespoons butter, divided

1 orange, juiced

Season the fish with salt and let it rest for 15 minutes. Dredge one side of the fish in sesame seeds and press them firmly into the flesh. In a sauté pan over medium-low heat, melt 4 tablespoons of the butter and cook until golden brown. Place the fish in the pan sesame seed side down. Cook without flipping until the fish is almost done and the sesame seeds are crisp and brown, then flip to finish cooking. Remove the fish from the pan. Add the remaining 2 tablespoons of butter and the orange juice. Swirl to incorporate and season with salt.

Steamed Scorpionfish with Lemongrass and Star Anise

SERVES 4

4 scorpionfish portions, skin off

Salt

3 lemongrass stalks, split

2 star anise pods

½ cup wine

4 tablespoons butter, melted

Season the fish with salt and let it rest for 15 minutes. In the bottom of a wide, shallow pot over medium-low heat, place the lemongrass and star anise to create an aromatic raft. Add the wine and enough water to cover the bottom of the pot. Bring to a simmer. Place the fish on top of the aromatics, cover, and cook until done, 7–10 minutes. Serve each portion with 1 tablespoon of butter and a spoonful of the remaining cooking liquid drizzled over it.

SEAGREENS

Seagreens, also known as seaweed or sea vegetables, are members of a very diverse group of organisms distantly related to plants that can grow in either saltwater or freshwater. The recipes below focus exclusively on the two commonplace saltwater varieties: kelp and dulse.

Sugar kelp is the most commonly available seagreen, is easy to use, and has a mild flavor. Its high level of natural sugars gives it an herbal, fruity taste. Sugar kelp is both harvested and farmed wild, in North America, and is available fresh, frozen, or dried. It is also called kombu, the principal flavoring agent of dashi broth. Fresh, thawed, or rehydrated leaves have a pleasant texture and crunch similar to a green bean. They make a wonderful addition to salads. Sugar kelp pairs particularly well with the spicy kick of raw onions, which flatters the mellow flavor of this seagreen and brings its sea charisma into focus.

Winged kelp has a palm frond–like shape, is mostly sold dried, and is best used as a subtle flavor addition to broths or stews to coax a boldness from all other ingredients with which it is paired. The dried product is also good simply crumbled over dishes such as roasted vegetables or autumn soups.

Deep violet-colored dulse is one of the most versatile of all the seagreens. Dried, either in flakes or long, thin sheets that are sometimes smoked, dulse promises a dark and brooding flavor (think dark chocolate). Dulse broths are best used in hearty dishes such as beef stew or lentil soup. A sprinkle of dulse flakes does wonders for dishes like minestrone, where it brings a mélange of ingredients into clear focus. Dulse sheets, crisped nicely into chips, make a great snack.

Creamed Kelp

SERVES 4–6 AS A SIDE DISH

    1 star anise pod

    2 ounces dried sugar kelp

    4 tablespoons butter

    2 onions, thinly sliced

    2 garlic cloves, sliced

    ½ cup cream

    1 lemon, zested

    Smoked sweet paprika

    Ground mace

    Salt

Fill a large pot with water, add the star anise, and boil for 5 minutes. Turn off the heat, add the kelp, and soak for 15 minutes. Drain off the water and discard the star anise. (This water can be used as a stock in another dish, if desired.) Tear the kelp into bite-size pieces and reserve. In a deep, heavy pot over medium-high heat, melt the butter. Add the onions and garlic and cook until they are beginning to brown, about 5 minutes. Add the reserved kelp and cook gently until warmed through. Reduce the heat to low and stir in the cream, lemon zest, a pinch of paprika, and a pinch of mace. Bring to a simmer, then remove from the heat, season with salt, and serve.

Seagreens Flatbread

SERVES 4 AS AN APPETIZER

    1 recipe Kelp-Walnut Pesto (page 26)

    1 pound pizza dough, store-bought or homemade

    1 pound blanched asparagus, cut into pieces

    Shaved Parmesan cheese

Roll out the pizza dough into a thin rectangle shape and place it on a dry baking sheet. Spread the Kelp-Walnut Pesto over the dough all the way to the edges. Scatter the asparagus evenly over the pesto. Slide the pan into a 450°F oven and cook until the dough is cooked and the edges crisped, about 15–20 minutes. Top the hot flatbread with Parmesan.

Seagreens Lasagna

SERVES 6-8

- 1 pound lasagna noodles, prepared according to package instructions
- 3 tablespoons extra-virgin olive oil
- 1 onion, diced
- ¼ cup dried dulse flakes, preferably smoked dulse
- 1 garlic clove, crushed
- 1 pound ground beef
- Salt
- 1 (28-ounce) can crushed tomatoes
- ½ tablespoon dried oregano
- Crushed red chile flakes
- 1 ounce dried kelp, rehydrated and cut into ribbons
- 14 ounces ricotta cheese

In a large pot over medium heat, warm the oil. Add the onion, dulse flakes, and garlic and cook until aromatic, about 2 minutes. Add the beef and cook until it begins to brown and is nearly cooked through. Season with salt and add the tomatoes, oregano, and chile flakes to taste. Bring to a simmer, then remove from the heat. In a baking dish, layer the ingredients in this order: half of the noodles, half of the beef mixture, all of the kelp, half of the ricotta, the remaining beef, the remaining noodles, and topped off with the remaining ricotta cheese. Cover and bake at 325°F until the sauce is bubbling and the cheese is lightly browned, about 45 minutes.

Kelp Salad with Orange and Fennel

SERVES 4-6

- 1 pound fresh or frozen kelp, or 2 ounces dried kelp, rehydrated, torn into bite-size pieces
- 3 oranges, cut into segments
- 1 fennel bulb, thinly sliced
- 1 Vidalia onion, thinly sliced
- 6 ounces radishes, thinly sliced
- 2 tablespoons sherry vinegar
- 2 tablespoons sesame oil
- 2 tablespoons vegetable oil
- Salt

In a large bowl, combine the kelp, orange segments, fennel, onion, radishes, vinegar, and oils. Season with salt and toss gently to combine. Let it sit for 10 minutes before serving.

SHAD
Fillet fish

Shad is a cult favorite along the eastern shores of the United States.

What's kept shad from wider acceptance is its complex bone structure, which features a second set of floating pin bones. Fortunately, most shad are sold filleted. If you find a whole one, the best deboning workaround is to slowly roast the fish, then mash it with butter, and pass the mixture through a sieve to remove the bones. The remaining purée is then potted and covered with a layer of coriander-scented butter and served as a spread.

The fillets have a reddish-gray oily meat and a delicate character with a mild brininess. It's delicious, but the real star of any shad is the roe. These large skeins, or egg sacs, come in pairs and are taken from the female fish as they migrate upstream to spawn. The color of the roe can vary from beigey-yellow to deep red or maroon, but that color is not representative of flavor or quality. Overripe roe with large, bead-like eggs that seem to be bursting from their thin

membrane will overcook quickly and be greasy. Underripe roe, called green roe, have very small beads that appear to be more of a single mass than individual berries; at this stage they can be quite bitter and lacking in velvety richness. Just-ripe eggs will appear plump and firmly packed in their skein—this is the roe that you want.

Both shad roe and shad fillets are best sautéed in butter and finished with something acidic. All the recipes can be adapted to use shad fillets.

Pan-Fried Shad Roe in Bacon Drippings

SERVES 4

4 shad roe portions

Salt

Flour

Freshly cracked black pepper

6 tablespoons bacon drippings, or a combination of drippings and butter

1 lemon, cut into wedges

Season the roe with salt and let it rest for 15 minutes. Roll in flour to coat and season one side with the pepper. In a sauté pan over medium heat, warm the bacon drippings. Place the roe in the pan peppered side down and cook for 2 minutes per side. Serve with lemon wedges.

Sautéed Shad Roe with Thyme and Bay Leaf

SERVES 4

4 shad roe portions

Salt

Flour

6 tablespoons butter

4 sprigs thyme

2 bay leaves

1 lemon, cut into wedges

Season the roe with salt and let it rest for 15 minutes. Roll the roe in flour to coat. In a sauté pan over medium heat, melt the butter with the thyme and bay leaves and cook until golden brown. Place the roe in the pan and cook on each side for 2 minutes. Serve with lemon wedges.

Sautéed Smoky Shad Roe

SERVES 4

4 shad roe portions

Salt

1 tablespoon smoked sweet paprika

1 teaspoon sugar

1 teaspoon onion powder

⅓ cup flour

6 tablespoons butter

1 lemon, cut into wedges

Season the roe with salt, paprika, sugar, and onion powder and let it rest for 15 minutes. Roll the roe in the flour to coat. In a sauté pan over medium heat, melt the butter. Place the roe in the pan and cook on each side for 2 minutes. Serve with lemon wedges.

Sautéed Shad Roe with Brown Butter, Raisins, and Tarragon

SERVES 4

4 shad roe portions

Salt

6 tablespoons butter, divided

2 tablespoons raisins

1 tablespoon chopped fresh tarragon

1 lemon, juiced

Season the roe with salt and let it rest for 15 minutes. In a sauté pan over medium heat, melt 2 tablespoons of the butter and cook until golden brown. Place the roe in the pan and cook for 2 minutes on one side, then flip and add the remaining 4 tablespoons of butter and the raisins. Cook for 2 minutes. Remove the roe and add the tarragon and lemon juice and season with salt. Stir to combine.

Sautéed Shad Roe with Sorrel Butter

SERVES 4

1 recipe Sorrel Butter (page 22)

4 shad roe portions

Salt

Flour

2 tablespoons butter

Season the roe with salt and let it rest for 15 minutes. Roll the roe in flour to coat. In a sauté pan over medium heat, melt the plain butter and cook until golden brown. Place the roe in the pan and cook for 2 minutes. Flip the roe and top each with 2 tablespoons of the Sorrel Butter and cook for 2 minutes.

Broiled Shad with
Pine Nut Butter

SERVES 4

> 1 recipe Pine Nut Butter (page 21)
>
> 4 shad portions, skin on and scored
>
> Salt
>
> Extra-virgin olive oil

Season the fish with salt and let it rest for 20 minutes. Preheat the broiler to medium and set a rack in the position closest to the heat. Place the fish skin side up on a baking tray. Drizzle with a bit of olive oil, and slide the tray under the broiler. Cook until done, 5–7 minutes, depending on thickness. Top with the Pine Nut Butter.

VARIATION

+ **Broiled Shad with Lime-Dill Butter.** Use Lime-Dill Butter (page 21) instead of Pine Nut Butter.

Grill-Smoked Shad
with Fennel Butter

SERVES 4

> 1 recipe Fennel Butter (page 20)
>
> 4 shad portions, skin on and scored
>
> 1 cup white wine
>
> ⅓ cup kosher salt
>
> ⅓ cup sugar
>
> Chopped chives

In a small saucepan over low heat, warm the wine, kosher salt, and sugar, and stir to dissolve. Add 1 cup of ice water, and chill. Place the fish in a baking dish, cover with the brine, and let it sit 30 minutes. Remove the fish from the brine and pat dry. Prepare a medium fire with all coals concentrated on one side of the kettle, and add wood chips to it. Place the fish skin side down directly over the hot coals and cook for 3 minutes. Rotate the grill grate so the fish sit opposite the coals, adding more chips to maintain moderate smoke. Cover the grill and cook until the fish is firm and cooked through. Remove from the grill and top with Fennel Butter. Garnish with chopped chives.

NOTE *If using a gas grill, preheat all burners to high. Place a handful of wood chips in an insert or in a makeshift foil pouch and place over the flame. Place the shad on one side of the hot grates and cook for 3 minutes. Turn off the burner directly under the fish, cover the grill, and cook until the fish is firm and cooked through.*

Grilled Shad with Lemon-
Chile-Mint Dressing

SERVES 4

> 1 recipe Lemon-Chile-Mint Dressing (page 36)
>
> 4 shad portions, skin on and scored

Reserve half of the Lemon-Chile-Mint Dressing for serving. Combine the other half with the fish and let it rest for 1–8 hours. Prepare a charcoal grill with a medium fire, concentrating the hot coals on one side of the kettle. Remove the fish from the marinade, and place it skin side down on the grill over the hottest part of the fire. Cook until the skin begins to char, about 2 minutes. Lift the entire grill grate and rotate it so the fish rests opposite the hot coals. Baste with marinade, cover the grill, and continue to cook over this indirect heat until the fish is done. Serve with the remaining dressing drizzled over the top.

NOTE *If using a gas grill, preheat all burners to medium. Place the shad on one side of the hot grates. Once it begins to char around the edges, turn off the burner directly under the fish, baste the fish with marinade, and cover the grill to finish cooking.*

SHARK
Meaty dense fish, steak fish

If shark were judged only on its culinary merits, it would be quite popular. But there is that whole *Jaws* thing, which turned us off them entirely. Early on in the commercial fishery for shark in America, shark oil was more valuable than the meat and was rendered from the shark's meat and livers, leaving the meat dry, coarse, and undesirable. As such, it most often made it only to the bait bucket while its skin was turned into fancy boots for fancy people. In wartime the government pushed people to eat it, and the unchecked appetite for their fins in soup led to the deplorable practice of cutting the fins from live animals, which rightly drew negative attention to killing sharks for food. The lengthy reproduction habits of sharks make them very susceptible to fishing pressures. Though they are targeted in some fisheries, they are often caught as bycatch to the tuna and swordfish industries. These factors all add up to a negative view of shark as seafood.

The mako and thresher, which swim in both the Atlantic and the Pacific Oceans, are the highest in quality. On average they are landed around 125 pounds. When at their best, they are the culinary equal to swordfish (page 408). The hammerhead shark, leopard shark, and blacktip shark are second-tier quality, as their meat is more coarse, less fatty, and somewhat muted in flavor.

Most large sharks are at their best culinary quality from late summer throughout early fall. Twenty species of sharks are targeted for food, and all must be handled properly to be edible. If the shark is not immediately bled and iced upon capture, rigor sets in and the meat becomes heavily tainted with an ammonia scent and a sharp flavor. Shark meat with anything resembling ammonization should be outright rejected. Don't try to fix broken fish.

Larger sharks are similar to swordfish and tuna in that they have a band of bloodline tissue running along their cartilaginous skeletal structures. When the shark is fresh, this line is neatly delineated from the pale gray to peachy-pink flesh. As the shark ages, the bloodline loses density and its structure becomes limp, sagging as its color fades into the surrounding meat.

When shark meat is perfectly fresh, it is equally as good under the broiler as on the grill. The rich marbling of fat running throughout the flesh bastes the meat as it cooks, preserving moisture and absorbing the flavor of the live flame. Shark is also good served cold, especially when the meat is poached and left to chill in its cooking liquid.

Braised Shark à la Barigoule

In this recipe, the shark and vegetables are braised and marinated in spiced broth.

SERVES 4

  1 recipe Basic Aioli (page 25), made with oil skimmed from the cooked dish

  4 shark portions, skin off

  Salt

  3 stalks celery, chopped

  2 carrots, sliced

  4 ounces mushrooms, cut in quarters

  2 garlic cloves, thinly sliced

  5 sprigs thyme

  1 teaspoon ground coriander seeds

  1½ cups white wine

  1 (14-ounce) can oil-packed halved artichoke hearts with their oil

  ½ lemon, thinly sliced

  1 cup extra-virgin olive oil

  Crushed red chile flakes (optional)

  Crusty bread for serving

Season the shark with salt and let it rest for 20 minutes. In a large pot over medium heat, combine the celery, carrots, mushrooms, garlic, thyme, coriander, wine, and ½ cup of water. Season lightly with salt and simmer until the alcohol smell dissipates, about 5 minutes. Add the artichoke hearts with their oil, lemon slices, and olive oil. Reduce the heat to low. Nestle the shark into the pot so it is barely submerged. Add the chile flakes, if using. Cover and cook for 25–30 minutes. Remove the pot from the heat and cool to room temperature. The flavors improve if allowed to chill overnight in the refrigerator. Use a ladle to skim off the olive oil and use it to make Basic Aioli. Serve at room temperature with crusty bread and the aioli.

Braised Shark Puttanesca

The shark is braised in a lively tomato sauce with capers and olives.

SERVES 4

  4 shark portions, skin off

  Salt

  6 tablespoons extra-virgin olive oil, divided

  1 (2-ounce) tin anchovies in oil

  4 garlic cloves, sliced

  4 dried árbol chiles, or ½ tablespoon crushed red chile flakes

  2 (14-ounce) cans fire-roasted diced tomatoes

  ¾ cup white wine

  2 tablespoons capers, rinsed and patted dry

  ¼ cup pitted cured black olives

  6 basil leaves, torn, for garnish

Season the shark with salt and let it rest for 20 minutes. In an ovenproof sauté pan over medium-high heat, warm 3 tablespoons of the olive oil, anchovies with their oil, garlic, and chiles, and cook until the anchovies melt. Add the tomatoes, wine, capers, and olives. Bring to a simmer and cook for 10 minutes. Nestle the shark into the sauce, and drizzle with the remaining 3 tablespoons of olive oil. Cover the pan and place in a 275°F oven for 30 minutes. Remove and let it rest for 10 minutes before serving scattered with torn basil leaves.

Broiled Shark with Orange and Rum Flambé

SERVES 4

    4 shark portions, skin off

    Salt

    Bay leaves

    1 orange, cut into segments

    4 tablespoons butter

    1½ ounces dark rum

Season the shark with salt and let it rest for 20 minutes. Preheat the broiler to medium and set the rack in the middle position. Heat a sauté pan over high heat until very hot. Place a layer of bay leaves on the bottom and place the shark on top of them. Arrange the orange segments and 1 tablespoon of butter on top of each portion. Slide the pan under the broiler and cook until done, 7–10 minutes, depending on thickness. Remove from the broiler. Add the rum and flambé by lighting with a match. Allow the alcohol to burn off before serving.

Fried Shark en Adobo

SERVES 4

    1 recipe Adobo Marinade (page 36)

    1 recipe Basic Aioli (page 25)

    4 shark portions, skin off and cut into 1-inch pieces

    Vegetable or peanut oil

    Cornmeal

    Salt

    ½ cup parsley leaves

    ½ cup mint leaves

    Fresno or serrano chiles, thinly sliced

Marinate the shark in the Adobo for 12–48 hours. Pour 3–4 inches of oil into a high-sided pan. Place over medium-high heat and warm the oil to 375°F. Remove the shark from the marinade. Working with a couple of pieces at a time, roll the shark in cornmeal, making sure to completely and evenly coat it. Use a slotted spoon to place the coated shark in the hot oil, holding it for 5 seconds before releasing it. Repeat the process, cooking the shark in small batches. Turn with a slotted spoon to ensure that both sides crisp evenly. Remove the pieces as they finish and place on paper towels to absorb excess oil. Season with salt. Transfer the cooked shark to a large platter and scatter with the herbs and chile slices. Serve with Basic Aioli.

Broiled Shark en Adobo

SERVES 4

> 1 recipe Adobo Marinade (page 34)
>
> 1 recipe Salsa Criolla (page 32)
>
> 4 shark portions, skin off and cut into 1-inch pieces

Marinate the shark in the Adobo for 12–48 hours. Preheat the broiler to medium and set the rack in the middle position. Remove the shark from the marinade, thread onto skewers, and place the skewers on a baking tray. Slide the tray under the broiler and cook, turning once, until done. Serve with Salsa Criolla.

Poached Shark Waldorf Salad

SERVES 4

> ½ cup Mayonnaise (page 29, or store-bought) or Basic Aioli (page 25)
>
> 4 shark portions, skin off
>
> Salt
>
> 1 cup white wine
>
> 2 tablespoons white wine vinegar
>
> 1 small shallot, sliced
>
> 1 teaspoon ground mace
>
> 30 black peppercorns
>
> 1 bay leaf
>
> 1 cup quartered grapes
>
> ¾ cup toasted walnut pieces
>
> 2 apples, peeled and diced
>
> 2 teaspoons chopped tarragon
>
> 1 celery heart (about 1 pound), thinly sliced

Season the shark with salt and let it rest for 20 minutes. In a pan just wide enough to hold the shark in a single layer, combine 2 cups of water with the wine, vinegar, shallot, mace, peppercorns, and bay leaf. Simmer over low heat for 5 minutes. Season the broth with salt and bring it to 170°F. Add the shark and cook about 6–8 minutes per ½ inch of thickness. Remove the pan from the heat and cool the shark in the poaching liquid. Transfer the shark to a plate and flake it into bite-size pieces. Combine the grapes, walnuts, apples, tarragon, celery, and flaked shark. Toss with Mayonnaise or Basic Aioli.

SHRIMP

Shrimp's popularity is due to its incredible versatility: its flavor melds into dishes better than just about any other seafood. Shrimp works well with most seasonings, but its incredible sweetness takes especially to citrus, bold spices, and fiery heat.

But not all shrimp are created equal. And though great farmed products are available, wild American shrimp pulled from the warm waters of Louisiana and the Gulf, where they are steeped in that region's traditions of hospitality, are worth seeking out.

There are three wild-caught species of shrimp widely available on the American market. Brown shrimp are caught mostly in Texas and are the largest of the three species. The waters in which they are predominantly caught are highly saline, and their flavor is correspondingly iodine. This distinctive tang, along with a taste generally described as "big," makes brown shrimp the most robustly flavored of the three major species. The white shrimp, caught mostly in Louisiana and Florida, is considered the highest quality, with the cleanest flavor and a snappy texture. Pink shrimp, caught mostly in Florida, is nearly equal in quality to the white shrimp.

One other wild shrimp of note is rock shrimp. This deep-water species harvested in Florida gets its name due to the hardness of its shell, which has to be peeled mechanically. The meat is small and tightly concentric, and when battered and deep-fried, it is commonly called popcorn shrimp.

Cold-water shrimp are not as well suited to moist-heat preparations (such as steaming) as are warm-water shrimp. However, when sautéed, griddled, grilled, or broiled, they provide a unique texture and unmatched sweetness. In this category are the spot prawn and side-stripe shrimp of the Pacific Coast. Northern shrimp from both the East and West Coasts is a small, sweet shrimp (70+ per pound) that is rarely available fresh. It can be found peeled and frozen or cooked and canned. This shrimp can be added to pasta sauces and seafood salads and mixed with mayonnaise for sandwiches.

At the market, shrimp are sold by size and measured by how many shrimp make up a pound. My recipes are written to accommodate medium shrimp, labeled as 16–20 count. The recipes will accommodate small shrimp (21–25 count) or large shrimp (10–15 count) with minute adjustments to stated cooking times.

Shrimp Boil

SERVES 4-6

    1 pound baby red potatoes

    2 large onions, quartered

    2 fennel bulbs, quartered

    2 jalapeño chiles, cut in half

10–15 thyme sprigs

    1 pound Andouille sausage, cut into chunks

    ½ cup kosher salt

    1 cup Old Bay spice

    2 (12-ounce) bottles lager beer

    1 lemon, halved

    4 pounds shrimp, head on and unpeeled

    Melted butter for serving

Fill a large covered pot with water. Place all ingredients except the beer and shrimp in a strainer basket and lower it into the pot. Over medium heat, bring the liquid to a simmer and cook for 10 minutes. Add the beer, increase the heat, bringing the water to a boil, and add the shrimp. Return to a boil, then turn off the heat and let it rest for 5 minutes to cook the shrimp. Remove the basket, drain, and serve with melted butter.

Shrimp and Peanut Boil

SERVES 4-6

    2 recipes Blackening Spice Mix
(page 33), divided

    2 pounds raw peanuts in their shells

    3 pounds shrimp, shell on and deveined

    ½ cup sea salt, divided

    2 (12-ounce) bottles beer

    1 pound baby red potatoes

    8 ears corn, shucked

    1 Fresno or serrano chile

    1 pound smoked sausage, such as
andouille or chorizo

    3 lemons, cut into quarters

    Melted butter

    Hot sauce

Soak the peanuts in cold water overnight. Toss the shrimp in half of the Blackening Spice Mix and let rest at least 30 minutes or overnight. Drain the peanuts and place them in a large stock pot with ¼ cup of the sea salt. Add the beer and 1 gallon of water. Place a plate over the peanuts to keep them submerged in the liquid, then bring the liquid to a simmer over medium-low heat. Simmer until the peanuts are soft, about 6 hours, adding more water (or beer) as needed to keep the peanuts covered.

When the peanuts are soft, add the potatoes, corn, and chile and cook until the potatoes are just tender, 10–15 minutes. Add the shrimp, sausage, lemons, and remaining Blackening Spice Mix. Cook over medium heat for 15 minutes. Turn off the heat and let it rest for 5 minutes. Strain off the cooking liquid, then pour all of the boiled goodness onto a large table covered with plenty of newspaper. Serve with bowls of melted butter, hot sauce, and lots of cold beer.

New Orleans BBQ Shrimp

SERVES 4–8

>   2 tablespoons Blackening Spice Mix
>   (page 33)
>   3 pounds shrimp, head on and unpeeled
>   Salt
>   1 lemon, halved
>   12 tablespoons butter, divided
>   2 garlic cloves, smashed
>   1 cup white wine
>   ½ cup Worcestershire sauce
>   2 tablespoons red wine vinegar
>   2 bay leaves
>   4 sprigs fresh tarragon
>   ¼ cup chopped flat-leaf parsley
>   Crusty bread for serving

Season the shrimp lightly with salt. Heat a large heavy skillet over high heat until smoking hot, then add the lemon halves, cut sides down, and shrimp to the dry pan. Cook for 1 minute on each side, then remove. Allow the pan to cool down, then add 8 tablespoons of the butter, the Blackening Spice Mix, and garlic. Cook over medium heat until the butter is melted. Add the white wine, Worcestershire sauce, vinegar, bay leaves, and tarragon and bring to a boil. Return the shrimp to the pan and cook until they are done, about 3–5 minutes. Add the remaining 4 tablespoons of butter and parsley and stir to combine. Serve immediately with lemon halves and crusty bread (and plenty of napkins).

Shrimp Aguachile

This is a type of spicy ceviche; the name literally means "chile water."

SERVES 4–6 AS AN APPETIZER

>   1 cup lime juice
>   1 Fresno or serrano chile, thinly sliced
>   2 tablespoons red wine vinegar
>   Salt
>   1 pound cooked shrimp, deveined and
>   sliced in half lengthwise
>   ¼ cup extra-virgin olive oil
>   1 red onion, thinly sliced, rinsed under
>   cold running water, and patted dry
>   1 cucumber, peeled, seeded and finely diced
>   Black pepper
>   2 avocados, peeled and thinly sliced

Combine the lime juice, chile, vinegar, and salt to taste. Add the shrimp and marinate in the refrigerator 1–4 hours. Add the olive oil, onion, and cucumber and toss well. Season with black pepper and serve over the avocados.

Shrimp Ceviche with Fennel and Mint

SERVES 4–6 AS AN APPETIZER

1 cup lime juice

2 Fresno or serrano chiles

2 stalks celery, thinly sliced

Salt

1 pound cooked shrimp, peeled, deveined, and sliced in half lengthwise

1 fennel bulb, thinly sliced

1 red onion, thinly sliced, rinsed under cold running water, and patted dry

¼ cup extra-virgin olive oil

¼ cup mint leaves, torn

1 teaspoon grated mace

Sliced endive, radicchio, and/or boiled sweet potatoes for serving

Combine the lime juice, chiles, celery, and salt to taste. Add the shrimp and marinate in the refrigerator 1–4 hours. Add the fennel, onion, olive oil, mint, and mace and toss to combine. Let it rest for 5 minutes, then divide among individual dishes and spoon any remaining vinaigrette over the shrimp. Serve immediately with slices of endive, radicchio, and/or boiled sweet potatoes.

Sautéed Shrimp with Crispy Mint and Caper Sauce

SERVES 4–6

1 recipe Crispy Mint and Caper Sauce (page 27)

2 pounds large shrimp, peeled and deveined

Salt

3 tablespoons extra-virgin olive oil or butter

Season the shrimp with salt and let them rest for 15 minutes. In a large sauté pan over high heat, warm the olive oil. Place the shrimp in the pan. Cook until the shrimp begin to turn pink, 2–3 minutes. Flip and cook until done, about 2 minutes. Toss with Crispy Mint and Caper Sauce and serve.

VARIATION

+ **Spicy Sautéed Shrimp Options.** Instead of Crispy Mint and Caper Sauce, toss the cooked shrimp with a generous amount of seasoning, such as Old Bay, Blackening Spice Mix (page 33), or Five Spice Mix (page 33) and salt.

Grilled Shrimp with Salt, Pepper, and Olive Oil

SERVES 4–6

2 pounds shrimp, head on and unpeeled

1 tablespoon extra-virgin olive oil

Salt

Black pepper

1 lemon, cut into wedges

Prepare a charcoal grill with a large fire. Toss the shrimp with olive oil and season generously with salt and pepper. Place the shrimp on the grill directly over the coals and cook undisturbed for 3 minutes. Flip the shrimp and cook until done, about 1–2 more minutes. Serve with lemon wedges.

NOTE *If using a gas grill, preheat all burners to high.*

Spice-Marinated Shrimp

SERVES 4

> 1 pound medium shrimp, peeled and deveined
>
> Salt
>
> 1 cup white wine
>
> 5 star anise pods
>
> 1 teaspoon crushed red chile flakes
>
> ¾ cup extra-virgin olive oil
>
> 1 orange, zest removed in wide strips
>
> 2 garlic cloves, grated
>
> 2 stalks rosemary
>
> ½ tablespoon cracked black peppercorns
>
> ½ tablespoon crushed fennel seeds
>
> 2–3 dried chiles, such as de árbol or Calabrian
>
> ¼ cup mixed chopped herbs, such as parsley, tarragon, or chives
>
> Toast points for serving

Season the shrimp with salt and let them rest for 15 minutes. In a pan just wide enough to hold the shrimp in a single layer, combine 2 cups of water with the wine and star anise. Simmer over low heat for 5 minutes. Season the broth with salt and bring it to 170°F. Add the shrimp and cook until they are firm, about 5 minutes. Remove the pan from the heat and let the shrimp cool in the poaching liquid to room temperature. In a small saucepan over low heat, warm the olive oil, zest, garlic, rosemary, peppercorns, fennel seeds, and chiles. When the oil is highly aromatic, remove from the heat and cool. Remove the shrimp from the liquid and pat dry. Combine the oil with the herbs and shrimp. Marinate 1–3 days. Serve with toast points dipped in the oil.

Sautéed Shrimp with Chimichurri

SERVES 4

> 1 recipe Chimichurri (page 26)
>
> 1 pound medium shrimp, peeled and deveined
>
> Salt
>
> 3 tablespoons extra-virgin olive oil

Season the shrimp with salt and let them rest for 15 minutes. In a large sauté pan over high heat, warm the olive oil. Place the shrimp in the pan. Cook until the shrimp begin to turn pink, 1–2 minutes. Flip and cook until done, about 1–2 minutes. Remove from the pan and toss with the Chimichurri. Serve warm or at room temperature.

Shrimp à la Grecque

The shrimp is cooked and marinated in a flavorful Mediterranean broth.

SERVES 4–6

> 2 pounds medium shrimp, peeled and deveined
>
> Salt
>
> ½ cup plus 3 tablespoons extra-virgin olive oil
>
> ½ cup white wine
>
> 3 tablespoons white wine vinegar
>
> ½ tablespoon ground coriander
>
> 1 tablespoon fennel seeds
>
> 6 sprigs fresh thyme
>
> 3 bay leaves
>
> ½ pound carrots, cut into ½-inch rounds
>
> 2 onions, cut into 1-inch wedges
>
> ½ pound small mushrooms

Season the shrimp with salt and let them rest for 15 minutes. In a sauté pan over high heat, warm 3 tablespoons of the olive oil. Add the shrimp and sear on one side. Remove from the pan. Reduce the heat to medium and add the remaining ½ cup of olive oil, wine, ½ cup of water, vinegar, coriander, fennel, thyme, bay leaves, and a good pinch of salt. Simmer for 5 minutes, then add the carrots, onions, and mushrooms. Cover the pan and simmer until the carrots are just tender. Nestle the shrimp into the sauce. Cover and cook over very low heat until the shrimp are cooked through, about 6–8 minutes. Remove from the heat and cool to room temperature. The flavors improve if the dish is chilled overnight in the refrigerator before being served at room temperature.

Shrimp al Ajillo

In this classic Spanish tapa preparation, the shrimp is bathed in a garlicky sauce.

SERVES 4–6

> 1½ pounds medium shrimp, peeled and deveined
>
> Salt
>
> ⅓ cup extra-virgin olive oil
>
> 8 garlic cloves, sliced
>
> 4 dried chiles, such as de árbol or Calabrian
>
> 2 bay leaves
>
> ½ cup wine
>
> 2 ounces brandy
>
> ½ lemon, juiced
>
> 3 tablespoons chopped parsley
>
> Crusty bread for serving

Season the shrimp with salt and let them rest for 15 minutes. In a sauté pan over high heat, warm the oil. Add the garlic, chiles, and bay leaves. Cook until the garlic begins to color. Carefully add the shrimp, toss to coat with oil, spread evenly in the pan, and cook, without stirring, until the shrimp begin to color, 2–3 minutes. Flip the shrimp, add the wine and brandy, and bring to a boil. Add the lemon juice and parsley and season generously with salt. Remove from the heat and stir. Serve with plenty of crusty bread.

Sautéed Shrimp and Grits

SERVES 4–6

4–6 servings grits, prepared per package
    instructions

1 pound medium shrimp, peeled
    and deveined

Salt

4 tablespoons butter

1 onion, finely diced

2 garlic cloves, sliced

1 tablespoon smoked sweet paprika

1 teaspoon crushed red chile flakes

1 lemon, zested and juiced

1 cup white wine

½ cup sour cream or cream cheese

¼ cup minced scallions

Season the shrimp with salt and let them rest for
15 minutes. In a sauté pan over medium heat,
melt the butter. Add the onion and garlic and
cook until the onion is softened, about 5 minutes.
Add the paprika, chile flakes, and zest and cook
for 1 minute. Add the shrimp, wine, and lemon
juice and toss to combine. Simmer until the
liquid is reduced by half and the shrimp are
cooked through, 5–6 minutes. Remove the pan
from the heat, add the sour cream and scallions,
and stir to combine. Spoon the grits into serving
dishes and top with the shrimp and their sauce.

Sautéed Shrimp with Preserved Lemon and Linguine

SERVES 4–6

1 pound medium shrimp, peeled, deveined,
    and sliced in half lengthwise

Salt

1 pound linguine, cooked al dente according
    to package instructions, reserving 1 cup
    of cooking liquid

4 tablespoons butter, divided

1 preserved lemon, sliced into thin strips

2 sprigs thyme, leaves picked

Crushed red chile flakes

Season the shrimp with salt and let them rest
for 15 minutes. In a sauté pan over medium
heat, melt 2 tablespoons of the butter. Add the
shrimp, preserved lemon, and thyme and cook
for 2 minutes. Add the pasta and reserved pasta
water and simmer until the liquid is mostly
absorbed. Finish the sauce with the remaining
2 tablespoons of butter and crushed red chile
flakes to taste.

Sautéed Shrimp with Lemon and Dill

SERVES 4–6

1½ pounds medium shrimp, peeled and deveined

Salt

6 tablespoons butter, divided

2 shallots, diced

½ cup white wine

1 lemon, juiced

¼ cup chopped dill

Crusty bread for serving

Season the shrimp with salt and let them rest for 15 minutes. In a large sauté pan over high heat, melt 2 tablespoons of the butter, add the shallots, and cook for 2 minutes. Add the shrimp and cook on one side for 2 minutes. Add the wine, remaining 4 tablespoons of butter, and lemon juice. Cook until the sauce is thick enough to coat the shrimp, about 4 minutes. Add the dill, toss, and serve with crusty bread.

Shrimp Griddled with Garlic and Worcestershire Sauce

SERVES 4–6

2 pounds large shrimp, head on and unpeeled

1 tablespoon kosher salt

2 garlic cloves, minced

2 tablespoons Worcestershire sauce

1 tablespoon of vegetable oil

1 lemon, cut into wedges

Combine the shrimp with salt, garlic, Worcestershire sauce, and oil and let it sit for 30 minutes. Place a griddle on the stovetop over high heat. When the griddle is smoking, add the shrimp and cook undisturbed for 4 minutes. Flip, cooking an additional 2 minutes. Remove from the heat and serve with lemon wedges.

SKATE
Flaky white fish, fillet fish

Skate have long been abundant in the Atlantic and Pacific Oceans. But it took high-profile French restaurants to bring this fish to our attention. Skate's ribbons of flesh are delicately strung together like a fan to accommodate its cartilaginous skeletal structure. These bottom-dwelling fish eat mollusks, crabs, and small fish. Skate, being that they are what they eat, taste very sweet and briny. When caught, they must be bled immediately, and the edible portions must be removed from the body in order to protect their wonderful flavor and quality.

Skate is almost always sold at market as "wings." These diamond-shaped pieces are the equivalent to fillets. Like flounder, skate have both a top and a bottom fillet (four fillets per animal). The top fillets on larger animals are about 50 percent thicker than the underside fillets. On smaller skate, the top fillets can sometimes be three times as thick as the bottom ones.

The skin should not be served because it has sharp thorns instead of scales and is covered with a thick layer of slime. This slime can be removed by soaking the entire wing in acidulated water for 20 minutes or by scrubbing with salt and a stiff brush. Skinning an uncooked skate wing is difficult. The easiest method is simply to cook it with the skin on and then peel it off with a spoon when it is ready to eat.

In all preparations, brining prior to cooking helps to maintain the structure of the flesh without sacrificing the tenderness for which it is so prized. Given its delicacy, it is best prepared sautéed, poached, or steamed, as these methods are less likely to cause the portions to break during cooking.

Skate cheeks, liver, and "bones" are added treats. The cheeks are like scallops. The liver is excellent poached in hard cider; pounded with butter, lemon juice, and salt; and served as a sauce for the skate itself or as a chilled potted spread served with warm butter-toasted crostini. The "bones," thin fanlike cartilage separating the top and bottom fillets, when soaked in a strong brine and then deep-fried, are as addictive as cracklins.

Broiled Skate with Orange and Rosemary

SERVES 4

    4 skate portions, skin off
    Salt
    1 orange, zested
    4 stalks rosemary
    4 tablespoons butter,
        cut into pieces
    1½ ounces rum

Season the skate with salt and the orange zest and let it rest for 15 minutes. Preheat the broiler to high and set the rack in the position closest to the heat. In the bottom of an ovenproof dish, arrange the rosemary in a single layer and place the skate on top. Put 1 tablespoon of butter on top of each serving, slide the dish under the broiler, and cook until the skate is done, 5–8 minutes, depending on thickness. Remove from the broiler. Add the rum and flambé by lighting it with a match. Allow the alcohol to burn off before serving.

Poached Skate Wing with Mustard Vinaigrette

SERVES 4

    4 skate portions, skin off
    Salt
    1 tablespoon whole grain mustard
    3 tablespoons red or white wine vinegar,
        divided
    2 tablespoons extra-virgin olive oil
    2 tablespoons chopped fresh tarragon
    1 small onion, sliced
    ½ lemon, thinly sliced
    2 tablespoons Pernod or dry vermouth

Season the skate with salt and let it rest for 15 minutes. In a small bowl, whisk together the mustard, 1 tablespoon vinegar, olive oil, and tarragon. In a wide pan, combine 2 cups water with the onion, lemon slices, Pernod or vermouth, and remaining 2 tablespoons vinegar. Simmer over low heat for 5 minutes. Season the broth with salt and bring it to 170°F. Working in batches, add the skate and cook until it is opaque and flakes under gentle pressure, about 7–8 minutes. Use a slotted spatula to gently transfer the skate to plates. Drizzle with the vinaigrette and serve.

Sautéed Skate Wing with Brown Butter, Walnuts, and Orange

SERVES 4

    4 skate portions, skin off
    Salt
    6 tablespoons butter, divided
    ¼ cup chopped walnuts
    1 orange, zested
    2 tablespoons chopped parsley
    1 tablespoon red wine vinegar

Season the skate with salt and let it rest for 15 minutes. In a sauté pan over high heat, melt 2 tablespoons of the butter. Add the skate and cook without flipping until almost done, then flip to finish cooking. Remove the skate and wipe the pan clean. Add the remaining 4 tablespoons of butter and the walnuts and cook until the butter is browned. Add the zest, parsley, and vinegar and swirl to combine.

Sautéed Cornmeal-Crusted Skate

SERVES 4

> 4 skate portions, skin off
>
> Salt
>
> 1 lemon, zested, cut into wedges
>
> ½ cup cornmeal
>
> 6 sprigs thyme, leaves picked and chopped
>
> 6 tablespoons butter or bacon drippings

Season the skate with salt and zest and let it rest for 15 minutes. Combine the cornmeal, thyme, and lemon zest. Dredge one side of the skate in the cornmeal mixture. In a sauté pan over medium heat, melt the butter or bacon drippings. Place the skate in the pan, cornmeal side down. Cook without flipping until almost done, then flip to finish cooking. Serve with lemon wedges.

Steamed Skate with Orange and Bay Leaf

SERVES 4

> 4 skate portions, skin off
>
> Salt
>
> 1 orange, thinly sliced
>
> 2 star anise pods
>
> ½ cup white wine
>
> 4 tablespoons butter, melted

Season the skate with salt and let it rest for 15 minutes. In the bottom of a wide, shallow pot over low heat, place the orange slices and star anise to create an aromatic raft. Add the wine and enough water to cover the bottom of the pot. Bring to a simmer. Place the skate on top of the aromatics, cover, and cook until done, 7–8 minutes. Serve each portion with 1 tablespoon of butter and a spoonful of the remaining cooking liquid drizzled over it.

SMELT
Small silver fish

These finger-size fish are similar in size to their silver-side anchovy cousins but have a more delicate flavor, and you'll never see them in a can. While you can find whole smelts fresh in the springtime, the more common product are frozen dressed smelts that have a microsheet of ice encapsulating them, which protects them from freezer burn. These fish are so small that they can be cooked straight from frozen.

Primarily a saltwater species, smelt also boast freshwater populations in the United States. East Coast rainbow smelt are mostly snagged recreationally in Maine, with most of the commercial catch coming from a freshwater fishery in Wisconsin. California has the largest saltwater fishery, and although these Western fish carry all of the culinary attributes of their East Coast counterparts, they do tend to run a little bigger.

Quality fresh or frozen smelts broadcast a strong and pleasant aroma of watermelon and cucumber, which is backed by the elegant scent of violet. These aromas, though robust, fade relatively quickly, leaving just the gentle, mildly sweet flavor of the flesh. Smelts take very well to pickling with strong spices, such as nutmeg and star anise, whose floral aspects revive the charisma of the fish.

The cook's main concern when using any of these species is simply their size, which determines the rigidity of the bones. Smaller fish less than 5–6 inches long can be grilled, broiled, fried, or sautéed whole. The bones in these little guys are very small, delicate, and wholly edible. The bones of the larger fish are less pleasant to eat. This process requires simply heading and gutting the fish, and then laying it belly side down and applying gentle pressure with your thumb as you slide it down the backbone. This pushes the fillets away from the bone structure, completely freeing one side and allowing you to grab the backbone and easily peel it away from the flesh.

One of the great joys of smelts are the roe. They are incredibly clean tasting—fresh but briny—with a creamy rich texture. When cooking a lot of fresh smelt, there is likely to be enough roe to make a little side dish. I like to toss the roe in cornmeal and fry it very quickly in butter. If I have only a handful of fish, I leave the roe inside the fish; as it cooks, it adds a wonderful floral aroma to the flesh and a beautiful creamy texture when eating.

380 **Broiled Smelts with Oregano and Lemon**

380 **Cornmeal-Crusted Smelts**

380 **Fried Smelts with Pine Nut Agrodolce**

381 **Pickled Smelts**

381 **Smelt Fritto Misto**

381 **Grilled Smelts with Red Wine–Shallot Vinaigrette**

Broiled Smelts with Oregano and Lemon

SERVES 4

1½ pounds smelts, dressed

    Salt

6 tablespoons butter

½ lemon, quartered and thinly sliced

8 sprigs fresh oregano, leaves picked,
    or 1 tablespoon dried

Season the fish with salt and let them rest for 15 minutes. Preheat the broiler to high and set the rack in the position closest to the heat. In an ovenproof sauté pan over medium heat, melt the butter, and cook until golden brown. Add the lemon slices and cook for 1 minute. Add the fish in a single layer and toss to coat with butter. Season with salt and oregano and place the pan under the broiler. Cook until the fish become crispy and the lemons char.

Cornmeal-Crusted Smelts

SERVES 4

1½ pounds smelts, dressed

    Salt

    Vegetable or peanut oil

    Flour

½ cup buttermilk

    Fine cornmeal

1 lemon, cut into wedges

Season the fish with salt and let them rest for 15 minutes. Pour 3–4 inches of oil into a high-sided pan. Place over medium-high heat and warm the oil to 375°F. Dredge one fish through the flour to coat, then dip it into the buttermilk and dredge through the cornmeal to evenly coat. Place one piece of coated fish at a time into the oil, and hold it for 5 seconds before releasing it. Repeat the process, cooking the fish in small batches. Turn the fish with a slotted spoon so all sides crisp evenly. Remove the fish as they finish and place on paper towels to absorb excess oil. Season with salt. Serve with lemon wedges.

Fried Smelts with Pine Nut Agrodolce

SERVES 4

1 recipe Pine Nut Agrodolce (page 30)

1–2 pounds smelts, dressed

    Salt

1 lemon, juiced

    Vegetable or peanut oil

½ cup flour, sifted

½ cup cornstarch, sifted

Season the fish with salt and lemon juice and let them rest for 15 minutes. Pour 3–4 inches of oil into a high-sided pan. Place over medium-high heat and warm the oil to 375°F. Combine the flour and cornstarch on a large plate and dredge one fish at a time in the mixture, coating both sides. Place one piece of coated fish at a time into the oil, and hold it for 5 seconds before releasing it. Repeat the process, cooking the fish in small batches. Turn the fish with a slotted spoon so all sides crisp evenly. Remove the fish as they finish and place on paper towels to absorb excess oil. Top the cooked fish with the Pine Nut Agrodolce.

VARIATION

+ **Lemon and Spice Smelts.** Replace Agrodolce with Lemon-Chile-Soy Sauce (page 29) used as a dipping sauce.

Pickled Smelts

MAKES 1 POUND

1 pound smelts, dressed

¼ cup kosher salt

¼ cup packed brown sugar

1 teaspoon mace

½ teaspoon nutmeg

6 crumbled bay leaves

¾ cup apple cider vinegar

In a bowl, toss the smelts with the salt, brown sugar, mace, nutmeg, and bay leaves. Tightly pack the fish together and let them rest for 24 hours. Wash the salt mixture from the fish and set them in a nonreactive dish. In a small pan over medium-high heat, combine the vinegar and ¾ cup of water and bring to a boil. Pour the vinegar mixture over the smelts. Cool to room temperature and then refrigerate 2 days. The fish will keep up to a week in the refrigerator.

Smelt Fritto Misto

SERVES 4

1 pound smelts, dressed

1 bunch scallions, cut into 3-inch pieces

1 lemon, thinly sliced

2–3 stalks celery, cut on a bias into 2-inch pieces

1 onion, quartered and peeled into individual leaves

Salt

Vegetable or peanut oil

1½ cups flour, sifted

3 tablespoons cornstarch, sifted

1 teaspoon garlic powder

2 teaspoons onion powder

2¼ cups seltzer water

Season the fish, scallions, lemon, celery, and onion with salt and let them rest for 15 minutes. Pour 3–4 inches of oil into a high-sided pan. Place over medium-high heat and warm the oil to 375°F. Make a batter by combining the flour, cornstarch, garlic powder, onion powder, seltzer water, and salt to taste. Whisk until smooth and use within 10 minutes. Dip one fish or vegetable at a time into the batter and place it in the oil, holding it for 5 seconds before releasing. Repeat the process, cooking the ingredients in batches. Turn with a slotted spoon to ensure that all sides crisp evenly. Remove the pieces as they finish and place on paper towels to absorb excess oil.

Grilled Smelts with Red Wine–Shallot Vinaigrette

SERVES 4

1 recipe Red Wine–Shallot Vinaigrette (page 37)

1½ pounds smelts, dressed

¼ cup chopped herbs, such as chervil, parsley, or tarragon

Reserve half of the Red Wine–Shallot Vinaigrette. Pour the other half over the fish and marinate for 1–8 hours. Remove the fish from the marinade and skewer the fish, 3–4 per skewer. Prepare a charcoal grill with a large fire. Place the skewers on the grill over the hottest part of the fire. Cook until the edges of the fish begin to crisp, 2–3 minutes. Gently flip the fish, brush with any remaining marinade and cook another 2–3 minutes. Serve with the remaining vinaigrette drizzled over the top and scattered with chopped herbs

The huge snapper family is known for the vibrant color swatch it boasts. Among them are brilliant reds, pretty pinks, and interesting violets.

Lucky for cooks, most snapper species sport a consistent and versatile culinary profile. Nearly every variety is firm in texture with whitish flesh, simple bone structure, and a sharp, sweet, and meaty flavor. Despite being relatively lean, most are resilient to high heat and retain their moisture as well as fattier fish do.

As many snapper species come to market weighing just 1–2 pounds, they are perfect for panfish preparations, using single-portion fillets or cooking whole on the grill or roasted in the oven or roasted in salt. However, many other snapper species do not reproduce until they are much larger in size; thus, we as consumers have a responsibility to use larger fillets that yield multiple portions each. Snapper are also great for braising, as well as for chowders and stews.

The bones of all snapper make for a good stock when very gently simmered. If allowed to boil, the stock can become heavy flavored, but can be brightened by a dash of lemon juice or the addition of aromatic fennel or ginger. Snapper livers are a delicacy when sautéed or pounded to a paste with butter and used to thicken soups or sauces.

Braised Snapper à la Barigoule

The snapper and vegetables are braised and marinated in a spiced broth.

SERVES 4

> 1 recipe Basic Aioli (page 25), made with oil skimmed from the cooked dish
>
> 4 snapper portions, skin off
>
> Salt
>
> 3 stalks celery, chopped
>
> 2 carrots, sliced
>
> 4 ounces mushrooms, cut in quarters
>
> 2 garlic cloves, thinly sliced
>
> 5 sprigs thyme
>
> 1 teaspoon ground coriander
>
> 1½ cups white wine
>
> 1 (14-ounce) can halved artichoke hearts in oil
>
> ½ lemon, thinly sliced
>
> 1 cup extra-virgin olive oil
>
> Crushed red chile flakes (optional)
>
> Crusty bread for serving

Season the fish with salt and let it rest for 15 minutes. In a large pot over medium heat, combine the celery, carrots, mushrooms, garlic, thyme, coriander, wine, and ½ cup of water. Season lightly with salt and simmer until the alcohol smell dissipates, about 5 minutes. Add the artichoke hearts with their oil, lemon slices, and olive oil. Reduce the heat to low. Nestle the fish into the pot so it is barely submerged. If desired, add the chile flakes. Cover and cook for 25–30 minutes. Remove the pot from the heat and cool to room temperature. The flavors improve if allowed to chill overnight in the refrigerator. Use a ladle to skim off the olive oil and use it to make Basic Aioli. Serve at room temperature with crusty bread and the aioli.

Braised Snapper Puttanesca

The snapper is braised in a lively tomato sauce with capers and olives.

SERVES 4

> 4 snapper portions, skin off
>
> Salt
>
> 6 tablespoons extra-virgin olive oil, divided
>
> 1 (2-ounce) tin anchovies in oil
>
> 4 garlic cloves, sliced
>
> 4 dried árbol chiles or ½ tablespoon crushed red chile flakes
>
> 2 (14-ounce) cans fire-roasted diced tomatoes
>
> ¾ cup white wine
>
> 2 tablespoons capers, rinsed and patted dry
>
> ¼ cup pitted cured black olives
>
> 6 basil leaves, torn, for garnish

Season the fish with salt and let it rest for 15 minutes. In an ovenproof sauté pan over medium-high heat, warm 3 tablespoons of the olive oil, anchovies with their oil, garlic, and chiles, and cook until the anchovies melt. Add the tomatoes, wine, capers, and olives. Bring to a simmer and cook for 10 minutes. Nestle the fish into the sauce, and drizzle with the remaining 3 tablespoons of olive oil. Cover the pan and place in a 275°F oven for 30 minutes. Remove and let it rest for 10 minutes before serving scattered with torn basil leaves.

Sautéed Snapper Provençal

SERVES 4

> 4 snapper portions, skin on, scored
>
> Salt
>
> 6 tablespoons extra-virgin olive oil
>
> 1 garlic clove, finely minced
>
> 1 (14-ounce) can fire-roasted, diced tomatoes, drained, or ¾ cup large diced tomatoes
>
> 2 tablespoons chopped green or black olives
>
> 1 tablespoon red or white wine vinegar

Season the fish with salt and let it rest for 15 minutes. In a sauté pan over medium-high heat, warm the olive oil. Place the fish in the pan skin side down. Cook without flipping until almost done, then remove the fish. Add the garlic and cook for 1 minute. Add the tomatoes, olives, and vinegar. Season with salt and simmer for 5 minutes. Turn off the heat and nestle the fish skin side up into the sauce to finish cooking, about 1 minute. Serve hot or at room temperature.

Stewed Snapper with Romesco

SERVES 4

> 1 recipe Romesco (page 31)
>
> 4 snapper portions, skin off
>
> Salt
>
> Rice for serving

Season the fish with salt and let it rest for 15 minutes. Pour the Romesco in a pan wide enough to comfortably fit the fish in a single layer. Nestle the fish into the sauce, cover, and place over low heat. Cook until the fish is flaky, about 12 minutes. Do not stir or shake the pan while cooking, as the fillets will break up. Check the sauce for seasoning. Serve over rice.

Broiled Snapper with Sour Cream and Dill

SERVES 4

> 3 tablespoons Mayonnaise (page 29, or store-bought)
>
> 4 snapper portions, skin off
>
> Salt
>
> 3 tablespoons sour cream
>
> 2 tablespoons fresh chopped dill

Season the fish with salt and let it rest for 15 minutes. Preheat the broiler to medium and set the rack in the position closest to the heat. Combine the sour cream, Mayonnaise, and dill. Place the fish on a greased baking tray. Spread the sour cream mixture evenly over the fish. Slide the tray under the broiler and cook until done, 7–10 minutes, depending on thickness.

Snapper Ceviche

SERVES 4 AS AN APPETIZER

> 1 pound snapper fillets, skin off, diced into ½-inch pieces
>
> Salt
>
> 1 cup lime juice
>
> 1–2 teaspoons crushed red chile flakes
>
> ½ cup toasted pecan pieces
>
> 3 shallots, thinly sliced, rinsed under cold running water, and patted dry
>
> ¼ cup extra-virgin olive oil
>
> ½ cup cilantro or chervil, leaves picked

Keep this dish cold at all times during preparation. Season the fish with salt and let it rest for 5 minutes. Combine the fish with the lime juice and chile flakes and let it rest for 30 minutes. Add the nuts and shallots and let it rest for another 10 minutes. Toss with the olive oil and cilantro and serve.

Snapper Crudo with Black Pepper and Orange

SERVES 4 AS AN APPETIZER

> 1 pound snapper fillets, skin off and sliced on the bias into ¼-inch-thick ribbons, avoiding any dark tissue
>
> Salt
>
> Extra-virgin olive oil, spicy is best
>
> Black pepper
>
> 1 orange, zested

Lay the fish on serving plates, season the fish with salt, and let it rest for 10 minutes. Drizzle with oil, and garnish with black pepper and zest.

Grilled Snapper on the Half-Shell with Sundried Tomato–Basil Butter

SERVES 4

> 1 recipe Sundried Tomato–Basil Butter (page 23)
>
> 1 (3- to 5- pound) whole snapper, filleted, pin bones removed, scales and skin left intact
>
> Salt
>
> 2 tablespoons butter, melted
>
> Black pepper

Prepare a charcoal grill with a medium fire. Season the flesh of the fish with salt and pepper and let it rest for 15 minutes. Place the fish scaly skin side down directly over the hot coals. Baste the fillets with the melted butter, cover, and cook until done, 12–15 minutes. Transfer to a serving platter, slather with the compound butter, and serve with instructions to eaters to spoon the fish off the skin, leaving the skin on the platter.

NOTE *If using a gas grill, preheat all burners to medium-high.*

Pine-Grilled Snapper with Gremolata

SERVES 4

> 1 recipe Gremolata (page 28)
>
> 4 snapper portions, skin on and scored
>
> Salt
>
> Extra-virgin olive oil
>
> Untreated pinecones

Season the fish with salt and let it rest for 15 minutes. Prepare a charcoal grill with a medium fire, concentrating the hot coals on one side of the kettle. Lightly brush the fish with oil and place it skin side down on the grill directly over the hot coals. Cook until the skin begins to char, about 3 minutes. Lift the entire grill grate and rotate it so the fish rests opposite the hot coals. Add the pinecones to the coals, cover the grill, and continue to cook over this indirect heat until the fish is done. Serve with Gremolata.

NOTE *If using a gas grill, preheat all burners to medium. Place the snapper on one side of the hot grates. Once it begins to char around the edges, turn off the burner directly under the fish, add the pinecones to the grates still above the flames, and cover the grill to finish cooking.*

Ember-Roasted Whole Snapper

SERVES 4-6

> 1 whole (4- to 6-pound) snapper, gutted, scales left intact
>
> Salt
>
> 4 sprigs thyme
>
> 2 garlic cloves, smashed
>
> 3 lemons, 1 thinly sliced and 2, halved
>
> Extra-virgin olive oil

Prepare a charcoal grill with a medium fire, concentrating the hot coals on one side of the kettle. Season the belly cavity of the fish with salt and stuff it with the thyme, garlic, and lemon slices. When the charcoal has burned to embers, place the fish directly on the coals. Place the halved lemons on the grill cut side down directly over the embers. Cover the grill and allow the fish to cook for 15 minutes, then flip the fish, adding wood chips (or more charcoal) to keep the fire going if necessary. Remove the lemon halves and reserve. Cover the grill and cook another 10–15 minutes. Check to see if the fish is cooked by inserting a knife along the backbone to reveal the flesh. It should be opaque when done. If more time is needed, cover the grill and cook another 5–10 minutes. Remove the fish to a platter. To serve, insert a spatula along the backbone of the fish and gently peel off sections of the fillet. Serve with the grilled lemon halves and a drizzle of olive oil.

Snapper en Papillote (cooked in parchment)

SERVES 4

> 4 snapper portions, skin off
>
> Salt
>
> 4 stalks celery, sliced
>
> 2 fennel bulbs, thinly sliced
>
> 4 canned artichoke hearts, drained and cut in quarters
>
> 1 small onion, sliced
>
> 1 cup white wine
>
> 4 tablespoons butter, cut into pieces, plus additional for greasing the parchment

Season the fish with salt and let it rest for 15 minutes. In a shallow pan, place the celery, fennel, artichokes, onion, and wine and season with salt. Cook until the vegetables are soft and the wine is nearly evaporated. Take four 18-inch squares of parchment paper and cut into heart shapes. Use butter to grease an 8-inch square area in the middle of each. Evenly divide the vegetables and remaining liquid among the parchment hearts, place the fish on top, and add 1 tablespoon of butter to each fillet. Fold the paper over, then crimp the edges tightly (empanada style) to form a pouch. Roast at 350°F for 10–12 minutes, depending on the thickness of the fish. Serve in the pouch and slice open just prior to eating.

Poached Snapper with Pine Nut Piccata

SERVES 4

> 1 recipe Pine Nut Piccata (page 30)
>
> 4 snapper portions, skin off
>
> Salt
>
> 1 cup white wine
>
> 8 garlic cloves, smashed
>
> 8–10 black peppercorns
>
> 6 allspice berries
>
> 2 sprigs thyme
>
> 1 bay leaf

Season the fish with salt and let it rest for 15 minutes. In a deep pan wide enough to hold the fish in a single layer, combine 1½ cups of water with the wine, garlic, peppercorns, allspice, thyme, and bay leaf. Simmer over low heat for 5 minutes. Season the broth with salt and bring it to 170°F. Add the fish and cook until it is opaque and flakes under gentle pressure, 4–6 minutes per ½ inch of thickness. Remove the fish from the liquid and serve with Pine Nut Piccata.

Poached Snapper with Cucumber Broth

SERVES 4

    4 snapper portions, skin off
    Salt
    2 large cucumbers, roughly chopped
    4 tablespoons butter, melted
    Black pepper

Season the fish with salt and let it rest for 15 minutes. In a blender, combine the cucumbers with 2 cups of water and blend until liquefied. Strain the liquid into a pan just wide enough to hold the fish in a single layer. Season the broth with salt and bring it to 170°F. Add the fish and cook until it is opaque and flakes under gentle pressure, 4–6 minutes per ½ inch of thickness. Divide the fish among four shallow bowls and top each with 1 tablespoon of butter. Spoon a few tablespoons of the broth over each portion and garnish with a scant amount of freshly ground black pepper.

Corned Snapper

SERVES 4

    4 snapper portions, skin on
    Salt
    4 tablespoons butter
    2 garlic cloves, grated
    1 cup white wine
    2 bay leaves
    1 lemon, juiced

Lightly season the fish with salt and let it rest for 8–12 hours. In a small saucepan over medium heat, melt the butter and add the garlic. Keep it warm. In a deep pan wide enough to hold the fish in a single layer, combine 1 cup of water with the wine and bay leaves. Simmer over low heat for 5 minutes. Season the broth with salt and bring it to 170°F. Add the fish skin side down and cook until it is opaque and flakes under gentle pressure, flipping the portions if necessary, for 4–6 minutes per ½ inch of thickness. Transfer the fish to a serving plate, add the lemon juice and 1 tablespoon of the poaching liquid to the reserved garlic butter, and spoon the sauce over the fish to serve.

Salt-Roasted Whole Snapper with Lemon and Herbs

SERVES 2

    3 pounds kosher salt
    1 (1½- to 2½-pound) whole snapper,
        scaled, gutted, skin on, and scored
    2 lemons, thinly sliced
    6 sprigs thyme
    6 stalks rosemary
    4 tablespoons butter, melted

Combine the salt with enough water so that it resembles wet sand. Place a thin layer on a baking sheet and top with half of the sliced lemons, half of the thyme, and half of the rosemary. Place the fish on top, then cover it with the remaining lemon slices, thyme, and rosemary. Pack on the remaining salt mixture to completely encase the fish. Roast at 375°F for 20–30 minutes. Remove the fish from the oven and let it rest for 5 minutes. Crack the salt crust and discard it. Discard the lemon, thyme, and rosemary from the top of the fish. Serve whole or peel off the skin before carefully transferring the top fillet to a platter. Remove and discard the backbone and transfer the bottom fillet without its skin to the platter. Drizzle the fish with melted butter.

Butter-Basted Snapper with Chile, Mint, and Ginger

SERVES 4

4 snapper portions, skin on and scored

Salt

6 tablespoons butter, divided

2 garlic cloves, minced

2 dried chiles, such as de árbol or Calabrian

20 mint leaves

1 tablespoon finely grated ginger

1 lemon, cut into wedges

Season the fish with salt and let it rest for 15 minutes. In a sauté pan over medium-high heat, melt 2 tablespoons of the butter. Place the fish in the pan skin side down and cook until the skin is beginning to brown. Flip the fish. Add the remaining 4 tablespoons of butter, garlic, chiles, mint, and ginger. Cook until the butter is frothy, then angle the pan toward you and use a spoon to continuously baste the fish with the butter until it is cooked through. Remove the fish from the pan. Discard the chiles, strain the butter, and reserve the crisped garlic and mint to scatter over the fish. Serve with lemon wedges.

Sautéed Snapper with Peppers and Mint

SERVES 4

4 snapper portions, skin on and scored

Salt

6 tablespoons extra-virgin olive oil or butter, divided

1 red bell pepper, seeded and cut into ½-inch strips

1 yellow bell pepper, seeded and cut into ½-inch strips

1 Fresno or serrano chile, minced (optional)

2 garlic cloves, minced

1 tablespoon ground mace

½ teaspoon ground mace

2 tablespoons chopped fresh mint

Season the fish with salt and let it rest for 15 minutes. In sauté pan over medium-low heat, warm 4 tablespoons of the oil or butter. Place the fish in the pan skin side down. Cook without flipping until almost done and remove the fish. Add the remaining 2 tablespoons of oil or butter, bell pepper, chile, and garlic, and cook until the pepper softens. Season with salt, vinegar, and mace and stir. Nestle the fish into the pepper uncooked side down and cook until done. Sprinkle with mint and serve hot or at room temperature.

Sautéed Sesame-Crusted Snapper with Brown Butter

SERVES 4

4 snapper portions, skin off

Salt

⅓ cup sesame seeds

6 tablespoons butter, divided

1 orange, juiced

Season the fish with salt and let it rest for 15 minutes. Dredge one side of the fish in sesame seeds and press them firmly into the flesh. In a sauté pan over medium-low heat, melt 4 tablespoons of the butter and cook until golden brown. Place the fish in the pan sesame seed side down. Cook without flipping until the fish is almost done and sesame seeds are crisp and brown, then flip to finish cooking. Remove the fish from the pan. Add the remaining 2 tablespoons of butter and the orange juice. Swirl to incorporate and season with salt.

Sautéed Snapper with Brown Butter, Thyme, and Orange

SERVES 4

> 4 snapper portions, skin on and scored
>
> Salt
>
> 6 tablespoons butter, divided
>
> 8 sprigs thyme, leaves picked
>
> 1 orange, zested and cut into segments

Season the fish with salt and let it rest for 15 minutes. In a sauté pan over medium heat, melt 2 tablespoons of the butter and cook until golden brown. Place the fish in the pan skin side down. Cook without flipping until almost done, then remove the fish, and wipe the pan clean. Add the remaining 4 tablespoons of butter and the thyme. Cook until the butter is dark brown. Add the orange zest and segments and season with salt. Stir gently to combine. Turn off the heat and return the fish to the pan uncooked side down to finish cooking.

Sautéed Snapper with Walnut and Lime

SERVES 4

> 4 snapper portions, skin on and scored
>
> Salt
>
> 6 tablespoons butter, divided
>
> ½ cup crushed walnuts
>
> 2 limes, juiced
>
> 2 tablespoons chopped cilantro

Season the fish with salt and let it rest for 15 minutes. In a large sauté pan over medium heat, melt 4 tablespoons of the butter. Place the fish in the pan skin side down. Cook without flipping until almost done, then remove the fish. Add the walnuts and cook until toasted. Add the lime juice and remaining 2 tablespoons of butter and bring to a simmer. Stir in the cilantro and season with salt. Turn off the heat and return the fish to the pan skin side up to finish cooking.

Sautéed Snapper with Cider–Brown Butter Sauce

SERVES 4

> 4 snapper portions, skin on and scored
>
> Salt
>
> 6 tablespoons butter, divided
>
> 1 lemon, juiced
>
> ½ cup apple cider or hard cider

Season the fish with salt and let it rest for 15 minutes. In a sauté pan over medium heat, melt 2 tablespoons of the butter and cook until golden brown. Place the fish skin side down in the pan. Cook without flipping until almost done, then remove the fish and wipe the pan clean. Add the remaining 4 tablespoons of butter and cook until golden brown. Add the lemon juice and cider, reduce until the sauce is thick. Season with salt. Turn off the heat and return the fish to the pan uncooked side down to finish cooking.

Sautéed Snapper with Bay Leaf

SERVES 4

> 4 snapper portions, skin on and scored
>
> Salt
>
> 8 tablespoons olive oil
>
> 8 bay leaves
>
> 4 garlic cloves, smashed

Season the fish with salt and let it rest for 15 minutes. In a sauté pan over medium-low heat, warm the olive oil. Add the bay leaves and garlic and cook until aromatic. Add the fish, skin side down. Cook until almost done, then flip to finish cooking. Discard the bay leaves and serve the fish topped with garlic and drizzled with some of the cooking oil.

Steamed Snapper with Lemongrass and Star Anise

SERVES 4

> 4 snapper portions, skin off
>
> Salt
>
> 3 stalks lemongrass, split
>
> 2 star anise pods
>
> ½ cup white wine
>
> 4 tablespoons butter, melted

Season the fish with salt and let it rest for 15 minutes. In the bottom of a wide, shallow pot over low heat, place the lemongrass and star anise to create an aromatic raft. Add the wine and enough water to cover the bottom of the pot. Bring to a simmer. Place the fish on top of the aromatics, cover, and cook until done, about 7–8 minutes. Serve each portion with 1 tablespoon of butter and a spoonful of the remaining cooking liquid drizzled over it.

SPOT
Fillet fish

Spot are small, feisty fish with a distinctive large, black spot near their gill opening. They are commonplace in shallow mid-Atlantic waters from April through November but are best in the fall, just before spawning, when their flesh is taut and fat. At full size, they weigh about a pound, making them a perfectly sized panfish. Spot's flavor can be a bit more assertive than other panfish, but when the fish is very fresh, the taste is both mild and sweet.

Sautéed Cornmeal-Coated Spot

SERVES 4

    4 portions spot, skin off
    Salt
    Milk
    Fine cornmeal
    8 tablespoons bacon drippings or butter
    1 lemon, cut into wedges

Season the fish with salt and let it rest for 15 minutes. Dip one side of the fish in milk then dredge that side in cornmeal to coat. In a large sauté pan over medium heat, warm the bacon drippings or butter. Place the fish in the pan cornmeal side down. Cook until the crust has crisped and the fish is cooked through, flipping each fillet if need be just for a few seconds. Serve with lemon wedges.

Sautéed Spot with Brown Butter, Raisins, and Tarragon

SERVES 4

    4 spot portions, skin on and scored
    Salt
    6 tablespoons butter, divided
    2 garlic cloves, finely minced
    2 tablespoons raisins
    1 lemon, zested and juiced
    2 tablespoons chopped fresh tarragon

Season the fish with salt and let it rest for 15 minutes. In a sauté pan over medium heat, melt 2 tablespoons of the butter and cook until golden brown. Place the fish skin side down in the pan. Cook without flipping until almost done, then remove the fish, and wipe the pan clean. Add the remaining 4 tablespoons of butter, garlic, and raisins. Cook until the butter is brown and the raisins plump. Add the lemon zest and juice and tarragon. Stir to combine and season with salt. Turn off the heat and return the fish to the pan uncooked side down to finish cooking.

Fried Whole Spot with Mint, Shallot, and Fish Sauce

SERVES 4

> 2 pounds spot, headed and gutted, skin scored
>
> Salt
>
> 1 lemon, juiced
>
> Vegetable or peanut oil
>
> Rice flour
>
> 2 tablespoons chopped fresh mint
>
> 1 shallot, thinly sliced
>
> 1 Fresno or serrano chile, thinly sliced
>
> 2 tablespoons Thai fish sauce

Season the fish with salt and lemon juice and let them rest for 15 minutes. Pour 2–3 inches of oil into a high-sided skillet large enough to hold two fish at a time. Place over medium-high heat and warm the oil to 350°F. Dredge one fish in rice flour, coating both sides. Slide the fish into the hot oil and hold for 5 seconds before releasing. Repeat the process with a second fish. Turn with a slotted spoon to ensure that both sides crisp evenly. Cook for 5–7 minutes total. Remove the fish when they finish cooking and place on paper towels to absorb excess oil. Repeat the process with the remaining fish. Transfer the fish to a serving platter. Scatter the mint, shallot, and chile over the fish. Drizzle with the fish sauce.

Spot en Escabeche

The cooked spot is marinated in vinegar and spices.

SERVES 4

> 2 pounds spot, headed and gutted, skin scored
>
> Salt

> Flour
>
> 1 cup plus 2 tablespoons extra-virgin olive oil
>
> 2 carrots, sliced into thin rounds
>
> 2 shallots, sliced into rings
>
> 4 garlic cloves, smashed
>
> 1 tablespoon smoked sweet paprika
>
> 1 teaspoon ground coriander
>
> 6 sprigs thyme or 3 stalks rosemary
>
> 1 orange, zest removed in wide strips
>
> ½ cup fruity white wine
>
> 1 tablespoon sherry vinegar
>
> ¼ cup chopped fresh herbs, such as chives, parsley, or tarragon
>
> Sliced baguette for serving

Season the fish with salt and let it rest for 15 minutes. Roll the fish in flour. In a sauté pan over medium heat, warm 2 tablespoons of the olive oil. Place the fish into the pan two at a time and cook without flipping until almost done, then flip to finish cooking. Repeat the process with the remaining fish. Alternatively, fish can be broiled. Transfer the cooked fish to a baking dish just large enough to hold them in one layer. Wipe the sauté pan clean. Heat the remaining 1 cup of olive oil. Add the carrots, shallots, and garlic and cook until the carrots begin to soften. Add the paprika, coriander, thyme or rosemary, and orange zest and cook for 2 minutes, until the aromas bloom. Add the wine and vinegar, season with salt, and simmer until reduced by half. Add the herbs. Stir to combine and pour over the cooked fish. Cool to room temperature. Wait at least 1 hour before serving. For best results, allow the fish to marinate overnight in the refrigerator before returning to room temperature. Serve with a sliced baguette.

SQUID

Swimming along every coast, squid is one of the great underappreciated resources we have in this country. Most people are familiar with it when prepared as flash-fried calamari. But it has much more culinary potential.

You're most likely to find squid frozen, and this can be a fantastic product. If you find it fresh, buy it! Fresh squid, sometimes called "dirty," are the whole animals, with their whisper-thin skin intact. The skin is the best indicator of freshness—it is a deep mottled purple, when very fresh, shifting to light purple-pink with shades of brown as it grows stale. This skin can be the very best part of fresh squid, as its depth of flavor intensifies that of the meat while pairing up with flavors of char and smoke perfectly. Squid is versatile not only in the flavors it pairs well with but also in the cooking methods that flatter it. From poached and served chilled, to flash-fried, to sautéed, to braised, to grilled, there isn't a method that doesn't work.

The meat of the animal comprises two distinct parts: the tubes (the hollow body) and tents (the tentacles or head). Any fishmonger selling whole squid should be happy to clean it for you, so ask for it to be prepared with the skin on—tubes and tents.

From a kitchen perspective, the parts cook the same and should be included equally in a dish, as they provide contrast in structure and presentation. When cooking squid, there is a definite rule to follow: cook them for just a couple of minutes or for more than 20, but never anything in between that time span, as they will toughen significantly. Lengthier cooking allows the squid to relax into a delightfully porous yet firm texture.

Braised Squid with Rosemary, White Wine, and Fennel

SERVES 4

1 cup Basic Fish Stock (page 61) or water

4 squid portions, tubes and tentacles

Salt

¼ cup extra-virgin olive oil

1 fennel bulb, cut into wedges

1 stalk rosemary

1 cup white wine

Crushed red chile flakes

2 tablespoons chopped fresh parsley

Crusty bread for serving

Season the squid with salt and let it rest for 15 minutes. In a heavy-bottomed sauté pan over high heat, warm the olive oil. Add the fennel and rosemary and cook without stirring until the fennel begins to brown, 3–4 minutes. Add the squid and sear it undisturbed until it begins to take on a bit of color, about 2 minutes. Add the wine, stock, a pinch (or more) of chile flakes, and salt. Reduce the heat to low and simmer until the squid is tender, about 25–35 minutes. Remove the squid and fennel, increase the heat, and reduce the liquid to ½ cup. Discard the rosemary and add the parsley. Spoon the sauce over the squid and serve warm with crusty bread.

Broiled Squid with Red Onion and Bay Leaf Flambé

SERVES 4

4 squid portions, tubes and tentacles

Salt

1 lemon, zested

6 tablespoons butter, melted

1 large onion, thinly sliced

2 bay leaves

1½ ounces Calvados or brandy

Season the squid with salt and the lemon zest and let it rest for 15 minutes. Preheat the broiler to medium and set the rack in the position closest to the heat. In a heavy-bottomed sauté pan over high heat, add the onion in a single layer (no fat is added yet). Cook without stirring for 3–4 minutes until they begin to char. Add the bay leaves and nestle the squid into the onion. Pour the butter over the squid and slide the dish under the broiler. Cook for 2–4 minutes. Remove from the broiler. Add the Calvados or brandy and flambé by lighting it with a match. Allow the alcohol to burn off and remove the bay leaves before serving.

Citrus-Fried Squid

SERVES 4

4 squid portions, cut into 1-inch rings and tentacle pieces

Salt

Vegetable or peanut oil

½ cup citrus juice

Flour

Panko

Season the squid with salt and let it rest for 15 minutes. Pour 3–4 inches of oil into a high-sided pan. Place over medium-high heat and warm the oil to 375°F. Dip a few pieces of squid into the citrus juice, then into flour to coat completely. Repeat the process if necessary to ensure that the pieces are thoroughly coated. Place the floured squid in the oil and hold it for 5 seconds before releasing it. Repeat the process, cooking the squid in small batches. Turn with a slotted spoon if necessary to ensure that the squid crisps evenly. Remove pieces as they finish and place on paper towels to absorb excess oil. Season with salt.

Wood-Grilled Squid with Cilantro-Pecan Pesto

SERVES 4

> 1 recipe Cilantro-Pecan Pesto (page 25)
>
> 4 squid portions, tubes and tentacles
>
> 1 tablespoon extra-virgin olive oil
>
> 4 garlic cloves, grated
>
> Salt

Toss the squid with the olive oil, garlic, and salt and let it rest for 15 minutes. Prepare a charcoal grill with a large fire accented with wood chunks, concentrating the hot coals on one side of the kettle. Place the squid on the grill directly over the fire. Cook for 1–2 minutes and then flip. Cook until the squid is lightly charred and caramelized and cooked through, about another 1–2 minutes. Serve immediately with Cilantro-Pecan Pesto.

NOTE *If using a gas grill, preheat all burners to high. Place a handful of wood chips in an insert or a piece of foil fashioned into a bowl on one side of the grill to create the smoke.*

Grilled Squid with Charred Lemon and Olive Oil

SERVES 4

> 4 portions squid, tubes and tentacles
>
> 1 tablespoon extra-virgin olive oil, plus additional for serving
>
> 4 garlic cloves, grated
>
> Salt
>
> 2 lemons, halved

Toss the squid with 1 tablespoon olive oil, garlic, and salt and let it rest for 15 minutes. Prepare a charcoal grill with a large fire accented with wood chunks, concentrating the hot coals on one side of the kettle. Place the lemons cut side down directly over fire and cook until deeply charred, about 5 minutes. Place the squid on the grill directly over the fire. Cook for 1–2 minutes and then flip. Cook until the squid is lightly charred and caramelized and cooked through, about another 2–3 minutes. Serve immediately with the charred lemons and a generous drizzle of olive oil.

NOTE *If using a gas grill, preheat all burners to high. Place a handful of wood chips in an insert or a piece of foil fashioned into a bowl on one side of the grill to create the smoke.*

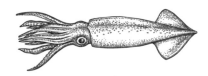

Seared Squid with Herbsaint Flambé

SERVES 4

> 4 squid portions, tubes and tentacles
> Salt
> 4 tablespoons butter
> 1½ ounces Herbsaint or Pernod

Season the squid with salt and let it rest for 15 minutes. In a sauté pan over medium-high heat, melt the butter and cook until golden brown. Place the squid in the pan. Cook without flipping until almost done, about 2–3 minutes, then flip to finish cooking. Turn off the heat. Add the Herbsaint and flambé by lighting with a match. Allow the alcohol to burn off before serving.

Poached Squid with Garlic-Parsley Oil

SERVES 4

> 1 recipe Garlic-Parsley Oil (page 27)
> 4 squid portions, tubes and tentacles, cleaned
> Salt
> 1 cup white wine
> 1 bay leaf
> Spicy salad greens for serving
> Lemon

Season the squid with salt and let it rest for 15 minutes. Place the squid in a pan just wide enough to hold it all in a single layer. Add the wine and the bay leaf and enough water to cover the squid. Season the broth with salt and bring it to 170°F. Cook until the squid is milky white in color and firm, about 3–4 minutes. Remove the squid from the poaching liquid, pat dry, and slice it as thinly as possible. Toss with the Garlic-Parsley Oil and serve over salad greens dressed with lemon.

Poached Squid Marinated with Chile, Mint, and Lemon

SERVES 4

> 4 squid portions, tubes and tentacles
> Salt
> 1 lemon, zest removed in wide strips, juiced
> 4 tablespoons sherry vinegar, divided
> 2 tablespoons black peppercorns
> 1 tablespoon coriander seeds
> 1 cup extra-virgin olive oil
> 2–3 dried chiles, such as de árbol or Calabrian
> ¼ cup chopped mint
> Toast for serving

Season the squid with salt and let it rest for 15 minutes. Place the squid in a pan just wide enough to hold it all in a single layer. Add the lemon juice, 2 tablespoons sherry vinegar, a generous amount of salt, black peppercorns, and coriander seeds. Add enough water to cover the squid. Season the broth with salt and bring it to 170°F. Cook until the squid is milky white in color and nearly firm, about 2–3 minutes. Remove the pan from the heat and cool the squid in the poaching liquid to room temperature. Remove the squid from the poaching liquid, pat dry, and slice it as thinly as possible. In a small saucepan over low heat, warm the olive oil, zest, and chiles. When the oil is highly aromatic, remove it from the heat and cool. Combine the oil with the squid, the remaining 2 tablespoons of vinegar, and mint. Marinate for at least 1 hour, though preferably 1–3 days. Serve with toast dipped in the marinade.

STRIPED BASS
Fillet fish (small), meaty dense fish (large)

Sometimes hailed as the king of fish, striped bass is much adored by fish lovers. It represents a great fisheries management story, too. Striped bass on the East Coast had reached dangerously low population levels in the 1980s and '90s, and an unprecedented multistate cooperative effort brought them back. It now supports important fisheries, both commercial and sport.

These fish can grow to epic size, and their fillets can be up to 2 inches thick. They have grayish-beige flesh that cooks up to a pretty white. They are almost always served with the beautiful skin on. The flake is fairly meaty, with a firm texture. While wild-caught striped bass is usually available, farm-raised is available year-round. These reared fish are actually a hybrid, a cross between wild striped bass and freshwater white bass. While the farmed version doesn't have the same robust flavor and texture as wild, it's still a very tasty fish.

Striped bass is great on the grill or sautéed, but I think the luscious and juicy meat of the fish is at its very best when poached in wine flavored with herbs and spices. These full-bodied flavors draw out a surprisingly gentle personality in the vigorous fish. If grilling, broiling, or sautéing, it's best to first marinate the fish. Frying is not a good application for this fish, as it is already so charismatic that adding so much richness only diminishes its robust personality.

The head and body make for a very richly flavored stock, but care must be taken to simmer as gently as possible to avoid a cloudy and murky-flavored liquid. I've found that it's best to slowly simmer the bones and head in butter in a large pot with the top on so that they gently steam through prior to the addition of water and wine. Though I don't always add celery to stock made of any other fish, here it helps to retain striped bass's crisp flavor.

Historically, the heads were regarded as the finest eating of the fish.

Striped Bass Braised with Sundried Tomatoes

SERVES 4

> 4 striped bass portions, skin off
>
> Salt
>
> 2 shallots, finely diced
>
> 4 thyme sprigs
>
> 3 whole cloves
>
> 1 orange, zested and juiced
>
> ¼ cup shredded sundried tomatoes
>
> 1 cup white or red wine
>
> 4 tablespoons butter, cut into pieces
>
> 2 tablespoons fresh chopped chives or tarragon
>
> Crusty bread for serving

Season the fish with salt and let it rest for 15 minutes. In a large skillet over medium heat, combine the shallots, thyme, cloves, orange zest and juice, sundried tomatoes, wine, and 1 cup of water. Simmer the liquid for 5 minutes. Add the fish, cover, and gently simmer until cooked through, about 12–15 minutes. Transfer the fish to a warm plate. Discard the thyme and cloves. Increase the heat to high and reduce the liquid to ¼ cup. Whisk in the butter, simmer until incorporated, add the chives or tarragon, and season with salt. Return the fish to the pan and stir to coat the fish. Serve with crusty bread.

Sautéed Striped Bass with Herbes de Provence

SERVES 4

> 1 recipe Herbes de Provence Mix (page 33)
>
> 4 striped bass portions, skin on and scored
>
> Salt
>
> 8 tablespoons extra-virgin olive oil
>
> 1 lemon, cut into wedges

Season the fish all over with salt and on the flesh side with Herbes de Provence Mix. Press the spices into the flesh and let it rest for 15 minutes. In a sauté pan over medium-low heat, warm the olive oil. Place the fish in the pan spice side down. Cook for 2 minutes, then flip to the skin side and continue to cook until done. Serve with the cooking oil drizzled over the top and lemon wedges.

Broiled Striped Bass with Lemon, Thyme, and Brandy Flambé

SERVES 4

    4 striped bass portions, skin on and scored
    Salt
    1 lemon, zested
    10 sprigs thyme or 5 stalks rosemary
    4 tablespoons butter, cut into pieces
    1½ ounces brandy

Season the fish with salt and lemon zest and let it rest for 15 minutes. Preheat the broiler to medium and set the rack in the position closest to the heat. In the bottom of an ovenproof dish, arrange the thyme. Place the fish on top, skin side up. Place 1 tablespoon of butter on top of each portion, slide the dish under the broiler, and cook until done, 6–10 minutes, depending on thickness. Remove from the broiler. Add the brandy and flambé by lighting it with a match. Allow the alcohol to burn off and discard the thyme before serving.

Grilled Striped Bass with Red Wine–Shallot Vinaigrette

SERVES 4

    1 recipe Red Wine–Shallot Vinaigrette
    (page 37)
    4 striped bass portions, skin on and scored

Reserve half of the Red Wine–Shallot Vinaigrette for serving. Combine the other half with the fish and let it marinate for 1–8 hours. Prepare a charcoal grill with a medium fire, concentrating the hot coals on one side of the kettle. Remove the fish from the marinade and place it skin side down on the grill over the hottest part of the fire. Cook until the skin begins to char, about 2 minutes. Lift the

entire grill grate and rotate it so the fish rests opposite the hot coals. Baste the fish with used marinade, cover the grill, and continue to cook over this indirect heat until the fish is done. Serve with the reserved vinaigrette.

NOTE *If using a gas grill, preheat all burners to medium-high. Place the striped bass on one side of the hot grates. Once it begins to char around the edges, turn off the burner directly under the fish, baste the fish with marinade, and cover the grill to finish cooking.*

Grilled Striped Bass with Peruvian Marinade

SERVES 4

    1 recipe Peruvian Marinade (page 37)
    4 striped bass portions, skin on and scored

Reserve one-third of the Peruvian Marinade for serving. Combine the remaining marinade with the fish and let it rest for 4–8 hours. Prepare a charcoal grill with a medium fire, concentrating the hot coals on one side of the kettle. Remove the fish from the marinade and place it skin side down on the grill over the hottest part of the fire. Cook until the skin begins to char, about 2 minutes. Lift the entire grill grate and rotate it so the fish rests opposite the hot coals. Cover the grill, baste the fish with any remaining used marinade, and continue to cook over this indirect heat until the fish is done. Serve with the reserved marinade drizzled over.

NOTE *If using a gas grill, preheat all burners to medium-high. Place the striped bass on one side of the hot grates. Once it begins to char around the edges, turn off the burner directly under the fish, baste the fish with marinade, and cover the grill to finish cooking.*

Poached Striped Bass with Green Goddess Dressing

SERVES 4

> 1 recipe Green Goddess Dressing (page 28)
>
> 4 striped bass portions, skin off
>
> Salt
>
> 1 cup white wine
>
> 2 tablespoons white wine vinegar
>
> 1 orange, zest removed in wide strips and juiced
>
> 5 cloves
>
> 5 juniper berries
>
> 1 bay leaf

Season the fish with salt and let it rest for 15 minutes. In a pan just wide enough to hold the fish in a single layer, combine 1 cup of water with the wine, vinegar, orange zest and juice, cloves, juniper, and bay leaf. Simmer over low heat for 5 minutes. Season the broth with salt and bring it to 170°F. Add the fish and cook until it is opaque and flakes under gentle pressure, 4–6 minutes per ½ inch of thickness. Transfer the fish to a plate and serve with Green Goddess Dressing.

Chilled Poached Striped Bass with Herb Vinaigrette

SERVES 4

> 4 striped bass portions, skin off
>
> Salt
>
> 3 shallots, thinly sliced, divided
>
> ¼ cup extra-virgin olive oil
>
> 1 tablespoon sherry vinegar
>
> ¼ cup chopped parsley or tarragon
>
> 1 cup white wine
>
> 2 tablespoons white wine vinegar
>
> 1 teaspoon ground mace
>
> 30 black peppercorns
>
> 1 bay leaf
>
> Spicy greens, such as arugula, endive, or radicchio, or 4 large heirloom tomatoes, sliced

Season the fish with salt and let it rest for 15 minutes. Make a vinaigrette with 2 of the sliced shallots, the olive oil, sherry vinegar, and parsley. Season with salt, and reserve. In a pan just wide enough to hold the fish in a single layer, combine 1 cup of water with the wine, white wine vinegar, 1 sliced shallot, peppercorns, and bay leaf. Simmer for 5 minutes. Season the broth with salt and bring it to 170°F. Add the fish and cook until it is opaque and flakes under gentle pressure, 4–6 minutes per ½ inch of thickness. Transfer the fish to a dish and combine with the vinaigrette. Discard the poaching liquid. Chill the marinating fish for 12–24 hours before serving at room temperature over spicy greens or sliced tomatoes.

Chilled Poached Striped Bass with Pine Nut Agrodolce

SERVES 4

> 1 recipe Pine Nut Agrodolce (page 30)
>
> 4 striped bass portions, skin off
>
> Salt
>
> 1 cup white wine
>
> 2 tablespoons white wine vinegar
>
> 1 small shallot, sliced
>
> 1 small carrot, sliced
>
> 10 whole black peppercorns
>
> 1 bay leaf

Season the fish with salt and let it rest for 15 minutes. In a pan just wide enough to hold the fish in a single layer, combine 1 cup of water with the wine, vinegar, shallot, carrot, peppercorns, and bay leaf. Simmer over low heat for 5 minutes. Season the broth with salt and bring it to 170°F. Add the fish and cook until it is opaque and flakes under gentle pressure, 4–6 minutes per ½ inch of thickness. Remove the pan from the heat and cool the fish in the poaching liquid to room temperature. To serve, remove the fish from the liquid, pat dry, and serve with Pine Nut Agrodolce.

Salt-Roasted Striped Bass with Orange and Rosemary

SERVES 2

> 3 pounds kosher salt
>
> 1 (1½- to 2½-pound) striped bass, scaled, gutted, and scored
>
> 2 oranges, thinly sliced
>
> 6 stalks rosemary, divided
>
> 4 tablespoons butter, melted, or extra-virgin olive oil

Combine the salt with enough water so that it resembles wet sand. Place a thin layer on a baking sheet and top with half of the orange slices and 4 stalks of rosemary. Place the fish on top of the rosemary. Place the remaining orange slices and rosemary on top of the fish. Pack on the remaining salt mixture to completely encase the fish. Roast at 375°F for 20–30 minutes. Remove the fish from the oven and let it rest for 5 minutes. Crack the salt crust and discard. Serve whole, or remove the oranges and rosemary and peel off the skin before transferring the top fillet to a platter. Remove and discard the backbone and transfer the bottom fillet without its skin to the platter. Drizzle the fish with melted butter.

Broiled Striped Bass with Lemon and Rosemary Flambé

SERVES 4

    4 striped bass portions, skin on and scored

    Salt

    1 lemon, zested and juiced

    10 stalks rosemary or 2–4 untreated
        pine boughs

    4 tablespoons butter

    1½ ounces Herbsaint or Pernod

Preheat the broiler to high and set the rack in the middle position. In an ovenproof dish, arrange the rosemary and place the fish on top, skin side up. Place 1 tablespoon of butter on top of each portion and broil for 6–10 minutes, depending on thickness. Remove from the broiler. Add the Herbsaint or Pernod and flambé by lighting with a match. Allow the alcohol to burn off. Drizzle with the lemon juice and discard the rosemary before serving.

Sautéed Striped Bass with Brown Butter, Raisins, and Tarragon

SERVES 4

    4 striped bass portions, skin on and scored

    Salt

    6 tablespoons butter, divided

    2 garlic cloves, finely minced

    2 tablespoons raisins

    1 lemon, juiced

    1 tablespoon chopped fresh tarragon

Season the fish with salt and let it rest for 15 minutes. In a sauté pan over medium heat, melt 2 tablespoons of the butter and cook until golden brown. Place the fish in the pan skin side down. Cook without flipping until almost done, then remove the fish, and wipe the pan clean. Add the remaining 4 tablespoons of butter, garlic, and raisins. Cook until the butter is very dark. Turn off the heat. Add the lemon juice and tarragon and season with salt. Stir to combine. Return the fish to the pan uncooked side down to finish cooking.

Steamed Striped Bass with Lemon and Pepper

SERVES 4

    4 striped bass portions, skin off

    Salt

    2 lemons, sliced

    15 black peppercorns

    ½ cup white wine

    4 tablespoons butter, melted

Season the fish with salt and let it rest for 15 minutes. In the bottom of a wide, shallow pot over low heat, place the lemons and peppercorns to create an aromatic raft. Add the wine and enough water to cover the bottom of the pot. Bring to a simmer. Place the fish on top of the aromatics, cover, and cook until done, about 7–8 minutes. Serve each portion with 1 tablespoon of butter and a spoonful of the remaining cooking liquid drizzled over it.

STURGEON
Meaty dense fish, steak fish

Sturgeon are a very slow-growing, long-lived fish of prehistoric pedigree—and they look the part, with thick armored plates running the length of their bodies and super-thick skin. But as other-worldly as they are, they are also the source of one of our world's greatest luxuries: caviar. Having survived for millions of years, wild sturgeon were almost exterminated because of our love of caviar.

The good news is that sturgeon fisheries in the Pacific Northwest are recovering, and sustainable farm-raised sturgeon and sturgeon roe are now being produced there as well. The flesh is a pale off-white, flecked with an egg-yolk-yellow fat that is very rich. The meat is finely grained, and its fillets are ivory in color, sometimes leaning to pink. Smaller fish can be cut into steaks, but sturgeon is most often sold as fillets, as the bones are few and easily removed.

Despite this richness, the meat has a tendency to dry out. It is so dense that the heat may not evenly penetrate it without overcooking the outer areas. Slow-cooking methods are often the most effective and also flatter sturgeon's mild flavor and aptly soften its meaty, veal-like texture. I particularly like to hot-smoke it, but sturgeon is as good for kebabs as it is in scaloppini preparations. Thick cuts can seize up and become coarse and dry

if exposed to high heat. If sautéing or grilling, I cut the fillet thinly on the bias, producing portions with a larger surface area. This counteracts the density of the fish and evens the cooking process. I also recommend starting any cooking process with the fish at room temperature to ease the penetration of heat.

Sturgeon's semisoft cartilaginous "bones" make an excellent stock—rich, gelatinous, and well textured. Behind caviar, the soft spinal cord is one of the most desirable parts of the fish. One method for removing the spine is unique: at the tail end, use a knife to sever and expose enough bone to gain a good grip; then, using a hook for leverage, pull the entire cord straight from the fish, leaving the flesh entirely intact. Long considered a delicacy in Russian and Chinese communities, the rich marrow is a wonderfully unique ingredient that can be adapted to any cuisine.

Braised Sturgeon in Spiced Coconut Broth

SERVES 4

4 sturgeon portions, skin off, sliced in 1-inch-thick sheets

Salt

3 tablespoons peanut oil, divided

1 lime, quartered

1 red onion, cut into ½-inch wedges

1 (1-inch) knob ginger, sliced

1 garlic clove, sliced

¾ pound carrots, cut into 1-inch pieces

¼ pound shiitake mushrooms, sliced

¼ cup slivered almonds

2 (14-ounce) cans unsweetened coconut milk

1 sprig basil

2 scallions, sliced on the bias

Rice for serving

Season the fish with salt and let it rest for 20 minutes. In a large sauté pan over high heat, warm 1 tablespoon of the oil. Add the lime and onion and cook undisturbed until the onion gets a nice char, almost burned, 3–5 minutes. Remove the onion and lime from the pan and reserve separately. Add the remaining 2 tablespoons of oil, ginger, garlic, carrots, mushrooms, and almonds. Sauté over medium heat until the almonds are toasted and the carrots just softened. Add the reserved onion and nestle the fish into the vegetables. Add the coconut milk and basil. Cover, turn the heat to low, and cook until the fish is done, 10–15 minutes. Discard the basil and ginger slices. Garnish with scallions and the reserved seared limes. Serve with rice.

Grilled Sturgeon with Rosemary and Butter

SERVES 4

4 sturgeon portions, skin off, sliced in 1-inch-thick sheets

Salt

1 stalk rosemary

8 tablespoons butter, melted

1 lemon, cut into wedges

Season the fish with salt and let it rest for 20 minutes. Prepare a charcoal grill with a medium fire, concentrating the hot coals on one side of the kettle. Use the rosemary stalk to brush the fish with butter. Place the fish on the grill directly over the hot coals. Cook until the edges begin to char, about 2 minutes. Lift the entire grill grate and rotate it so the fish rests opposite the hot coals. Constantly baste the fish with the rosemary and butter. Cover the grill and continue to cook over this indirect heat until the fish is done. Serve with lemon wedges and any remaining butter drizzled over the top.

NOTE *If using a gas grill, preheat all burners to medium-high. Place the sturgeon on one side of the hot grates. Once it begins to char around the edges, turn off the burner directly under the fish and cover the grill to finish cooking.*

Grilled Sturgeon Sandwich

SERVES 4

> 1 recipe Tartar Sauce (page 32)
>
> 4 sturgeon portions, skin off, sliced in 1-inch-thick sheets
>
> Salt
>
> Extra-virgin olive oil
>
> 4 potato buns
>
> 1–2 cups coleslaw
>
> 1 large tomato, sliced

Season the fish with salt and let it rest for 20 minutes. Prepare a charcoal grill with a medium fire, concentrating the hot coals on one side of the kettle. Drizzle the fish with olive oil. Place the fish on the grill directly over the hot coals. Cook until the edges begin to char, about 2 minutes. Lift the entire grill grate and rotate it so the fish rests opposite the hot coals. Cover the grill and continue to cook over this indirect heat until the fish is done. Assemble the sandwiches by topping each bun with a piece of grilled fish, Tartar Sauce, coleslaw, and tomato slices.

NOTE *If using a gas grill, preheat all burners to medium-high. Place the sturgeon on one side of the hot grates. Once it begins to char around the edges, turn off the burner directly under the fish and cover the grill to finish cooking.*

Grilled Sturgeon Kebabs with Cilantro-Yogurt Dressing

SERVES 4

> 1 recipe Cilantro-Yogurt Dressing (page 35)
>
> 4 sturgeon portions, skin off, cut into 1-inch pieces

Thread 3–4 pieces of fish onto each skewer. Repeat until all the fish is used. Place the skewers in a baking dish. Set aside half of the dressing for serving. Pour the other half over the fish and let it marinate up to 8 hours. Prepare a charcoal grill with a medium fire, concentrating the hot coals on one side of the kettle. Remove the skewers of fish from the marinade and place them on the grill directly over the hot coals. Cook until the edges begin to char, about 2 minutes. Turn the kebabs and lift the entire grill grate and rotate it so the fish rests opposite the hot coals. Brush the kebabs with any remaining marinade, cover the grill, and continue to cook over this indirect heat until the fish is done. Serve with the reserved dressing.

NOTE *If using a gas grill, preheat all burners to medium-high. Place the kebabs on one side of the grill, and cook until the edges of the fish begin to char. Turn the kebabs and turn off the burner directly below them. Brush kebabs with marinade, cover the grill, and continue to cook over this indirect heat until the fish is done.*

Broiled Sturgeon with Peruvian Marinade

SERVES 4

> 1 recipe Peruvian Marinade (page 37)
>
> 4 sturgeon portions, skin off, sliced in 1-inch-thick sheets
>
> 4 tablespoons butter, cut into pieces

Combine the marinade and fish and let it rest up to 8 hours. Preheat the broiler to medium and set the rack in the position farthest from the heat. Remove the fish from the marinade and place it on a baking tray. Slide the tray under the broiler and cook until done, 7–10 minutes, depending on thickness. Pour the remaining marinade into a small pan set over high heat and bring to a boil. Add the butter and swirl to combine. Serve the sauce drizzled over the fish.

Chilled Poached and Spice-Marinated Sturgeon

SERVES 4

> 4 sturgeon portions, skin off, sliced in 1-inch-thick sheets
>
> Salt
>
> 1 cup white wine
>
> 5 black peppercorns
>
> 5 star anise pods
>
> ¾ cup extra-virgin olive oil
>
> 1 orange, zest removed in wide strips
>
> 2 stalks rosemary
>
> ½ tablespoon coarsely ground black pepper
>
> ½ tablespoon crushed fennel seeds
>
> 2–3 dried chiles, such as de árbol or Calabrian
>
> 2 tablespoons sherry vinegar
>
> ¼ cup chopped fresh herbs, such as chives, parsley, or tarragon
>
> Toast points

Season the fish with salt and let it rest for 20 minutes. In a pan just wide enough to hold the fish in a single layer, combine 1 cup of water with the wine, peppercorns, and star anise. Simmer over low heat for 5 minutes. Season the broth with salt and bring it to 170°F. Add the fish and cook until it is firm to the touch and flakes under gentle pressure, 10–12 minutes. Remove the pan from the heat and cool the fish in the poaching liquid to room temperature. In a small pan over low heat, warm the olive oil. Add the zest, rosemary, pepper, fennel seeds, and the chiles. When the oil is highly aromatic, remove the pan from the heat, add the vinegar, and cool to room temperature. Remove the fish from the liquid and pat dry. Pour the oil over the poached fish, add the herbs, and marinate for 1–3 days. Serve the fish on toast points dipped in the marinade oil.

SWORDFISH
Steak fish, meaty dense fish

With a rich, buttery, steak-like texture, this giant fish has a mild flavor despite its richness. The color of swordfish flesh varies greatly. Smaller fish tend toward a paler ivory color with little dots, like stitching, running through the meat. As they grow, they can gain a pinkish-orange or peachy color, depending upon their diet. This variation makes shopping fun but does not indicate much difference in the flavor. The major factor affecting quality is the fat content, and the highest-quality fish will have a very fine marbling of translucent fat, which gives it much of its flavor. The bloodline—the dark-colored tissue coursing through the center—is more highly flavored and not to everyone's taste. It can easily be removed after cooking.

The fattest swordfish are taken in the North Pacific waters in the late summer and early fall, when their migrations from Mexico hit their northernmost peak. In the Atlantic, they peak in flavor by middle to late October; in Hawaii, from April to July. These ocean giants feed principally on squid, menhaden, and mackerel, and their flesh reflects an equally rich, fatty character and lustrous quality. Because of this, swordfish taken at their peak freeze well. In fact, it can be preferable to use a properly frozen fish caught at the peak of flavor rather than a fresh but insipid specimen taken in early spring after a lean winter.

The most important thing to look for when buying swordfish is the vibrancy and compactness of the red-tissue bloodline. When fresh, it is brilliant red with a brownish hue. As it ages, its color fades to a limp brown and leaches this color into the surrounding flesh. Whether buying steaks or loins, look for this ribbon of flesh to be bright cherry red.

As with tuna, the greatest proportion of a swordfish's fat is stored in its belly, giving it the most flavor and character. It's best braised with aromatics. After 2 hours of very low, gentle cooking, a hefty 2- to 3-pound belly portion will be tender and silky. The loin muscles of swordfish also braise well, though the texture is similar to that of chicken breast and it can dry out quickly. The most important rule of swordfish is to never overcook it, as its musculature firms and becomes chewy and unappetizingly cotton-like, even sandy, in texture.

A 1-inch-thick slice of loin is best for grilling. For braising, ask for the belly and other trim pieces. There's no reason to start with a perfectly butchered loin if you're going to cut it into chunks anyway, plus the best part is the belly. And for sautéing or broiling, use loin cuts that are about ½ inch thick. This thickness gives a cook a better chance at rendering a finished temperature that maintains the meat's moisture and quality.

Always cook swordfish from room temperature to allow even heat penetration. The fish is often cooked with its skin on, but the skin is never eaten and is easily removed before or after cooking.

Swordfish in Tomato Sauce

SERVES 4

1 recipe Basic Aioli (page 25), using oil
    skimmed from the braising liquid

4 swordfish portions, skin off

Salt

1 cup extra-virgin olive oil

6 garlic cloves, crushed

1 onion, diced

Crushed red chile flakes

1 orange, zested and juiced

2 bay leaves

2 (14-ounce) cans fire-roasted tomatoes

Crusty bread

Season the fish with salt and let it rest for 20 minutes. In a large pot over medium heat, warm the oil. Add the garlic and cook until it is lightly browned. Add the onion and a good pinch of chile flakes and cook until the onion begins to soften. Add the orange zest and juice, bay leaves, 1 cup water, and tomatoes. Season with salt and simmer for 10 minutes. Nestle the fish into the sauce, reduce the heat to low, and cover. Cook until the fish is very tender, 1–1½ hours. Remove from the heat and cool to room temperature. Use a ladle to skim the olive oil from the surface and refrigerate the stew until cold. Use the oil to make Basic Aioli. Gently rewarm the fish in the sauce and serve with crusty bread and Basic Aioli.

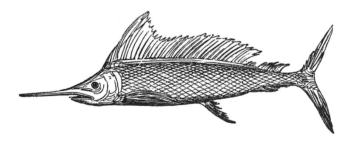

Braised Swordfish with Oregano

SERVES 4

    4 swordfish portions, skin off

    Salt

    2 tablespoons extra-virgin olive oil

    1 garlic clove, thinly sliced

    1 tablespoon dried oregano

    Black pepper

    ¼ cup extra-virgin olive oil

    1 cup white wine

    2 tablespoons butter

    3 tablespoons chopped fresh parsley

Season the fish with salt and let it rest for 20 minutes. In a pan just large enough to hold the fish, warm the olive oil over medium heat. Add the garlic, oregano, and a few turns of black pepper, and sauté until aromatic. Add the wine and 1 cup of water and bring to a simmer. Cook for about 5 minutes. Nestle the fish into the liquid so that it is barely submerged, and turn the heat to low. Cook until the fish begins to flake under gentle pressure, about 20–25 minutes, then remove to a plate and keep warm. Return the pot to the stove and reduce the liquid to ½ cup. Add the butter and parsley and stir to combine. Pour the sauce over the fish and serve.

Braised Swordfish à la Barigoule

In this recipe, the swordfish and vegetables are braised and marinated in spiced broth.

SERVES 4

    1 recipe Basic Aioli (page 25), made with oil skimmed from the cooked dish

    4 swordfish portions, skin off

    Salt

    3 stalks celery, chopped

    2 carrots, sliced

    4 ounces mushrooms, cut in quarters

    2 garlic cloves, thinly sliced

    5 sprigs thyme

    1 teaspoon ground coriander seeds

    1½ cups white wine

    1 (14-ounce) can halved artichoke hearts in oil

    ½ lemon, thinly sliced

    1 cup extra-virgin olive oil

    Crushed red chile flakes (optional)

    Crusty bread

Season the fish with salt and let it rest for 20 minutes. In a large pot over medium heat, combine the celery, carrots, mushrooms, garlic, thyme, coriander, wine, and ½ cup of water. Season lightly with salt and simmer until the alcohol smell dissipates, about 5 minutes. Add the artichoke hearts with their oil, lemon slices, and olive oil. Reduce the heat to low. Nestle the fish into the pot so it is barely submerged. If desired, add the chile flakes. Cover and cook for 25–30 minutes. Remove the pot from the heat and cool to room temperature. The flavors improve if allowed to chill overnight in the refrigerator. Use a ladle to skim off the olive oil and use it to make Basic Aioli. Serve at room temperature with crusty bread and the aioli.

Braised Swordfish in Spiced Coconut Broth

SERVES 4

> 4 swordfish portions, skin off
>
> Salt
>
> 3 tablespoons peanut oil, divided
>
> 1 lime, cut into quarters
>
> 1 medium red onion, cut into wedges
>
> 1 knob ginger, sliced
>
> 1 garlic clove, sliced
>
> ¾ pound small carrots, cut into 1-inch pieces
>
> ¼ pound shiitake mushrooms, sliced
>
> ¼ cup slivered almonds
>
> 2 (14-ounce) cans unsweetened coconut milk
>
> 1 sprig basil
>
> Scallions, sliced
>
> Rice for serving

Season the fish with salt and let it rest for 20 minutes. In a large sauté pan, heat 1 tablespoon of the oil over high heat. Add the lime and onion. Let it cook undisturbed until the onion gets a nice char, almost burned, about 3–5 minutes. Remove the onion and lime from the pan and reserve separately. Add the remaining 2 tablespoons of oil, ginger, garlic, carrots, mushrooms, and almonds. Sauté until aromatic and the carrots are just softened. Add the reserved onion and nestle the fish into the vegetables. Add the coconut milk and basil. Cover, reduce the heat to low, and cook until the fish is done, about 20 minutes. Discard the basil and ginger slices. Garnish with sliced scallions and the reserved seared lime. Serve with rice.

Grilled Swordfish with Peruvian Marinade

SERVES 4

> 1 recipe Peruvian Marinade (page 37)
>
> 4 swordfish portions, skin off

Reserve one third of the Peruvian Marinade for serving. Combine the remaining marinade with the fish and let it rest for 4–8 hours. Prepare a charcoal grill with a medium fire, concentrating the hot coals on one side of the kettle. Remove the fish from the marinade and place it on the grill over the hot coals. Cook until the edges begin to char, about 2 minutes. Lift the entire grill grate and rotate it so the fish rests opposite the hot coals. Baste with marinade, cover the grill, and continue to cook over this indirect heat until the fish is done. Serve with the reserved marinade.

NOTE *If using a gas grill, preheat all burners to medium-high. Place the swordfish on one side of the hot grates. Once it begins to char around the edges, turn off the burner directly under the fish, baste the fish with marinade, and cover the grill to finish cooking.*

VARIATION

+ **Red Wine–Shallot Vinaigrette Marinated Swordfish.** Substitute Red Wine–Shallot Vinaigrette (page 37) for the Peruvian Marinade.

Grilled Swordfish with Turmeric

SERVES 4

> 4 swordfish portions, skin off
> Salt
> Black pepper
> ¼ cup extra-virgin olive oil
> 1 tablespoon ground turmeric
> Crushed red chile flakes
> 1 lemon, cut into wedges

Season the fish with salt and black pepper. In a small saucepan over low heat, warm the olive oil, turmeric, and chile flakes until the aromas bloom. Cool to room temperature, pour the marinade over the fish, and let it marinate for 1 hour. Prepare a charcoal grill with a medium fire, concentrating the hot coals on one side of the kettle. Remove the fish from the marinade and place it on the grill over the hot coals. Cook until the edges begin to char, about 2 minutes. Lift the entire grill grate and rotate it so the fish rests opposite the hot coals. Baste the fish with any remaining marinade, cover the grill, and continue to cook over this indirect heat until the fish is done. Serve with lemon wedges.

NOTE *If using a gas grill, preheat all burners to medium-high. Place the swordfish on one side of the hot grates. Once it begins to char around the edges, turn off the burner directly under the fish, baste it with marinade, and cover the grill to finish cooking.*

Sautéed Swordfish with Madeira, Walnuts, and Raisins

SERVES 4

> 4 swordfish portions, skin off
> Salt
> 6 tablespoons butter, divided
> ¼ cup chopped walnuts
> 2 tablespoons raisins
> ½ cup Madeira, a drier style such as Sercial or Verdelho

Season the fish with salt and let it rest for 20 minutes. In a sauté pan over medium heat, melt 2 tablespoons of the butter. Place the fish in the pan. Cook without flipping until almost done, then remove the fish. Add the remaining 4 tablespoons of butter, the walnuts, and raisins and cook until the nuts are toasted and the raisins plump. Add the Madeira, season with salt, and stir to combine. Turn off the heat and place the swordfish uncooked side down in the sauce to finish cooking. Cook until done.

Chilled Poached and Spice-Marinated Swordfish

SERVES 4

    4 swordfish portions, skin off
    Salt
    1 cup white wine
    5 black peppercorns
    5 star anise pods
    ¾ cup extra-virgin olive oil
    1 orange, zest removed in wide strips
    2 stalks rosemary
    ½ tablespoon coarsely ground black pepper
    ½ tablespoon crushed fennel seeds
    2–3 dried chiles, such as de árbol or Calabrian
    ¼ cup chopped fresh herbs, such as chives, parsley, or tarragon
    Toast points for serving

Season the fish with salt and let it rest for 20 minutes. In a pan just wide enough to hold the fish in a single layer, combine 1 cup of water with the wine, peppercorns, and star anise. Simmer over low heat for 5 minutes. Season the broth with salt and bring it to 170°F. Add the fish and cook until it is opaque and flakes under gentle pressure, 10–12 minutes. Remove the pan from the heat and cool the fish in the poaching liquid to room temperature. In a small pan over low heat, warm the olive oil. Add the zest, rosemary, peppercorns, fennel seeds, and chiles. When the oil is highly aromatic, remove the pan from the heat and cool to room temperature. Remove the fish from the liquid and pat dry. Pour the oil over the poached fish, add the herbs, and marinate for 1–3 days. Serve the fish on toast points dipped in the marinade.

Butter-Basted Smoky Swordfish

SERVES 4

    4 swordfish portions, skin off
    Salt
    2 tablespoons smoked sweet paprika
    6 tablespoons butter, divided
    2 garlic cloves, crushed
    2 sprigs thyme
    1 lemon, cut into wedges

Season the fish all over with salt and on one side with paprika and let it rest for 20 minutes. In a large sauté pan over medium heat, melt 2 tablespoons of the butter. Place the fish in the pan paprika side down and cook for 2 minutes. Flip the fish and cook another 4 minutes. Increase the heat to medium-high and add the remaining 4 tablespoons of butter, garlic, and thyme. Cook until the butter is frothy, angle the pan toward you, and use a spoon to continuously baste the fish with the butter until cooked through. Remove the fish from the pan, strain the butter, and reserve the crisped garlic and thyme to scatter over the fish. Serve with lemon wedges.

TAUTOG
Meaty dense fish, fillet fish

The nickname it goes by in New York is blackfish. This moniker alludes to the fish's most common appearance: a thick mottled skin that is mostly black, though it can range from gray to a dark brownish green, depending on its habitat. The fish live along the coast around rock jetties, reefs, and pilings. Tautog's diet is directly mirrored in the flavor of its flesh: delicate and nuanced, with the brine of an oyster and the sweetness of crab. Its texture is firm and snappy. Tautog is a great stand-in for grouper.

It is sometimes called chowder fish because it stews well and integrates with other flavors easily. Because it lives on rocky bottoms and around wrecks, it has a very thick skin with heavy scales to protect it from abrasion and injury. The scales are quite difficult to remove, including a strip of them running along the lateral line that is quite stubbornly attached. I do not serve the skin. However, cooking with the skin on adds to the flavor and protects it from drying out.

The flesh runs far into the head, extending nearly over the eyes. This is all usable meat. The cheeks are small, but on larger fish they are certainly worth carving out. The meat of the fillet itself is a glowing pearly white with a faint purple hint. Though the fish is moderately lean, it has a rich flavor and silky texture. The bones are among the very best of any species for making a stock that is clear and brightly flavored. To capture the full essence, simmer the split head and bones in butter, keeping the pan lid on, to gently steam them in their own juice before adding wine, peppercorns, and fennel to round out the concentrated essence. Tautog does not take well to smoking, as the flavors contrast in a tinny and unflattering way.

Broiled Tautog with Citrus-Herb Crust

SERVES 4

>   4 tautog portions, skin off
>   Salt
>   1 cup panko
>   2 tablespoons chopped parsley
>   1 tablespoon chopped fresh thyme leaves
>   1 orange, zested
>   1 lemon, zested
>   6 tablespoons butter, melted

Season the fish with salt and let it rest for 20 minutes. Preheat the broiler to medium and set the rack in the middle position. Combine the panko, parsley, thyme, orange zest, lemon zest, and butter. Place the fish on a baking dish and cover with the panko mixture, patting it down gently. Place under the broiler and cook until the fish is done and the crust is lightly browned, 7–10 minutes, depending on thickness.

Tautog Ceviche with Orange, Pernod, and Parsley

SERVES 4

>   1 pound tautog fillets, skin off, diced into ½-inch pieces
>   Salt
>   1 cup lime juice
>   1 orange, zested and segmented
>   1 tablespoon Pernod or Herbsaint
>   3 shallots, thinly sliced, rinsed under cold running water and patted dry
>   ¼ cup extra-virgin olive oil
>   ½ cup parsley, leaves picked

Keep this dish cold at all times during preparation. Season the fish with salt and let it rest for 5 minutes. Combine the fish with the lime juice, orange zest, Pernod or Herbsaint, and shallots and let it rest for 40 minutes. Add the olive oil, orange segments, and parsley and toss. Let rest for another 10 minutes before serving

Grilled Tautog on the Half Shell

SERVES 4

>   1 recipe Horseradish Butter (page 20)
>   1 (3- to 5-pound) whole tautog, gutted and filleted, but scales and skin intact
>   Salt
>   Black pepper
>   2 tablespoons butter, melted
>   1 cup picked herbs, such as chervil, parsley, tarragon, and/or mint

Season the fish with salt and pepper and let it rest for 20 minutes. Prepare a charcoal grill with a medium fire. Place the fish scaly skin side down directly over the hot coals. Baste the fillets with the melted butter. Cover and cook until done, about 12–15 minutes. Transfer to a serving platter, slather with the Horseradish Butter, top with the herbs, and serve with instructions to eaters to spoon the fish off the skin, leaving the skin on the platter.

NOTE *If using a gas grill, preheat all burners to medium-high.*

Chilled Poached Tautog with Citrus Vinaigrette

SERVES 4

4 tautog portions, skin off

Salt

1 cup white wine

2 tablespoons white wine vinegar

1 orange, zested in wide strips and juiced

2 shallots, 1 sliced, 1 minced

1 small carrot, sliced

10 black peppercorns

1 bay leaf

1 sprig fresh rosemary

2 teaspoons grainy mustard

2 tablespoons lemon juice

¼ cup extra-virgin olive oil

2 tablespoons chopped tarragon or chives

2 apples, cored and thinly sliced

3 heads Belgian endive, cut into
½-inch strips

Season the fish with salt and let it rest for 20 minutes. In a pan just wide enough to hold the fish in a single layer, combine 1 cup of water with the wine, vinegar, orange juice and zest, sliced shallot, carrot, peppercorns, bay leaf, and rosemary. Simmer over low heat for 5 minutes. Season the broth with salt and bring it to 170°F. Add the fish and cook until it is opaque and flakes under gentle pressure, 5–7 minutes per ½ inch of thickness. Remove the pan from the heat and let cool to room temperature in the poaching liquid. Transfer the fish to a serving plate and flake it into bite-size pieces. Strain the poaching liquid into a pan, reduce over high heat to 4 tablespoons, and whisk in the minced shallot, mustard, lemon juice, olive oil, and tarragon or chives. Toss the apples and endive with the vinaigrette and serve with the fish.

Poached Tautog with Gremolata

SERVES 4

1 recipe Gremolata (page 28)

4 tautog portions, skin off

Salt

1 cup white wine

2 tablespoons white wine vinegar

1 small shallot, sliced

1 small carrot, sliced

10 whole black peppercorns

1 bay leaf

Spicy greens

Season the fish with salt and let it rest for 20 minutes. In a pan just wide enough to hold the fish in a single layer, combine 1 cup of water with the wine, vinegar, shallot, carrot, peppercorns, and bay leaf. Simmer over low heat for 5 minutes. Season the broth with salt and bring it to 170°F. Add the fish and cook until it is opaque and flakes under gentle pressure, 5–7 minutes per ½ inch of thickness. Remove the fish from the liquid. Serve with Gremolata and a salad of spicy greens.

Sautéed Tautog with Chermoula

SERVES 4

1 recipe Chermoula (page 26)

4 tautog portions, skin off

Salt

4 tablespoons butter

Season the fish with salt and let it rest for 20 minutes. In a sauté pan over medium heat, melt the butter. Place the fish in the pan. Cook without flipping until almost done, then flip to finish cooking. Serve with Chermoula.

Blackened Tautog

SERVES 4

> 1 recipe Blackening Spice Mix (page 33)
>
> 4 tautog portions, skin off
>
> Salt
>
> 4 tablespoons butter, melted, divided
>
> ¼ cup vegetable oil
>
> 1 lemon, cut into wedges

Lightly season the fish with salt and let it rest for 20 minutes. Heat a cast iron skillet or heavy-bottomed sauté pan over high heat until it is screaming hot. Combine 2 tablespoons of the butter and all of the oil in a bowl and brush each portion so the fish glistens all over. Dredge one side of each portion in Blackening Spice Mix, coating evenly. Place the fish in the pan spice side down and drizzle half of the remaining butter-and-oil mixture over the top. Reduce the heat to medium-low and cook without flipping until a dark crust forms, then flip to cook through. Drizzle with the remaining butter and serve with lemon wedges.

Tautog au Poivre Flambé

SERVES 4

> 4 tautog portions, skin off
>
> Salt
>
> 1½ tablespoons black peppercorns, coarsely ground
>
> 1½ tablespoons fennel seeds, crushed
>
> 4 tablespoons butter
>
> 1½ ounces cognac or brandy

Season the fish with salt on both sides and on one side with the pepper and fennel. Press the seasonings into the flesh and let it rest for 20 minutes. In a sauté pan over medium heat, melt the butter and cook until golden brown.

Place the fish pepper side down in the pan. Cook without flipping until almost done, then flip to finish cooking. Turn off the heat. Add the cognac or brandy and flambé by lighting with a match. Allow the alcohol to burn off before serving.

Sautéed Tautog Marinated with Sage and Orange

SERVES 4

> 1½ pounds tautog fillets, skin off, cut into 2-inch sections
>
> Salt
>
> 1 orange, zest removed in large strips and juiced
>
> 1¼ cups extra-virgin olive oil, divided
>
> 2 tablespoons raisins
>
> 3 sprigs fresh sage, leaves picked
>
> 6 garlic cloves, smashed
>
> 2 onions, thinly sliced top to bottom
>
> 1 cup white wine vinegar, or ½ cup sherry vinegar
>
> Flour
>
> Crusty bread for serving

Season the fish with salt and the orange juice and let it rest for 20 minutes. In a large pot over medium heat, combine 1 cup of the olive oil, orange zest, raisins, sage, and garlic and cook until the raisins begin to plump and the sage crisps. Add the onions, season generously with salt, and cook until the onions are wilted, about 5 minutes. Add the orange juice, vinegar and ¾ cup of water and simmer for 15 minutes. Roll the fish in flour. In a sauté pan over medium heat, warm the remaining ¼ cup of oil. Add the fish and fry until one side is brown and crisp, then flip to finish cooking. Transfer the fish to a baking dish and pour the hot vinaigrette over it. Cool to room temperature. Cover and refrigerate for at least a couple of hours and up to 3 days. Serve at room temperature with crusty bread.

TILAPIA
Fillet fish, flaky white fish

Tilapia are not native to the United States even though they are one of the most frequently consumed fish in the United States. The vast majority of tilapia are farm-raised in ponds. The quality of this fish is wholly a reflection of the water quality from which it comes. Those from brackish or clear waters will have a far more distinguished and clean flavor than those coming from muddy waters. Be careful to understand the source of the tilapia you buy, as not all tilapia is produced sustainably. Choose one from a grower whose aquaculture practices are considered sustainable. It is one of the best environmental choices that we can make when shopping for dinner if you are certain of its source.

Tilapia is perfect for the home cook because it is accessible on many levels. It is widely available and inexpensive, stays fresh for a long time, and is almost always sold as skinless fillets. Best used as a gateway fish, tilapia have little fat, a very mild flavor, and a toothsome texture that make them a good canvas for the ingredients with which they are paired. These tilapia recipes dial up the interesting flavor factor.

Stewed Tilapia with Chickpeas and Garlic Toast

SERVES 4

    1 cup Basic Fish Stock (page 61), or
      vegetable stock

    4 tilapia portions, skin off

    Salt

    2 tablespoons extra-virgin olive oil

    3 onions, sliced

    2 (14-ounce) cans chickpeas with
      their liquid

    1 teaspoon nutmeg

    ¼ cup parsley, chopped

    Baguette, sliced, for serving

    2 garlic cloves, sliced in half

Season the fish with salt and let it rest for 15 minutes. In a large pot over medium heat, warm the olive oil. Add the onions and cook until caramelized, about 20 minutes. Mash ½ cup of the chickpeas and their liquid into a paste and add it with the remaining chickpeas, nutmeg, reserved liquid, and stock to the pot. Season with salt, bring to a simmer, and cook until slightly thickened. Add the fish, cover, and reduce the heat to low. Cook until the fish is done, 8–10 minutes. Remove it from the heat and stir in the parsley. Serve with baguette slices that have been rubbed with garlic.

Broiled Tilapia with Ginger, Garlic, and Scallions

SERVES 4

    3 tablespoons Mayonnaise (page 29, or
      store-bought)

    4 tilapia portions, skin off

    Salt

    2 garlic cloves, grated

    1 tablespoon grated fresh ginger

    1 lime, juiced

    Hot sauce

    Soy sauce

    ¼ cup minced scallions

Season the fish with salt and let it rest for 15 minutes. Preheat the broiler to high and set the rack in the position closest to the heat. Whisk together the Mayonnaise, garlic, ginger, lime juice, a dash of hot sauce, and a dash of soy sauce. Fold in the scallions. Place the fish on a baking tray. Spread the mayonnaise mixture evenly over the fish. Slide the tray under the broiler and broil until done, 5–7 minutes, depending on thickness.

Broiled Tilapia with Spinach-Parmesan Crust

SERVES 4

> 1 cup Mayonnaise (page 29, or store-bought)
>
> 4 tilapia portions, skin off
>
> Salt
>
> 3 tablespoons cooked, drained, and chopped spinach
>
> 2 tablespoons grated Parmesan cheese
>
> 2 garlic cloves, grated
>
> 1 lemon, juiced

Season the fish with salt and let it rest for 15 minutes. Preheat the broiler to high and set the rack in the position closest to the heat. Whisk together the Mayonnaise, spinach, cheese, garlic, and lemon juice. Place the fish on a baking tray. Spread the mayonnaise mixture evenly over the fish. Slide the tray under the broiler. Broil until the fish is done and the topping is browned, 5–8 minutes, depending on thickness.

Tilapia Ceviche with Fennel and Mint

SERVES 4 AS AN APPETIZER

> 1 pound tilapia fillets, skin off, cut into ½-inch pieces
>
> Salt
>
> 1 cup lime juice
>
> 1 Fresno or serrano chile
>
> 2 stalks celery, thinly sliced
>
> 1 red onion, thinly sliced, rinsed under cold running water, and patted dry
>
> 1 fennel bulb, thinly sliced
>
> ¼ cup extra-virgin olive oil
>
> ¼ cup torn mint leaves
>
> 1 teaspoon grated mace for garnish

Keep this dish cold at all times during preparation. Season the fish with salt and let it rest for 5 minutes. Combine the fish with the lime juice and chile and let it rest for 30 minutes. Add the celery, onion, and fennel and let it rest another 10 minutes. Add the olive oil and mint and toss. Garnish with mace.

Roasted Tilapia with Marinara

SERVES 4

> 1 recipe Marinara Sauce (page 29), room temperature
>
> 4 tilapia portions, skin off
>
> 4 tablespoons extra-virgin olive oil
>
> Crusty bread for serving

Season the fish with salt and let it rest for 15 minutes. Pour the Marinara Sauce into a baking dish just large enough to hold the fish. Nestle the fish into the sauce and drizzle with the olive oil. Cover the dish with foil or a lid and slide it into a 275°F oven for about 20–25 minutes. Remove and let it rest for 10 minutes before serving with crusty bread.

Beer-Battered Tilapia

SERVES 4

>   1 recipe Traditional Remoulade Sauce
>   (page 31)
>
>   4 tilapia portions, skin off, cut
>   into 2-inch pieces
>
>   Salt
>
>   Vegetable or peanut oil
>
>   ¾ cup flour, sifted
>
>   ¾ cup cornstarch, sifted
>
>   ¾ cup beer
>
>   2 tablespoons vegetable oil
>
>   1 egg, separated
>
>   Malt vinegar for serving

Season the fish with salt and let it rest for 15 minutes. Pour 3–4 inches of oil into a high-sided pan. Place over medium-high heat and warm the oil to 375°F. Make a batter by combining the flour, cornstarch, beer, oil, and egg yolk. Beat the egg white to soft peaks and fold into the batter. Season with salt to taste. Dip one piece of fish at a time into the batter, place it into the oil, and hold it there for 5 seconds before releasing it. Repeat the process, cooking a couple of pieces at a time. Turn with a slotted spoon to ensure that both sides crisp evenly. Remove the fillets as they finish and place on paper towels to absorb excess oil. Serve with the Remoulade Sauce and malt vinegar.

VARIATIONS

+ **Curried Fried Tilapia.** Add 2 teaspoons of curry powder to the salt when seasoning at the beginning.

+ **Tilapia en Adobo.** Marinate the fish in Adobo (page 34) for 2 hours, drain, and pat the fish dry before coating the fish with batter.

+ Use Green Goddess Dressing (page 28), Basic Aioli (page 25), Tartar Sauce (page 32), or Dill Crème Fraîche (page 27) in place of the Traditional Remoulade Sauce.

Citrus-Crusted Fried Tilapia

SERVES 4

>   4 tilapia portions, skin off, cut
>   into 2-inch pieces
>
>   Salt
>
>   Vegetable or peanut oil
>
>   ½ cup citrus juice
>
>   Flour
>
>   Panko

Season the fish pieces with salt and let them rest for 15 minutes. Pour 3–4 inches of oil into a high-sided pan. Place over medium-high heat and warm the oil to 375°F. Dip the pieces of fish into the juice, then into flour to coat both sides, then into juice again, and finally into panko to coat both sides. Place each breaded piece in the oil and hold it for 5 seconds before releasing it. Repeat the process, cooking the fish a couple of pieces at a time. Turn with a slotted spoon to ensure that both sides crisp evenly. Remove the fillets as they finish and place on paper towels to absorb excess oil. Season with salt.

Chilled Poached Tilapia with Shaved Vegetable Salad

SERVES 4

 4 tilapia portions, skin off

 Salt

 1 cup white wine

 2 tablespoons white wine vinegar, divided

 1 small shallot, sliced

 1 teaspoon ground mace

30 black peppercorns

 1 bay leaf

 1 teaspoon mustard powder

 ¼ cup extra-virgin olive oil

 1 shallot, finely minced

 ½ cup fresh chervil or tarragon, 2 tablespoons chopped, remainder of leaves picked from stems

 1 large sweet onion, thinly sliced

 2 carrots, peeled into long strips with a peeler

 4 ounces radishes, thinly sliced

Season the fish with salt and let it rest for 15 minutes. In a pan just wide enough to hold the fish in a single layer, combine 1 cup of water with the wine, 1 tablespoon of the vinegar, shallot, mace, peppercorns, and bay leaf. Simmer over low heat for 5 minutes. Season the broth with salt and bring it to 170°F. Add the fish and cook until it is opaque and flakes under gentle pressure, 4–6 minutes per ½ inch of thickness. Remove the pan from the heat and cool the fish in the poaching liquid. Transfer the fish to a serving plate and flake it into bite-size pieces. Strain the poaching liquid into a small pan, reduce over high heat to 4 tablespoons, and whisk in the mustard, remaining 1 tablespoon of vinegar, olive oil, shallot, chopped chervil or tarragon, and half of the vinaigrette. Coat the flaked fish with sauce. Combine the onion, carrots, radishes, and picked herb leaves and toss with the remaining vinaigrette. Serve the dressed fish over the salad.

Blackened Tilapia

SERVES 4

 1 recipe Blackening Spice Mix (page 33)

 4 tilapia portions, skin off

 Salt

 4 tablespoons butter, melted, divided

 ¼ cup vegetable oil

 1 lemon, cut into wedges

Lightly season the fish with salt and let it rest for 15 minutes. Heat a cast iron skillet or heavy-bottomed sauté pan over high heat until it is screaming hot. Combine 2 tablespoons of the butter and all of the oil in a bowl and brush each portion so the fish glistens all over. Dredge one side of each portion in Blackening Spice Mix, coating evenly. Place the fish in the pan spice side down and drizzle half of the remaining butter-and-oil mixture over the top. Reduce the heat to medium-low and cook without flipping until a dark crust forms, then flip to cook through. Drizzle with the remaining butter and serve with lemon wedges.

Tilapia en Saor
(sweet-sour vinaigrette)

SERVES 4-6

> 1½ pounds tilapia, skin off
>
> Salt
>
> ¾ cup extra-virgin olive oil, divided
>
> 3 tablespoons pine nuts or slivered almonds
>
> 2 tablespoons raisins
>
> 1 small onion, thinly sliced
>
> 1 red bell pepper, finely diced
>
> 1 small eggplant, ½-inch dice, about 2 cups
>
> ¼ cup red wine vinegar
>
> 1 tablespoon brown sugar
>
> Baguette for serving

Season the fish with salt and let it rest for 15 minutes. In a sauté pan over medium heat, warm ¼ cup of the olive oil. Place the fish in the pan and cook, turning once when slightly brown, until done, 5–7 minutes. Alternatively, the fish can be grilled. Remove the fish from the pan. Add the remaining ½ cup of olive oil over high heat, add the pine nuts (or slivered almonds) and raisins, and cook until the nuts are golden brown and the raisins plump. Add the onion and bell pepper and cook until the pepper begins to soften. Add the eggplant and cook until it has softened and has absorbed much of the oil. Stir in the vinegar and brown sugar and season with salt. Turn off the heat and nestle the cooked fish into the sauce. The flavors improve if allowed to chill overnight in the refrigerator and then brought to room temperature before serving. At a minimum, let it sit at least 1 hour before serving at room temperature with slices of baguette.

Pan-Fried Tilapia Marinated
with Sage and Orange

SERVES 4-6

> 1½ pounds tilapia fillets, skin off, cut into 2-inch sections
>
> Salt
>
> 1 orange, zest removed in large strips and juiced
>
> 1¼ cups extra-virgin olive oil, divided
>
> 2 tablespoons raisins
>
> 3 sprigs fresh sage, leaves picked
>
> 6 garlic cloves, smashed
>
> 2 onions, thinly sliced, top to bottom
>
> 1 cup white wine vinegar or ½ cup sherry vinegar
>
> Flour
>
> Crusty bread for serving

Season the fish with salt and let it rest for 15 minutes. In a large pot over medium heat, combine 1 cup of the olive oil, orange zest, raisins, sage, and garlic and cook until the raisins begin to plump and the sage crisps. Add the onions, season generously with salt, and cook until the onions are wilted, about 5 minutes. Add the orange juice, vinegar and ¾ cup of water and simmer for 15 minutes. Roll the fish in flour. In a sauté pan over medium heat, warm the remaining ¼ cup of oil. Add the fish and fry until one side is brown and crisp, then flip to finish cooking. Transfer the fish to a baking dish and pour the onion marinade over it. Cool to room temperature. Cover and refrigerate for at least a couple of hours and up to 3 days. Serve at room temperature with crusty bread.

Stir-Fried Tilapia with Red Onion and Ginger

SERVES 4

> 4 portions tilapia, cut into ½-inch slices on the bias
>
> Salt
>
> ¼ cup peanut or vegetable oil, divided
>
> 1 red onion, thinly sliced
>
> 2 garlic cloves, thinly sliced
>
> 1 tablespoon ginger, grated
>
> 3–4 stalks celery, thinly sliced on the bias
>
> 2 tablespoons brown sugar
>
> 3 tablespoons soy sauce
>
> 3 tablespoons white wine
>
> Cornstarch

NOTE *If possible, flavor the fish with cold smoke for just a few minutes.*

Season the fish with salt and let it rest for 15 minutes. In a large sauté pan over high heat, warm 2 tablespoons of the oil until it shimmers. Add the onion, garlic, ginger, and celery. Cook, stirring occasionally, until the onion begins to singe and the celery is al dente. In a small bowl, combine the brown sugar, soy sauce, and wine. Add the liquid to the pan and toss vigorously for 30 seconds before removing the glazed vegetables from the pan. Wipe out the pan, place over medium-high heat, and warm the remaining 2 tablespoons of oil. Toss the tilapia in cornstarch to coat and add the fish to the pan. Cook without turning until almost cooked through, then flip and cook for 30 seconds to finish. Transfer the fish to a platter and cover with the vegetable mixture.

Tilapia Tacos

SERVES 4

> 1 recipe Orange-Coriander Vinaigrette (page 37) or Lemon-Chile-Mint Dressing (page 36)
>
> 1 pound tilapia fillets, skin off
>
> 1 recipe Pico de Gallo (page 30) or store-bought salsa
>
> Sour cream
>
> 2 avocados, sliced
>
> ½ cup cilantro, leaves picked
>
> ¼ head cabbage, shaved, or coleslaw
>
> 16 corn tortillas

Season the fish with salt and let it rest for 15 minutes. Grill, roast, broil, or poach the fish until cooked. Flake the fish into bite-size pieces and toss with the vinaigrette or dressing. Set out bowls of Pico de Gallo, sour cream, avocado, cilantro, and shredded cabbage. Warm the tortillas in a dry heavy-bottomed pan over medium heat until crisped yet pliable. Keep them warm in a kitchen towel. For each taco, stack two tortillas together. Let everyone build their own tacos just the way they like.

TILEFISH
Fillet fish

All six species of tilefish swimming along the Eastern Seaboard claim a smooth, fine-grained texture and delicate flavor, reminiscent of the best characteristics of halibut but with the gamey moxie of a striped bass. I have always been charmed by its tender-but-firm meat and its buttermilk-sour-sweet aroma that foreshadows a complex but playful flavor that is as opulent as a scallop and is often compared to lobster. Its predominantly crustacean-based diet gives tilefish this confident, charismatic flavor.

The skin is very thick, and, though it is edible, the high heat needed to give it a pleasant texture is not in the best interest of the flesh. It has a relatively thick band of red muscle tissue, or bloodline, though this is soft in flavor and contrasts well with the ashen-white flesh. Its unique firmness makes it a good choice for stews and braises. The taut texture also makes it a wonderful candidate for salt curing. But I find tilefish best bathed in a dense brine before being slowly hot-smoked and sliced very thin. The flavors of highly aromatic wood with a hint of spice, such as alder or cherry, provide the fish a perfect point of flattery.

Braised Tilefish Puttanesca

The tilefish is braised in a lively tomato sauce with capers and olives.

SERVES 4

> 4 tilefish portions, skin off
>
> Salt
>
> 4 tablespoons extra-virgin olive oil, divided
>
> 1 (2-ounce) tin anchovies in oil
>
> 4 garlic cloves, sliced
>
> 4 dried árbol chiles, or ½ tablespoon crushed red chile flakes
>
> 2 (14-ounce) cans fire-roasted diced tomatoes
>
> ¾ cup white wine
>
> 2 tablespoons capers, rinsed and patted dry
>
> ¼ cup pitted cured black olives
>
> 6 basil leaves, torn, for garnish

Season the fish with salt and let it rest for 15 minutes. In an ovenproof sauté pan over medium-high heat, warm 3 tablespoons of the olive oil, anchovies with their oil, garlic, and chiles, and cook until the anchovies melt. Add the tomatoes, wine, capers, and olives. Bring to a simmer and cook for 10 minutes. Nestle the fish into the sauce and drizzle with the remaining 3 tablespoons of olive oil. Cover the pan and place it in a 275°F oven for 30 minutes. Remove and let it rest for 10 minutes before serving scattered with torn basil leaves.

Grilled Tilefish with Charred Tomato Vinaigrette

SERVES 4

> 1 recipe Charred Tomato Vinaigrette (page 35), divided
>
> 4 tilefish portions, skin on and scored

Reserve half of the Charred Tomato Vinaigrette for serving. Combine the other half with the fish and let it marinate for 1–8 hours. Prepare a charcoal grill with a medium fire, concentrating the hot coals on one side of the kettle. Remove the fish from the marinade and place it on the grill skin side down over the hot coals. Cook until the edges of the fish begin to crisp, about 2 minutes. Lift the entire grill grate and rotate it so the fish rests opposite the hot coals. Baste the fish with any remaining marinade, cover the grill, and cook over this indirect heat until the fish is done. Serve with the reserved vinaigrette.

NOTE *If using a gas grill, preheat all burners to medium-high. Place the tilefish on one side of the hot grates. Once it begins to char around the edges, turn off the burner directly under the fish, baste the fish, and cover the grill to finish cooking.*

Poached Tilefish with Lemon-Chile-Mint Dressing

SERVES 4

    1 recipe Lemon-Chile-Mint Dressing (page 36)

    4 tilefish portions, skin off

    Salt

    1 cup white wine

    ¼ cup red wine vinegar

    2 small shallots, sliced

    2 teaspoons ground mace

    30 black peppercorns

    1 bay leaf

    1 orange, zested in wide strips and juiced

    1 sprig fresh rosemary

Season the fish with salt and let it rest for 15 minutes. In a deep pan just wide enough to hold the fish in a single layer, combine 1 cup of water with the wine, vinegar, shallots, mace, peppercorns, bay leaf, orange zest and juice, and rosemary. Simmer over low heat for 5 minutes. Season the broth with salt and bring it to 170°F. Add the fish and cook until it is opaque and flakes under gentle pressure, about 5–7 minutes per ½ inch of thickness. Transfer to a plate and serve with Lemon-Chile-Mint Dressing.

Poached Tilefish with Cider, Apples, and Thyme

SERVES 4

    4 tilefish portions, skin off

    Salt

    1 cup dry hard cider

    2 sprigs fresh thyme

    1 apple, peeled and finely diced

    4 tablespoons cold butter, cut into pieces

Season the fish with salt and let it rest for 15 minutes. In a pan just wide enough to hold the fish in a single layer, combine 1 cup of water with the cider and thyme. Simmer on low heat for 5 minutes. Season the broth with salt and bring it to 170°F. Add the fish and cook until it is opaque and flakes under gentle pressure, 5–7 minutes per ½ inch of thickness. Transfer the fish to a plate and keep warm. Discard the thyme stems. Return the pan to the stove over high heat and reduce the liquid to ¼ cup. Turn off the heat, add the apple and the butter, swirl to incorporate it, season with salt, and spoon it over the fish.

Slow-Roasted Whole Tilefish with Bay and Orange

SERVES 4

    1 (3- to 4-pound) whole tilefish, scaled and gutted

    2 tablespoons kosher salt

    2 oranges, zested and thinly sliced

12 bay leaves

    1 teaspoon crushed fennel seeds

    1 teaspoon ground coriander

    1 teaspoon black pepper

    Extra-virgin olive oil

Season the fish cavity with salt and stuff with the orange slices and bay leaves. Combine the kosher salt with the fennel seeds, coriander, zest, and black pepper. Season the fish all over with the spice mixture. Drizzle with the olive oil. Roast in a 300°F oven for 40–50 minutes. Check to see if the fish is cooked by inserting a knife along the backbone to reveal the flesh. It should be opaque when done.

Butter-Basted Tilefish with Garlic and Thyme

SERVES 4

    4 tilefish portions, skin on and scored

    Salt

    6 tablespoons butter, divided

    6 sprigs thyme

    2 garlic cloves, minced

    1 lemon, zest removed in wide strips

Season the fish with salt and let it rest for 15 minutes. In a sauté pan over medium-high heat, melt 2 tablespoons of the butter. Place the fish in the pan skin side down and sear until well colored. Reduce the heat to medium and flip the fish. Add the remaining 4 tablespoons of butter, thyme, garlic, and lemon zest. Cook until the butter is frothy, angle the pan toward you, and use a spoon to continuously baste the fish with the butter until cooked through. Remove the fish from the pan, strain the butter, discard the lemon zest, and reserve the crisped garlic and thyme leaves to scatter over the fish.

Grilled Tilefish with Pine Nut Butter

SERVES 4

    1 recipe Pine Nut Butter (page 21)

    4 tilefish portions, skin on and scored

    Extra-virgin olive oil

    2 lemons, halved

Season the fish with salt and let it rest for 15 minutes. Prepare a charcoal grill with a medium fire, concentrating the hot coals on one side of the kettle. Brush the fish with olive oil, and place it skin side down on the grill directly over the coals. Cook until the skin begins to char, 3–4 minutes. Lift the entire grill grate and rotate it so the fish rests opposite the hot coals. Place the lemons on the grill, cut side down, directly over the hot coals. Cover the grill and continue to cook until the fish is done and the lemons are charred. Serve with Pine Nut Butter over the top and the lemons.

NOTE *If using a gas grill, preheat all burners to medium-high. Place the tilefish on one side of the hot grates. Once it begins to char around the edges, turn off the burner directly under the fish and cover the grill to finish cooking.*

TRIGGERFISH
Fillet fish

The name *triggerfish* is a reference to the first spine of the fish's dorsal fin. When touched, the bone-hard spike springs into vertical position like something out of a James Bond movie. The Latin family name roughly translates to "similar to a crossbow." There are many members of the triggerfish family, but few are marketable. The gray triggerfish, queen triggerfish, and ocean triggerfish are culinary peers that all swim in the Atlantic, are caught as bycatch of the snapper fishery, and are rarely distinguished from one another.

But triggerfish stand apart from other food fish because of their incredibly tough skin and zealously adherent scales. Don't be put off by how difficult it is to access the fillets hiding beneath that armor-like skin, as the flesh is sweet and tender, with a wonderfully buttery aroma. Once the skin has been removed, triggerfish are easily filleted like any other similar fish, turning out well-shaped fillets. When the fish is cooked, the flesh is off-white and glisteningly moist, with a high fat content and a tender, beautiful flake.

The relatively thin fillets sear well, taking on color without drying out. The very fatty flesh is self-basting when broiled or grilled. Butter intensifies the fish's sweetness, adding a nutty characteristic and balance; when cooked in butter it smells like roasted pecans and an ocean breeze. Olive oil highlights the milder oceanic and herbal flavors in the fish. It is also one of the very best candidates for braising, as its fillets maintain their structure and the flavor is agreeable with almost anything you pair it with.

Broiled Jamaican Jerk Triggerfish

SERVES 4

- 1 recipe Jerk Seasoning Mix (page 33), divided
- 4 triggerfish portions, skin off
- Salt
- 4 tablespoons butter, plus additional for greasing the baking sheet

Season the triggerfish with salt and the Jerk Seasoning Mix and let it rest for 20 minutes. Preheat the broiler to medium and set the rack in the position closest to the heat. Grease a baking sheet lightly with butter, place the fish on it, and top each portion with 1 tablespoon of butter. Slide the baking sheet under the broiler and cook until done, 6–9 minutes, depending on thickness.

Triggerfish Braised in Cinnamon and Tomato

SERVES 4

    4 triggerfish portions, skin off
    Salt
    4 tablespoons butter, divided
    2 tablespoons extra-virgin olive oil
    4 garlic cloves, smashed
    2 sticks cinnamon
  10 sprigs thyme
    1 (14-ounce) can fire-roasted tomatoes
    1 cup white wine or stock
    Baguette, sliced, for serving

Season the fish with salt and let it rest for 20 minutes. In a sauté pan over medium heat, melt 2 tablespoons of the butter and the olive oil. Add the garlic, cinnamon, and thyme and sauté for about 2 minutes. Add the tomatoes, wine, and a pinch of salt. Bring to a simmer and reduce the heat to low. Place the fish in the pan, cover, and cook until done, about 8–10 minutes. Carefully remove the fish from the pan and simmer the sauce until slightly thickened. Add the remaining 2 tablespoons of butter and stir to combine. Discard the cinnamon and thyme. Pour the sauce over the fish and serve with a sliced baguette.

Chilled Poached and Spice-Marinated Triggerfish

SERVES 4

    4 triggerfish portions, skin off
    Salt
    1 cup white wine
    5 black peppercorns
    5 star anise pods
    ¾ cup extra-virgin olive oil
    1 orange, zest removed in wide strips
    2 stalks rosemary
    ½ tablespoon crushed fennel seeds
2–3 dried chiles, such as de árbol or Calabrian
    1 tablespoon sherry vinegar
    ¼ cup chopped herbs, such as chives, parsley, or tarragon
    Toast points for serving

Season the fish with salt and let it rest for 20 minutes. In a pan just wide enough to hold the fish in a single layer, combine 1 cup of water with the wine, peppercorns, and star anise. Simmer over low heat for 5 minutes. Season the broth with salt and bring it to 170°F. Add the fish and cook until it is opaque and flakes under gentle pressure, 4–6 minutes for each ½ inch of thickness. Remove the pan from the heat and cool the fish in the poaching liquid. In a small pan over low heat, warm the olive oil. Add the zest, rosemary, fennel seeds, and chiles. When the oil is highly aromatic, remove the pan from the heat and cool to room temperature. Remove the fish from the liquid and pat dry. Pour the oil over the poached fish, add the vinegar and herbs, and marinate for 1–3 days. Serve the fish on toast points dipped in the marinade.

Sautéed Triggerfish with Brown Butter and Sage

SERVES 4

> 4 triggerfish portions, skin off
>
> Salt
>
> 6 tablespoons butter, divided
>
> 20 small sage leaves
>
> 1 lemon, juiced

Season the fish with salt and let it rest for 20 minutes. In a large sauté pan over medium heat, warm 2 tablespoons of the butter until golden brown. Place the fish in the pan. Cook without flipping until almost done, then remove the fish. Add the remaining 4 tablespoons of butter and the sage. Cook until the butter is dark brown and the sage is crisp. Add the lemon juice and season with salt. Turn off the heat and return the fish to the pan uncooked side down to finish cooking.

Pan-Fried Cornmeal-Coated Triggerfish

SERVES 4

> 4 triggerfish portions, skin off
>
> Salt
>
> Fine cornmeal
>
> 6 tablespoons bacon drippings or butter
>
> 1 lemon, cut into wedges

Season the fish with salt and let it rest for 20 minutes. Dredge the fish on one side in cornmeal. In a sauté pan over medium heat, warm the bacon drippings. Place the fish in the pan cornmeal side down. Cook without flipping until almost done, then flip to finish cooking. Serve with lemon wedges.

Butter-Basted Triggerfish with Chile and Mint

SERVES 4

> 4 triggerfish portions, skin off
>
> Salt
>
> 6 tablespoons butter, divided
>
> 2 garlic cloves, minced
>
> 2 dried chiles, such as de árbol or Calabrian
>
> 20 mint leaves
>
> 1 lemon, cut into wedges

Season the fish with salt and let it rest for 20 minutes. In a sauté pan over medium-high heat, melt 2 tablespoons of the butter. Place the fish in the pan and cook until the edges begin to brown. Flip the fish. Add the remaining 4 tablespoons of butter, garlic, chiles, and mint. Cook until the butter is frothy, then angle the pan toward you and use a spoon to continuously baste the fish with the butter until it is cooked through. Remove the fish from the pan. Discard the chiles, strain the butter, and reserve the crisped garlic and mint to scatter over the fish. Serve with lemon wedges.

TRIPLETAIL
Fillet fish

Atlantic tripletail has recently become a darling of Southern chefs, and rightfully so. It is an unattractive but impressively built fish, with a body of pronounced heft. These fish are compact, looking as if they'd swum into a wall too many times. The fish appears to have three tail fins, but it's simply an illusion made by the anal and dorsal fins extending nearly as far back as the tail fin.

Their regional nicknames include black perch in Charleston and flasher in New York. Its West Coast twin, the Pacific tripletail, swims at the very southern edge of our coast and does not appear to support any fishery. It is identical to the Atlantic tripletail for every purpose other than scientific description.

If the fish's cruel countenance doesn't turn you off, you'll be amply rewarded by its thick, pearly white fillets and smooth, lustrous flakes. The thickness of the fillets is similar to that of a prime cut of grouper or halibut, although the tripletail's texture is softer and its flavor is more brackish, with a lingering sweet aftertaste. It is such an excellent food fish that it is best served simply, flattered with nothing more than a lemon wedge. Long underappreciated by chefs, Atlantic tripletail is finding new champions in its home waters.

Braised Tripletail with Fennel

SERVES 4

4 tripletail portions, skin off

Salt

6 tablespoons butter, divided

3 fennel bulbs, sliced into 1-inch wedges

2 oranges, juiced

1 cup white wine

2 tablespoons chopped fresh chives or parsley

Season the fish with salt and let it rest for 15 minutes. In a large pot over medium-high heat, melt 2 tablespoons of the butter. Add the fennel and cook until it begins to brown. Add the orange juice and wine. Season with salt, reduce the heat to medium, cover, and simmer until the fennel is barely softened, 5–7 minutes. Place the fish in with the fennel and reduce the heat to low. Cover and cook for 9–10 minutes. Remove the fish and fennel. Reduce the remaining liquid to a syrup and whisk in the remaining 4 tablespoons of butter and chives. Drizzle the sauce over the fish and fennel, and serve warm or at room temperature.

Grilled Tripletail on the Half Shell with Sriracha Butter

SERVES 4

1 recipe Sriracha Butter (page 22)

1 (3- to 5-pound) whole tripletail, gutted, and filleted, but scales and skin intact

Salt

Black pepper

4 tablespoons butter, melted

1 cup picked herbs, such as chervil, parsley, tarragon, and/or mint

Season the fish with salt and pepper and let it rest for 15 minutes. Prepare a charcoal grill with a medium fire. Place the fish scaly skin side down directly over the hot coals. Baste the fillets with the melted butter. Cover and cook until done, about 12–15 minutes. Transfer to a serving platter, slather with the Sriracha Butter, top with the herbs, and serve with instructions to eaters to spoon the fish off of the skin, leaving the skin on the platter.

NOTE *If using a gas grill, preheat all burners to medium-high.*

Salt-Roasted Tripletail with Lemon and Bay

SERVES 2

3 pounds kosher salt

1 (1½- to 2½-pound) whole tripletail, scaled, gutted and scored

2 lemons, thinly sliced

12 bay leaves

4 tablespoons butter, melted, or extra-virgin olive oil

Combine the salt with enough water so that it resembles wet sand. Place a thin layer on a baking sheet and top with half of the lemon slices and half of the bay leaves. Place the fish on top and arrange the remaining lemon slices and bay leaves on top of the fish. Pack on the remaining salt mixture to completely encase the fish. Roast at 375°F for 20–30 minutes. Remove the fish from the oven and let it rest for 5 minutes. Crack the salt crust and discard. Serve whole, or remove the lemons and bay leaves and peel off the skin before carefully transferring the top fillet to a platter. Remove and discard the backbone and transfer the bottom fillet without its skin to the platter. Drizzle the fish with melted butter or extra-virgin olive oil.

Sautéed Tripletail with Brown Butter, Orange, and Rosemary

SERVES 4

> 4 tripletail portions, skin off
> Salt
> 6 tablespoons butter, divided
> 2 garlic cloves, finely minced
> 2 stalks rosemary, leaves picked
> 1 orange, zested and cut into segments

Season the fish with salt and let it rest for 15 minutes. In a large sauté pan over medium heat, melt 2 tablespoons of the butter and cook until golden brown. Place the fish in the pan. Cook without flipping until almost done, then remove the fish, and wipe the pan clean. Add the remaining 4 tablespoons of butter, garlic, rosemary, and zest. Cook until the butter is dark brown and the rosemary is crisped. Add the orange segments and season with salt. Stir gently to combine. Turn off the heat and return the fish to the pan uncooked side down to finish cooking.

Blackened Tripletail

SERVES 4

> 1 recipe Blackening Spice Mix (page 33)
> 4 tripletail portions, skin off
> Salt
> 4 tablespoons butter, melted, divided
> ¼ cup vegetable oil
> 1 lemon, cut into wedges

Lightly season the fish with salt and let it rest for 15 minutes. Heat a cast iron skillet or heavy-bottomed sauté pan over high heat until it is screaming hot. Combine 2 tablespoons of the butter and all of the oil in a bowl, and brush each portion so the fish glistens all over. Dredge one side of each portion in Blackening Spice Mix, coating evenly. Place the fish in the pan spice side down and drizzle half of the remaining butter-and-oil mixture over the top. Reduce the heat to medium-low and cook without flipping until a dark crust forms, then flip to cook through. Drizzle with the remaining butter and serve with lemon wedges.

TROUT
Orange-fleshed fish, fillet fish

Trout is widely available. It's delicious, and it's one of the most versatile fish on the market. I love cooking trout whole, as it makes for such a great plate presentation. But it is more often sold head on and butterflied, and these fish are great for stuffed preparations. Skin-on, boneless fillets are a quick-cooking trick every cook should keep on the weeknight rotation.

Trout's broad flavor and lack of brininess pair very well with butter-based sauces that have a slight acidity.

Most of the trout sold in this country comes from farms in the middle and western states, but there is a large cottage industry of small trout farmers distributed around the country as well, making fresh trout available in nearly every market. Try looking for a producer in your area. You can't beat driving over to a local farm and having your fish pulled directly from the water for freshness!

Smoked trout, which is available from many small local producers as well, makes for an easy and luxurious garnish for soups and salads. If you're game to try a new technique, smoke a fresh one yourself (page 438).

Pan-Fried Cornmeal-Crusted Trout

SERVES 4

    4 trout portions, skin on and scored

    Salt

    Fine cornmeal

    6 tablespoons bacon drippings or butter

    1 lemon, cut into wedges

Season the fish with salt and let it rest for 15 minutes. Dredge the fish in cornmeal. In a sauté pan over medium heat, warm the bacon drippings. Place the fish in the pan skin side down. Cook without flipping until the crust begins to crisp, then flip to finish cooking. Serve with lemon wedges.

Whole Grilled Trout with Orange-Pistachio Piccata

SERVES 2–4

> 1 recipe Orange-Pistachio Piccata (page 29)
>
> 2 whole trout, butterflied
>
> Salt
>
> 1 orange, thinly sliced
>
> 8 sprigs thyme
>
> Extra-virgin olive oil

Season the trout with salt, stuff the bellies with the orange slices and thyme, and let it rest for 15 minutes. Prepare a charcoal grill with a medium fire, concentrating the hot coals on one side of the kettle. Drizzle the fish with olive oil and place on the grill over the hot coals. Cook until the edges of the fish begin to char, about 2 minutes. Gently flip the fish over. Lift the entire grill grate and rotate it so the fish rests opposite the hot coals. Cover the grill and continue to cook over this indirect heat until the fish is done. Discard the orange slices and thyme. Serve with Orange-Pistachio Piccata.

NOTE *If using a gas grill, preheat all burners to medium-high. Place the trout on one side of the hot grates. Once it begins to char around the edges, turn off the burner directly under the fish and cover the grill to finish cooking.*

Chilled Poached and Spice-Marinated Trout

SERVES 4

> 4 trout portions, skin on
>
> Salt
>
> 1 cup white wine
>
> 5 black peppercorns
>
> 5 star anise pods
>
> Crushed red chile flakes
>
> ¾ cup extra-virgin olive oil
>
> 1 orange, zest removed in wide strips
>
> 2 stalks rosemary
>
> ½ tablespoon crushed fennel seeds
>
> 2–3 dried chiles, such as de árbol or Calabrian
>
> 1 tablespoon sherry vinegar
>
> ¼ cup chopped herbs, such as chives, parsley, or tarragon
>
> Toast points for serving

Season the fish with salt and let it rest for 15 minutes. In a pan just wide enough to hold the fish in a single layer, combine 1 cup of water with the wine, peppercorns, and star anise. Simmer over low heat for 5 minutes. Season the broth with salt and bring it to 170°F. Add the fish and cook until it is opaque and flakes under gentle pressure, 4–6 minutes. Remove the pan from the heat and cool the fish in the poaching liquid to room temperature. In a small pan over low heat, warm the olive oil. Add the zest, rosemary, fennel seeds, and chiles. When the oil is highly aromatic, remove the pan from the heat and cool to room temperature. Remove the fish from the liquid, remove the skin from the fish, and pat fillets dry. Pour the oil over the poached fish, add the herbs, and marinate for 1–3 days. Serve the fish with toast points dipped in the marinade oil.

Sautéed Trout with Brown Butter, Apples, and Thyme

SERVES 4

4 trout portions, skin on

Salt

6 tablespoons butter, divided

2 garlic cloves, finely minced

4 sprigs thyme, leaves picked

1 apple, peeled and diced in ½-inch pieces

2 tablespoons apple cider vinegar

2 tablespoons chopped fresh tarragon or chives

Season the fish with salt and let it rest for 15 minutes. In a large sauté pan over medium heat, melt 2 tablespoons of the butter and cook until golden brown. Place the fish in the pan skin side down. Cook without flipping until almost done, then remove the fish. Add the remaining 4 tablespoons of butter, garlic, thyme, and apple. Cook until the butter is dark brown and the thyme is crisped. Add the vinegar and herbs and season with salt. Stir to combine. Turn off the heat and return the fish to the pan uncooked side down to finish cooking.

Sautéed Trout Almondine

SERVES 4

4 trout portions, skin on

Salt

6 tablespoons butter, divided

2 garlic cloves, finely minced

¼ cup sliced almonds

1 lemon, juiced

Season the fish with salt and let it rest for 15 minutes. In a sauté pan over medium heat, melt 2 tablespoons of the butter and cook until golden brown. Place the fish in the pan skin side down. Cook without flipping until almost done, then remove the fish. Add the remaining 4 tablespoons of butter, garlic, and almonds. Cook until the almonds are browned. Add the lemon juice and season with salt. Stir to combine. Turn off the heat and return the fish to the pan uncooked side down for fillets to finish cooking. Serve with sauce poured over the top.

Hot-Smoked Trout

MAKES ABOUT 1 POUND

    4 trout fillets, skin on

⅓ cup kosher salt

⅓ cup packed brown sugar

    1 orange, juiced

10 juniper berries

    1 tablespoon fennel seeds

    1 cinnamon stick

¼ cup Pernod or other anise-flavored liqueur, divided

In a saucepan over medium heat, simmer 1 cup of water with the salt, brown sugar, orange juice, juniper, fennel seeds, and cinnamon for 5 minutes. Add 3 cups of cold water and 2 tablespoons of the Pernod to the brine and stir. Place the fish in a glass or ceramic baking dish, pour the brine over, and refrigerate for 2 hours. Remove the fish from the liquid, pat dry, and brush with the remaining 2 tablespoons of Pernod. Refrigerate the fish uncovered on a wire rack overnight. Cold-smoke the fish skin side down for 1–2 hours at as low a temperature as possible (below 100°F). Increase the temperature to 150°F and smoke for another 2 hours. Remove from the smoker and cool to room temperature. Tightly wrap the fillet in plastic and refrigerate overnight before using.

VARIATIONS

+ **Allspice Smoked Trout.** Add 2 tablespoons of allspice berries to the smoking wood.

+ **Herb-Scented Smoked Trout.** When removing the fish from the smoker, immediately cover with fresh basil or mint leaves to gently perfume the fish. Remove the leaves prior to serving.

Hot-Smoked Trout Cobb Salad

SERVES 4

1 pound flaked Hot-Smoked Trout (at left), or purchased

1 recipe Cilantro-Yogurt Dressing (page 35)

6 plum tomatoes, cut into quarters

1 large head endive, chopped

1 or 2 bunches watercress, thick stems trimmed

2 avocados, thinly sliced

4 hard-boiled eggs, sliced

   Salt

   Black pepper

Flake the trout into bite-size pieces. Toss the tomatoes and trout with half of the Cilantro-Yogurt Dressing and let it rest for 20 minutes. Set up four plates with equal portions of endive, watercress, avocados, and hard-boiled eggs. Drizzle the remaining dressing over the salads and season with salt and pepper. Top with the marinated smoked fish and tomatoes.

Hot-Smoked Trout with Roasted Apples and Watercress

SERVES 4

>   1 pound Hot-Smoked Trout (page 438, or purchased)
>
>   1 recipe Bay Leaf–Garlic Vinaigrette (page 35)
>
>   3 apples, cored and cut into wedges
>
>   2 tablespoons honey
>
>   2 tablespoons extra-virgin olive oil
>
>   2 bunches watercress, thick stalks trimmed
>
>   ½ cup parsley, leaves picked
>
>   ½ cup chervil, leaves picked
>
>   1 lemon, zested and juiced
>
>   Salt

Flake the smoked fish into bite-size pieces, toss with half of the Bay Leaf–Garlic Vinaigrette, and reserve. Toss the apples with the honey and the olive oil and spread on a baking tray. Set the broiler to high and place the rack in the position closest to the heat. Slide the tray under the broiler and cook until the apples brown and are nearly tender. Toss the watercress, parsley, and chervil with the remaining vinaigrette plus lemon juice and zest. Season with salt. Plate the salad and top with the warm apples and smoked fish.

Smoked Trout Quiche

SERVES 4

>   1 (9-inch-wide and 2-inch-deep) pie crust
>
>   1 pound Hot-Smoked Trout (page 438, or purchased)
>
>   3 cups half-and-half
>
>   6 large eggs
>
>   3 tablespoons chopped fresh tarragon or 1 tablespoon dried tarragon
>
>   1 lemon, zested
>
>   Salt
>
>   Spicy greens for serving

In a pan over low heat, combine the smoked trout and half-and-half. Simmer for 5 minutes. Remove the fish and flake it in bite-size pieces into the pie shell set on a baking tray. Cool the half-and-half to room temperature. Whisk the eggs, half-and-half, tarragon, lemon zest, and salt to taste. Pour the batter into the shell, slide the tray into a 375°F oven, and bake until set, 30–45 minutes. Cool to room temperature and serve with a salad of spicy greens.

TUNA
Steak fish

Tuna is a wide-ranging species. They range in size from the diminutive bonito to the giant bluefin. Enabled by their bullet-shaped bodies, they swim long distances at great speeds, so where they are captured and landed varies far and wide in both the Atlantic and Pacific Oceans. The color of their flesh spans from deep red to pale pink, and their flavor can be mild to sharp, with many variations along the way. But for the purpose of cooking with this book, there are three kinds of tuna: fatty, lean and canned.

The rich, fatty-textured tunas, such as bigeye, bluefin, and yellowfin, can also be identified by their dark red coloration and have a silky texture and a smooth taste. They work well in raw preparations such as crudo, tartare, and sushi and can stand up to higher-heat cooking methods like grilling or searing.

The leaner school of tuna includes albacore and blackfin. Given the lower fat content (but still quite high in relation to other seafood), these varieties can have a vigorous flavor that often carries a sharp acidity. These species are better suited for gentle cooking methods like poaching or slow roasting. Though some species might be better than others for particular preparations, all tunas in either category will work in the recipes that follow.

The single best way to detect the freshness and quality of any tuna is to inspect the dark red bloodline tissue that cross-sects the four loins and runs along the spine and rib bones. In very fresh fish, this tissue is firm and compact and its color is even and full. As any tuna ages, this tissue will leach its color into the lighter flesh of the loin. As the fish begins to fade, the bloodline's own color will become more brown than red.

You likely have encountered bright, super-pink, and perfectly consistently colored frozen tuna steaks. This unnatural color indicates that the fish has been treated by a process called tasteless smoke. Also known as carbon monoxide, this gas, harmless in this context, acts as a color preservative and enhancer. While treated fish is typically not the highest-quality product, it is quite versatile, tasty, and perfectly safe to eat.

Many types of tuna come in cans, but I do not distinguish among them in these recipes. I do specify that the tuna be packed in oil versus water, however. The flavor of the fish leaches into the medium in which it is packed. While tuna water most of the time simply goes down the drain, the oil packed in a tuna can be used in salad dressings and sautéed dishes.

There are at the time of writing significant issues surrounding tuna and sustainability, especially with bluefin. I choose to include them here, as this book is a reference and not meant as a contemporary commentary. Additionally, there are tuna fisheries that do act sustainably but unfortunately are working with stocks of fish that know no boundaries and are subject to overfishing elsewhere.

TUNA
Fresh

Gravlax-Style Tuna with Herbs

MAKES ABOUT 2 POUNDS

> 1 recipe Red Wine–Shallot Vinaigrette (page 37)
>
> 2 pounds tuna steaks, 2-inches-thick
>
> 2 cups kosher salt
>
> 2 cups sugar
>
> 2 tablespoons cracked peppercorns

Combine the tuna with half of the Red Wine–Shallot Vinaigrette and let it rest for 4 hours. Reserve the other half of the vinaigrette for serving. Wash off the marinade and pat the fish dry. Combine the salt, sugar, and peppercorns. Completely coat the marinated tuna with the salt mixture. Refrigerate for 24 hours. Remove from the cure, rinse away the excess salt, pat dry, and air-dry in the refrigerator on a wire rack for 24 hours. Wrap in plastic wrap and store in the refrigerator for up to 1 week. To serve, slice very thinly and arrange as you would carpaccio and serve with the remaining vinaigrette (see Salmon Gravlax Carpaccio with Herbs and Nuts, page 333).

Wood-Grilled Tuna with Cilantro-Chile-Lime Butter

SERVES 4

> 1 recipe Cilantro-Chile-Lime Butter (page 20)
>
> 4 tuna portions
>
> Salt
>
> Extra-virgin olive oil

Season the fish with salt and let it rest for 15 minutes. Prepare a charcoal grill with a medium fire, concentrating the hot coals on one side of the kettle. Add several chunks of smoking wood to the fire. Drizzle the fish with olive oil and place it on the grill over the hot coals. Cook until the edges of the fish begin to char, about 2 minutes. Flip the fish and cook another 1–2 minutes. Serve slathered with Cilantro-Chile-Lime Butter.

NOTE *If using a gas grill, preheat all burners to high. Place a handful of wood chips in an insert or a piece of foil fashioned into a bowl on one side of the grill to create the smoke. Place the tuna on one side of the hot grates. Once it begins to char around the edges, flip the fish to finish cooking for another 1–2 minutes.*

VARIATION

+ **Wood-Grilled Tuna with Pine Nut Butter.** Substitute Pine Nut Butter (page 21), for the Cilantro-Chile-Lime Butter.

Grilled Tuna with Herbes de Provence

SERVES 4

> 1 recipe Herbes de Provence Mix (page 33)
>
> 4 tuna portions, skin off
>
> Salt
>
> Extra-virgin olive oil
>
> 1 lemon, cut into wedges

Season the fish with salt and Herbes de Provence Mix and let it rest for 15 minutes. Prepare a charcoal grill with a medium fire, concentrating the hot coals on one side of the kettle. Drizzle the fish with olive oil and place it on the grill over the hot coals. Cook until the edges of the fish begin to char, about 2 minutes. Flip the fish and cook another 1–2 minutes. The tuna should be about medium doneness. Serve with lemon wedges.

NOTE *If using a gas grill, preheat all burners to high. Place the tuna on one side of the hot grates. Once it begins to char around the edges, flip the fish to finish cooking for another 1–2 minutes.*

Sautéed Tuna with Brown Butter, Lemon, and Herbs

SERVES 4

> 4 tuna portions, skin off
>
> Salt
>
> 6 tablespoons butter, divided
>
> 4 sprigs thyme, leaves picked
>
> 1 lemon, zested and juiced
>
> 3 tablespoons chopped fresh chives or parsley

Season the fish with salt and let it rest for 15 minutes. In a large sauté pan over high heat, melt 2 tablespoons of the butter and cook until golden brown. Place the fish in the pan. Cook for 1–2 minutes. Flip the fish and cook another 1–2 minutes, then remove the fish and wipe the pan clean. The tuna should be about medium doneness. Add the remaining 4 tablespoons of butter, thyme, and zest. Cook until the butter is dark brown and the thyme is crisped. Add the lemon juice and chives or parsley, and season with salt. Stir to combine. Slice the fish and serve with the sauce spooned over the top

Grilled Tuna with Orange-Walnut Vinaigrette

SERVES 4

> 1 recipe Orange-Walnut Vinaigrette (page 37)
>
> 4 tuna portions
>
> Salt

Season the fish with salt and let it rest for 15 minutes. Prepare a charcoal grill with a medium fire, concentrating the hot coals on one side of the kettle. Place the fish on the grill over the hot coals. Cook until the edges of the fish begin to char, about 2 minutes. Flip the fish and cook another 1–2 minutes. Serve with the vinaigrette.

NOTE *If using a gas grill, preheat all burners to high. Place the tuna on one side of the hot grates. Once it begins to char around the edges, flip the fish to finish cooking for another 1–2 minutes.*

VARIATION

+ **Great Butters and Marinade for Grilled Tuna.** Meyer Lemon-Pepper Butter (page 21); Preserved Lemon-Mint Butter (page 22); Creamy Lime-Almond Dressing (page 36).

Sautéed Tuna au Poivre Flambé

SERVES 4

  4 tuna portions

  Salt

1½ tablespoons black peppercorns,
  coarsely ground

1½ tablespoons fennel seeds, crushed

  4 tablespoons butter

1½ ounces Pernod or Herbsaint

Season the fish on both sides with salt and on one side with the peppercorns and fennel seeds. Gently press the seasonings into the flesh and let it rest for 15 minutes. In a sauté pan over medium-high heat, melt the butter and cook until golden brown. Place the fish pepper side down in the pan. Cook for 1–2 minutes, then flip and cook another 1–2 minutes. Turn off the heat. The tuna should be about medium doneness. Add the Pernod or Herbsaint and flambé by lighting with a match. Allow the alcohol to burn off before serving.

Seared Tuna with Five Spice Rub

SERVES 4

  1 recipe Five Spice Mix (page 33)

  4 tuna portions

  Salt

  3 tablespoons vegetable oil or butter

  1 lime, cut into wedges

Season the fish on both sides with salt and on one side with Five Spice Mix. Press the spices into the flesh and let it rest for 15 minutes. In a large sauté pan over medium-high heat, warm the oil or butter. Place the fish in the pan spice side down. Sear until the fish begins to color. Flip and continue to cook another 1–2minutes. The tuna should be about medium doneness. Serve with lime wedges.

Oil-Poached Tuna

This recipe produces a perfect stand-in for the canned tuna in any recipe.

SERVES 4–6

  1 onion, thinly sliced

  1 carrot, thinly sliced

  1 fennel bulb, thinly sliced

  5 sprigs thyme

  1 bay leaf

  1 cinnamon stick

  Ground coriander

  Black pepper

  1 pound tuna

  Extra-virgin olive oil

  1 tablespoon sherry vinegar or
  1 lemon, juiced

In a saucepan, combine the onion, carrot, fennel, thyme, bay leaf, cinnamon, a pinch of ground coriander, and a generous amount of black pepper. Place the fish on top. Add enough olive oil to just cover. Place the pan over low heat until the oil reaches 160°F. Remove from the heat and allow it to cool to room temperature. Strain and reserve the oil. Flake the fish into large pieces and toss with the vegetables, sherry vinegar, and a few spoonfuls of the oil. The tuna is now ready to be used in salads, sandwiches, appetizers, pastas, etc.

Broiled Tuna with Ginger and Mint Flambé

SERVES 4

> 4 tuna portions
>
> Salt
>
> 1 (1-inch) knob ginger, thinly sliced
>
> 20 mint leaves
>
> 4 tablespoons butter
>
> 1½ ounces Pernod

Season the fish with salt and let it rest for 15 minutes. Preheat the broiler to medium and set the rack in the position closest to the heat. In the bottom of an ovenproof dish, arrange the ginger and mint leaves in a single layer and place the fish on top. Add butter to the fish, slide the dish under the broiler, and cook, flipping once until done, 4–5 minutes, depending on thickness and desired doneness. Remove from the broiler. Add the Pernod and flambé by lighting it with a match. Allow the alcohol to burn off, and discard the ginger and mint leaves before serving.

Tuna Tartar

SERVES 4-6

> 1 pound tuna, diced into 1-inch pieces
>
> Salt
>
> ¼ cup lime juice
>
> 1 orange, zested and juiced
>
> 2 tablespoons soy sauce
>
> 1–2 Fresno or serrano chiles, thinly sliced
>
> 1 red onion, thinly sliced, rinsed under cold running water, and patted dry
>
> ½ cup slivered or sliced almonds, toasted
>
> 2 tablespoons almond oil, roasted peanut oil, or sesame oil
>
> 2 tablespoons chopped cilantro
>
> ½ teaspoon ground mace or nutmeg
>
> Black pepper

Keep this dish cold at all times during preparation. Season the fish with salt and let it rest for 5 minutes. Combine the fish with the lime juice, orange zest and juice, soy sauce, and chiles and let it rest for 5 minutes. Add the onion, almonds, almond oil, cilantro, and mace, and toss to combine. Season with black pepper and serve.

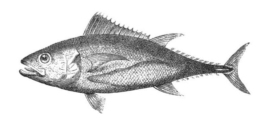

Poached Albacore with Fennel, Apple, and Radish Salad

SERVES 4

4 garlic cloves, crushed

¼ cup tarragon leaves, stems reserved

Salt

4 albacore tuna portions, skin off

2 tablespoons minced shallots

1 tablespoon chopped fresh thyme

1½ tablespoons lemon juice

2 teaspoons Dijon mustard

¼ cup extra-virgin olive oil

3 cups baby kale or arugula leaves

1 cup thinly sliced radishes

1 fennel bulb, trimmed and thinly sliced

1 apple, thinly sliced

In a pan just wide enough to hold the fish in a single layer, combine 4 cups of water with the garlic and tarragon stems. Simmer over low heat for 5 minutes. Season the broth with salt and bring it to 160°F. Add the fish and cook until it is opaque and flakes under gentle pressure, 4–6 minutes for each ½ inch of thickness. Remove the pan from the heat and cool the fish in the poaching liquid. Remove the fish from the liquid and flake into large chunks. Combine the shallots, thyme, lemon juice, and mustard in a large bowl. While whisking constantly, drizzle the oil into the bowl. Toss half of the vinaigrette with the flaked fish. Toss the remaining vinaigrette with the kale or arugula, radishes, tarragon leaves, fennel, and apple and season with salt. Divide the salad among four plates and top with tuna.

TUNA
Canned

Tuna Melt

SERVES 4

¼ cup Mayonnaise (page 29, or store-bought)

2 (5-ounce) cans tuna in oil, drained, or 1 recipe Oil-Poached Tuna (page 444)

Pinch of celery salt

Hot sauce (optional)

4 slices pumpernickel or whole grain bread

Cheddar cheese, sliced

Preheat the broiler to medium and set the rack in the middle position. Flake the fish into a bowl and add the Mayonnaise, celery salt, and hot sauce, if desired. Gently stir to combine. Place the bread slices on a baking tray. Divide the fish among the bread and cover each with slices of cheese. Slide the tray into the oven or under the broiler and cook until the fish is warmed through and the cheese is melted.

Pasta with Tonnato Sauce

SERVES 4

- ¼ cup Mayonnaise (page 29, or store-bought)
- 2 (5-ounce) cans tuna in oil or 1 recipe Oil-Poached Tuna (page 444)
- 1 lemon, juiced
- 2 tablespoons capers, rinsed
- ½ cup extra-virgin olive oil
- 1 pound linguine, cooked al dente according to package instructions, reserve 1 cup of cooking liquid
- ¼ cup chopped fresh herbs, such as chervil, chives, or parsley

In a food processor, blend the tuna in its oil, lemon juice, Mayonnaise, capers, olive oil, and ¼ cup of cold water. Add a bit more water if needed to achieve a smooth purée. Place the pasta and reserved pasta water in a large pan over medium heat. Bring the liquid to a boil, then stir in the sauce. Reduce heat to low and cook until the pasta has absorbed most of the water and the sauce is thick. Garnish with the herbs.

VARIATION

+ Use the sauce to garnish cooked chicken, veal, or pork dishes.

Tuna Noodle Casserole

SERVES 4–6

- 1 (10-ounce) package flat egg noodles, prepared according to package instructions and drained
- 6 tablespoons butter, plus more for buttering the baking dish
- 2 (5-ounce) cans tuna in oil or 1 recipe Oil-Poached Tuna (page 444), drained, oil reserved
- 1½ cups bread crumbs or cracker crumbs
- 1 onion, diced
- 2 garlic cloves, sliced
- 3 tablespoons flour
- 3½ cups milk
- Salt
- 2 teaspoons Dijon mustard

In a saucepan over medium heat, melt the butter and the oil from the tuna. Mix about 3 tablespoons of the melted butter/oil with the bread crumbs and set aside. To the saucepan, add the onion and garlic and cook until the onion softens, about 5 minutes. Add the flour and cook, stirring frequently, for 1 minute. Gradually pour the milk into the pan, whisking constantly, and bring to a simmer. Cook until smooth and thick, about 15 minutes. Season with salt and stir in the tuna and mustard. Toss the noodles with the sauce. Transfer the mixture to a buttered baking dish and top with the reserved bread crumbs. Bake at 375°F until golden brown and bubbling, 15–20 minutes.

VARIATION

+ **Other Casserole-Friendly Seafood.** Substitute canned salmon or mackerel for the tuna.

Tuna and Potato Salad

SERVES 4–6

> 1 cup Basic Aioli (page 25) or Mayonnaise (page 29, or store-bought)
>
> 6 eggs, hard-boiled
>
> 3 (5-ounce) cans tuna in oil or 1 recipe Oil-Poached Tuna (page 444)
>
> 1 pound white potatoes, peeled but kept whole
>
> 2 large carrots, peeled and cut into 1-inch pieces
>
> 1 bay leaf
>
> Salt
>
> 1 cup peas, frozen or fresh

In a bowl, lightly mash the eggs and tuna with its oil. Add the Basic Aioli or Mayonnaise and stir to make a chunky paste. In a large saucepan, combine the potatoes, carrots, and bay leaf. Cover with cold water and season well with salt. Place over high heat and boil the vegetables until they are tender. Add the peas for the last couple of minutes of cooking. Drain and cut the potatoes into 1-inch pieces. While the vegetables are still warm, toss them with the tuna mixture, being careful not to mash the potatoes or carrots. Let it rest for at least 1 hour before serving at room temperature.

Tuna with Chickpeas and Hot Sauce

SERVES 4

> ½ pound Oil-Poached Tuna (page 444) or 3 (5-ounce) cans tuna in oil
>
> 2 (14-ounce) cans chickpeas, drained, with ¼ cup liquid reserved
>
> 2 shallots, finely diced
>
> 1 lemon, zested and juiced
>
> Extra-virgin olive oil
>
> Hot sauce

In a bowl, combine the tuna with its oil, chickpeas with the reserved liquid, shallots, and lemon zest and juice. Toss to gently flake the fish. Add the olive oil and hot sauce to taste.

Poached Tuna and Chickpea Sandwich

SERVES 4

¼ cup Mayonnaise (page 29, or
    store-bought)

2 (5-ounce) cans tuna in oil or ½ pound
    Oil-Poached Tuna (page 444)

Salt

1 (14-ounce) can chickpeas, drained,
    ¼ cup liquid reserved

1 tablespoon hot pepper relish

½ lime, juiced

½ tablespoon fresh tarragon, chopped

Whole wheat toast for serving

Flake the fish into large chunks. In a bowl, mash
the chickpeas and their reserved liquid with a
fork. Add the reserved tuna oil, Mayonnaise,
pepper relish, and lime juice. Fold in the fish.
Stir in the tarragon and serve open-faced on
whole wheat toast.

Poached Tuna Crostini

SERVES 4-8 AS AN APPETIZER

2 (5-ounce) cans tuna in oil or ½ pound
    Oil-Poached Tuna (page 444)

Baguette, sliced on the bias into
    ½-inch pieces

Extra-virgin olive oil

1 (14-ounce) can white beans, drained,
    with ¼ cup liquid reserved

4 tablespoons butter

1 shallot, finely diced

Salt

Flake the tuna into large chunks. Arrange the
baguette slices on a baking sheet, drizzle with oil
from the tuna, and bake in a 350°F oven until
slightly browned. Remove from the oven and cool
on a baking sheet. In a small pan over medium
heat, warm the beans and their reserved liquid,
butter, and shallot. Mash the beans to a chunky
paste, fold in the chunked tuna, and season with
salt. Spoon atop the crostini and serve.

URCHIN

The Joy of Cooking describes sea urchins as having a "subtle, yet briny and complex flavor, something like an undiscovered species of oyster." An apt description for sure, but, like that of an oyster, an urchin's flavor depends on the time of year and the locale in which it is caught. In Maine, divers brave cold waters when spiny green sea urchins are at their peak of flavor to capture them for export to Japan, where the seafood is called *uni* and is very popular in sushi. Sea urchins are best between late summer and the end of winter, their peak coinciding with Christmas.

Only the roe or gonads are eaten. Most often, only these parts are found in the market, although occasionally you might find whole, live urchin for sale. Edible urchin parts need no additional preparation before using. There are five segments of these, generally arranged in a star pattern, in each urchin. To access these, the urchin is held upside down and scissors are used to cut a wide circle in the bottom portion of the shell. The juices and brown tissues are poured off, leaving just the desired parts. Urchins are measured in quality by color and texture. Bright yellow, firm, and sweet ones are the highest grade; muted yellow and softer texture make up the middle grade; and those that are dark in color, very soft, and often bitter are the lowest grade.

The texture is fatty, sometimes described as slippery. Though they are most often eaten raw or pounded into butter with herbs, with simply a few drops of lemon, there is a small industry of salt-drying urchins, which are then grated over dishes as a seasoning.

Sea Urchin with Olive Oil and Basil

SERVES 4–6 AS AN APPETIZER

12–24 crostini

12–24 basil leaves, approximately the size of each roe

12–24 sea urchin roes

    2 tablespoons extra-virgin olive oil

    1 lemon, juiced

Layer each crostini with a basil leaf topped with an urchin roe, and drizzle with olive oil and lemon juice.

Sea Urchin with Red Pepper Salsa

SERVES 4–6 AS AN APPETIZER

12–24 sea urchin roes

1 sweet red pepper, finely diced

1 shallot, finely diced

1 orange, zested and juiced

1 teaspoon red wine or sherry vinegar

3 tablespoons extra-virgin olive oil

Toasted bread rubbed with garlic

Arrange the roe on a platter. Combine the pepper, shallot, orange juice and zest, vinegar, and olive oil. Scatter the salsa over the roe and serve with toasted bread rubbed with garlic.

Pasta with Creamy Sea Urchin

SERVES 4

6 tablespoons butter, softened, divided

1 garlic clove, grated

2 shallots, finely diced

4 ounces sea urchin roe

1 lemon, zested and juiced

1 pound linguine, cooked al dente according to package instructions, reserve 1 cup of cooking liquid

Salt

3 tablespoons chopped fresh herbs, such as chervil or chives

Crushed red chile flakes

In a sauté pan over medium heat, melt 2 tablespoons of the butter. Add the garlic and shallots. Cook until the shallots are golden brown. In a bowl, mash the roe with the lemon zest and juice and the remaining 4 tablespoons of butter until it is a smooth paste. Add the pasta and cooking liquid to the sauté pan and simmer until the pasta is fully cooked. Remove from the heat, add the sea urchin paste, and stir to combine. Garnish the pasta with herbs and chile flakes.

WAHOO
Steak fish

While *white tuna* is not a legal name for wahoo, nonetheless it is an apt description of its flesh. Wahoo is actually the largest member of the mackerel family. This deep-water open-ocean fish is well known in the cuisines of the Caribbean and Hawaii, where it is known as *ono*, which means "good to eat." Wahoo is available year-round as bycatch of the tuna industry but is better known in the summer, when it comes nearer to shore and is caught in a number of fisheries as well as recreationally.

These mirror-bright silver fish with azure bands are between 10 and 50 pounds on average. Much like tuna, the rich texture of wahoo is defined by concentric rings. The fish is lean compared to red-fleshed tunas but still very rich, with a smooth, creamy mouthfeel. Its flavor is not nearly as robust as tuna, but it cooks and presents in much the same way.

When cut, wahoo has a sea-green opalescence. The bloodline, when fresh, is bright cherry red, though as the fish ages it takes on a browner hue. It is best when cooked rare or medium, much the way most tuna is. It's very good steamed, as its dense but porous meat absorbs flavors very well, especially highly aromatic spices such as star anise, clove, and cinnamon and vegetables such as fennel and celery. Its skin is edible, though it can be very chewy on fish larger than 20 pounds. It has very fine scales that are easily removed. Its liver, which is very dense and fatty, makes a fine meal served on its own, poached or even grilled and then sliced thinly and topped with an herb salad.

Seared Wahoo with Five Spice Mix

SERVES 4

1 recipe Five Spice Mix (page 33)

4 wahoo portions, skin off

Salt

3 tablespoons butter

1 lime, cut into wedges

Season the fish with salt all over and on one side with Five Spice Mix. Press the spices into the flesh and let it rest for 15 minutes. In a large sauté pan over medium-high heat, melt the butter. Place the fish in the pan spice side down. Sear until the fish begins to color, about 1–2 minutes. Flip and continue to cook the remaining sides for approximately 30–45 seconds, until the fish is medium rare. Serve with the cooking butter drizzled over the top and lime wedges.

Wahoo Crudo with Chile and Lime

SERVES 4

- 1 pound wahoo fillet, skin off, bloodline sliced away and discarded, and flesh cut into ¼-inch-thick ribbons
- Salt
- Extra-virgin olive oil
- 1 lime, juiced
- Crushed red chile pepper

Lay the fish on serving plates and season with salt and let rest for 10 minutes. Drizzle with oil, and garnish with a few drops of lime juice and a pinch of crushed red chile pepper.

Wahoo Ceviche with Grapefruit

SERVES 4

- 1 pound wahoo fillet, skin off, bloodline sliced away and discarded, and flesh cut into ½-inch cubes
- Salt
- ½ cup lime juice
- 2 pink grapefruit, 1 juiced and cut into segments
- 1 teaspoon honey or maple syrup
- 1–2 Fresno or serrano chiles, thinly sliced
- 1 red onion, thinly sliced and rinsed under cold running water and patted dry
- ¼ cup extra-virgin olive oil
- ½ cup basil, leaves picked and torn
- ¼ cup mint, leaves picked and torn
- Black pepper

Keep this dish cold at all times during preparation. Season the fish with salt and let it rest for 5 minutes. Combine the fish with the lime juice, grapefruit juice, honey, and chiles and let it rest for 20 minutes. Add the onion, olive oil, grapefruit

segments, basil, and mint, and toss gently. Let it rest another 5 minutes. Season with black pepper before serving.

Wahoo Tartare with Nutmeg, Mint, and Lemon

SERVES 4

- 1 pound wahoo fillet, skin off, bloodline sliced away and discarded, and flesh cut into ½-inch cubes
- 2 tablespoons soy sauce
- 2 lemons, zested and juiced
- 1 Fresno or serrano chile, finely minced
- 2 tablespoons nut oil or sesame oil
- ½ teaspoon of ground nutmeg
- 2 tablespoons finely sliced mint
- Toasted bread for serving
- Garlic

Keep this dish cold at all times during preparation. Combine the fish with the soy sauce, lemon zest, chile, nut oil, and nutmeg and let it rest for 20 minutes. Just before serving, stir in the lemon juice and mint. Serve with toasted bread brushed lightly with garlic.

Sautéed Wahoo with Chermoula

SERVES 4

 1 recipe Chermoula (page 26)

 4 wahoo portions, skin off

 Salt

 3 tablespoons butter or extra-virgin olive oil

Season the fish with salt and let it rest for 15 minutes. In a large sauté pan over medium-high heat, melt the butter. Place the fish in the pan. Cook until the fish begins to color, about 1–2 minutes. Flip and continue to cook the remaining sides for approximately 30–45 seconds, until the fish is medium rare. Slice the fish on the bias and serve with Chermoula.

Grilled Wahoo with Crispy Mint and Caper Sauce

SERVES 4

 1 recipe Crispy Mint and Caper Sauce (page 27)

 4 wahoo portions, skin off

 Salt

 3 tablespoon extra-virgin olive oil or butter

Season the fish with salt and let it rest for 15 minutes. Prepare a charcoal grill with a medium fire, concentrating the hot coals on one side of the kettle. Brush the fish with the olive oil and place it on the grill over the hot coals. Cook until the edges of the fish begin to char, about 2 minutes. Flip and continue to cook the remaining sides for approximately 30–45 seconds, until the fish is medium-rare.

NOTE *If using a gas grill, preheat all burners to medium-high.*

WEAKFISH
Fillet fish

This general name can refer to any of four species also known collectively as seatrout, though none are actually related to trout. These are a popular game fish in the mid-Atlantic through Gulf regions and are enjoyed equally at the table. They have a finely grained flesh with little connective tissue, which gives them a pleasantly soft texture. The flavor is complex and assertive without being strong. Their skin has a delicious flavor on its own and adds nuance to the fillet. The skin is necessary in most preparations in order to maintain the integrity of the fillet.

The meat is pink-hued and cooks to a very slight grayish-white. Its flesh absorbs flavors well, so preparations such as poaching and steaming flatter it. It's also a great candidate for marinating prior to preparation, as this will help to both firm and flavor the fish.

Broiled Weakfish with Cilantro-Pecan Pesto

SERVES 4

> 1 recipe Cilantro-Pecan Pesto (page 26)
> 4 weakfish portions, skin on
> Salt

Season the fish with salt and let it rest for 15 minutes. Preheat the broiler to high and set the rack in the position closest to the heat. Place the fish on a baking tray, skin side up. Slide the tray under the broiler and cook until done, 6–9 minutes, depending on thickness. Serve with Cilantro-Pecan Pesto.

Broiled Herb-Marinated Weakfish

SERVES 4

> 1 recipe Sicilian Herb Sauce (page 32)
> 4 weakfish portions, skin on

Combine the fish with half of the Sicilian Herb Sauce and marinate for 1–8 hours. Preheat the broiler to medium and set the rack in the position closest to the heat. Remove the fish from the marinade and place it skin side up on a baking tray. Slide the tray under the broiler and cook until done, 6–9 minutes, depending on thickness. Serve with the remaining sauce.

Salt-Roasted Weakfish with Lemon and Thyme

SERVES 2

3 pounds kosher salt

1 (2- to 3-pound) weakfish, scaled, gutted, and scored

2 lemons, thinly sliced

8 sprigs thyme

4 tablespoons butter, melted, or extra-virgin olive oil

Combine the salt with enough water so that it resembles wet sand. Place a thin layer on a baking sheet, and top with half of the lemon slices and half of the thyme. Place the fish on top and arrange the remaining lemon slices and thyme on top of the fish. Pack on the remaining salt mixture to completely encase the fish. Roast at 375°F for 20–30 minutes. Remove the fish from the oven and let it rest for 5 minutes. Crack the salt crust and discard. Serve whole, or remove the lemons and thyme and peel off the skin before carefully transferring the top fillet to a platter. Remove and discard the backbone and transfer the bottom fillet without its skin to the platter. Drizzle the fish with melted butter.

Sautéed Weakfish with Brown Butter, Raisins, and Tarragon

SERVES 4

4 weakfish portions, skin on and scored

Salt

6 tablespoons butter, divided

2 garlic cloves, finely minced

2 tablespoons raisins

1 tablespoon chopped fresh tarragon

1 lemon, juiced

Season the fish with salt and let it rest for 15 minutes. In a sauté pan over medium heat, melt 2 tablespoons of the butter and cook until golden brown. Place the fish in the pan skin side down. Cook without flipping until almost done, then remove the fish and wipe the pan clean. Add the remaining 4 tablespoons of butter, garlic, and raisins. Cook until the butter is very dark. Add the tarragon and lemon juice, and season with salt. Stir to combine. Turn off the heat and return the fish to the pan uncooked side down to finish cooking.

Sautéed Weakfish with Lime-Dill Butter

SERVES 4

1 recipe Lime-Dill Butter (page 21)

4 weakfish portions, skin on and scored

Salt

2 tablespoons butter

Season the fish with salt and let it rest for 15 minutes. In a sauté pan over medium heat, melt the butter and cook until golden brown. Place the fish in the pan. Cook without flipping until almost done, then turn off the heat and flip the fish to finish cooking. Top each portion with 2 tablespoons of Lime-Dill Butter.

Grilled Weakfish with Anchovy-Horseradish Butter

SERVES 4

1 recipe Anchovy-Horseradish Butter (page 19)

4 weakfish portions, skin on and scored

Salt

Extra-virgin olive oil

Season the fish with salt and let it rest for 15 minutes. Prepare a charcoal grill with a medium fire, concentrating the hot coals on one side of the kettle. Brush the fish with olive oil and place it skin side down on the grill over the hot coals. Cook until the edges begin to char, about 2 minutes. Lift the entire grill grate and rotate it so the fish rests opposite the hot coals. Cover the grill and continue to cook over indirect heat until the fish is done. Top each portion with 2 tablespoons of the Anchovy-Horseradish Butter.

Sautéed Weakfish au Poivre with Herbs

SERVES 4

4 weakfish portions, skin on and scored

Salt

1½ tablespoons black peppercorns, crushed

1½ tablespoons fennel seeds, crushed

4 tablespoons butter

¼ cup chopped parsley, chervil, or chives

1 lemon, cut into wedges

Season the fish on both sides with salt and on the flesh side with the pepper and fennel seeds. Gently press the seasonings into the flesh and let it rest for 15 minutes. In a sauté pan over medium heat, melt the butter and cook until golden brown. Place the fish pepper side down in the pan. Cook without flipping until almost done, then flip to finish cooking. Gently peel back and discard the skin. Scatter the parsley over the fish and serve with lemon wedges.

Seared Jamaican Jerk Weakfish

SERVES 4

1 recipe Jerk Seasoning Mix (page 33)

4 weakfish portions, skin on and scored

Salt

4 tablespoons butter

1 lime, cut into wedges

Season the fish with salt on both sides and on the skin side with the Jamaican Jerk Seasoning. Press the spices into the fish and let it rest for 15 minutes. In a large sauté pan over medium heat, melt the butter. Place the fish in the pan skin side down. Sear until a dark crust forms. Flip and continue to cook until done. Serve with the cooking butter drizzled over the top and lime wedges.

WHITING
Flaky white fish, small silver fish

Whiting is a colloquial name that applies to many different unrelated species, but in this book it is used to describe a species of hake (see page 210). It is labor-intensive to prepare these small fish, but they are quite delicious and appealing when fresh, though they age very quickly. They are limp in texture and prone to damage when handling. They can be dressed for serving whole (head, fins, and scales removed), or they can be filleted like other small silver fish by placing the fish on a board in a swimming position and pressing down along the backbone to flatten the fish. The bones can be stripped away from the fillets at this point. Whiting must always be served with its skin on, as it would readily fall apart without it.

They have a delicate white flesh and are similar to haddock in flavor and to hake in texture.

Broiled Whole Whiting with Lemon and Herbs
SERVES 4

4–8 whole whiting, scaled and gutted

    Salt

2 lemons, thinly sliced

5 stalks rosemary

5 sprigs thyme

8 tablespoons butter, melted

Season the fish with salt and let it rest for 15 minutes. Preheat the broiler to high and set the rack in the position closest to the heat. Line a baking dish with the lemon slices and herbs. Place the fish in swimming position on top of the lemons, drizzle with half of the butter, and slide the tray under the broiler. Baste with remaining butter after about 3 minutes. Cook until done, 6–9 minutes, depending on thickness.

Beer-Battered Whiting
SERVES 4

1 recipe Traditional Remoulade Sauce (page 31)

4 whiting portions, skin on, cut into 2-inch pieces

    Salt

Vegetable or peanut oil

¾ cup flour, sifted

¾ cup cornstarch, sifted

¾ cup beer

2 tablespoons vegetable oil

1 egg, separated

Season the fish with salt and let it rest for 15 minutes. Pour 3–4 inches of oil into a high-sided pan. Place over medium-high heat and warm the oil to 375°F. Make a batter by combining the flour, cornstarch, beer, vegetable oil, and egg yolk. Beat the egg white to soft peaks and fold it into the batter. Season with salt to taste. Dip one piece of fish at a time into the batter, place it in the oil, and hold it there for 5 seconds before releasing it. Repeat the process, cooking the fish in small batches. Turn with a slotted spoon if necessary to evenly render both sides golden and crispy. Remove the pieces as they finish and place on paper towels to absorb excess oil. Serve with Remoulade Sauce.

Flip to finish cooking. Remove the fish from the pan. Add the remaining ½ cup of olive oil, pine nuts, and raisins and cook until the pine nuts are golden brown and the raisins plump. Add the onion and bell pepper and cook until the pepper begins to soften. Add the eggplant and cook until it has softened and has absorbed much of the oil. Stir in the vinegar and brown sugar, and season with salt. Turn off the heat and nestle the cooked fish into the sauce. The flavors improve if allowed to chill overnight in the refrigerator and then brought to room temperature before serving. But at a minimum, let it sit at least 1 hour before serving at room temperature with slices of baguette.

Whiting en Saor (sweet-sour vinaigrette)

SERVES 4

    1½ pound whiting fillets, skin on
        Salt
    ¾ cup extra-virgin olive oil, divided
        Flour
    3 tablespoons pine nuts or slivered almonds
    2 tablespoons raisins
    1 small onion, thinly sliced
    1 red bell pepper, finely diced
    1 small eggplant, ½-inch dice, about 2 cups
    ¼ cup red wine vinegar
    1 tablespoon brown sugar
        Baguette for serving

Season the fish with salt and let it rest for 15 minutes. In a sauté pan over medium heat, warm ¼ cup of the olive oil. Lightly dust the fish with flour and place it in the pan skin side down and cook without flipping until almost done.

Whiting with Sage and Brown Butter

SERVES 4

    4 whiting portions, skin on
        Salt
        Flour
    6 tablespoons butter, divided
    2 garlic cloves, finely minced
    20 small sage leaves

Season the fish with salt and let it rest for 15 minutes. In a sauté pan over medium heat, melt 2 tablespoons of the butter and cook until golden brown. Lightly coat the fish in flour and place the fish in the pan, skin side down. Cook without flipping until almost done, then flip to finish cooking. Remove the fish from the pan and wipe the pan clean. Add the remaining 4 tablespoons of butter, garlic, and sage leaves. Cook over medium heat until the butter is golden brown and the sage leaves are crispy.

Whiting with Pine Nut Piccata
SERVES 4

1 recipe Pine Nut Piccata (page 30)

4 whiting portions, skin on

Salt

6 tablespoons butter

Flour

Season the fish with salt and let it rest for 15 minutes. In a sauté pan over medium heat, melt the butter and cook until golden brown. Lightly coat the fish in flour and place the fish in the pan skin side down. Cook without flipping until almost done, then flip to finish cooking. Serve with Pine Nut Piccata scattered over the top of each portion.

WOLFFISH
Flaky white fish, fillet fish, orange-fleshed fish

These monstrous creatures of the deep are now rare in American markets because of historical overfishing. But a small amount of product is still imported from northern European waters, and if you find it, snap it up.

A couple different species fall under this market name, and all of them share the same culinary character. The meaty, dense flesh is akin to monkfish with its snappy elastic texture, but when cooked it also yields into a rich and delicately textured flake like that of sablefish. Its qualities are also akin to salmon.

Wolffish is extremely versatile in the kitchen. It takes as well to earthy and robust flavors as it does to a simple garnish of drizzled olive oil. Should you ever come across wolffish cheeks, treat yourself to them; they are a particular delight. They cook up more like pork belly than one might expect and take to braising as well as any seafood.

Beer-Battered Wolffish

SERVES 4

1 recipe Louisiana Remoulade (page 31)

4 wolffish portions, skin off, cut into 2-inch pieces

Salt

Vegetable or peanut oil

¾ cup flour, sifted

¾ cup cornstarch, sifted

¾ cup beer

2 tablespoons vegetable oil

1 egg, separated

Season the fish with salt and let it rest for 20 minutes. Pour 3–4 inches of oil into a high-sided pan. Place over medium-high heat and warm the oil to 375°F. Make a batter by combining the flour, cornstarch, beer, vegetable oil, and egg yolk. Beat the egg white to soft peaks and fold into the batter. Season with salt to taste. Dip one piece of fish at a time into the batter, place it in the oil, and hold it there for 5 seconds before releasing it. Repeat the process, cooking the fish in small batches. Turn with a slotted spoon if necessary to evenly render both sides golden and crispy. Remove the pieces as they finish and place on paper towels to absorb excess oil. Serve with Louisiana Remoulade.

Wolffish au Poivre Flambé

SERVES 4

4 wolffish portions, skin off

Salt

1½ tablespoons black peppercorns, crushed

1½ tablespoons fennel seeds, crushed

4 tablespoons butter

1½ ounces Cognac or dark rum

Season the fish with salt on both sides and on one side with the pepper and fennel seeds. Gently press the seasonings into the flesh and let the fish rest for 20 minutes. In a sauté pan over medium heat, melt the butter and cook until golden brown. Place the fish pepper side down in the pan. Cook without flipping until almost done, then flip to finish cooking. Turn off the heat. Add the Cognac or dark rum and flambé by lighting with a match. Allow the alcohol to burn off before serving.

Sautéed Wolffish with Garlic and Fresh Tomato

SERVES 4

4 wolffish portions, skin off

Salt

6 tablespoons extra-virgin olive oil, divided

3 garlic cloves, thinly sliced

1 cup chopped fresh tomatoes

Season the fish with salt and let it rest for 20 minutes. In a sauté pan over medium heat, warm 2 tablespoons of the olive oil. Place the fish in the pan. Cook without flipping until almost done, then remove the fish. Add the remaining 4 tablespoons of olive oil and garlic and cook until the garlic is soft, about 2 minutes. Add the tomatoes, bring the sauce to a simmer, and season with salt. Cook for about 3–4 minutes until the tomatoes just begin to break down. Turn off the heat and return the fish to the pan uncooked side down to finish cooking.

WRASSE
Fillet fish

Despite being a little-known family of fish, it claims among it some of the very best-eating fish there are. Specifically, the Spanish hogfish and the hog snapper (no relation to the snapper family), are prized by both anglers and eaters. They have a very pleasant firm flesh that softens but maintains its integrity when cooked. The flavor is distinctly crab-like in its sweetness. The skin, however, can be bitter and its thickness and hard-to-remove scales make it not edible. I do like to cook the fish with the skin on (scales, too) in preparations such as grilling, removing and discarding before serving.

Beer-Battered Wrasse

SERVES 4

>   4 wrasse portions, skin off, cut into
>   2-inch pieces
>   Salt
>   Vegetable or peanut oil
>   ¾ cup flour, sifted
>   ¾ cup cornstarch, sifted
>   ¾ cup beer
>   2 tablespoons vegetable oil
>   1 egg, separated

Season the fish with salt and let it rest for 20 minutes. Pour 3–4 inches of oil into a high-sided pan. Place over medium-high heat and warm the oil to 375°F. Make a batter by combining the flour, cornstarch, beer, 2 tablespoons of vegetable oil, and egg yolk. Beat the egg white to soft peaks and fold into the batter. Season with salt to taste. Dip one piece of fish at a time into the batter, place it in the oil, and hold it there for 5 seconds before releasing it. Repeat the process, cooking the fish in small batches. Turn with a slotted spoon if necessary to evenly render both sides golden and crispy. Place on paper towels to absorb excess oil.

Steamed Wrasse with Braised Fennel and Bay

SERVES 4

>   4 wrasse portions, skin off
>   Salt
>   6 tablespoons butter
>   2 fennel bulbs, cut into ½-inch slices
>   4 bay leaves
>   1 cup white wine

Season the fish with salt and let it rest for 20 minutes. In a wide, shallow pot over medium-high heat melt 3 tablespoons of butter. Add the fennel and sauté for 3 minutes. Add the bay leaves, wine, and ½ cup of water and reduce the heat to low. Season with salt and bring to a simmer. Place the fish on top of the fennel, cover, and cook until done, 7–10 minutes. Transfer the fish and fennel to a plate. Increase the heat, bring the liquid to a boil, and reduce until it is a thick glaze. Stir in the remaining 3 tablespoons of butter and toss the fennel with the glaze, season with salt, and serve with the fish.

WRECKFISH
Fillet fish, meaty dense fish

Wreckfish are relatively new arrivals to the culinary scene. I first discovered them when I was searching for a sustainable substitute for grouper. At the time, I believe only a single boat, maybe two, was fishing for this species. I got into a bit of a bidding war over them with a couple of other mid-Atlantic chefs, and when I was lucky enough to be the winning chef, I could say without much doubt that we were the only restaurant in America serving wreckfish that night.

These fish are plump and full in their shape and typically landed weighing around 30–40 pounds. Juveniles are found at the top of the water column, aggregating around floating objects, whereas adults live deep down on rocky bottoms and other habitats such as shipwrecks, from which they derive their shared common name, wreckfish. There they feed mostly on small fish and crustaceans, which gives them a sweet, crab-like flavor.

In the kitchen, its flesh is tinged pink and gray, becoming bone-white in color when cooked. Its raw, slightly fibrous texture eases into a moist and tender one. The richness of flavor is due more to its sweetness than fattiness. Olive oil, more so than butter, heightens wreckfish's flavor. Its skin is far too tough to serve, though it is helpful in preparation to maintain moisture.

The bones of the wreckfish, especially the head, are intensely flavored and gelatinous, making a clean, brightly flavored stock, but it's quite rare that you'll buy a whole fish. I prefer the fattier belly sections, as they are thick enough to yield attractive portions and have less of the dense connective tissue than the top fillets.

The fish are at their peak in the late fall and early winter, which is fortunate, as these fish lend themselves perfectly to the layered flavors of cold-weather cooking. I will often stew it with large chunks of autumn squash and walnuts. The squash breaks down and thickens the braising liquid, while the walnuts offer a textural counterpoint. These woodsy and hearty flavors accentuate an entirely different side of this fish's personality.

Braised Wreckfish in Spiced Coconut Broth

SERVES 4

> 4 wreckfish portions, skin off
>
> Salt
>
> 3 tablespoons peanut oil, divided
>
> 1 lime, cut into quarters
>
> 1 medium red onion, cut into wedges
>
> 1 (1-inch) knob ginger, sliced
>
> 1 garlic clove, sliced
>
> 1 pound small carrots, cut into 1-inch pieces
>
> ¼ pound shiitake mushrooms, sliced
>
> ¼ cup slivered almonds
>
> 2 (14-ounce) cans unsweetened coconut milk
>
> 1 sprig basil
>
> Scallions, sliced
>
> Rice for serving

Season the fish with salt and let it rest for 20 minutes. In a large sauté pan, heat 1 tablespoon of the oil over high heat. Add the lime and onion. Cook undisturbed until the onion gets a nice char, almost burned, 3–5 minutes. Remove the onion and lime from the pan and reserve separately. Add the remaining 2 tablespoons of peanut oil, ginger, garlic, carrots, mushrooms, and almonds. Sauté until aromatic and just softened. Add the reserved onion and nestle the fish into the vegetables. Add the coconut milk and basil. Cover, reduce the heat to low, and cook until the fish is done, about 10 minutes. Discard the basil and ginger slices. Garnish with sliced scallions and the reserved seared limes. Serve with rice.

Wreckfish Braised with Sundried Tomatoes

SERVES 4

> 4 wreckfish portions, skin off
>
> Salt
>
> 2 shallots, finely diced
>
> 4 sprigs thyme
>
> 3 whole cloves
>
> 1 orange, zested and juiced
>
> ¼ cup shredded sundried tomatoes
>
> 1 cup white or red wine
>
> 4 tablespoons butter, cut into pieces
>
> 3 tablespoons fresh chopped chives or tarragon
>
> Crusty bread for serving

Season the fish with salt and let it rest for 20 minutes. In a large sauté pan over medium heat, combine the shallots, thyme, cloves, orange zest and juice, sundried tomatoes, wine, and 1 cup of water. Simmer the liquid for 5 minutes. Add the fish and gently simmer until cooked through, 12–15 minutes. Transfer the fish to a warm plate. Discard the thyme and cloves. Increase the heat and reduce the liquid to ½ cup. Whisk in the butter and chives, and season with salt. Return the fish to the pan and stir to coat. Serve with crusty bread.

Grilled Wreckfish with Anchovy-Herb Butter

SERVES 4

> 1 recipe Anchovy-Herb Butter (page 19)
>
> 4 wreckfish portions, skin off
>
> Salt
>
> Extra-virgin olive oil

Season the fish with salt and let it rest for 20 minutes. Prepare a charcoal grill with a medium fire, concentrating the hot coals on one side of the kettle. Drizzle the fish with olive oil. Place the fish on the grill over the hot coals. Cook until edges begin to char, about 2 minutes. Lift the entire grill grate and rotate it so the fish rests opposite the hot coals. Cover and continue to cook over this indirect heat until the fish is done. Serve slathered with Anchovy-Herb Butter.

NOTE *If using a gas grill, preheat all burners to medium-high. Place the wreckfish on one side of the hot grates. Once it begins to char around the edges, turn off the burner directly under the fish and cover the grill to finish cooking.*

Sautéed Wreckfish with Brown Butter, Coriander, and Orange

SERVES 4

   4 wreckfish portions, skin off

   Salt

   3 tablespoons coriander seeds, crushed

   6 tablespoons butter, divided

   2 garlic cloves, finely minced

   1 orange, zested and juiced

   Black pepper

Season the fish on both sides with salt and on one side with coriander and let it rest for 20 minutes. In a sauté pan over medium heat, melt 2 tablespoons of the butter and cook until golden brown. Place the fish in the pan coriander side down. Cook without flipping until almost done, then remove the fish, and wipe the pan clean. Add the remaining 4 tablespoons of butter and the garlic, and cook until brown. Add the zest, season with black pepper, and cook for 30 seconds. Add the orange juice and season with salt. Turn the heat off. Return the fish to the pan uncooked side down to finish cooking.

Wreckfish Tacos

SERVES 4

   1 pound wreckfish fillets, skin off

   1 recipe Orange-Coriander Vinaigrette (page 37) or Lemon-Chile-Mint Dressing (page 36)

   1 recipe Pico de Gallo (page 30) or store-bought salsa

   Sour cream

   2 avocados, sliced

   ½ cup cilantro, leaves picked

   ¼ head cabbage, shaved, or coleslaw

   16 corn tortillas

Season the fish with salt and let it rest for 15 minutes. Grill, roast, broil, or poach the fish until cooked. Flake the fish into bite-size pieces and toss with the vinaigrette. Set out bowls of Pico de Gallo, sour cream, avocado, cilantro, and shredded cabbage. Warm the tortillas in a dry heavy-bottomed pan over medium heat until crisped yet pliable. Keep them warm in a kitchen towel. For each taco, stack two tortillas together. Let everyone build their own tacos just the way they like.

Bottarga

Bottarga is the Italian name for salted, cured fish roe, typically of gray mullet or bluefin tuna and featured in Mediterranean cuisine. The dense orange to brown slabs range from several inches to more than a foot long. Bottarga is often used as a garnish to dishes such as when grated onto pasta or salads. It can also be the featured ingredient, but a little goes a long way. Just a couple thin shavings are enough to make a huge flavor impact.

Bottarga Vinaigrette on Roasted Radicchio

SERVES 4 AS A SIDE DISH

   1 recipe Orange-Coriander Vinaigrette
   (page 37)

   3 tablespoons bottarga, finely grated, divided

   2 heads radicchio, cut into wedges

   2 tablespoons extra-virgin olive oil

   Salt

   Black pepper

   ¼ cup chopped fresh herbs, such as chives,
   parsley, or tarragon

   1 orange, zested

Combine 2 tablespoons of the bottarga with the Orange-Coriander Vinaigrette. Brush the radicchio wedges with the olive oil. Set the broiler to medium and position the rack in the middle position. Heat a heavy sauté pan until smoking hot. Place the radicchio cut side down and slide the pan under the broiler. Cook until the radicchio is slightly charred and wilted. Remove the radicchio to serving plates and season lightly with salt and pepper. Drizzle with the vinaigrette mixture. Garnish with the herbs, zest, and the remaining 1 tablespoon of grated bottarga.

Buttered Pasta with Bottarga

SERVES 4

   1 pound linguine

   Salt

   6 tablespoons butter

   1 lemon, zested and juiced

   1 bay leaf

   3 tablespoons chives, chopped

   Black pepper

   4 tablespoons bottarga, finely grated

In a pot over high heat, boil the linguine in salted water until al dente, according to the package instructions. Strain the pasta and reserve 1 cup of the cooking liquid. In the same pot over medium heat, bring the reserved pasta water, butter, lemon juice, and bay leaf to a boil. Add the cooked pasta. Simmer until the pasta is fully cooked and coated in sauce. Remove the bay leaf and toss with the lemon zest and chives. Season with black pepper and garnish with bottarga.

Marinated Bottarga

SERVES 4 AS AN APPETIZER

  2–3 ounces bottarga

   Pinch mace

   Crushed red chile flakes

   1 lemon, zested

   4 tablespoons extra-virgin olive oil

   1 shallot, thinly sliced, rinsed under
   cold running water, and patted dry

   2 sprigs mint, leaves torn

   Belgian endive leaves or crostini

Slice the bottarga into ⅛-inch-thick sheets and place on a platter. Sprinkle with the mace, chile flakes, and zest and cover with olive oil. Marinate for 1 hour. Garnish with shallots and mint. Serve with endive leaves or crostini.

Index

About the Author

Before leaving the restaurant industry to pursue his interests in sustainable food systems, award-winning chef **Barton Seaver** created three top seafood restaurants in Washington, DC. Since then, he has written seven seafood-centric books, including *The Joy of Seafood*, *American Seafood*, *Two If By Sea*, *For Cod and Country*, and *Where There's Smoke*. Seaver has contributed to *Coastal Living*, *The Coastal Table*, *Cooking Light*, *Every Day with Rachael Ray*, *Fine Cooking*, *Fortune*, *Martha Stewart's Whole Living*, *The New York Times*, *O: The Oprah Magazine*, *Saveur*, and the *Washington Post*, among many others. He has appeared on CNN, NPR, 20/20, and the TED Talk stage. Seaver hosted the national television program *In Search of Food* on the Ovation Network and *Eat: The History of Food* on National Geographic TV. He is also the founder of the Coastal Culinary Academy, a multiplatform initiative that seeks to increase seafood consumption through seafood-specific culinary education for all levels of cooks.